PERSPECTIVES ON CONTRACT LAW

ASPEN PUBLISHERS

PERSPECTIVES ON CONTRACT LAW

Fourth Edition

Randy E. Barnett
Carmack Waterhouse Professor of Legal Theory
Georgetown University Law Center

Wolters Kluwer

Law & Business

AUSTIN   BOSTON   CHICAGO   NEW YORK   THE NETHERLANDS

To contact Customer Care, e-mail customer.care@aspenpublishers.com,
call 1-800-234-1660, fax 1-800-901-9075, or mail correspondence to:

> Aspen Publishers
> Attn: Order Department
> PO Box 990
> Frederick, MD 21705

Printed in the United States of America.

1 2 3 4 5 6 7 8 9 0

ISBN 978-0-7355-8297-2

Library of Congress Cataloging-in-Publication Data

Perspectives on contract law / [edited by] Randy E. Barnett. — 4th ed.
   p. cm.
  ISBN 978-0-7355-8297-2
  1. Contracts — United States. I. Barnett, Randy E.
  KF801.A7P42 2009
  346.7302 — dc22

                                                         2009028613

About Wolters Kluwer Law & Business

Wolters Kluwer Law & Business is a leading provider of research information and workflow solutions in key specialty areas. The strengths of the individual brands of Aspen Publishers, CCH, Kluwer Law International and Loislaw are aligned within Wolters Kluwer Law & Business to provide comprehensive, in-depth solutions and expert-authored content for the legal, professional and education markets.

CCH was founded in 1913 and has served more than four generations of business professionals and their clients. The CCH products in the Wolters Kluwer Law & Business group are highly regarded electronic and print resources for legal, securities, antitrust and trade regulation, government contracting, banking, pension, payroll, employment and labor, and healthcare reimbursement and compliance professionals.

Aspen Publishers is a leading information provider for attorneys, business professionals and law students. Written by preeminent authorities, Aspen products offer analytical and practical information in a range of specialty practice areas from securities law and intellectual property to mergers and acquisitions and pension/benefits. Aspen's trusted legal education resources provide professors and students with high-quality, up-to-date and effective resources for successful instruction and study in all areas of the law.

Kluwer Law International supplies the global business community with comprehensive English-language international legal information. Legal practitioners, corporate counsel and business executives around the world rely on the Kluwer Law International journals, loose-leafs, books and electronic products for authoritative information in many areas of international legal practice.

Loislaw is a premier provider of digitized legal content to small law firm practitioners of various specializations. Loislaw provides attorneys with the ability to quickly and efficiently find the necessary legal information they need, when and where they need it, by facilitating access to primary law as well as state-specific law, records, forms and treatises.

Wolters Kluwer Law & Business, a unit of Wolters Kluwer, is headquartered in New York and Riverwoods, Illinois. Wolters Kluwer is a leading multinational publisher and information services company.

To Lon Fuller, for inspiring generations of contracts scholars

CONTENTS

Preface: Answering the Great Questions of Contract Law

The study of contract law in the first year of law school presents students and their teachers with a host of fascinating — or at least vexatious — questions: What is a promise? How should the default rules of contract law be chosen? Which promises should be enforced? Why is there a doctrine of consideration? What purpose is served by the doctrine of promissory estoppel? When should someone be excused from a contractual obligation? What is the appropriate form of relief for breach of contract? What is the appropriate measure of money damages? When should parol evidence be considered by a court?

These are among the great questions of contract law. Although no student escapes the first year of contracts without confronting them, many students are never exposed to the answers provided by generations of contracts scholars. The fact that you are reading this page means that you or your professor (or both) are interested in these answers. In the chapters that follow, you will read articles that have achieved the status of "classics" as well as more recent writings that criticize them or that present their own novel answers. For most questions, more than one answer appears to give you a taste of the existing scholarly debate and permit you to compare competing approaches.

The Fourth Edition represents a substantial reboot of this collection. Writings by a new generation of contracts scholars are now featured alongside the favorites from previous editions and a few new contributions by more senior scholars. In Chapter 2, Marco Jimenez offers his take on efficient breach. There is a new Chapter 3 on how default rules should be chosen with excerpts of articles by Ian Ayres and Robert Gertner and by me. A new section of Chapter 9 is devoted to the continuing discussion of the model of "contract as promise" with writings by Seana Valentine Shiffrin, Charles Fried, and Aditi Bagchi. Chapter 10 now includes Curtis Bridgeman's important defense of Judge Cardozo's analysis of consideration in *Allegheny College v. Chautauqua County Bank*. Chapters 11 and 12 reflect the growing interest in the concept of intent to contract, with articles by Dori Kimel and Gregory Klass. And Chapter 18 features two new contributions to the long-running debate over relational contract theory by Ethan Leib and Dori Kimel.

All the articles in this book were selected and edited to ensure they would be accessible to law students. If your professor does not assign these excerpts to be read before class, as I often do, you might well consider reading them *after* your professor has introduced the relevant issue in class. Once you have wrestled with a problem on your own, you will be in a better position to appreciate how the scholars whose works are included here have attempted to resolve that problem.

Finally, you should realize that the ideas presented by these contract scholars are not just for the idle hours of contracts professors. In practice, a lawyer must operate on three levels: *theory, doctrine,* and *facts.* By "doctrine," I mean the specific legal rules that most people identify as "the law." Although competent lawyers must be able to apply the existing rules to the complex factual circumstances of their clients' situations, doctrine and facts are not enough. Lawyers and judges must also have a grasp of how the rules "hang together" in a coherent framework. Only in this way can they *predict* what the rules are before looking them up—which is of great assistance in guiding their legal research and making quick decisions on their feet. And only in this way can they make legal claims when there is no doctrine on their side, or when the doctrine is in conflict with their position. In sum, while competent lawyers know the rules, excellent lawyers understand how the rules fit together and why they are warranted. And legal theory provides this understanding.

People are used to making a radical distinction between theory and practice. Everyone has heard and probably used the expression, "It sounds good in theory, but it won't work in practice," but few stop and consider what this expression means. Suppose you have what you think is a pretty good theory of how to build a bridge. You then build the bridge according to your theory and it collapses. Would you not revise your theory, no matter how good it had sounded? Practice revealed your theory to be defective, so your theory has to be revised. Your new theory should sound even better than your original. A theory of bridge building that does not work in practice is a bad theory.

This is because *theories are problem-solving devices*. This aspect of theories has two implications: First, we *evaluate* a theory by seeing how well it solves the problem for which it was conceived. If this is a practical problem — as most legal problems are — then a theory must work in practice to be a good theory. But we do not evaluate theories solely in the abstract. Instead, we compare a theory's problem-solving ability to that of other theories that address the same problem. We then commit ourselves to the "best" of the available theories, knowing that a theory that is better still may yet come along. Second, we *care about* a theory only if we care about the underlying problem it is supposed to address. We simply would have no interest in a bridge-building theory unless, for some reason, we are interested in the problem of building bridges.

In sum, legal theories provide answers to questions that we care about answering — in this case the great questions of contract law. Excellent judges and lawyers, as opposed to merely competent ones, have an intuitive grasp of whole fields of law. In formulating their theories, contract scholars are often simply trying to articulate, evaluate, and reshape these intuitions. Although we would be lost without our intuitions, we know our intuitions are not infallible. Among the many purposes served by a legal education is the opportunity it provides — for some their *only* opportunity — to examine the writings of legal scholars who are trying to improve our intuitions. Reading the contract scholarship in this book can help you refine *your* intuitions about contract law so that they will be sound in practice as well as in theory — and, like a well-built bridge, the legal arguments you construct in class and in practice will stand.

Randy E. Barnett
Georgetown University Law Center

July 2009

ACKNOWLEDGMENTS

My thanks to Professor Marco Jimenez for his insightful feedback on the Third Edition and his suggestions for revisions, many of which I adopted.

Footnotes in the articles have been renumbered consecutively within each article.

Andersen, Eric G., A New Look at Material Breach in the Law of Contracts, 21 U.C. Davis L. Rev. 1073 (1988). Copyright © 1988 by The Regents of the University of California. Reprinted with permission.

Ayes, Ian and Robert Gertner, Filling Gaps in Incomplete Contracts: An Economic Theory of Default Rules, 99 Yale L.J. 87 (1989).

Bagchi, Aditi, Contracts *versus* Promise. © Aditi Bagchi 2009.

Barnett, Randy E., Consenting to Form Contracts, 71 Fordham L. Rev. 627 (2002). Reprinted with permission of Fordham Law Review.

Barnett, Randy E., Rights and Remedies in a Consent Theory of Contract, in Liability and Responsibility (R. G. Frey & Christopher W. Morris, eds.). Copyright © 1991. Reprinted with permission.

Barnett, Randy E., The Sound of Silence: Default Rules and Contractual Consent, 78 Va. L. Rev. 821 (1992).

Fried, Charles, The Convergence of Contract and Promise, 120 Harv. L. Rev. F. 1 (2007).

Friedman, Daniel, The Efficient Breach Fallacy, 18 J. Legal Studies 1 (1989). Copyright © 1989. Reprinted with permission.

Fuller, Lon L., Consideration and Form. This article originally appeared at 41 Colum. L. Rev. 799 (1941). Reprinted with permission.

Fuller, Lon L., and Perdue, William R., Jr., The Reliance Interest in Contract Damages, 46 Yale L.J. 52 (1936). Copyright © 1936. Reprinted with permission of The Yale Law Journal Company and Fred B. Rothman and Company.

Hillman, Robert A., Court Adjustment of Long-Term Contracts: An Analysis Under Modern Contract Law, 1987 Duke L.J. (1987). Copyright © 1987 by Duke University School of Law. Reprinted with permission.

Holmes, Eric Mills, The Four Evolutionary Stages of Promissory Estoppel, from Restatement of Promissory Estoppel, 32 Willamette L. Rev. 263 (1996). Copyright © 1996. Reprinted with permission.

Jimenez, Marco J., The Value of a Promise: A Utilitarian Approach to Contract Law Remedies, 56 UCLA L. Rev. 59 (2008).

Kelly, Michael, The Phantom Reliance Interest, 1992 Wis. L. Rev. 1755 (1992). Copyright © 1992 by The Board of Regents of the University of Wisconsin System. Reprinted by permission of the Wisconsin Law Review.

Kennedy, Duncan, From the Will Theory to the Principle of Private Autonomy: Lon Fuller's "Consideration and Form," 100 Colum. L. Rev. 94, 168-174 (2000). Copyright © 2000. Reprinted with permission.

Kimel, Dori, From Promise to Contract: Towards a Liberal Theory of Contract 136-142 (2005). Copyright © 2003, 2005 Dori Kimel.

Kimel, Dori, The Choice of Paradigm for Theory of Contract: Reflections on the Relational Model, 27 Oxford J. Legal Stud. 233 (2007).

Klass, Gregory, Intent to Contract, 95 Va. L. Rev. (forthcoming).

Knapp, Charles L., Enforcing the Contract to Bargain, 44 N.Y.U. L. Rev. 673 (1969). Copyright © 1969. Reprinted with permission.

Kronman, Anthony T., Disclosure, Information, and the Law of Contracts, 7 J. Legal Studies 1 (1978). Copyright © 1978. Reprinted with permission.

Leib, Ethan J., Contracts and Friendships, 59 Emory Law Journal (forthcoming).

Posner, Richard A., Economic Analysis of Law (4th ed. 1992). Copyright © 1992 by Richard A. Posner. Reprinted with permission.

Rakoff, Todd D., Contracts of Adhesion: An Essay in Reconstruction, 96 Harv. L. Rev. 1173 (1983). Copyright © 1983 by the Harvard Law Review Association. Reprinted with permission.

Ricks, Val D., Mutual Mistake: Half-Civilian Mongrel, Consideration Reincarnate, 58 La. L. Rev. 663 (1998). Reprinted with permission.

Schwartz, Alan, The Case for Specific Performance, 89 Yale L.J. 271 (1979). Copyright © 1979. Reprinted by permission of The Yale Law Journal Company and Fred B. Rothman and Company.

Scott, Robert E., The Case for Formalism in Relational Contract, 94 Nw. U. L. Rev. 847, 847-862, 871-876 (2000). Copyright © 2000. Reprinted with permission.

Shiffrin, Seana Valentine, The Divergence of Contract and Promise, 120 Harv. L. Rev. 708 (2007).

Siprut, Joseph, The Peppercorn Reconsidered: Why a Promise to Sell Blackacre for Nominal Consideration Is Not Binding, But Should Be, 97 Nw. U. L. Rev. 1809 (2003). Reprinted by special permission of Northwestern University School of Law, Northwestern Law Review.

Summers, Robert S., The General Duty of Good Faith, 67 Cornell L. Rev. 810 (1982). Copyright © 1982 by Cornell University. All Rights

Reserved. Reprinted with permission by Cornell University and Fred B. Rothman and Company.

Tiersma, Peter Meijes, On the Nature of Offer, Acceptance, and Promise, 26 U.C. Davis L. Rev. 1 (1992). Copyright © 1992 by The Regents of the University of California. Reprinted with permission.

Williams, Patricia J., Alchemical Notes: Reconstructing Ideals from Deconstructed Rights, 22 Harv. C.R.-C.L. L. Rev. 401, 406-408 (1987). Reprinted with permission.

Yorio, Edward and Thel, Steve, The Promissory Basis of Section 90, 101 Yale L.J. 111, 129-144, 151, 160-167 (1991). Copyright © 1991. Reprinted by permission of The Yale Law Journal Company and William S. Hein Company from The Yale Law Journal, Vol. 101, pages 111-167.

PERSPECTIVES ON CONTRACT LAW

I

ENFORCING PRIVATE AGREEMENTS

HOW SHOULD DAMAGES FOR BREACH OF CONTRACT BE MEASURED?

Traditionally, the normal remedy for breach of contract is an award of monetary damages. Judges and lawyers must decide how much money is appropriate. Fairness to both parties argues against both *over* compensation and *under* compensation. By what standards are we to decide what level of compensation is appropriate?

The term "path-breaking" can be applied to many of the articles in this book. Nonetheless, by consensus, Lon L. Fuller and William R. Perdue's article, *The Reliance Interest in Contract Damages*, is the most famous and oft-cited article on contract law ever written. In it, Fuller and Perdue contend that we cannot ascertain the appropriate measure of damages without understanding the function that contract damage awards are supposed to perform. They identify three purposes or "interests" as central: the expectation interest, the restitution interest, and the reliance interest. This tripartite division of damage interests has come to permeate subsequent judicial decisions and scholarly writings, achieving the status of gospel. Also well-accepted, though more controversial, is their paradoxical contention that the normal award of expectation damages is justified primarily on the ground that it serves the reliance interest.

In a 1983 phone conversation with William Perdue, Professor Jay Feinman confirmed that, although the article was coauthored by Perdue (then a student at Duke Law School, where Fuller taught) Fuller was entirely responsible for the article's theoretical aspects. Perdue was Fuller's research assistant; he performed the case research for the article and did initial drafts of some sections of the article's second part, which concerned existing case law. Following his graduation from Duke, Perdue entered law practice in New York and is now retired. Fuller eventually became the Carter Professor of Jurisprudence at Harvard Law School. He died in 1978 and this book is dedicated to his memory.

Michael Kelly, a law professor at the University of San Diego, has had the temerity to challenge the centrality and even the coherence of the reliance interest concept. In his article, *The Phantom Reliance Interest in Contract Damages*, he claims that there are not one but three distinct concepts of the reliance interest, none of which plays much — if any — role in actual cases. What is called the reliance interest is really a modified version of expectation damages.

Professor Richard Craswell of Stanford Law School goes farther than Professor Kelly to contest Fuller and Perdue's basic approach of assessing damages by looking at the "interests" of the parties to the transaction. Rather, in *Against Fuller and Perdue*, he contends we should consider the incentives for the behavior of these and other parties created by different measures of damages under different factual circumstances. As an alternative to the tripartite interests scheme, Craswell proposes we take the expectation interest as the baseline, and then assess damage awards above or below this baseline depending on the incentives we wish to create.

Study Guide: Study carefully the three damage "interests." Why do you think courts and commentators have found this distinction to be so helpful? According to Fuller and Perdue, why is the expectation interest the normal measure of contract damages? Why do they think that the expectancy should provide a ceiling or "cap" on the recovery of out-of-pocket expenses incurred in reliance on the contract?

THE RELIANCE INTEREST IN CONTRACT DAMAGES*

Lon L. Fuller and William R. Perdue, Jr.

The proposition that legal rules can be understood only with reference to the purposes they serve would today scarcely be regarded as an exciting truth. The notion that law exists as a means to an end has been commonplace for at least half a century. There is, however, no justification for assuming, because this attitude has now achieved respectability, and even triteness, that it enjoys a pervasive application in practice. Certainly there are even today few legal treatises of which it may be said that the author has throughout clearly defined the purposes which his definitions and distinctions serve. We are still all too willing to embrace the conceit that it is possible to manipulate legal concepts without the orientation which comes from the simple inquiry: toward what end is this activity directed? Nietzsche's observation, that the most common stupidity consists in forgetting what one is trying to do, retains a discomforting relevance to legal science.

In no field is this more true than in that of damages. In the assessment of damages the law tends to be conceived, not as a purposive ordering of human affairs, but as a kind of juristic mensuration. The language of the decisions sounds in terms not of command but of discovery. We *measure* the *extent* of the injury; we determine whether it was *caused* by the defendant's act; we *ascertain* whether the plaintiff has included the *same item* of damage twice in his complaint. One unfamiliar with the unstated premises which language of this sort conceals might almost be led to suppose that Rochester produces some ingenious instrument by which these calculations are accomplished.

It is, as a matter of fact, clear that the things which the law of damages purports to "measure" and "determine" — the "injuries," "items of damage," "causal connections," etc. — are in considerable part its own creations, and that the process of "measuring" and "determining" them is really a part of the process of creating them. This is obvious when courts work on the periphery of existing doctrine, but it

---

*From Lon L. Fuller and William R. Perdue, Jr., The Reliance Interest in Contract Damages, Pt. 1, 46 Yale L.J. 52 (1936).

is no less true of fundamental and established principles. For example, one frequently finds the "normal" rule of contract damages (which awards to the promisee the value of the expectancy, "the lost profit") treated as a mere corollary of a more fundamental principle, that the purpose of granting damages is to make "compensation" for injury.[1] Yet in this case we "compensate" the plaintiff by giving him something he never had. This seems on the face of things a queer kind of "compensation." We can, to be sure, make the term "compensation" seem appropriate by saying that the defendant's breach "deprived" the plaintiff of the expectancy. But this is in essence only a metaphorical statement of the effect of the legal rule. In actuality the loss which the plaintiff suffers (deprivation of the expectancy) is not a datum of nature but the reflection of a normative order. It appears as a "loss" only by reference to an unstated *ought*. Consequently, when the law gauges damages by the value of the promised performance it is not merely measuring a quantum, but is seeking an end, however vaguely conceived this end may be.

It is for this reason that it is impossible to separate the law of contract damages from the larger body of motives and policies which constitutes the general law of contracts. It is, unfortunately for the simplicity of our subject, impossible to assume that the purposive and policy-directed element of contract law has been exhausted in the rules which define contract and breach. If this were possible the law of contract damages would indeed be simple, and we would have but one measure of recovery for all contracts. Of course this is not the case. What considerations influence the setting up of different measures of recovery for different kinds of contracts? What factors explain the rather numerous exceptions to the normal rule which measures damages by the value of the expectancy? It is clear that these questions cannot be answered without an inquiry into the reasons which underlie (or may underlie) the enforcement of promises generally.

In our own discussion we shall attempt first an analysis of the purposes which may be pursued in awarding contract damages or in

---

1. "In fixing the amount of these damages, the general purpose of the law is, and should be, to give compensation: — that is, to put the plaintiff in as good a position as he would have been had the defendant kept his contract." Williston, Contracts (1920) §1338.

"enforcing" contracts generally; then we shall attempt to inquire to what extent, and under what circumstances, these purposes have found expression in the decisions and doctrinal discussions. As the title suggests, the primary emphasis will be on what we call "the reliance interest" as a possible measure of recovery in suits for breach of contract.

THE PURPOSES PURSUED IN
AWARDING CONTRACT DAMAGES

It is convenient to distinguish three principal purposes which may be pursued in awarding contract damages. These purposes, and the situations in which they become appropriate, may be stated briefly as follows:

First, the plaintiff has in reliance on the promise of the defendant conferred some value on the defendant. The defendant fails to perform his promise. The court may force the defendant to perform his promise. The court may force the defendant to disgorge the value he received from the plaintiff. The object here may be termed the prevention of gain by the defending promisor at the expense of the promisee; more briefly, the prevention of unjust enrichment. The interest protected may be called the *restitution interest*. For our present purposes it is quite immaterial how the suit in such a case be classified, whether as contractual or quasi-contractual, whether as a suit to enforce the contract or as a suit based upon a rescission of the contract. These questions relate to the superstructure of the law, not to the basic policies with which we are concerned.

Secondly, the plaintiff has in reliance on the promise of the defendant changed his position. For example, the buyer under a contract for the sale of land has incurred expense in the investigation of the seller's title, or has neglected the opportunity to enter other contracts. We may award damages to the plaintiff for the purpose of undoing the harm which his reliance on the defendant's promise has caused him. Our object is to put him in as good a position as he was in before the promise was made. The interest protected in this case may be called the *reliance interest*.

Thirdly, without insisting on reliance by the promisee or enrichment of the promisor, we may seek to give the promisee the value of the expectancy which the promise created. We may in a suit for specific performance actually compel the defendant to render the promised performance to the plaintiff, or, in a suit for damages, we may make the defendant pay the money value of this performance. Here our object is to put the plaintiff in as good a position as he would have occupied had the defendant performed his promise. The interest protected in this case we may call the *expectation interest.*

It will be observed that what we have called the *restitution interest* unites two elements: (1) reliance by the promisee, (2) a resultant gain to the promisor. It may for some purposes be necessary to separate these elements. In some cases a defaulting promisor may after his breach be left with an unjust gain which was not taken from the promisee (a third party furnished the consideration), or which was not the result of reliance by the promisee (the promisor violated a promise not to appropriate the promisee's goods). Even in those cases where the promisor's gain results from the promisee's reliance it may happen that damages will be assessed somewhat differently, depending on whether we take the promisor's gain or the promisee's loss as the standard of measurement. Generally, however, in the cases we shall be discussing, gain by the promisor will be accompanied by a corresponding and, so far as its legal measurement is concerned, identical loss to the promisee, so that for our purposes the most workable classification is one which presupposes in the restitution interest a correlation of promisor's gain and promisee's loss. If, as we shall assume, the gain involved in the restitution interest results from and is identical with the plaintiff's loss through reliance, then the restitution interest is merely a special case of the reliance interest; all of the cases coming under the restitution interest will be covered by the reliance interest, and the reliance interest will be broader than the restitution interest only to the extent that it includes cases where the plaintiff has relied on the defendant's promise without enriching the defendant.

It should not be supposed that the distinction here taken between the reliance and expectation interests coincides with that sometimes taken between "losses caused" (damnum emergens) and "gains prevented" (lucrum cessans). In the first place, though reliance ordinarily results in "losses" of an affirmative nature (expenditures of labor and money) it is also true that opportunities for gain may be foregone in reliance on a promise. Hence the reliance interest must be interpreted as at least potentially covering "gains prevented" as well as "losses caused." (Whether "gains prevented" through reliance on a promise are properly compensable in damages is a question not here determined. Obviously, certain scruples concerning "causality" and "foreseeability" are suggested. It is enough for our present purpose to note that there is nothing in the definition of the reliance interest itself which would exclude items of this sort from consideration.) On the other hand, it is not possible to make the expectation interest entirely synonymous with "gains prevented." The disappointment of an expectancy often entails losses of a positive character.

It is obvious that the three "interests" we have distinguished do not present equal claims to judicial intervention. It may be assumed that ordinary standards of justice would regard the need for judicial intervention as decreasing in the order in which we have listed the three interests. The "restitution interest," involving a combination of unjust impoverishment with unjust gain, presents the strongest case for relief. If, following Aristotle, we regard the purpose of justice as the maintenance of an equilibrium of goods among members of society, the restitution interest presents twice as strong a claim to judicial intervention as the reliance interest, since if A not only causes B to lose one unit but appropriates that unit to himself, the resulting discrepancy between A and B is not one unit but two.

On the other hand, the promisee who has actually relied on the promise, even though he may not thereby have enriched the promisor, certainly presents a more pressing case for relief than the promisee who merely demands satisfaction for his disappointment in not getting what was promised him. In passing from compensation for change of position to compensation for loss of expectancy we pass, to use Aristotle's terms again, from the realm of corrective justice to that of distributive justice. The law no longer seeks merely to heal a disturbed status quo, but to bring into being a new situation. It ceases to act defensively or restoratively, and assumes a more active role. With the transition, the justification for legal relief loses its self-evident quality. It is as a matter of fact no easy thing to explain why the normal rule of contract recovery should be that which measures damages by the value of the promised performance. Since this "normal rule" throws its shadow across our whole subject it will be necessary to examine the possible reasons for its existence. It may be said parenthetically that the discussion which follows, though directed primarily to the normal measure of recovery where damages are sought, also has relevance to the more general question, why should a promise which has not been relied on ever be enforced at all, whether by a decree of specific performance or by an award of damages?

It should also be said that our discussion of "reasons" does not claim to coincide in all particulars with the actual workings of the judicial mind, certainly not with those of any single judicial mind. It is unfortunately very difficult to discuss the possible reasons for rules of law without unwittingly conveying the impression that these "reasons" are the things which control the daily operations of the judicial process. This has had the consequence, at a time when men stand in dread of being labelled "unrealistic," that we have almost ceased to talk about reasons altogether. Those who find unpalatable the rationalistic flavor of what follows are invited to view what they read not as law but as an excursus into legal philosophy, and to make whatever discount that distinction may seem to them to dictate.

WHY SHOULD THE LAW EVER PROTECT THE EXPECTATION INTEREST?

Perhaps the most obvious answer to this question is one which we may label "psychological." This answer would run something as follows: The breach of a promise arouses in the promisee a sense of injury. This feeling is not confined to cases where the promisee has relied on the promise. Whether or not he has actually changed his position because of the promise, the promisee has formed an attitude of expectancy such that a breach of the promise causes him to feel that he has been "deprived" of something which was "his." Since this sentiment is a relatively uniform one, the law has no occasion to go back of it. It accepts it as a datum and builds its rule about it.

The difficulty with this explanation is that the law does in fact go back of the sense of injury which the breach of a promise engenders. No legal system attempts to invest with juristic sanction all promises. Some rule or combination of rules effects a sifting out for enforcement of those promises deemed important enough to society to justify the law's concern with them. Whatever the principles which control this sifting out process may be, they are not convertible into terms of the degree of resentment which the breach of a particular kind of promise arouses. Therefore, though it may be assumed that the impulse to assuage disappointment is one shared by those who make and influence the law, this impulse can hardly be regarded as the key which solves the whole problem of the protection accorded by the law to the expectation interest.

A second possible explanation for the rule protecting the expectancy may be found in the much-discussed "will theory" of contract law. This theory views the contracting parties as exercising, so to speak, a legislative power, so that the legal enforcement of a contract becomes merely an implementing by the state of a kind of private law already established by the parties. If *A* has made, in proper form, a promise to pay *B* one thousand dollars, we compel *A* to pay this sum simply because the rule or *lex* set up by the parties calls for this payment. Uti lingua nuncupassit, ita jus esto.[2]

It is not necessary to discuss here the contribution which the will theory is capable of making to a philosophy of contract law. Certainly some borrowings from the theory are discernible in most attempts to rationalize the bases of contract liability. It is enough to note here that while the will theory undoubtedly has some bearing on the problem of contract damages, it cannot be regarded as dictating in all cases a recovery of the expectancy. If a contract represents a kind of private law, it is a law which usually says nothing at all about what shall be done when it is violated. A contract is in this respect like an imperfect statute which provides no penalties, and which leaves it to the courts to find a way to effectuate its purposes. There would, therefore, be no necessary contradiction between the will theory and a rule which limited damages to the reliance interest. Under such a rule the penalty for violating the norm established by the contract would simply consist in being compelled to compensate the other party for detrimental reliance. Of course there may be cases where the parties have so obviously anticipated that a certain form of judicial relief will be given that we can, without stretching things, say that by implication they have "willed" that this relief should be given. This attitude finds a natural application to promises to pay a definite sum of money. But certainly as to most types of contracts it is vain to expect from the will theory a ready-made solution for the problem of damages.

---

2. "A legal transaction is the exercise of the creative power which the private will possesses in legal matters. The individual commands, and the law adopts his command as its own." Windscheid, Lehrbuch Des Pandektenrechts (9th ed. 1906) §68, n.la.

A third and more promising solution of our difficulty lies in an economic or institutional approach. The essence of a credit economy lies in the fact that it tends to eliminate the distinction between present and future (promised) goods. Expectations of future values become, for purposes of trade, present values. In a society in which credit has become a significant and pervasive institution, it is inevitable that the expectancy created by an enforceable promise should be regarded as a kind of property, and breach of the promise as an injury to that property. In such a society the breach of a promise works an "actual" diminution of the promisee's assets — "actual" in the sense that it would be so appraised according to modes of thought which enter into the very fiber of our economic system. That the promisee had not "used" the property which the promise represents (had not relied on the promise) is as immaterial as the question whether the plaintiff in trespass *quare clausum fregit* was using his property at the time it was encroached upon. The analogy to ordinary forms of property goes further, for even in a suit for trespass the recovery is really for an expectancy, an expectancy of possible future uses. Where the property expectancy is limited (as where the plaintiff has only an estate for years) the recovery is reduced accordingly. Ordinary property differs from a contract right chiefly in the fact that it lies within the power of more persons to work a direct injury to the expectancy it represents. It is generally only the promisor or some one working through or upon him who is able to injure the contract expectancy in a direct enough manner to make expedient legal intervention.

The most obvious objection which can be made to the economic or institutional explanation is that it involves a *petito principii*. A promise has present value, why? Because the law enforces it. "The expectancy," regarded as a present value, is not the cause of legal intervention but the consequence of it. This objection may be reinforced by a reference to legal history. Promises were enforced long before there was anything corresponding to a general system of "credit," and recovery was from the beginning measured by the value of the promised performance, the "agreed price." It may therefore be argued that the "credit system" when it finally emerged was itself in large part built on the foundations of a juristic development which preceded it.

The view just suggested asserts the primacy of law over economics; it sees law not as the creature but as the creator of social institutions. The shift of emphasis thus implied suggests the possibility of a fourth explanation for the law's protection of the unrelied-on expectancy, which we may call *juristic*. This explanation would seek a justification for the normal rule of recovery in some policy consciously pursued by courts and other lawmakers. It would assume that courts have protected the expectation interest because they have considered it wise to do so, not through a blind acquiescence in habitual ways of thinking and feeling, or through an equally blind deference to the individual will. Approaching the problem from this point of view, we are forced to find not a mere explanation for the rule in the form of some sentimental, volitional, or institutional datum, but articulate reasons for its existence.

What reasons can be advanced? In the first place, even if our interest were confined to protecting promises against an out-of-pocket loss, it would still be possible to justify the rule granting the value of the expectancy, both as a cure for, and as a prophylaxis against, losses of this sort.

It is a cure for these losses in the sense that it offers the measure of recovery most likely to reimburse the plaintiff for the (often very numerous and very difficult to prove) individual acts and forbearances which make up his total reliance on the contract. If we take into account "gains prevented" by reliance, that is, losses involved in foregoing the opportunity to enter other contracts, the notion that the rule protecting the expectancy is adopted as the most effective means of compensating for detrimental reliance seems not at all far-fetched. Physicians with an extensive practice often charge their patients the full office call fee for broken appointments. Such a charge looks on the face of things like a claim to the promised fee; it seems to be based on the "expectation interest." Yet the physician making the charge will quite justifiably regard it as compensation for the loss of an opportunity to gain a similar fee from a different patient. This foregoing of other opportunities is involved to some extent in entering most contracts, and the impossibility of subjecting this type of reliance to any kind of measurement may justify a categorical rule granting the value of the expectancy as the most effective way of compensating for such losses.

The rule that the plaintiff must after the defendant's breach take steps to mitigate damages tends to corroborate the suspicion that there lies hidden behind the protection of the expectancy a concern to compensate the plaintiff for the loss of the opportunity to enter other contracts. Where after the defendant's breach the opportunity remains open to the plaintiff to sell his services or goods elsewhere, or to fill his needs from another source, he is bound to embrace that opportunity. Viewed in this way the rule of "avoidable harms" is a qualification on the protection accorded the expectancy, since it means that the plaintiff, in those cases where it is applied, is protected only to the extent that he has in reliance on the contract foregone other equally advantageous opportunities for accomplishing the same end.

But, as we have suggested, the rule measuring damages by the expectancy may also be regarded as a prophylaxis against the losses resulting from detrimental reliance. Whatever tends to discourage breach of contract tends to prevent the losses occasioned through reliance. Since the expectation interest furnishes a more easily administered measure of recovery than the reliance interest, it will in practice offer a more effective sanction against contract breach. It is therefore possible to view the rule measuring damages by the expectancy in a quasi-criminal aspect, its purpose being not so much to compensate the promisee as to penalize breach of promise by the promisor. The rule enforcing the unrelied-on promise finds the same justification, on this theory, as an ordinance which fines a man for driving through a stop-light when no other vehicle is in sight.

In seeking justification for the rule granting the value of the expectancy there is no need, however, to restrict ourselves by the assumption, hitherto made, that the rule can only be intended to cure or prevent the losses caused by reliance. A justification can be developed from a less negative point of view. It may be said that there is not only a policy in favor of preventing and undoing the harms resulting from reliance, but also a policy in favor of promoting and facilitating reliance on business agreements. As in the case of the stop-light ordinance we are interested not only in preventing collisions but in speeding traffic. Agreements can accomplish little, either for their makers or for society, unless they are made the basis for action. When business agreements are not only made but are also acted on, the division of labor is facilitated, goods find their way to the places where they are most needed, and economic activity is generally stimulated. These advantages would be threatened by any rule which limited legal protection to the reliance interest. Such a rule would in practice tend to discourage reliance. The difficulties in proving reliance and subjecting it to pecuniary measurement are such that the business man knowing, or sensing, that these obstacles stood in the way of judicial relief would hesitate to rely on a promise in any case where the legal sanction was of significance to him. To encourage reliance we must therefore dispense with its proof. For this reason it has been found wise to make recovery on a promise independent of reliance, both in the sense that in some cases the promise is enforced though not relied on (as in the bilateral business agreement) and in the sense that recovery is not limited to the detriment incurred in reliance.

The juristic explanation in its final form is then twofold. It rests the protection accorded the expectancy on (1) the need for curing and preventing the harms occasioned by reliance, and (2) on the need for facilitating reliance on business agreements. From this spelling out of a possible juristic explanation, it is clear that there is no incompatibility between it and the economic or institutional explanation. They view the same phenomenon from two different aspects. The essence of both of them lies in the word "credit." The economic explanation views credit from its institutional side; the juristic explanation views it from its rational side. The economic view sees credit as an accepted way of living; the juristic view invites us to explore the considerations of utility which underlie this way of living, and the part which conscious human direction has played in bringing it into being. . . .

THE DIVERGENCE OF MEASURE
AND MOTIVE AND THE PROBLEM
OF MIXED MOTIVES

We have already intimated the nature of the principal difficulty which is encountered in any analysis of the purposes of contract law. This difficulty consists in the fact that it is impossible to assume that when a court enforces a promise it necessarily pursues only one purpose and protects one "interest," or that the purpose or interest which forms the rationale of the court's action necessarily furnishes the measure of the promisee's recovery.[3] In actuality not only may a court consider itself in a given case as vindicating more than one of the three contract "interests" we have distinguished, but even where it is reasonable to

---

3. A failure to take into account what may be called motivational cross-currents seems to constitute the principal defect of Professor Cohen's valuable article, The Basis of Contract, 46 Harv. L. Rev. 553 (1933).

suppose that a single interest furnishes the exclusive *raison d'etre* of legal intervention it is still possible that for reasons of convenience and certainty the court may choose a measure of recovery which differs from that suggested by the interest protected. . . .

With this preliminary survey of the three contract interests, we are now ready to turn our attention more directly to the interest which is the chief subject of this inquiry, the reliance interest.

THE RELATION BETWEEN THE RELIANCE INTEREST AND THE OTHER CONTRACT INTERESTS

The abstract definitions which we have given of the three contract "interests" would seem on casual reading to be mutually exclusive. Yet here as everywhere in the law we are plagued by the borderline cases. Not only does there exist, as we have shown in our last section, an ambiguity concerning these interests from a psychological or motivational point of view, so that it is difficult to tell which of them a court is "really" seeking to vindicate, but there is also an ambiguity in them even from an analytical or definitional point of view.

The reliance interest is, as we have already pointed out, generally broad enough to cover all of the cases coming under the restitution interest. It is also broad enough to embrace some cases not covered by that interest. The problem of the relation between these two interests hinges, therefore, chiefly on the problem of defining this surplus area of the reliance interest. Since this area consists of the cases in which the promisee has detrimentally relied on a promise without thereby benefiting the promisor, it is obvious that the extent of this area will depend upon the scope given the concept "benefit." If we define benefit narrowly by insisting on an "actual" increase in the promisor's "assets" then the field of cases covered by the reliance interest but excluded from the restitution interest will be relatively large. Thus if *A* were hired by *B* to cast spells, we might, assuming *A* devoted himself assiduously to his task, be able to find detrimental reliance by *A* without any corresponding "benefit" to *B*. At the other extreme lies a conception which would view as a "benefit" anything for which the promisor bargained and was willing to pay a price. If this conception of "benefit" were accepted in its extreme form only a relatively narrow field would be left for the reliance interest. Any bargained-for reliance would automatically fall within the restitution interest. Excluded from the restitution interest we should find only two kinds of reliance: (1) reliance on promises which are not bargains (as under §90 of the Contracts Restatement), and (2) unbargained-for reliance on bargain promises (reliance "outside the contract," as for example in "passing up" other offers). The field occupied by these two types of reliance would, so far as legal effect is concerned, be even further narrowed by the application of such notions as "causality" and "foreseeability." Hence it is clear that any conception which made "benefit" equivalent to "bargained-for act" would leave only an extremely limited field as the exclusive hegemony of the reliance interest.

The inescapable flexibility of the concept "benefit" means that drawing the line between the reliance and restitution interests is in the end a rather arbitrary affair. By substituting for "benefit" a stricter term like "enrichment" we shift the line in one direction; by substituting a looser term like "performance received by the promisor" we shift it in the other. In view of the fact that the line is set ultimately by a kind of definitional fiat it is remarkable that it should have become customary to think of restitution as a remedy entirely distinct from the usual suit on a contract. Where "the contract" is regarded as furnishing a kind of conduit for the ordinary suit, it becomes an obstruction in the way of restitution and must be removed by "rescission." That in this legal hydromechanics sight should be lost of the purposes underlying the remedies involved can occasion no wonder. . . .

In distinguishing between the reliance and the expectation interests we encounter not so much a shifting line of division as a miscellaneous group of cases which seem equally happy in either category. These two interests will furnish identical, or nearly identical, measures of recovery in at least three kinds of cases.

First, where the plaintiff's reliance takes the form of acts essential to the enforcement of the contract by him (such as partial performance of the contract or necessary preparations to perform) and the defendant breaks or repudiates the contract before complete performance has taken place, it is possible to classify the plaintiff's suit as resting either on the expectation interest alone, or on a combination of the expectation and reliance interests. If a building contractor has finished half the structure when the property owner puts an end to the contract the contractor's declaration may list two items of damage: (1) expenditures actually made in performing or preparing to perform, and (2) the profit which he would have made on the whole contract. This looks like a combination of the reliance and the expectation interests, and it will necessarily be so analyzed if we restrict the scope of the expectation interest to what may be called the net expectancy, in other words, if we make "the expectation interest" and "the lost profit" synonymous. But in cases where the plaintiff has undertaken performance or preparations to perform a profitable contract before the defendant's breach it involves no distortion to say that the plaintiff's expectancy is really twofold and includes (1) reimbursement for what has been done, and (2) a profit in addition. This broader expectancy we may call the *gross expectation interest*. Using this broader concept the contractor's suit in the case supposed will appear to be founded entirely on the expectation interest. The possibility of subsuming a recovery for the value of part performance under the expectation interest is indicated by the fact that it is possible to state, entirely in terms of the expectancy, measures of recovery which would, if all the relevant data were available, yield the same sum as the formula measuring recovery by the reasonable value of what has been done plus the profit. Examples of such measures would be: (a) payment for work done at the contract rate, plus the profit lost on the unperformed portion of the contract, (b) the full contract price less the cost of completion.

Secondly, where the reliance interest is conceived to embrace the loss of the opportunity to enter similar contracts with other persons, the reliance and expectation interests will have a tendency to approach one another, the precise degree of their correspondence depending upon the extent to which other opportunities of a similar nature were open to the plaintiff when he entered the contract on which suit is brought. The physician who by making one appointment deprives himself of the opportunity of making a precisely similar appointment with another patient presents a case of a complete correspondence between the reliance and expectation interests. The tendency of the expectation and reliance interests to coalesce in cases of this sort has the consequence that the same item of damages may often be classified under either heading. Thus where the defendant's breach of contract results in the plaintiff's property remaining idle for a period, the courts in awarding the plaintiff the rental value of the premises have sometimes considered that they were granting reimbursement for the loss of opportunity to employ the property for other purposes (the reliance interest), and sometimes that they were granting compensation for the loss of the profits which would have been made had the defendant performed his promise (expectation interest).

Thirdly, the reliance and the expectation interests will coincide in those cases where the breach of a contract results not simply in the loss of the promised value but in some direct harm. A farmer buys a cow warranted to be free from disease. The cow is in fact diseased and contaminates the purchaser's whole herd. So far as the item of direct loss is concerned (the contamination of the herd) it is not possible to draw a distinction between the reliance and the expectation interests. This loss would not have occurred either if the defendant had not broken his contract, or if the plaintiff had not entered and relied on the contract.

SHOULD THE EXPECTATION INTEREST
SET THE LIMIT OF RECOVERY?

In the contracts upon which suit is brought the value of the expectancy ordinarily exceeds the reliance interest. It is possible, however, that the reliance interest may offer the plaintiff a more generous measure of recovery than the expectation interest. In such cases should the value of the expectancy be regarded as setting a limit on recovery? The sections of the German Civil Code which accord protection to the reliance interest provide that the recovery shall in no event exceed the expectation interest. The covert treatment accorded the reliance interest in our law makes it impossible to expect so explicit and general an answer to the problem as it arises in the common law. There are not lacking, however, intimations of a view similar to that taken in the German Code. Is there any basis for this notion that recovery based on reliance should never be allowed to exceed the value of the expectancy? . . .

To pass on this question it is necessary to inquire what things may bring it about that the reliance interest exceeds the "reasonable value" of the defendant's promised performance. The most obvious possibility is that the plaintiff has entered a losing contract. A manufacturer has undertaken to construct a machine for $1,000 failing to foresee that it will be necessary at a cost of $1,500 to tear down and replace a wall of his plant in order to remove the machine when it is completed. If the manufacturer here should seek to recover the full reliance interest ($1,500 plus the cost of materials and labor on the machine) the obvious objection might seem to be that he is trying to shift the burden of his own improvidence to the other party. In answer it may be pointed out that he will have no opportunity to do this unless the other party has first been guilty of a breach of contract. If the buyer promptly pays the $1,000 agreed upon as the purchase price no suit by the manufacturer will be possible; if the manufacturer is going to be able to sue at all, it will be because the purchaser is in default. The question then really becomes, should default by the defendant have the consequence of entitling the plaintiff to shift to him the loss which he would have suffered if the defendant had performed the contract? Is this a proper penalty to impose for contract breach? Probably in most cases it would not be so regarded. . . .

But does an excess of the reliance over the expectation interest necessarily imply that the plaintiff has entered a losing bargain? In the old case of Nurse v. Barns the defendant "in consideration of £10" promised to give the plaintiff the use of certain premises for a period of six months. Relying on this promise the plaintiff laid in a stock of goods. The defendant then failed to perform his promise. Because his expenditures for goods were thus rendered vain the plaintiff lost £500, which he was permitted to recover from the defendant. Here there was nothing to indicate that the plaintiff entered a losing bargain; on the contrary it was expressly found that the lease was worth just what the plaintiff agreed to pay for it.

It is obvious that we need a distinction between the two types of reliance. Certain acts of reliance are in a loose sense the "price" of whatever benefits the contract may involve for the plaintiff. This type of reliance we shall call "essential reliance." Under this heading would be included the performance of express and implied conditions in bilateral contracts, the performance of the act requested by an offer for a unilateral contract, preparations to perform in both of the cases just mentioned, and the losses involved in entering the contract itself, as, for instance, in foregoing the opportunity to enter other profitable contracts. As to this kind of reliance ("essential reliance") if we do not limit recovery by the "contract price" we are permitting the plaintiff to shift to the defendant his own contractual losses, when the defendant is guilty of nothing more reprehensible than breach of contract.

In contrast to "essential reliance" is the kind of reliance involved in Nurse v. Barns, which we shall call "incidental reliance." The plaintiff's reliance there (laying in a stock of goods) followed naturally, and, we may assume, foreseeably, from the contract. It did not, however, consist of acts necessary to the perfection of the plaintiff's rights on the contract; it cannot be regarded as the "price" of the defendant's performance. To shift the burden of such reliance to the defendant in an amount exceeding "the full contract price" is not to shift to the defendant the plaintiff's contractual losses. In such a case therefore there appears no valid reason to limit the plaintiff's recovery by the expectation interest measured "objectively." If there is to be any limit at all it must be according to some standard more generous than the "contract price."

Should there be any limit on recovery in cases like Nurse v. Barns? Suppose it had been shown in that case that the business contemplated by the plaintiff would have been operated at a loss and that this loss would have exceeded the amount which the plaintiff sought to recover as reimbursement for his reliance. If the plaintiff is in such a situation permitted to recover, it is obvious that we are in effect shifting to the defendant the loss which the plaintiff would have incurred in the venture undertaken in reliance on the contract. To prevent this we must limit the plaintiff's recovery by the expectation interest measured "subjectively," that is, with reference to the profit or loss reasonably to be anticipated from the completed business. In practice this limitation will be of slight significance since in cases like Nurse v. Barns it will seldom be possible to judge with any accuracy what the fate of the venture would have been had it not been interrupted by the defendant's failure to perform his contract.

We may summarize the conclusions reached so far in the following terms. A claim based upon "essential reliance" should normally be limited by the expectation interest measured "objectively," because an excess of the reliance interest over the reasonable value of the thing promised by the defendant would indicate that the plaintiff had entered a losing bargain. To permit a recovery beyond the "full contract price" would be to permit the plaintiff to shift his contractual losses to the defendant. Where "incidental reliance" is involved there is no reason to limit recovery by "the full contract price," that is, the "objective" expectancy. On the other hand, the plaintiff should no more be permitted to shift to the defendant the losses incurred in a venture undertaken in reliance on the contract than he should be permitted to compel the defendant to stand the loss he incurred in entering the contract itself. Accordingly, in cases where reimbursement for "incidental reliance" is sought recovery should be limited by the expectation interest measured "subjectively." In practice this limitation will generally be too indefinite, however, to be of great significance. All of these points are contained by implication in a very simple formula: *We will not in a suit for reimbursement for losses incurred in reliance on a contract knowingly put the plaintiff in a better position than he would have occupied had the contract been fully performed.* . . .

STUDY GUIDE: *Why does Professor Kelly call the reliance interest a "phantom"? What does he propose take its place when the normal expectation measure is too uncertain to be calculated?*

THE PHANTOM RELIANCE INTEREST
IN CONTRACT DAMAGES*

Michael B. Kelly

In 1936 Fuller and Perdue revolutionized the way scholars thought about contract damages by publishing their seminal work, The Reliance Interest in Contract Damages. They identified three basic interests contract law might seek to protect: the restitution interest, the reliance interest, and the expectation interest. This taxonomy continues to provide the foundation for discussions of contract damages. They pointed out that purpose and practice need not mirror one another, that courts could employ rules couched in the language of one interest as a means of pursuing the normative goals dictated by another. Penetrating behind the language courts used to decide contract cases, they argued that the reliance interest provided the normative justification for contract remedies calculated using expectation measures. Damage awards that permitted the plaintiff to recover profit merely used profit as a proxy for the gains prevented because one party, in reliance on a promise,

---

*From Michael B. Kelly, The Phantom Reliance Interest in Contract Damages, 1992 Wis. L. Rev. 1755.

elected to forego other opportunities that would have produced similar profit.

The dominance of the expectation interest virtually compelled Fuller and Perdue to claim a subtle role for the reliance interest. The expectation interest is and was "the basic principle for the measurement of [contract] damages."[1] Yet by divorcing purpose from practice, Fuller and Perdue created the reliance interest as a phantom. The language of courts did not reveal it. It operated, if at all, as an invisible, unacknowledged force that explained contract damage awards. It lurked in the shadows of judicial reasoning, motivating recoveries that courts naively attributed to the expectation interest.

Not content with this invisible role, Fuller and Perdue described situations in which the reliance interest deserved explicit recognition. Having identified this powerful explanation of contract law, they sought ways in which it might apply directly to produce better reasoned damage awards. By expressly recognizing the reliance interest as a third option, intermediate between restitution and expectation, they found a compromise alternative to the all or nothing version of contract remedies advanced by Williston in the Restatement of Contracts.

Scholars have resoundingly endorsed and extended this enterprise. They refer to the Fuller and Perdue work as a "landmark," the most influential piece of contract scholarship in this century. The Second Restatement of Contracts accepted many of Fuller and Perdue's suggestions. Contracts casebooks recognize the possibility of denying recovery for the plaintiff's expectation. Cases cite Fuller and Perdue as authority for limited recoveries. Some scholars, suggesting that the reliance interest offers the only legitimate basis for enforcing contracts, have proposed expanding the role of reliance as a measure of recovery.

Despite scholarly acclaim, the reliance interest plays virtually no role in the calculation of damages in contract cases. A recent survey of cases awarding damages based on promissory estoppel found that, even in this bastion of the reliance interest, courts generally award the expectation interest when it can be ascertained with the requisite degree

---

1. E. Allan Farnsworth, Contracts §12.8 (2d ed. 1990) (also, §12.16 refers to the reliance interest as an "Alternative Measure of Damages"); John E. Murray, Murray on Contracts §117 (3d ed. 1990) ("the expectation interest is paramount in contract remedies"). . . .

of certainty. The reliance interest may play a modest role, filling in as an ascertainable measure of damages when, for whatever reason, the court refuses to award the full expectation interest. Yet even when courts deny recovery of the expectation interest for lack of certainty, the award frequently represents an effort to come as close as possible to the expectation interest rather than recourse to a different theoretical framework.

This Article rejects the reliance interest as a measure of contract damages.[2] As applied by the courts, the reliance interest does not fulfill the normative goals defined by Fuller and Perdue. In creating the reliance interest, Fuller and Perdue divorced purpose and practice more completely than they ever admitted; they divorced the reliance interest as applied from the reliance interest as defined. Only the mystique surrounding the reliance interest and the confusing use of that title to describe several different approaches conceal the remarkable differences between the reliance interest in theory and the reliance interest in practice. . . .

I.   THE METAMORPHOSIS OF
THE RELIANCE INTEREST

Fuller and Perdue defined the theoretical ideal of the reliance interest: the position the plaintiff (or nonbreaching party) would have occupied if the contract had not been formed. Their normative justification of the reliance interest rested on that ideal construct. . . .

. . . Throughout their article, Fuller and Perdue use the phrase as if it had a single meaning. They placed *the* reliance interest as a middle step in a three part taxonomy of interests in contract law. They created one normative justification for the reliance interest. They entitled their article The Reliance Interest in Contract Damages.

---

2. The Article focuses only on contract damages. As a normative theory, the reliance interest might explain other aspects of contract law, such as the selection of which promises to enforce. In addition, reliance expenditures may play a role when courts calculate restitution recoveries.

But the taxonomy created by Fuller and Perdue contains too few categories. . . . The reliance interest breaks down into three different subdivisions:

(1) *The Pure Reliance Interest*, measured by the position the plaintiff would have occupied if the defendant had not entered the contract, including lost opportunities;

(2) *Reliance Limited by Expectation*, measured by the pure reliance interest, unless the pure reliance interest would exceed the expectation interest, in which case recovery would be limited to the expectation interest;

(3) *The Expenditure Measure*, awarding out-of-pocket expenditures (but denying any compensation for either profit or lost opportunities), unless out-of-pocket expenditures would exceed the expectation interest, in which case recovery would be limited to the expectation interest.

To understand the reliance interest in practice, one must consider which of the reliance interests is under consideration.

The multiple meanings attached to "the reliance interest" cloud the usefulness of that interest in considering contract damages. Fuller and Perdue built their normative justification for the reliance interest around the pure reliance interest. But that interest would permit recovery of amounts in excess of the expectation interest, producing damage awards virtually no one supports. Thus, Fuller and Perdue spent little time discussing the pure reliance interest as a practical remedy. It receded early in their article.

Reliance limited by expectation might garner more support but in practice almost never differs from expectation. As long as the actual contract presents the only practical estimate of the value of opportunities foregone, the expectation interest will dominate recoveries. Cases in which lost opportunities supplant the expectation interest are exceedingly rare. The reliance interest only explains cases when it coincides with the expectation interest. This suggests that continued reference to the reliance interest adds nothing to practical consideration of contract damage awards.

More significant, however, is the fascination of scholars with the expenditure measure. Almost invariably, suggestions that courts employ "the reliance interest" mean courts should deny plaintiff profits (in some or all cases). Fuller and Perdue urged that result in part 2 of their article. Farnsworth suggested it in his well-regarded treatise on contract law. Courts seeking to apply the reliance interest frequently simply add up the expenses and stop, as if that were the complete and only inquiry before them.

The failure to acknowledge the difference between the reliance interest defined by Fuller and Perdue and the expenditure measure leaves the reliance interest in a normative limbo. Whatever justification one might devise for putting the plaintiff in the position she would have occupied if the contract had never been formed, one cannot transfer that justification automatically to a recovery defined by the position the plaintiff would have occupied if the contract had been performed, but without the profit (if any) she would have gained from that performance. The sole purpose of this measure is to reduce the size of recoveries, a purpose that does not justify itself and seems to lack any tie to an accepted theory of contract law.

Consider the practical implications of each subcategory, assuming (with Fuller and Perdue) that lost opportunities cannot be measured independently but must be estimated by reference to profit on the actual contract. Each measure then can be recharacterized:

(1) *The Pure Reliance Interest* becomes *Expectation or Expenditures, whichever is higher*: Award the expectation interest (as an estimate of reliance including lost opportunities) unless the expenditures exceed expectation, in which case all expenditures are recoverable (since they would not have been incurred but for the promise).

(2) *Reliance Limited by Expectation* becomes *The Expectation Interest*: Award the expectation interest, either as an estimate of reliance including lost opportunities or as a limit on recovery of expenditures in losing contracts.

(3) *The Expenditure Measure* becomes *Expectation or Expenditures, whichever is lower*: Award the expenditures incurred, unless the expectation interest would produce a smaller recovery, in which case expectation serves as a limit on the recovery of expenditures.

The Expenditure Measure thus produces a curious rule: Courts should award the smallest recovery they can rationalize, choosing either the plaintiff's expenditures or the expectation interest. The rule lacks any obvious normative justification, any link to the plaintiff's precontract position. Yet that is the rule courts and scholars urge when they speak of the reliance interest.

It seems difficult to justify either the first or the third approach, once the practical implications are recognized. Each involves an incredibly one-sided remedy, forcing one party to bear the risk of a bad deal without benefiting from the converse risk of a good deal. The pure reliance interest puts that risk on the defendant, who must pay all of the plaintiff's expenditures if the plaintiff made a bad deal, and pay expenditures plus profit if the plaintiff made a good deal. Conversely, the expenditure measure places the same burden on the plaintiff, who must bear any losses for a bad deal, yet cannot receive the benefits of a good deal.

Contract law revolves around agreements among parties allocating the risks of a business transaction. A measure of damages that allocates the risks entirely to one party overlooks that central function of contracts. The expectation interest permits the parties to allocate risks among themselves and enforces that allocation. The pure reliance interest retains at least some recognition of the risk allocation function by permitting the nonbreaching party to recover if she could have guarded against the risk the breaching party assumed by dealing with a different party originally. It may afford the plaintiff too much protection by also relieving her of risks she assumed under the agreement. The expenditure measure, however, deprives the plaintiff of any protection against the risks she allocated to the other party. She cannot enforce the deal she made, nor can she recover her opportunity to obtain protection from a different contract partner. By consistently favoring the breaching party, the expenditure measure loses any connection to the normative theory Fuller and Perdue espoused — or any plausible normative explanation of contract law. . . .

III.   QUESTIONING THE NORMATIVE GOALS OF THE RELIANCE INTEREST

As noted above, reliance scholars almost never support the pure reliance interest. They uniformly deviate from the retrospective focus of the reliance interest in one class of cases: when the plaintiff entered a bad contract with the defendant.[3] In those situations, they argue that the expectation interest should serve as a limit on the plaintiff's recovery.

I intend no criticism of the result produced by limiting recoveries to the expectation interest. The arguments favoring this approach have persuaded courts and scholars for over a century. Indeed, this Article argues that the expectation interest dominates contract damage awards, necessarily producing the same result.

A problem arises, however, when one tries to reconcile this result with the reliance interest as defined by Fuller and Perdue. While the result flows easily from an expectation theory, it seems a square expectation peg forced into a round reliance hole when it appears in Fuller and Perdue's work. Nothing in the normative theory of restoring the precontract position explains the result. Fuller and Perdue do not argue that the plaintiff would have lost the money spent in reliance even if the defendant had not entered into the contract. Thus, the normative call for compensating the plaintiff for all expenditures and lost opportunities seems equally strong in cases involving bad contracts.

This limitation suggests that the reliance interest selected an inappropriate goal at the very first stage of its analysis. The reliance interest looks backward, seeking to restore to the plaintiff all the assets, including opportunities, she possessed at the time she entered the contract. The expectation interest takes a fundamentally different view of the plaintiff's rightful position. It looks forward, seeking to secure for the plaintiff all the assets (or liabilities) she would have possessed at the time both parties completed performance.

Willingness to deviate from the reliance interest's goal casts doubt on the desirability of that goal in the first place. Imposing an inherently prospective limitation on an inherently retrospective remedy seems inconsistent. One devoted to restoration of the past steps out of character to admit an exception based only on what the future would have brought. If courts should employ a prospective measure to bad contracts, perhaps they should employ a prospective measure to all contracts.

The doubts increase as one recognizes that courts, even if following reliance theory, do precisely that — they employ a prospective measure

---

3. I shall use "bad contracts" to refer to both losing contracts and contracts that produce smaller profits than alternatives the plaintiff could have obtained.

for all contracts. The prospective limitation collapses the reliance interest into the expectation interest. When the contract would be profitable, courts should award the expectation interest (ostensibly because profit serves as a surrogate for the opportunities the plaintiff relinquished to enter the contract). When the contract would generate a loss, the court should award the expectation interest (to prevent parties from becoming better off after a breach than they would have been if the contract had been performed). The reliance interest compromises its mission just at the point that it begins to differ from expectation. When, exactly, does the reliance interest produce a better recovery?

Fuller and Perdue do not explain why one set of contracts deserves different treatment. Nor do they explain why the identifying feature of that different set is the prospect of loss, a fact completely divorced from the nature or extent of the reliance involved. The problem is complex, for the justification requires two points. One cannot stop at proving that the expectation measure should apply to bad contracts. Alone, those reasons imply that the expectation measure should apply to all contracts. Nor can one simply show that the reliance measure should apply to some contracts, for the reasons again apply to all contracts. . . .

IV.   A PRACTICAL APPROACH
TO CONTRACT DAMAGES

Eliminating the reliance interest from the language of contract damages may leave a void in the way courts conceptualize contract remedies. Courts frequently resort to "the reliance interest" as an "alternative" measure of damages in cases where they cannot or will not award the plaintiff lost profits, such as when the plaintiff cannot prove with reasonable certainty that the venture would have produced a profit. Any proposal to eliminate the references to reliance should indicate how the courts should treat those cases.

The expectation interest can duplicate existing outcomes with one simple clarification: Courts should presume, subject to refutation by either party, that a contract would have produced zero profit for the plaintiff. In other words, the court should start by awarding the plaintiff enough money to break even on the contract or the venture of which the contract was a part. If the evidence indicates with the necessary degree of certainty that the plaintiff either would have earned a profit or would have suffered a loss if the defendant had performed, the court can add profits or subtract losses to reach the expectation interest.

For example, assume a writer accepted $20,000 in exchange for a promise to produce a movie script. If the writer failed to deliver a script, we could assume that the movie would have broken even. If so, the producer would have recovered its $20,000, but would have made no profit on that investment. The producer could try to prove the movie would have been the next Star Wars. The writer could try to prove the movie would have been the next Ishtar. But absent persuasive evidence either way, the court should stay with the original presumption: Cover expenses but award zero profit.[4]

The presumption of zero profit seems reasonable. Most people enter into contracts expecting to make a profit.[5] They know they will incur costs in their own performance, but each party believes that the return, however measured and in whatever form, will exceed the cost.[6] As long as the plaintiff is correct in that belief, she will receive a value sufficient to compensate for all expenditures and then some. Even if the plaintiff cannot quantify "and then some," it seems fair to start with a rebuttable presumption that the plaintiff at least would have broken even. Thus, the expectation interest supports full compensation for expenditures.

With very few exceptions, this approach does not change, but merely describes, the outcome of existing cases. Courts already insist upon evidence of profits before allowing their recovery. Similarly, courts already require the defendant to prove that plaintiff would have incurred losses. The presumption of zero profit duplicates that allocation of the burden of proof, but it produces that result without ever mentioning the reliance interest. Courts need not look backward to find the remedy; they can look forward to find the break-even point.

---

4. Mistletoe Express Serv. of Oklahoma City, Oklahoma v. Locke, 762 S.W.2d 637 (Tex. App. 1988).

5. . . . If a person values her money (or other things the money can buy) more than she values the good or service another offers in exchange (or the profit she might produce using that good or service), she seems unlikely to agree to an exchange. Agreement provides prima facie evidence that she expects a profit (or consumer surplus) from the transaction. Thus, contracts facilitate the movement of goods and services to the persons who value them most. . . .

6. The beauty of contract lies in the fact that both parties may be correct.

Courts need not administer alternative remedies; a single rule covers all contract damages.[7]

The similarity of results should come as no surprise. In cases where the plaintiff cannot recover profits, courts usually employ the expenditure measure. The expenditure measure, however, is merely a subset of the expectation interest. Every recovery based upon the expectation interest includes expenditures: The plaintiff must break even (by recovering expenditures) before she can profit (by recovering any additional amount she would have gained if defendant had performed). In cases where the profit cannot be measured (or for some other reason should not be awarded) the expectation interest with a presumption of zero profit produces a measure nearly identical to the expenditure measure.

The expectation of zero profit will differ from the expenditure measure in some ways. First, the presumption will clarify the prospective nature of the remedy. That prospective focus will produce different results for at least two types of damage claims: claims for expenditures incurred before the contract with the defendant was formed; and claims for unallocated overhead expenses. The reliance interest can and should provide compensation in many of these cases, but the retrospective approach to damages embodied in the expenditure measure tends to lead (or mislead) courts into denying these elements of damage. A presumption of a break even recovery will clarify the need to include these items in the damage award when they can be proven. In some cases, however, the expectation of zero profit may permit a plaintiff to recover under circumstances where the reliance interest would deny recovery. The expectation of zero profit is an expectation measure. Those who share the intuition that precontract expenditures and unallocated overhead deserve full compensation in all cases ultimately prefer the expectation interest over the reliance interest.

Second, the presumption may reduce at least one category of mistakes courts make: those involving election of remedies. By viewing the reliance interest and the expectation interest as alternative remedies, courts sometimes reach curious results that neither interest would support.

---

7. I resort to the convenient classification that differentiates damages from restitution. Restitution remains an alternative approach to contract recovery. Only the reliance interest becomes subsumed into the expectation interest.

A unified approach to damages, one focused only on the expectation interest with a presumption of zero profit, seems likely to avert some, if not all, of these errors. . . .

A. Precontract Expenditures

Precontract expenditures differentiate the expectation interest and the reliance interest more clearly than any other single element of damages.[8] Looking backward, the reliance interest concludes that the plaintiff would have incurred those expenditures even if the defendant had not made the promise in question. Thus, to put the plaintiff in the position she would have occupied if the defendant had not made the promise, the court must leave the burden of those expenditures on the plaintiff. Put another way, the plaintiff did not incur the expenditures in reliance on the contract. Looking forward, the expectation interest (with a presumption of zero profit) presumes that the plaintiff's venture would have produced revenue sufficient to cover all expenses, regardless of when they were incurred. If the defendant's breach prevents the plaintiff from realizing that revenue, the defendant should make good all expenses incurred, putting the plaintiff in approximately the position she would have occupied if the defendant had performed. While the expectation interest would prefer to measure the future more directly (by estimating the profit), when that proves impractical the presumption serves as a surrogate that brings us as close as we can come to the expectation interest.

Consider a simple example. In Anglia Television Ltd. v. Reed, the plaintiff incurred substantial expenses in preparing to produce a television play. About ten days before filming would have begun, the plaintiff entered a contract with Robert Reed to play the lead. A few days later, Mr. Reed's agent canceled because he had inadvertently committed

---

8. One might suggest that profit differentiates the two interests more clearly, but as long as the reliance interest employs profit as a measure of lost opportunities, that element does not differentiate the two interests at all. The differences emerge most clearly when profit cannot be recovered because of uncertainty. Then, and only then, does reliance look backward, since the forward looking surrogate for lost opportunities disappears. The expectation interest, meanwhile, continues to look forward to locate the break-even point.

Mr. Reed to two conflicting projects. Efforts to locate another acceptable actor failed, forcing the plaintiff to cancel the project.

The plaintiff did not even seek lost profits. It could not prove how much television stations might have paid for the film. But the plaintiff did seek to recover expenditures made before it entered the contract with Mr. Reed, a claim Mr. Reed resisted.

At first glance, the reliance interest strongly favors Mr. Reed's position. If the promise had not been made, Anglia nonetheless would have incurred all the preliminary expenses. That money was spent before Mr. Reed agreed. His promise had nothing to do with the loss.[9]

The expectation interest, however, favors Anglia. If Mr. Reed had performed the contract, Anglia would have produced the film. Assuming Anglia could have sold it for an amount at least equal to cost of production, it would have received revenues sufficient to recoup all the expenses, even those incurred before Mr. Reed agreed to perform.[10]

Lord Denning awarded Anglia the full amount sought — all of the expenses, whenever incurred. The court couched the decision in terms of "wasted expenditures," language one might ordinarily associate with the reliance interest. Indeed, Lord Denning spoke of alternative remedies: "It seems to me that a plaintiff in such a case as this had an election; he can either claim for his loss of profits; or for his wasted expenditure. But he must elect between them. He cannot claim both." The result, however, suggests a judicial preference for protecting the expectation interest. The two interests would produce divergent results. The court chose the result most consistent with the expectation interest. . . .

. . . In Chicago Coliseum Club v. Dempsey, the plaintiff sought to promote a boxing match between Jack Dempsey, then the heavyweight

---

9. Put another way, the expenditures were not made in reliance on a promise Mr. Reed had not yet made. This situation presents a clear example of how the reliance interest injects causation into contract damages. The expenditures were not caused by Mr. Reed. They were made independently of his promise and of his breach. His breach converted expenditures that would have been productive (and, presumably, would have been recouped on the sale of the film) into expenditures that were wasted, with no opportunity for recoupment. But neither the promise nor the breach caused the expenditures.

10. The presumption may require some faith in the judgment of the plaintiff. But absent evidence to rebut that presumption, it seems better to presume the break-even point than to presume losses.

champion, and Harry Wills. Plaintiff signed Wills first, promising him at least $50,000. Dempsey later signed a contract for the fight. Dempsey breached the contract. The plaintiff never paid Wills and, apparently, lacked the resources to pay any judgment Wills might obtain against it. The court refused to allow recovery of expenses incurred before the contract on which the plaintiff allegedly relied.

The expectation interest would produce a different result. If the court starts with the assumption that revenues from the fight would equal (but not exceed) expenditures,[11] the precontract expenditures form a proper element of the damage award. They, too, would have been paid by the revenues from the fight. . . .

The expectation of zero profit simplifies litigation by providing a clear criterion for determining which expenses the plaintiff may recover. That criterion comports with reliance principles in a great many cases. It recognizes lost opportunities without demanding speculation concerning the value those opportunities would have provided. In so doing, it brings the existing law much closer to a normatively defensible version of the reliance interest. Die-hard reliance advocates may prefer an approach that retains the flexibility to reduce recoveries in a few cases where even zero profit seems excessive but where the defendant cannot prove that the plaintiff would have suffered losses if the contract had been per-formed. On balance, the cost of litigation required to effectuate that approach seems likely to outweigh any advantages it may have over the expectation of zero profit. . . .

C.   Costly Errors in Applying the Expenditure Measure

It would be vain to hope for judicial perfection. Opportunities for misapplication will arise with some regularity even for simple rules.

---

11. Plaintiff failed to prove that the fight would have generated a profit. . . . The court could not assume a profit. The court apparently did not consider the gate receipts of Dempsey's fight with Tunney in Philadelphia that same Fall (about $1.9 million) or in Chicago the following Fall (about $2.6 million). . . . While these figures may not prove that plaintiff could have promoted a fight with equal skill or that Wills would draw as large and lucrative a crowd as Tunney, they certainly suggest that a fight involving Dempsey, even after he lost the world title in the first Tunney fight, could produce substantial revenues. That lends credence to the presumption that the plaintiff could break even, even if it could not prove a profit.

Yet, everything else being equal, one might prefer rules that create the least confusion, at least when there is any reliable basis for predicting which rules will create more or less confusion.

A unified measure of damages focusing on the expectation interest with a presumption of zero profit offers some advantages over a remedial structure involving alternative remedies. The unified structure maintains a single, familiar approach. It avoids issues of election of remedies. It avoids confusion regarding overlapping remedies. It minimizes concern for strategic choices among remedial alternatives. And it helps judges focus on a single objective.

One can demonstrate the misapplication of the reliance interest in several types of cases. One might start, of course, with the cases discussed earlier in this Part. If Lord Denning intended to apply a reliance measure in *Anglia*, he failed. By failing to ask the proper question — "Where would plaintiff be if the defendant had not made the promise?" — Lord Denning missed the appropriate application of the reliance measure.[12] And if he did not — if the reliance interest supports the recovery of precontract expenditures — then the court[s] in *Dempsey* must have erred in reaching the contrary conclusion. . . .

V.   CONCLUSION

Fuller and Perdue produced a masterpiece of legal scholarship. Their article deserves the praise that has been heaped upon it over the years. They opened our eyes to new ways to think about contract damages. They explained the law in terms of the institutions it serves, revealing new justifications for principles the law long had taken for granted. They provided a taxonomy of remedial objectives. They helped generations of lawyers think about the normative justifications of contract law.

Fuller and Perdue's article works considerably less well as a prescription for the calculation of contract damages. Their ambivalence toward opportunities lost in reliance on the promise produced significant

---

12. Of course, Lord Denning may have been dissatisfied with the implications of the reliance measure and may have rejected that inquiry in order to reach the normatively superior result of an expectation interest based on a presumption of zero profits.

inconsistencies in their approach. Instead of creating a unified reliance interest, they spawned a trio of approaches, each with a claim to the name reliance: the pure reliance interest, reliance limited by expectation, and the expenditure measure. Only the pure reliance interest lives up to the normative claims Fuller and Perdue made. But the pure reliance interest never found favor in the courts or subsequent scholarship. Fuller and Perdue themselves abandoned it in favor of, first, reliance limited by expectation and, later, the expenditure measure. Without even an attempt to apply the normative rationale to the lesser versions of reliance, Fuller and Perdue progressively modified the reliance interest in ways that consistently decreased the plaintiff's recovery.

Given the tendency of reliance language to reduce contract damages in ways that lack any normative basis, it is fortunate that the courts rarely employ reliance language. Scholars, however, continue to urge greater use of the reliance interest as a measure of damages. The tendency of reliance measures to undercompensate plaintiffs, even by the normative standards Fuller and Perdue identified, make reliance a poor model for contract remedies.

The goals of the reliance interest may be better served if we banish the language of reliance from discussions of contract damages. With very few (and fairly minor) exceptions, the expectation interest meets the normative goals set by the reliance interest — at least in those cases where courts have shown any inclination to base recoveries on reliance at all. We need only fix recoveries at the level of zero profit unless one party can prove that performance would have produced profits or losses. This presumption of zero profit captures the essence of existing contract law. In addition, the presumption can clarify and add consistency to the judicial treatment of precontract expenses and unallocated overhead. The expectation of zero profit, however, is the least important contribution this Article offers.

Primarily, this Article sounds a cautionary note, a warning against blind expansion of recoveries based on reliance. Invocation of the reliance interest conjures the spirit of Fuller and Perdue. Their well-deserved prestige and the normative arguments they presented attach to any proposal waving the flag of reliance, but the normative rationale does not inhere in the word "reliance." Proposals to expand reliance remedies deserve close scrutiny to ascertain their relationship to the normative goals they invoke. Even legends like Fuller and Perdue themselves failed to link their specific proposals to their normative rationale. We mortals who follow in their footsteps deserve no greater deference, incantations of reliance notwithstanding.

STUDY GUIDE: *How does Professor Craswell's "incentives" approach differ from the "interests" approach of Fuller and Perdue? Why does he think it is preferable? How competent are courts in accomplishing the objectives he sets for them? (This will be a recurring question about "efficiency" theories we shall read in this book.) In light of his criticisms, why does he pick the "expectation interest" as the baseline measure of damages? How does his "framework" differ from theirs?*

BEYOND FULLER AND PERDUE?*

Richard Craswell

INTRODUCTION

In 1936, Lon Fuller and William Perdue published an article they called, "The Reliance Interest in Contract Damages." In the history of contract law, and of American legal thought in general, this article stands as a towering classic. It changed forever the way we think about monetary remedies for breach of contract. It also exemplified Fuller's particular brand of jurisprudence, showing the power of his critique of formalism. . . .

While Fuller and Perdue's article centered around three distinct "interests," Fuller's own thinking may have been rather broader. In a letter to Karl Llewellyn, written six years after the article was published, Fuller downplayed the specific "interests" themselves, and spoke in terms more suggestive of a continuous range of remedies. He referred instead to a "hierarchy" of contract interests, which he said could be "sloganized" as extending from restitution to reliance to expectation,

---

*From Richard Craswell, Against Fuller and Perdue, 67 U. Chi. L. Rev. 99 (2000).

but which also included "a number of little midstations ... along the way." He then concluded:

> I consider the contribution made in my article on the reliance interest to lie, not in calling attention to the reliance interest itself, but in an analysis which breaks down the Contract-No-Contract dichotomy and substitutes *an ascending scale* of enforceability.

This language suggests something closer to a continuous scale of remedies, rather than three discrete "interests."

Whatever Fuller may have intended, though, those three remedial "interests" receive most of the attention today. For example, the *Restatement (Second) of Contracts* begins its sections on remedies by announcing that all remedies "serve to protect one or more of the following interests of a promisee," followed by definitions of Fuller and Perdue's three interests. Almost every casebook begins its materials on remedies in the same way. . . . In academic scholarship, many law-and-economics analyses begin with these same three remedies, as do any number of non-economic writings. It is this use of Fuller and Perdue's three "interests" that I wish to criticize here. . . .

ECONOMICS

Economic analysis is consequentialist: it asks what consequences will follow from adopting this remedy or that. Moreover, to economists, the best way to predict the likely consequences is to understand the *incentives* that a given remedy creates. The steady expansion of the economic analysis of contract remedies has thus come from the identification of more and more incentives that might be affected by the law's choice of remedy, and which thus would have to be considered in any normative evaluation. Of course, to the extent that the legal remedy is merely a default rule that the parties are allowed to alter, economic analysts have also been concerned about the effect of the default rule on contractual negotiations. But even when the parties are likely to leave the default remedy in place, there are a number of incentives that are relevant from an economic perspective.

To take the most obvious example, the threat of a larger remedy might deter a promisor from deliberately breaking her promise, while a reduction in the remedy might reduce that incentive. This effect — the effect on the incentive to perform a contract or to break it — has since become famous as the "theory of efficient breach." However, subsequent economic analysis has identified any number of other incentives that might also be affected by the legal remedy.

For example, the size of the remedy may also affect a promisor's incentive to take precautions against accidents that might leave her unable to perform her contract, as when stiffer penalties for breach of warranty give manufacturers an incentive to build more reliable products. The remedy may also affect the *promisee's* incentives to avoid relying too much (or too little) on the promised performance, or to take other precautions to protect himself against the effects of breach. The damage rules may also affect the promisee's incentive to take steps to mitigate his losses *after* a breach by the promisor. More broadly, the damage rules may affect both parties' incentives to think carefully about a contract before signing it, or to think differently about which parties to contract with (and at what price), or to spend more time searching for other parties who might be willing to contract. The damage rule can also affect the degree of risk to which each party is exposed, an important consideration whenever the parties are not risk-neutral.

Interestingly, a few of these effects may support the expectation remedy, thus coinciding with one of Fuller and Perdue's "interests." For example, expectation damages may give promisors just the right incentive to choose between performing and breaking a contract (the "efficient breach" effect), at least when subsequent renegotiation between the parties is unlikely. Expectation damages may also provide the right incentive to take precautions against any contingencies that would leave the promisor unable to perform. And if the promisee is risk-averse while the promisor is risk-neutral or risk-preferring, expectation damages can also provide the best allocation of risk between the two parties.

There is, however, no reason to suppose that the totality of economic effects will *always* favor an award of expectation damages. For example, if both parties are risk-averse, the optimal allocation of risk will usually be achieved by a remedy that is somewhat less than the full expectation measure (although it will not necessarily equal the reliance measure). Similarly, the incentives to research the relevant contingencies prior to signing a contract may also be optimized by a remedy that is below the expectation measure — though for this effect, too, the optimal remedy could be either above or below the reliance measure. In other cases, if there is a significant probability that a breach of contract will not be detected or will not be brought to trial, the optimal remedy could exceed the expectation measure. On the other hand, some systems of imperfect enforcement might require lower damage measures, to correct what might otherwise be a tendency toward overdeterrence. And in markets with informed customers, lower damages might suffice because promisors may already have optimal incentives, even if the law's remedy is below the expectation level.

More fundamentally, whenever different amounts of damages would be optimal for each of the different incentives to be optimized, the measure that is optimal when *all* of the relevant incentives are considered will often be some hybrid or intermediate number. For example, if the potential breacher's incentives to perform or to take appropriate precautions would be optimized by full expectation damages, but if the nonbreacher's attitude toward risk leads him to prefer less than full insurance, the measure that best accommodates both of those goals will normally be more than would be chosen if insurance were the only relevant goal, but less than what would be chosen if precautions alone were relevant. Once this has been recognized, it is not too far-fetched to say that the measure of damages that is truly optimal — optimal, that is, when *all* of the relevant factors have been considered — could lie anywhere on the real number line.

To lawyers who think of remedies as protecting discrete, identifiable "interests," the prospect of a continuum of remedies to choose from may seem odd. To economists who view remedies in instrumental terms, though, there is nothing at all odd about this. After all, most instruments — be they legal rules, electrical devices, or even physical tools like hammers or crowbars — can produce slightly larger or smaller effects by being tweaked in one direction. Indeed, if the exact consequences one wants to produce vary from one use of these tools to another, this sort of tweaking will often be needed. From an instrumental perspective, the focus is entirely on the *effect* one wants to produce, not on the "interest" one wants to protect.

My point thus is not merely that modern economics does not necessarily support any of the three remedies that Fuller and Perdue considered (though often it will not). The more fundamental point is that economics does not even approach the question in the same way that Fuller and Perdue did, for economics does not begin by asking what "interest" the law should protect. To be sure, if the optimal award from an economic standpoint turned out to be (say) 63 percent of expectation damages, we could always *define* that amount as a recognizable "interest" of the promisee, and then announce that the law aimed to protect the promisee's "63 percent expectation interest." But that definition would be entirely arbitrary, adding nothing to any normative case for that remedy. The normative case, at least from an economic standpoint, would still consist of whatever effects had led to the initial conclusion that 63 percent of expectation damages was the appropriate "interest" for the law to recognize.

The same would be true even if the best combination of incentives happened to be produced by a remedy that did correspond to one of Fuller and Perdue's three interests. For example, suppose (as may well be true) that, at least in certain cases, a remedy of expectation damages yields the best combination of overall incentives. That would give us an economic argument for expectation damages — but this economic argument would not rest on the fact that expectation damages happen to coincide with a somewhat less arbitrary "interest" of the promisee. From an economic perspective, an "interest" of 100 percent of expectation damages is no less arbitrary than an "interest" of 63 percent of expectation damages, or than any other number (at least at the beginning of the analysis). While economic analysis may conclude that one of those numbers is superior to the others, its justification for that conclusion owes nothing to Fuller and Perdue's framework. . . .

BEYOND FULLER AND PERDUE?

The question, then, is what should replace that classification. . . . Fuller and Perdue's lasting impact has come from their framework for organizing our thinking and our teaching about remedies for breach. This is the aspect of Fuller and Perdue that I have criticized, so it is this aspect — the framework for organizing our thinking and teaching — that requires replacement. That is, if we take the existing legal rules (and the remedies they define) as given, is it useful to organize or to classify those rules according to whether they serve the expectation, reliance, or restitution "interests"? Or would some other classification be a more useful way of organizing our thinking and teaching? . . .

A useful organizing framework should group together the different remedies in a way that highlights the most important differences and similarities, even while recognizing that there will always be some similarities between various remedies that are not grouped together (and always some differences among those that are). Part of the attraction of Fuller and Perdue's framework is precisely that it did provide, for two generations of legal scholars, a thematic way of grouping together various remedies that would otherwise have to be seen as an unorganized laundry list. Framed in this way, the question is whether there is any alternative grouping that can do this better than Fuller and Perdue's.

As should by now be obvious, I believe that there is. . . . [S]ome remedies seem usefully understood as attempting to approximate the plaintiff's expectation interest as nearly as the available evidence allows — including some remedies that may be designated "reliance" damages, but which actually serve to estimate the expectation interest. Other remedies seem to aim for compensation *above* the expectation interest: not just in the case of punitive damages, but also in the case of some ways of measuring expectation or restitution damages. Still other remedies attempt to limit the plaintiff to something *below* his expectation interest — including some cases awarding reliance or restitution damages, and most of the cases employing the doctrines that limit expectation damages.

Admittedly, the choice of expectation damages as the dividing line that separates the other two categories is to some extent arbitrary. Still, any classification requires a dividing line of some sort, and since contract law still treats expectation damages as the standard remedy, there is pedagogical value in using that remedy as the starting point. In addition, the expectation remedy has a number of effects (perhaps more than any other single remedy) that are relevant from a normative standpoint, which make that remedy a convenient baseline for policy analysis as well. For example, in many situations the expectation remedy — if calculated correctly — creates the right incentives for the promisor to take precautions against accidents that would prevent performance. It may also create the right incentive for promisees [sic] who are choosing between performance or breach; and in some situations, it may provide promisees with their preferred level of insurance. Significantly, though, expectation damages have these effects only if they are measured so as to leave the nonbreacher truly indifferent between receiving damages and receiving the promised performance. For this reason, I take this "true" measure of expectation damages, and not expectation damages as they might be measured by a court, as the dividing line between my two outer categories. . . .

In short, the classification that I propose has three parts: (1) remedies above expectation, (2) remedies that approximate expectation, and (3) remedies below expectation. The middle category, remedies that approximate the expectation interest, is essentially the same as Fuller and Perdue's (and the traditional category that preceded them), so I cannot claim any improvement in that regard. But the first category — encompassing remedies *above* the expectation interest — is clearly an advance over Fuller and Perdue, since they saw the expectation interest as the largest possible remedy (except in the unusual case of a losing contract, where expectation might be exceeded by reliance and restitution). As a result, Fuller and Perdue's three categories do not help us talk about the many other remedies that exceed, and often intentionally exceed, the expectation interest. At the same time, my third category (remedies that aim *below* the expectation interest) should also be viewed as an advance over Fuller and Perdue. While Fuller and Perdue provided two categories for remedies that fall below the expectation interest — restitution and reliance — my third category is even broader, to reflect the many other sub-expectation remedies besides those two.

Of course, such a classification might seem both obvious ("above, below, and equal to expectation — what's so novel about that?") and useless ("why do we need such a classification anyway?"). In response to the obviousness charge, note that this classification does group the remedies in ways that do not always follow existing doctrinal lines. For example, this classification puts some of the cases awarding reliance damages in the "below expectation" category, and others in the category of remedies that approximate the expectation interest. It also puts some restitution cases in the "above expectation" category, and others in the category for remedies "below expectation." Even the cases that purport to award expectation damages will sometimes fall in the "above" category and sometimes in the "below" category, depending on how the damages are measured and on what limiting doctrines are applied. Obvious as such a division may seem, then, this is not how existing remedies are conceived doctrinally. . . .

If a finer grain is desired, . . . there are many ways to subdivide my outer categories to provide more structure. Those who prefer doctrinal subdivisions could . . . simply list all of the legal doctrines that could produce the effect described by each category. Using this approach, the "below expectation" category could list each of the doctrines that limit expectation damages (the foreseeability requirement, the mitigation requirement, the requirement of proof with certainty, and the various categorical exclusions of attorneys' fees and other losses), along with *some* uses of the reliance and restitution measure, in cases when those fell below the measurable expectation damages. Similarly, the "above expectation" category could list punitive damages; *some* uses of restitution and reliance (when those exceeded the best measure of the expectation interest); some liquidated damage clauses; and some cases employing particular measures of expectation damages (such as the cost-of-completion measure, in cases when that measure exceeded the plaintiff's subjective valuation of complete performance).

Alternatively, rather than following these doctrinal lines, for some purposes it might be better to subdivide each category according to the *reason* for aiming above or below the expectation measure. For example, the economic analysis discussed earlier has identified four or five reasons that might (in appropriate circumstances) justify an award below the expectation ideal. A lower award might strengthen the promisee's incentives to take his own precautions to reduce the consequences of breach, especially if the promisee was the better cost-avoider. A lower award might also better match the promisee's taste for insurance, if he was not very risk-averse; or it might prevent what would otherwise be the cross-subsidization of some promisees by others. In some cases, lower awards might prevent what would otherwise be a problem of overdeterrence. And in markets where reputations were believed to work well, lower awards (up to and including complete nonenforcement) might reduce the costs of operating the legal system, without giving up anything desirable in terms of incentives. To this list, those who wish could add non-economic justifications as well—for instance, lower awards might express a social judgment that the promisor was not really at fault, or that the fault was divided between promisor and promisee. Conceivably, lower awards might in some cases produce a desired distributional effect.

On the other end, there is a similarly small list of reasons that might justify remedies that exceed the expectation measure. Most of the economic justifications focus either on the need to make up for imperfect enforcement, or on the desire to alter the parties' bargaining positions (should an occasion for breach arrive) in a way that improves their ex ante incentives, or — a related concern — on the desirability of protecting certain rights with property rules rather than liability rules. The list of non-economic reasons for large awards is similarly small, being limited to the desire to punish the breacher, to make an expressive statement of condemnation, or — again, *perhaps* — the desire to produce a particular distributional effect.

Of course, there are many other ways to subdivide these categories, and others may have different ways of doing it. In some sense, what ultimately matters is the amounts that courts actually award, and how we classify those amounts is a matter of our own convenience. My main claim, however, is that Fuller and Perdue's classification is *not* a convenient way of classifying them, for almost any purpose that might be relevant.

2

ARE SOME BREACHES
OF CONTRACT EFFICIENT?

We are accustomed to thinking of a breach of contract as a bad thing that is to be discouraged. Certainly that is the layperson's view of the matter. So strong is this intuition that to claim that some breaches of contract may be "efficient" and, for this reason, a good thing to be encouraged may strike one as bizarre, if not perverse. Yet this very argument has been advanced by some legal economists.

Suppose that you and I enter a contract. Later on I am presented with an opportunity from which I may profit if I break my contract with you. Suppose further that my profit exceeds the amount of money it would take to compensate you according to the expectation measure of damages. Provided I fully compensate you, doesn't this mean that breaching the contract would make me better off, while leaving you no worse off than had I performed? Would not the "state of the world" be improved if I were to breach our contract?

This, in a nutshell, is the concept of "efficient breach." In his book, *The Economic Analysis of Law*, this concept is presented and defended by Judge Richard A. Posner, Chief Judge of the United States Court of Appeals for the Seventh Circuit. Prior to assuming the bench, Judge Posner was a law professor at the University of Chicago. He remains the most prolific legal scholar in the country.

Challenging this view are Professor Daniel Friedmann of the Tel-Aviv University in Israel and Marco Jimenez of the Stetson University College of Law. In *The Efficient Breach Fallacy*, Friedman he argues that the concept of efficient breach is inconsistent with that of the entitlement or property rights of the victim of the breach. For Friedmann, the issue is which party to the original contract is entitled to the gain to be achieved by the second transfer. And he contests the claim that efficiency results from breaking a contract under these circumstances. In *A Utilitarian Critique of Wealth Maximization Theory*, Professor Jimenez contends that the alleged efficiency of the efficient breach theory depends on improperly conflating "wealth" as measured by dollars and "utility" or the subjective intrinsic value that the parties attach to receiving performance. There is good reason, he maintains, to doubt that allowing so-called efficient breaches actually enhances social welfare.

STUDY GUIDE: If a breach of contract makes one person better off, while harming no one else in the process, why should not such a contract be breached? Does the efficient breach argument rest in any assumptions about the legal system and its competence to make damage awards? Is this a concept that "works well in theory, but not in practice"? Is a legal theory that does not work in practice a good theory?

FUNDAMENTAL PRINCIPLES OF CONTRACT DAMAGES*

Richard A. Posner

When a breach of contract is established, the issue becomes one of the proper remedy. There are a bewildering variety of possibilities, which in rough order of increasing severity can be arrayed as follows:

(1)   the promisee's reliance loss (the costs he incurred in reasonable reliance on the promisor's performing the contract);

(2)   the expectation loss (loss of the anticipated profit of the contract);

---

*From Richard A. Posner, Economic Analysis of Law 117-120 (4th ed. 1992).

(3)   liquidated damages (damages actually specified in the contract as the money remedy for a breach);

(4)   consequential damages (ripple effects on the promisee's business from the breach);

(5)   restitution (to the promisee of the promisor's profits from the breach);

(6)   specific performance (ordering the promisor to perform on penalty of being found in contempt of court);

(7)   a money penalty specified in the contract, or other punitive damages.

It makes a difference in deciding which remedy to grant whether the breach was opportunistic. If a promisor breaks his promise merely to take advantage of the vulnerability of the promisee in a setting (the normal contract setting) where performance is sequential rather than simultaneous, we might as well throw the book at the promisor. An example would be where *A* pays *B* in advance for goods and instead of delivering them *B* uses the money in another venture. Such conduct has no economic justification and ought simply to be deterred. An attractive remedy in such a case is restitution. The promisor broke his promise in order to make money — there can be no other reason in the case of such a breach. We can deter this kind of behavior by making it worthless to the promisor, which we do by making him hand over all his profits from the breach to the promisee; no lighter sanction would deter.

Most breaches of contract, however, are not opportunistic. Many are involuntary; performance is impossible at a reasonable cost. Others are voluntary but (as we are about to see) efficient — which from an economic standpoint is the same case as that of an involuntary breach. These observations both explain the centrality of remedies to the law of contracts (can you see why?) and give point to Holmes's dictum that it is not the policy of the law to compel adherence to contracts but only to require each party to choose between performing in accordance with the contract and compensating the other party for any injury resulting from a failure to perform.[1] This dictum, though overbroad, contains an

---

1. Oliver Wendell Holmes, The Path of the Law, 10 Harv. L. Rev. 457, 462 (1897) ("The duty to keep a contract at common law means a prediction that you must pay damages if you do not keep it — and nothing else").

important economic insight. In many cases it is uneconomical to induce completion of performance of a contract after it has been broken. I agree to purchase 100,000 widgets custom-ground for use as components in a machine that I manufacture. After I have taken delivery of 10,000, the market for my machine collapses. I promptly notify my supplier that I am terminating the contract, and admit that my termination is a breach. When notified of the termination he has not yet begun the custom grinding of the other 90,000 widgets, but he informs me that he intends to complete his performance under the contract and bill me accordingly. The custom-ground widgets have no operating use other than in my machine, and a negligible scrap value. To give the supplier a remedy that induced him to complete the contract after the breach would waste resources. The law is alert to this danger and, under the doctrine of mitigation of damages, would not give the supplier damages for any costs he incurred in continuing production after notice of termination.

But isn't the danger unreal if the Coase Theorem is true? There are only two parties, and there is a price for the supplier's forbearing to stand on his contract rights—indeed a range of prices—that will make both parties better off. But this is just another example of bilateral monopoly; transaction costs will be high even though (in a sense, because) there are only two parties.

Now suppose the contract is broken by the seller rather than the buyer. I really need those 100,000 custom-ground widgets for my machine but the supplier, after producing 50,000, is forced to suspend production because of a mechanical failure. Other suppliers are in a position to supply the remaining widgets that I need but I insist that the original supplier complete his performance of the contract. If the law compels completion (specific performance), the supplier will have to make arrangements with other producers to complete his contract with me. Probably it will be more costly for him to procure an alternative supplier than for me to do so directly (after all, I know my own needs best); otherwise he would have done it voluntarily, to minimize his liability for the breach. To compel completion of the contract (or costly negotiations to discharge the promisor) would again result in a waste of resources, and again the law does not compel completion but confines the victim to simple damages.

But what are simple contract damages? Usually the objective of giving the promisor an incentive to fulfill his promise unless the result would be an inefficient use of resources (the production of the unwanted widgets in the first example, the roundabout procurement of a substitute supplier in the second) can be achieved by giving the promisee his expected profit on the transaction. If the supplier in the first example receives his expected profit from making 10,000 widgets, he will have no incentive to make the unwanted 90,000. We do not want him to make them; no one wants them. In the second example, if I receive my expected profit from dealing with the original supplier, I become indifferent to whether he completes his performance.

In these examples the breach was committed only to avert a larger loss, but in some cases a party is tempted to break his contract simply because his profit from breach would exceed his profit from completion of the contract. If it would also exceed the expected profit to the other party from completion of the contract, and if damages are limited to the loss of that profit, there will be an incentive to commit a breach. But there should be. Suppose I sign a contract to deliver 100,000 custom-ground widgets at 10¢ apiece to *A* for use in his boiler factory. After I have delivered 10,000, *B* comes to me, explains that he desperately needs 25,000 custom-ground widgets at once since otherwise he will be forced to close his pianola factory at great cost, and offers me 15¢ apiece for them. I sell him the widgets and as a result do not complete timely delivery to *A*, causing him to lose $1,000 in profits. Having obtained an additional profit of $1,250 on the sale to *B*, I am better off even after reimbursing *A* for his loss, and *B* is also better off. The breach is Pareto superior. True, if I had refused to sell to *B*, he could have gone to *A* and negotiated an assignment to him of part of *A*'s contract with me. But this would have introduced an additional step, with additional transaction costs — and high ones, because it would be a bilateral-monopoly negotiation. On the other hand, litigation costs would be reduced.

Could not the danger of overdeterring breaches of contract by heavy penalties be avoided simply by redefining the legal concept of breach of contract so that only inefficient terminations counted as breaches? No. Remember that an important function of contracts is to assign risks to superior risk bearers. If the risk materializes, the party to whom it was assigned must pay. It is no more relevant that he could not have prevented the risk from occurring at a reasonable, perhaps at any, cost than that an insurance company could not have prevented the fire that destroyed the building it insured. The breach of contract corresponds to the occurrence of the event that is insured against.

STUDY GUIDE: *According to Professor Friedmann, why is the concept of efficient breach a "fallacy"? What does his analysis suggest about the relationship between the concept of entitlements or property rights and the concept of contract?*

THE EFFICIENT BREACH FALLACY*

Daniel Friedmann

The only universal consequence of a legally binding promise is that the law makes the promisor pay damages if the promised event does not come to pass. In every case it leaves him free from interference until the time for fulfillment has gone by, and therefore free to break his contract if he chooses.[1]

So wrote Oliver Wendell Holmes in his seminal discussion of contract remedies in The Common Law. That position, while widely discussed, is not acceptable as a normative (nor, as will be shown, as a positive) account of the question of contract remedies. Stated in a phrase, the weakness of Holmes's approach lies in its conclusion that the remedy provides a perfect substitute for the right, when in truth the purpose of the remedy is to vindicate that right, not replace it. Holmes's analysis mistakenly converts the remedy into a kind of indulgence that the wrongdoer is unilaterally always entitled to purchase. As with any unifying ideal, Holmes's proposition is difficult to confine to the contract cases to which it was originally applied. Why not generalize the proposition so that every person has an "option" to transgress another's rights and to violate the law, so long as he is willing to suffer the consequences? The legal system could thus be viewed only as establishing a set of prices, some high and some low, which then act as the only constraints to induce lawful conduct.

The modern theory of "efficient breach" is a variation and systematic extension of Holmes's outlook on contractual remedy. It assumes that

---

*From Daniel Friedmann, The Efficient Breach Fallacy, 18 J. Leg. Stud. 1 (1989).
1. O. W. Holmes, Jr., The Path of the Law, in Collected Legal Papers 167, 175 (1920); and O. W. Holmes, Jr., The Common Law, 300-301 (1881).

role because of the dominance that it gives to the expectation measure of damages in cases of contract breach: the promisor is allowed to breach at will so long as he leaves the promisee as well off after breach as he would have been had the promise been performed, while any additional gain is retained by the contract breaker. . . .

I. ENTITLEMENT AND ECONOMIC EFFICIENCY

Proponents of the efficient breach theory have embraced Holmes's approach and endowed it with economic apparel and terminology. In their view, if the promisor's profits from the breach exceed the loss to the promisee, the breach is to be permitted or even encouraged on the ground that it leads to maximization of resources.[2] Under this theory of efficient breach, the promisor is given the option not to perform his contract as long as he is prepared to pay plaintiff his expectation damages, that is, a sum necessary to make the plaintiff indifferent between the performance of the contract and the damages so paid. The theory of efficient breach is that the defendant will exercise this option only if the gains from breach are greater than the moneys so paid over. The pristine form of the theory implies that the plaintiff is left as well off from the breach as before, while the defendant is made better off. If so, the program of expectations damages, if faithfully implemented, satisfies not only the Kalder-Hicks standard of hypothetical compensation but the more restrictive Pareto standards of efficiency as well: not only is there a net social gain for the contracting parties, but no one is left worse off after breach than before. Consequently, under either view of efficiency the optimal level of damages is that which compensates the plaintiff only for this loss, and no more.

Originally, this theory was religiously preached and was hardly capable of suffering any qualification. Its modern version, as formulated in the latest (1986) edition of Posner's Economic Analysis of Law, evidences a certain retreat from this extreme position. A distinction is drawn between "opportunistic breach" and other breaches of contract. Breaches in the latter category still enjoy respectability and, if considered efficient, are lauded. Opportunistic breaches have lost the patronage

---

2. Richard A. Posner, Economic Analysis of Law 107 (3d ed. 1986).

of the efficient breach theory and are harshly denounced. The distinction is unsatisfactory[3] and in fact undermines much of the efficient breach theory. Indeed, Posner states that the opportunistic contract breaker should be made to "hand over all his profits from the breach to the promisee." Recovery of these gains is diametrically opposed to the efficient breach theory, the essence of which is that the promisor should be allowed or even encouraged to commit a breach whenever his gains exceed the promisee's loss. The theory clearly assumes that the promisor should be allowed to keep his gain, for otherwise he would lose interest in committing the breach that is supposedly so desirable. It is not explained why opportunistic breaches should be discouraged even if they are efficient. Is it because they are morally reprehensible? Is morality more important than efficiency? Or is it because they undermine the institution of contract in general? . . .

The essence of the theory is "efficiency." The "right" to break a contract is not predicated on the nature of the contractual right, its relative "weakness," or its status as merely in personam, as opposed to the hardier rights in rem. Rather it is on the ground that the breach is supposed to lead to a better use of resources. The theory, therefore, is, in principle, equally applicable to property rights, where it leads to the adoption of a theory of "efficient theft" or "efficient conversion."[4] To see the point, observe how this account of efficiency plays out in two cases. In the first, A promises to sell a machine to B for $10,000 but then turns around and sells it instead to C for $18,000. In the second, B owns a machine for which he has paid $10,000, which A takes and sells to C for $18,000.

---

3. Opportunism means taking advantage of the promisee's vulnerability. Posner regards the vulnerability mainly as created by the sequential character of performance under the contract. Hence, if A pays in advance for goods or services to be supplied by B in the future, A is vulnerable until B performs. . . . However, the sequence in which the performances are to be made is only one relevant factor. Thus, suppose A paid part of the price in advance while B has not yet performed. Although A has already partly performed, B may be more vulnerable if his need to receive the remaining part of A's payment is greater than A's need for B's promised performance. In fact, vulnerability is a matter of degree. The greater the need for the other party's performance and the more difficult it is to obtain a substitute, the greater the vulnerability.

4. On the "efficient theft," see Ian R. Macneil, Efficient Breach Contract: Circles in the Sky, 68 Va. L. Rev. 947, 963 (1982). . . .

To keep matters simple, assume that *B* values the machine at exactly $12,000 in both cases. If the willful contract breach is justified in the first case, then the willful conversion is justified in the second. In the first, *B* gets $2,000 in expectation damages and is released from paying the $10,000 purchase price. In the second, *B* obtains damages for conversion equal to $12,000 because he has already paid the $10,000 purchase price to his seller. The two cases thus look identical even though they derive from distinct substantive fields.

No doubt in the contract situation, *A* may negotiate with *B* a release from his contractual obligation. But this, in Posner's view, would lead to additional transaction costs. It is, therefore, preferable to permit the "efficient breach." But the property example is indistinguishable on this ground, for in the second, *A*, when he takes the machine from *B*, avoids the transaction cost of having to purchase it from him. The similarity between the two situations (breach of contract and conversion) becomes more striking if the converter did not wrongfully deprive the owner of his possessions. Thus, suppose that *A* is a bailee who keeps *B*'s goods. *C* offers *A* for the goods an amount that exceeds their value to *B*. *A* can negotiate with *B* for the purchase of the goods and, if he is successful, sell them to *C* at a profit. The cost of this transaction could be saved, just as in the contract example, if *A* were allowed to sell the goods to *C*, while limiting his liability to *B*'s expectation-like damages. Nevertheless, the better rule, which has been universally adopted by Anglo-American law, is that the plaintiff is entitled to recover in restitution the proceeds of the sale from the defendant who converted the plaintiff's property and sold it to a third party. Efficient breach theory does not provide an explanation why the promisee in a contract of sale should not be accorded similar rights.

There are, of course, refinements. Where the promisor is a merchant engaged in selling these types of goods, he may be in a better position to find a buyer willing to pay a higher price for them, so that his transaction costs may be somewhat lower. This however, is not necessarily the case, and in any event it does not justify the breach. Again, the situation can be compared to conversion. The fact that *A*, for example, is a car dealer who is likely to know that *C* is an excellent buyer for *B*'s car does not justify him to take *B*'s car from his driveway in order to sell it to *C*. Nor if *B*'s car has been left with *A* for repairs can *A* sell it to *C*.

The real issue in both the conversion and the breach situation is who should benefit from *C*'s willingness to pay a high price for the goods owned by *B* (the conversion example) or promised to him (the breach example). In principle, there should be in both situations only one transaction; in my view it should be between *C* and *B* (the owner or the promisee). If *A* promised to sell a piece of property to *B* for $10,000 and *C* is willing to have it for $18,000, he should negotiate its purchase from *B*. *A* is simply not entitled to sell to *C* something he has promised to return or transfer to *B*, and *A* is therefore not the right party to negotiate with. Consequently, if *C* negotiates such a purchase, he may be exposed to liability toward *B*, the promisee.[5] Similarly, with a bailment, *C* must negotiate with *B* (the owner) and not with the bailee. Hence, the question of additional transaction costs does not arise.

It is, of course, conceivable that a person (in the above example, *A*) would like to take advantage of a potential transaction between two other parties (*B* and *C*). In some instances this can legitimately be done. *A* may know that *C* is the best buyer for *B*'s property (or for the property promised to *B*), while *B* and *C* are unaware of each other. *A* may buy the property from *B* and sell it to *C*, or he may reach an agreement (with *B* or *C* or with both) for the payment of a commission. If this is done, the inevitable result would be that the transfer from *B* to *C* would involve two or more transactions (and, arguably, additional transaction costs). This course of dealing is not objectionable. What is, however, objectionable is an attempt by *A* to obtain through the commission of a wrong (breach of contract or a tort such as conversion) the benefit of a transaction that should have been concluded between *B* and *C*.

Moreover, the efficient breach rule is inefficient on its own terms. Neither it nor the analogous efficient conversion rule has the desired effect of minimizing either the number of transactions or, more decisively, the total amount of transaction costs. In fact, these rules may often lead to an increase in total transaction costs. In the above contract example, the breach is likely to require two transactions instead of one. If *A* performs his contract with *B*, there will be only one additional transaction, that between *B* and *C*. If, however, *A* is "allowed" to break

---

5. In some cases, *C*'s conduct may amount to interference with contractual relations. Even if it does not, *B* may in the appropriate case get specific performance against *C* if *C* was aware of the contract between *A* and *B*. . . . Moreover, if *C* has not perfected his title, specific performance may be granted against him although he was not aware of the contract (between *A* and *B*). . . .

his contract with B, there will be two transactions: one between A and C over the sale of property promised to B, and the other a dispute between A and B regarding the measure of damages. The implied assumption in Posner's analysis is that the payment of damages by A to B entails no transaction costs. This, however, is totally unrealistic. The payment of damages is hardly ever a standard of the type the parties are routinely engaged in. It is likely to follow protracted negotiations, or even litigation, over difficult questions of fact and law. Finally, the breach may lead to an expensive tort action for inducement of breach of contract by the promisee (B) against the third party (C). This claim may breed another transaction between C and A regarding A's liability for losses suffered by C.

Hence, the set of remedies that deter breach (such as specific enforcement, injunction, punitive damages or restitution of gains acquired through breach of contract) are likely to reduce the number of transactions as compared to situations in which expectation damages provide the sole remedy. It is, of course, conceivable that the promisor (A) will commit a breach when these rules are in place, forcing the promisee to claim specific performance or restitution of gains.

Here, too, transaction costs will be positive, and it is difficult in the abstract to say whether they are greater with either specific performance or restitution than they are with expectation damages. Nonetheless, there is good reason to believe that the frequency of breach will be reduced where specific performance and restitution are provided, if only because the defendant has less to gain from breach. The *total* level of transaction costs should accordingly be reduced when the plaintiff is provided with strong protection against breach of contract.

The relaxation of contract remedies also has deleterious effects on the willingness of parties to enter into mutually beneficial contracts in the first place. If the legal system imposes severe limitations on specific performance (irrespective of whether they are based on the right to break the contract theory or its modern "efficient breach" offshoot), it undermines the parties' faith in getting what they bargained for, and the consequence is inefficiency and a waste of resources.[6] If a party in

---

6. See also Alan Schwartz, The Case for Specific Performance, 89 Yale L.J. 271 (1979), who points out that the availability of specific performance would not generate greater transaction costs than the damages remedy . . . and that it would actually produce certain efficiency gains. . . .

need of contracting with another cannot rely on the contract to guarantee performance, then he may turn to another more costly and less efficient means (for example, becoming a self-supplier or vertically integrating with his supplier) to gain greater assurance that he will get what he seeks.[7]

This insistence on the respect of both property and contract rights will cause some hardship where there is bargaining breakdown and the parties cannot agree on the terms under which property should be sold. Thus, suppose that *A* can profitably use a machine that is owned by *B* or promised to him. *A* cannot get the machine elsewhere. *B*, who has no use for the machine, is willing to sell or rent it, but the parties cannot agree on the price. If *A* takes *B*'s machine (or *B*'s contractual right to receive it), he could gain use of a machine that would otherwise remain idle. Hence, greater efficiency. But this obviously cannot be allowed. The inefficiency resulting from failure of the bargaining process is inherent in the market system. If failure to reach an agreement created a license to take another's property (including contractual rights), then a complete breakdown of the market economy could follow. Why negotiate with a determined owner to buy something that can be taken, subject only to a court's subsequent appraisal of its value? Hence, in the context of a sale of existing property, the contract situation is (as far as efficiency is concerned) indistinguishable from the property situation.

STUDY GUIDE: What role does (and should) intrinsic value play in a court's determination of contract remedies? Can a breach of contract ever be efficient and, if so, under what circumstances? How much confidence do you have in a judge's ability to distinguish between efficient and inefficient breaches? What implication does your answer have on the way courts should award remedies for the breach of contract? Hint: What does this analysis suggest for the enforcement of liquidated damages clauses or ordering specific performance?

---

7. Compare E. Allan Farnsworth, Contract 812 n.4 (1982), suggesting that an "enterprise that does not wish to be subjected to the risks inherent in its supplier's freedom to break its contract" may assure itself of a source of supply by acquiring its supplier. This clearly demonstrates how freedom to break a contract (if such freedom is to be allowed) results in inefficiency.

A UTILITARIAN CRITIQUE OF WEALTH MAXIMIZATION THEORY*

Marco J. Jimenez

Law and economics (L&E), or wealth maximization theory (WMT), is a consequentialist theory of justice holding that those actions that increase wealth are just and should be allowed, whereas those actions that decrease wealth are unjust and should be forbidden. . . . [Consider Richard] Posner's famous illustration of an efficient breach:

> Suppose I sign a contract to deliver 100,000 custom-ground widgets at $0.10 apiece to A, for use in his boiler factory. After I have delivered 10,000, B comes to me, explains that he desperately needs 25,000 custom-ground widgets at once since otherwise he will be forced to close his pianola factory at great cost, and offers me $0.15 apiece for 25,000 widgets. I sell him the widgets and as a result do not complete timely delivery to A, who sustains $1000 in damages from my breach. Having obtained an additional profit of $1250 on the sale to B, I am better off even after reimbursing A for his loss. Society is also better off. Since B was willing to pay me $0.15 per widget, it must mean that each widget was worth at least $0.15 to him. But it was worth only $0.14 to A — $0.10, what he paid, plus $0.04 ($1000 divided by 25,000), his expected profit. Thus the breach resulted in a transfer of the 25,000 widgets from a lower valued to a higher valued use.[1]

Society, it would seem, is better off. But is it? . . . .

A. The Concept of Value

[A]ccording to WMT, courts should substitute dollar values for intrinsic values (that is, utility) not because maximizing dollars maximizes utility (it does not), but because dollars are easier to measure, and therefore maximize, than utility. To be sure, L&E scholars would reject this characterization of WMT, and argue that the utilitarian concept of

---

* From Marco J. Jimenez, The Value of a Promise: A Utilitarian Approach to Contract Law Remedies 56 UCLA L. Rev. 59 (2008).

1. See Richard A. Posner, Economic Analysis of Law 57 (1972).

welfare (happiness) is both analytically distinct from, and inferior to, the WMT concept of welfare (value or dollars). This distinction, however, cannot be maintained, because the very basis upon which the WMT concept of value rests is quintessentially utilitarian.

To see why, let us return to Judge Posner's widget hypothetical, and examine more carefully the claim that the breach there was efficient, in that it left the parties and society better off. If we examine this argument closely, it will be noted that the linchpin holding it together is the utilitarian assumption that the each widget was only worth $0.14 to A, which was arrived at by adding the $0.10 A paid for each widget to the $0.04 in damages[2] that would be awarded to A as a result of the breach. But there is no evidence supporting the conclusion that A only valued these widgets at $0.14 each, and thus no basis for equating value with price, because, although it is true that it is impossible to objectively measure the actual value A assigned to the widgets . . . , it is almost certain that he valued them more than $0.14. To see why, note that the efficient breach calculation above ignored, among other things, the intrinsic value (or utility) A may have attached to P's actual performance by failing to take into account such factors as the "personal element ([including,] for example, embarrassment or humiliation resulting from breach of contract),"[3] the inconvenience and emotional stress caused by the breach, the possible loss of customers from A (who could not meet customer demand) to B (who could), and the possible resulting damage to A's reputation, just to name a few of the more obvious considerations that would bear in significant ways on A's intrinsic value. These costs may be reflected in the price, but they need not be, especially — and this point has been largely ignored by WMT theorists — where A is a good negotiator.

To see why, suppose that A, taking into account his expected profit, but also factoring in the intrinsic value he assigned to performance (as discussed above), really valued P's widgets at $0.20, not $0.10. Further, assume that A was a good negotiator, and was able to talk P into selling him the widgets for $0.10 (we would not expect a good negotiator to pay

---

2. This amount, of course, would be limited by the doctrines of avoidability, certainty, and foreseeability.

3. Lawrence M. Friedman, Contract Law In America — A Social And Economic Case Study 21 (1965).

his highest price, would we?). Now, assume that B approaches P, as before, and offers him $0.15 apiece per widget, a price above which A would have gladly paid had P been a better (or A been a worse) negotiator. Could we now hold that allowing P to breach his contract with A was efficient? The answer, of course, is no,[4] and this illustrates nicely one of the more bizarre results of using market price (as opposed to the promisee's subjective valuation) as the basis for awarding contract damages: It tends to punish more severely those individuals that wealth maximization theorists should most want to reward (for example, good bargainers) because it is to them that wealth maximization theorists look to make their theory work by moving goods to those individuals who value them most.

Indeed, the better A can negotiate, the more surplus he or she will create in wealth maximization terms (by paying a lower price than is reflective of the true intrinsic value he or she attached to the promisor's performance), which would, in turn, not only make it more likely that an efficiently made contract be inefficiently breached, but would practically ensure that the judicially determined expectation measure of damages would be undercompensatory in most cases in which it was awarded. This outcome results because the larger the surplus A creates,[5] the greater the probability a third party such as B will swoop in and appropriate it by maneuvering between A's true intrinsic value and the contract price.[6] This outcome can be illustrated by returning to the widget hypothetical discussed above, where we can see that any breach by the promisor would be inefficient whenever it was the case that B valued the widgets less than A did, but more than the contract price (for example between $0.11 and $0.19 in the pianola hypothetical). And this, in turn, would often happen whenever A was a particularly good negotiator. Thus, for example, if we assume that A valued the widgets at

---

4. Unless, of course, it was the case that B happened to value the widgets even more than A did (in other words, more than $0.20 per widget).

5. Measured here as the difference between the true intrinsic value that A attached to the widgets and the price he or she actually paid.

6. A striking corollary to this is that such a theory could also operate to reward bad bargainers (like P) by leaving third parties (like B) more room to negotiate between the actual contract price and A's true intrinsic value, which would, in effect, reward P (by giving him a better price) for poorly negotiating his contract while punishing A (by giving him a price below his true intrinsic value) for his superior negotiating skills.

$0.20, then the breach at $0.15 (which was postulated in the widget hypothetical) would clearly be inefficient, and the award of $1000 would undercompensate A by not giving him the benefit of his bargain, which is, after all, the very purpose of contract law damages. Even more strikingly, under this regime, bad bargainers (such as the seller of the widgets above) may be rewarded because third parties (such as B) have more room to negotiate between the previously negotiated contract price (which would be low in proportion to the seller's poor bargaining skills) and A's true intrinsic value,[7] which would, in effect, reward the bad bargainer for poorly negotiating his contract (by giving him a better price than he originally bargained for), while simultaneously punishing A for his superior negotiating skills (by giving him a price below his true intrinsic value). To be sure, the greater the difference between the promisor's poor bargaining skills and the promisee's superior bargaining skills, the more pronounced the distinction will become, much to the chagrin of the wealth maximization theorist wishing to promote efficiency.

In the previous example, the contract price of $0.10 failed to fully capture the intrinsic value the promisee attached to the promisor's performance (that is, the intrinsic value represented by the difference between $0.10 and $0.20), but it at least captured some of that value (that is, the intrinsic value represented by the difference between $0 and contract price, or $0.10). There are, however, some situations in which the damages awarded under a WMT approach are not related at all, and sometimes even inversely related, to utility. This illustration can most clearly be shown in those instances where a party enters into an agreement that can simultaneously be characterized as both a "winning" utilitarian contract and a "losing" wealth maximization contract, which is to say, a contract that simultaneously increases a party's utility while decreasing that party's wealth.

Consider, for example, a vain homeowner who contracts with a sculptor to erect a colossal (and, in the minds of many, hideous) concrete statue of himself in the front lawn of his $500,000 home, the completion of which would dramatically increase the homeowner's intrinsic value, or utility, while reducing the dollar value of his home to $300,000. If the

---

7. Which must always be higher than the price actually paid. . . .

sculptor begins to build the statue but then breaches by abandoning the project when a more lucrative opportunity presents itself, the homeowner bringing suit will find that he is compensated quite differently under a regime seeking to maximize utility rather than wealth. Under the first regime, a utility-maximizing court would be most likely to award the homeowner specific performance[8] or "cost of completion" damages,[9] both of which would give the homeowner (or allow the homeowner to get) exactly what he bargained for — a colossal (even if, in the eyes of many, ugly) statue of himself in his front yard, even though doing so would reduce the dollar value of his home. On the other hand, a court that operated under the WMT framework would be most likely to refuse to award the cost of completion remedy (because it would operate to decrease the wealth of society and the parties to the contract), and opt instead for "dimunition in value,"[10] or the difference between the dollar value of the home before the breach ($500,000) and after the breach ($300,000). Because this amount is negative — in other words, because the sculptor's breach actually saved the homeowner $200,000 — the court will refuse to award any damages at all, even though the promisee not only contemplated — but contracted for — a loss in dollar value to his property in exchange for an increase in utility at the time of entering into the contract. To be sure, an exchange of wealth for utility was not only the sole purpose of this particular promisee's contract, but, as can be shown, is the sole purpose of nearly every legally enforceable contract that is freely entered into by consenting adults.

Be that as it may, a wealth maximization theorist would probably shrug her shoulders at the above analysis, and would certainly be puzzled by all the discussion surrounding utility and intrinsic value, [arguing] that these concepts are fraught with problems still unsolved, and cannot hope to serve as a meaningful basis upon which calculating damages for the breach of contract may rest. Indeed, even if a wealth

---

8. Although, if the contract is characterized as a personal services contract, the court would be unlikely to award this remedy as doing so would violate public policy. See, e.g., Lumley v. Wagner, (1852) 42 Eng. Rep. 687, 693 (Q.B.).

9. See, e.g., Groves v. John Wunder Co., 286 N.W. 235, 245 (Minn. 1939) (awarding cost of completion damages).

10. See, e.g., Peevyhouse v. Garland Coal Mining Co., 382 P.2d 109, 114 (Okla. 1962) (awarding loss in value damages) . . . .

maximization theorist agreed with the above analysis and conceded that WMT's reliance on the expectancy does not perfectly capture a promisee's intrinsic value, she would likely dismiss it as a moot point, arguing that a judge, being unable to measure intrinsic value, cannot use this concept as the basis for determining damages for the breach of contract. She might then conclude . . . that wealth maximization theory, and the expectancy interest, even with its shortcomings, is the best practical alternative for solving the sticky issue of determining damages for the breach of contract, and it was largely because of this reason that wealth replaced utility as the maximand in the first place.

But what are these dollars that serve as the foundation of wealth maximization theory? What, really, is this maximand called wealth? To be sure, monetary value is nothing more than the average price (or market price) of a good or service, determined through the forces of supply and demand, of numerous individuals coming together in a marketplace and, through their transactions, revealing their idiosyncratic preferences, or utilities, which are in turn reflected in collective averages known as price. And during this revelatory process, it can be shown that consumers who subjectively value a good or service offered in the marketplace more than the market price attached to that good or service will buy it, and those who value the good or service less than the market price will not. To see why, consider the following example.

Suppose Johnny goes to a car dealership to buy a car, and there sees a Honda Accord selling for $20,000 that he likes very much. What forces will determine whether Johnny buys that car or walks off the lot? There are numerous psychological forces at work, to be sure, but it is safe to say that Johnny will buy the car if, at the time of making his decision, he intrinsically values the car more than the market values the car (for example, more than the average value, or price, placed on the car by the collective agreement of every participant in the market). In other words, if Johnny's intrinsic value, or utility, exceeds the monetary value, or price, placed on the car by the market, Johnny will buy the car. Why? Because he will attach more satisfaction, or intrinsic value, to owning the car, than he would lose by parting with the $20,000 dollars, and people, who are defined by wealth maximization theorists as "rational maximizers of their satisfaction," should logically engage in such satisfaction-maximizing transactions.

If, on other hand, Johnny intrinsically values the car at only $15,000, while society values it at $20,000, Johnny will not buy the car. Why?

Because the satisfaction or utility Johnny would derive from keeping the $20,000 would exceed the utility he would derive from buying the car. But would Johnny buy the car if he intrinsically valued it at exactly $20,000, and saw the car selling for exactly that price? The answer is still no, because if Johnny would derive the same amount of utility from keeping the money in his pocket as he would by purchasing the car, then the transaction costs alone, as measured in terms of utility, of reaching into his back pocket to pull out his wallet would disincentivize him from doing so (unless, of course, he derived utility from pulling out his wallet, in which case he might buy the car after all).

It can thus be seen, then, that Johnny's decision to purchase or not purchase the car was determined exclusively by reference to utility, and not wealth. Indeed, the dollar amount attached to a good need not (and usually will not) reflect the intrinsic value that a particular individual will attach to a good, but will operate instead to facilitate exchange by allowing a party to compare his or her intrinsic value to the collective average intrinsic value (or price) that a marketplace attaches to that good. And, it can further be shown that, like Johnny, an individual will buy the good in question if, at the time of the transaction, they associate a higher intrinsic value to the good (or a lower intrinsic value to their dollars) than does the market, whereas the individual will not buy (or will become a seller of) the good where the opposite is true. Dollars, then, simply serve as a convenient medium of exchange by which to facilitate this comparison between intrinsic and market values, and have no intrinsic value of their own of which to speak — a relatively straightforward point that should not need mentioning but for the fact that it is all too frequently forgotten. . . .

[W]hat I understand wealth maximization theorists to be saying is that, because we cannot directly measure (and therefore maximize) intrinsic value, we ought instead to capture it as best we can by maximizing the medium of exchange (for example, dollars) that best approximates this value. And, if this is correct, then what the wealth maximization theorist is really concerned about is not maximizing the medium of exchange at all, but rather maximizing intrinsic value, or the satisfaction that individuals attach to the medium of exchange. Therefore, the wealth maximization theorists' desire to maximize dollars should only be understood as valid to the extent that it functions as a proxy for maximizing satisfaction. And if . . . utilitarians are unable to measure and intersubjectively compare different levels of satisfaction, the wealth maximization theorists' decision to substitute dollars for utility seems to be an entirely sensible one.

It should be clear, then, that expressing the concept of value through the concept of wealth as measured by a medium of exchange (such as, dollars) is meaningful in proportion to the extent that the medium of exchange actually reflects intrinsic value, and in inverse proportion to the extent that it does not. This outcome results because . . . the medium of exchange is meaningless except to the extent it reflects individual expressions of utility. It should thus be clear that no theory, including WMT, can be based on the underlying premise that wealth is pursued for its own sake, because, as we have seen, wealth must be pursued as a means of satisfying intrinsic value, or "utility." Indeed, although wealth maximization theorists insist upon a firm separation between the concepts of utility and wealth, even they are unable to escape employing the utilitarian concept of value in furtherance of their wealth maximization aims. Consider, for instance, the following example:

> [Suppose] I offer you $5 for a bag of oranges, you accept, and the exchange is consummated. We can be confident that the wealth of society has been increased. Before the transaction you had a bag of oranges worth less than $5 to you and I had $5; after the transaction you have $5 and I have a bag of oranges worth more than $5 to me. We are both richer, as measured by the money value we attach to the goods in question.[11]

The above example insists that the transaction is beneficial from a wealth maximization perspective because it increases the wealth of society and the wealth of the parties. And "wealth," it will be recalled, has been defined by wealth maximization theorists as the "value in dollars or dollar equivalents . . . of everything in society."[12] So far, so good. But how, exactly, can it be that an exchange of dollars for oranges resulted in an increase in wealth? The key move is made in the third sentence, where the author resorts to the utilitarian concept of "worth"

---

11. Richard A. Posner, Utilitarianism, Economics, and Legal Theory, 8 J. Legal Stud. 103, 120 (1979).
12. Id. at 119.

(that is, intrinsic value) to justify the claim that society's wealth ("dollars or dollar equivalents") has increased. Parsing the language more carefully, we note that two very different concepts of worth (that is, the utilitarian concept of intrinsic value and the wealth maximization concept of "dollars or dollar equivalents") are being used interchangeably with one another, the utilitarian concept of intrinsic value carrying the weight at the very moment the wealth maximization concept of value begins to break down. If we disambiguate these two concepts of value and more accurately reconstruct the above example, however, what we are told is that, in essence, a society and both parties to the transaction are wealthier because the party who sold the oranges intrinsically valued them less than he or she intrinsically valued the $5, and the party who bought them intrinsically valued them more than he or she intrinsically valued the $5.

But when we look at the matter from this perspective, what we see is that something significant has happened from a utilitarian perspective (that is, the intrinsic values of both parties to the transaction has been increased), while little that is remarkable has happened from the perspective of wealth maximization theory. Why? Because, as measured in terms of dollars or dollar equivalents, we observe that, before the transaction, there existed one bag of oranges and one $5 bill. After the transaction, we still observe the same bag of oranges and the same $5 bill — and nothing more. Society's wealth, as measured in terms of dollars, is exactly the same as it was before. If the parties are better off at all, they are better off only in the utilitarian sense of the word. And indeed, this is exactly what the explanation embedded in the example above really suggests has changed: Society and the parties are better off in the utilitarian sense because each party was able to exchange something intrinsically worth less to them for something intrinsically worth more to them. As a result of this transaction, the goods have moved from a lower-value to a higher-value use in a utilitarian sense because each party valued the thing he or she gave up less than the thing he or she received in return. Both parties feel better off, and are better off after the exchange than they were before the exchange, but again, only in utilitarian terms. In terms of dollars, however, the collective wealth of the parties and of society is exactly the same as what it was before (the money and the oranges have simply changed hands). Even more notably, in terms of dollars, one of the parties is actually richer than he or she was before by $5), while one of the parties is now poorer than he or she was before by $5, a result that simply cannot be explained on the basis of wealth maximization theory alone.

Indeed, it can at this time be said that a party will only contract for land, goods, or services if that party believes, at the time of entering into the contract, that he or she will derive more utility from the land, good, or service to be obtained than the disutility he or she will suffer from having to give up the thing required to obtain it (for example land, goods, services, or money). To be sure, it must therefore be the case that, in the absence of duress, fraud, unconscionability, and the like, transactions that are voluntarily entered into (and protected via the mechanism of contract) are agreed to because the utility (and not the wealth) that the person acquiring the land, good, or service expects to gain exceeds the utility (and not the wealth) that the person expects to lose in giving up the consideration required to obtain it, and that the utility or intrinsic value referred to above is, in all cases, necessarily subjective.[13] . . .

[O]ne immediate implication [of the distinction between wealth and utility] is that, in an action brought for damages for the breach of contract, an award of an objective expectation remedy is an illusion and will rarely fully compensate a party for the thing for which he or she contracted. This is because, by definition, the person who entered into the contract must have, at the time of contracting, intrinsically valued the land, good, or services he or she contracted for more than he or she valued the consideration he or she had to give up to obtain it, and therefore more than the market price attached to the land, good, or service, which is what courts often use to calculate expectation damages. . . .

In sum, then, it is clear that utility, or intrinsic value, is almost always a more accurate measure of the true value an individual places on a good or service than is its price. And because intrinsic value is more accurate, if we are really interested in maximizing the welfare or utility of individuals and/or society, courts that rely on money damages via the

---

13. For purposes of argumentation, this Article assumes, along with wealth maximization theorists, that individuals act rationally and properly evaluate their own satisfactions, two assumptions that have (rightly) come under attack as of late by behavioral economists. While this condition probably holds true much of the time, there are undoubtedly important exceptions where it does not. . . .

expectancy as a crude proxy for utility will never fully succeed in doing so. . . .

B.   The Problem of Measurement

. . . [T]he above analysis reveals a hierarchy of remedies that courts should employ when compensating promisees in breach of contract cases: First, where parties have stipulated damages in a liquidated damages provision, courts should give serious weight to these expressed ex ante intentions, and enforce these clauses to the exclusion of all other remedies.[14] This is because these clauses constitute the only device available to a party wishing to reveal his or her utility to a court by accurately pricing the ex ante intrinsic value he or she assigns to the other party's performance. In addition, enforcing such clauses not only takes seriously the parties' original intent by allowing courts to enforce the parties' original allocation of risk — including specifically the risk of nonperformance — but a failure to do so will result in a forfeiture to the party who paid a risk premium for a clause that was not enforced. Further, it is only through the enforcement of such clauses that truly efficient breaches are even possible, for it is only in such cases that courts can be sure that a promisor paying a liquidated sum to a promisee is not failing to capture accurately the promisee's ex ante intrinsic value or any unforeseeable or uncertain damages that may be suffered by the promisee as a result of the promisor's breach, unless the promisee himself failed to disclose these risks to the promisor at the time of entering into the contract. . . .

---

14. This statement should not be read to mean, however, that liquidated damages provisions, where they exist, should be enforced absolutely. Rather, this remedy, like all remedies proposed in this Article, should be subject to the same qualifications as the specific performance remedy . . . (that is, the traditional contract law defenses and the doctrines of good faith and fair dealing). Thus, for instance, under this regime, one need not fear the demands of a promisee seeking the enforcement of a penalty clause allowing him to cut a pound of flesh from the promisor for the latter's breach of contract, as such a provision would clearly violate public policy. William Shakespeare, The Merchant Of Venice, Act 4, Sc. 1.

Second, this hierarchy suggests awarding specific performance where the parties did not themselves provide for a liquidated damages provision, because, as discussed earlier, the promisee will get exactly what he or she bargained for ex ante, including any ex ante intrinsic value he or she attached to the promisor's performance, while at the same time shielding the promisee from damages that were unforeseeable or uncertain at the time of entering into the contract, but that are nonetheless real.[15]

And last, this hierarchy suggests awarding expectation damages only where, first, the parties have not themselves already provided for a liquidated damages provision, or second, where, on public policy grounds or otherwise, a court is unable to award the remedy of specific performance. . . .

CONCLUSION

This Article shows that, within contract law itself, utilitarian analysis — and not wealth maximization theory — ought to be the coin of the consequentialist realm. This is because wealth maximization theory's dependence on the utilitarian concept of value renders it unable to stand on its own terms, and makes it intelligible only as a utilitarian substitute. Such a substitute, however, is not needed within contract law, where the parties, through the processes of consent-based bargain and exchange, are able to capture (via contract) and reflect (to a court and to each other) their respective ex ante utilities. . . .

---

15. Once again, it must be emphasized that nothing stated here should suggest awarding specific performance where there are valid contractual defenses available to the promisor, such as impossibility, impracticability, or frustration of purpose. . . .

3

HOW SHOULD DEFAULT RULES BE CHOSEN?

By now everyone acknowledges the legal realist insight that all contracts are, by necessity, incomplete to some degree. The inevitability of incompleteness reflects, to borrow a distinction from H.L.A. Hart, both our "relative ignorance of fact" and "our relative indeterminacy of aim."[1]

Parties drafting a contract cannot foresee every future event or know precisely how their own purposes may change; they cannot negotiate terms specifically to cover all contingencies. As a result, their manifested agreement will be silent as to these matters. As the duration of a contract is extended, the knowledge problem facing the parties is likely to increase and the completeness of their agreement to decrease. Contractual incompleteness also arises because settling in advance even those contingencies that can be foreseen is costly. Many foreseeable contingencies, given their low probability, are better left unnegotiated ex ante in the hopes that they will not materialize or will be handled cooperatively ex post if they do. And, as we shall see, strategic considerations may lead one or both parties to remain silent about a particular issue.

The received wisdom concerning contractual incompleteness is reflected in the concept of "gap-filler," a legal realist term that has

---

1. H.L.A. Hart, The Concept of Law 125 (1961).

dominated contract discourse for several decades. According to this view, no contract is without its "gaps." Much of what is taught as the law of contract can be conceived as publicly provided "background" rules or principles that fill the inevitable gaps in the private law made by contracting parties.

This gap-filling conception of contract law has tended to undermine support for consent as the basis of contractual obligation. Gap-filling terms — sometimes referred to as "implied-in-law" — are said to be imposed by the legal system for reasons of principle or policy rather than consented to by the parties. That such implied-in-law terms are based on the parties' consent has long been thought to be pure fiction. If the publicly provided rules of contract law almost always operate where there is a gap in the manifestation of assent, then consequently a gap-filling provision must be coercively imposed on parties who have not, by assumption, consented to its imposition. Furthermore, if the central problem of contract theory is to decide how gaps in manifested assent should be filled, then the consent of the parties plays no role in the choice of gap-fillers. In this manner, the pervasiveness of contractual incompleteness and the concept of gap-fillers makes consent look quite irrelevant to the main issues of contract theory.

Since the 1990s, however, the rhetoric of gap-filling was increasingly supplanted by a new and powerful heuristic device: the concept of default rules. The default rule approach analogizes the way that contract law fills gaps in the expressed consent of contracting parties to the way that word-processing programs set our margins for us in the absence of our expressly setting them for ourselves. A word-processing program that required us to set every variable needed to write a page of text would be more trouble than it was worth. Instead, all word-processing programs provide default settings for such variables as margins, type fonts, and line spacing and leave it to the user to change any of these default settings to better suit his or her purposes.

What makes the default rule approach to gap-filling distinctive in both word processing and contract law is that default rules are binding in the absence of manifested assent to the contrary — which means that a manifested assent to the contrary will displace the default rule. Any gap-filling rule that cannot be displaced by manifested assent is not properly called a default rule at all, but is called an "immutable" rule — that is, some other kind of contract law background norm that may fill a gap in assent or may even displace the manifested assent of the parties.

By this criterion, many of the provisions of Article 2 of the Uniform Commercial Code (U.C.C.) are default rules, because they apply "unless otherwise agreed." Eighteen of the twenty-eight provisions of Part 3 of Article 2, which specify the "General Obligation and Construction of Contract," contain this or comparable language. Moreover, section 1-102(4) specifies that "[t]he presence in certain provisions of this Act of the words 'unless otherwise agreed' or words of similar import does not imply that the effect of other provisions may not be varied by agreement under subsection (3)."

The default rule approach is not, of course, limited to the U.C.C. Outside the areas of fraud, duress, and unconscionability, few of the cases in law school casebooks would have arisen had the parties included an express clause in their agreement to govern the problem that arose between them. In almost every case, the silence of the parties creates a gap that the default rules of contract law are used to fill.

In this chapter, we read an excerpt from an influential article by Yale law professor Ian Ayres and University of Chicago business school professor Robert Gertner. In "Filling Gaps in Incomplete Contracts: An Economic Theory of Default Rules," they prominently introduced the rhetoric of "default" and "immutable" rules into the literature and offered some proposals on how default rules should be set. In particular, they took issue with a common argument that the gap-filling background rules of contract should reflect what a majority of contracting parties would want, thereby putting the onus on the minority of parties to contract around the rules. Sometimes, they said, we should adopt "penalty default" rules that most parties do not want, but that force parties to reveal information to each other when they are negotiating to deviate from the default rule.

In my article, "The Sound of Silence: Default Rules and Contractual Consent," I expand upon their approach to contend that there is good reason for default rules to correspond to the "common sense" of unsophisticated parties, as contrasted with repeat players. I also take issue with the claim made by Richard Craswell that an approach that bases the enforcement of contracts on the consent of the parties to be legally bound has nothing to say about how default rules should be chosen. Both excerpts use for an example, the default rules provided by the case of *Hadley v. Bexendale*.

STUDY GUIDE: *First, make sure you understand the difference between a default rule and an immutable rule. Second, make sure you understand the difference between two types of default rules: majoritarian default rules and penalty default rules. Under what circumstances do Professors Ayres and Gertner favor the use of penalty defaults? How does the rule of Hadley v. Baxendale illustrate the concept of and rationale for penalty defaults?*

FILLING GAPS IN INCOMPLETE CONTRACTS*

Ian Ayres and Robert Gertner

INTRODUCTION

The legal rules of contracts and corporations can be divided into two distinct classes. The larger class consists of "default" rules that parties can contract around by prior agreement, while the smaller, but important, class consists of "immutable" rules that parties cannot change by contractual agreement. Default rules fill the gaps in incomplete contracts; they govern unless the parties contract around them. Immutable rules cannot be contracted around; they govern even if the parties attempt to contract around them. . . .

[A]lthough the academy recognizes the analytic difference between default and immutable rules, a detailed theory of how defaults should be set has yet to be proposed. Indeed, the lack of agreement over even what to call the "default" concept is evidence of the underdeveloped state of default theory. Default rules have alternatively been termed background, backstop, enabling, fallback, gap-filling, off-the-rack, opt-in, opt-out, preformulated, preset, presumptive, standby, standard-form and supplementary rules.

This Article provides a theory of how courts and legislatures should set default rules. We suggest that efficient defaults would take a variety of forms that at times would diverge from the "what the parties would have contracted for" principle. To this end, we introduce the concept of "penalty defaults." Penalty defaults are designed to give at least one

---

*From Ian Ayres and Robert Gertner, Filling Gaps in Incomplete Contracts: An Economic Theory of Default Rules, 99 Yale L.J. 87 (1989).

party to the contract an incentive to contract around the default rule and therefore to choose affirmatively the contract provision they prefer. In contrast to the received wisdom, penalty defaults are purposefully set at what the parties would not want — in order to encourage the parties to reveal information to each other or to third parties (especially the courts). . . .

An essential component of our theory of default rules is our explicit consideration of the sources of contractual incompleteness. We distinguish between two basic reasons for incompleteness. Scholars have primarily attributed incompleteness to the costs of contracting. Contracts may be incomplete because the transaction costs of explicitly contracting for a given contingency are greater than the benefits. . . .

This Article also proposes a second source of contractual incompleteness that is the focus of much of our analysis. We refer to this source of incompleteness as strategic. One party might strategically withhold information that would increase the total gains from contracting (the "size of the pie") in order to increase her private share of the gains from contracting (her "share of the pie"). By attempting to contract around a certain default, one party might reveal information to the other party that affects how the contractual pie is split. Thus, for example, the more informed party may prefer to have inefficient precaution rather than pay a higher price for the good. While analysts have previously explained incomplete contracting solely in terms of the costs of writing additional provisions, we argue that contractual gaps can also result from strategic behavior by relatively informed parties. By changing the default rules of the game, lawmakers can importantly reduce the opportunities for this rent-seeking, strategic behavior. In particular, the possibility of strategic incompleteness leads us to suggest that efficiency-minded lawmakers should sometimes choose penalty defaults that induce knowledgeable parties to reveal information by contracting around the default penalty. The strategic behavior of the parties in forming the contract can justify strategic contractual interpretations by courts.

Our analysis therefore moves beyond the received wisdom that default rules should simply be what the majority of contracting parties would have wanted. In choosing among default rules, lawmakers should be sensitive to the costs of contracting around, and the costs of failing to contract around, particular defaults. . . .

I. PENALTY DEFAULT RULES

A.   The Zero-Quantity Default

The diversity of default standards can even be seen in contrasting the law's treatment of the two most basic contractual terms: price and quantity. Although price and quantity are probably the two most essential issues on which to reach agreement, the U.C.C. establishes radically different defaults. If the parties leave out the price, the U.C.C. fills the gap with "a reasonable price."[2] If the parties leave out the quantity, the U.C.C. refuses to enforce the contract.[3] In essence, the U.C.C. mandates that the default quantity should be zero.

How can this be? The U.C.C.'s reasonable-price standard can be partly reconciled with the received wisdom that defaults should be set at what the parties would have contracted for. But why doesn't the U.C.C. treat a missing quantity term analogously by filling the gap with the reasonable quantity that the parties would have wanted? Obviously, the parties would not have gone to the expense of contracting with the intention that nothing be exchanged.

We suggest that the zero-quantity default cannot be explained by a "what the parties would have wanted" principle. Instead, a rationale for the rule can be found by comparing the cost of ex ante contracting to the cost of ex post litigation. The zero-quantity rule can be justified because it is cheaper for the parties to establish the quantity term beforehand than for the courts to determine after the fact what the parties would have wanted.

It is not systematically easier for parties to figure out the quantity than the price ex ante, but it is systematically harder for the courts to figure out the quantity than the price ex post. To estimate a reasonable

---

2. U.C.C. §2-305(1) reads: "The parties if they so intend can conclude a contract for sale even though the price is not settled. In such a case the price is a reasonable price at the time for delivery. . . ." U.C.C. §2-305(1) (1976).

3. U.C.C. §2-201 states that a "contract . . . is not enforceable under this [provision] beyond the quantity of goods shown. . . ." U.C.C. §2-201(1) (1976). The official comment adds that "[t]he only term which must appear is the quantity term which need not be accurately stated but recovery is limited to the amount stated." U.C.C. §2-201(1) (official comment) (1978).

price, courts can largely rely on market information of the type "How much were rutabagas selling for on July 3?" But to estimate a reasonable quantity, courts would need to undertake a more costly analysis of the individual litigants of the type "How much did the buyer and seller value the marginal rutabagas?"

The U.C.C's zero-quantity default is what we term a "penalty default." Because ex ante neither party would want a zero-quantity contract, such a rule penalizes the parties should they fail to affirmatively specify their desired quantity. Because the non-enforcement default potentially penalizes both parties, it encourages both of them to include a quantity term.

B.   Toward a More General Theory of Penalty Defaults

Penalty defaults, by definition, give at least one party to the contract an incentive to contract around the default. From an efficiency perspective, penalty default rules can be justified as a way to encourage the production of information. The very process of "contracting around" can reveal information to parties inside or outside the contract. Penalty defaults may be justified as 1) giving both contracting parties incentives to reveal information to third parties, especially courts, or 2) giving a more informed contracting party incentives to reveal information to a less informed party.

The zero-quantity default, for instance, gives both contracting parties incentives to reveal their contractual intentions when it would be costly for a court to discover that information ex post. This justification — that ex ante contracting can be cheaper than ex post litigation — can also explain the common law's broader rule that "for a contract to be binding the terms of the contract must be reasonably certain and definite." . . .

Lawmakers should select the rule that deters inefficient gaps at the least social cost. When the rationale is to provide information to the courts, the non-enforcement default is likely to be efficient. . . . In contrast, when the rationale is to inform the relatively uninformed contracting party, the penalty default should be against the relatively informed party. This is especially true when the uninformed party is also uninformed about the default rule itself. If the uninformed party does not know that there is a penalty default, she will have no opportunistic incentives.

In some situations it is reasonable to expect one party to the contract to be systematically informed about the default rule and the probability of the relevant contingency arising. If one side is repeatedly in the relevant contractual setting while the other side rarely is, it is a sensible presumption that the former is better informed than the latter. Consider, for example, the treatment of real estate brokerage commissions when a buyer breaches a purchase contract. Such contracts typically include a clause which obligates the purchaser to forfeit some given amount of "earnest" money if she breaches the agreement. How should the earnest money be split between the seller and the broker if their agency contract does not address this contingency? Some courts have adopted a "what the parties would have wanted" approach and have awarded all the earnest money to the seller. We agree with this outcome, but for different reasons. The real estate broker will more likely be informed about the default rule than the seller. Indeed, the seller may not even consider the issue of how to split the earnest money in case of default. Therefore, if the efficient contract would allocate some of the earnest money to the seller, the default rule should be set against the broker to induce her to raise the issue. Otherwise, if the default rule is set to favor the broker, a seller may not raise the issue, and the broker will be happy to take advantage of the seller's ignorance. By setting the default rule in favor of the uninformed party, the courts induce the informed party to reveal information, and, consequently, the efficient contract results.

Although social welfare may be enhanced by forcing parties to reveal information to a subsidized judicial system, it is more problematic to understand why society would have an efficiency interest in inducing a relatively informed party to a transaction to reveal information to the relatively uninformed party. After all, if revealing information is efficient because it increases the value created by the contract, one might initially expect that the informed party will have a sufficient private incentive to reveal information — the incentive of splitting a bigger pie. This argument ignores the possibility, however, that revealing information might simultaneously increase the total size of the pie and decrease the share of the pie that the relatively informed party receives. If the "share-of-the-pie effect" dominates the "size-of-the-pie effect," informed parties might rationally choose to withhold relevant information.[4]

Parties may behave strategically not only because they have superior information about the default, but also because they have superior information about other aspects of the contract. We suggest that a party who knows that a particular default rule is inefficient may choose not to negotiate to change it. The knowledgeable party may not wish to reveal her information in negotiations if the information would give a bargaining advantage to the other side.

How can it be that by increasing the total gains from contracting (the size-of-the-pie effect) the informed party can end up with a smaller share of the gains (the share-of-the-pie effect)?[5] This Article demonstrates how relatively informed parties can sometimes benefit by strategically withholding information that, if revealed, would increase the size of the pie. A knowledgeable buyer, for example, may prefer to remain indistinguishable from what the seller wrongly perceives to be the class of similarly situated buyers. By blending in with the larger class of contractors, a buyer or a seller may receive a cross-subsidized price because the other side will bargain as if she is dealing with the average member of the class. A knowledgeable party may prefer to remain in this inefficient, but cross-subsidized, contractual pool rather than move to an

---

4. Withholding socially valuable private information to obtain private gains is common. Companies may withhold information about innovations from competitors to increase profits; car buyers may withhold information about particular options or accessories that they value if this information signals to car dealers a greater willingness to pay for the underlying automobile; and professional athletes may withhold information about injuries to increase their salaries, even though as a result their team may inefficiently hire reserves.

5. If, under a given set of default rules, a seller wants to sell a sweater that she values at $50 to a buyer who values it at $150, then without contracting around any of the defaults the parties' agreement will create $100 of value. The total gain from contracting, in other words, will be $100. The parties will split this gain in value between themselves by bargaining for a price between $50 and $150. Suppose, however, that the buyer (and only the buyer) has information that would make the sweater worth $200 to him if the seller would take on a duty that is outside of the default provisions and that would cost the seller $10. The total gains from this non-default exchange would be $140 ($200 - $50 - $10). How could the buyer lose by revealing information that increased the size of the pie by $40? If the parties accept the default provisions and negotiate a $100 price (implying that each party receives a $50 share of the total gains), how can it be that revealing the value-enhancing information — by contracting for the non-default duty — would reduce the buyer's share to less than $50 (implying that the negotiated price would exceed $150 and that the seller's share would exceed $90)?

efficient, but unsubsidized, pool. If contracting around the default suffi-ciently reduces this cross-subsidization, the share-of-the-pie effect can exceed the size-of-the-pie effect because the informed party's share of the default pie was in a sense being artificially cross-subsidized by other members of the contractual class. . . .

C. Penalty Defaults in Action

1. Uncompensated Damages in *Hadley v. Baxendale*

An example of how a penalty default can restrict rent-seeking beha-vior can be seen in the venerable case, *Hadley v. Baxendale*.[6] In *Hadley* a miller in Gloucester contracted with a carrier to have a broken crank shaft transported to Greenwich. The shipment was delayed, and the miller sued the carrier for consequential damages of the profits lost while the mill was inoperative. The court, holding that only foreseeable consequential damages should be awarded, reversed a damage award and remanded for a new trial.

The holding in *Hadley* operates as a penalty default. The miller could have informed the carrier of the potential consequential damages and contracted for full damage insurance.[7] The *Hadley* default of deny-ing unforeseeable damages may not be consistent with what fully informed parties would have wanted. The miller's consequential damages were real and the carrier may have been the more efficient bearer of this risk. As a general matter, millers may want carriers to compensate them for consequential damages that carriers can prevent at lower cost.[8] The default can instead be understood as a purposeful indu-cement to the miller as the more informed party to reveal that information to the carrier. Informing the carrier creates value because

---

6. 9 Ex. 341, 156 Eng. Rep. 145 (1854). . . .

7. There is some evidence that the miller in fact attempted to inform the carrier of the probable damages. Thus, it may be difficult for parties to contract around the *Hadley* default. . . .

8. The efficient risk-sharing agreement between symmetrically-informed shippers (e.g., the miller in this case) and carriers will depend upon their relative attitudes toward risk, the ability of the carrier to prevent the damages, and the ability of the shipper to mitigate damages in case of breach. . . .

if the carrier foresees the loss, he will be able to prevent it more efficiently. At the same time, however, revealing the information to the carrier will undoubtedly increase the price of shipping. Nonetheless, so long as transaction costs are not prohibitive, a miller with high consequential damages will gain from revealing this information and contracting for greater insurance from the carrier because the carrier is the least-cost avoider.

This is not to say that there could not be an equally efficient market response if *Hadley* had gone the other way. If the default required carriers to compensate for unforeseeable consequential damages, low-damage millers would have the incentive to raise the issue of consequential damages. In a competitive industry, the uninformed carrier, in effect, assumes she is facing an average-damage miller and charges a price accordingly. The market price will reflect the expected cost of insuring high-damage millers. A low-damage miller will want to contract for less-than-average insurance and, therefore, a lower price. But the gains from contracting around the default may be insignificant if the proportion of millers with high damages is small. Furthermore, it may be very difficult for a low-damage miller to determine how much of the price is an implicit insurance premium for millers with higher damages.

Thus, there may be situations in which the low-damage millers fail to contract for the low-insurance/low-price contract. In the resulting equilibrium, carriers may charge a price representing their average cost of serving both high- and low-damage millers and take an average amount of precaution (which will be relatively low if there are relatively few high-damage millers). . . .

It is important to consider another channel for information revelation. The uninformed party, the carrier, may attempt to learn the expected damages of the informed parties, the millers, by offering a menu of insurance contracts. The millers might then be induced to self-select the insurance contract that is optimal for their expected damages. The problem faced by uninformed parties trying to induce information revelation, however, is that in many situations the necessary menu is more complicated than in the common carrier example. Devising a menu that induces information revelation may require a great deal of sophistication by the uninformed party and may entail large transaction costs.

The main lesson to draw from our discussion of *Hadley* is that there may be strategic reasons for parties' choosing not to reveal information.

If the default rule awarded all consequential damages, to be sure, the low-damage millers would want to distinguish themselves from the high-damage millers. But the high-damage millers may intentionally choose to withhold information that would make their contracts more efficient. An informed party may not realize the full social value of revealing the information and, hence, her private benefits from revealing may diverge from the social benefits of having the information revealed. As elaborated below, by not distinguishing themselves, informed parties may be able to free-ride on the lower-cost qualities of others and thereby contract at a subsidized price. To counteract this strategic behavior, courts should choose defaults that are different from what the parties would have wanted. . . .

D. Summary

Penalty defaults stand as stark counter-examples to the proposition that courts should simply choose defaults that the parties would have wanted. Particularly when individual parties have private incentives to withhold information, it may be desirable for the law to give them a nudge. The possibility that efficient defaults will at times be used to reflect what most people want while at other times be used to encourage the revelation of information is analogous to the disparate uses of presumptions in the laws of evidence. In both instances, the law is sometimes chosen to promote the revelation of information.

Finally, having shown that lawmakers will sometimes want to set defaults that encourage one or both parties to reveal information, we now should warn lawmakers that they should sometimes protect the private incentives to become informed. In some instances forcing parties to reveal information will undermine their incentives to obtain the information in the first place. Lawmakers therefore should not impose penalty defaults that have a net effect of reducing the amount of socially useful information. But in some instances, a particular party may need to acquire certain types of information before contracting, so that forcing disclosure would have minimal disincentive effects. . . .

STUDY GUIDE: *How does the concept of default rule undermine the picture of gap-filling contract law rules being imposed on parties without their consent for reasons of principle or policy? In what respect does the consensual nature contract influence the choice of default rules supplied by contract law? What is a "conventionist" default rule and how does it differ from a majoritarian default rule? Once again, consider how the rule of Hadley v. Baxendale illustrates the analysis.*

THE SOUND OF SILENCE: DEFAULT RULES AND CONTRACTUAL CONSENT*

Randy E. Barnett

... I had grasped the significance of the silence of the dog, for one true inference invariably suggests others. . . . Obviously the midnight visitor was someone whom the dog knew well.

— Sherlock Holmes

INTRODUCTION: INCOMPLETE CONTRACTS AND CONSENT

... The rhetoric of default rules is in the process of becoming the terminology of choice for contract theorists. Yet the implications of this subtle conceptual shift for the debate concerning the underlying basis of contractual obligation — especially the role of consent — have yet to be explored. The idea of filling gaps in manifested consent with default rules calls into question the neat dichotomy between terms that are assented to and those that are imposed by the legal system. It suggests yet another category of terms that, although supplied by courts or legislatures when there is a gap in manifested assent, nonetheless reflect the consent of the parties.

Terms supplied by default rules are not a product of the expressed or implied-in-fact consent of the parties as these two notions have traditionally been understood, and may therefore be considered genuinely implied-in-law. But neither are terms supplied by default rules invariably imposed on the parties by the legal system for reasons of principle

---

*From Randy E. Barnett, The Sound of Silence: Default Rules and Contractual Consent, 78 Va. L. Rev. 821 (1992).

or policy as are terms supplied by immutable contract rules or by tort law. In a very real sense, such terms can be and often are indirectly consented to by parties who could have contracted around them — but did not.

In this Article, I want to challenge the received wisdom of "gap-filling in the absence of consent" by showing how the concept of default rules bolsters the theoretical importance of consent. I will accomplish this by expanding and refining my analysis of a "consent theory of contract." I propose that the concept of default rules reveals consent to be operating at two distinct levels of contract theory. First, the presence of consent to be legally bound is essential to justify the legal enforcement of any default rules. Second, nested within this overall consent to be legally bound, consent also operates to justify the selection of particular default rules.

With consent operating on both of these levels, contract terms supplied by default rules can be seen to occupy a previously undifferentiated middle ground between the traditional categories of implied-in-fact and implied-in-law terms. Under certain circumstances, it is not at all fictitious to characterize a choice to remain silent and let default rules operate as an expression of consent, albeit a more inchoate or indirect expression than what we associate with expressed or implied-in-fact terms. And, even when parties cannot be said to have consented by their silence to the enforcement of particular default rules, enforcement may still be justified on the grounds of consent when default rules are chosen to reflect the commonsense or conventional understanding of most parties.

As will become apparent, the concept of default rules entails a very practical implication for how contract law is taught in law school. We should replace the traditional dichotomy of expressed or implied-in-fact contract terms that are "really" consented to and implied-in-law contract terms that are "really" imposed on the parties with a more realistic trichotomy. In the first category are terms that are a product of direct consent (expressed or implied-in-fact terms), in the second are terms that are a product of indirect consent (implied-in-law default rules), and in the third are terms that are imposed upon the parties without any consent (implied-in-law immutable terms). With this reconfiguration, the set of implied-in-law terms that represent a genuine imposition on the parties is much smaller than is commonly assumed. . . .

A.   "Conventionalist" Default Rules and Subjective Agreement

[A consent theory views contracts as] part of an entitlements scheme that performs a vital boundary-defining function, facilitating the orderly use of local and personal knowledge. Entitlements cannot perform this function unless persons can obtain knowledge of their requirements so that they can regulate their own behavior and reliably predict how others will behave. Because we never have direct and reliable access to the hidden or subjective intentions of others, we can only rely on the reasonable meaning conveyed by a party's words and behavior. . . .

[Nevertheless, a consent theory of contract law] is not indifferent to the fact that the objective meaning of consent is likely to correspond to the subjectively held intentions of the parties. Indeed, some of the functions performed by . . . freedom of contract depend on this correspondence. For example, one of the functions of freedom *to* contract is to enable persons to exchange entitlements they have for those that they subjectively prefer, thereby making them better off. One of the functions of freedom *from* contract is to require persons who seek to acquire the resources belonging to others to take into account the subjective preferences of the present right-holder. To perform either of these functions our objective interpretation of assent should mirror as nearly as possible (subject to other constraints) the subjective intentions of the parties.

When there is a gap in manifested intent, it may be a true gap, in which case neither party has any subjective intentions. In this situation, both parties' (nonexistent) subjective intentions will be satisfied equally by any default rule. It is also possible, however, even likely, that there are mutually shared tacit subjective intentions that cannot be established and that influence the meaning of what has been manifested. As Lon Fuller (no lover of legal fictions) explained:

> Words like "intention," "assumption," "expectation" and "understanding" all seem to imply a conscious state involving an awareness of alternatives and a deliberate choice among them. It is, however, plain that there is a psychological state which can be described as a "tacit assumption" that does not involve a consciousness of alternatives. The absent-minded professor stepping from his office into the hall as he reads a book "assumes" that the floor of the hall will be there to receive him. His conduct is conditioned and directed by this assumption, even

though the possibility that the floor has been removed does not "occur" to him, that is, is not present in his conscious mental processes.[9]

Fuller's insights are supported by modern psychological research focusing on the relationship between conscious and nonconscious thought processes. This relationship can better be understood by considering an analogy to video games that create fictional "worlds" sometimes called "virtual realities." Only a portion of the game's world appears on the screen (in "consciousness") at any particular time, but the portion that remains out of sight still "exists" (though "nonconsciously"). The off-screen portion bears a constant "spatial" relationship to the portions of the world that is on the screen notwithstanding that it does not exist anywhere literally as a picture. Similarly, when using a word processor, the rest of one's document still exists even though a portion of each page appears on the screen at any one time and the balance exists as magnetically recorded computer code, not actual text.

Finally, consider an analogy to fiction. We can say with confidence that certain things are "true" about the fictional world of Sherlock Holmes and other things are "false" even when there is no reference to these facts in any of Conan Doyle's stories.

> What is true in the story is much, much more than what is explicitly asserted in the text. It is true that there are no jet planes in Holmes' London (though this is not asserted explicitly or even logically implied in the text), but also true that there are piano tuners (though — as best I recall — none is mentioned, or, again, logically implied). In addition to what is true and false in the story, there is a large indeterminate area: while it is true that Holmes and Watson took the 11:10 from Waterloo Station to Aldershot one summer's day, it is neither true nor false that that day was a Wednesday ("The Crooked Man").[10]

Fictitious worlds are constructs of which only a fraction appears explicitly at any given time. Similarly, the human mind can be viewed as creating a "virtual reality," an elaborate construct of the external world.

---

9. Lon L. Fuller & Robert Braucher, Basic Contract Law 555 (1964). . . .
10. [Daniel C. Dennett, Consciousness Explained 79 (1991).]

Only a tiny fraction of this construct is present in consciousness at any given time.

Contracts, too, can be understood as the enterprise of projecting into the future an imagined "world." As Steven Burton and Eric Andersen have explained: "Two persons can cooperate by jointly imagining a possible world and, by entering an agreement with a promise on at least one side, committing themselves to each other to bring that world into being by their actions."[11] Of most relevance here is that this projected "world of contract" is usually the same as the present world of the parties in all respects except for the changes explicitly identified by the agreement. The parties silently assume that which "is" will continue to exist. Significantly, much of what they assume is true of the present is only a tacit or subconscious assumption. In other words, contracting parties are often silent — even to themselves — about what they in fact believe.

This does not mean that these silent assumptions are not real. Rather, they represent the immense "iceberg" of personal knowledge that lies submerged beneath the exposed "tip" of knowledge evident both to oneself and to others. . . . [B]ecause these assumptions are tacit and often nonconscious, they are notoriously difficult to prove directly — even the person possessing this sort of knowledge may be unaware of it. Moreover, tacit assumptions are by definition unexpressed, and thus they are evidenced by some linguistic formulation. Indeed, tacit assumptions serve to modify the normal meaning of what has been manifested. . . .

In light of this, the parties' subjective consent is most likely to be satisfied by a default rule that interprets manifested consent to reflect the commonsense or conventional expectations that likely are part of the tacit assumptions of particular parties. Where there is an unexpressed (and possibly nonconscious, but nonetheless genuine) tacit assumption shared by both parties, it almost invariably reflects the commonsense expectations of the relevant community. "Common sense," as used here, simply means the sense of things that most people share in common. In the example given by Fuller, people commonly expect that the floor of the hallway that was outside their office door when they entered

---

11. [Steven J. Burton & Eric G. Andersen, The World of a Contract, 75 Iowa L. Rev. 861, 864 (1990).]

will still be there when they leave. That expectation is part of their elaborate and largely nonconscious mental construct of the world. The fact that this belief is unexpressed and nonconscious — one does not ordinarily think about it — does not mean that one does not believe it and, if asked, would not say that one believed it.

This simple insight is crucial to the choice of default rules. Suppose it was legally relevant to adopt a rule that would best capture most people's subjective, but unexpressed and possibly nonconscious understanding concerning the floor outside their office. A rule reflecting the parties' tacit expectations that the floor outside their office still exists is functionally superior to a rule that reflects some other assumption about the state of the floor. Because tacit factual assumptions color every manifestation of consent, contractual enforcement will correspond to the subjective intentions of the parties only to the extent that default rules comport with the factual assumptions prevailing in the community of discourse to which the parties belong.

Neither when silence represents a true gap because the parties have no tacit assumption about the world, nor when it represents a tacit assumption that is actually shared by the parties, do we face the problem for which the objective theory is the solution: one party relying on the reasonable meaning of behavior while the other party has a subjective intention that differs from this meaning. Although the objective theory attempts to resolve disputes that arise from the subjective disagreement of contracting parties, situations where silence represents the subjectively-held tacit assumptions of both parties are situations of subjective agreement between the parties. The objective theory of contract is inapposite to this situation. . . .

Given that a default rule reflecting the commonsense expectations within the relevant community of discourse is likely to satisfy the parties' intentions as well (in the case of a true gap) or better (in the case where shared tacit subjective assumptions are present) than any rival default rule, there is a strong reason to prefer it. This is particularly true in light of the fact that the legal system usually cannot know whether it is facing a situation of true gaps or tacit assumptions. . . . [I]n a world of limited access to personal knowledge of intentions, default rules reflecting the commonsense expectation within the relevant community of discourse will lead to fewer interpretive mistakes than some other type of rule. . . . The conventional understanding is evidence, perhaps the best and only evidence, of what parties with mutual subjective tacit intentions concerning a matter arising in a gap in the manifestation of consent actually agreed to. . . .

B.   "Conventionalist" Default Rules and Subjective Disagreement

Suppose, however, that parties do not share the same factual assumptions about the world. To see how a consent theory may contribute to the proper choice of background rules in such circumstances, consider . . . the two default rules provided by the case of *Hadley v. Baxendale*. According to [Richard] Craswell, a consent theory is irrelevant to determining, for example, whether expansive liability for all foreseeable losses should be imposed on Federal Express (which would then have to expressly limit its responsibility) or whether Federal Express should confront a default rule of limited liability (that would apply unless the customer expressly bargains for more expansive liability). In Craswell's view, this choice must be based on some notion of efficiency or some other substantive theory, but not on consent.[12]

A consent theory is indifferent to the choice of default rules, however, only on the assumption that it is rational for both parties to incur the costs of learning the existing default rule and of bargaining around it. If this were always the case, from the perspective of consent, we could equally well place the burden on a promisee or on the promisor to expressly bargain around the default allocation of liability. But this assumption about rationality is often unwarranted.

With small one-shot transactions it may be irrational for either party to pay a lawyer to provide information concerning the default rules. Put another way, in light of the stakes involved, it may be rational for the parties to remain ignorant of the background rules. Under these circumstances, for reasons previously discussed, a conventionalist default rule

---

12. [See Richard Craswell, Contract Law, Default Rules, and the Philosophy of Promising, 88 Mich. L. Rev. 489, 528 (1989) ("Theories that explain the binding force of promises by pointing to the value of individual freedom . . . may well be valid answers to the question of why promises are binding. But . . . freedom can usually be served equally well by any background rule, so some other value must be introduced to explain why any one rule ought to be chosen over any other").]

based on the commonsense expectations of most persons would be most likely to accurately reflect the tacit subjective agreement of these rationally ignorant parties. In this manner, a gap between manifested consent and subjective assent would likely be narrowed.

In some common and definable circumstances, the cost of obtaining knowledge of the background rules of contract law can justify adopting a conventionalist default that reflects the commonsense understanding of rationally ignorant parties. In situations where the commonsense meaning embodied in a conventionalist default rule reflects the subjective understanding of only one of the parties, such a rule operates as what Ayres and Gertner call a "penalty default." . . .

Although Ayres and Gertner see the device of penalty defaults as serving a variety of informational purposes, a consent theory offers a particular justification for using conventionalist default rules as penalty defaults. When one party is rationally ignorant of the background rules of contract and the other party is not — that is, the other party is either knowledgeable or irrationally ignorant — default rules can reduce the instances of subjective disagreements arising between parties who otherwise are manifesting mutual consent.

Compare repeat players, like Federal Express, who can amortize the cost of obtaining knowledge of the background rules over a great many transactions, with the one-shot user of express mail for whom it would be irrational to hire a lawyer to discover what the normal default rule governing liability was. In other words, it is rational for many parties to remain ignorant — "rationally ignorant," as it were — of the background legal rule. Because they would simply assume that, by its silence concerning liability for breach, Federal Express is implicitly consenting to liability for all foreseeable losses when it expressly promises to "absolutely, positively" get your package delivered overnight — this, after all, is the commonsense meaning of these words — these rationally ignorant parties would fail to bargain for increased liability.

Under circumstances where it is rational for one party to obtain knowledge of the default rules and the other party to remain ignorant of them, the substance of the default rules is highly relevant to any effort to reduce the incidence of subjective disagreement between the parties. Where, for example, the default rule is something other than the commonsense or conventional expectation held by persons in the position of the rationally ignorant party, and such terms favor the interests of the rationally informed party, then, although they hold different intentions, both parties are likely to remain silent on this issue. The rationally ignorant party will not expressly bargain around the default rule because she does not expect an undesirable rule. The rationally informed party will not expressly bargain for the default rule, because the favorable rule will apply by default. In this way, the silence of the parties will mean different things to each party and a subjective disagreement between the parties will result.

When a "misunderstanding" arises concerning the meaning of the terms of the parties' agreement and it is engendered by the choice of a default rule that is counter-intuitive for the rationally ignorant party, rational ignorance of the law may be an excuse. Adopting a convention-alist default rule that reflects the commonsense expectation of the community of discourse of which the rationally ignorant party is a member would reduce the instances of this sort of subjective disagree-ment. Such a rule functions as a penalty default, creating an incentive for the rationally informed party to express a preference for the term that deviates from this common sense. In this way, the rationally informed party is induced to inform by its bargaining behavior the rationally ignorant party of the terms of their agreement and reduce the incidence of subjective disagreement.

For example, a default rule in favor of awarding damages for all foreseeable losses caused by breach requires rationally knowledgeable Federal Express to notify the rationally ignorant customer by its bargain-ing behavior — that is, with its form contract — that it seeks to deviate from the commonsense norm of liability for foreseeable loss. With such an express clause, those consumers who are not harmed much by late delivery get the benefit of a lower price, while those needing extra protection must compensate Federal Express for its increased risk by purchasing insurance for nondelivery. Although it may be rational to remain ignorant of the background rules if knowledge of these rules can be obtained only by consulting a lawyer, the same cannot be said of the costs of reading a sufficiently clear, explicit agreement. . . .

What is true of the measure of relief for breach holds true for the form of relief as well. The commonsense meaning of a commitment to perform is that the promisor is obliged to actually perform. Most persons untutored in the fine points of contract law think they are bargaining for performance, not the option of the promisor to perform or pay expecta-tion damages. Rationally ignorant promisees will assume that the commonsense expectation governs their transaction. Should they desire a specific performance remedy, they will not bargain for a different clause because they are unaware that such bargaining is necessary.

In this situation, a default rule limiting relief to money damages would fail to induce bargaining behavior to clarify the matter. Assuming the promisor desires the damages remedy, she will knowingly or unknowingly obtain this implied clause without having to pay extra for it. Unlike the typical cause of contractual incompleteness, this communicative discrepancy is not based on any ignorance concerning the future, but on ignorance of the default rules provided by the legal system, coupled with the fact that this knowledge does not come free. On the other hand, a default rule that the provider of goods or corporate services, for example, would have to specifically perform such services unless an express clause limits liability to money damages would either (a) give both parties what they really want or (b) force the party seeking to limit relief to money damages to educate the rationally ignorant consumer as to what has really been consented to. . . . [G]iven this conventional expectation, a consent theory of contract recommends a presumption in favor of specific performance of sales contracts.

Both the *Hadley* and specific performance examples illustrate that, when the cost of obtaining knowledge of the default rule supplied by a legal system is sufficiently high (as it typically is for one-shot players), the rationally ignorant party is most likely to interpret the other party's silence as meaning consent to a default rule that conforms to the normal commonsense expectation. Therefore, when one-shot players are contracting with each other or with repeat players, the default rule should reflect this everyday common sense and the onus should fall upon the repeat player to contract around the rule. This choice of default rules induces one party to educate the other so that the manifested agreement is brought into closer correspondence with the subjective intent. . . . Thus, contrary to Craswell, a consent theory does say something quite significant about the choice of default rules. . . .

4

WHEN SHOULD COURTS ORDER SPECIFIC PERFORMANCE?

Though the award of money damages may be the rule, it is not the exclusive remedy for breach of contract. In his book, *The Common Law*, Oliver Wendell Holmes, Jr., observed that "[t]he only universal consequence of a legally binding promise is that the law makes the promisor pay damages if the promise event does not come to pass." By making this statement about the universality of damages, however, Holmes did not deny that specific performance could and should be available as a remedy for *some* breaches of contract.

The articles in this chapter discuss whether money damages should remain the presumptive form of relief. After all, parties bargain for performance, not damages. Why then should they not be entitled, at least presumptively, to have performance awarded? This question is addressed by Richard Posner in *The Economic Analysis of Law*. Posner defends the traditional rule favoring money damages from the standpoint of efficiency. Professor Alan Schwartz of the Yale Law School takes issue with this analysis in *The Case for Specific Performance*. He contends that a presumption favoring specific performance would be efficient and preferable for that reason to the current approach.

STUDY GUIDE: *Notice the close connection between Judge Posner's analysis of the efficiency of specific performance with the concept of "efficient breach" he defends in Chapter 2. Notice also the practical problem of administration created by an order of specific performance. Traditionally, this has been among the most important reasons why judges were reluctant to order specific performance.*

SPECIFIC PERFORMANCE*

Richard A. Posner

When a court decrees specific performance, it orders the party who has broken the contract to perform, on penalty of being held in contempt of court if he does not. Logical as this remedy may seem, in Anglo-American law it is exceptional. The promisee must, as the dictum of Holmes quoted earlier suggests, make do with damages[1] — unless damages are difficult to compute because of a lack of good market substitutes for the performance of the contract breaker.

The exception has swallowed the rule in the case of contracts for the sale of real estate — and rightly so, it would seem. Suppose I have a contract to buy a house and the seller defaults. The estimation of damages may be very difficult, since . . . I may value the house more than the market does. To remit a purchaser to damages in such cases might result in a systematic under-valuation of the costs of breach, since a court will perforce be guided by market price and be skeptical of a buyer's claim that the house is worth more to him.

Although this problem is solved by decreeing specific performance, another economic problem is created. The fact that the seller defaulted may indicate that there is another transaction that increases value by even more than would completion of the sale to me; if so, we want to encourage the breach. The results of decreeing specific performance are

---

*From Richard A. Posner, Economic Analysis of Law 130-132 (4th ed. 1992).

1. This is a general rule of equitable remedies. The commonest equitable remedy is an injunction, and an order of specific performance of a contract is simply one type of mandatory injunction (an injunction that orders someone to do something rather than to refrain from doing something). The discussion in the text is generalizable to most equitable remedies.

not catastrophic, since the seller can always pay the buyer to surrender the right of specific performance and presumably will do so if a substitute transfer would yield a higher price. But the additional negotiation will not be costless. This is clearest in a case of physical impossibility where discharge is nevertheless unwarranted because the promisor had agreed to assume the risk of impossibility. Suppose the promisee could obtain a decree ordering the promisor to complete the performance due under the contract. Although the promisor could pay the promisee to remove the injunction (as an alternative to suffering the penalties, potentially of great severity, for disobeying an injunction), the amount of the payment would bear no relation to the costs to the promisee of the promisor's failure to perform. Indeed, since an injunction could require the promisor to incur possibly unlimited costs (infinite, in a case of true physical impossibility) to comply with the contract, the promisor might, depending on the costs of defying an injunction, have to yield his entire wealth to the promisee in order to obtain a release from his obligation — and this even though nonperformance might have imposed only trivial costs on the promisee. The promisor is unlikely to have to pay *that* much; the lesser of his wealth and of the cost of defying the injunction would merely be the upper limit of the range within which bargaining would occur between the parties to the contract (what would be the lower limit?). But this just means that the availability of injunctive relief in this case creates a bilateral monopoly . . . , which is a source of high transaction costs. Although this is no problem in the case of an opportunistic breach — by definition, completion of performance by the contract breaker is not impossible or even uneconomical — specific performance is not necessary in that case; restitution will do just as well and will require less supervision by the court.

This discussion suggests another reason for preferring damages remedies to specific performance. The damages remedy is, for the court, a one-shot deal; the court enters judgment, and the sheriff goes and sells some of the defendant's assets if the defendant refuses to pay the judgment voluntarily. But specific performance, like other equitable remedies, requires the court to keep the case on its docket until performance is complete so that if necessary it can respond to the plaintiff's argument that the defendant is failing to perform in good faith. Since the costs of the court system are not borne fully by the parties (as we shall see in due course), the costs of specific performance are to some extent externalized by the parties to the contract.

STUDY GUIDE: *What is Professor Schwartz's answer to the administrative problems associated with compelling specific performance? Can you see the relevance of the concept of "subjective value" to his efficiency analysis? Does his response to Judge Posner also apply to the concept of efficient breach? How does Professor Schwartz answer objections to specific performance based on "liberty concerns"?*

THE CASE FOR SPECIFIC PERFORMANCE*

Alan Schwartz

It is useful to begin by examining the paradigm case for granting specific performance under current law, the case of unique goods. When a promisor breaches and the promisee can make a transaction that substitutes for the performance the promisor failed to render, the promisee will be fully compensated if he receives the additional amount necessary to purchase the substitute plus the costs of making a second transaction. In some cases, however, such as those involving works of art, courts cannot identify which transactions the promisee would regard as substitutes because that information often is in the exclusive possession of the promisee. Moreover, it is difficult for a court to assess the accuracy of a promisee's claim. For example, if the promisor breaches a contract to sell a rare emerald, the promisee may claim that only the Hope Diamond would give him equal satisfaction, and thus may sue for the price difference between the emerald and the diamond. It would be difficult for a court to know whether this claim is true. If the court seeks to award money damages, it has three choices: granting the price differential, which may overcompensate the promisee; granting the dollar value of the promisee's foregone satisfaction as estimated by the court, which may overcompensate or undercompensate; or granting restitution of any sums paid, which undercompensates the promisee. The promisee is fully compensated without risk of overcompensation or undercompensation if the remedy of specific performance is available to him and its use encouraged by the doctrine that damages must be foreseeable and certain.

---

*From Alan Schwartz, The Case for Specific Performance, 89 Yale L.J. 271 (1979).

If specific performance is the appropriate remedy in such cases, there are three reasons why it should be routinely available. The first reason is that in many cases damages actually are undercompensatory. Although promisees are entitled to incidental damages,[1] such damages are difficult to monetize. They consist primarily of the costs of finding and making a second deal, which generally involves the expenditure of time rather than cash; attaching a dollar value to such opportunity costs is quite difficult. Breach can also cause frustration and anger, especially in a consumer context, but these costs also are not recoverable. . . .

In addition, problems of prediction often make it difficult to put a promisee in the position where he would have been had his promisor performed. If a breach by a contractor would significantly delay or prevent completion of a construction project and the project differs in important respects from other projects — for example, a department store in a different location than previous stores — courts may be reluctant to award "speculative" lost profits attributable to the breach.

Second, promisees have economic incentives to sue for damages when damages are likely to be fully compensatory. A breaching promisor is reluctant to perform and may be hostile. This makes specific performance an unattractive remedy in cases in which the promisor's performance is complex, because the promisor is more likely to render a defective performance when that performance is coerced, and the defectiveness of complex performances is sometimes difficult to establish in court. Further, when the promisor's performance must be rendered over time, as in construction or requirements contracts, it is costly for the promisee to monitor a reluctant promisor's conduct. If the damage remedy is compensatory, the promisee would prefer it to incurring these monitoring costs. Finally, given the time necessary to resolve lawsuits, promisees would commonly prefer to make substitute transactions promptly and sue later for damages rather than hold their affairs in suspension while awaiting equitable relief. The very fact that a promisee requests specific performance thus implies that damages are an inadequate remedy.

The third reason why courts should permit promisees to elect routinely the remedy of specific performance is that promisees possess better information than courts as to both the adequacy of damages

---

1. E.g., U.C.C. §2-715(1).

and the difficulties of coercing performance. Promisees know better than courts whether the damages a court is likely to award would be adequate because promisees are more familiar with the costs that breach imposes on them. In addition, promisees generally know more about their promisors than do courts; thus they are in a better position to predict whether specific performance decrees would induce their promisors to render satisfactory performances.

In sum, restrictions on the availability of specific performance cannot be justified on the basis that damage awards are usually compensatory. On the contrary, the compensation goal implies that specific performance should be routinely available. This is because damage awards actually are undercompensatory in more cases than is commonly supposed; the fact of a specific performance request is itself good evidence that damages would be inadequate; and courts should delegate to promisees the decision of which remedy best satisfies the compensation goal. Further, expanding the availability of specific performance would not result in greater exploitation of promisors. Promisees would seldom abuse the power to determine when specific performance should be awarded because of the strong incentives that promisees face to seek damages when these would be even approximately compensatory.

III. SPECIFIC PERFORMANCE AND EFFICIENCY

... [I]f specific performance were routinely available, promisors who wanted to breach would often be compelled to "bribe" promisees to release them from their obligations. The negotiations required might be more complex and costly than the post-breach negotiations that occur when breaching promisors have merely to pay promisees their damages. Professor Richard Posner argues, therefore, that restricting specific performance reduces "post-breach" negotiation costs. ...

... For example, suppose that a buyer (*B1*) contracts with a seller (*S*) to buy a widget for $100. Prior to delivery, demand unexpectedly increases. The widget market is temporarily in disequilibrium as buyers make offers at different prices. While the market is in disequilibrium, a second buyer (*B2*) makes a contract with *S* to purchase the same widget for $130. Subsequently, the new equilibrium price for widgets is $115. If specific performance is available in this case, *B1* is likely to demand it, in order to compel *S* to pay him some of the profit that *S* will make from breaching. *B1* could, for example, insist on specific performance unless *S* pays him $20 ($15 in substitution damages plus a $5 premium).[2] If *S* agrees, *B1* can cover at $115,[3] and be better off by $5 than he would have been under the damage remedy, which would have given him only the difference between the cover price and the contract price ($15). Whenever *S*'s better offer is higher than the new market price, the seller has an incentive to breach, and the first buyer has an incentive to threaten specific performance in order to capture some of the seller's gains from breach.

The post-breach negotiations between *S* and *B1* represent a "deadweight" efficiency loss; the negotiations serve only to redistribute wealth between *S* and *B1*, without generating additional social wealth. If society is indifferent as to whether sellers or buyers as a group profit from an increase in demand, the law should seek to eliminate this efficiency loss. Limiting buyers to the damage remedy apparently does so by foreclosing post-breach negotiations.

This analysis is incomplete, however. Negotiation costs are also generated when *B1* attempts to collect damages. If the negotiations by which first buyers (*B1* here) capture a portion of their sellers' profits from breach are less costly than the negotiations (or lawsuits) by which first buyers recover the market contract differential, then specific performance would generate lower post-breach negotiation costs than damages. This seems unlikely, however. The difference between the contract and market prices is often easily determined, and breaching sellers have an incentive to pay it promptly so as not to have their extra profit consumed by lawyers' fees. By contrast, if buyers can threaten specific performance and thereby seek to capture some of the sellers' profits from breach, sellers will bargain hard to keep as much of the profits as they can. Therefore, the damage remedy would probably result in quick payments by breaching sellers while the specific performance

---

2. *B1* would not require *S* to convey the widget to him for resale to *B2* at $130 because if *S* breached his contract with *B2, B2* would then buy a widget in the open market for $115. Only *S* can sell to *B2* at $130, because *B2* has contracted only with *S* to purchase at that price.

3. To "cover" is to make a substitute purchase. See U.C.C. §2-712(1). "Cover costs" refer not to the price paid for the substitute, but rather to the costs incurred in locating the substitute and making a second transaction.

remedy would probably give rise to difficult negotiations.[4] Thus the post-breach negotiation costs associated with the specific performance remedy would seem to be greater than those associated with the damage remedy.

This analysis makes the crucial assumption, however, that the first buyer, *B1*, has access to the market at a significantly lower cost than the seller; though both pay the same market price for the substitute, *B1* is assumed to have much lower cover costs. If this assumption is false, specific performance would not give rise to post-breach negotiations. Consider the illustration again. Suppose that *B1* can obtain specific performance, but that *S* can cover as conveniently as *B1*.[5] If *B1* insists on a conveyance, *S* would buy another widget in the market for $115 and deliver on his contracts with both *B1* and *B2*. A total of three transactions would result: *S–B1; S–B2; S2–S* (*S*'s purchase of a second widget). None of these transactions involves post-breach negotiations. Thus if sellers can cover conveniently, the specific performance remedy does not generate post-breach negotiation costs.

The issue, then, is whether sellers and buyers generally have similar cover costs. Analysis suggests that they do. Sellers as well as buyers have incentives to learn market conditions. Because sellers have to "check the competition," they will have a good knowledge of market prices and quality ranges. Also, when a buyer needs goods or services tailored to his own needs, he will be able to find such goods or services more cheaply than sellers in general could, for they would first have to ascertain the buyer's needs before going into the market. However, in situations in which the seller and the first buyer have already negotiated a contract, the seller is likely to have as much information about the buyer's needs as the buyer has. Moreover, in some markets, such as those for complex machines and services, sellers are likely to have a comparative advantage over buyers in evaluating the probable quality of

---

4. Similarly, a liquidated damage clause with a very high payoff would also produce negotiations. This is because, if the clause is enforceable, the payoff would exceed any profit the promisor could realize from breach, but the promisee has an incentive to permit breach in return for a share of this profit. . . .

5. When the contract between *S* and *B1* involves the sale of goods, *S* of course covers by purchasing similar goods in the market. When the contract involves services, *S* covers by providing a delegate to render the promised performance. Buyers are required to accept the delegate unless the promisor's performance is in some sense unique. . . .

performance and thus would have lower cover costs. Therefore, no basis exists for assuming that buyers generally have significantly lower cover costs than sellers. It follows that expanding the availability of specific performance would not generate higher post-breach negotiation costs than the damage remedy. . . .

IV. SPECIFIC PERFORMANCE AND LIBERTY

The analysis thus far indicates that none of the efficiency arguments against expansion of the availability of specific performance are persuasive, except in the rare cases in which the difficulty of supervision defense properly applies. There is, however, another basis for objection to specific performance. A moral objection to expansion of the availability of this remedy can be raised on the ground that requiring performance interferes with the promisor's liberty more than requiring the payment of money. If this liberty interest takes precedence over the goals that specific performance serves, the equitable remedy should be prohibited or restricted.[6] The liberty interest objection consequently cannot be evaluated fully without a theory that would either reconcile or enable choice to be made among four arguably relevant goals of contract law: (i) to permit a promisor freely to choose the terms under which to contract, including an implied term providing for specific performance; (ii) to prevent a promisor from the possibly undue compulsion of having to perform; (iii) to minimize the costs of undercompensation; (iv) to give the promisee the performance he bought because he is morally entitled to it. Developing such a meta-theory is beyond the scope of this Article, but fortunately it is not necessary to deal with most of the liberty interest arguments.

To begin, a promisor's liberty interest is not seriously compromised by a specific performance decree if the promisor sells roughly fungible

---

6. The distinction in French law between "obligations to do and not to do" and "obligations to convey" reflects this concern. Breach of the former is compensable only in damages, whereas breach of the latter may be remedied by an order equivalent to specific performance. Different remedies apply because "[i]t was considered less onerous to owe money than to be liable to compulsion actually to perform an act or forbearance." Treitel [Remedies for Breach of Contract, in VII International Encyclopedia of Comparative Law 13 (1976)].

goods or is in the business of selling unique goods. In either circumstance, the goods are assets to the promisor much like cash; requiring their delivery is not relevantly different from requiring the delivery of cash. Similarly, requiring a sizable corporation that renders services to perform for a given promisee does not violate the corporation's associational interests or the associational interests of its employees.

Liberty interests are affected, however, in the case of an individual promisor who performs personal services. In part for this reason, current law does not allow specific performance to be granted in this case.[7] Liberty interests might also be implicated if a promisor were required to deliver goods or realty to which he has a sentimental attachment, on the ground that his liberty comprehends the right to define himself partly in terms of the possession of tangible things. The law, however, commonly awards specific performance in such cases; goods which have sentimental associations for the promisor may not have close substitutes for the promisee,[8] while all realty is presumed unique.

The liberty interest objection thus poses no barrier to expanding the availability of specific performance to sales of roughly fungible goods and corporate services. But it does suggest eliminating use of the remedy in some cases in which it now is available. This suggestion is premature, however. To limit specific performance with regard, say, to unique goods would first require the development of a coherent theory of the "personality aspect" of property ownership. It must then be shown that protection of the liberty interest to which the theory gives rise is more important than the goals that specific performance is thought to serve. Until this showing is made, liberty motivated exceptions to a rule of specific performance on promisee request should not be created.

---

7. See Lumley v. Wagner, 42 Eng. Rep. 687 (1852) (personal services contract enforced by enjoining performance elsewhere rather than by requiring specific performance); Restatement §379 (same).

8. For example, "[h]eirlooms, family treasures . . . , a grandfather's clock . . . , a baby's worn-out shoe, or faithful old Dobbin the faithful horse . . . ," Restatement §361 Comment e, are goods with "sentimental associations" that may justify a grant of specific performance. Id. §361(b). Such items may have sentimental associations for promisors as well as promisees.

II

MUTUAL ASSENT

5

IS THERE A DUTY TO NEGOTIATE A CONTRACT IN GOOD FAITH?

In the famous case of Texaco v. Pennzoil, within days of reaching a preliminary agreement to sell its assets to Pennzoil, Getty Oil entered a contract to sell its assets instead to Texaco. Pennzoil then sued Texaco for tortious interference with its contract with Getty. The question arose as to whether there ever was a contract between Pennzoil and Getty for Texaco to have interfered with or whether, instead, there was merely what the common law called an "agreement to agree." Such agreements are traditionally unenforceable as contracts.

Courts are reluctant to enforce preliminary agreements that still require additional negotiations because doing so might require courts to make up terms and impose them on the parties. Moreover, with preliminary agreements, one or both parties may not have thought themselves bound to a final agreement, and enforcing such an agreement would impose a contract contrary to the consent of the party opposing enforcement. Either of these prospects appears to violate the parties' "freedom from contract." Such enforcement might also inhibit parties from entering into the sorts of preliminary agreements that enable them to invest their energies in negotiating what may be a very complex transaction.

The traditional approach is what might be termed "all-or-nothing." Either Pennzoil had a fully enforceable contract to buy Getty, or it had no contract at all. In *Enforcing the Contract to Bargain*, Professor Charles Knapp of the University of California, Hastings College of Law argues that an intermediate contract might well exist even if no final enforceable agreement was reached. He calls this a "contract to bargain." Such a contract obligates both parties to negotiate in good faith but does not obligate them to reach a final agreement.

The common law recognized no duty of good faith negotiations between persons who have yet to reach an agreement. By and large, this remains true today. Professor Knapp's proposal is not to impose such a duty on negotiating parties, but to recognize that negotiating parties can *blind themselves* to a duty of good faith negotiations.

STUDY GUIDE: Consider why courts have been reluctant to enforce "agreements to agree." Would Professor Knapp's proposal address these concerns? What would constitute a breach of such an agreement? The failure to reach an agreement? What would the appropriate remedy be for such a breach?

ENFORCING THE CONTRACT TO BARGAIN*

Charles L. Knapp

I.   INTRODUCTION

A.   Purpose and Scope of the Study

The main theme of the discussion which follows will be that the common law has failed to deal adequately with many cases in which the parties to a negotiation have reached partial agreement on the terms of their eventual exchange. Such a thesis obviously requires some indulgence on the reader's part, and a certain amount of irreverence

---

*From Charles L. Knapp, Enforcing the Contract to Bargain, 44 N.Y.U. L. Rev. 673 (1969).

as well; to put the reader in the proper frame of mind it may be well to begin with two selections from Professor Corbin's treatise, probably the single most authoritative work in the area of contract law today:

> Frequently agreements are arrived at piecemeal, different terms and items being discussed and agreed upon separately. As long as the parties know that there is an essential term not yet agreed on, there is not a contract; the preliminary agreements on specific items are mere preliminary negotiation building up the terms of the final offer that may or may not be made. . . . Further illustrations are to be found in the so-called contract to make a contract. . . . If the document or contract that the parties agree to make is to contain any material term that is not already agreed on, no contract has yet been made; and the so-called "contract to make a contract" is not a contract at all.[1]

No one can go to the moon.[2]

The common law of contracts assumes in general that there is a clear theoretical distinction between what the law calls a "contract" and the relation between those who have merely entered negotiations looking to the formation of a contract. The important difference between the initial stage of preliminary negotiation and the state of contract itself is, of course, that in the latter each party has enforceable rights against the other. Even though these rights may be conditional, and may never become rights to immediate performance, they nevertheless exist in the contemplation of the law — and they exist as soon as the contract comes into being.

Correlative to (but not necessarily dictated by) the proposition that creation of a contract relation results in the immediate existence of rights, is the converse: until the stage of contract is reached, no rights exist because none have been created. One common expression of their proposition is the rule that an offer may be withdrawn at any time until its acceptance, with no liability on the part of the withdrawing offeror.

---

1. 1 A. Corbin, Contracts §29, at 82-85 (rev. ed. 1963).
2. 6 A. Corbin, Contracts §1325, at 337 (rev. ed. 1963). The quoted language is found in the course of an explanation of the term "objective impossibility," and — in one sense, at least — was true when written. Professor Corbin was of course all too aware of the obvious point being made here. . . .

... Thus, for a common law lawyer, characterizing a particular negotiation situation is likely to be a choice between two alternatives — contract or no-contract. ...

The distinction between contract and non-contract could be phrased in another way, based on the presence or absence of legally enforceable duties. The person who becomes a party to a contract assumes a duty to go forward with the contemplated transaction. ... One who is not yet bound by a contract, however, has no such duty to go forward. He is at liberty to withdraw completely from the proposed transaction at any time, for any reason. He may choose to enter into a substitute transaction of a similar nature with some third party, or, indeed, to refrain from action altogether — in either case without being answerable to the abandoned party for any disappointment to the latter's expectations, however severe this may have been.

Such at least would be the view of the common law. It seems likely, however, that there are in fact many situations in which at some stage of negotiations the views of the negotiating parties as to their own "duty to go forward" would be somewhere between the two extremes described. Most of these cases would be among those customarily put in two of the traditional pigeonholes of contract law — the "agreement to agree" cases and the "formal contract contemplated" cases. The first of these categories is comprised primarily of transactions which have reached the stage of full agreement on many, perhaps most, terms of the proposed exchange of performances, plus agreement that an agreement *should* and probably *will* later be reached on the remaining terms. The second category includes those cases in which agreement has been reached on many terms of the proposed exchange (probably at least enough to suggest that the parties considered the extent of remaining potential disagreement to be negligible), but it is nevertheless evident that the parties to the negotiation expect to sign later a detailed, formal, written document containing all the terms earlier agreed upon.

In each of these situations, the common law court considers the basic question to be whether at the time the dispute arose a contract had been made. In the "agreement to agree" case, the parties often have failed to achieve "contract" status simply because they did not reach a bargain complete and final enough to be worthy of (and capable of) legal recognition and enforcement. The intention of the parties not to have a binding contract is perhaps clear, but not of crucial importance. In the "formal contract contemplated" situation, however, the parties may have arrived at an agreement complete enough to satisfy even a demanding court, but the court is wary of enforcing the agreement because it doubts that the parties really intended their promises to be initially enforceable. Here the intention of the parties as to enforceability is said to be of paramount importance.

The draftsmen of the Uniform Commercial Code have undertaken to amend basic rules of contract law in a number of areas where courts have unjustifiably imposed on innocent businessmen the judges' own ideas of what does or does not constitute a sufficiently complete contract. In line with this approach they have modified the "agreement to agree" rule to a considerable degree, so that now under the Code a contract may be found despite a substantial degree of "indefiniteness." The "written contract contemplated" rule, on the other hand, survives today in much the same form as when it was first enunciated. This may be due to the fact that it appears by its very nature to give effect to the real intention of the parties, rather than ignoring it.

It is suggested that in a number of cases, the "agreement to agree" rule — even as liberalized by the U.C.C. — and the "written contract contemplated" rule both run counter to the intentions and expectations of the parties at the time of the transaction under scrutiny. This is because the common law's dichotomy of contract/no-contract does not exhaust the catalog of possible intentions. . . .

The hypothesis here will be . . . : that in at least a substantial number of the "agreement to agree" and "formal contract contemplated" cases, the parties — at the relevant stage of negotiations — do consider themselves "morally" or "ethically" bound, but only in a limited way.

In the typical "agreement to agree" case, the parties have clearly intended to make some sort of "bargain" — they contemplate an exchange of performances, not simply a one-sided, gratuitous transfer. However, for some reason, they have postponed a present decision on one or more details of that exchange, such as the time for performance, the precise price to be paid, the terms of payment, or the amounts or varieties of particular goods to be furnished within an overall agreed amount — the possible range of such items is as broad as the whole scope of contracting activity.

At this stage of negotiation, there are a number of possible states of mind which the negotiating parties may have on the question of whether each is "bound" to the other (using "bound" here in the sense of bound by what each would regard as good business ethics):

(1) Each may regard himself and his opposite number as perfectly free for any reason whatsoever to refuse to reach agreement

on the outstanding points, and to withdraw from the transaction without being bound to proceed farther with the exchange (except to pay some reasonable amount for any performance which may have already been rendered and received). This is also apt to be the answer of traditional contract common law to the question of whether any legally enforceable bond has been created: that no contract has yet come into existence, and thus no rights exist other than those arising from a duty to make restitution for benefits actually received. No expectation damages can be recovered, because no reasonable expectations have yet been created; no reliance damages can be recovered, because no reliance on such an incomplete transaction is deserving of protection.

(2) Each may regard himself and his opposite number as being fully bound to the proposed exchange unless an excuse exists which would have been sufficient to excuse performance of an ordinary executory contract. Under their view even an eventual failure to reach agreement on the "postponed" points would not of itself be sufficient justification for withdrawal; an impartial arbiter could properly decree the standard of performance in the remaining areas of non-agreement. On the question of whether any legally enforceable bond has been created, this second view might also be the answer given by traditional contract law, based on the assumption that the agreement of the parties is complete, though imperfectly expressed. On any matters left open the parties should, if necessary, be bound in accordance with a standard to be set either by some designated impartial third party or by a court. This approach overcomes the objection that the agreement is too incomplete by finding it no more incomplete than many other perfectly unremarkable commercial contracts in which one or more terms of performance have to be supplied by the court in deciding questions of enforcement.

(3) Finally, it is possible that each of the negotiating parties really regards himself and the other party not as completely bound, but nonetheless as "committed to the deal," and bound to the extent actual agreement is eventually reached. The parties are bound to try in good faith to reach some agreement and not to withdraw from the proposed exchange for any reason other than the eventual failure to reach such agreement. Implicit in this view of the facts are a number of assumptions: (1) that each party to the negotiations considers the proposed exchange beneficial and has indicated to the other that he can properly

be regarded as "committed" to it; (2) that there is a mutual recognition by the parties that important points of substance remain to be decided at some later time, possibly in the light of changing or emergent conditions, but that an immediate decision on such matters would be premature and possibly damaging to one party or the other if conditions should develop in an unanticipated way; (3) and finally, that both parties regard the points remaining to be decided as being potential "deal-upsetters" — so material that failure to reach agreement must excuse further performance.

This third view of the transaction is one which has no common law counterpart. If the parties are legally bound to each other, they have impliedly agreed to submit to the court's judgment any terms which for some reason they omitted, left unclear, or reserved for future agreement. If the parties have not so bound themselves, however, they are not bound at all — no contract exists, only an "agreement to agree," and each party is free at any time, and for any reason to say "I choose to go no farther with this deal."

In the typical "formal contract contemplated" case, the parties have clearly intended a bargain; they have also reached the stage of agreement on at least a number of the material terms of the proposed exchange. However, for some reason, they both apparently contemplate the later execution of a full, formal written document. At this stage of the negotiations, there are once again a number of possible views which the parties may entertain as to the extent to which each of them is "bound," by good business ethics, to the proposed exchange of performances:

(1) Each may regard himself as not bound to anything at all unless and until a formal writing is signed by him, and, further, as being free to refuse to sign that writing for any reason whatsoever. This is one possible view which the law may take as to the extent of the obligation created by the negotiations to date — none at all. A legal conclusion of this sort, which will be presented as the reflection of the parties' intention, is made more likely by the presence of factors such as the following: (a) the contract is of a type which requires writing for enforceability under the Statute of Frauds; (b) the contract contemplated involves large sums of money; (c) the contract has many details; (d) the contract is an unusual one, for which a standard form is not available or appropriate; (e) the parties were apparently unwilling to proceed with any performance until the formal document was prepared and signed. There are many cases in which it is impossible to believe

that the parties intended any liability to attach to either side until final execution of the contemplated formal document.

(2) Each party may really feel that the "formal" document is only a "formality" — some sort of ritual, desirable for one or more reasons, but in no sense a prerequisite to a "binding" agreement.

This second view is, again, not an unlikely one for the law to adopt on the issue of whether in a particular case a binding legal obligation has been created. The likelihood of such an outcome is increased where: (a) no independent policy of the law requires a writing for enforceability, or, if it does, the parties have exchanged letters, telegrams or other writing in which the agreed-upon terms are sufficiently reflected; (b) the proposed contract appears relatively simple, and does not involve long-term obligations; (c) the contemplated "formal" contract is a standard-form document, which itself contains the details necessary for a contract of their sort; or (d) the parties themselves, without waiting for the formality of execution, have proceeded to perform, in way that suggests they believed full and binding agreement to have been reached.

In each of the two preceding characterizations of the "formal contract contemplated" situation, the parties may have actually reached agreement on every detail of their proposed exchange. In any such case where at the relevant point in negotiation there remain terms on which agreement has not been expressly reached, there is yet a third possibility.

(3) It is possible that the principals have carried the "deal" as far as they can, and that they are relying on their agents (almost always including lawyers, but possibly also accountants and other experts) to complete the process of agreement. In this view of the facts, the purpose of preparing the formal document is not simply to postpone creation of an obligation, or even to provide evidence of its existence or terms, but rather to afford these experts an opportunity to add to the total agreement such protection against various risks as they think necessary or prudent. On this assumption, the principals are likely to feel ethically bound to the outlines of the deal as they have hammered it out, the withdrawal of either one based simply on dissatisfaction with those outlines being regarded by both as admittedly unjustified. The principals, however, are likely to consider themselves still morally free to withdraw if and when it should appear that the "second team" of bargainers have raised a substantial issue on which they are unable to

agree and which the principals, when apprised of the difficulty, are likewise unable to resolve.

As with the "agreement to agree" discussed above, this third, middle view of the intention of the parties has no common law counterpart. It is similar to the first view in that the execution of a formal writing, or, at least, full agreement on each of its terms, is the point at which the completely binding contract is created. In the eyes of the parties, however, a significant narrowing of the "moral right" to withdraw has occurred at a much earlier time (although immediate commencement of performance is still to be viewed as risky, in light of the continuing possibility of eventual disagreement followed by justified withdrawal).

B.   The Contract to Bargain

The preceding discussion has preserved the distinction between the "agreement to agree" situation and the "formal-contract-contemplated" situation, resting the distinction on the nature of the reason for delaying agreement: where the delay is to await the concurrence of further events which control the future agreement, the relationship is termed an "agreement to agree"; where the delay is to permit negotiations which will settle the details of a transaction already fully agreed upon in its "essential" terms, the case has been referred to as one where a "formal contract" is "contemplated." Of course, the boundary between the two categories is not always clearly ascertainable, and a given case may be well characterized as falling in either — or indeed, in both.

For our purposes, therefore, it will be sufficient to further describe and define the two "middle" positions outlined above, in order to stress the essential similarity between them and the difference between these two categories and other, more conventional analyses. Thus, it has been suggested that in each of the two hypothetical cases above, the parties have reached agreement to such a degree that they regard themselves as bound to each other to the extent that they neither can withdraw for an "unjustified" reason, and yet still agree enough that neither will be compelled to perform if — after good faith bargaining — actual agreement cannot be reached. This situation, if recognized at law in the manner suggested, might be most accurately denominated a "contract to bargain." This nomenclature seems accurate for the following reasons: (1) Use of the word "contract" stresses the fact that the relationship, to at least some extent, entails binding obligations, the breach of which will give rise to a legal remedy. (2) Use of the term "bargain" emphasizes that such a contract imposes neither an absolute duty to perform the contemplated exchange, nor even an absolute duty to *agree* to perform it. Rather it creates a present duty to "bargain" — to engage, in good faith, in the process of attempting to reach agreement on the terms of the proposed exchange, for as long as may reasonably be required under the circumstances.[3]

As used herein, therefore, the term "contract to bargain" will be used to describe any situation where two or more parties have commenced negotiations looking toward a particular exchange, have reached actual agreement on some important terms of the proposed exchange, have delayed agreement on other terms of real importance, but have nevertheless mutually signified their willingness to be regarded as "committed" to the entire proposed exchange. Each regards withdrawal by the other — for a reason other than failure to reach agreement on the remaining points — as unjustified, and worthy of both moral and legal condemnation. . . .

IV.   SOME ASPECTS OF THE CONTRACT TO BARGAIN

A.   Intention

What manifestation of intention will serve to create a contract to bargain? The essential question is whether the parties have expressed both satisfaction with and commitment to the essential terms of the proposed transaction, to the extent that each would reasonably regard the other as unjustified in withdrawing for any reason other than a failure — after negotiation in good faith — to arrive at a complete and final agreement. The . . . cases suggest that the most likely source of

---

3. Use of the verb form "to bargain" (rather than "contract of bargain" or just "bargain contract") is intentional, in the hope of stressing the process of bargaining which remains to be performed, rather than the agreement (if any) which will result therefrom.

such manifestations of intention will be a writing or a series of writings executed by the parties. The common law, of course, has traditionally insisted that elaborate writings . . . should be without any legal effect whatsoever.

Nonetheless, a contract to bargain should not be held to exist merely because the parties have reduced one or more fully negotiated terms — however important — to writing. The additional element of willingness to be bound must also appear, either from the words of the writing itself or from the surrounding circumstances at the time of its preparation.[4] In light of the legal and practical significance attributed to the execution of a written agreement, however, it is not unreasonable to suggest that since the parties have taken the trouble to embody their partial agreement in a signed writing, the court should at least recognize the possibility that they intended to create some binding relation.[5]

No court, however, should lightly engage in speculation about the possible intention of the parties; the burden of proof should be on the proponent of a contract to bargain, just as it is on the proponent of any contract. On the other hand, the burden of proof should be no greater than for any other contract, and — leaving aside such requirements as the Statute of Frauds — the proponent should not be precluded from relying on oral manifestations of intention.

B. Good Faith Bargaining

What sort of conduct will be regarded as "bad faith" in the context of a contract to bargain? . . . Withdrawal merely because a better offer

---

4. This is, of course, one important difference between the contract to bargain and the conventional contract; in the latter, the intention to be legally bound need not be affirmatively shown as a separate element of the agreement, but will be inferred from its completion. . . . In the case of the contract to bargain, however, where the intention to be at least partially bound is the factor distinguishing the agreement from mere negotiation, it seems necessary to have plaintiff demonstrate such an intention as a part of his case, although such intention may be inferred from surrounding circumstances, and need not be spelled out expressly in the terms of the agreement itself.

5. Although the existence of a memorandum of terms agreed upon may itself have important consequences, . . . there is a vast difference, so far as evidence of intention to contract is concerned, between a mere notation of agreed-on-terms and a formal document executed by both parties.

has been received from a third party . . . seems the most obvious case of bad faith. Somewhat less obvious, but an example of bad faith nevertheless, would be a withdrawal . . . for no reason other than a change of heart.[6] On the other hand, withdrawal after substantial negotiations have failed to produce agreement on the reserved terms . . . should not be regarded as bad faith, and should produce no liability on the part of the withdrawing party.[7]

Consideration of the "good faith" standard for performance of the contract to bargain suggests two related objections which may be raised to judicial recognition of such contracts. The device may be used to penalize a party merely for "insufficient bargaining." There is, of course, some danger that a party's withdrawal from a contemplated transaction after what he regards as a complete breakdown of negotiations might later be viewed as a failure to bargain long enough or "reasonably" enough, thus constituting a breach of contract. Plaintiff, however, bears the burden of proof both as to the existence of a contract and as to its breach. In the absence of any additional factors to indicate bad faith (such as acceptance of a better offer from a third party), a court might well find that plaintiff had failed to demonstrate lack of good faith.

This leads to the second objection that whenever an extraneous factor, such as a better offer from a third party, makes withdrawal

---

6. The statement in the text is perhaps a bit too glibly dogmatic; there may be cases where plaintiff can properly be held to have borne the risk of defendant's decision to forego the transaction altogether, but not the risk of his entering into a substitute transaction.

7. There is a statutory duty to bargain in good faith in the area of labor contracts. . . . One suggested definition of "bad faith" in this context is a "desire not to reach an agreement." . . . [S]ee Cox, The Duty to Bargain in Good Faith, 71 Harv. L. Rev. 1401, 1417 n.57. . . . This statutory duty does not depend for its existence on any agreement of the parties and is very different from the duty which should be imposed by a contract to bargain. It may be, however, that some labor cases can provide useful analogies for the court faced with a contract to bargain case. Professor Cox has noted, for instance, that the following types of conduct have been held to be evidence of employer bad faith: "Stalling the negotiations by unexplained delays in answering correspondence and by the unnecessary postponement of meetings," "repudiating the commitments made by the company's bargaining representative after it had led the union to believe that he had full authority to conclude an agreement," "withholding agreement upon trivial matters," "failure to make counter proposals," "[advancing] demands so obviously intolerable to the union as to suggest a purpose to obstruct negotiations." Cox, supra, at 1418-1422. All these appear to have potential application to the commercial contract to bargain.

from the contract materially advantageous to one party, that party runs the risk of being held liable even if he withdraws from the transaction only after extensive bargaining has failed to produce a complete agreement. Two factors, however, seem to minimize the likelihood of such occurrences. One is the possibility of creating a record of bargaining sufficient to demonstrate that agreement clearly could have been reached had the plaintiff really desired it; second, even those courts willing to recognize the contract to bargain will do so with extreme caution, and only where the justice of plaintiff's claim is virtually beyond question. These two factors suggest that a contract to bargain is likely to be enforced only where there has been either a unilateral withdrawal from negotiations or at least an insistence on terms so clearly unreasonable that they could not have been advanced with any expectation of acceptance, coupled with some demonstrable advantage to be gained by defendant in avoiding the contemplated transaction.

C.   Remedy for Breach

What sort of remedy should be available for the breach of a contract to bargain? No definitive answer will be attempted here; indeed, there is respectable authority for avoiding such an attempt.[8] The suggestion has already been made that the damage remedy in such a case should extend at least to reimbursement of the plaintiff's reliance expenditures; . . . The harder question is whether the plaintiff's remedy should always be confined to reliance, or should in some cases extend to full compensation for lost expectation. The cases suggest certain factors which bear on this question.

Contract law generally imposes a requirement that damages claimed must be proved with reasonable certainty. In the case of a contract to bargain, there may be greater uncertainty than in the usual case because of the failure to agree on a number of terms; this may prevent the award of an expectation remedy. In some cases, however, the main terms of performance, including quantity, quality and price, may have been so

---

8. Restatement (Second) of Contracts §90 (Tent. Draft No. 2, 1965) (remedy in promissory estoppel case may be limited "as justice requires"). Comment e to this section makes some suggestions as to the application of this very vague standard.

agreed upon by the time of breach that an expectation remedy can be computed with as much certainty as is usually required. . . . Of course the disappointed seller may also have incurred expenditures which can be proved with certainty and could form the basis for his remedy; however, the fact that he is clearly entitled to his reliance remedy should not preclude him from instead seeking his expectation remedy, any more than it does in the ordinary contract case.

Moreover, in many such cases, a full remedy for the plaintiff can be justified as necessary merely to protect the reliance interest. If plaintiff were the seller of goods or services, and defendant's withdrawal from the transaction allowed plaintiff to make a substitute sale of the same goods or comparable services, the plaintiff could properly claim the difference between defendant's proposed price and the price actually realized on the later sale. The plaintiff's remedy is actually earned by his reliance on the initial prospect of a sale to defendant. In cases where the plaintiff is the prospective buyer rather than the seller of goods or services, protection of his reliance interest again requires compensation for the higher price he ultimately is forced to pay. . . .

The preceding discussion has been concerned with the various measures of damages that might be employed for breach of a contract to bargain. Should such an agreement ever be specifically enforced?

Because of the peculiar nature of the contract to bargain, it is apparent that two types of specific performance are theoretically possible: specific performance of the bargaining process to which defendant had committed himself in the contract, and specific performance of the end-transaction which was to be shaped by the parties pursuant to their initial contract. It seems highly unlikely that a court would grant specific performance of the former type, given the inevitable lapse of time and the likely estrangement of the parties. In many cases an adequate remedy will be available without resorting to enforced bargaining; a court which recognizes the contract to bargain under Section 2-204 of the Commercial Code would probably not regard specific enforcement of this type as being "appropriate," even if no other remedy appeared "adequate."

What then of the second possibility? Should a court ever order specific performance of the exchange on terms which in its opinion would have been agreed on by the parties if good faith bargaining had actually taken place? The discussion above suggests that it should not, since the parties are not consenting to a third party's determination of what constitutes reasonable agreement as to the open terms. It has already been suggested that in some cases the essential terms of the contemplated exchange will have been so far agreed upon that a court could properly frame an expectation remedy in damages. In some cases the terms of that exchange will — by the time of defendant's breach — have been agreed upon in such detail that a court would be justified in rendering a decree of specific performance. If specific performance of the exchange is to be an available remedy for breach of the contract to bargain — even if only in exceptionally clear cases — does the contract to bargain amount to a "reasonable terms" contract, under another name?

Reference to Section 2-305 of the Uniform Commercial Code demonstrates that there is indeed an important distinction between the two types of contract. In the kind of "reasonable price" contract envisioned by 2-305(1), the parties are bound even if they are unable, after good faith negotiation, to agree on such a price. Once the contract has been made, therefore, a legal remedy becomes available to any party who is later disappointed by failure to consummate the exchange. In the contract to bargain case, a remedy would not be available unless the defendant was somehow at fault for the failure to agree. A genuine breakdown in negotiations will not discharge the "reasonable price" contract of 2-305(1); it would, however, discharge the contract to bargain. . . .

For years, the "contract to make a contract" has been as firmly fixed in the affairs of men as the moon in its track, and yet, because of a seemingly unavoidable logical contradiction, has been as remote from our legal system as the moon seemed to Professor Corbin. The draftsmen of the Code have now bridged this abyss of contradiction; any judge persuaded to cross it will find the step a short one, and the terrain on the far side not as unfamiliar as might have been expected.

6

DOES A PROMISE DIFFER FROM AN OFFER?

Traditionally contract law distinguished between bilateral and unilateral contracts. The modern view, as embodied in the Restatement (Second) of Contracts is that bilateral and unilateral contracts differ only in their manner of acceptance: Whereas bilateral contracts are formed when an offer is accepted by a promise, unilateral contracts are formed when an offer is accepted by performance. Although most offers may be rejected until accepted, the Restatement (Second) has imposed restrictions on the revocation of some offers that contemplate acceptance by performance when those offers have been relied upon. In sum, it converts some offers that solicit acceptance by performance into limited option contracts.

In his article, *Reassessing Unilateral Contracts: The Role of Offer, Acceptance, and Promise*, Professor Peter Meijes Tiersma of Loyola-Marymount University questions whether the new understanding of offer and acceptance makes sense. He maintains that the traditional distinction between bilateral and unilateral contracts did not refer exclusively to the manner by which offers are accepted. Although bilateral contracts are formed when *offers* are accepted, Professor Tiersma argues that unilateral contracts are enforceable *promises* that need no acceptance. He closely examines the difference between a promise and an offer; his study reveals much that is interesting about promises, offers,

121

and acceptances. It also suggests why the power of a promisee to revoke a unilateral contract up until the time when performance has been completed and tendered might properly be restricted.

STUDY GUIDE: When reading the next article, keep in mind the definitions of "promise" and "offer" provided by Restatement (Second) of Contracts. Section 2 defines a promise as "a manifestation of intention to act or refrain from acting in a specified way, so made as to justify a promise in understanding that a commitment has been made." Section 3 defines an offer as "the manifestation of willingness to enter into a bargain, so made as to justify another person in understanding that his assent to that bargain is invited and will conclude it." How does an offer differ from a promise? How does this difference explain the distinction between bilateral and unilateral contracts?

ON THE NATURE OF OFFER, ACCEPTANCE, AND PROMISE*

Peter Meijes Tiersma

This Article takes as its central premise that contract law is conceptually based on private obligations fashioned by the parties themselves. The law, to varying degrees, enforces a contract because it wishes to effectuate the agreement of the parties, or because it wishes to protect the parties' reasonable reliance on the agreement. In these situations the crucial question is how the parties themselves understand and use concepts such as offer, acceptance, and promise. Not all promises or agreements are legally recognized as contracts, of course, and the law may impose an obligation where there has been no agreement. But because contract law is heavily dependent on relations created by the parties themselves, it must be finely attuned to how people create obligations and how they expect those obligations to operate. Only by understanding how speech acts like offer, acceptance, and promise function is it possible to determine how well the present doctrine of contract

---

* From Peter Meijes Tiersma, Reassessing Unilateral Contracts: The Role of Offer, Acceptance, and Promise, 26 U.C. Davis L. Rev. 1 (1992).

formation fits the intent of those who make agreements. Fortunately, the philosophy of language has made great strides in illuminating these concepts during the past few decades.

A. Brief Introduction to Speech Acts

Speech act theory is a philosophical approach to language, based in large part on the work of J. L. Austin and John Searle.[1] The theory attempts to explain how the utterances of a speaker are related to, and have an impact on, the surrounding world. Searle posits that each attempt to communicate is some type of *speech act*. Beyond offer, acceptance, and promise, speech acts include asserting, claiming, declaring, commanding, and many others.

Often, a speech act like promising can be identified by the use of the verb "promise," as in "I promise to take you sailing tomorrow." Unfortunately, it is not always this simple. Sometimes a speaker makes a promise without using the verb "promise," as in "I will take you sailing." Obviously, it may not be clear whether such a sentence is a promise or merely an expression of intent ("I assert that I intend to take you sailing tomorrow"). In addition, the word "promise" is sometimes used in a nonpromissory way to add emphasis to an utterance or to make a threat. Neither "I promise to kick your butt if you lay a hand on my car" nor "I promise you she's home today" performs the speech act of promising, despite the use of the word.

Searle posits that there are five basic types of action that a person can perform by speech, as reflected in five different classes of speech acts. These classes are *representatives, directives, commissives, expressives*, and *declarations*. Although most lawyers have not been trained in speech act theory, they are intuitively aware that many legal issues depend on whether an utterance is one type of speech act or another. For example, if someone says, "This table costs fifty dollars," the force of the utterance is ambiguous — it might have the force of stating or asserting ("I *assert* that the price of this table is fifty dollars"), or of

---

1. See generally J. L. Austin, How to Do Things with Words (J. O. Urmson ed., 1962); John R. Searle, Speech Acts: An Essay in the Philosophy of Language (1969). . . .

offering ("I *offer* you this table for fifty dollars"). The legal consequences depend on which speech act the court decides was involved. Similarly, if I consider lending money to John, and his father says, "Don't worry, he's good for the money," the father may have made an assertion regarding John's financial condition ("I *assert* that John can pay it back") or he might have guaranteed the debt ("I *guarantee* that John will pay it back").

Important for present purposes is the category of commissive speech acts. Promises and offers belong to this category of speech acts. Commissives share the feature that they allow individuals to *commit* themselves to some future undertaking.[2] It is important to bear in mind that by performing a commissive speech act like a promise, I do not just state or express my intent to do something in the future. If I state that I intend to go sailing tomorrow, I have simply stated what my plans are by using a *representative* speech act. You could not blame me for changing my plans later. On the other hand, if I *promise* to go sailing, I *commit* myself to a future course of action, and not carrying out this action would indeed be blameworthy. As the philosopher J. L. Austin has written, "But now, when I say 'I promise,' a new plunge is taken: I have not merely announced my intention, but, by using this formula (performing this ritual) I have bound myself to others, and staked my reputation, in a new way."[3] Yet while both promise and offer/acceptance create commitment, they do so in different ways, as I will now explain.

B. Offer and Acceptance

The speech act analysis of offer is quite similar to its legal definition. Although the terminology may be unfamiliar, lawyers would recognize Searle and Vanderveken's description of an offer as "a promise that is conditional on the hearer's acceptance. An offer becomes binding

---

2. . . . Other commissives are represented by the verbs *consent, bid, guarantee*, and *bet*. . . .

3. J. L. Austin, Other Minds, in Philosophical Papers 76, 99 (J. O. Urmson & G. J. Warnock eds., 3d ed. 1979).

only on acceptance. Roughly speaking the logical form of an offer is: this speech act commits me to perform a certain course of action if it is accepted by the hearer."[4]

Like offer, acceptance is a commissive speech act. Acceptance is a response to a limited set of other speech acts, including not only offers, but also invitations and applications. "Thus if one receives an offer, invitation, or application one can accept or reject it, and in each case the acceptance commits the speaker in certain ways."[5] Searle and Vanderveken also observe that the content of an acceptance is determined by the speech act to which it is a response, known to the law as the "mirror image" rule.

This symbiosis of offer and acceptance creates what Searle and Vanderveken call "reciprocal" speech acts. "One's offer becomes binding only if it is accepted, and one can accept an offer only if it has been made and has not been withdrawn."[6] Similarly, Michael Hancher classifies offer and acceptance, along with certain others, as *cooperative* speech acts that require the participation of at least two actors to become effective. The reciprocal or cooperative relationship distinguishes offer and acceptance from most other speech acts. The majority of speech acts require only one speaker, who can perform the speech act unilaterally.

Within the realm of contract law, the bilateral agreement is obviously a prototypical example of an obligation that arises by means of the reciprocal or cooperative speech acts of offer and acceptance. The offer is a proposal for a bargain. That bargain goes into effect when the other party accepts its terms. There must, therefore, be two participants to this cooperative act: the offeror who makes the proposal, and the offeree, the person to whom the offer is made and who can, through acceptance, make the terms binding on both parties. Bilateral agreements are therefore "bilateral" not only in the sense that both parties are under an obligation to perform, but also in that it takes two people to create the reciprocal obligations.

---

4. [John R. Searle & Daniel Vanderveken, Foundations of Illocutionary Logic 195-196 (1985)].

5. Searle & Vanderveken, *supra* note 63, at 195-196.

6. Searle & Vanderveken, *supra* note 63, at 196.

C.   Promise

A promise is a speech act by which the speaker places herself under an obligation to carry out a particular future course of action. The literature on promise is extensive. This Article will focus on those features of promise that are critical to understanding unilateral contracts. The most important of these is that a promise commits the speaker when made. As soon as I promise a friend to go hiking tomorrow by saying "I promise to go hiking with you tomorrow," I am under an obligation to do so. I cannot change my mind later without breaking my promise.[7]

A related observation is that a promise, in contrast to an offer, does not require acceptance to commit the promisor. The promisee might acknowledge the promise in some sense, but does not need to assent to it. If I write you a letter promising that I will visit next month, I obligate myself to do so regardless of whether you respond. You might tell me that my coming is convenient, but it would be unusual and certainly superfluous for you to write, "I accept your promise."

There are thus critical differences between offer and promise. As one commentator has noted, " 'Promise' and 'offer' do not run on the same track, though the words are sometimes used synonymously. An offer looks to an acceptance or a rejection in a way a promise does not. . . . A promise, on the other hand, contemplates a unilateral performance by the promisor, and the offeror is committed as soon as he makes the promise."[8] For our purposes, there are two ways to create commitment, i.e., to bind oneself to a future course of action. One means is by the speaker unilaterally stating that she "promises" to do a particular action in the future, or uses words to like effect. From that point on, the speaker is committed to doing so.[9] The other means of committing

---

7. In this sense a promise is very different from a will. My testament, though made today, does not go into effect until I die, and I am free to change it as I wish until then.

8. [Robert Samek, Performative Utterances and the Concept of Contract, 43 Australasian J. Phil. 196, 204-205 (1965).]

9. The Restatement's definition of "promise" recognizes that commitment is critical to this concept by defining promise as "a manifestation of intention to act or refrain from acting in a specified way, so made as to justify a promisee in understanding that a commitment has been made." Restatement (Second) of Contracts §2(1) (1979).

oneself is through offer and acceptance. Here, commitment requires two parties, one to offer and one to accept. The offer is binding only after acceptance, at which point both parties are committed to its contents.

D. Conditions

A promise can, of course, be conditional. If so, the promisor does not need to perform until the condition occurs. Nonetheless, he is obliged at the time he makes the promise to perform the promised act if and when the condition has been fulfilled. Suppose, for instance, that I promise my friend to go hiking tomorrow if it is a nice day. I am under an obligation today to go hiking if the condition is met tomorrow. Surely I cannot renege before the condition has been fulfilled without breaking my promise. Even if the condition does not occur, I have promised. If it rains tomorrow, I cannot say that we are not going hiking because I never promised anything. Rather, I must say that although I promised to go hiking, it was subject to the condition that it had to be a nice day. Because it rained, my duty to carry out the promised act never matured.

The duties that arise by offer and acceptance can, of course, also be conditional. A typical example is an insurance contract for earthquake damage to a residence. The policyholder is under a duty to pay the premium regularly. The insurer's duty is to pay for any damage to the policyholder's house, but that duty is conditional. The insurer only pays if the house is damaged by an earthquake. It is also possible for both parties' duties to be conditional. For example, two or more parties might make a contract to form a joint venture to build a water desalination plant, but both parties' duties might be conditioned on factors like approval from the county, obtaining financing, and so forth.

Although the duties that arise from an accepted offer may be conditional, it is important to distinguish this situation from the observation that offers are inherently conditional, especially since the term "conditional promise" is often used indiscriminately in both contexts. True conditional promises contain a condition on the *maturation of duty* that determines whether and when the duty to which someone has committed himself must be carried out. I will refer to this as a *conditional duty*. In contrast, the statement that offers are "conditional promises" refers to a condition on the *commitment* itself and determines whether or not a person becomes committed in the first place. I refer to this as *conditional commitment*.[10]

Conditional commitment is one of the critical features that distinguishes an offer from a promise. The obligation created by an offer is inherently subject to acceptance. There is no commitment to any duty until the reciprocal speech acts have been successfully performed. Until an offer is accepted, the proposal binds no one and can be withdrawn unilaterally. On the other hand, the commitment of a promise, by its very nature, *cannot* be conditional. The speaker either commits herself by a promise or does not. As soon as the speech act is properly performed, the speaker is bound to carry out the promised act. Consequently, a promise cannot be revoked at the will of the maker. When the promise contains an unconditional duty, that duty will mature at some time in the future, barring an unforeseen event that makes performance impossible or otherwise excuses it. Likewise, when making a promise with a conditional duty, the speaker commits herself at the time of the speaking of the promissory words. But the maturation of the duty to perform is uncertain. The speaker is surely committed, but must perform only if some future event occurs. If the condition is met, however, the promisor's failure to abide by its terms is a breach.

III. APPLYING THE ANALYSIS

A. Unilateral Contracts Are Not Formed by Offer and Acceptance

As explained in the preceding sections, several critical distinctions separate offer/acceptance from promise as vehicles for creating commitment. These differences can be summarized as follows:

1. An offer must be accepted; a promise need not.
2. An offer does not commit the speaker until it has been accepted and is thus revocable until then; a promise commits the speaker when it is made and is not freely revocable.

---

10. Part of the reason for the persistence of the traditional view may be that writers have often used the terms "offer" and "promise" without carefully distinguishing them, commonly referring to an offer as a "promise" or "conditional promise." . . .

3. Two parties must perform the "ritual" of offer and acceptance to create commitment; a promise is made unilaterally.
4. With offer and acceptance, the offeror and acceptor are both bound, whereas with promise only the promisor is bound.

In this section, we will see that unilateral contracts fit the criteria for promise rather than those for offer and acceptance. As a consequence, an "offer" of a unilateral contract is in fact a promise or set of promises rather than a true offer. . . .

1.   Unilateral Contracts Do Not Require Acceptance

According to the generally accepted view, unilateral contracts, like bilateral contracts, require formation by offer and acceptance. The offeror, who can invite the offeree to accept in any way that pleases him, requires that the offeree accept the offer not by saying "I accept," but rather by completing a particular act. For example, if I run a restaurant, I might tell a waitress that I will give her a bonus if she sells ten special desserts. In the traditional theory of unilateral contracts, my promise does not become binding until all ten desserts have been sold because this is what I, the "master" of my offer, desire. Before that time I am at least theoretically free to revoke at my pleasure, even after the waitress has sold nine desserts and has said "I accept" a dozen times.[11]

Of course, saying "I accept" is the prototypical way of accepting. The Restatement defines acceptance as a "manifestation of assent" to the terms of the offer.[12] And it defines an "offer" as inviting "assent" to a proposed bargain; indeed, the offeror intends that "assent" by the offeree will conclude the bargain.[13] If acceptance is assent to the terms of a bargain, the offeree should be able to accept the offer in any way

---

11. Of course, the law may protect the promisee with an option contract. But the general principle that I can revoke at any time before completed performance is the only logical view in the traditional framework, even according to the second Restatement. See Restatement (Second) of Contracts §45 (1979).

12. Id. §50(1).

13. Id. §24.

that is comprehensible to the offeror as assent. She might explicitly say that she accepts. Or she might begin to do the requested performance in such a way that the offeror can infer that she is symbolically communicating assent. All of these manners of acceptance are consistent with viewing an offer as a speech act that commits the speaker to a proposal once the other party — via the speech act of acceptance — also commits herself.[14] . . .

Obviously, "acceptance" of a unilateral offer by completing the requested act is not a "manifestation of assent." If a unilateral contract must be accepted, saying "I accept" or symbolically assenting by beginning performance in such a way that the offeror will notice would be perfectly sufficient. But a manifestation of assent by itself never suffices to constitute acceptance of a unilateral contract.

Although lawyers have become accustomed to the notion that an offeror "invites" the offeree to "accept" by performance, consider how strange this must sound to the uninitiated: "I offer to pay you $100 to repair my bicycle. I invite you to accept this offer, but do not want your promise to repair my bicycle. You may accept only by completing the job, and I do not consider myself obligated in any way until then." More natural — and hence more likely to reflect how people actually structure their commercial relations — is the following: "I promise to pay you $100 to repair my bicycle. You don't need to accept or to promise anything. I just want you to do the work, if possible. I will pay you after you have finished the entire job." . . .

The traditional view of unilateral contracts is quite correct in holding that the unilateral "offeror" does not want words of acceptance. Where it went astray was in presupposing that commitment can only arise by offer and acceptance. Because with unilateral contracts there is no real speech act of acceptance, it was necessary to label some other act or event an "acceptance" if the offer/acceptance model was to remain intact. The traditional theory chose to identify completed performance as "acceptance." Several commentators subsequently recognized that full performance does not resemble acceptance in any reasonable sense of that word. Unfortunately, rather than question the hegemony

---

14. Of course, the offeror may dictate that the proposal be accepted in a particular way, such as waving a flag, but with bilateral agreements, the acceptance, whatever its mode, must be an act of communication. . . .

of the offer and acceptance model, they strove to find acceptance elsewhere, as in reliance or beginning performance. In reality, the fact that the offeror does not want words of acceptance simply means that no acceptance is necessary to make the promise binding.

We may conclude, therefore, that with respect to not needing acceptance, unilateral contracts resemble promises rather than offers.

2. Unilateral Contracts Commit the Speaker from the Time the Promise Is Made

The second criterion that distinguishes offers from promises is that offerors commit themselves only after acceptance, and can therefore freely revoke until that time. With a promise, on the other hand, there is no need for acceptance. The promise is an unconditional act of commitment that goes into effect immediately and therefore cannot be freely revoked.

Although the traditional view posits that the unilateral offeror does not wish to be bound until he has obtained full performance and can freely revoke until that time, the modern rule of Restatement section 45 is less clear. Practically speaking, when the offeree commences or tenders performance, revocation is no longer possible. Oddly, however, the Restatement seems to free the offeror from commitment until the offeree finishes performance.[15] Section 45 therefore assumes, like the traditional rule, that the offeror has not committed himself until completed performance, but by imposing an option contract it prevents him from revoking after the offeree begins to do the requested act.

Closer examination reveals how unlikely it is that someone would make an offer of the type envisioned by the traditional theory or the Restatement. . . .

. . . [N]o reasonable person would intentionally create the sort of agreement that the traditional theory of unilateral contracts assumes. Suppose that a person, asserting his freedom to contract and his mastery over his offer, specifically intends to make a promise that will bind him not at the time he makes it, but only after the other party has completed a particular act in exchange. In other words, this promisor wishes to

---

15. See Restatement (Second) of Contracts §24 comment a (1979).

create the traditional unilateral contract. For example, he might tell the offeree that if she paints his house, he will—once she is finished—commit himself to paying her $1000. He makes it clear that he does not wish to be bound until she is completely finished, explaining to her that before she is finished he may revoke with impunity. What rational person would even buy the paint if she believed the speaker had not committed himself? No one would realistically begin to perform such an agreement. Nor should the law give damages to an offeree injured by acting so rashly; expending money and effort on the basis of such a non-promise is hardly justifiable reliance, and the law is loath to protect fools.

The primary purpose of unilateral contracts, such as reward offers or promises to pay a commission to a real estate broker, is to motivate the offeree to do the requested act. In other words, their goal is precisely to induce reliance. Obviously, an "offer" to pay someone to paint a fence or find a lost dog provides precious little inducement if it remains freely revocable until full performance. An offer to pay that becomes irrevocable after the offeree commences performance (the Restatement approach) is more apt to entice the offeree, but even beginning performance costs time and effort, and the offeree must take the risk that she will forfeit money she spends on *preparations* to perform if the offeror revokes before she can commence.[16] Clearly, the offeror is most likely to induce reliance if he commits himself at the time of the making of the unilateral contract. He can only do this by the speech act of promising, rather than offering. The presence of commitment justifies the promisee's preparation or initial performance. If the law truly believes that the offeror is master of his offer, it should recognize that when he truly wants the promisee to perform a particular act, he will make a promise, thus binding himself from inception. . . .

Obviously, no reasonable person can expect another to carry out a requested act if he has not committed himself to rewarding her for her efforts. Why, therefore, has the law so long insisted that the offeror does not intend to be bound until completed performance, a position

---

16. Perhaps a more serious problem is that it is highly unlikely that most offerees know the rule of §45. Unlike the mechanisms of offer and acceptance, which rest on social institutions of which most people are aware, §45 is an ad hoc solution to the injustice of the traditional rule and does not necessarily pretend to mirror what the parties intend to accomplish.

even maintained, albeit with little enthusiasm, by the second Restatement? The answer lies, I believe, in the fact that with many unilateral contracts, in particular those like rewards and brokerage agreements, offerors do not want to contribute their part of the bargain until they have received all that they asked for in exchange. Partial performance of a proposal to pay a reward or broker's commission is useless to the offeror, who simply wants a lost pet found or a house sold. He does not want to pay for failed or incomplete efforts. But this is no reason to assume that the offeror does not wish to commit herself until full performance.

Recall the distinction between *conditional commitment* and a *conditional duty*. Obviously, the offeror's *duty to perform* is contingent on the offeree performing her part of the contract. Therefore, he need not pay her until she has found his dog or produced a ready, willing and able buyer for his house. At the same time, however, the offeror is unconditionally committed to pay if and when the condition is met. There is no reason to posit, as does the present rule, that the offeror intends to commit himself only after "acceptance" by full performance. . . .

3.   Unilateral Contracts Are Formed Unilaterally

One of the other distinctions between offers and promises is that offers require two people to perform reciprocal speech acts — offer and acceptance — before commitment arises. In contrast, promises require only one person, who commits himself unilaterally.

Unilateral contracts once again fit the criteria for promising because, as the name suggests, they can be formed unilaterally. To a great extent, this relates to the points made in the previous sections that unilateral contracts do not need acceptance and are immediately binding. If the unilateral "offeror" can commit herself, effective immediately, to a particular course of action, as the previous sections argue, there is no substantial role for the "offeree" to play in the creation of commitment.

Of course, the law may insist that until someone acts in reliance on the unilateral offer, it will not consider the offer *legally* binding. In other words, the law may not recognize that the offeror has committed himself through a promise unless another person will be injured if the offeror reneges. After all, people commit themselves every day to unenforceable promises. This is not a question of when commitment arises, however, but simply one of when the law will enforce a promise. For present purposes it suffices to note that the offeree does not need to do anything to commit the offeror. By finding, for instance, a willing purchaser for a house, the broker does not complete or bring into fruition the seller's act of commitment. The fact that the broker invested time and money looking for a buyer indicates that the buyer had already committed himself. The offeree merely completes the act that fulfills the condition on the offeror's duty to perform.

Thus, not only completed performance but also reliance by the offeree is irrelevant to the creation of commitment. Reliance is important because it signals that the offeree will be injured if the offeror does not honor his commitment. In some instances the law may not want to award damages for breach of a promise until someone has relied on it and thus been injured, as under Restatement section 90. Yet both with section 90 cases and with unilateral contracts, commitment must usually exist before reliance is reasonable. And the commitment in these cases is, of necessity, created by the unilateral speech act of the promisor.

4. Unilateral Contracts Bind Only One Party

The final criterion distinguishing offers from promises is that offers, when accepted, bind both parties, while promises bind only their maker. Of course, even under the traditional theory, unilateral contracts are just like promises in this respect.

By now it should be clear that unilateral contracts arise by means of the speech act of promise rather than through offer and acceptance. The next section will explore the nature of this promise.

B. Unilateral Contracts as Conditional Promises

In reality, a unilateral contract is nothing more than a type of conditional promise. The promisor commits himself to doing a particular act on the condition that the promisee first perform another act in exchange. Semantically, it takes roughly the following form: *I promise that I will do X if you (first) do Y.* Most or all traditional unilateral agreements can be phrased in this way: "I promise that I will pay you $1000 if you paint my house"; "I promise to pay you six percent of the sale price if you find a ready, willing and able buyer for my house within three months"; or "I promise to pay you $100 if you find and return my lost dog." Note that this structure is quite similar to more general conditional promises like "I promise to go hiking with you tomorrow if it is a nice day."

As with other conditional promises, it is not the commitment of a unilateral agreement that is conditional, but the promisor's duty to perform. Because this is a promise — a unilateral act of commitment — the speech act of acceptance is not required. The promise, if correctly made, is an effective act of commitment when spoken.

Viewing unilateral contracts as conditional promises rather than as offers reflects more accurately the expectations of the parties. My promise to pay if you find a buyer for my house binds me from the time I utter the words. Because I have committed myself, you can quite reasonably begin to look for a buyer. This, of course, is precisely what brokers do. But my duty to pay the money does not mature until you fulfill the condition by finishing the task, even though commitment exists from the beginning. Once again, this conforms to my expectation that I will not have to pay you unless you actually find a qualified buyer.

Consequently, the question when someone is initiating a business deal is not whether the offer invites the offeree to accept by a return promise, or by performance. Instead, the critical issue is whether the speaker is making an offer or a promise. Does he wish to induce the addressee to do what is requested, without further ado? In that case he must have made a promise, since it would be unreasonable to expect the addressee to begin unless he had committed himself. A promise is particularly appropriate where the speaker does not really care if the promisee commits herself to perform, or if the promisee cannot promise because the performance (e.g., finding a lost dog) is too speculative. On the other hand, if the speaker wants the addressee to commit herself to doing the act in the future, either because she cannot begin immediately, or because he wants assurance that she will complete the task, he has made an offer that must be accepted before commitment arises. . . .

D.   Implications for the Theory of Contract Formation

As explained in the preceding sections, some important distinctions separate unilateral from bilateral contracts. Most of those distinctions relate to when and how commitment arises. By fixating on offer and acceptance, the law has failed to recognize that parties can commit themselves to a proposal in more than one way. A likely reason that unilateral contracts were forced into the offer-and-acceptance model is that agreements arising through an accepted offer have normally been enforced in Anglo-American contracts law. "Mere" promises, on the other hand, have traditionally been deemed unenforceable, with certain specific exceptions. To place unilateral contracts in the same category as bilateral contracts in terms of offer and acceptance thus permitted the law to distinguish enforceable agreements from generally unenforceable simple promises. Unfortunately, although this parallelism was attractive, it was also misleading. Because crucial differences exist in the formation of unilateral and bilateral contracts, the distinction between the two remains relevant.

Despite these differences, the similarities between unilateral and bilateral contracts are ultimately of far greater significance. Contracts, whether unilateral or bilateral, share the attribute that both are formed by speech acts of commitment, usually either a promise or offer/acceptance, through which one or both parties place themselves under an obligation to carry out a future act. Therefore, *the method of formation should not determine what renders a proposed bargain enforceable.* It is in this sense that Llewellyn's argument against the dichotomy between unilateral and bilateral contracts is especially cogent. The essential issue is whether a person has committed herself to do something in the future, or in Llewellyn's terms, whether a business deal is "on."

Of course, Uniform Commercial Code section 2-204 has gone a long way in this direction by providing that a contract for the sale of goods may be made "in any manner sufficient to show agreement, including conduct by both parties which recognizes the existence of such a contract," and even if the moment of its making is undetermined.[17] Likewise, the Restatement provides that a manifestation of mutual assent may exist "even though neither offer nor acceptance can be

---

17. U.C.C. §2-204 (1990).

identified and even though the moment of formation cannot be determined."[18] The proposal in this Article goes beyond these rules by positing that the presence of commitment, rather than mere agreement or mutual assent, is critical to contract formation. Once there is commitment, reliance on that commitment is reasonable and injury will result if the promisor does not adhere to his promise.

Focusing on the presence of commitment, instead of merely offer and acceptance, will allow the law to respond better to challenges posed by modern large-scale dealmaking. Many such "deals" are complex transactions that do not fit well in the offer and acceptance framework. Their terms do not normally arise by a relatively complete proposal being offered to the other party, but result rather from a long process of negotiation, the results of which may be encompassed in several documents. Final agreement is reached roughly simultaneously at the closing, during which parties sign and exchange the documents. Despite the clear presence of commitment, it may be impossible to pinpoint offer and acceptance in such modern business transactions. Likewise, contract formation should be possible when, in the presence of two parties, a third person suggests the terms for an agreement and the parties, without further ado, simultaneously agree. Again, offer and acceptance are absent, but there is plainly commitment. What is therefore critical to the formation of a contract is not specifically offer and acceptance, or even agreement, but some act of commitment. . . .

---

18. Restatement (Second) of Contracts §22(2) (1979).

7

WHEN SHOULD PAROL EVIDENCE OF CONTRACTING PARTIES' INTENTIONS BE CONSIDERED BY A COURT?

Few doctrines are as initially mysterious to students as the parol evidence rule. Allowing courts to rely on evidence of the parties' intentions that is extrinsic to their written contract would seem to undermine the usefulness of such integrated writings. On the other hand, denying parties the opportunity to present such evidence may lead to decisions that distort rather than respect their intentions.

The best place to begin to understand the appropriate use of extrinsic evidence is to consider what is meant by the "meaning" of a contract. For the use of extrinsic evidence is less threatening when interpreting the meaning of the terms that are included in a writing than when it is used to contradict these terms.

In his article, *"Meaning" in the Law of Contract*, the late Professor E. Allan Farnsworth of Columbia University examines the definition of "meaning." In particular, he distinguishes between contract terms that are *ambiguous* and those that are *vague*. A term is ambiguous when it might properly be used to describe two very different things, whereas a term is vague when it is not clear whether it applies to a particular thing or not. (Don't worry, he gives plenty of examples of each.) Professor Farnsworth describes the common sources of ambiguity and vagueness in contracts. He then argues that using extrinsic evidence of the parties' intent is appropriate to discern the meaning of ambiguous and vague terms. Doing so is not to contradict the writing but to interpret it.

STUDY GUIDE: *What is the difference between interpreting and contradicting a writing? Why should parol evidence be used for the former purpose and not the latter? What is the difference between the traditional approach to the parol evidence rule and the more liberal approach? Does the liberal approach carry with it any dangers for contracting parties?*

"MEANING" IN THE LAW OF CONTRACTS*

E. Allan Farnsworth

Although contract disputes often turn on the interpretation of contract language, this subject has received relatively little attention, especially when compared to that lavished on the interpretation of statutory language. This article will examine some of the conflicting assumptions American courts make in interpreting contract language, and will offer some suggestions for change. . . .

"Interpretation" will be used here in this modern sense to refer to the process by which courts determine the "meaning" of the language. We are not concerned with overriding legal rules which may render contract language ineffective after it has been interpreted. Nor are we concerned with "gap filling" by which the absence of contract language is remedied. Our concern is exclusively with contract language and its "meaning." . . .

The object of contract law is to protect the justifiable expectations of the contracting parties themselves, not those of third parties, even reasonable third parties. . . . "Meaning" for the purpose of contract

---

*From E. Allan Farnsworth, "Meaning" in the Law of Contracts, 76 Yale L.J. 939 (1967).

interpretation should therefore be defined as: (1) that to which either party refers, where it can be determined and where it can be established that it is the same as that to which the other party refers, or believes or has reason to believe the first party to be referring; and, only failing this, (2) that to which either party has reason to believe the other to be referring. Interpretation then becomes the process applied to the language of the parties by which this meaning is determined. It is sometimes supposed, however, that language can be so clear that no recourse need be had to external circumstances to determine its meaning. Are there circumstances under which the meaning of language is so "plain" that some other definition of that term is appropriate?

THE SEARCH FOR PLAIN MEANING

In Semantics

The very concept of plain meaning finds scant support in semantics, where one of the cardinal teachings is the fallibility of language as a means of communication. Waismann lamented that,

> Ordinary language simply has not got the "hardness," the logical hardness, to cut axioms in it. It needs something like a metallic substance to carve a deductive system out of it such as Euclid's. But common speech? If you begin to draw inferences it soon begins to go "soft" and fluffs up somewhere. You may just as well carve cameos on a cheese *soufflé*.[1]

Much of this softness of language comes from the differing ways in which we learn to use words, for the use of a symbol for communication is ordinarily preceded by an elaborate process of conditioning which may vary greatly with the individual. According to Skinner, a leading figure among psychologists and philosophers who study language learning, this process takes place in roughly the following manner. In late infancy children begin to emit sounds in a random way, to

---

1. Waismann, How I See Philosophy, in Logical Positivism 345 (A. Ayer ed. 1959).

babble. The parents show pleasure when they hear patterns that sound like words among the random noises. Their display of pleasure serves as a reward for the child, which reinforces both his ability and desire to repeat these sound-patterns. In this way a vocabulary is acquired. The child learns to use this vocabulary correctly and to respond to words themselves as stimuli by associating words with the stimuli presented at the time of a rewarded bit of babbling. A rudimentary form of trial and error serves to weed out irrelevant stimuli.[2]

This account of language learning shows two reasons why vagueness pervades language. First, each person learns words on the basis of different sets of stimuli. To borrow Quine's example of the word "red," some will have learned this word in situations where red was sharply contrasted with other colors that differ greatly; others will have learned it by being rewarded for distinguishing red from other reddish colors. It seems clear that the former group will use "red" more freely than the latter group. Second, the abilities of people to group stimulations into sets differ somewhat. Thus, some children will simply respond "red" when either a red object or a crimson object comes into view and will remain incapable of distinguishing them.

Quine has built upon Skinner's theory of language learning to explain the concept of vagueness. According to Quine, "stimulations eliciting a verbal response, say 'red,' are best depicted as forming not a neatly bounded class but a distribution about a central *norm.*"[3] The idea of a central norm is useful in explaining the concept of vagueness, for a word is vague to the extent that it can apply to stimuli that depart from its central norm.

Contract language abounds in perturbing examples of vagueness. The parties provide for the removal of "all the dirt" on a tract; may sand from a stratum of subsoil be taken?[4] An American seller and a Swiss buyer agree upon the sale of "chicken"; is stewing chicken "chicken"?[5] Vagueness may even infect a term that has an apparently precise connotation. The parties contract for the sale of horsemeat

---

2. B. Skinner, Verbal Behavior (1960).

3. W. Quine, Word and Object 85 (1960). See also id. at 126.

4. See Highley v. Phillips, 176 Md. 463, 5 A.2d 824 (1939) (held: yes).

5. See Frigaliment Importing Co. v. B.N.S. Intl. Sales Corp., 190 F. Supp. 116 (S.D.N.Y. 1960) (held: for seller).

scraps "Minimum 50% protein"; may evidence be admitted to show that by trade usage scraps containing 49.5% or more conform?[6]

Ambiguity, properly defined, is an entirely distinct concept from that of vagueness. A word that may or may not be applicable to marginal objects is vague. But a word may also have two entirely different connotations so that it may be applied to an object and be at the same time both clearly appropriate and inappropriate, as the word "light" may be when applied to dark feathers.[7] Such a word is ambiguous.

Whether an ambiguity arises may depend upon the medium of communication. Some ambiguities (ordinarily homonyms), such as "beer" and "bier" arise only in speech and disappear in writing; others such as "tear" (a rip or a drop), arise only in writing and disappear in speech. Speech will do much to remove the ambiguity from sentences such as, "Do you think that one will do?" which can be read aloud in a variety of ways by stressing a different word each time. Gestures also play a part in normal face-to-face conversation, and habits of speech have been shown to change when conversation is over a telephone and normal gesture reinforcement is lost. Ambiguity may arise in a telegram because of the lack of punctuation which would ordinarily be supplied in a letter. And even given an ambiguity, it may be resolved by its context: one drinks a beer, not a bier, and sheds a tear (drop) not a tear (rip).

Ambiguities may be classified into those of term and those of syntax. As Young has pointed out, true examples of ambiguity of term are rare in contract cases. A contract specifies "tons"; are they to be long or short tons? A charter party provides that a vessel must be "double-rigged," which by usage can refer to either two winches and two booms per hatch, or four of each per hatch; how many must the vessel have? An important variety of ambiguity of term, for our purposes, is proper name ambiguity, the kind of ambiguity that plagued Shakespeare's Cinna,[8] the kind of ambiguity that we deliberately create when we

---

6. See Hurst v. Lake & Co., 141 Ore. 306, 16 P.2d 627 (1932) (held: yes).
7. The example is from W. Quine, Word and Object 129 (1960).
8. Cinna: I am Cinna the poet. . . . I am not Cinna the conspirator!
  Second Plebian: It is no matter, his name's Cinna; pluck but his name out of his heart and turn him going.

  Julius Caesar, III, iii.

name a child after someone. It was this kind of ambiguity that was involved in the celebrated case of the ships "Peerless."

An ambiguity of syntax is, in the strictest sense, an ambiguity of grammatical structure, of what is syntactically connected with what. A classic example is, "And Satan trembles when he sees/The weakest saint upon his knees," in which the ambiguity is that of pronominal reference.

Ambiguity of syntax is probably a more common cause of contract disputes than is ambiguity of term. An insurance policy covers any "disease of organs of the body not common to both sexes"; does it include a fibroid tumor (which can occur on any organ) of the womb? A contract provides that, "Before the livestock is removed from the possession of the carrier or mingled with other livestock, the ship-per . . . shall inform in writing the delivery carrier of any visible injuries to the livestock"; is it enough that he notify before mingling although after removal?[9]

Syntactical ambiguity is often the result of inadequate punctuation. Note, for example, the confusion that sometimes results from contracts concluded by an unpunctuated telegram. Sometimes the ambiguity is caused by the dropping of words to make shorthand expressions. A contract for the sale of "approx. 10,000" heaters adds "All in perfect condition"; is this, as buyer contends, an express warranty ("All *to be* in perfect condition") or, as seller contends, a limitation on the quantity ("All *that are* in perfect condition")?[10] . . .

Ambiguity in contracts may also result from inconsistent or con-flicting language. A buyer agrees to pay "at the rate of $1.25 per M" for all the timber on a designated tract, and that "the entire sale and purchase price of said lumber is $1,400.00"; how much must he pay for 4,000 M feet?[11] In many of these cases the conflict is between language in a form contract and that added by the parties for the par-ticular transaction. A printed warranty in the sale of a house requires

---

9. See Atlantic Coast Line R. Co. v. Holman, 33 Ala. App. 319, 33 So. 2d 365 (1946), *rev'd*, 250 Ala. 1, 33 So. 2d 367 (1947). . . . The lower court read it: "*either* before the livestock is removed from the possession of the carrier, *or* before it is mingled with livestock" and answered in the negative. 33 Ala. App. at 322, 33 So. 2d at 367 (emphasis added).

10. See Udell v. Cohen, 282 App. Div. 685, 122 N.Y.S.2d 552 (1953) (mem. dec.) (held: parol evidence admissible to resolve ambiguity).

11. See Hardin v. Dimension Lumber Co., 140 Ore. 385, 13 P.2d 602 (1932).

the owner to give notice of breach "within one year from . . . the date of initial occupancy" and also provides that "notice of nonconformity must be delivered no later than January 6, 1957," the date having been inserted by hand; when must the buyer give notice if he moves in on May 16, 1955?[12]

It would be wrong to assume that the failure of contract language to dispose of a dispute that later arises is invariably due to some inherent fallibility of language as a means of communication. The parties may simply not have foreseen the problem at the time of contracting. An insurance contract on a motor vessel covers "collision with any other ship or vessel"; is a collision with an anchored flying boat included?[13] Or one or both may have foreseen the problem but deliberately refrained from raising it during the negotiations for fear that they might fail — the lawyer who "wakes these sleeping dogs" by insisting that they be resolved may cost his client the bargain. An elderly lady enters a home for the aged, paying a lump sum, to be returned to her "if it should be found advisable to discontinue her stay" during a two-month probationary period; must the home refund her money if she dies within that time?[14] Or both may have foreseen the problem but chosen to deal with it only in general terms, delegating the ultimate resolution of particular controversies to the appropriate forum. A contract for the sale of wool requires "prompt" shipment from New Zealand to Philadelphia; does shipment in 52 days conform?[15] It is interesting to note that while either ambiguity or vagueness may result from the other causes just suggested, only vagueness is suitable for use in such a conscious attempt at delegation.

Having seen, then, that vagueness and ambiguity represent different concepts and that for various reasons they pervade contract language, we now pursue the search for "plain meaning" into the field of contract interpretation itself.

---

12. See McNeely v. Claremont Management Co., 210 Cal. App. 2d 749, 27 Cal. Rptr. 87 (1962).

13. See Polpen Shipping Co. v. Commercial Union Assurance Co., [1943] 1 K.B. 161 (1942) (held: no).

14. See First Natl. Bank v. Methodist Home, 181 Kan. 100, 309 P.2d 389 (1957) (held: yes).

15. See Kreglinger & Fernau v. Charles J. Webb Sons Co., 162 F. Supp. 695 (E.D. Pa. 1957) (held: yes).

In Contract Interpretation

The concept of a plain meaning of language has found a more hospitable climate in the field of contract law than it has in semantics. The problem is not, however, that courts engaged in interpreting contracts have assumed that there is always a fixed connection between a word and its referent. While they may have made that assumption for the interpretation of such formal instruments as wills and deeds, they seem not to have done so for the interpretation of informal contracts, since from earliest times courts have been willing to vary the meaning of words according to custom or usage. . . .

While courts engaged in contract interpretation, then, have not adopted the idea that there is *always* a fixed and inevitable connection between word and object, they have found it difficult to rid themselves of the influence of this view. They have tended to attribute a definitive quality to written words. This tendency is exemplified by the parol evidence rule, which deserves close examination in light of the points we have just discussed.

Of the parol evidence rule, Thayer wrote: "Few things are darker than this, or fuller of subtle difficulties."[16] Typically, the rule is called into play where the parties have reduced their contract to writing after oral or written negotiations in which they have given assurances, made promises, or reached understandings. When, in the event of litigation, one of them seeks to introduce evidence of these negotiations to support his version of the contract, he will be met with this rule which, if it applies, will preclude his reliance on such "parol evidence," that is to say, on prior oral or written or contemporaneous oral negotiations. . . .

For the rule to apply at all, a court must first conclude that the parties regarded the documents as a sort of exclusive memorial of their transaction, an "integration." This happens if the parties adopt a writing as the final, complete, and exclusive expression of their agreement. Once it is judicially determined that the agreement is "integrated," then the parol evidence rule applies, and prior oral or written and contemporaneous oral agreements are "inoperative to add to or to vary the agreement."[17] It is generally recognized, however, that this prohibition

---

16. J. Thayer, A Preliminary Treatise on Evidence 390 (1898).
17. Restatement §237. On partial integration, see Restatement §§228 and 229.

against addition and variation does not necessarily preclude resort to parol evidence when it is offered for the purpose of interpretation of language. Here there are two conflicting views.

Under the older and more restrictive, parol evidence may only be used for the purpose of interpretation where the language in the writing is "ambiguous." The decision to admit parol evidence, that is, consists of two steps: first, one decides whether the language is ambiguous; second, if it is ambiguous, then one admits parol evidence only for the purpose of clearing up that ambiguity. This is the view adopted both by Williston and by the Restatement of Contracts. . . . Accordingly, the Restatement provides that in the absence of ambiguity, the standard of interpretation to be applied to an integration is "the meaning that would be attached . . . by a reasonably intelligent person" familiar with all operative usages and knowing all the circumstances other than oral statements by the parties about what they intended the words to mean.[18]

Under the newer and more liberal view championed by Corbin, the parol evidence rule is not applicable at all to matters of interpretation. On this view there is only one standard, applicable alike to integrated and unintegrated agreements, and parol evidence is always admissible in either of these two cases so long as it is used for the purpose of interpretation. The court need not first determine that the language is "ambiguous." This latter version of the rule seems more meaningful.[19]

The principal instance in which the two views give conflicting results occurs when the parties reach an oral understanding whose meaning differs from what would be inferred by the Restatement's "reasonably intelligent person." This can be illustrated by [an] example based on the *Peerless* case.

> . . . *A*, by an agreement evidenced by an integration, contracted to sell *B* goods shipped from Bombay "ex Peerless." There were two steamers of the name "Peerless" sailing from Bombay at materially different times. *A* and *B* orally agreed that they were referring to Peerless No. 1, but a reasonably intelligent person acquainted with all operative

---

18. Restatement §230.

19. Corbin, The Interpretation of Words and the Parol Evidence Rule, 50 Cornell L.Q. 161 (1965). This view seems to be supported by Uniform Commercial Code §2-202, which states the parol evidence rule so as to forbid contradiction but not interpretation, without regard to "ambiguity."

usages and knowing all the circumstances, other than the oral agreement, would have referred to Peerless No. 2.

Under the more restrictive view, it will be remembered, the court must determine whether "Peerless" as used in the writing is ambiguous. Assuming that it would conclude that it is not, parol evidence would be excluded. And since the reasonably intelligent person would have referred to Peerless No. 2, the court will find that to be the meaning of "Peerless." Under the more liberal view, however, since the purpose for which the evidence is offered is clearly that of "interpretation" of "Peerless," the court will admit evidence of the oral agreement and find the "meaning" of "Peerless" to be Peerless No. 1.

Under the more restrictive view, therefore, the parties do not have absolute freedom to attach special meanings to ordinary words. This view is kin to the much discredited "plain meaning" rule in the field of statutory interpretation, which excludes from consideration the statute's legislative history where the meaning of the statutory language is "plain." For if parol evidence may only be used to interpret the language of an integrated agreement where that language is ambiguous, the effect is to exclude the "transactional history" of the contract where the meaning of the integration is "plain."

The problem then becomes one of determining what constitutes ambiguity for this purpose. . . .

The more liberal view is more persuasive. This view makes it unnecessary to determine whether the language of an integrated writing is "plain" as opposed to "ambiguous" or "vague." Instead the task is to characterize the process involved as that of "interpreting" the writing on the one hand, or as that of "adding to" or "varying" it on the other. The distinction can be justified on the ground that although the writing is an integration and the parties have assented to it as a complete and exclusive statement of terms, the imprecise nature of language still leaves room for interpretation.

The question is then, when does "interpretation" end and "addition" or "variation" begin? The answer under the definition of "interpretation" arrived at earlier must be, interpretation ends with the resolution of problems which derive from the failure of language, that is to say with the resolution of ambiguity and vagueness. Accordingly, even under the liberal view, parol evidence is admissible only where vagueness or ambiguity is claimed. In many cases this will produce the same result as the restrictive view — that parol evidence is admissible only where the meaning of the writing is not "plain." The principal departure is that while the restrictive view confines the court to the language of the integration itself and requires it to decide whether there is ambiguity or vagueness, the liberal view simply requires the court to look to the purpose for which the parol evidence is sought to be introduced, without the necessity of deciding beforehand whether the language is, in fact, ambiguous or vague. The significance of this difference will be more apparent after a discussion of some of the cases in which courts have wrestled with these problems.

Many of the cases in which courts claim to have rejected the more liberal view and excluded parol evidence which was offered for the purpose of interpretation turn out on careful analysis to be cases in which the evidence was not actually offered for this purpose at all. In Imbach v. Schultz,[20] for example, an integrated deposit receipt for a real estate deal contained an agreement to pay "as commission on closing the sum of Eighteen Thousand Five Hundred (18,500) dollars, or one-half the deposit in case same is forfeited by purchaser." The sum was written and the words "on closing" were interlined in ink on a printed form. When the purchaser defaulted, the broker claimed one half of the $15,000 deposit, or $7,500. The seller maintained that he had an understanding with the broker that nothing was to be paid unless the sale was closed. The Supreme Court of California held it error to admit this. Parol evidence is not admissible when it is offered, as here, to give the terms of the agreement a meaning to which they are not reasonably susceptible. . . . But here the evidence was not offered for the purpose of *interpretation* of the language of the contract. No term was claimed to be vague or ambiguous. Rather, the evidence was offered to establish an additional term that plainly contradicted the terms of the integrated writing.

Where, in contrast to the case just discussed, parol evidence is offered purely for the purpose of interpretation, courts have generally been ready to admit it, at least after a finding of "vagueness" or "ambiguity." Asheville Mica Co. v. Commodity Credit Corp.[21] is typical. The CCC and the General Service Administration both had contracts

---

20. 58 Cal. 2d 585, 377 P.2d 272, 27 Cal. Rptr. 1690 (1962).
21. 335 F.2d 768 (2d Cir. 1964).

to buy mica from the plaintiff. The CCC agreed to match any increase in "the unit prices under GSA's purchase contracts." The plaintiff negotiated new contracts with the GSA, but the CCC refused to match these prices, claiming that the term "GSA's purchase contracts" referred only to contracts in existence at the time the contracts with the CCC were made. The federal court of appeals reversed the district court, which had held that the contract sued upon was "so clear on its face as to preclude resort to oral testimony. . . ." The court of appeals relied on parol evidence and approved Corbin's view that parol evidence is always admissible for the purpose of interpretation. Since the purpose for which the evidence was offered was to clear up the claimed vagueness of the word "contracts" and to show that the new contracts were "contracts," the court was correct in its conclusion that only interpretation was involved. Although on this view it was unnecessary for the court to find vagueness or ambiguity, it gratuitously added that "the provision in question is not wholly unambiguous" since it was not limited to existing contracts with GSA.[22]

Upon elimination of the first group of cases in which the rejection of the more liberal view has concerned controversies not actually involving interpretation, and of the second group where courts admitted parol evidence offered for the purposes of interpretation, there remains, of course, a hard core of cases in which the more liberal view has been rejected. American Sumatra Tobacco Corp. v. Willis[23] is an example. A tobacco grower was sued on his contract to sell his "entire crop . . . to be grown by me on about 30 acres." He offered parol evidence to show that he had two farms, that only one of them was referred to by the contract, and that his crop had failed on that farm. The court held that this evidence should have been excluded under the parol evidence rule. Parol evidence was "not admissible to vary, alter, or contradict the terms of a complete and unambiguous written contract." Under the more liberal view this unsatisfactory result would have been avoided. The evidence would have been admitted since it was offered for the purpose of interpretation; that is, to resolve a claimed ambiguity in the term "30 acres." Applicability of the parol evidence rule would have turned simply upon a determination of the purpose for which the

---

22. . . . . Strictly speaking, vagueness rather than ambiguity was in issue.
23. 170 F.2d 215 (5th Cir. 1948).

evidence was offered, not upon a decision as to whether or not the term was ambiguous.

A similar problem arises in connection with what are sometimes referred to as "private conventions" as to interpretation. Holmes argued against accepting parol evidence of such conventions where the language was "plain," and rejected the notion that the parties to a contract, making sense as it was written, could show that they had orally agreed "that when they wrote five hundred feet it should mean one hundred inches, or that Bunker Hill Monument should signify Old South Church."[24] But as applied to cases of private conventions as well as generally, the unhappy effect of this more restrictive view is to impose upon contracting parties interpretations that were expected by neither of them. It has been suggested that reformation is the proper remedy in these cases. These are not, however, situations where the parties have mistakenly used words which they did not intend, and so where reformation is appropriate to insert the correct words. These are situations where the parties have used the very words intended by them, but have used them in a way not sanctioned by the usage of others. Reformation is neither a necessary nor even an appropriate remedy; judicial interpretation is sufficient.

It is increasingly difficult to justify the restrictive view of the parol evidence rule. Once it is recognized that all language is infected with ambiguity and vagueness, it is senseless to ask a court to determine whether particular language is "ambiguous" or "vague" as opposed to "plain." But it is possible to give content to the terms "ambiguity" and "vagueness," and it does make sense to ask a court to determine whether evidence is offered for the purpose of resolving ambiguity or vagueness. By limiting "interpretation" to the resolution of ambiguity or vagueness, we can give meaningful content to the more liberal rule.

---

24. Holmes, The Theory of Legal Interpretation, 12 Harv. L. Rev. 417, 420 (1899). See Holmes's earlier statement on this point in Goode v. Riley, 153 Mass. 585, 586, 28 N.E. 228 (1891). . . .

8

SHOULD FORM CONTRACTS
BE ENFORCED?

Form contracts are pervasive in the modern commercial world. Yet at least since 1943, when Friedrich Kessler dubbed them "contracts of adhesion," form contracts have been under fire by law professors. Their complaint? As every reader of these words has personally experienced, forms are typically offered on a take-it-or-leave-it basis and their individual terms are not negotiated by the parties. Critics contend that, because parties have no choice but to agree to the form in its entirety, the individual terms lack the sort of subjective assent present in genuinely bargained-for transactions. Moreover, because those who present the form are well aware that they largely go unread, form contracts lack even the objective assent of those who sign them. In this chapter we consider the merits of this critique.

In his influential article, *Contracts of Adhesion: An Essay in Reconstruction*, Harvard law professor Todd Rakoff considers whether form contracts deserve to be accorded the same presumption of enforceability as contracts in which the manifestation of assent is negotiated. Although he identifies many important benefits of form contracts, Rakoff favors a presumption of invalidity for all "invisible terms" in the form that do not meet certain court-determined standards.

In *Consenting to Form Contracts*, I explain how form contracts are supported by a proper conception of contractual consent and contest

153

Rakoff's proposed treatment of what he calls "invisible terms." I contend that such terms should be enforced if they are not radically unexpected.

STUDY GUIDE: *What "institutional" role does Professor Rakoff think is played by form contracts? Why does he think they do not merit the same respect as fully negotiated contracts? How do the parties' consent and contractual freedom figure in his analysis? How does he distinguish between "visible" and "invisible" terms? How does this approach differ from that of unconscionability?*

CONTRACTS OF ADHESION: AN ESSAY IN RECONSTRUCTION*

Todd D. Rakoff

A NEW ANALYSIS

A.   The Practice of Using Contracts of Adhesion

The development and use of contracts of adhesion represents one facet of the domination of the modern economy by business organizations. Firms create standard form contracts in part to stabilize their external market relationships, and in part to serve the needs of a hierarchical and internally segmented structure. Adherents' responses to contracts of adhesion are intelligible only within this institutional context. Each dimension of the problem will be examined in turn.

1.   The Firm and the Market. — A dominant feature in the growth of the modern business firm over the past century and a half has been the

---

*From Todd D. Rakoff, Contracts of Adhesion: An Essay in Reconstruction, 96 Harv. L. Rev. 1174 (1983).

replacement of market transactions by managerial coordination. In the production of goods, for example, the path from raw material to consumer commonly has been reduced by vertical integration to require only one, or a very few, transactions. Similarly integrated systems exist in many other sectors of economic life. In part, this phenomenon reflects the fact that market transactions are not cost free. It takes money to develop the relevant information, negotiate the deal, and draft the contract. But there is more. Dealing with an outsider in the marketplace introduces uncertainties into the productive process: suppliers may not ship materials as needed; buyers may delay payments and thus threaten cash flow. Internal administration of the sequential steps involved in production and distribution, and internal processing of the inevitable disputes, allow for greater coordination and predictability, and hence lower costs. When complete integration is not possible, output and requirements contracts, franchise arrangements, and the like will often help to accomplish the same goals.

Integration has its limits, however. At the end of the economic chain is a market between the firm and the consumer that, absent rationing, will remain a market. Yet here, too, the firm will attempt to tame the market; it will try to reduce the costs of contract formation, minimize uncertainty and liability for uncertainty, and gain some command over the remaining disputes.

Standard form documents, if legally enforceable, provide a means by which business firms can administer transactions that occur on the firms' "final" markets in an effort to achieve these goals. Standardization is valuable; it reduces transaction costs. The possibilities transcend mere standardization, however, for firms can draft the terms so as to stabilize the incidents of doing business. Encyclopedic force majeure clauses, for example, help to avoid the risks of aberrant events. Limits on liability for consequential damages allow the firm to reduce the potential losses on any transaction and to calculate better the risks that remain. Short time limits for making claims and filing suit facilitate the closing of accounts and reduce the need for contingency funds. Finally, if legal liabilities are set lower than the obligations that the firm recognizes in its actual practice, the gap can provide room to maneuver in the face of inevitable adversity. The enterprise can build a reputation for allowing customers substantial recourse in matters of return, repair, or alteration without committing itself to maintain the policy in any particular case.

At some point, the firm's interest in freeing itself from external constraints begins to merge with the professional ethos of the legal draftsman. The lawyer drafts to protect the client from every imaginable contingency. The real needs of the business are left behind; the standard applied is the latitude permitted by the law. Ultimately, the document becomes unintelligible even to the normal businessman.

Thus, standardization saves money, and the drive to stabilize or control market relations, abetted by the lawyer's craft, goes far to explain why standard forms often contain complex terms unfavorable to the adhering party. These factors do not, however, suffice to explain why firms present form terms on a take-it-or-leave-it basis, or why customers do not challenge that demand. For firms do spend much time and money on sales efforts and are often willing to negotiate concessions on one or more specific points. A salesman and a buyer of, say, a major household appliance will haggle at length over its price and perhaps over whether the sale will be for cash or for credit; yet both will assume that the remaining terms will be provided by the seller's standard form. It is sometimes said that this failure to dicker about all but a few terms simply reflects the consumer's "natural" lack of interest. Yet substantial matters, such as the conditions of the buyer's right of return or the seller's right of repossession, may be at stake. The apparently unprotesting acquiescence of the customer would appear to have deeper causes.

2. *The Form and the Firm.* — The use of standard form documents to govern relations with the external market is only one aspect of the institutional dynamic. Modern business firms are typically organized by departments and through hierarchies. The characteristics of such firms counsel the adoption of standard forms and rigidify allegiance to them.

Form documents promote efficiency within a complex organizational structure. First, the standardization of terms, and of the very forms on which they are recorded, facilitates coordination among departments. The costs of communicating special understandings rise rapidly when one department makes the sale, another delivers the goods, a third handles collections, and a fourth fields complaints. Standard terms make it possible to process transactions as a matter of routine; standard forms, with standard blank spaces, make it possible to locate rapidly whatever deal has been struck on the few customized items. Second, standardization makes possible the efficient use of expensive managerial and legal talent. Standard forms facilitate the diffusion to underlings of management's decisions regarding the risks the organization is prepared to bear, or make it unnecessary to explain these matters to subordinates at all. Third, the use of form contracts serves as an automatic check on the consequences of the acts of wayward sales personnel. The pressure to produce may tempt salesmen to make bargains into which the organization is unwilling to enter; the use of standard form contracts to state the terms of the deal obviates much of the need for, and expense of, internal control and discipline in this regard.

No less importantly, form documents help to solidify the organization's internal power structure. In private organizations, as in public bureaucracies, discretion is power — and this is true of discretion at the bottom of the hierarchy as well as at the top. As subordinates are given wider discretion, they become more difficult to discipline, because standards of performance are less clear. From the point of view of an organization that desires to maintain internal hierarchy, the most desirable salespeople are nearly interchangeable: they sell a standard product at a standard price on standard terms. When price is negotiable, the employee's status increases somewhat. If all terms were negotiable, a much greater degree of training and ability — and consequently of status and reward — would be required. Instead, the routinization of transactions through the use of standard forms reserves discretion for positions further up the organizational hierarchy.

Many of the terms often included in contracts of adhesion bear out this analysis. The flavor of hierarchy suffuses the common provisions disavowing an agent's authority to vary the terms of the document or stipulating that acceptance will occur only on approval by a superior or the home office. Clauses requiring that modifications be written or that notices be given in a specified manner seem designed in good part to accommodate bureaucratic office procedures. Even terms that appear to have quite independent purposes may have latent organizational functions as well. Apart from its obvious role in litigation, a clause transforming a vague legally implied term ("a reasonable time") into a precise one ("ten days") may simultaneously serve to inform subordinates of the decision made by managerial and legal personnel. Similarly, it has been suggested that one reason enterprises routinely disclaim liability for consequential damages is the difficulty of keeping track of the communicated special needs of the customer that are made relevant by the test of Hadley v. Baxendale.

The take-it-or-leave-it approach to form contracts is thus fundamentally grounded not only on the efficiencies of mass distribution, but also on substantial institutional rigidities. Firms do not want to negotiate individualized contracts, because doing so entails bearing not only the costs of the particular negotiations, but also the economic and institutional costs of modifying an organizational structure geared to the standardized terms.

Accordingly, no assumption of even partial market control is needed to explain why firms use contracts of adhesion. Even in a competitive market, firms will refuse to bargain their standard terms in situations in which two individuals would find it worthwhile to dicker over identical matters. The contrary thesis in essence assumes that the internal structure of a firm is irrelevant to the problem of explaining the firm's market behavior, including its contracting practices, and therefore concludes that any refusal of a firm to bargain when an individual would do so must be based on market power in the usual sense. This thesis is tenable only on the supposition that the force of the market is so strong and so precise that all participants will be compelled to act exactly as would individual human beings. When the market itself is populated primarily by firms, as a great many markets are, such a supposition seems far-fetched. If discipline by competition is assumed, it is competition among institutions that is at issue.

Conversely, the prevalence of contracts of adhesion does not prove that competition is absent. The fact that any given firm will seek to do business only on the basis of its own document does not exclude the possibility that other firms will offer different mixes of form terms. Accordingly, one must still ask whether adherents, who stand on the other side of the market, can generate sufficient pressure to discipline the drafting parties by shopping among the various packages.

3.   The Form and the Adherent. — Customers know well enough that they cannot alter any individual firm's standard document. They are largely members of the society that spawns business firms, and they understand the institutional arrangements behind the take-it-or-leave-it stance. If they do not, and if they attempt to bargain the form terms, the salesman will explain his lack of authority to vary the form. Haggling, the customer finds, requires penetrating the hierarchical structure of the firm in the hope of finding someone who will deal — a daunting and perhaps prohibitively costly endeavor. And there may in fact be no one at any level who is willing to bargain. "We cannot make an exception for one customer" — the language of standardization becomes a moral claim. Ultimately, in transactions involving organizational hierarchies, bargaining ceases to be the expected, or even appropriate, consumer behavior.

Shopping is still possible. But for most consumer transactions, the close reading and comparison needed to make an intelligent choice among alternative forms seems grossly arduous. Moreover, many of the terms concern risks that in any individual transaction are unlikely to eventuate. It is notoriously difficult for most people, who lack legal advice and broad experience concerning the particular transaction type, to appraise these sorts of contingencies. And the standard forms — because they are drafted to cover many such contingencies — are likely to be long and complex, even if each term is plainly stated. Once form documents are seen in the context of shopping (rather than bargaining) behavior, it is clear that the near-universal failure of adherents to read and understand the documents they sign cannot be dismissed as mere laziness. In the circumstances, the rational course is to focus on the few terms that are generally well publicized and of immediate concern, and to ignore the rest. The ideal adherent who would read, understand, and compare several forms is unheard of in the legal literature and, I warrant, in life as well.[1]

Customers do shop some terms, but within a limited compass. That compass is defined largely by immediacy of impact (cash or credit), by ease of comparability (size of downpayment), and, to a certain extent, by the customs and practices of the trade (warranty terms in some industries at some times). As the last example indicates, businesses can and occasionally do undertake to combat otherwise-rational consumer apathy in order to "sell" new form terms.[2] This is an expensive proposition, however, because the firm must both underwrite the additional risks comprehended by the new term and bear the cost of stimulating shopping behavior. At times, special business needs will make the expense

---

1. It is sometimes argued that in a competitive market even a small net gain or loss of customers can be a sufficient stimulus to lead to a change in the standard terms offered. . . . This assertion seems wrong, because the institutional costs of changing forms and procedures are greater than would be warranted by the profits to be made by satisfying the demands of marginal customers. . . .

2. The example most often invoked in the legal literature is the periodic eruption of warranty battles among the automobile manufacturers. . . .

worthwhile. Ordinarily, it is preferable to compete in regard to terms that already engage the customers' attention — most notably price.

The predictable consequence is that over time more and more risks are shifted to the adhering party. Drafting parties introduce contracts of adhesion to minimize their exposure to external risks and to further internal organizational aims. Adherents respond not by reading, but instead by focusing on a few terms. The firms compete in regard to those items. The incentive for the firms is to save whatever they can with defensive form terms and employ the savings to compete with respect to the shopped terms. Strong competition, far from ameliorating the situation, will only exacerbate it. As early as 1930, Llewellyn observed that the practice of contracting by standard form tends to the "accumulation of seller-protective instead of customer-protective clauses," even in "highly competitive" industries. As he later pointed out, this happens "often by whole lines of trade."

A possible, perhaps common response for consumers is to concentrate on business reputation in selecting the firms with which they will deal. They consider, for example, a seller's apparent willingness to take back unsatisfactory merchandise, or an insurance company's reputation for settling claims without requiring extensive documentation or hiding behind "technical" clauses. What is revealing is that, in making such general evaluations, customers try to protect the very interests addressed by the more important of the form clauses — yet they remain apparently unconcerned about contractual clauses that limit or deny their legal recourse should they suffer exactly the injuries they fear. This emphasis on practice rather than terms is consistent with, and perhaps based on, an assumption that a firm's routine will often be more favorable to the adherent than the form document would require. Such an assumption may well be valid, because businessmen concerned with fostering goodwill do not always stand on a document that was from the beginning overdrafted by lawyers. Nevertheless, the adherent's recourse is now based solely on the willingness of the drafting party to process a dispute in a routine and reasonable way. The discretion of the organization has taken the place of rights enforceable by law.[3]

---

3. No doubt even in bargained-out contracts between individuals, the parties will rely to a large extent on each other's good faith in the event of a dispute. But the assumption is that the law will stand as a backup should good faith fail, and that the existence of this sanction will encourage good faith in the first place.

There is little that the individual adherent can do to improve his position. From the standpoint of ordinary contract law, the obvious failure of adherents to read and understand form documents appears to be the core problem involved in the use of contracts of adhesion. On fuller examination, this failure proves to be merely the most visible symbol of a pervasive and complex institutional practice. Once the practice comes to exist generally, the fact that a particular adherent reads and understands the particular form that he signs is irrelevant. The internal rigidity of the firm will itself be likely to prevent a knowledgeable adherent's objection to any form term from generating bargaining behavior, even if the objection is coupled with a threat to take his trade elsewhere. Yet the effect is magnified when both the adherent and the drafter know, or at least sense, that other adherents are not attempting to bargain, for then the request that the firm change its standard practice becomes mere eccentricity. Similarly, that the adherent reads one form does not establish that he has read or shopped many others, or that it would be rational for him to do so. But even if a particular adherent undertakes that task, the widespread ethos of not shopping form terms submerges his effort and contributes to the likelihood that, regarding most matters, the terms on all the various forms will be protective of the drafting parties. Shopping can protect shoppers only when it is a widespread activity. When contracts of adhesion become commonplace, even the individual who reads and understands is, and may well perceive himself to be, essentially helpless.[4] The consumer's experience of modern commercial life is one not of freedom in the full sense posited by traditional contract law, but rather one of submission to organizational domination, leavened by the ability to choose the organization by which he will be dominated.

> ***4.   The Power of the Form.*** — The foregoing analysis shows that the practice of using contracts of adhesion, and the consequences of that practice, are best seen neither as results of the exercise of monopoly power nor merely as concomitants of mass production and mass distribution, but rather as circumstances intimately linked to the specific

---

4. Although this is not the place to discuss general programs of statutory reform, the argument suggests that mandatory "disclosure" obligations may have less effect than is supposed. To be effective, "disclosure" must not simply increase cognition: it must lead to alteration of ingrained institutional patterns of action. . . .

organizational form in which mass production and distribution most typically occur in our society. This appears to be the only explanation that accounts for all the crucial aspects of the situation: the standardization of documents in a great many industries for a great many types of transactions, the use and acceptance of form contracts on a take-it-or-leave-it basis, the failure of adherents to read or understand the documents they sign, and the tendency of forms to become very protective of the drafting party. Moreover, this theory connects the practice of standard form contracting with the general course of business history over the last century and a half—that is, with the growth of large business organizations and the parallel substitution of management for bargaining in the marketplace.

Accordingly, the legally supported practice of using contracts of adhesion must be viewed as an institution that itself generates and allocates power—not market power in the traditional sense, but power nonetheless. It is no longer sufficient to view the contract of adhesion as a mere legal form operating as a transmission belt of monopoly power. The use of form documents, if legally enforceable, imparts to firms—even to those otherwise harnessed by the pressures of competition—a freedom from legal restraint and an ability to control relationships across a market. The legal support afforded to the practice must be evaluated with this consequence in mind. . . .

B.   Evaluation of the Practice . . .

2.   The Ordering of Power and Freedom. —(a) "Freedom of Contract."—Contract law has long been recognized as one of the most powerful statements of the nature of freedom in our society. The enforcement of contracts of adhesion certainly liberates drafting parties from legal restraints. At the same time, however, exploitation of that freedom leads to the imposition of terms on adherents. We must consider what approach to contracts of adhesion most nearly comports with the meaning and demands of freedom in modern conditions.

In an earlier age, the quest for contractual freedom formed part of the historical movement by which the modern market economy grew and, often with the aid of governmental power, replaced a social order organized substantially by status and rife with legal and customary restrictions on the power to contract. In the legal discourse of the past century or so, however, "freedom of contract" has had a much narrower and somewhat different meaning. Contract law, and the other fields of private law, are presumed adequate to prevent social coercion in the now-established market economy. The aid of the state is no longer needed to clear away the rubble of prior legal orders. "Freedom of contract" now consists in the absence of governmental meddling except when a substantial public policy justifies that intervention. It is defined in terms of the separation of the market and the state, private and public law; at its fullest reach, it is the doctrine of laissez faire.

Although the set of public policies that justify governmental action is no longer restricted to a minimal list, this conception of freedom of contract continues to impel courts to base arguments on the presence or absence of specific affirmative reasons to intervene. By using such a framework to deal with contracts of adhesion, however, the judiciary errs both in valuing highly a claim to freedom that is inapposite and in overlooking the elements of liberty that are actually at stake.

Refusal to enforce a contract of adhesion, the courts say, trenches on freedom of contract. Implicit in the argument is an equating of the drafting organization with a live individual. For what gives value to uncoerced choice — the type of freedom that the courts have in mind — is its connection to the human being, to his growth and development, his individuation, his fulfillment by doing. But enforcement of the organization's form does not further these fundamental human values; the standard document grows out of and expresses the needs and dynamics of the organization. To see a contract of adhesion as the extension and fulfillment of the will of an individual entrepreneur, entitled to do business as he sees fit, is incongruous. To argue that such a contract represents the cooperative expression of the freedom of all or most of the individuals who comprise the organization is unpersuasive. Most commercial hierarchies are far from being sufficiently participatory to make that claim more than a reified abstraction; form documents are designed by a very few hands, often those of lawyers. Once it is recognized that contracts of adhesion arise from the matrix of organizational hierarchy, the argument for enforcement of form terms as a recognition of "freedom of contract" in its usual sense is unsupportable.

Emphasis on the standard analysis also obscures the manner in which individual freedom really is at stake. A conception of contractual freedom modeled on the opposition between individual and state is inadequate in industrialized, organized, and institutionalized society.

Institutions other than the state can and do dominate the individual within the framework of private law as ordinarily conceived. We are accustomed to seeing this danger in certain facets of economic life, such as the labor relationship in modern industry, and to recognizing that elimination of such domination, where it exists, is as much a fulfillment of liberty as is the limitation of governmental control. In considering the types of disputes that typically arise concerning contracts of adhesion, however, we often miss the point.

What the courts should say is that enforcing boilerplate terms trenches on the freedom of the adhering party. Form terms are imposed on the transaction in a way no individual adherent can prevent, and a major purpose and effect of such terms is to ensure that the drafting party will prevail if the dispute goes to court. The adhering party is remitted to such justice as the organization on the other side will provide. As Professor Kessler well said, the use of contracts of adhesion enables firms "to legislate in a substantially authoritarian manner without using the appearance of authoritarian forms."[5]

Of course, the realistic alternative to the drafter's term is not a term chosen by the individual adherent, or even by adherents as a class; a solution will be imposed by the law if not by the drafter. Compared, however, to the drafters of forms, judges, legislators, and administrative officials are impartial. They fill roles that encourage them to take a broader view of the common good. Legislators, at least, are subject to popular political control — and the decisions of administrators and judges, ultimately, to legislators. If government is at all legitimate, it is legitimate for the purpose of framing generally applicable legal rules. That cannot be said of the form draftsman.

As the courts would have it, the question presented in determining the enforceability of a contract of adhesion is whether the adherent makes a sufficient claim based on public policy or simple fairness to override the drafting party's claim based on the value of free choice. This way of framing the issue is erroneous; individual freedom, insofar as it is at stake, supports the claim of the adhering party not to have the drafter's terms imposed on him. Indeed, once we recognize that the legal enforcement of form terms provides the basis for domination of this sort,

---

5. [Kessler, Contracts of Adhesion — Some Thoughts About Freedom of Contract, 43 Colum. L. Rev. 629, 640 (1943).] . . .

we seem pushed toward the conclusion that such terms should be completely unenforceable.

Such a conclusion would, however, be premature. The idea of liberty relates not only to individual human development and fulfillment, but to the preservation of a democratic society as well. If business firms play an important part in maintaining such a society, and if their ability to do so depends significantly on the use of standard forms, perhaps enforcement of the forms can be justified. . . .

TOWARD THE DEVELOPMENT OF
NEW DOCTRINE

A.   The Pattern of the Issues . . .

2.   Separating Visible and Invisible Terms. — . . . [O]nly some of the terms contained within a standard form contract will embody the evils associated with their use. The next step, therefore, is to distinguish the form terms that are usually innocuous from those that tend to be abused even in a competitive market. The legal validity of the former set should be determined by applying the "ordinary" rules of contract law; the validity of the latter set, by applying the principle that such terms ought not to be enforced without affirmative justification.

In language an adherent might use, we must separate the "visible" terms of the contract from the "invisible" ones. Bargained terms are, of course, visible; but a term does not become invisible merely because it was presented by the drafting party on a take-it-or-leave-it basis. If we follow the dynamics of the practice we have investigated, we must also include within the set of visible terms those for which a large proportion of adherents (although not necessarily all) may be expected to have shopped; for bargaining is not essential to protect adherents as long as shopping concerning the particular term takes place. Considered by themselves, then, the visible terms of a contract of adhesion are most often those that would constitute the entire explicit contents of a very simple ordinary contract, with the price term (dickered or not) being the paradigmatic example. The invisible terms are, quite simply, all the rest.

Of course, distinguishing between the visible and invisible terms may not be a simple task. Although it is not especially difficult to identify the bargained terms in any concrete case, deciding which terms are to be considered shopped is much harder. Whether the particular adherent before the court actually shopped is not dispositive, for only when adherents in general read, understand, and shop for alternative terms do the evils associated with invisible terms disappear. Thus, the history of the actions of the parties — the most common stuff of legal proof — is not a sufficient guide; a court must consider the practices of adherents as a class.

At first blush, the task may seem hopelessly formidable. But many common legal standards assume that similar knowledge concerning social practices is accessible and manageable. "Reasonable men," "reasonable reliance," and "reasonable disclosure" simply do not exist in a social vacuum. Indeed, the traditional rules applicable to form documents themselves depend on such knowledge; one cannot apply the traditional version of the parol evidence rule, for example, without some sense of what most people — definitely not the parties before the court — would "naturally" have included in a written document. Thus, developing and applying a "customary shopper" standard is a problem of the sort typically thought fit for legal resolution. The answer, it is true, will turn in part on an appreciation of current ordinary practice that is not based on courtroom evidence, and in part — especially in changing circumstances — on a sense of what would be reasonable practice. But these are questions informed by everyday experience; as long as any unusual facts can be introduced as evidence, there seems to be no reason to fear oversimplified or insensitive categorization. Some difficulty may arise in fields in which shopping practices are rapidly changing, perhaps under the impact of advertising. Because the purpose of demonstrating that a term is visible is to make the term more likely to be binding, it may well make sense to put the burden of persuasion on the form drafter to show that shopping practices have changed, or that sales practices have shifted to such an extent that new shopping practices are reasonable.

In the court's consideration of what constitutes the "customary shopper," the type of market will of course be relevant. For example, in commercial markets in which the adherents are typically businesses, it may well be found that a greater number of terms are visible. It is often thought — and courts sometimes assert — that doctrines concerning contracts of adhesion are only for consumers, in the popular sense of that term, and that any contract entered into by a sophisticated business should be enforced down the line. In evaluating that assertion, however, we must recognize that much turns on what constitutes "sophistication" in the matter at hand. Present law certainly does not say that only consumers, and never businesses, can take advantage of the new doctrines that temper the traditional rules. And many of the opinions that deny relief to commercial adherents do not rely on any such broad principle. Rather, they are at pains to point out that the adherent was represented by a person likely to be knowledgeable about the types of documents used or the problems likely to arise, or that the deal was sufficiently large to make it worthwhile for the adhering party to become knowledgeable concerning the particular clause at issue. These judicial statements may overemphasize the circumstances of the case at hand, as contrasted with the shopping behavior of adherents in general, but they illustrate how the proposed analysis naturally supports the intuitive idea that deals between commercial parties should be upheld more often than consumer transactions, even if the terms appear on form documents. Commercial parties with greater expertise, and with more at stake in individual deals, can reasonably be expected to shop or bargain for a greater number of terms. When this rationale is not applicable, deals between businesses ought not to be treated differently.

The concept of the "customary shopper," as applied to consumers or to businesses, recognizes that it is not only common, but also reasonable in light of the institutional dynamics for adherents to shop only some of the terms of a prospective transaction. It is thus at odds with the traditional conceptions underlying the imposition of a "duty to read," and with some of the more recent doctrinal formulations that retain traces of that approach. For example, courts sometimes state that one of the factors helpful, or perhaps necessary, in showing that the term at issue is adhesive, is proof that no other drafting party in the same industry was offering a more favorable corresponding term. The point, presumably, is to show what would have happened had the adherent shopped for a better deal. If, however, it would be unreasonable for adherents to shop the term in question, the doctrine taxes the adhering party with the hypothetical consequences of what would have been unreasonable behavior. The asserted relevance of the inquiry depends on the erroneous assumption that the practice of using contracts of adhesion, far from having any internal logic, creates problems only when coupled with an independent distortion of the marketplace.

Similarly, courts err when they treat a contract consisting largely of form terms as they would a negotiated deal simply because one of the terms has in fact been bargained out. The existence of a single negotiated term — if it is a normally visible term, and especially if it is the price term — shows at most that the drafting party does not, compared with the adhering party, possess overwhelming economic power. It does not show that just because the adherent had some "bargaining power," he ought rationally to have negotiated every term. To the contrary, the institutional process makes it both likely and reasonable that shopping or even bargaining behavior with respect to a few terms of the deal will coexist with the imposition of invisible terms for the rest of the transaction.

In sum, the division of form terms into visible and invisible classes is administrable. And the distinction is valuable, because it brings the law into better congruence with the institutional roots of form contracting than do doctrines based on the supposed existence of monopoly power or, more generally, on the exercise of "superior bargaining power." . . .

4.   Preparing to Judge the Invisible Terms. — In most cases, the terms that a drafting party stipulates to fill in the transaction type will be invisible and hence, under the proposed analysis, presumptively unenforceable. If nothing further appears, the case should be decided by application of background law. But even if the drafting party tries to show that an invisible term should be upheld, the court cannot evaluate that showing without determining how the case would come out absent the form clause; for the showing must be particularized, and the degree of deviance from the background rule as well as the reasons supporting both the background and form terms would appear always to be relevant. Therefore, before the invisible terms can be judged, the background law and its application to the particular case must be known.

It is a routine task — not necessarily effortless, but often shouldered — for the legal system to construct the implied term applicable to a particular facet of a given type of transaction. Case law principles, statutory and administrative sources, and appropriate custom and practice furnish the building materials. In many situations, the basic outline of the implied term already exists in the law, either in the form of a generally applicable norm or as a term routinely added to simple negotiated transactions of the given type. In those cases, all that is needed is application of the rule to the particular circumstances, considered apart from the existence of a form term on point. Nevertheless, form terms come already spelled out and applied to particular transactions. One might contend that the present proposal, if it requires such constant reference to background law, will so increase the burden of litigation for the judiciary and parties alike that it will not be worth the effort. Decision on the basis of the presumed validity of the form term might be thought to save an extended inquiry into precedent, and especially into trade usage and commercial circumstance. Moreover, one might assert that it is easier in a motion proceeding to rule on the enforceability of a form term than on the applicability of a rule of law, and therefore that the present proposal will increase the need for going to trial.

These objections might have some force if the present suggestion were to be contrasted with a strict application of the Willistonian rules governing standard form contracts. Existing law, however, has already — quite rightly — departed from that approach. In comparison to present law, with its inclination to introduce alleviating doctrines into a great number of cases, the additional burden seems at most marginal. For example, courts that treat form contracts under the rubric of "unconscionability" already consider commercial practice and context legally relevant, following generally the approach required by the Uniform Commercial Code within its domain.[6] Similarly, the courts can hardly hope to determine whether a form term is "very unfair" without having at least some idea of what result background law would stipulate. The range of relevant inquiry is already quite extensive.

The proposed method would alter present practice in two, or possibly three respects. First, if a determination of the legally implied term were seen as a necessary part of assessing the drafter's work, and not as part of an alleviating doctrine, the burden of proof on matters such as commercial usage might more naturally be put on the drafting party. This change is hardly cause for alarm; indeed, it responds to some of the concerns that ordinarily influence the assignment of at least the initial burden of production, in that the drafting party has greater knowledge of the industry and a greater stake in the validity of the form.

Second, judges would have to make a more precise determination of the background rule at issue and of its application to the facts than is often required under present practice. This process may sometimes

---

6. See, e.g., Williams v. Walker-Thomas Furniture Co., 350 F.2d 445 (D.C. Cir. 1965).

require investigation into unusual commercial situations and usages that may not be fully explored in the record. But judges can always use the mechanisms generally available for reaching decisions on sparse information; they can decide a case on the record presented (with a clear indication that the holding is subject to reconsideration in a later case), and they can decide it by application of burdens of production or persuasion. . . .

If the applicable background law, once it has been determined, yields the same result as the form term, the court ought to render judgment on the basis of the legally implied rule alone and treat the form term as an irrelevancy. Exclusive reliance on the background rule has two symbolic but important purposes. First, enforcement of an invisible term, even when justified, represents acquiescence by the law in the imposition of terms on adherents. When application of the rules provided by legitimate governmental authority will give the same result, no such acquiescence should even be considered. Second, the approach taken in litigated cases becomes part of the basis on which many other claims will be abandoned, settled, or mediated. The judicial nod at the drafting party's "freedom of contract" is not harmless, even if nothing in the case turns on it. Present case law is already rife with general pronouncements favoring form draftsmen, pronouncements that when put to the test turn out to have been overstated. If the basic presumption of the law has been altered, a marked shift in approach is particularly desirable to signal the change.

If the form term differs from the legally implied term in a way that would alter the outcome of the case, it is still possible that decision should rest solely on the force of background law. There have always been rules of law beyond the reach of even the most completely dickered contract. Prohibitions on wilfully harmful or grossly negligent behavior are traditional examples. Attempts to circumvent these norms are "void as against public policy." The modern cases holding "due-on-sale" clauses in mortgages void as unreasonable restraints on alienation take the same form.

However, because the use of contracts of adhesion represents a distinct social institution not adequately encapsulated by the difference between "public" policy and "private" contract, one must go beyond these generally applicable notions. That a particular background rule can be varied by a dickered term does not imply that it can be altered by a form; accordingly, it is not sufficient to assess only the degree of

importance of the substantive rule in comparison to the force of a negotiated agreement. The question — or better, questions — of freedom as
applied specifically to contracts of adhesion must also be addressed.

*STUDY GUIDE: In the next excerpt, what distinction is offered to dis-
tinguish "invisible terms" that should not be enforced from those that
should? What is meant by "nested consent"? How can there be "real"
consent to terms that one has not read and is not expected to have read?
Are you persuaded by this defense of the "terms later" practice sanctioned by Judge Easterbrook in ProCD and Gateway? By this analysis is
there something that Gateway did not do that it should have done?*

CONSENTING TO FORM CONTRACTS*

Randy E. Barnett

There is a remarkable dissonance between contract theory and practice on the subject of form contracts. In practice, form contracts are
ubiquitous. From video rentals to the sale of automobiles, form contracts
are everywhere. Yet contract theorists are nothing if not suspicious of
such contracts, having long ago dubbed them pejoratively "contracts of
adhesion." Indeed, I would wager that a plurality of contracts teachers
would favor a judicial refusal to enforce form contracts altogether — or
could not explain exactly why they would reject such a suggestion.

In this essay, I will identify one theoretical source of the common
antipathy towards form contracts and why it is misguided. I contend
that the hostility towards form contracts stems, in important part,
from an implicit adoption of a promise-based conception of contractual
obligation. I shall maintain that, when one adopts (a) a consent theory of
contract based not on promise but on the manifested intention to be
legally bound and (b) a properly objective interpretation of this consent,
form contracts can be seen as entirely legitimate — though some form
terms may properly be subject to judicial scrutiny that would be inappropriate with nonform agreements. In this regard, I shall endorse the
much-maligned approach of the United States Supreme Court in its

---

*From Randy E. Barnett, Consenting to Form Contracts, 71 Fordham L. Rev. 627
(2002).

decision in Carnival Cruise Lines v. Shute. With this account of form contracts in mind we can better appreciate the wisdom of that other maligned contracts case: Hill v. Gateway 2000, Inc.[1] . . .

Because most terms in a form contract are rarely read, it is considered a fiction to think one has promised — either subjectively or objectively under the modern view — to perform according to a term of which the other party knows good and well one is unaware. Despite this, most contracts professors and practitioners also know that form contracts make the world go round. Psychologists tell us that the human mind will strive mightily to resolve the dissonance between two incompatible ideas. In this case, some resolve the conflict between theory and practice by rejecting form contracts because consent is lacking, while others are led to reject consent as the basis of contract and then, because consent is unnecessary, also reject form contracts in favor of government-supplied terms. By either route, then, form contracts are disdained.

Nowhere was this dissonance between the theory and practice more tellingly displayed than in Todd Rakoff's classic treatment of form contracts in *Contracts of Adhesion: An Essay in Reconstruction*. It is almost as though Rakoff's piece is comprised of two separate articles. The first explains at length all the reasons why form contracts, so disparaged by his peers, are beneficial, if not essential, to the market economy. . . . In what seems almost like a second and different article, he argues that only visible terms should be enforced as written. Invisible terms should presumptively be supplanted by terms supplied by statute or by the courts.[2] . . .

---

1. Since I will be evaluating and partially defending the court's decision in *Gateway*, I should disclose that in 1999 I was retained and compensated by Gateway to express an opinion to the American Law Institute and the National Conference of Commissioners on Uniform State Laws on the merits of proposed revisions of Article 2 of the Uniform Commercial Code that would have effectively reversed the holding of that case. I have had no further relationship with Gateway since then.

2. While I think Rakoff's distinction between terms that one has a sufficient interest in reading and those about which it is rational to remain ignorant was a critical advance on previous theory, I think his decision to call the former terms "visible" and the latter "invisible" was unfortunate. After all, the terms one may rationally fail to read are not *literally* invisible; rather, they were unread and unshopped. Unread terms *could* be read if a party so chose; literally invisible terms cannot. [This passage was moved from elsewhere in the article — ED.]

There are a great many things one can say about this recommendation. For one, it assumes that courts, legislatures, or the American Law Institute are capable of writing gap-filling terms that better serve the interests of both contracting parties than is the author of the form. Imposing terms more favorable to the party disfavored in the form will raise the cost of the transaction to the other party — and not just the monetary cost. By so doing, this may ultimately disserve the party who is supposed to be the beneficiary of government intervention. It might work to the ultimate advantage of the "adherent" to consent to a "one-sided" term and rely on the other party to deliver voluntarily what may not be required of it under the terms of the form.[3] It is very hard for third parties writing terms of contracts to know whether they are really improving the situation for the adherent. However, if we lack confidence that any particular intervention is actually beneficial to the adherent, the principal justification of intervention is greatly weakened to say the least.

Furthermore, the terms that will actually be imposed on the parties are even more removed from the transaction than is a form. If anything, the problem of rational ignorance will be greatly exacerbated. Parties would no longer be weighing the probability of a suit against the cost of reading the form in front of them; they now would have to weigh this probability against the cost of hiring a lawyer to tell them what is in case law or a statute and predict, if prediction is possible, how a background rule will be applied by a future court. Surely this proposal moves an agreement much farther from the consent of the parties and towards a regime in which the legal system supplies terms that others think best.

Nevertheless, Todd Rakoff provided important and previously overlooked reasons why form contracts are useful and why they do not automatically implicate the same problems addressed by the doctrine of unconscionability. His unfortunate choice of terminology

---

3. For an example of this phenomenon in the feed and grain trade, see Lisa Bernstein, Merchant Law in a Merchant Court: Rethinking the Code's Search for Immanent Business Norms, 144 U. Pa. L. Rev. 1765 (1996). There, she provides a "theory of legally unenforceable agreements" explaining why it may be in one party's interest to agree to a "one-sided" legal commitment while relying on the good faith of the other party to do more than it was obligated to do under the contract. See *id.* at 1787-95. Bernstein's analysis responds directly to Rakoff's claim that courts and legislatures can provide default rules that are superior to those provided by one party and consented to by the other.

notwithstanding, the substance of his distinction between visible and invisible terms in forms is a highly useful one, as we shall see in the next part.

FORM CONTRACTS AND CONSENT TO BE LEGALLY BOUND

A.   The Consensual Basis for Enforcing Form Contracts

Suppose that the enforcement of private agreements is not about promising, but about manifesting consent to be legally bound. Suppose the reason why we enforce certain commitments, whether or not in the form of a promise, is because one party has manifested its consent to be legally bound to perform that commitment.[4] According to this theory, the assent that is critical *to the issue of formation or enforceability* is not the assent to perform or refrain from performing a certain act — the promise — but the manifested assent to be legally bound to do so.

Consider the Uniform Written Obligations Act, which has been in effect in Pennsylvania since 1927:

> A written release or promise, hereafter made and signed by the person releasing or promising, shall not be invalid or unenforceable for lack of consideration, if the writing also contains an additional express statement, in any form of language, that the signer intends to be legally bound.

Here the promise (or release) is enforceable if accompanied by a separate statement indicating that the signatory intends to be legally bound. It is this statement that substitutes for consideration and provides the element of enforceability.

Now think of click license agreements on web sites. When one clicks "I agree" to the terms on the box, does one usually know what

---

4. By referring to consent as "the reason," I do not mean to suggest that there are not several important reasons why consent to be legally bound ought to be the central principle of contractual enforceability. . . .

one is doing? Absolutely. There is no doubt whatsoever that one is objectively manifesting one's assent to the terms in the box, whether or not one has read them. The same observation applies to signatures on form contracts. Clicking the button that says "I agree," no less than signing one's name on the dotted line indicates unambiguously: I agree to be legally bound by the terms in this agreement.

If consent to be legally bound is the basis of contractual enforcement, rather than the making of a promise, then consent to be legally bound seems to exist objectively. Even under the modern objective theory, there is no reason for the other party to believe that such subjective consent is lacking. Even if one does not want to be bound, one knows that the other party will take this conduct as indicating consent to be bound thereby.

If this sounds counterintuitive, as it will to many contracts professors, consider the following hypothetical. Suppose I say to my dearest friend, "Whatever it is you want me to do, write it down and put it into a sealed envelope, and I will do it for you." Is it categorically impossible to make such a promise? Is there something incoherent about committing oneself to perform an act the nature of which one does not know and will only learn later? To take another example, is there some reason why a soldier cannot commit himself to obey the commands of a superior (within limits perhaps), the nature of which he will only learn about some time in the future? Hardly. Are these promises *real*? I would say so and cannot think of any reason to conclude otherwise. What is true of the promises in these examples is true also of contractual consent in the case of form contracts.

If contractual enforcement is not about the promise to do or refrain from doing something, but is about legally committing oneself to perform the act described in the envelope, there is no reason, in principle, why this consent cannot be considered real. Therefore there is no reason, in principle, why such consent cannot be objectively manifested to another person. This reveals the nested nature of consent. The particular duty consented to — the promise or commitment — is nested within an overall consent to be legally bound. The consent that legitimates enforcement is the latter consent to be legally bound.

Suppose now that instead of the promise being in an unopened envelope, it is contained in an unread scroll box on a computer screen. Does this make the act of clicking "I agree" below the box any less a manifestation of consent to be bound by the unread terms therein than did the promise to perform the unknown act described in the envelope? I cannot see why. Whether or not it is a fiction to say someone is making the promise in the scroll box, it is no fiction to say that by clicking "I agree" a person is consensually committing to these (unread) promises.

True, when consenting in this manner one is running the risk of binding oneself to a promise one may regret when later learning its content. But the law does not, and should not, bar all assumptions of risk. Hard as this may be to believe, I know of people who attach waxed boards to their feet and propel themselves down slippery snow and tree covered mountains, an activity that kills or injures many people every year. Others (for fun) freely jump out of airplanes expecting their fall to be slowed by a large piece of fabric that they carry in a sack. (I am not making this up). Some ride bicycles on busy streets with automobiles whizzing past them. It seems to me that if people may legally choose to engage in such unnecessarily risky activities — and these choices are not fictions — they may legally choose to run what, to me, is the much lesser, and more necessary, risk of accepting a term in an unread agreement they may later come to regret.

B.   The Limits on Enforcing Form Contracts

Does the justification for enforcing form contracts based on the existence of a manifested intention to be legally bound entail that any and every term in a form contract is enforceable? I do not think so. To begin with, as with negotiated terms, there are limits to what the obligation can be. It cannot be a commitment to violate the rights of others or (in my view) to transfer or waive an inalienable right. But the enforcement of some form terms may be subject to additional constraints that would not apply to expressly negotiated terms.

While it does manifest consent to unread terms as well as read terms, I believe there is a qualification implicit in every such manifestation of consent to be legally bound. Call it the "your-favorite-pet" qualification. If a term of the sort that Rakoff calls "invisible" (insofar as it is rational to remain ignorant of its content) specifies that in consequence of breach one must transfer custody of one's beloved dog or cat, it could surely be contended by the promisor that "while I did agree to be bound by terms

I did not read, I did not agree to *that*." As Andrew Kull has explained in the context of the defenses of mistake, impossibility, and frustration:

> Common sense sets limits to a promise, even where contractual lan-
> guage does not. Though a promise is expressed in unqualified terms, a
> person does not normally mean to bind himself to do the impossible, or
> to persevere when performance proves to be materially different from
> what both parties anticipated at the time of formation. Faced with the
> adverse consequences of such a disparity, even a person who has pre-
> viously regarded his promise as unconditional is likely to protest that he
> never promised to do *that*. . . . The force of the implicit claim is hard to
> deny: I did not mean my promise to extend to this circumstance; nor did
> you so understand it; to give it that effect would therefore be to enforce a
> contract different from the one we actually made.[5]

If, therefore, a realistic interpretation of what clicking "I agree" means is "I agree to be legally bound to (unread) terms that are not radically unexpected," then that — *and nothing more* — is what has been consented to objectively. To appreciate this better, consider the following three possible interpretations of clicking "I agree."

1. By clicking "I agree" I am expressing my intent to be bound only by the visible price and quantity terms and none of the terms in the box above. (In the case of free software, I am agreeing to nothing whatsoever when I click "I agree" though I know that the other party does not wish me to use the software without agreeing to these terms).[6]
2. By clicking "I agree" I am expressing my intent to be bound by any term that is in the box above no matter how unexpected such a term may be.
3. By clicking "I agree" I am expressing my intent to be bound by the terms I am likely to have read (whether or not I have done

---

5. Andrew Kull, Mistake, Frustration, and the Windfall Principle of Contract Remedies, 43 Hastings L.J. 1, 38-39 (1991).
6. This suggests that the contract lacks the objective consent of the software distributor.

so) and also by those unread terms in the agreement above that I am not likely to have read but that do not exceed some bound of reasonableness.

Options 1 and 2 have the advantage of certainty, but sacrifice the consent of the parties. Option 1 is agreement not only to visible terms, but to terms supplied by statute or some future judge which are much farther removed from the consent of the parties than the terms in the scroll box. Option 2 is easy to administer but unlikely to reflect the subjective and, for this reason, the objective meaning of "I agree."

If option 3 is the most likely meaning of clicking "I agree," as I think it is, then two things follow. First, in Rakoff's terminology, "invisible" terms that are unlikely to be read, as well as "visible" terms, can and should be enforced. Second, "invisible" terms that are beyond the pale should not be enforced unless they are brought to the attention of the other party who manifests a separate agreement to them. While option 3 does, therefore, require judicial scrutiny, it requires much less judicial scrutiny than option 1 (the option preferred by Rakoff, and probably by most contracts scholars) which permits courts to provide all the terms of the agreement beyond the few that are visible.

Discerning whether or not an "invisible" term is radically unexpected would require an inquiry much like what law and economics analysis provides. Namely, is this the sort of term that a reasonable person *would have* agreed to had the matter been expressed? Or perhaps the better formulation is that, *if most reasonable persons would not have agreed to such a term, then the other party cannot assume consent to be bound to such a term unless it is made visible.* In this way, hypothetical consent is perhaps the best way we have to determine actual consent to unread terms.

Option 3 was the approach taken by the Supreme Court in Carnival Cruise Lines v. Shute, a case involving a forum selection clause in a form contract on the back of a cruise ticket. While rejecting the proposition that a non-negotiated forum-selection clause is never enforceable simply because it is nonnegotiated, the Court emphasized that such "clauses contained in form passage contracts are subject to judicial scrutiny for fundamental fairness." In essence, the Court rejected options 1 and 2 in favor of option 3. "Fundamental fairness" can be viewed as a surrogate for highly unexpected terms. Nobody expects the Spanish Inquisition.[7]

Does an inquiry into the fundamental fairness of terms reflect a rejection of freedom of contract? Hardly. We must never forget that it is a form contract the Court is expounding. The issue is what the parties have (objectively) agreed to. If I am right, parties who sign forms or click "I agree" are manifesting their consent to be bound by the unread terms in the forms. They would rather run the risk of agreeing to unread terms than either (a) decline to agree or (b) read the terms. Refusing to enforce *all* of these terms would violate their freedom *to* contract. But parties who click "I agree" are not realistically manifesting their assent to radically unexpected terms. Enforcing such an unread term would violate the parties' freedom *from* contract.

Refusing to enforce a term a court finds to be radically unexpected does not prevent both parties from contracting on that basis. All a party who seeks to have such an unexpected term enforced need do is make it visible to the other party. The term would then be expected and, barring the application of some other limiting doctrine, should be enforced. This is analogous to the rule of Hadley v. Baxendale, which requires that special notice be given of any consequences of breach that are unusual and therefore not normally foreseeable or expected. Like the rule in *Hadley*, the "fundamental fairness" test should be viewed as a way to distinguish what was actually consented to from what was

---

7. See Monty Python, The Spanish Inquisition Sketch, available at http://www .montypython.net/scripts/spanish.php:

Chapman: (slightly irritatedly and with exaggeratedly clear accent) One of the cross beams has gone out askew on the treddle.

Cleveland: Well what on earth does that mean?

Chapman: I don't know—Mr. Wentworth just told me to come in here and say that there was trouble at the mill, that's all—I didn't expect a kind of Spanish Inquisition.

(JARRING CHORD) (The door flies open and Cardinal Ximinez of Spain (Palin) enters, flanked by two junior cardinals. Cardinal Biggles (Jones) has goggles pushed over his forehead. Cardinal Fang (Gilliam) is just Cardinal Fang.)

Ximinez: NOBODY expects the Spanish Inquisition! Our chief weapon is surprise . . . surprise and fear . . . fear and surprise. . . . Our two weapons are fear and surprise . . . and ruthless efficiency. . . . Our three weapons are fear, surprise, and ruthless efficiency . . . and an almost fanatical devotion to the Pope. . . . Our four . . . no . . . Amongst our weapons. . . . Amongst our weaponry . . . are such elements as fear, surprise. . . . I'll come in again.

radically unexpected and therefore not objectively agreed to, rather than a vehicle for overriding the consent of the parties.

What is true of terms unread because of rational ignorance is also true of terms unread because they are supplied later, an issue that was raised in the cases of ProCD, Inc. v. Zeidenberg and Hill v. Gateway 2000, Inc. *ProCD* involved what is called a shrink-wrap, or box-top, agreement in which the terms are contained inside a box that one cannot read until one gets home from the store and opens the box. In *ProCD*, the court held that the terms of the software license were agreed to. In *Gateway*, the parties agreed to the sale of a computer over the phone. The written terms of the sale were later delivered to the buyer in the box along with the computer, both of which he was free to accept or reject. In *Gateway*, the court upheld the enforceability of the agreement that followed the telephone transaction. In both of these transactions there was an initial "agreement" — the store purchase and the phone order — and terms to follow later.

At first blush, there is one seemingly big difference between clicking agreement to (unread) terms in a scroll box and agreeing to (unread) terms in a form one has yet even to receive. With the scroll box, a party *could* read the terms if he or she so chose and reject them by refusing to click "I agree." With terms arriving later in a box, one cannot read them until one receives them. In such a case, it seems appropriate that one be given the opportunity to decline such terms by returning the goods. The court in both *ProCD* and *Gateway* emphasized the existence of this option.

Requiring an opportunity to decline the terms received later seems, however, to reveal a defect in the argument I have offered here. Why insist on the opportunity to decline the terms? If the enforceability of a commitment is not based on the appearance that one has subjectively made a promise, but on the consent to be legally bound, and if, as I have argued, one can consent to be legally bound to terms one has not read — and that the other party knows one has not read — then why does one need a right to decline these terms? Have they not already been consented to? For that matter, why even send the terms along with the item, since one has already consented to them initially when buying the software or ordering the computer over the phone?

Such a line of questioning would misconstrue my claim. I argued above that, in principle, one *can* consent to terms one does not read. By the same token, *in principle*, I think one can consent to terms one is not even shown in advance. The main point of this essay is that there is nothing incoherent or illogical about claiming that consent to be legally bound in these situations is real — not fictitious. I was not claiming, however, that anyone actually *does* consent to such terms. That is a factual or empirical question that needs to be answered not in principle, but in practice.

In practice it is difficult to definitively establish the true implicit meaning of actions when parties do not make their intentions explicit. One way we typically do this is to ask counterfactual questions. For example, do we think a person buying a computer over the phone would say they agree to *any* unseen term no matter how unexpected it may be, or to any term they have never even had an opportunity to read? The result of such counterfactual (or hypothetical) exercises is to establish the likely meaning of silence and establish a default rule that then puts the onus on a dissenting party seeking to get an express agreement to the contrary.[8]

This suggests that, while it is *possible* for a computer buyer to consent to numerous terms she not only did not read, but could not read because she never received them, such an interpretation may be an entirely unrealistic assessment of actual transactions. I think the act of purchasing software or ordering a computer over the phone is more realistically portrayed as the first step of a process of consent that is not finalized until there is an opportunity to inspect the terms, even if such opportunity is never exercised. By insisting on this, the court in *ProCD* and *Gateway* can be seen as viewing the manifestation of consent as a combination of the initial purchase or phone order and the act of retaining the software or computer.

That a manifestation of consent has two parts at two different times is far from novel. In the famous case of Hobbes v. Massasoit Whip Co., the seller sent conforming eel skins used to make whips to the buyer, who then kept them. The Supreme Judicial Court of Massachusetts found that this constituted acceptance of the eel skins because of the prior relationship or understanding of the parties. "The plaintiff was not

---

8. A counterfactual inquiry by a court or jury is a sensible method to discover the probable meaning of silence by consumers because judges and jurors are consumers too. What they think most people would mean by their silence is a good indicator of what most people do mean. Of course if parties are not typical consumers but members of a trade, their silence may have a different meaning and evidence of this should be examined.

a stranger to the defendant," wrote Justice Holmes,

> even if there was no contract between them. He had sent eel skins in
> the same way four or five times before, and they had been accepted
> and paid for. On the defendant's testimony, it was fair to assume that
> if it had admitted the eel skins to be over 22 inches in length, and fit
> for its business, as the plaintiff testified and the jury found that they
> were, it would have accepted them; that this was understood by the
> plaintiff; and, indeed, that there was a standing offer to him for such
> skins.
>
> In such a condition of things, the plaintiff was warranted in sending the
> defendant skins conforming to the requirements, and even if the offer was
> not such that the contract was made as soon as skins corresponding to its
> terms were sent, sending them did impose on the defendant a duty to act
> about them; and silence on its part, coupled with a retention of the skins
> for an unreasonable time, might be found by the jury to warrant the
> plaintiff in assuming that they were accepted, and thus to amount to an
> acceptance.

In *Gateway*, the parties were not strangers to each other. In the
absence of the phone order, Gateway could not simply send the buyer
a computer and take his failure to return it as consent to the purchase.
The phone order imposed a duty on the buyer to accept or return the
computer and accompanying terms. As in *Hobbes*, the transaction must
be viewed in its entirety to assess the reasonable meaning of the buyer's
silence.

From this perspective, the only genuinely controversial issue of
Gateway is whether the court should have upheld the enforceability
of the form in the absence of some express notice to phone buyers
that a form would be sent to them later.[9] There are some compelling
reasons for requiring that notice be given. If most consumers would be
surprised by the existence of additional form terms in the box, a default
rule requiring notice that a form will follow in the box is more likely to
lead to manifestations of assent that reflect the subjective assent of the
parties than a contrary rule requiring no disclosure.

---

9. The comparable issue in *ProCD* is whether there should be some explicit notice
on the box that a form agreement is on the software inside.

As I have explained elsewhere,[10] we can expect that repeat-player-sellers will have low cost access to a default rule requiring them to notify buyers that a form agreement will follow later in the box and can inexpensively comply with the rule. In contrast one-time-player-buyers are unlikely to know of a background rule permitting forms to follow without notice, and for this reason are unlikely even to ask whether such will occur. According to this analysis, a default rule requiring disclosure by sellers is more likely to reduce any gap between objective consent and subjective assent and is to be preferred for that reason.

All Gateway or other sellers need do to obtain enforcement of their form is to tell consumers on the phone that the form will follow in the box. They no more need to read aloud all the terms to follow than the software company needs to read aloud all the terms in the scroll box above the button labeled "I agree." Both formalities perform the same function: putting the other party on notice that it is agreeing to other terms that it may or may not read.

Moreover, withholding consent until the form is delivered is prudent because it locks the other party into some terms rather than agreeing to a blank slate. It also provides an incentive for the other party to offer more reasonable terms that marginal parties who do read their forms will not reject. For this reason too, we may infer from their silence that most parties are withholding their consent until they have actually received the terms and had an opportunity to reject them even if they never plan to read the terms themselves.

In sum, just as persons can manifest their intent to be bound by terms they have not read in a scroll box, they can manifest their intent to be bound by terms they will receive later in the box containing the goods they are buying. The empirical question is whether or not they *have* so consented. The presence of notice that more terms are to follow resolves any uncertainty as to the existence of consent and greatly reduces the risk of any misunderstanding. And if repeat-player-sellers know that one-shot-player-buyers would be surprised to learn additional terms are forthcoming, they cannot take the failure to return the computer as an objectively manifested consent to the terms in the box.

---

10. See [Randy E. Barnett, The Sound of Silence: Default Rules and Contractual Consent, 78 Va. L. Rev. 821, 885-894 (1992)].

Apart from what it suggests about whether notice of terms to follow and opportunity to accept or decline them should be required, the last discussion establishes that any such requirement is entirely consistent with the main thesis of this article: One can consent to be legally bound even to terms in form contracts of which one is rationally ignorant, whether the unread terms are in a box on a computer screen, in a box purchased in the store and opened later, or in a box sent later by UPS. Nothing in principle prevents a competent individual from assuming the risk that they later will dislike one of the unread terms in the box, though there are limits on what one can consent to in this manner. Barring a showing that these terms were radically unexpected, or that some other defense applies, the enforcement of even the "invisible" terms of form contracts can be justified on the basis of consent — real consent properly understood — not a fiction.

III

ENFORCEABILITY

9

WHICH COMMITMENTS SHOULD BE ENFORCED?

Professor Melvin Eisenberg has written that "[t]he first great question of contract law is . . . what kinds of promises should be enforced." This question assumes, of course, that *any* commitment should be enforced — an assumption that has always been widely accepted. Contract scholars assume that some commitments merit enforcement and debate how we distinguish the enforceable from the unenforceable commitment. Several different answers to the question of enforceability have been given. None has been accepted as the exclusive descriptive or normative account of contractual enforcement.

The 1933 article, *The Basis of Contract*, by the late Professor Morris Cohen of Yale Law School is a classic overview of the competing answers that have been offered to this question. In many respects, his critique of these theories has never been surpassed and many of the weaknesses he attributes to each of these theories may be observed still in contemporary scholarship. With the publication in 1981 of Harvard law professor Charles Fried's book Contact as Promise, a renewed emphasis was placed on the first of Cohen's bases for contract: the sanctity of promises. This development was reinforced by philosophers who have long struggled with the morality of promise keeping and who have tended to assume that contracts are an extension of this morality.

In her 2007 article, *The Divergence of Contact and Promise*, U.C.L.A. law professor Seana Shiffrin defends and develops this approach by critiquing contract law for its divergence from what the morality of promise-keeping requires. In his reply, *The Convergence of Contract and Promise*, Charles Fried disputes that contract law diverges from promise to the extent alleged by Shiffrin though, where it does, he agrees with her that contract law should be reformed to achieve greater convergence. Finally, in *Contract* versus *Promise*, Professor Aditi Bagchi of the University of Pennsylvania Law School questions the whole model of "contract as promise" by highlighting the differences between the institutions of promise and contract and describing how invoking the institution of contract can undermine, rather than reinforce, the institution of promising. (In Chapter 11, Dori Kimel will rely on a story by Patricia Williams to illustrate some additional reasons why contract is different than promise.)

A.   SIX REASONS FOR ENFORCING PROMISES

STUDY GUIDE: *Make sure you understand each reason why commitments should be enforced and its corresponding weakness. Are these reasons mutually exclusive? How might one combine some or all of them into a general theory of contractual enforceability? How could such a general theory deal with conflicts among the competing rationales? Should theories such as those presented by Professor Cohen be used to decide actual contracts disputes? If so, why do judges not discuss them? If not, then how should the issue of enforceability be decided by courts? Of what relevance are these theories to that decision-making process?*

THE BASIS OF CONTRACT*
Morris R. Cohen

The nature of contract has been much discussed by lawyers interested in specific technical doctrines, and by moralists, economists, and

---

*From Morris R. Cohen, The Basis of Contract, 4 Harv. L. Rev. 553 (1933).

political theorists interested in general social philosophy. There is still need for some effort to combine these points of view. The bearings of general philosophy become more definite through its applications, and the meaning of a technical doctrine receives illumination when we see it in the light of those wider ideas of which it is the logical outcome.

This large and important task is obviously beyond the limits of a short paper. But a few suggestions may indicate something of the scope of the problem. . . .

III.   THE JUSTIFICATION OF CONTRACT LAW

A.   The Sanctity of Promises

Contract law is commonly supposed to enforce promises. Why should promises be enforced?

The simplest answer is that of the intuitionists, namely, that promises are sacred *per se*, that there is something inherently despicable about not keeping a promise, and that a properly organized society should not tolerate this. This may also be said to be the common man's theory. Learned writers ignore this because of their interest in showing the evil consequences of allowing promises to be broken. But the intuitionists can well object that to judge the goodness of an act by its consequences is an obvious evasion by postponing the issue. For when we inquire which consequences are good and which are bad, we face the same question over again. . . .

Now there can be no doubt that common sense does generally find something revolting about the breaking of a promise, and this, if a fact, must be taken into account by the law, though it may be balanced by other factors or considerations. In any case, let us not ignore the fact that judges and jurists, like other mortals, do frequently express this in the feeling that it would be an outrage to let one who has broken his promise escape completely.

. . . If . . . we find ourselves in a state of society in which men are, as a matter of fact, repelled by the breaking of promises and feel that such practice should be discouraged or minimized, that is a primary fact which the law must not ignore.

But while this intuitionist theory contains an element of truth, it is clearly inadequate. No legal system does or can attempt to enforce all promises. Not even the canon law held all promises to be sacred. And when we come to draw a distinction between those promises which should be and those which should not be enforced, the intuitionist theory, that all promises should be kept, gives us no light or guiding principle.

Similar to the intuitionist theory is the view of Kantians ... that the duty to keep one's promise is one without which rational society would be impossible. There can be no doubt that from an empirical or historical point of view, the ability to rely on the promises of others adds to the confidence necessary for social intercourse and enterprise. But as an absolute proposition this is untenable. The actual world, which assuredly is among the possible ones, is not one in which all promises are kept, and there are many people — not necessarily diplomats — who prefer a world in which they and others occasionally depart from the truth and go back on some promise. It is indeed very doubtful whether there are many who would prefer to live in an entirely rigid world in which one would be obliged to keep *all* one's promises instead of the present more viable system, in which a vaguely fair proportion is sufficient. Many of us indeed would shudder at the idea of being bound by every promise, no matter how foolish, without any chance of letting increased wisdom undo past foolishness. Certainly, some freedom to change one's mind is necessary for free intercourse between those who lack omniscience.

For this reason we cannot accept Dean Pound's theory that all promises in the course of business should be enforced. He seems to me undoubtedly right in his insistence that promises constitute modern wealth and that their enforcement is thus a necessity of maintaining wealth as a basis of civilization. My bank's promise to pay the checks drawn to my account not only constitutes my wealth but puts it into a more manageable form than that of my personal possession of certain goods or even gold. Still, business men as a whole do not wish the law to enforce every promise. Many business transactions, such as those on a stock or produce exchange, could not be carried on unless we could rely on a mere verbal agreement or hasty memorandum. But other transactions, like those of real estate, are more complicated and would become too risky if we were bound by every chance promise that escapes us. Negotiations would be checked by such fear. In such cases men do not want to be bound until the final stage, when some formality like the signing of papers gives one the feeling of security, of having taken proper precautions. The issue obviously depends upon such factors as the relative simplicity of a given transaction, the speed with which it must be concluded, and the availability of necessary information.

At various times it has been claimed that mere promises as such received legal force in Hebrew, Greek, early German, and canon law. None of these claims can be justified.

All biblical references to binding promises are either to those involving an oath or promise to God or else they assume, as a matter of course, some formality such [as] a striking of hands and pledge or security. Greek covenants, or agreements, had to be in writing or to be recorded and were not free from other formalities. The binding character of promises could not have been absolute to a people to whom Odysseus was a hero.

Though . . . the early Germans attached great importance to keeping one's word, . . . the evidence collected . . . shows that the Germans, like other peoples, held promises binding only if some real object passed hands or some formal ceremony took place. Otherwise, pledge or security was required.

More substantial is the case for the canon law, which undoubtedly went further than any other system to enforce bare promises. The Council of Carthage in 348 B.C. made all written agreements binding and this later to the action *ex nudo pacto* before the courts of the Church. But the use of the oath was a distinctive ceremony and as it was binding in conscience, that is, in one's relation to God, it did not always afford relief to the promisee. The latter was at times even compelled by the ecclesiastical judge to release the promisor. And through the extension of the power of temporal rulers, as well as of bishops, to pass on the validity of the promise under oath, the legal effectiveness of the latter was whittled away.

B.   The Will Theory of Contract

According to the classical view, the law of contract gives expression to and protects the will of the parties, for the will is something inherently worthy of respect. Hence such authorities as Savigny, Windsheid, Pothier, Planiol, Pollock, Salmond, and Langdell hold that the first essential of a contract is the agreement of wills, or the meeting of minds.

The metaphysical difficulties of this view have often been pointed out. Minds or wills are not in themselves existing things that we can look at and recognize. We are restricted in our earthly experience to the observation of the changes or actions of more or less animated bodies in time and space; and disembodied minds or wills are beyond the scope and reach of earthly law. But while this objection has become familiar, it has not been very effective. The force of the old ideas, embodied in the traditional language, has not always been overcome even by those who like Langdell and Salmond profess to recognize the fictional element in the will theory.

Another line of objection can be found in the incompatibility of the classical theory with the consequences that the law attaches to an offer. Suppose that I offer to buy certain goods from A at a given price, and, following his refusal, give him a week's time to reconsider it. If I change my mind the next day but fail to notify him, a contractual obligation will none the less arise if five days later he notifies me that he has accepted my terms. Here obviously there is never a moment of time when the two parties are actually in agreement or of one mind. Yet no one denies that the resulting rights and duties are identical with those called contractual. It does not help the classical theory to say that I am under a legal duty to notify A (the offeree) and that if I fail to perform this duty in a proper way, the law will treat my change of mind as a nullity, *as if* it had never happened. The phrase italicized indicates that we are moving in the realm of fiction (or better, rights and duties imposed by law) and not in the realm of fact. No one denies that the contractual obligation should attach in this case; but there is in point of fact no actual agreement or meeting of minds. The latter, then, is not always necessary for a legal contract.

The logical inconsistency of the classical theory is not cured if we say that the law protects not the will but the expression or declaration of the will. Suppose that in the case mentioned I make a solemn declaration of the revocation of my offer, or write a letter but fail to communicate it. The law, in refusing to give effect to my declared revocation, is not protecting my expressed will, but is enforcing a duty on me in the interest of the general security of business transactions.

A more important objection to the theory that every contract expresses the consensus or agreed wills of the two parties is the fact that most litigation in this field arises precisely because of the advent of conditions that the two parties did not foresee when they entered into the transaction. Litigation usually reveals the absence of genuine agreement between the parties *ab initio*. If both parties had foreseen the difficulty, provision would have been made for it in the beginning when the contract was drawn up. When courts thus proceed to interpret the terms of the contract they are generally not merely seeking to discover the actual past meanings (though these may sometimes be investigated), but more generally they decide the "equities," the rights and obligations of the parties, in such circumstances; and these legal relations are determined by the courts and the jural system and not by the agreed will of the contesting parties.

Planiol and others have argued that while certain effects of a contract may not have been foreseen by the parties, nevertheless these are effects following from the original objective and are therefore the will of the two contractors. But to argue that, because the law fixes certain obligations, you did foresee something that in fact you did not see is a confusion which would be too ridiculous to criticize were it not so prevalent in juristic discussions. The confusion between what exists in fact and what ought to be according to our theory occurs also in other fields of liability. An employer is held liable for the negligence of an agent, even where he may have specifically warned the agent against it. For instance, a man instructs his servant to exercise his two horses in his field, since the animals are too spirited to be taken on the street. The servant takes the horses into the street, where they commit some damage. The master is held liable. Now the theory holds that the man who caused the damage is liable. Therefore, the master, being liable, is declared to be the "cause" of the damage. In truth, however, he is the "cause" because he is liable, and not *vice versa*. So in contracts men are liable for things that they did not actually foresee; and to say that they intended or willed these results is a fiction designed to save the will theory.

The obvious limitations of the will theory of contract has caused a reaction that takes the form of positivism or behaviorism: Away with the whole notion of will! — the only realities are specific acts to which the law attaches certain consequences, that is, if you do something by word or mouth, by writing, or by any other act that someone else takes [as] a promise, then the latter can, under certain conditions, bring an action. In its extreme form, this appears in what Dean Pound calls the state of strict law, which, like everything called primitive, is always with us. A developed system of law, however, must draw some distinction between voluntary and involuntary acts. Mr. Justice Holmes thinks that even a dog discriminates between one who stumbles over him and one who kicks him. The whole of the modern law of contract, it may be argued, thus does and should respond to the need of greater or finer discrimination in regard to the intentional character of acts. The law of error, duress, and fraud in contract would be unintelligible apart from such distinction.

C.   The Injurious-Reliance Theory

Though this seems the favorite theory today, it has not as yet been adequately formulated, and many of those who subscribe to it fall back on the will theory when they come to discuss special topics in the law of contract. The essence of the theory, however, is clear enough. Contractual liability arises (or should arise) only where (1) someone makes a promise explicitly in words or implicitly by some act, (2) someone else relies on it, and (3) suffers some loss thereby.

This theory appeals to the general moral feeling that not only ought promises be kept, but that anyone innocently injured by relying on them is entitled to have his loss "made good" by the one who thus caused it. If, as Schopenhauer has maintained, the sense of wrong is the ultimate human source of the law, then to base the obligation of the promise on the injury of the one who has relied on it, is to appeal to something really fundamental.

This theory also appeals powerfully to modern legal theorists because it seems to be entirely objective and social. It does not ask the court to examine the intention of the promisor. Instead, the court is asked to consider whether what the defendant has said or done is such that reasonable people generally do rely on it under the circumstances. The resulting loss can be directly proved and, to some extent, even measured. In emphasizing the element of injury resulting from the breach, the whole question of contract is integrated in the larger realm of obligations, and this tends to put our issues in the right perspective and to correct the misleading artificial distinctions between breach of contract and other civil wrongs or torts.

Nevertheless, this theory is not entirely consistent with existing law, nor does it give an altogether satisfactory account of what the law should do.

Contractual obligation is not coextensive with injurious reliance because (1) there are instances of both injury and reliance for which there is no contractual obligation, and (2) there are cases of such obligation where there is no reliance or injury.

(1) Clearly, not all cases of injury resulting from reliance on the word or act of another are actionable, and the theory before us offers no clue as to what distinguishes those which are. There is, first, the whole class of instances of definite financial injury caused by reliance on an explicit promise made in social relations, such as dinner parties and the like. Suppose I say to A, "If you agree to meet my friends and talk to them about your travels in Africa, I will hire an appropriate room in a hotel and give a dinner in your honor." A agrees but fails to come, or notifies me too late to prevent my financial loss. Here the law gives me no redress. Cases like these are often said to be properly ruled out on the ground that those who make them do not intend to be legally bound. And doubtless people generally know enough law to know that they cannot collect damages in such cases. But this argument is rather circular, since liability does not generally depend on knowledge or ignorance of the law. Men are held liable in many cases where they do not intend to be bound legally. There are doubtless good reasons why there should be no legal liability for "social" promises; but our theory does not account for them.

Even clearer are those cases where someone advertises goods for sale or a position to be filled, and, when I come, tells me that he has changed his mind. The fact that I have suffered actual loss from relying on this public statement does not in this case give me a cause of action. The law does not help everyone who has relied on the word or act of another.

(2) In formal contracts, such as promises under seal, stipulation in court, and the like, it is clearly not necessary for the promisee to prove reliance and injury. Certain formalities are binding *per se*. Consider also an ordinary agreement to sell something. Suppose that the defendant, who refuses to receive the goods, offers to prove that the vendor did not expect the deal to go through and had told others that he did not care whether it did or not. Would that be a bar to recovery? Actual reliance, it seems, is not always a necessary element in the case. The reliance of the promisee may be as "constructive" or fictional as the intention of the promisor. Nor does the plaintiff have to prove actual damage through the defendant's refusal to live up to his promise and take the goods. To be sure, where the law recognizes no loss, only nominal damages are usually awarded. But the fact that the plaintiff receives judgment is of practical, as well as of theoretic, importance. Clearly, the law favors the

carrying-out of promises even in cases where there is no actual reliance or actual loss from nonperformance.

(3) Finally, the recovery that the law allows to the injured promisee is not determined by what he lost in relying on the promisee, but rather by what he would have gained if the promise had been kept. There are obviously many cases where the injured party is subsequently no worse after the breach than if the contract had never been made. He has thus not been in fact injured. And yet he may recover heavy damages if he would have gained heavily by the performance of the contract. The policy of the law, then, is not merely to redress injuries but also to protect certain kinds of expectation by making men live up to certain promises.

There can be no question about the soundness of the injurious-reliance theory in accounting for a dominant phase of the law of contract, and the foregoing difficulties may thus seem petty. But they do call attention to fundamental obscurities in the very idea of "reliance" as well as in the criteria of "injury." The injurious-reliance theory, like others, calls attention to a necessary element but does not give an adequate account of the whole of the law of contract. Its merits become clearer when its claims are properly limited.

D.   The Equivalent Theory

Popular sentiment generally favors the enforcement of those promises which involve some *quid pro quo*. It is generally considered unfair that after *A* has given something of value or rendered *B* some service, *B* should fail to render anything in return. Even if what *A* did was by way of gift, *B* owes him gratitude and should express it in some appropriate way. And if, in addition, *B* has promised to pay *A* for the value or services received, the moral sense of the community condemns *B*'s failure to do so as even more unfair. The demand for justice behind the law is but an elaboration of such feelings of what is fair and unfair.

The equivalent theory of contract has the advantage of being supported by this popular sentiment. This sentiment also explains the primacy of *real* contracts.

While a legal theory must not ignore common sense, it must also go beyond it. For common sense, while generally sound at its core, is almost always vague and inadequate. Common sentiment, for instance, demands an equivalent. But what things are equivalent? It is easy to answer this in regard to goods or services that have a standard market value. But how shall we measure things that are dissimilar in nature, or in a market where monopolistic or other factors prevent a fair or just price? Modern law therefore professes to abandon the effort of more primitive systems to enforce material fairness within the contract. The parties to the contract must themselves determine what is fair. Thereby, however, the law loses a good deal of support in the moral sense of the community.

Though legal historians like Ames are right in insisting that the common-law doctrine of consideration did not originate in the law's insistence on equivalence in every contract, the latter idea cannot be eliminated altogether. It colors the prevailing language as to consideration, and especially the doctrine that in a bilateral contract, each promise is consideration for the other. If a bare promise is of no legal validity, how can it be of any profit to the promisee or of any detriment to the promisor? Clearly, two things that are valueless cannot become of value by being exchanged for each other. The real reason for the sanctioning of certain exchanges of promises is that thereby certain transactions can be legally protected, and when we desire to achieve this result we try to construe the transactions as an exchange of promises. Consideration is in effect a formality, like an oath, the affixing of a seal, or a stipulation in court.

E. Formalism in Contract

The recognition of the formal character of consideration may help us to appreciate the historical myopia of those who speak of a seal as "importing" consideration. Promises under seal were binding (because of the formality) long before the doctrine of consideration was ever heard of. The history of forms and ceremonies in the law of contract offers an illuminating chapter in human psychology or anthropology. We are apt to dismiss the early Roman ceremonies of *mancipatio, nexum,* and *sponsio,* the Anglo-Saxon *wed* and *borh,* or the Frankish ceremonies of *aramitio, wadiatio,* and of the *festuca,* as peculiar to primitive society. But reflection shows that our modern practices of shaking hands to close a bargain, signing papers, and protesting a note are, like the taking of an oath on assuming office, not only designed to make evidence secure, but are in large part also expressions of the fundamental human need for formality and ceremony, to make sharp distinctions where otherwise lines of demarcation would not be so clearly apprehended.

Ceremonies are the channels by which the stream of social life creates its ceaseless flow through the sands of human circumstance. Psychologically, ceremonies function as habits; socially, they are customary ways of doing things; ethically, they have what Jellinek has called the normative power of the actual, that is, they control what we do by creating a standard of respectability or a pattern to which we feel bound to conform. The daily obedience to the act of the government, which is the basis of all political and legal institutions, is thus largely a matter of conformity to established ritual or form of behavior. For the most part, we obey the law or the policeman as a matter of course, without deliberation. The customs of other people seem to us strange and we try to explain them as ceremonies symbolic of things that are familiar or seem useful to us. But many of our own customs can appear to an outsider as equally nonrational rituals that we follow from habit. We may justify them as the sacred vessels through which we obtain the substance of life's goods. But the maintenance of old forms may also be an end in itself to all those to whom change from the familiar is abhorrent.

F.   Contract and the Distribution of Risks

Mr. Justice Holmes has suggested that a legal promise may be viewed as a wager: I assure you of a certain event (which may or may not be within my control) and I pay in case of failure.

This view has not found much favor. The first objection that has been urged against it is that when men make a contract, they contemplate its performance rather than its breach. This is hardly fatal. Men can and do sometimes deliberately plan to pay damages in certain contingencies rather than carry out their legal promises. It might even be said that the law sometimes encourages that attitude. Thus, up to the period of the Reform Bill, English law definitely put obstacles in the way of the lessee of land for a term of years who wanted any relief other than damages. On the other hand, Mr. Justice Holmes fails to dispose of the objection that the law does in some cases — in civil law countries more even than in our equity courts — compel specific performance. Moreover, his theory fails to attain its expressed objective, namely, to dispose of the view that a contract is a qualified subjection of one will to another. For the paying of damages does not flow from the promisor's willingness, but is the effect of the law's lending its machinery to the promisee.

Nevertheless, when taken in a wider sense in connection with Mr. Justice Holmes's general philosophy concerning the risk in all human affairs, his theory is illuminating and important.

All human transactions are directed to a future that is never free from elements of uncertainty. Every one of our ventures, therefore, involves the taking of a risk. When I board a train to go home I am betting my life that I will get to my destination. Now a contract or agreement may be viewed as an agreement for the distribution of anticipated gains or losses. If I agree to sell certain goods or services I expect that I shall be paid in good United States money and that with this money I shall be able to acquire certain other goods. I do not generally take into account the possibility that the purchasing power of the American dollar may be radically reduced when I receive my pay. That contingency is generally not thought of or else deemed too remote, yet certain bondholders do think of it and specify payment in gold of a certain standard. Now the human power to foresee all the consequences of an agreement is limited, even if we suppose that the two parties understand each other's meaning to begin with. Disputes or disagreements are therefore bound to come up; and the law of contract may thus be viewed as an attempt to determine the rights and duties of the two parties under circumstances that were not anticipated exactly in the same way by the two contracting parties, or at any rate were not expressly provided for in an unambiguous way. One can therefore say that the court's adjudication supplements the original contract as a method of distributing gains and losses.

From this point of view, we may look upon the law of contract as a number of rules according to which courts distribute gains and losses corresponding to the equities of such cases; and the pretense that the result follows exclusively from the agreement of the two parties is fictional. Just as the process of interpreting a statute is really a process of subsidiary legislation, so is the interpretation of a contract really a method of supplementing the original agreement by such provisions as are necessary to determine the point at issue.

If we view the law of contract as directed to strengthening the security of transactions by enabling men to rely more fully on promises, we see only one phase of its actual workings. The other phase is the determination of the rights of the contracting parties as to contingencies that they have not foreseen, and for which they have not provided. In this latter respect the law of contract is a way of enforcing some kind of distributive justice within the legal system. And technical doctrines of contract may thus be viewed as a set of rules that will systematize decisions in this field and thus give lawyers and their clients some guidance in the problem of anticipating future decisions. Thus, for instance, if the question arises as to who should suffer a loss caused by the destruction of goods in transit, the technical doctrine of when title passes enables us to deal with the problem more definitely. In any case, the essential problem of the law of contract is the problem of distribution of risks. The other phase, namely, the assurance that what the parties have actually agreed on will be fulfilled, is a limiting principle.

B. CONTRACT AS PROMISE

STUDY GUIDE: *How does Professor Shiffrin view the relationship of promise to contract? In what ways does she think contract law diverges from the morality of promise keeping?*

THE DIVERGENCE OF CONTRACT AND PROMISE*

Seana Valentine Shiffrin

INTRODUCTION

In U.S. law, a contract is described as a legally enforceable promise. So to make a contract, one must make a promise. One is

---

*From Seana Valentine Shiffrin, The Divergence of Contract and Promise, 120 Harv. L. Rev. 708 (2007).

thereby simultaneously subject to two sets of norms — legal and moral. As I argue, the legal norms regulating these promises diverge in substance from the moral norms that apply to them. This divergence raises questions about how the moral agent is to navigate both the legal and moral systems. . . . By claiming that contract diverges from promise, I mean that although the legal doctrines of contract associate legal obligations with morally binding promises, the contents of the legal obligations and the legal significance of their breach do not correspond to the moral obligations and the moral significance of their breach. . . .

This Article approaches these topics by exploring the demands and tensions to which contract law, in particular, subjects moral agents. It starts from the more general premise that law must be made compatible with the conditions for moral agency to flourish — both because of the intrinsic importance of moral agency to the person and because a just political and legal culture depends upon a social culture in which moral agency thrives. The content and normative justifications of a legal practice . . . should be capable of being known and accepted by a self-consciously moral agent. Legal rules must be constructed and justified in ways that take into account the fact that law embodies a system of rules and practices that moral agents inhabit, enforce, and are subject to alongside other aspects of their lives, especially their moral agency. . . .

B.   What Accommodating Moral Agency Requires

[T]he legal system should be fashioned, justified, and interpreted to accommodate the opportunity for the governed to lead a full and coherently structured moral life. What does this commitment entail in the case of contract? I start from the following premise: when a legal practice is pervasive and involves simultaneous participation in a moral relationship or practice, the content and normative justification for the legal practice must be acceptable to a reasonable moral agent with a coherent, stable, and unified personality. Law's justification should not depend upon its being opaque or obscure or upon the ignorance, amorality, or split personality of the citizens it governs. From this basic premise follow three more specific principles that regulate the interrelation between moral norms and legal norms, at least in those pervasive, regular contexts that involve the simultaneous participation of moral agents in parallel legal and moral relationships or practices.

First, what legal rules directly require agents to do or to refrain from doing should not, as a general matter, be inconsistent with leading a life of at least minimal moral virtue. "Minimal moral virtue" should be understood in a way that does not presuppose any particular comprehensive conception of the good or ideal of virtue.

Second, the law and its rationale should be transparent and accessible to the moral agent. Moreover, their acceptance by the agent should be compatible with her developing and maintaining moral virtue. Although knowledge of the justifications of law is not required or expected of every citizen, understanding the law's rationale should not present a conflict for the interested citizen qua moral agent. This is not merely because the agent is subject to the law and that to which she is subject should be justifiable to her. Within a democratic society, the law should be understood as ours — as authored by us and as the expression of our joint social voice. This second principle governs both the reasons that actually motivate government agents to impose and enforce divergent rules, as well as the strongest available justifications for the divergence. Examination of the latter reveals whether the divergence is intrinsically problematic. . . .

Third, the culture and practices facilitated by law should be compatible with a culture that supports morally virtuous character. Even supposing that law is not responsible for and should not aim to enforce virtuous character and interpersonal moral norms, the legal system should not be incompatible with or present serious obstacles to leading a decent moral life. A principled requirement that the law facilitate a culture that is compatible with moral virtue need not go so far as to enforce moral virtue. In some circumstances, this goal may better be realized by doing quite the opposite. One may facilitate moral virtue by affording opportunities to be virtuous and by refraining from offering strong incentives or encouragements to misbehave; direct enforcement of virtue for its own sake, in some contexts, can be counterproductive — particularly when it is a necessary aspect of the virtuous conduct that it be voluntary and that it be evident to others that it is voluntarily performed.

The remainder of my discussion investigates whether the divergence of contract from promise can satisfy these principles. . . . [I] argue that although contract law does not violate the first principle by issuing directives that contradict moral requirements, it may violate the second and third principles. Defenses of the rules of contract law often invoke rationales the acceptance of which is incompatible with maintaining one's moral convictions. Further, the rules themselves may contribute to a culture that challenges moral agency.

II.   THE DIVERGENCE OF PROMISE AND CONTRACT

I now turn to the particulars of the divergence between contract and promise. I focus specifically on the ways in which contract law expects less of the promisor and more of the promisee than morality does. Chiefly, I examine the treatment of remedies in contract and promise, although I occasionally draw on other helpful examples.

[T]he argument proceeds in three steps that correspond to the three principles for accommodating moral agency just articulated. First, contract and promise diverge in some significant ways, although not by directly generating inconsistent directives. Second, some of the standard arguments for the doctrines' divergence are exactly the sort of justifications that a virtuous agent could not accept. Third, even though some reasons for the divergence may be acceptable to a virtuous agent, the divergence itself may risk another difficulty by contributing to a culture that may be in tension with the conditions for the maintenance of moral character. . . .

U.S. contract law represents that a contract is an enforceable promise. Contracts do not merely resemble promises in that both involve voluntary agreements, usually concerning future activity, and often use identical language. . . . In U.S. law, promises are embedded within contracts and form their basis. The Restatement of Contracts defines a contract as "a promise . . . for the breach of which the law gives a remedy, or the performance of which the law in some way recognizes as a duty."[1] The Restatement's definition of a promise is not technical. It invokes the familiar notion of the communication of an intention, the content and context of which justify the recipient in believing that a commitment has been made through its communication. The language of promises, promisees, and promisors saturates contract law — in decisions, statutes, and the Restatement. It also permeates the academic

---

1. Restatement (Second) of Contracts §1 (emphasis added).

literature through its common characterization of contracts as the law of enforceable promises and by its formulation of the foundational questions of contract as which promises to enforce, why, and how. Notably, in U.S. law, promises of the right sort may form the basis for a contract without an additional intention to enter into a legally binding arrangement.[2] Suppose we start by taking the law's self-description seriously and conceive of contracts as resting upon promises per se. As I argue below, a virtuous agent could not accept this self-description as accurate while also accepting the justification and structure of some of the divergence of contract from morality.

A.   The Divergence Between Promise and Contract

As I have already observed, U.S. contract law diverges from the morality of promises. Contract law would run parallel to morality if contract law rendered the same assessments of permissibility and impermissibility as the moral perspective, except that it would replace moral permissibility with legal permissibility and it would use its distinctive tools and techniques to express and reflect those judgments. For example, typically, a promisor is morally expected to keep her promise through performance. Absent the consent of the promisee, the moral requirement would not be satisfied if the promisor merely supplied the financial equivalent of what was promised. Financial substitutes might be appropriate if, for good reason, what was promised became impossible, or very difficult, to perform. Otherwise, intentional, and often even negligent, failure to perform appropriately elicits moral disapprobation. If contract law ran parallel to morality, then contract

---

2. See Restatement (Second) of Contracts §21 ("Neither real nor apparent intention that a promise be legally binding is essential to the formation of a contract, but a manifestation of intention that a promise shall not affect legal relations may prevent the formation of a contract."). In other countries, the presumption sometimes runs the other way. For instance, in British law, the intention to enter into legal relations is presumed for promises between commercial entities but must be positively proved for social and familial promises to become contracts. . . . American law also evinces reluctance to enforce certain sorts of familial promises, though this resistance is not articulated through a doctrine that there must be additional intent to enter into legal relations.

law would — as the norms of promises do — require that promisors keep their promises as opposed merely to paying off their promisees. The only difference is that it would require this as a legal, and not merely a moral, matter.

1. Specific Performance and Damages. — Contract law, however, diverges from morality in this respect. Contract law's dominant remedy is not specific performance but expectation damages. Usually, the financial value of the performance is demanded from the promisor, but actual performance is not required (even when it is possible), except in special circumstances. Further, intentional promissory breach is not subject to punitive damages, that is, to those legal damages that express the judgment that the behavior represents a wrong. Notably, U.S. law typically makes damages for emotional distress and attorney's fees unavailable upon breach.

There are two further examples of the divergence over the significance of performance. First, one cannot obtain an order of specific performance even when one successfully alleges anticipatory repudiation. Even prior to the directed time of performance, a court is unlikely to direct specifically that the promised performance should occur. On the contrary, moral observers would direct that the performance should occur as promised, unless the promisee waives. The difference between the moral and legal reaction to breach does not appear only after the specified time for performance elapses.

Second, under the *Hadley* rule, promisors are liable only for those consequential damages that could reasonably have been foreseen at the time of the contract's formation. From a moral perspective, this is quite strange. If one is bound to perform but without excuse voluntarily elects to breach one's duty, a case could be made that the promisor should be liable for all consequential damages. If foreseeability should limit this liability at all, what would matter morally is what was foreseeable at the time of breach rather than at the time of formation. Whereas the former reflects the idea that breach is a wrong for which the promisor must take responsibility, the latter fits better with the idea that the contract merely sets a price for potential promissory breach.

The law thereby fails to use its distinctive powers and modes of expression to mark the judgment that breach is impermissible as opposed to merely subject to a price. For this reason, I find unpersuasive the possible rejoinder that contract and promise deliver the same primary judgments — namely, that breach of promise is wrong — but that they diverge only with respect to legal and moral remedies. There are standard legal remedies (as well as legal terms) that signify that a wrong has been done. In other areas of private law, remedies such as punitive damages and specific performance are more commonly invoked. Contract has a distinctive remedial regime that not only diverges from its moral counterpart, but also reflects an underlying view that promissory breach is not a wrong, or at least not a serious one.

2. Mitigation. — The mitigation doctrine provides another example of divergence. Contract law requires the promisee to mitigate her damages. It fails to supply relief for those damages she could have avoided through self-help, including seeking another buyer or seller, advertising for a substitute, or finding a replacement. As a general rule, morality does not impose such requirements on disappointed promisees. True, morality does not look sympathetically upon promisees who stay idle while easily avoidable damages accumulate. But this is a far cry from what contract expects of the promisee and what it fails to demand of the breaching promisor. Following the norms of promising, promisors would not readily expect the promisee to accept a substitute for the promised performance, at least not without a strong excuse or justification for nonperformance. Were a substitute unavoidable or justified, promissory norms would ordinarily place the burden on the promisor, rather than the promisee, to locate and provide it. It may sometimes be permissible for the promisor to ask the promisee to shoulder this burden when the substitute is much easier for the promisee to obtain or when the promisor is ill-suited to select a replacement (as when the promisee's judgment is necessary for the replacement to serve the promisee adequately). Still, even in such cases, it would usually be unacceptable for the promisor to insist were the promisee to refuse.

The difficulties in measuring and fully compensating for the costs incurred in mitigation provide another rationale for the moral stance and trouble some scholars have with respect to the current legal rule. But concerns about whether compensation can be full and adequate do not exhaust the moral reasons for declining to impose a strong responsibility to mitigate on the promisee. It is morally distasteful to expect the promisee to do work that could be done by the promisor when the occasion for the work is the promisor's own wrongdoing. That expectation is especially distasteful when its rationale is that it makes the promisor's wrongdoing easier, simpler, more convenient, or less costly.

Might it be objected that the promisee, while within her rights to refuse, should not, morally, refuse a promisor's request that she mitigate? It might be thought to be stingy and overly punitive to refuse such a request. If so, it might be maintained that the mitigation doctrine does in fact run parallel to morality.

Sometimes it can be morally wrong for the promisee to refuse to mitigate, especially when the costs of refusal are very steep and disproportionate to the seriousness of what is promised. But whether it is morally wrong for the promisee to refuse may depend on a number of factors to which the law is insensitive, including the closeness of the relationship, the history of the relationship, the reason for breach, the reason the promisor wants to shift the burden, and how cumbersome mitigation activities would be.

It might be suggested that the law's insensitivity to these factors is the byproduct of the need to formulate a clear rule. This is not an entirely satisfying diagnosis. The law is capable of fashioning clear, but more sensitive, rules in other equally complex contexts. Furthermore, it is unclear why, if a blunt rule is necessary, it should be fashioned to favor systematically the breaching promisor and not the promisee. Not only is the promisor the party responsible for the breach, but the wrong committed by the unreasonably reluctant mitigator-promisee is not the sort that is typically the appropriate object of legal enforcement. This wrong may fall within the category of wrongs the law should allow because interference in this particular domain might preclude recognizable realization of the virtuous thing to do — namely, to be gracious and forgiving in the face of another's wrong.

3. Punitive and Liquidated Damages. — Not only are punitive damages unavailable as a response to garden-variety, intentional breach, but willing parties are not permitted to elect them in advance through legally enforceable agreements. It is a delicate question whether this bar exhibits true divergence. On the one hand, agents typically cannot specify the moral seriousness of their conduct and, in particular, their misconduct: the moral status of conduct that is truly misconduct is usually independent of agents' attitudes or will. This feature of morality might lend support to the view that the rule in contracts runs parallel to morality.

On the other hand, promises occupy an interesting part of moral territory because, through them, agents themselves can alter the moral valence of some future conduct. A promise may render an action mandatory and important, when it otherwise would have been optional and, perhaps, unimportant. This created status can then be undone yet again through the consent and waiver of the promisee.

Further, although I have been speaking of promises in a rather univocal way, a number of different sorts of commitments are available to agents. Parties can have tacit understandings that have many of the features of formal, strict promises. Certain sorts of affirmations or agreements constitute commitments that can be promise-like without using the most formal terms of promising. Within our moral practices of promising, agents can signify an understanding that there is a commitment but that it is fairly loose and flexible; it is not illusory, but it is subject to change for lesser reasons than would normally be acceptable for standard promises. Consider the following commitment: "I promise to be there if I can, but life is complicated right now and I can't commit for sure." The issuer is surely bound to appear if her schedule is free and her car and legs function; she is bound to turn down new, unanticipated, and conflicting requests for commitment or attendance; but she is not duty-bound to attend if it turns out that working late is necessary to meet a preexisting deadline. We are also able to signal when such looseness and flexibility is out of order, such as when one makes a solemn commitment to be there no matter what. One might regard the ability to specify punitive damages as a very rough legal counterpart to the poorly defined mechanisms through which parties mark a particular promissory relation as especially serious or not. If so, then the law does show divergence by disallowing enforceable specifications of liquidated damages that exceed rough approximations of market value. As I say, though, this would be a rather rough method of capturing this aspect of promising — both because it might better be captured through more clearly specified content within the contract, for example through conditions of performance, and because it marks a departure from the more general inability of moral agents to specify for themselves the significance of their own moral failures and the appropriate remedies. . . .

V.   TOWARD AN ALTERNATIVE CONCEPTION

. . . So what is the purpose of a legal regime dedicated to the enforcement of some subset of promises? Suppose one did not start from a purely instrumental point of view. Would generally morally compliant and highly proficient agents who are not shy about making and keeping promises have reasons to establish a system of contract?

I believe they would. In . . . addition to the work they may do in facilitating cooperation or the pursuit of parties' ends or projects, promises play a significant moral function in interpersonal relationships. Promises and their availability provide a concrete (and I believe indispensable) way for parties to reaffirm their equal moral status and respect for each other under conditions in which possibly divergent present or future interests create vulnerability. The promissory commitment represents an effort to disable and manage some of the hazardous mechanisms and effects of power, hierarchy, and vulnerability. These reasons may be extended to illuminate the function of promises between nonintimates as well. . . .

One might then understand contract as the public complement to the private promissory relationship. In creating a contract, the parties render public their efforts to manage morally their disparate interests, as well as the associated latent or emergent vulnerabilities this disparity may create or feed. Creation of a contract invites this relationship to be witnessed, recognized, and scrutinized by the public. The purpose of rendering the relationship public might vary according to circumstance and content. In some cases, contracts provide assurance — going public is meant to assuage concerns that one or more parties have about the security of the arrangement. Motivations like these are familiar in both business contexts and familial contexts, including the public promises involved in marriage. But the emphasis on contract as primarily a mode of assurance, a response to the worry that things may go wrong, is exaggerated. Contract law may play an important function even outside nonideal moral circumstances. Parties may well seek to create contracts for reasons that are not predominantly grounded in fear, lingering distrust of their promissory partners, or even more innocuous concerns about inadvertent breach.

For other parties, by contrast, going public may be a demonstration of feelings of strong security in the relationship and in the reliability of the commitment; one or both parties may be so confident of the commitment that they are happy to render it public and regard their willingness to do so as a symbol of their good intentions. Again, motivations like these are familiar in both business contexts and familial contexts, including the public promises involved in marriage.

In other cases, contract serves a positive gap-filling function; parties may come to the essence of an agreement but rely on public rules designed to provide reasonable accommodations of the parties' interests and any relevant public interest to resolve open questions. In still other cases, given what is at issue in the agreement — for example, the use of important resources — going public may be mandatory because public oversight of such resources is necessary to protect broader interests.

Except in cases of the latter type, why should the public attend to these commitments and expend effort to enforce them, as well as establish norms that fill in the gaps that promissory parties fail to anticipate or resolve? A partial answer refers to reasons quite familiar from our discourse about contract. First, although promises solve and manage certain dynamics of vulnerability, they also generate new vulnerabilities. The public has an interest in protecting parties from the consequences and harm caused by breaches that result from these vulnerabilities. Second, and more broadly, the reinforcement of equal status facilitated by promises takes on a political value when made public. In addition to the political interest in a culture of taking commitment seriously, there are reasons to affirm and support such public declarations of equal status and such good faith efforts to manage diversity and vulnerability morally. That such a system also tends to create efficient systems of economic exchange is an important side benefit that may affect many of our decisions about how to structure the institution, but only in ways complementary to our other moral purposes.

This quick articulation is admittedly vague, but it provides a flavor of a set of rationales that could supply normative, moral reasons for an institution of contract without relying upon any direct aim to enforce interpersonal morality or to encourage virtuous behavior. Contract, on this view, is not an effort to get people to act virtuously, to prompt people to keep their promises for the right reasons, to ensure that private relationships go as well as possible, or to get people to make promises when morally appropriate to do so. It is not an effort to legalize as much as possible the interpersonal moral regime of promising, but rather to provide support for the political and public values associated with promising.

Understood in this way, a variety of the divergent aspects of contract law make sense, especially those associated with evidentiary concerns. Requirements of writing — for example, the parol evidence rule or the statute of frauds — may be understood more generally in terms of the conditions of making something verifiable to outside assessors and the public. The unconscionability and public policy doctrines manifest the limits on what commitments the public can support, given the underlying purpose of supporting equality as well as our other social aims. The doctrines of mistake and impracticability presuppose notions of reasonable risk that represent our sense of which endeavors and which assumptions of risk are worth our affirmation and efforts. These characterizations refer back to public, legally normative values, but they are not in implicit or explicit tension with the view that the underlying moral promises are binding.

Although this normative conception of the purposes of contract law can readily support some divergences between promise and contract, it may be inconsistent with some others discussed [here], such as the general unavailability of punitive damages in contract. At the least, some standard arguments for these doctrines are in tension with the maintenance of the conditions of moral agency. Given the overriding nature of our moral commitments, as well as the dependence of a well-functioning democracy on a flourishing moral culture, there may be reason to reexamine these doctrines and their justifications, and to strive for greater convergence between promise and contract.

Many legal theorists have been particularly troubled by the idea of separating criminal law, tort, or constitutional law from moral concerns. Some have been more sanguine about conceiving of contract law as an amoral domain driven by aims entirely insensitive or indifferent to the concerns of interpersonal morality. I suspect that quite the opposite is true. Contract law cannot properly be regarded as an amoral domain in the least. . . . [T]he nesting of promise into the self-conception of contract, the ubiquity of promises and contracts, and the elemental role of commitment in social life require a legal approach to contract that is deliberately sensitive to the demands of interpersonal morality.

STUDY GUIDE: *In what respect does Professor Fried think contract law converges with promises where Professor Shiffrin thinks they diverge?*

THE CONVERGENCE OF CONTRACT
AND PROMISE*

Charles Fried

I agree with the general tenor and many of the details of Professor Seana Shiffrin's lucid and closely reasoned account of the relation between standard contract doctrine and the morality of promising. In this brief Response, I take up two points with which I disagree. First, Professor Shiffrin argues that contract doctrine, by making expectation damages rather than specific performance the general or default remedy for breach, diverges from what the morality of promising requires. Second, she makes a similar argument about contract doctrine's imposition of the burden of mitigating damages on the disappointed promisee. In respect to these two arguments she repeats what I think is a frequently made but mistaken argument in the economic literature on promising, which uses these very examples to claim that contract doctrine is not and should not be rooted in the morality of promising, but rather in the economics of efficiency. Professor Shiffrin does not argue for that conclusion. Rather, she would move contract doctrine into closer alignment with what she considers to be the requirements of the morality of promising.

I begin with a general account, one with which I do not suppose Professor Shiffrin would fundamentally disagree, of what I mean by morality and the morality of promising. Every society of any size and complexity, and certainly any such society that seeks the advantages of modernity — such as specialization of functions, accomplishment of time-extended tasks, provision for the future, and accumulation and transmission of knowledge — requires rules to guide the conduct of individuals and to specify the institutions and mechanisms by which those rules are identified, interpreted, enforced, and changed. I think it is an affectation and a quibble to deny these rules the name of law. And to do their work, such systems of rules must display a significant degree of regularity, comprehensibility, and stability. . . .

---

*From Charles Fried, The Convergence of Contract and Promise, 120 Harv. L. Rev. F. 1 (2007).

Morality is concerned with how people should lead their lives and how they should treat each other. The precepts of morality for that reason will address many of the same aspects of behavior that are the subject of rules of law. By morality I do not mean what people think is the way they should live and how they should treat each other, nor how some person or group of persons think people should live their lives. Morality does not in the first degree describe attitudes, beliefs, or demands about these things, any more than mathematics in the first degree is about what people think, teach, or ordain about the domain of numbers and abstract relations. In both cases there is a fact of the matter: the gratuitous infliction of pain is wrong; $2 + 2 = 4$. Only in the second degree is there a subject matter of what people believe and have believed on these scores, and how they come to believe these things. Those inquiries belong to the history, the sociology, the psychology of morals or mathematics, but they are not moral or mathematical inquiries except incidentally. I understand Professor Shiffrin's article to be about morality in the first degree. How else to understand her talk of morality being about people living virtuous lives?

Morality takes as a premise that persons have goals and projects of many sorts. Some of these goals and projects implicate other persons only in the sense that they divert that person's energy from goals that do implicate others. Other goals and projects implicate other persons either by getting in the way of those other persons reaching their goals or by enlisting them in the actor's pursuit. The last is an important, perhaps the most important, subset of human pursuits. That subset may be further subdivided into two different kinds of pursuits: first, those in which an actor enlists others instrumentally in the attainment of his goal, and second, those in which the other person is a constitutive, intrinsic element in that goal. Examples of the first include objectives in pursuit of which the use of a machine or an animal would do as well as the use of the other person; examples of the second are any goal that made reference in its very definition to the feelings or activity of another, for instance acts of love, friendship, or sadistic cruelty.

Morality addresses all of these sets and subsets of human activity and human relations. It condemns a way of life indifferent to the well-being of others, and even more strongly condemns pursuits that are constituted by the frustration, humiliation, or destruction of others. By contrast, it enjoins each actor to respect the other's humanity — that is, the feeling, judging, and striving nature of other persons — and celebrates pursuits that involve others not only without disrespecting them (that is, "using" them in Kantian terminology), but also by furthering their own pursuits as they further the actor's pursuit. A string quartet is a paradigmatic example of the last. Trust is the relation between persons who respect each other. It is a relation of mutual respect among persons pursuing individual and common goals. Promising is a deliberate invocation of trust, and breaking a promise is a betrayal of that trust and therefore is immoral.[3] Judging by her other work and the tenor of this article, when Professor Shiffrin invokes morality and the morality of trust, I take her to mean something like this.

When Professor Shiffrin and I (in *Contract as Promise*) relate the legal institution of contract to the moral institution of promising, we see contract as not only an analogy to promising. We see . . . contract as rooted in, and underwritten by, the morality of promising. . . . Law can be, should be, but need not be a set of institutions that underwrite, facilitate, and enforce the demands and aspirations of morality in our dealings with each other. It is therefore entirely appropriate that various legal institutions resemble the moral institutions which they partially instantiate. Contract and promise are like that. It is because the legal institution of contract is grounded in the moral institution of promise — as the standard legal doctrine of the subject cited by Professor Shiffrin testifies — that we both expect congruence between the two, but also demand an explanation when the two diverge. It is that divergence that is Professor Shiffrin's subject. . . .

The divergence that most excites Professor Shiffrin is contract law's preference for expectation damages when, she supposes, the morality of promising would demand specific performance. . . . In the end, what I suspect lends Professor Shiffrin's complaint plausibility is the well-known fact that rarely do expectation damages make the disappointed promisee completely whole. If he is forced to sue, he will usually not get back his lawyer's fees and court costs, not to mention that he has had to bear the risk of an unjustly unfavorable outcome in that suit. All this is avoided in the case in which the defaulting promisor at the outset offers

---

3. This is a sketch of an argument worked out at greater length in Charles Fried, Contract As Promise 14–17 (1981), and more recently in Charles Fried, Modern Liberty And the Limits of Government 69–70 (2007). The argument is explicitly and intrinsically Kantian. . . .

full compensation measured by the promisee's expectation. That is what the promisor *should* do. That is what morality demands and efficiency does not require otherwise.

The unfairness of saddling the disappointed buyer with his litigation costs is a defect of the American system of justice generally. Unlike the much fairer British system in which the loser pays the winner's costs, American "justice" makes a shibboleth of each party paying his own costs — a shibboleth reversed only in special cases designated by statute. As *Contract as Promise* is not committed to the Panglossian mantra that all is most just in this most just of all possible worlds, I think here is a ripe occasion for reforming the law,[4] though the reform has arrayed against it the formidable political forces of the bar, who wrap themselves in the mantle of equal access to the courts when what they are really concerned about is drumming up more business.

As for the risk of a mistaken outcome that the disappointed promisee is forced to encounter when the defaulting promisor does not tender expectation damages at the outset, that is where Professor Shiffrin's plea for punitive damages has some plausibility.

My argument that expectation damages rather than specific performance is the remedy generally required both by the morality of promising and the efficiency analysis of contract law loses its force when we consider a contract/promise that explicitly provides for specific performance in the event of breach. We do not see many such contractual provisions, and if we did I suspect they would usually relate to performances that are unique or otherwise hard to value, and that is just when both contract law and the moral argument I have been making would require specific performance. But what if we have such a clause in an ordinary sale-of-goods case? Then I am in trouble. I would be inclined to fall back on the nonpromissory and somewhat theoretically desperate notion that unreasonable or unconscionable provisions need not be respected. But the possibility raises a more satisfactory account — that Professor Shiffrin and I really do not disagree that much because in the vast number of cases, the contract does not address

---

4. Another place where morality points the way to the reform of actual legal institutions is in respect to gratuitous promises that — if made with sufficient seriousness and reflection — should be as enforceable as those supported by consideration. Professor Shiffrin and I agree about this. . . .

the issue one way or the other. Then my rule favoring expectation damages becomes merely a default rule, filling a gap in the explicit bargain, and there is no necessary conflict with Professor Shiffrin's analysis.

A further supposed divergence between the morality of promising and contract law that attracts Professor Shiffrin's attention is the disappointed promisee's duty to mitigate his damages. The economist has little trouble explaining this rule of contract law: it is the promisee who is in the best position to seek out and implement opportunities to mitigate the disappointment he has suffered as a result of the breach. But that explanation does not and should not satisfy Professor Shiffrin, the moralist of promise. Yet here she makes another mistake. She rightly sees promising as a moral and not just an economic institution, but she fails to take into account that promising is not all there is to morality — something I suspect in different contexts she understands perfectly well. Morality, for instance, recognizes a duty to save another from serious loss when the actor can do so with little trouble, risk of loss, or harm to himself. The common law does not — except when the person in peril and his potential rescuer have some prior relation, and then law and morality do converge. But is not the disappointed promisee in a position analogous to that of the Good Samaritan, and is not the relation of trust that the moral institution of promising creates between them enough to make the two parties neighbors rather than strangers? The morality of promising is not all there is to morality. Promising is an entailment of the general morality of human concern and respect. Finally, I should say that both in law and morals, the duty of mitigation only arises when the effort is not great, and, I would add (though it is not clear the law follows here), when the defaulting promisor has acted straightforwardly, announced his intentions, and offered compensation. . . .

In the end it is not the divergence between contract and promise that is striking but their convergence, and the convergence of both with the economic/efficiency explanation for legal institutions. Moralists often scorn efficiency-like arguments, and economists — who confuse morality with superstition — try to show up moralists as implausible sticklers. But the convergence tells us a good deal about morality and economics. Normative economics is about furthering human goods. Morality too is a human enterprise, and its special case, promising, underwrites human cooperation in furthering human goods, but on terms of equality, trust, and mutual respect. When law diverges from these terms, it should be changed.

STUDY GUIDE: *How does Professor Bagchi think that contract law is quite different than promising? How does she think the invocation of contract law undermines the institution of promising? Who do you think more accurately describes the relationship between contract and promise? Shiffrin and Fried or Bagchi?*

CONTRACT *VERSUS* PROMISE*

Aditi Bagchi

Contract has been conceptualized as a species of promise. Most famously, Charles Fried has argued that contracts should be enforced because they are promises.[5] ... [A]nd Seana Shiffrin has suggested ways in which the obligations of contract and promise diverge, a problem only because those subject to contractual obligations are ostensibly also subject to the norms of promise.[6] As Shiffrin and others have pointed out, "U.S. contract law represents that a contract is an enforceable promise" and "the language of promises, promisees, and promisors saturates contract law" and its surrounding literature.

Treating contractual promise as a kind of promise highlights certain important aspects of contracting, including the communication of a commitment to future action and the delegation of partial authority over future conduct to another person. ... Perhaps because of their familial relations, [however,] the similarities between contract and promise are often too easily assumed and often over-emphasized. The result has been to obscure essential differences between legally binding and everyday, or what I will call "private" promises. The moral character of a private promise depends on the fact that it is not only freely made but

---

*From Bagchi, Aditi, Contract v. Promise (September 2, 2007). U. of Penn Law School, Public Law Research Paper No. 07-35. Available at SSRN: http://ssrn.com/abstract=1012150.
5. See generally Charles Fried, Contract as Promise (1981).
6. Seana Shiffrin, The Divergence of Contract and Promise, 120 Harv. L. Rev. 708 (2007).

also freely kept. Most contractual promises are not intended to have and (by definition) do not have this voluntary character. . . .

The reasons for enforcing contract are sometimes taken to be derivative from the reasons to keep one's promise, or the reasons to support an institution of promise are taken to be reasons to support an institution of contract. Contractual obligation is then thought to reinforce promissory obligation. But private promises which are given the status of contract are not thereby elevated. A private promise marked as contractual actually loses (at least some of) its promissory quality. The reasons for keeping and relying upon a private promise are in part replaced rather than merely augmented by the reasons for keeping and relying upon a contract.

In most contracts, one of the two following scenarios is likely: In the first, the agreement between contractual promisor and contractual promisee is not taken to be an exchange of private promise, and thus the law readily recognizes it as a contract. In the second, because the agreement between the promisor and promisee is of a character that the law is reluctant to imbue with legal status, the parties must go out of their way to signal that theirs is a legal rather than a private affair. In both scenarios, the promisor essentially opts out of the private practice of promising when she assigns to a third party the authority to coerce performance of her promise. Similarly, the promisee essentially opts out of the practice of promising by demanding or accepting that what would otherwise be a private promise is instead converted to a legally binding commitment.

Why does contract begin where private promise ends? Because the objective reasons that apply to promisor and promisee are replaced once what was a promise is subject to legal intervention. In making a private promise, a promisor ordinarily creates a sufficient reason to perform the content of her promise: the very fact of her promise. To the extent she simultaneously creates a second sufficient reason — liability in the case of breach — the first reason does no work, or, there is no way for the independent sufficiency of the first reason to manifest itself objectively.

Similarly, in being made a private promise, a promisee is given a ground for belief that the promisor will perform: again, the fact of promise. To the extent the promisee is given independent assurance of performance, she cannot objectively rely on the fact of promise alone. Because private promises, but not all promises, are intended not only to assume obligation but to communicate the re-ordering of interests in which that obligation consists, it is important for the reasons created by private promise to do observable work for both promisor and promisee.

Some contractual promises co-exist with private promises of the same content. But their co-existence is uneasy, because invoking the specter of the law undermines the moral commitment contained in a promise from the perspective of both promisor and promisee. The content of that commitment is possible only within a close personal relationship. It entails a combining of interests that were previously separately held by promisor and promisee. In a private promise, the promisor undertakes to give the promisee's relevant interests weight equal to or greater than her own. Contract, by contrast, turns on the separateness of these interests. The specter of legal liability creates a reason for performance that stems from the separateness rather than the unity of interests between promisor and promisee. A sincere intent on the part of the promisor to perform for reasons unrelated to legal obligation does not dissipate this tension any more than a sincere intent on the part of the more powerful party in a dispute to resolve that dispute fairly would render her unilateral decision just.

The tension between contracting and private promising is evident when one considers which commitments usually take the contractual form. The typical contract is a commercial, arms-length bargain, and those are the agreements the law most readily recognizes as contractual. The law is reluctant to enforce commitments made within the context of personal relationships, i.e., in precisely those contexts in which one would expect private promise to reign. To the extent contract liability — and not the unity of interest accomplished by promise — might either motivate the promisor to perform or assure the promisee of performance, any accompanying personal promise is corrupted.

My aim is not to characterize private promise as more valuable than contract, but rather to suggest that by appreciating the difference between them, we can better mark the appropriate domain of contract law. . . . [G]iven that I see contract and private promise as fundamentally different, I do not follow those who argue that contract law is or should be patterned on promissory norms. But nor am I arguing that, because contract and promise are fundamentally different, promissory norms should have nothing to do with contract law. I agree with Shiffrin that we should start from the premise that "law must be

made compatible with the conditions for moral agency to flourish."
Unlike Shiffrin, I believe that contract law's accommodation of promise
usually entails steering clear of private promise. . . .

I. THE SEPARATE DOMAINS OF CONTRACT
AND PRIVATE PROMISE

A. The Character of Private Promising

Charles Fried has argued that the principle of autonomy requires that
individuals be able to bind themselves by promising. . . . Autonomy, on
the part of both promisor and promisee, is promoted by a practice of
promising.[7] . . . I suggest here that by enforcing certain promises, the
state makes it more difficult for individuals to make private
promises. . . . It may be that moral autonomy is well served by the enforcement of many kinds of promises, notably promises to strangers. The
heart of my argument is that, whatever its advantages, enforcing private
promises is in other respects too costly from a moral point of view to
justify the legal enforcement of those promises in the usual case.

The moral cost of enforcing private promises stems from the character of the relationships within which those promises are usually made.
Not all non-commercial promises are made within the context of personal relationships, but most are. Most people do not make self-styled
promises to strangers. One might stop there and understand a private
promise just as a promise which, unlike a contractual promise, feeds off

---

7. Randy Barnett seems to make a similar move when he argues that "freedom to
contract stipulates that persons should have the power to alter by their consent their legal
relations." Randy Barnett, Some Problems with Contract as Promise, 77 Cornell L. Rev.
1022, 1024 (1992). It is not clear why freedom of contract should be defined thus, or in
particular, how this conception of freedom of contract follows from the moral value of
our capacity to enter moral commitments. In any case, it is worth noting that, as I am only
addressing the default rules of enforceability, there is nothing in what I am saying that
would preclude the law from recognizing as enforceable certain private promises where
the promisor and promisee jump through enough hoops. Thus, under my approach,
nobody would lack the ability to render a commitment binding where the other party
consented to that arrangement; but as the relationship between the parties appears more
intimate, the parties would have to do more to definitively demonstrate that they intend
their arrangements to have legal force.

of the special relationship which caused the promisor to make her promise in the first place.

But as important as the effect of the relationship on the initial decision to make a promise is its effect on the nature of the promise likely to be made. It is often observed by those of varying views of promising that a promise creates or adds to the relationship between promisor and promisee. We should distinguish between the effect of the promise on the relationship and the moral effect of the relationship on the promise, i.e., how the nature of the moral commitment embodied in a promise between intimates differs from the nature of a moral commitment made by one stranger to another.

Because a promise represents a voluntary undertaking, a promisor's intentions are critical to determining the content of her promise. But a promisor will not normally spell out the intended normative consequences of her promise. Rather, she invokes a convention, which is in turn used by others — including her promisee — to understand the nature and scope of her commitment. Elaborating the commitment is in part an exercise in the interpretation of the promisor's communicative acts, but because a promisor by definition partakes in a pre-existing convention of promise, she cannot fully control the content of that commitment short of abandoning the practice of promise all together. A promise made within the context of a private relationship, unless expressly identified as something other than a private promise, will normally obligate the promisor according to promissory norms applicable to such private promises.

Unsurprisingly, the moral commitment made by an intimate is in some ways greater than that by a stranger. Perhaps surprisingly, in other respects, the moral commitment implied by a promise within a close relationship is less rigorous. Experience belies the frequent, implicit claim that a promise is the functional equivalent of an inexorable command to perform; it alters but does not eliminate deliberation at the stage of performance. While even a private promise involves a delegation of authority to the promisee, it is only a partial delegation of authority in a narrow sense. The obligation created by a private promise is not simply to perform a specified action, but to regard the decision whether to perform that act, in the future, in a particular manner. A private promisor is normally obligated to give greater weight to her promisee's interests than her own — how much greater weight will depend on the nature of the promise and the relationships within which it takes place.

Because the weight we are obligated to give each other's interests is an important dimension of our normative relations to one another, a private promise does alter the promisor's normative status vis a vis her promisee. Inasmuch as she must defer not only to the promisee's interests but also the promisee's understanding of those interests, because those will control the specific content of her duty, she has indeed delegated partial authority over her future action. But the promisor herself has not ceded authority over her future actions entirely. The promise will require deliberation to execute. The promisor must consider not just whether to keep the promise, but what exactly the promise requires of her once future facts reveal themselves. She is, however, bound to regard those future facts differently than she likely would in the absence of her promise. . . .

Why does the existence of a personal relationship between promisor and promisee make a difference? After all, to give equal weight to another's interests is to maximize joint interests, and economic theories of law are about interest maximization too. There are two important differences. First, interest maximization in the context of economic theory adopts primarily an ex ante perspective. . . . It is because the norms that apply between strangers turn on establishing the right incentives at the time of promise and not just at the time of performance, and also on minimizing the cost of resolving their disputes, that the scope of parties' obligations depends on what was communicated or known and what prevailed in the market at the time of promise. The ex ante perspective is appropriate to strangers. Because intimates know more about each other, they can more reliably assess and act on a richer account of each other's evolving interests; to this extent this hold true, they can adopt and continually update an ex post view.

The last point relates to a second. Interest combination between intimates is often accompanied by some measure of joint consumption or voluntary internal redistribution. There is no such presumption in a contracts case. It would be unfair for the court to adopt an aggregation approach with respect to two individual parties where that approach results in clear distributive consequences and there is no reason to believe the imbalance will be corrected. This is because the contract does not create a community within which there are specific grounds or mechanisms for subsequent redistribution between the parties. To maximize the combined interests of two contracting parties is no less arbitrary than reallocating resources between five randomly selected persons in order to employ those resources most efficiently. By contrast, contract rules set from an ex ante perspective maximize the welfare of a non-arbitrarily defined political community, within which distribution also takes place. In private promise, the unity of interest created by promise against the background of already partially unified interests makes the distribution of gains and losses less important. . . .

[T]he notion of combining interests is . . . only practical or appealing among intimates. We often take into account others' interests, and kind and generous persons give the interests of others more weight than unkind and selfish persons. But to treat someone else's interests as just as important as one's own in one's private decision-making is a rare thing. The effect of a promise between intimates is to unify the interests of promisor and promisee with respect to the content of the promise. Going forward, a private promisor keeps a promise because it is the unified interest of promisor and promisee. The promisor may no longer act on her interests alone. This is rare.

The effect of intimacy on the character of a promise feeds back into the nature of the relationship. As others have observed, behaving trustworthily and in a trusting manner promotes trust. Combining interests in one sphere has the effect of unifying interests in other spheres. Indeed, this is often the reason for making promises in the first place.

But this effect is only achieved inasmuch as the promisee can see that the promisor acts from unified interests. This is so because in most cases, the promise is supposed to enact a change in the calculation of interests (recall that promises are usually made between those who are close and seek to become closer). That change must be manifest somehow. While it may be possible for a person to harbor an interest in literature without ever acting on that interest by reading, it is less plausible to say that one has acquired an interest in literature where there has been no behavioral change.

Layering contractual obligation over the commitment contained in a private promise makes it difficult for the promisor to treat her promisee's interest as of equal or greater weight than her own, and makes it more difficult for the promisee to act on the belief that the promisor will give her interests appropriate weight. Performance of a private promise is not usually in the promisor's interest except inasmuch as she chooses to act on the promisee's interests, either because of the commitment to do so contained in her promise or because she is moved by those interests again at the time of performance. But a contractual promise creates a selfish reason for performance. Not only does it create a reason that speaks to the promisor's own interests, it is a reason that turns on the divergence of interest between promisor and promisee. Similarly, the promisee who would otherwise rely on the unity of her promisor's interests with her own will now rely instead on the legal priority of her interests over the promisor's. Even if the promisee intends to excuse the promisor from performance in circumstances where performance would be morally but not legally excused, to the extent that intent is not manifest in the contract's terms, the promisee will find herself in the position of exercising power over the promisor that is incompatible with the unity a promise would otherwise accomplish. The contract has a separating effect that undermines the unifying effect of promise. . . .

Notably, it is the character of the relationship within which private promises are normally made, and not their commonly unilateral character, which fundamentally distinguishes them from contract. The unilateral character of many private promises reflects that fact that the promisor undertakes to act from unified motives and therefore need not link the promisee's interest to a separate interest on the part of the promisor. While private promises may take the form of mutual promise, what constitutes reciprocity between the interests of separate persons amounts to internal symmetry within unified interests. Importantly, unity of interest with respect to the content of a given promise does not precede the promise but is the product of it. That is, while a relationship within which some unity of interest exists forms the backdrop against which a private promise is normally made, the promise itself extends that unity by establishing unity of interest with respect the content of the promise. A private promise thus feeds on a background relationship that may have been previously buttressed through promise, but it does not depend on the exchange form.

Although private promise may be either unilateral or bilateral, contract is necessarily bilateral. A particular contractual promise may not be explicitly linked to a reciprocal promise (and therefore may not qualify as bilateral in contract terms), but a promise motivated by self-interest always contemplates some return. Sometimes the return is reliance that is useful to the promisor; sometimes the return is improved performance of outstanding promises; sometimes the return is credibility that will allow the promisor flexibility in future economic dealings with the promisee or others. But as there is no unity of interest with respect to the content of a contractual promise, the promisor must have a reason to make the promise that is separate from the promisee's interest in obtaining it.

While I believe the most appropriate way to understand the divergence of contract and private promise lies in the unity of interests created by private promise, which is absent and indeed inappropriate outside personal relationships, one need not buy this specific conception of private promise in order to appreciate the more general point that private promise is unlike contract in (1) the nature of the obligation undertaken and (2) its effect on the relationship within which it takes places, and that as a result, (3) voluntary performance is essential to private but not legal promise. That divergence is neglected in contract theory. But there is no reason to expect that the same rules should govern all communicated commitments.

Just as private promise is the stuff of personal relationships, contract structures ordinary commercial exchange. Commercial exchange takes place between separately self-interested parties who do not undertake to promote the other's good but only to perform on terms that serve their own interests. If some parts of the law are designed for a nation of devils, contract law is best suited to a nation of strangers. It ensures that parties behave respectfully, i.e., in accordance with just rules that serve the public interest. Like a too stringent cleaner, when those rules are applied to parties who are not strangers (or rather, to the degree contracting parties are not strangers), they may leave unpleasant marks on the parties' relationship. Just as law designed for devils may have perverse results when applied to angels, so too will law designed for strangers produce unfortunate effects on intimates.

10

DOES THE DOCTRINE OF CONSIDERATION HAVE A FUNCTION?

The doctrine of consideration has long been the bane of law students. Its very name is perplexing. What is "consideration" and why do you need it to enforce a commitment? One way to get a handle on the doctrine is to study its historical development. Another is to examine the function the doctrine is supposed to perform.

The most influential statement of this function was provided by Lon Fuller in his article, *Consideration and Form*, in which he argues that consideration is a formality, much like the seal. He identifies the three functions of formality—the evidentiary, cautionary, and channeling functions—as well as several substantive reasons why commitments should be enforced. The most theoretically insightful, and most difficult, part of his presentation is his attempt to account for the relationship between form and substance. In essence, he argues that the more substantive reasons exist for enforcing a commitment the less we need such formalities as the doctrine of consideration; and as the substantive grounds for enforcement are reduced simply to the exercise of the parties' autonomy, the greater is the need for a formal embodiment of their intentions. Fuller's analysis is aimed at responding to those who would do away with the requirement of consideration altogether. Tellingly, he concludes that as long as the problems addressed by the doctrine of consideration exist, we shall need some such doctrine.

In *The Ideological Subtext of "Consideration and Form,"* Professor Duncan Kennedy puts Lon Fuller's article in historical and ideological perspective. As part of a much longer article describing how legal thinking moved from a model of deduction of rules from first principles or natural rights to a model of "conflicting considerations" of public policy, Professor Kennedy maintains that Fuller's article helped the doctrine of consideration make that transition. In so doing, and in emphasizing the centrality of "private autonomy" at the expense of other considerations, Fuller also shielded contract law and "freedom of contract" from the more radical assault that was permeating legal scholarship at the time. Professor Kennedy is the Carter Professor of Jurisprudence at Harvard Law School, the same chair formerly held by Lon Fuller.

In *Consideration and Contextual Formalism,* Florida State law professor Curtis Bridgeman contributes several important ideas to the study of consideration. First, and most obviously, he disputes the common reading of Justice Benjamin Cardozo's 1927 decision in *Allegheny College v. Chautauqua County Bank.* Bridgeman contends that the decision does not represent a precursor of modern-day promissory estoppel, but was a contextually sensitive application of the modern bargain theory of consideration. Second, his treatment of the case reveals important nuances of the modern doctrine of consideration, in contrast both with promissory estoppel and conditioned gifts. Finally, he takes up the issue of the formalism versus realism. Curtis attributes to Cardozo a "contextual formalism" that is both "anti-realist" in that it adheres to formal rules of law and also distinct from the rigid formalism associated with Christopher Columbus Langdell in that it is consciously sensitive to the factual contexts in which these rules are applied.

STUDY GUIDE: What is the "problem" for which the doctrine of consideration is the "solution"? Consider the commodities exchanges in which millions of dollars of sales take place in a "pit" by persons shouting at each other at the top of their lungs. Why are the normal formalities of contract not needed? How does Fuller's discussion of the substantive bases of contract differ from that of Morris Cohen? In particular, how does his discussion of the private autonomy differ from Cohen's discussion of the will theory and Fuller's own discussion in The Reliance Interest in Contract Damages *that appears in Chapter 1?*

Finally, note to what degree Fuller's analysis would recommend changes in current doctrine, particularly with respect to "moral" and "nominal" consideration. What does Fuller mean in his discussion of moral consideration when he questions the metaphor of $0+0=0$ and suggests instead the metaphor of $\frac{1}{2}+\frac{1}{2}=1$? Could this metaphor be applied to Morris Cohen's analysis of the different bases of contract as well?

CONSIDERATION AND FORM*

Lon L. Fuller

§1.   Introduction. — What is attempted in this article is an inquiry into the rationale of legal formalities, and an examination of the common-law doctrine of consideration in terms of its underlying policies. That such an investigation will reveal a significant relationship between consideration and form is a proposition not here suggested for the first time; indeed the question has been raised (and sometimes answered affirmatively) whether consideration cannot in the end be reduced entirely to terms of form.

That consideration may have both a "formal" and a "substantive" aspect is apparent when we reflect on the reasons which have been advanced why promises without consideration are not enforced. It has been said that consideration is "for the sake of evidence" and is intended to remove the hazards of mistaken or perjured testimony which would attend the enforcement of promises for which nothing is given in exchange. Again, it is said that enforcement is denied gratuitous promises because such promises are often made impulsively and without proper deliberation. In both these cases the objection relates, not to the content and effect of the promise, but to the manner in which it is made. Objections of this sort, which touch the form rather than the content of the agreement, will be removed if the making of the promise is attended by some formality or ceremony, as by being under seal. On the other hand, it has been said that the enforcement of gratuitous promises is not an object of sufficient importance to our social and economic order to justify the expenditure of the time and energy necessary to accomplish it. Here the objection is one of

---

* From Lon L. Fuller, Consideration and Form, 41 Colum. L. Rev. 799 (1941).

"substance" since it touches the significance of the promise made and not merely the circumstances surrounding the making of it.

The task proposed in this article is that of disentangling the "formal" and "substantive" elements in the doctrine of consideration. Since the policies underlying the doctrine are generally left unexamined in the decisions and doctrinal discussions, it will be necessary to postpone taking up the common-law requirement itself until we have examined in general terms the formal and substantive bases of contract liability.

I.   THE FUNCTIONS PERFORMED BY LEGAL FORMALITIES

§2.   The Evidentiary Function. — The most obvious function of a legal formality is, to use Austin's words, that of providing "evidence of the existence and purport of the contract, in case of controversy." The need for evidentiary security may be satisfied in a variety of ways: by requiring a writing, or attestation, or the certification of a notary. It may even be satisfied, to some extent, by such a device as the Roman *stipulatio*, which compelled an oral spelling out of the promise in a manner sufficiently ceremonious to impress its terms on participants and possible bystanders.

§3.   The Cautionary Function. — A formality may also perform a cautionary or deterrent function by acting as a check against inconsiderate action. The seal in its original form fulfilled this purpose remarkably well. The affixing and impressing of a wax wafer — symbol in the popular mind of legalism and weightiness — was an excellent device for inducing the circumspective frame of mind appropriate in one pledging his future. To a less extent any requirement of a writing, of course, serves the same purpose, as do requirements of attestation, notarization, etc.

§4.   The Channeling Function. — Though most discussions of the purposes served by formalities go no further than the analysis just presented, this analysis stops short of recognizing one of the most important functions of form. That a legal formality may perform a function not yet described can be shown by the seal. The seal not only insures a

satisfactory memorial of the promise and induces deliberation in the making of it. It serves also to mark or signalize the enforceable promise; it furnishes a simple and external test of enforceability. This function of form Ihering described as "the facilitation of judicial diagnosis," and he employed the analogy of coinage in explaining it.

> Form is for a legal transaction what the stamp is for a coin. Just as the stamp of the coin relieves us from the necessity of testing the metallic content and weight — in short, the value of the coin (a test which we could not avoid if uncoined metal were offered to us in payment), in the same way legal formalities relieve the judge of an inquiry *whether* a legal transaction was intended, and — in case different forms are fixed for different legal transactions — *which* was intended.

In this passage it is apparent that Ihering has placed an undue emphasis on the utility of form for the judge, to the neglect of its significance for those transacting business out of court. If we look at the matter purely from the standpoint of the convenience of the judge, there is nothing to distinguish the forms used in legal transactions from the "formal" element which to some degree permeates all legal thinking. Even in the field of criminal law "judicial diagnosis" is "facilitated" by formal definitions, presumptions, and artificial constructions of fact. The thing which characterizes the law of contracts and conveyances is that in this field forms are deliberately used, and are intended to be so used, by the parties whose acts are to be judged by the law. To the business man who wishes to make his own or another's promise binding, the seal was at common law available as a device for the accomplishment of his objective. In this aspect form offers a legal framework into which the party may fit his actions, or, to change the figure, it offers channels for the legally effective expression of intention. It is with this aspect of form in mind that I have described the third function of legal formalities as "the channeling function."

In seeking to understand this channeling function of form, perhaps the most useful analogy is that of language, which illustrates both the advantages and dangers of form in the aspect we are now considering. One who wishes to communicate his thoughts to others must force the raw material of meaning into defined and recognizable channels; he must reduce the fleeting entities of wordless thought to the patterns of conventional speech. One planning to enter a legal transaction faces a similar problem. His mind first conceives an economic or sentimental objective, or, more usually, a set of overlapping objectives. He must then, with or without the aid of a lawyer, cast about for the legal transaction (written memorandum, sealed contract, lease, conveyance of the fee, etc.) which will most nearly accomplish these objectives. Just as the use of language contains dangers for the uninitiated, so legal forms are safe only in the hands of those who are familiar with their effects. Ihering explains that the extreme formalism of Roman law was supportable in practice only because of the constant availability of legal advice, *gratis*.

As a final and very obvious point of comparison between the forms of law and those of language, we may observe that in both fields the actual course of history is determined by a continuous process of compromise between those who wish to preserve the existing patterns and those who wish to rearrange them. Those who are responsible for what Ihering called "the legal alphabet" — our judges, legislators, and text-writers — exercise a certain control over the usages of business, but there are times when they, like the lexicographer, must acquiesce in the innovations of the layman. The mere fact that the forms of law and language are set by a balance of opposing tensions does not, of course, insure the soundness of the developments which actually occur. If language sometimes loses valuable distinctions by being too tolerant, the law has lost valuable institutions, like the seal, by being too liberal in interpreting them. On the other hand, in law, as in language, forms have at times been allowed to crystallize to the point where needed innovation has been impeded.

§5. Interrelations of the Three Functions. — Though I have stated the three functions of legal forms separately, it is obvious that there is an intimate connection between them. Generally speaking whatever tends to accomplish one of these purposes will also tend to accomplish the other two. He who is compelled to do something which will furnish a satisfactory memorial of his intention will be induced to deliberate. Conversely, devices which induce deliberation will usually have an evidentiary value. Devices which insure evidence or prevent inconsiderateness will normally advance the desideratum of channeling, in two different ways. In the first place, he who is compelled to formulate his intention carefully will tend to fit it into legal and business categories. In this way the party is induced to canalize his

own intention. In the second place, wherever the requirement of a formality is backed by the sanction of the invalidity of the informal transaction (and this is the means by which requirements of form are normally made effective), a degree of channeling results automatically. Whatever may be its legislative motive, the formality in such a case tends to effect a categorization of transactions into legal and non-legal.

Just as channeling may result unintentionally from formalities directed toward other ends, so these other ends tend to be satisfied by any device which accomplishes a channeling of expression. There is an evidentiary value in the clarity and definiteness of contour which such a device accomplishes. Anything which effects a neat division between the legal and the non-legal, or between different kinds of legal transactions, will tend also to make apparent to the party the consequences of his action and will suggest deliberation where deliberation is needed. Indeed, we may go further and say that some minimum satisfaction of the desideratum of channeling is necessary before measures designed to prevent inconsiderateness can be effective. This may be illustrated in the holographic will. The necessity of reducing the testator's intention to his own handwriting would seem superficially to offer, not only evidentiary safeguards, but excellent protection against inconsiderateness as well. Where the holographic will fails, however, is as a device for separating the legal wheat from the legally irrelevant chaff. The courts are frequently faced with the difficulty of determining whether a particular document — it may be an informal family letter which happens to be entirely in the handwriting of the sender — reveals the requisite "testamentary intention." This difficulty can only be eliminated by a formality which performs adequately the channeling function, by some external mark which will signalize the testament and distinguish it from non-testamentary expressions of intention. It is obvious that by a kind of reflex action the deficiency of the holographic will from the standpoint of channeling operates to impair its efficacy as a device for inducing deliberation.

Despite the close interrelationship of the three functions of form, it is necessary to keep the distinctions between them in mind since the disposition of borderline cases of compliance may turn on our assumptions as to the end primarily sought by a particular formality. Much of the discussion about the parol evidence rule, for example, hinges on the question whether its primary objective is channeling or evidentiary. . . .

§6.   When are Formalities Needed? The Effect of an Informal Satisfaction of the Desiderata Underlying the Use of Formalities. — The analysis of the functions of legal form which has just been presented is useful in answering a question which will assume importance in the later portion of this discussion when a detailed treatment of consideration is undertaken. That question is: In what situations does good legislative policy demand the use of a legal formality? One part of the answer to the question is clear at the outset. Forms must be reserved for relatively important transactions. We must preserve a proportion between means and end; it will scarcely do to require a sealed and witnessed document for the effective sale of a loaf of bread.

But assuming that the transaction in question is of sufficient importance to support the use of a form if a form is needed, how is the existence of this need to be determined? A general answer would run somewhat as follows: *The need for investing a particular transaction with some legal formality will depend upon the extent to which the guaranties that the formality would afford are rendered superfluous by forces native to the situation out of which the transaction arises —* including in these "forces" the habits and conceptions of the transacting parties.

Whether there is any need, for example, to set up a formality designed to induce deliberation will depend upon the degree to which the factual situation, innocent of any legal remolding, tends to bring about the desired circumspective frame of mind. An example from the law of gifts will make this point clear. To accomplish an effective gift of a chattel without resort to the use of documents, delivery of the chattel is ordinarily required and more donative words are ineffective. It is thought, among other things, that mere words do not sufficiently impress on the donor the significance and seriousness of his act. In an Oregon case,[1] however, the donor declared his intention to give a sum of money to the donee and at the same time disclosed to the donee the secret hiding place where he had placed the money. Though the whole donative act consisted merely of words, the court held the gift to be effective. The words which gave access to the money which the donor had so carefully concealed would presumably be accompanied by the same sense of present deprivation which the act of handing over the

---

1. Waite v. Grubbe, 43 Ore. 406, 73 Pac. 206 (1903). . . .

money would have produced. The situation contained its own guaranty against inconsiderateness.

So far as the channeling function of a formality is concerned it has no place where men's activities are already divided into definite, clear-cut business categories. Where life has already organized itself effectively, there is no need for the law to intervene. It is for this reason that important transactions on the stock and produce markets can safely be carried on in the most "informal" manner. At the other extreme we may cite the negotiations between a house-to-house book salesman and the housewife. Here the situation may be such that the housewife is not certain whether she is being presented with a set of books as a gift, whether she is being asked to trade her letter of recommendation for the books, whether the books are being offered to her on approval, or whether — what is, alas, the fact — a simple sale of the books is being proposed. The ambiguity of the situation is, of course, carefully cultivated and exploited by the canvasser. Some "channeling" here would be highly desirable, though whether a legal form is the most practicable means of bringing it about is, of course, another question.

What has been said in this section demonstrates, I believe, that the problem of "form," when reduced to its underlying policies, extends not merely to "formal" transactions in the usual sense, but to the whole law of contracts and conveyances. Demogue has suggested that even the requirement, imposed in certain cases, that the intention of the parties be express, rather than implied or tacit, is in essence a requirement of form. If our object is to avoid giving sanction to inconsiderate engagements, surely the case for legal redress is stronger against the man who has spelled out his promise than it is against the man who has merely drifted into a situation where he appears to hold out an assurance for the future.

II.   THE SUBSTANTIVE BASES OF CONTRACT LIABILITY

§7.   Private Autonomy. — Among the basic conceptions of contract law the most pervasive and indispensable is the principle of private autonomy. This principle simply means that the law views private individuals as possessing a power to effect, within certain limits, changes in their legal relations. The man who conveys property to

another is exercising this power; so is the man who enters a contract. When a court enforces a promise it is merely arming with legal sanction a rule or *lex* previously established by the party himself. This power of the individual to effect changes in his legal relations with others is comparable to the power of a legislature. It is, in fact, only a kind of political prejudice which causes us to use the word "law" in one case and not in the other, a prejudice which did not deter the Romans from applying the word *lex* to the norms established by private agreement.

What has just been stated is not presented as an original insight; the conception described is at least as old as the Twelve Tables. But there is a need to reaffirm it, because the issue involved has been obfuscated through the introduction into the discussion of what is called "the will theory of contract." The obfuscation has come partly from the proponents of that theory, but mostly from those who have undertaken to refute it and who, in the process of refutation, have succeeded in throwing the baby out with the bath.

The principle of private autonomy may be translated into terms of the will theory by saying that this principle merely means that the will of the parties sets their legal relations. When the principle is stated in this way certain consequences may seem to follow from it: (1) that the law must concern itself solely with the actual inner intention of the promisor; (2) that the minds of the parties must "meet" at one instant of time before a contract can result; (3) that the law has no power to fill gaps in an agreement and is helpless to deal with contingencies unforeseen by the parties; and even (4) that the promisor must be free to change his mind at any time, since it is his will which sets the rule. Since these consequences of the will theory are regarded as unacceptable, the theory is assumed to be refuted by the fact that it entails them.

If we recognize that the will theory is only a figurative way of expressing the principle of private autonomy, we see to what an extent this "refutation" of the will theory really obscures the issues involved. In our country a law-making power is vested in the legislature. This fact is frequently expressed by saying that the will of the legislature is the law. Yet from this hackneyed metaphor we do not feel compelled to draw a set of conclusions paralleling those listed above as deriving from the will theory of contract. Specifically, we do not seek the "actual, inner" intention of individual legislators; we do not insist, except in a very formal way, on proof that a majority of the legislators were actually of one mind at one instant of time; we do not hesitate to fill gaps in defective statutes; and, finally, we do not permit a majority of those who voted for a particular law to nullify it by a later informal declaration that they have changed their minds.

The principle of private autonomy, properly understood, is in no way inconsistent with an "objective" interpretation of contracts. Indeed, we may go farther and say that the so-called objective theory of interpretation in its more extreme applications becomes understandable only in terms of the principle of private autonomy. It has been suggested that in some cases the courts might properly give an interpretation to a written contract inconsistent with the actual understanding of either party.[2] What justification can there be for such a view? We answer, it rests upon the need for promoting the security of transactions. Yet security of transactions presupposes "transactions," in other words, acts of private parties which have a law-making and right-altering function. When we get outside the field of acts having this kind of function as their *raison d'être*, for example, in the field of tort law, any such uncompromisingly "objective" method of interpreting an act would be incomprehensible. . . .

   §8.   What Matters Shall be Left to Private Autonomy? — From the fact that a principle of private autonomy is recognized it does not follow that this principle should be given an unlimited application. Law-making by individuals must be kept within its proper sphere, just as, under our constitutional system, law-making by legislatures is kept within its field of competence by the courts. What is the proper sphere of the rule of private autonomy?

   In modern society the most familiar field of regulation by private autonomy is that having to do with the exchange of goods and services. Paradoxically, it is when contract is performing this most important and pervasive of its functions that we are least apt to conceive of it as a kind of private legislation. If *A* and *B* sign articles of partnership we have little difficulty in seeing the analogy between their act and that of a legislature. But if *A* contracts to buy a ton of coal from *B* for eight dollars, it seems absurd to conceive of this act as a species of private law-making. This is only because we have come to view the distribution of goods through private contract as a part of the order of nature, and we

---

2. 1 Williston, Contracts (rev. ed. 1936) §95.

forget that it is only one of several possible ways of accomplishing the same general objective. Coal does not have to be bought and sold; it can be distributed by the decrees of a dictator, or of an elected rationing board. When we allow it to be bought and sold by private agreement, we are, within certain limits, allowing individuals to set their own legal relations with regard to coal.

The principle of private autonomy is not, however, confined to contracts of exchange, and historically it perhaps found its first applications outside the relationship of barter or trade. As modern instances of the exercise of private autonomy outside the field of exchange we may cite gratuitous promises under seal, articles of partnership, and collective labor agreements. In all these cases there may be an element of exchange in the background, just as the whole of society is permeated by a principle of reciprocity. But the fact remains that these transactions do not have as their immediate objective the accomplishment of an exchange of values.

. . . When the principle of private autonomy is extended beyond exchange, can it legitimately be referred to as a "substantive basis of contract liability"? When we say that the contracting parties set the law of their relationship are we not giving a juristic construction of their act rather than a substantive reason for judicial intervention to enforce their agreement? . . . Though occasional philosophers may seem to dispute the proposition, most of us are willing to concede that some kind of regulation of men's relations among themselves is necessary. It is this general desideratum which underlies the principle of private autonomy. Whenever we can reinforce this general need for regulation by a showing that in the particular case private agreement is the best or the only available method of regulation, then in such a case "the principle of private autonomy" may properly be referred to as a "substantive" basis of contract liability.

§9.   Reliance. — A second substantive basis of contract liability lies in a recognition that the breach of a promise may work an injury to one who has changed his position in reliance on the expectation that the promise would be fulfilled. Reliance as a basis of contract liability must not be identified with reliance as a measure of the promisee's recovery. Where the object of the court is to reimburse detrimental reliance, it may measure the loss occasioned through reliance either

directly (by looking to see what the promisee actually expended in reliance on the promise), or *contractually* (by looking to the value of the promised performance out of which the promisee presumably expected to recoup his losses through reliance). If the court's sole object is to reimburse the losses resulting from reliance, it may be expected to prefer the direct measure where that measure may be applied conveniently. But there are various reasons, too complicated for discussion here, why a court may find that measure unworkable and hence prefer the contractual measure, even though its sole object remains that of reimbursing reliance.[3]

What is the relation between reliance and the principle of private autonomy? Occasionally reliance may appear as a distinct basis of liability, excluding the necessity for any resort to the notion of private autonomy. An illustration may be found in some of the cases coming under Section 90 of the Restatement of Contracts. In these cases we are not "upholding transactions" but healing losses caused through broken faith. In another class of cases the principle of reimbursing reliance comes into conflict with the principle of private autonomy. These are the cases where a promisee has seriously and, according to ordinary standards of conduct, justifiably relied on a promise which the promisor expressly stipulated should impose no legal liability on him. In still other cases, reliance appears not as an independent or competing basis of liability but as a ground supplementing and reinforcing the principle of private autonomy. For example, while it remains executory, a particular agreement may be regarded as too vague to be enforced; until it has been acted on, such an agreement may be treated as a defective exercise of the power of private autonomy. After reliance, however, the court may be willing to incur the hazards involved in enforcing an indefinite agreement where this is necessary to prevent serious loss to the relying party. The same effect of reliance as reinforcing the principle of private autonomy may be seen in much of the law of waiver. Finally, in some branches of contract law reliance and the principle of private autonomy appear not as reinforcing one another so as to justify judicial intervention where neither alone would be sufficient, but as alternative and independently sufficient bases for imposing liability in the same case.

---

3. See Fuller and Perdue, The Reliance Interest in Contract Damages (1936-1937) 46 Yale L.J. 52, 66-67 and *passim*.

This is perhaps the situation in those cases where the likelihood that reliance will occur influences the court to impose liability on the promisor. On the one hand, we may say that the likelihood of reliance demonstrates that the parties themselves viewed their transaction as an exercise of private autonomy, that they considered that it set their rights and were prepared to act accordingly. On this view, the law simply acquiesces in the parties' conception that their transaction determined their legal relations. On the other hand, we may say that the likelihood that reliance will occur is a sufficient reason for dispensing with proof that it occurred in fact, since where reliance takes negative and intangible forms it may be difficult to prove. On this theory enforcement of the promise is viewed either as protecting an actual reliance which has probably occurred, or as a kind of prophylactic measure against losses through reliance which will be difficult to prove if they occur.

§10.   *Unjust Enrichment.* — In return for *B*'s promise to give him a bicycle, *A* pays *B* five dollars; *B* breaks his promise. We may regard this as a case where the injustice resulting from breach of a promise relied on by the promisee is aggravated. The injustice is aggravated because not only has *A* lost five dollars but *B* has gained five dollars unjustly. If, following Aristotle, we conceive of justice as being concerned with maintaining a proper proportion of goods among members of society, we may reduce the relations involved to mathematical terms. Suppose *A* and *B* have each initially ten units of goods. The relation between them is then one of equivalence, $10:10$. *A* loses five of his units in reliance on a promise by *B* which *B* breaks. The resulting relation is $5:10$. If, however, *A* paid these five units over to *B*, the resulting relation would be $5:15$.[4] This comparison shows why unjust enrichment resulting from breach of contract presents a more urgent case for judicial intervention than does mere loss through reliance not resulting in unjust enrichment.

Since unjust enrichment is simply an aggravated case of loss through reliance, all of what was said in the last section is applicable here. When the problem is the quantum of recovery, unjust enrichment may be measured either *directly* (by the value of what the promisor received), or *contractually* (by the value of the promised equivalent). So too, the

---

4. Cf. Aristotle, Nicomachean Ethics, 1132a-1132b.

prevention of unjust enrichment may sometimes appear openly as a distinct ground of liability (as in suits for restitution for breach of an oral promise "unenforceable" under the Statute of Frauds), and at other times may appear as a basis of liability supplementing and reinforcing the principle of private autonomy (as where the notion of waiver is applied "to prevent forfeiture," and in cases where the inference of a tacit promise of compensation is explained by the court's desire to prevent unjust enrichment).

§11.   Substantive Deterrents to Legal Intervention to Enforce Promises. — I have spoken of "the substantive bases of contract liability." It should be noted that the enforcement of promises entails certain costs which constitute substantive objections to the imposition of contract liability. The first of these costs is the obvious one involved in the social effort expended in the legal procedure necessary to enforcement. Enforcement involves, however, another less tangible and more important cost. There is a real need for a field of human intercourse freed from legal restraints, for a field where men may without liability withdraw assurances they have once given.[5] Every time a new type of promise is made enforceable, we reduce the area of this field. The need for a domain of "free-remaining" relations is not merely spiritual. Business deals can often emerge only from a converging series of negotiations, in which each step contains enough assurance to make worthwhile a further exchange of views and yet remains flexible enough to permit a radical readjustment to new situations. To surround with rigid legal sanctions even the first exploratory expressions of intention would not only introduce an unpleasant atmosphere into business negotiations, but would actually hamper commerce. The needs of commerce in this respect are suggested by the fact that in Germany, where the code makes offers binding without consideration, it has become routine to stipulate for a power of revocation.

§12.   The Relation of Form to the Substantive Bases of Contract Liability. — Form has an obvious relationship to the principle of private

---

5. Cf. Cohen, The Basis of Contract (1933) 46 Harv. L. Rev. 553, 573. . . .

autonomy. Where men make laws for themselves it is desirable that they should do so under conditions guaranteeing the desiderata described in our analysis of the functions of form. Furthermore, the greater the assurance that these desiderata are satisfied, the larger the scope we may be willing to ascribe to private autonomy. A constitution might permit a legislature to pass laws relating to certain specified subjects in an informal manner, but prescribe a more formal procedure for "extraordinary" enactments, by requiring, for example, successive readings of the bill before it was put to a vote. So, in the law of contracts, we may trust men in the situation of exchange to set their rights with relative informality. Where they go outside the field of exchange, we may require a seal, or appearance before a notary, for validity of their promises.

When we inquire into the relevance of form to liability founded on reliance or unjust enrichment, it becomes necessary to discriminate between the three functions of form. As to the desiderata implied in the evidentiary and cautionary functions it is clear that they do not lose their significance simply because the basis of liability has shifted. Even in the law of torts we are concerned with the adequacy of the proof of what occurred in fact, and (sometimes, at least) with the degree of deliberation with which the defendant acted. It is true that in the law of torts these considerations are not usually effectuated in the same way that they are in contract law. This is due to the fact that the channeling function of form becomes, in this field, largely irrelevant, for this function is intimately connected with the principle of private autonomy and loses its significance in fields where that principle has no application. To the extent, then, that the basis of promissory liability shifts from the principle of private autonomy to the reimbursement of reliance or the prevention of unjust enrichment, to that extent does the relevance of the channeling function of form decrease. This function loses its relevance altogether at that indefinite point at which it ceases to be appropriate to refer to the acts upon which liability is predicated as a "transaction."

III.   THE POLICIES, "FORMAL" AND "SUBSTANTIVE," UNDERLYING THE COMMON-LAW REQUIREMENT OF CONSIDERATION

§13.   Reasons for Refusing to Enforce the Gratuitous and Unrelied-on Promise. — *A* promises to give *B* $100; *B* has in no way

changed his position in reliance on this promise, and he has neither given nor promised anything in return for it. In such a situation enforcement of the promise is denied both in the common law and in the civil law. We give as our reason, "lack of consideration"; the civilians point to a failure to comply with statutory formalities. In neither case, of course, does the reason assigned explain the policies which justify excluding this promise from enforcement. An explanation in terms of underlying policies can, however, be worked out on the basis of the analysis just completed.

Looking at the case from the standpoint of the substantive bases of contractual liability we observe, first of all, that there is here neither reliance nor unjust enrichment. Furthermore, gratuities such as this one do not present an especially pressing case for the application of the principle of private autonomy, particularly if we bear in mind the substantive deterrents to judicial intervention. While an exchange of goods is a transaction which conduces to the production of wealth and the division of labor, a gift is, in Bufnoir's words, a "sterile transmission."[6] If on "substantive" grounds the balance already inclines away from judicial intervention, the case against enforcement becomes stronger when we draw into account the desiderata underlying the use of formalities. That there is in the instant case a lack of evidentiary and cautionary safeguards is obvious. As to the channeling function of form, we may observe that the promise is made in a field where intention is not naturally canalized. There is nothing here to effect a neat division between tentative and exploratory expressions of intention, on the one hand, and legally effective transactions, on the other. In contrast to the situation of the immediate gift of a chattel (where title will pass by the manual tradition), there is here no "natural formality" on which the courts might seize as a test of enforceability.

§14. The Contractual Archetype — The Half-Completed Exchange. — A delivers a horse to *B* in return for *B*'s promise to pay

---

6. Propriété et Contrat (2d ed. 1924) 487. This remark of Bufnoir's cannot be taken too literally; the element of exchange is a variable one, and there are few human relationships which do not involve a degree of reciprocity. It should be recalled that the practice of exchanging goods has commonly emerged in primitive societies out of a system of donations with, as Llewellyn says, "a felt obligation to reciprocate."

him ten dollars; *B* defaults on his promise, and *A* sues for the agreed price. In this case are united all of the factors we have previously analyzed as tending in the direction of enforcement of a promise. On the substantive side, there is reliance by *A* and unjust enrichment of *B*. The transaction involves an exchange of economic values and falls therefore in a field appropriately left to private autonomy in an economy where no other provision is made for the circulation of goods and the division of labor, or where (as perhaps in primitive society) an expanding economy makes the existing provision for those ends seem inadequate. On the side of form, the delivery and acceptance of the horse involve a kind of natural formality, which satisfies the evidentiary, cautionary, and channeling purposes of legal formalities.

Describing this situation as "the contractual archetype," we may take it as our point of departure, dealing with other cases in terms of the degree of their deviation from it. Naturally, all kinds of nuances are here possible, and some minor departures from the pattern were the occasion for dispute in the early history of the action of debt. We are concerned here, however, chiefly with two major deviations from the archetype: the situation of the executory exchange, and the situation of reliance without exchange.

§15.   The Wholly Executory Exchange. — *B* promises to build a house for *A,* and *A,* in return, promises to pay *B* $5,000 on the completion of the house. *B* defaults on his promise, and *A,* without having had occasion to pay anything on the contract, sues *B* for damages. . . . It is now generally assumed that so far as consideration is concerned the executory bilateral contract is on a complete parity with the situation where the plaintiff has already paid the price of the defendant's promised performance. Yet if we examine the executory bilateral contract in terms of the policies underlying consideration, it will become apparent that this assumption is unjustified, and that Lord Holt in reality overshot the mark in his assertion that "where the doing a thing will be a good consideration, a promise to do that thing will be so too."[7]

---

7. Thorp v. Thorp, 12 Mod. 455, 459, 88 Eng. Rep. 1448, 1450 (K.B. 1702).

Where a bilateral contract remains wholly executory the arguments for judicial intervention have been considerably diminished in comparison with the situation of the half-completed exchange. There is here no unjust enrichment. Reliance may or may not exist, but in any event will not be so tangible and direct as where it consists in the rendition of the price of the defendant's performance. On the side of form, we have lost the natural formality involved in the turning over of property or the rendition and acceptance of services. There remains simply the fact that the transaction is an exchange and not a gift. This fact alone does offer some guaranty so far as the cautionary and channeling functions of form are concerned, though, except as the Statute of Frauds interposes to supply the deficiency, evidentiary safeguards are largely lacking. This lessening of the factors arguing for enforcement not only helps to explain why liability in this situation was late in developing, but also explains why even today the executory bilateral contract cannot be put on complete parity with the situation of the half-completed exchange.

In the situation of the half-completed exchange, the element of exchange is only one factor tending toward enforcement. Since that element is there reinforced by reliance, unjust enrichment, and the natural formality involved in the surrender and acceptance of a tangible benefit, it is unnecessary to analyze the concept of exchange closely, and it may properly be left vague. In the executory bilateral contract, on the other hand, the element of exchange stands largely alone[8] as a basis of liability and its definition becomes crucial. Various definitions are possible. We may define exchange vaguely as a transaction from which each participant derives a benefit, or, more restrictively, as a transaction in which the motives of the parties are primarily economic rather than sentimental. Following Adam Smith, we may say that it is a transaction which, directly or indirectly, conduces to the division of labor. Or we may take Demogue's notion that the most important characteristic of exchange is that it is a situation in which the interests of the transacting parties are opposed, so that the social utility of the contract is guaranteed in some degree by the fact that it emerges as a compromise of those

---

8. I say "largely alone" because there is always the possibility that the court will be influenced by actual reliance on the bargain or by the probability that reliance has taken place or will occur.

conflicting interests. The problem of choosing among these varying conceptions may seem remote and unimportant, yet it underlies some of the most familiar problems of contract law. For example, suppose a nephew promises his uncle that he will not smoke until he is twenty-one, and the uncle promises him $5,000 as a reward if he will keep his promise. Where the nephew sues after having earned the reward by following the prescribed line of conduct recovery has been permitted.[9] But would such an agreement be enforced as an executory bilateral contract? Could the uncle, for example, sue the nephew for smoking a cigarette? In answering this question it is at once apparent that we are faced with the necessity of defining the particular kind of exchange which is essential to the enforcement of a bilateral contract. A similar problem underlies many of the cases involving "illusory promises."

Like consideration, exchange is a complex concept. To the problem of executory exchange we may, within a narrower compass, apply the same general approach that we have applied to the problem of consideration as a whole. Here our "archetype" is the business trade of economic values in the form of goods, services, or money. To the degree that a particular case deviates from this archetype, the incentives to judicial intervention decrease, until a point is reached where relief will be denied altogether unless the attenuated element of exchange is reinforced, either on the formal side by some formal or informal satisfaction of the desiderata underlying the use of legal formalities, or on the substantive side by a showing of reliance or unjust enrichment, or of some special need for a regulation of the relations involved by private autonomy.

§16.   Transactions Ancillary to Exchanges. — There are various transactions which, though they are not themselves immediately directed toward accomplishing an exchange, are necessary preliminary steps toward exchanges, or are ancillary to exchanges in process of realization. Among these we may mention offers, promises of unpaid sureties, and what Llewellyn has described as "going-transaction adjustments" such as are involved in unilateral concessions or promises of extra compensation granted during performance of a bilateral contract.

---

9. Hammer v. Sidway, 124 N.Y. 538, 27 N.E. 256 (1891). . . .

Because of their connection with exchanges, these transactions, in varying degrees, participate in the underlying grounds, both "formal" and "substantive," which justify the enforcement of exchanges. Thus, for example, if it were thought that exchanges could in practice only be arranged through the device of preliminary offers and that offers could be effective only if made irrevocable, then the substantive grounds for enforcing bilateral contracts of exchange would extend to offers. Again, a promise of extra compensation to a man already under contract to build a house at a fixed price participates to some extent in the "formal" guaranties which justify the enforcement of exchanges. From the standpoint of the "channeling" function, for example, such a promise receives a certain canalization from being related to an existing business deal. There is not here to the same degree as in purely gratuitous promises a shadowy no-man's land in which it is impossible to distinguish between the binding promise and tentative or exploratory expressions of intention. . . .

§17.   Unbargained-for Reliance. — An uncle promises to give his nephew one thousand dollars; in reliance on this promise the nephew incurs an indebtedness he would not otherwise have incurred. In this case we have a change in position which is not bargained for as the price of the uncle's promise. Where the element of exchange is removed from a case, the appeal to judicial intervention decreases both in terms of form and of substance. The appeal is diminished substantively because we are no longer in the field which is in modern society the most obviously appropriate field for the rule of private autonomy. From the formal standpoint, when we lose exchange, we lose the formal guaranties which go with the situation of exchange. (See §§14 and 15, supra.)

Section 90 of the Contracts Restatement provides in effect that a promise which has given rise to unbargained-for reliance may or may not be enforced, depending on the circumstances of the case. The section makes explicit only two criteria bearing on the question whether relief should be granted, namely, the seriousness of the promisee's reliance and its foreseeability by the promisor. On the basis of the analysis presented in this article, the following additional inquiries would be relevant: (1) Was the promise prompted wholly by generosity, or did it emerge out of a context of tacit exchange? (See §§15 and 16, supra.) (2) Were the desiderata underlying the use of formalities satisfied in any degree by the circumstances under which the promise was made? (See §6, supra.) As bearing on the second question, we may ask whether the promise was express or implied, and whether after the promise was made the promisee declared to the promisor his intention of acting on it.[10]

§18.   Nominal Consideration. — It has been held that a promise to make a gift may be made binding through the payment of a "nominal" consideration, such as a dollar or a cent. The proper ground for upholding these decisions would seem to be that the desiderata underlying the use of formalities are here satisfied by the fact that the parties have taken the trouble to cast their transaction in the form of an exchange. The promise supported by nominal consideration then becomes enforceable for reasons similar to those which justify the enforcement of the promise under seal. (See §12, supra.) From the standpoint of such an analysis any such distinction is taken in Schnell v. Nell[11] and Section 76(c) of the Contracts Restatement is wholly out of place. . . .

§20.   Moral Obligation as Consideration. — Courts have frequently enforced promises on the simple ground that the promisor was only promising to do what he ought to have done anyway. These cases have either been condemned as wanton departures from legal principle, or reluctantly accepted as involving the kind of compromise logic must inevitably make at times with sentiment. I believe that these decisions are capable of rational defense. When we say the defendant was morally obligated to do the thing he promised, we in effect assert the existence of a substantive ground for enforcing the promise. In a broad sense, a similar line of reasoning justifies the special status accorded by the law to contracts of exchange. Men *ought* to exchange goods and services; therefore when they enter contracts to that end, we enforce those contracts. On the side of form, concern for formal guaranties justifiably diminishes where the promise is backed by a moral obligation to do the thing promised. What does it matter that the promisor may have

---

10. In this sense, the "acceptance" of the promise of a gratuity may be significant, even though the Restatement of Contracts in §85 exempts promises made enforceable under §90 from the requirement of mutual assent. . . .

11. 17 Ind. 29 (1861).

acted without great deliberation, since he is only promising to do what he should have done without a promise? For the same reason, can we not justifiably overlook some degree of evidentiary insecurity?

In refutation of the notion of "moral consideration" it is sometimes said that a moral obligation plus a mere promise to perform that obligation can no more create legal liability than zero plus zero can have any other sum than zero. But a mathematical analogy at least equally appropriate is the proposition that one-half plus one-half equals one. The court's conviction that the promisor ought to do the thing, plus the promisor's own admission of his obligation, may tilt the scales in favor of enforcement where neither standing alone would be sufficient. If it be argued that moral consideration threatens certainty, the solution would seem to lie, not in rejecting the doctrine, but in taming it by continuing the process of judicial exclusion and inclusion already begun in the cases involving infants' contracts, barred debts, and discharged bankrupts. . . .

§22.   The Future of Form. — Despite an alleged modern tendency toward "informality," there is little reason to believe that the problem of form will disappear in the future. The desiderata underlying the use of formalities will retain their relevance as long as men make promises to one another. Doubt may legitimately be raised, however, whether there will be any place in the future for what may be called the "blanket formality," the formality which, like the seal, suffices to make any kind of promise, not immoral or illegal, enforceable. It is not that there is no need for such a device. The question is whether with our present-day routinized and institutionalized ways of doing business a "blanket formality" can achieve the desiderata which form is intended to achieve. The net effect of a reform like the Uniform Written Obligations Act, for example, will probably be to add a line or two to unread printed forms and increased embarrassment to the task of judges seeking a way to let a man off from an oppressive bargain without seeming to repudiate the prevailing philosophy of free contract. Under modern conditions perhaps the only devices which would be really effective in achieving the formal desiderata would be that of a nominal consideration actually handed over, or a requirement that the promise be entirely in the handwriting of the promisor. As the holographic will shows, even the second of these devices would be inadequate from the standpoint of the "channeling" function.

§23.   The Future of Consideration. — ... It has sometimes been proposed that the doctrine of consideration be "abolished." Such a step would, I believe, be unwise, and in a broad sense even impossible. The *problems* which the doctrine of consideration attempts to solve cannot be abolished. There can be little question that some of these problems do not receive a proper solution in the complex of legal doctrine now grouped under the rubric "consideration." It is equally clear that an original attack on these problems would arrive at some conclusions substantially equivalent to those which result from the doctrine of consideration as now formulated. What needs abolition is not the doctrine of consideration but a conception of legal method which assumes that the doctrine can be understood and applied without reference to the ends it serves. When we have come again to define consideration in terms of its underlying policies the problem of adapting it to new conditions will largely solve itself.

STUDY GUIDE: When reading the following keep in mind that, in this excerpt, Professor Kennedy is largely situating Fuller's "Consideration and Form" into the intellectual and ideological discussion of its day and describing its powerful influence on subsequent contracts scholarship. Note also that, though the term "ideological" is considered pejorative by some, it is not by Professor Kennedy, who has long maintained that most, if not all, legal scholarship — including his own — is ideological or "political."

THE IDEOLOGICAL SUBTEXT OF "CONSIDERATION AND FORM"*

Duncan Kennedy

I will try to analyze the political subtext of "Consideration and Form" in a way that brings ideological intentions, conscious and unconscious, much more to the fore. My conclusion is that the article (and I would say "The Reliance Interest" as well) is not political by

---

*From Duncan Kennedy, From the Will Theory to the Principle of Private Autonomy: Lon Fuller's "Consideration and Form" 100 Colum. L. Rev. 94 (2000).

omission, . . . but aggressively ideological — an intervention in the legal politics of the time, and, as it turned out, an important influence on the politics of legal theory in the Cold War period.

A.   THE ABSENCE OF DISTRIBUTIVE JUSTICE FROM FULLER'S ANALYSIS OF THE CONTRACT CORE

At the time Fuller wrote, there was no unconscionability doctrine in American law. There were a variety of devices by which judges more or less overtly manipulated doctrine to achieve transactional fairness. There were extant fascist and communist critiques of the consequences for weak groups of a freedom of contract regime. There was also a well developed right wing position that freedom of contract was the legal manifestation of a natural right of individuals to do what they wanted so long as they didn't interfere with the like rights of others.

Finally, there was the position of the advocates of the "socialization" of contract, some more or less right (often Catholic) and some more or less left, methodologically anti-individualist but also anti-collectivists, advocates neither of laissez-faire nor of socialism in the sense of nationalization or planning. They wanted regulation, including judicially enforced compulsory terms, self-policing within trades, and the creation of administrative agencies armed with low level criminal rather than private law sanctions to police expert-generated standards of good practice. Methodologically, this tendency fluctuated between what Karl Klare has usefully dubbed "social conceptualism" (unproblematic derivation of a particular rule from a particular policy) and "balancing." Fuller's work is mainly in dialogue with these people.[1]

A basic condition of the existence of this group's moderately regulatory legislative and administrative law program was that the courts, during the classical period, had very self consciously given up the role of overtly policing bargains for substantive fairness. Horwitz has shown that consideration doctrine was understood by an important part of the

---

1. See Karl E. Klare, Contracts Jurisprudence and the First Year Casebook, 54 N.Y.U. L. Rev. 876, 880 (1979); Karl E. Klare, Judicial Deradicalization of the Wagner Act and the Origins of Modern Legal Consciousness, 1937-1941, 62 Minn. L. Rev. 265, 280 (1978).

pre-Civil War elite as a vehicle for assuring some minimum of substantive fairness in transactions, that is, as a guarantee that there
wouldn't be too much of a difference between the values of the things
exchanged. This approach faded with the century, in part at least
because of the fading of just price notions in the face of the devastating
critique of the economists, and in part because of the "subversive"
implications of judicial or other governmental review of the fairness
of the bargains between bosses and workers and between farmers and
the various intermediaries between them and consumers.[2]

The representative of this notion in modern contract law is the idea
that once there is consideration there is no doctrine of "inadequacy."
That the courts will not look into the adequacy of the consideration
means that the courts will not set out to police the distributive fairness
of the exchange system.

Fuller takes this so much for granted that he never mentions this rule
in his elaborate discussion of the various subrules of the system. . . .

Though he doesn't mention adequacy, Fuller is well aware that the
principle of private autonomy implicates issues of distributive justice.
He recognizes, first, that there are "limits" to the appropriate "sphere"
of application of the principle of private autonomy, by which he means
that it should be limited to the economy, as opposed, say to the family,
where non-market norms do and should apply.

Second, within the economic sphere, there is no reason to honor
contracts that reflect not private autonomy but private "heteronomy,"
meaning that they are imposed on one party by the other. But Fuller
simply puts to one side the question of when and how to decide whether
we are in the area of autonomy or that of heteronomy, as well as the
question of how the legal system should respond when heteronomy is
established. This means, as Rakoff pointed out about "The Reliance
Interest,"[3] that "Consideration and Form" puts aside the principal
ideological issues of the day, ideological issues that were understood
by the legal elite as of consuming importance for the future of the legal
system.

---

2. See [Morton J. Horwitz, The Transformation of American Law, 1780-1860, at
180-185 (1977)].

3. See [Todd D. Rakoff, Fuller and Perdue's The Reliance Interest as a Work of
Legal Scholarship, 1991 Wis. L. Rev. 203, 243-244].

But it means much more than that, in both articles. When we are talking about the domain that is left for the principle of private autonomy once we have spun off labor law, insurance, etc., as heteronomous, the possibly conflicting considerations are protection of reliance and prevention of unjust enrichment. Reliance is understood to be a "tort concept." Unjust enrichment is the classical legal thought category of the retention by the promisor of a benefit conferred by the promisee. The criterion of injustice is whether the promisor has retained something of the promisee's, in spite of his own breach.

   . . . [T]his meant that the opposing principles had impeccable private law pedigrees, albeit from the side of private law theory associated with the will of the state rather than the will of the parties. In the Aristotelian scheme, both reliance and restitution belong to the category of commutative justice. They restore the status quo ante, as that was defined by the pre-existing legal rights of the parties. There is no element of distributive justice involved. This meant that while Fuller made an extremely important contribution to the internal critique of the will theory, and to the rise of the notion that contract is in part a matter of public policing of private conduct through the tort principle, he gave his contribution a particular twist.

   He comes across as representing the right wing of the socialization-of-contract tendency. . . . By getting rid of labor law and acknowledging that protecting will was no more than a policy rather than a legally binding principle that could be a fountain of deductions, it was possible to save the baby — the apolitical, ethical, commutative, core of contract law.

   The trick here is to acknowledge that in setting boundaries to the sphere of private autonomy we have to make complex judgments about whether the parties are acting freely or one is merely dictated to — that is, whether we are dealing with autonomy or heteronomy. And there is no question that the choice whether to include a domain within the private autonomy sphere is a question of public law, a choice of a "principle of social order" for the domain in question, rather than a simple choice to enforce natural rights, for instance.

   Moreover, within the sphere of private autonomy, autonomy is not autonomous: The principle may occasionally have to yield to generally harmonious but also possibly conflicting formal or substantive considerations. But here's the rub: The interests or principles or purposes or ends or functions that oppose private autonomy within its sphere are *non-ideological*. While it is pretty clear that defining the scope of the

sphere involves public law — a political decision — it is equally clear
that within the sphere the acknowledged conflicts are between ethical
principles and practical objectives that no one could possibly object to.
The occasional conflicts can be seen as dilemmas for moral reasoning
rather than as threatening political confrontations.

B.   TRACES OF THE DISTRIBUTIONAL ISSUE IN FULLER'S TREATMENT OF THE CORE

But while it seems that the technique of segregating, first the family
and then domains of private heteronomy, including all of labor law, has
gotten rid of distributional questions in the core, this turns out to be not
quite possible. The first sign is that in the discussion of the application of
consideration doctrine to releases of claims, there is an aside to the effect
that "[a]mong the counter-currents which pull [against enforcement
is] . . . the peculiar background surrounding the surrender of personal-
injury claims."[4] . . .

On the next page, the trace gets stronger in the discussion of the pre-
existing duty rule, as applied to modifications of contracts that unilaterally favor one party. Here Fuller points out, following Ames, Corbin,
and Llewellyn, that the refusal to enforce a modification may well reflect
a judicial reaction against the possibility of duress (e.g., the contractor
threatens to abandon the job in midstream unless his compensation is
increased). But rather than suggesting, as they did, a doctrinal solution
to the duress problem that would allow enforcement in easy cases,
Fuller ducks: "These cases involve factors extrinsic to the problems
under discussion here. Among those factors are the effects of improper
coercion. . . ."[5]

A page further on, Fuller surrenders, briefly. The dealer/jobber relationship "calls increasingly for some kind of judicial regulation to
prevent hardship and oppression."[6] Behind this series of examples
lurks the general question whether and how to control the principle of

---

4. Fuller, Consideration and Form, at 821.
5. Id. at 822.
6. Id. at 823.

private autonomy in the politically important fields of the labor contract, landlord-tenant, agricultural tenure, consumer law, and so forth. But you have to look carefully.

On the formal side, there is a quite similar dance of avoidance and acknowledgment. Fuller uses, as the central example of how different formal requirements will be appropriate for different factual situations, the contrast between a contract between merchants on an exchange and a door-to-door sale. He suggests that the housewife buying from the door-to-door salesman may sign and be legally bound under the duty to read doctrine, although in fact she has no idea of what she is getting herself into. "Some 'channeling' here would be highly desirable, though whether a legal form is the most practicable means of bringing it about is, of course, another question."[7] Maybe he was thinking of the kind of right of revocation within a time certain that eventually was adopted by statute in many jurisdictions. So it is clear to him that the choice of form can have distributional consequences. But there is no more than that to indicate his thinking about how distributional considerations should be taken into account by the decision maker. . . .

C.   COMPLETING THE CONFLICTING CONSIDERATIONS MODEL BY THE RETURN OF THE SOCIAL

To my mind, the work that moves contract theory from Fuller's intermediate position to the fully developed modern conflicting considerations model[8] has to do with deciding what besides private autonomy is at stake, given that neither protecting reliance nor preventing unjust enrichment comes close to summarizing the various considerations that in fact come into play against autonomy. This involved reintroducing

---

7. Id. at 806.

8. [Elsewhere in his article, Professor Kennedy summarizes his thesis "that the current understanding of American legal academics is that each and every one of the valid legal norms that makes up our legal system (including private, public, and international law) can be understood as the product of what I will call 'conflicting considerations.' Every rule can be understood as representing a choice in the colloquial lawyers' sense of a 'policy question.' We resolve such questions by balancing conflicting considerations . . ." rather than by deduction from axiomatic first principles which characterized the older "classical model."]

the social, with its ideological baggage. The traces of the social Fuller left in "Consideration and Form" expanded to a bridgehead, and then into a reorganization. I plan to continue the narrative through this phase, but for reasons of space, I will give no more than the briefest sketch of these developments here.

The main actors seem to have been Friedrich Kessler in his article on contracts of adhesion[9] and Kessler and Fine, in their article on *culpa in contrahendo*,[10] and then Stewart Macaulay in his articles on Justice Traynor[11] and on lost credit cards,[12] with Ian Macneil coming along to wrap it all up in the first edition of his radically anti-formalist contracts casebook.[13] Kessler, Macaulay, and Macneil represent the post-World War II integration of the Demogue/Gardner/Fuller strand in contract theory with no fewer than three others.

The first, associated with Robert Hale and John Dawson, emphasized that the distributive outcome of cooperative but also conflictual relations in the production and sale of goods depends on the ground rules of contract and tort that govern the conduct of the cooperators when they decide to conflict. The second strand developed the case for consumer protection in products liability, landlord-tenant, consumer credit, franchising, and generalized unconscionability, all areas still governed by contract law after the Progressive and New Deal reformers spun public utilities, insurance, labor, banking, and securities law off into separate regulatory domains. The third strand worked at teasing out the ideological, rather than merely ethical issues involved in choosing standard contract rules to apply to parties with equal bargaining power.

---

9. See Friedrich Kessler, Contracts of Adhesion — Some Thoughts About Freedom of Contract, 43 Colum. L. Rev. 629 (1943).

10. See [Friedrich Kessler & Edith Fine, Culpa in Contrahendo, Bargaining in Good Faith, and Freedom of Contract: A Comparative Study, 77 Harv. L. Rev. 401 (1964)].

11. See Stewart Macaulay, Justice Traynor and the Law of Contracts, 13 Stan. L. Rev. 812 (1961).

12. See Stewart Macaulay, Private Legislation and the Duty to Read — Business Run by IBM Machine, the Law of Contracts and Credit Cards, 19 Vand. L. Rev. 1051 (1966).

13. See [Ian R. Macneil, Cases and Materials on Contracts: Exchange Transactions and Relationships (1971)].

Eventually contract doctrine was the site, not of the old "will theory versus social law" debate, but of an even more mildly ideologized debate between conservatives touting freedom of contract, on one side, and liberals advocating policing bargains in the interests of weak parties, on the other. They carried on the debate using the full repertoire of formal arguments, substantive arguments, including rights, morality, and efficiency, and institutional competence arguments about the appropriate roles of judges, administrators, and legislatures. And the criterion for decision was balancing. . . .

We can see the contracts scholarship of the period up to 1970 as Cold War, as opposed to 1930s, theory, in two senses. First, everyone assumed that there were communist and fascist extremes, but that they had nothing to do with the debate, except that they were occasionally invoked as destinations on one's opponent's slippery slope to serfdom. Moreover, not even moderate socialism or Catholic right wing organicism could much risk raising their heads, for fear of compromising their moderate, respectable spokespeople within the "vital center." Second, the conflict within the center was between liberal regulatory reform, pursued often obliquely and always ad hoc, and conservative free market holding of the line, or foot dragging, pursued in the same fashion. There was no aggressive conservative deregulatory program — that impulse was directed at the New Deal statutes, as in the Taft-Hartley Act — and most prestigious judges had been appointed by liberal presidents and governors.

The integration of the field around the dichotomy "freedom of contract" versus "good faith and fair dealing," "regulation," "socialization," "planning," "intervention," or "policing," reflected this post-World War II change of focus. It was no longer the contrast between private autonomy and fascism or communism, but rather the intra-free world choice between liberal and conservative approaches to the mixed capitalist economy. Since World War II, law has mirrored the general political debate. After 1970, there emerged both a more radical left and a more radical right tendency in legal scholarship, patently tied to developments outside law. This is what creates the perennial sense of danger: that ad hoc, semioticized conflicting considerations analysis of legal problems will turn out to be no more than a vehicle for ideology — liberal or conservative, radical or hard right, not communist or fascist; and it is one of the things that motivates the reconstruction projects that characterize the period from 1970 to the present.

Of reconstruction, I will say no more here than that the proliferation of projects has ironically defeated the purpose of the projects. Rather than helping us out of our sense of the ad hoc, post hoc, ideological character of conflicting considerations analysis, their proliferation leads us to array them on the very ideological spectrum they claim is irrelevant in good legal analysis.[14]

STUDY GUIDE: Pay close attention to how Professor Curtis distinguishes between the old benefit/detriment conception of consideration and modern bargained-for consideration, and how promissory estoppel fits into this picture. Why is the promise in Allegheny College not a conditioned gift? Notice his emphasis on "subscription and acceptance" in contrast with "offer and acceptance." Why is that significant? Finally, what does he mean by "contextual formalism"? How does Cardozo's opinion in Wood v. Lucy, Lady Duff Gordon illustrate this approach? How does it differ from either "realism" or the "formalism" attributed to Langdell?

---

14. Just as a thought experiment, without benefit of citation, and obviously subject to grievous error and misunderstanding, not to speak of hurtful accidental omission, I would array the projects as follows: I would place Allan Farnsworth, Farnsworth on Contracts (1998), in the center-right position that Fuller himself occupied in 1941. To his right are the conservative projects based on morals, rights, or efficiency, including those of Richard Epstein, Charles Fried, Randy Barnett, Farber and Matheson, Richard Posner, and Alan Schwartz. To his left, there are, first, the Fuller loyalists of the center, including Melvin Eisenberg, Robert Summers, Stanley Henderson, and Robert Hillman. Then come the more progressive modernists in the Fuller tradition, including Patrick Atiyah, Todd Rakoff, and Charles Knapp, and liberal law and economics types, such as Guido Calabresi, Michael Schill, Jon Hanson, and Christine Jolls. Further to the left are left reconstructionists, for example Roberto Unger and Margaret Radin. Also on the left are the critical legal studies contract scholars who pushed for bringing the ideological out of the shadows: myself, Karl Klare, Frances Olsen, Clare Dalton, Mary Joe Frug, Jay Feinman, Elizabeth Mensch, Peter Gabel, and James Mooney, among others.

CONSIDERATION AND CONTEXTUAL FORMALISM*

Curtis Bridgeman

[INTRODUCTION: *ALLEGHENY COLLEGE* REVISITED]

Allegheny College v. Chautauqua County Bank[1] is one of those chestnuts of contract law that almost everyone teaches even though it is not obvious why. The case involves a promise to make a gift to a college and a request that the gift be memorialized in the name of the donor. After making a partial payment early, the donor had a change of heart and did not wish to pay the balance. Upon her death, the college sued her estate and won despite the objection that the promise was unsupported by consideration and therefore unenforceable. The issue presented in the case is very narrow and is, in any event, now moot in those jurisdictions that follow the Second Restatement's position on charitable subscriptions.[2] Two reasons combine to explain the case's current status. First, Judge (later Justice) Cardozo wrote the opinion in characteristically memorable language. Second, his opinion discusses consideration and promissory estoppel at a time (and in influential New York) when both doctrines were in flux. Even if the holding of the case itself is narrow, its author, time, and place are thought to make it important historical reading for those who are interested in twentieth century contract doctrine. . . .

That said, almost everyone complains about the opinion, despite (or in some cases, perhaps because of) its illustrious author . . . Most scholarly treatment of the case has focused on his discussion of consideration and its relation to promissory estoppel. In particular, the puzzle thought to be posed in the case concerns whether the opinion rules in favor of Allegheny College on the doctrine of promissory estoppel or on the doctrine of consideration. Subsidiary questions concern how the two relate to one another and whether Cardozo was intellectually dishonest about the grounds for his decision.

---

*From Curtis Bridgeman, *Allegheny College* Revisited: Cardozo, Consideration, and Formalism in Context, 39 U.C. Davis L. Rev. 149 (2005).

1. Allegheny Coll. v. Nat'l Chautauqua County Bank, 159 N.E. 173 (N.Y. 1927).

2. "A charitable subscription . . . is binding . . . without proof that the promise induced action or forbearance." Restatement (Second) of Contracts § 90(2) (1981).

However, those are not the best questions to ask about *Allegheny College*. In fact, a close reading will answer them fairly easily. Cardozo's opinion decides the case based on the doctrine of consideration — this much is generally accepted these days, though usually tentatively. But what is not appreciated is that, as a case of consideration, it is relatively easy. Or rather, what is controversial about the finding of consideration is not what scholars have taken to be the tough issue: was value given for the promise? Value was given, according to Cardozo. The tough issue for him concerned whether the benefactor's promise was given *in order to induce that value*. If Cardozo's opinion stretches any doctrine, it is on the issue of inducement, which in turn raises an issue of offer and acceptance. Could the promise in question reasonably be construed as an offer to give money *in exchange for* (at least in part) a commemoration, or was that commemoration just a *condition* on the gift? Cardozo invoked promissory estoppel to show that the answer to this question could not be deduced from some formal or abstract notion of offer and acceptance, but instead had to be informed by a reconstruction of what, in context, the parties probably had in mind. When deciding whether a specification by a donor is seeking a return promise or setting a condition on a gift, one must consider the type of transaction at issue: charitable subscriptions. Interpreting the meaning of ambiguous actions and statements depends, in other words, on recognizing, as case law concerning promissory estoppel had already done, that charitable donations are quite different from commercial exchanges. . . .

Properly understood, then, *Allegheny College* is a subtle and insightful, but narrow decision about bargaining in the context of charitable subscriptions and consequently should not be included in the promissory estoppel section of casebooks. Indeed, much of the confusion about the case probably stems from it being thus improperly presented. Understood in its proper context, the case is much less controversial. It emphasizes that the move from the benefit/detriment test for consideration to the bargained-for theory of consideration requires that a promise be given in order to induce a certain action. Action in reliance on a promise (in this case, an implied action and an implied promise) is not sufficient for consideration, *even if it is something that the promisor demonstrably desires*, unless the promisor makes the promise in order to induce that action. But if a party does give a promise, at least in part, in order to induce a return promise or action, then the promise (and the return promise) is enforceable, even though the primary motivation for the promise may be altruistic. . . .

The case is not an attempt to excuse charities from formalities just because we favor them as a matter of public policy, but rather insists that we not ignore the context in which charitable subscriptions take place. Cardozo is known for his attention to context in commercial transactions and was influential in the U.C.C.'s move to be more flexible toward the way business is actually conducted. In *Allegheny College*, he is attentive to how charitable subscriptions are solicited and promised. The opinion is not an attack on the doctrine of consideration, but an appeal to a formalism that considers the context of transactions and tries to see them from the point of view of the parties involved — the kind of formalism to which, partly thanks to Cardozo, we are already more accustomed in commercial law. . . .

III. RE-EXAMINING *ALLEGHENY COLLEGE*

. . . To understand Cardozo's decision requires that we shift the focus away from promissory estoppel's requirement that the promisee rely on a promise to his detriment and toward promissory estoppel's lack of a requirement that the promisor make her promise in order to induce such reliance. Although in most promissory estoppel cases the reliance by the promisee is an alternative grounds for recovery, another way to look at the cause of action is as a way of relaxing the bargained-for requirement from consideration doctrine. Promissory estoppel requires that there be a detriment to the promisee that is the result of the promisor's promise. Under the benefit/detriment test for consideration as articulated in *Hamer v. Sidway*,[3] such a detriment alone would have been sufficient for consideration. But by Cardozo's day, consideration also required that the promisor give the promise *in order to induce the detriment*. As we shall see, his discussion of promissory estoppel makes clear that he is thinking of the doctrine not as a separate cause of action, but as a rethinking of the inducement requirement for consideration. When donors place conditions on their gifts, the transaction may rise

---

3. 27 N.E. 256 (1891).

to the level of an exchange enforceable by both sides, even if the donor's primary motivation is altruistic.

After laying out the facts in the two opening paragraphs, Cardozo begins his analysis in the third paragraph by noting that in the law of charitable subscriptions, "we have found consideration present where the general law of contract, at least as then declared, would have said that it was absent." Whatever the requirements of consideration are, they have been relaxed for charitable subscriptions. He then in the fourth paragraph lays out the general understanding of what constitutes consideration. He cites the famous case of *Hamer v. Sidway* and its benefit/detriment test. But he cautions that the benefit/detriment test is "little more than a half truth." The whole truth requires a "supplementary gloss," namely that the "promise and the consideration must purport to be the motive each for the other." In other words, the promise must be given in order to induce the consideration and vice versa.

Having thus stated the rule, in the fifth paragraph he argues that the "half-truths of one generation tend at times to perpetuate themselves in the law as the whole truth of another." Despite the fact that the modern conception of consideration requires not only that there be a detriment (or a benefit), but also that the promise must have been given in order to induce that detriment, the doctrine of promissory estoppel has "gone far in obliterating this distinction." He declines to say whether or not promissory estoppel has thus modified the bargained-for test as a general rule, but claims that it has at least done so with respect to charitable subscription cases. Cardozo goes on in the sixth paragraph to cite several cases enforcing charitable subscriptions, even though the consideration requirement as traditionally understood had arguably not been met. He suggests that those decisions may have been motivated by a public policy that loosens some of the formalities of contract law to favor charities, particularly when those formalities are arguably merely the result of "historical accidents of practice and procedure." But while Cardozo recognizes that "the pressure of exceptions has led to irregularities of form," he explicitly denies that he is trying to do away with consideration.

The reason the opinion strikes so many people as intellectually deceitful is because Cardozo cites other promissory estoppel cases that look factually dissimilar from the case he is deciding, since those cases all involve actual reliance. The point of his discussing promissory estoppel, though, is not to suggest that this is a case ripe for estoppel analysis, but merely to prepare us to relax our idea of what counts as an exchange. The most important feature of those cases, for Cardozo's purposes, is not that there was reasonable reliance, but that there was a promise enforced even though it was questionable whether or not each promise was given in order to *induce* the promisee's reliance. Imagine for a moment that when it received Johnston's $1000, Allegheny College made an express promise to create the scholarship fund. As discussed above, finding an implied return promise from the college here may be problematic, but not for consideration purposes. The problem, in other words, would not be a lack of anything on the promisee's side, but rather that the return promise was not the result of a bargained-for exchange, i.e., Johnston arguably did not make her own promise *in order to elicit* such a return promise, whether or not it was actually given. Cardozo's biggest challenge was not finding reliance or an obligation on the part of Allegheny College, but rather finding that Johnston gave her promise at least partly to induce the college to obligate itself by means of a promise to her.

After softening up his reader on the issue of inducement in charitable subscription cases, Cardozo writes the following key transitional paragraph, which I quote . . . in its entirety:

> It is in this background of precedent that we are to view the problem now before us. The background helps to an understanding of the implications inherent in subscription and acceptance. This is so though we may find in the end that without recourse to the innovation of promissory estoppel the transaction can be fitted within the mould of consideration as established by tradition.

"This background of precedent" has not been offered in order to confuse the reader, as many modern commentators have argued. Instead, the background helps us to understand that these transactions take place in a different context from commercial transactions and that courts have recognized this difference to be salient for legal analysis. The issue in this case is determining the "implications inherent in subscription and acceptance." Surprisingly, almost nothing is made in the literature about his phrase "subscription and acceptance." The words are chosen carefully and are meant to indicate that we are dealing with a special application of the basic rules of offer and acceptance, an application specific to charitable donations. The "background of precedent" is mentioned to show us that subscription and acceptance are not treated as rigorously as offer and acceptance in a commercial setting. In the last sentence, Cardozo tells us that the case may thus be decided on traditional consideration grounds after all, i.e., by *offer* and acceptance as traditionally understood, but only because, as he has already sought to establish, the law is not so strict when it comes to *subscription* and acceptance.

The opinion then turns to the case at hand, reasoning that, in accepting Johnston's $1000 advance payment, the college assumed a duty (by implication, promised) to memorialize her with that money. That in itself is not quite enough, however, because such requirements could have been built into Johnston's pledge as a mere condition on her gift rather than as a demand for a promise. One factor to consider in deciding whether "words of condition . . . indicate a request for consideration or state a mere condition in a gratuitous promise" is whether the occurrence of the condition would be a benefit to the promisor. Cardozo readily concludes that the establishment of a memorial fund honoring the donor would be "beneficial to the promisor." Here he reminds us that we need not compare how beneficial it is in comparison to the value of the promise, since courts need not inquire into the adequacy of consideration. He also notes that it might be more beneficial than one would at first think. "The longing for posthumous remembrance is an emotion not so weak as to justify us in saying that its gratification is a negligible good." Whereas Williston's famous tramp[4] performed a condition that simply made the giving easier on the promisor, Johnston was to receive something valuable in return for her promise. Thus, there is good reason to think she gave her promise at least in part in order to get that value.

According to this reading, Cardozo was not trying to undermine consideration doctrine at all. He was not even advocating for the

---

4. In his treatise, Professor Williston gave the following, now famous, example to illustrate the difference between a condition on a gift and consideration:

> If a benevolent man says to a tramp: 'If you go around the corner to the clothing shop there, you may purchase an overcoat on my credit,' no reasonable person would understand that the short walk was requested as the consideration for the promise, but that in the event of the tramp going to the shop the promisor would make him a gift. Yet the walk to the shop is in its nature capable of being consideration. It is a legal detriment to the tramp to make the walk, and the only reason why the walk is not consideration is because on a reasonable construction, it must be held that the walk was not requested as the price of the promise, but was merely a condition of a gratuitous promise.

broad treatment of charitable subscription cases eventually adopted in the Second Restatement, according to which gift promises to charities are enforceable even without reliance, though this opinion is sometimes cited as supporting that rule. Rather, the holding is the very narrow one that, when a party promises money to a charity and includes conditions that can be said to benefit the promisor and the promisee accepts part of that money without objecting to those conditions, we are justified in finding adequate consideration to bind both parties. The condition on the gift is crucial to the decision. The donee implicitly promises to do as the donor wishes, and the donor is understood as having bargained for the donee's promise to carry out those wishes. We are perhaps stretching what counts as a donor offering a promise in exchange for a benefit, since it is likely that the donor's primary motivation is altruistic. But even if that is true, the law has in the past treated charitable subscription cases differently by permitting such stretching. The earlier cases show that, when we are dealing with charities, we are not so strict about what counts as bargaining, and we should not worry if the bargain made here does not look exactly like a bargain made in a normal commercial setting. When parties give to charities, they are not necessarily bargaining in an entirely self-interested way, but in some cases there will be enough self-interest for us to enforce their promises nonetheless. Just because an exchange is not a commercial exchange does not mean it is not to be taken seriously . . . .

IV.   CONTRACTS IN OTHER CONTEXTS

Before his career on the bench, Cardozo practiced law for over twenty years, mostly in the area of commercial transactions. As a judge, he was able to bring his understanding of business transactions to bear on the cases he heard, so that he was better able to see the transactions from the point of view of the parties involved at the time of their agreement. Often the result was that he found an enforceable agreement where a more narrow interpretation of contract doctrine might have found the contract to be unenforceable for failure to meet one formality or another. While it is easy to see this approach as an attack on formalist requirements, Cardozo was actually respecting the formalities of contract law even as he recognized that nominally similar transactions, in the real world, are often importantly distinct. There are many examples of contracts cases where Cardozo showed an acute sensitivity to commercial contexts — too many to cover in this project. I will instead focus on one famous case as representative of his approach: *Wood v. Lucy, Lady Duff-Gordon.*[5]

In *Wood*, the designer Lady Duff Gordon signed an agreement giving her manager, Otis Wood, an exclusive right to market her designs and give her endorsements to others. In return for this exclusive right, Wood was to give half of the profits from such sales and endorsements to Gordon. Wood eventually sued, claiming that Gordon had broken her promise by placing her endorsement on "fabrics, dresses and millinery" without his knowledge and without sharing the profits with him. Gordon responded that the contract was unenforceable for lack of consideration because Wood never promised anything in return for Gordon's promise of an exclusive right.

In the opinion, Cardozo conceded that Wood had never made an express promise, but argued that the agreement contained an implied promise by Wood to "use reasonable efforts to place the defendant's endorsements and market her designs." Such a promise could be "fairly to be implied" from the nature of the agreement. The defendant gave an exclusive privilege for at least a year, something she would presumably not do for free, and with the exclusive agency came the duties of an agent. The contract contained numerous recitals, including that Wood's business was "adapted to the placing of such endorsements . . . ." Even more significant, according to Cardozo, were the terms under which Gordon was to be compensated: her only compensation was to be based on one-half of the money from the profits "resulting from the plaintiff's efforts. Unless he gave his efforts, she could never get anything" from her endorsements.

It is tempting to conclude that Cardozo's finding of an implied promise in *Wood* is based on abstract notions of fairness. It might seem unjust for Gordon to have made a formal, written promise and then have renounced that promise later when a better deal came along. Cardozo opines that "[t]he law has outgrown its primitive stage of formalism when the precise word was the sovereign talisman, and every slip was fatal. It takes a broader view to-day." It may sound as though Cardozo was allowing fairness to trump the formalities of

---

5. Wood v. Lucy, 118 N.E. 214 (N.Y. 1917).

contract law, but Cardozo's opinion is not a triumph of fairness over formalism. Rather, Cardozo insisted on seeing the contract as the parties themselves saw it at the time it was signed, even if it "imperfectly expressed" their understanding. Inferring that Wood implied a promise not only makes the contract fair, it also makes the contract make sense. As Cardozo put it, "[w]ithout an implied promise, the transaction cannot have such business 'efficacy as both parties must have intended that at all events it should have.'" We may "fairly" infer a promise by Wood not because that is the way by which we can achieve a fair result, but rather because, without such a promise, the transaction does not make business sense. In other words, assuming a promise was implied is a fair interpretation of the parties' intentions rather than just necessary to a fair outcome. The "broader view" that the law takes today — indeed, one must wonder if it were ever otherwise — is that we ought to apply these formal requirements of contract law in a way that makes sense with respect to the kind of transaction at issue. This was a business agreement — in particular an agency agreement — and we should interpret the contract and decide whether the formal requirements for enforceability have been met with that fact in mind. When looked at from a business perspective rather than from a too-narrow lawyerly perspective, it is clear that both parties intended to be bound in *Wood* even though they did not express their intentions clearly . . . .

CONCLUSION: CARDOZO AND CONTEXTUAL FORMALISM

Grant Gilmore once argued that Cardozo so "delighted in weaving gossamer spider webs of consideration," that he had rendered the term "consideration" "meaningless."[6] In particular, Gilmore concluded that "a judge who could find 'consideration' in . . . the *Allegheny College* case could, when he was so inclined, find consideration anywhere." . . . Realists like Gilmore (and to a much lesser extent, Corbin) who made it their mission to undermine classical formalism were eager to argue that, although Cardozo paid lip service to the formalities of contract law, his decisions were not really supportable on those grounds. Posner went

---

6. [Grant Gilmore, The Death of Contract 69 (Ronald K. L. Collins ed., 1995).]

further and openly argued — indeed, made it the thesis of an entire book on Cardozo — that Cardozo's real skill as a jurist was not legal analysis but rather rhetoric: the ability to figure out who ought to win a case and then fool enough of his colleagues on the court to go along by using his magnificent rhetorical gifts to couch his results in language pleasing to formalist ears.[7] Thus, while undermining Cardozo's stated reasoning of his decisions, such realists claim him as one of their own.

More sophisticated understandings of Cardozo and of the legal realist movement in general recognize that these matters are not so simple. If we must place a historical label on his work, "pre-realist" or "proto-realist" would be more accurate, and indeed John Goldberg persuasively argues that "[p]resent-day scholars interested in developing an adequate anti-Realist theory of law ... could hardly do better than to undertake a careful examination of [Cardozo's] work."[8] If it is tempting to think of Cardozo as an anti-formalist realist rather than as an anti-realist, it is only because we have inherited from the realists an uncharitable picture of formalism. The formalism characterized by its vigorous critics probably never existed and certainly was not the doctrine of those most famously painted as formalists. . . . It was easy for the realists to paint Cardozo as an anti-formalist when he tells us the law "has outgrown its primitive stage of formalism,"[9] but finding an actual theorist who can fairly be said to personify such a primitive form of formalism where "the precise word was the sovereign talisman, and every slip was fatal" proves to be nearly impossible . . . .

Rather than discussing how accurately Cardozo could be called a formalist in the whole, I would like simply to look at one common description of classical formalism, understood as "mechanical jurisprudence." According to this understanding of formalism, the label "contextual formalism" might at first seem to be a contradiction in terms. It is commonly said that formalists decide cases based on logical deductions from abstract rules. In its extreme versions, formalism is completely insensitive to results, even absurd or unjust ones. In an oft-quoted passage, Christopher Columbus Langdell opined that the fact that contract's mailbox rule might in some cases "produce not

---

7. [Richard A. Posner, Cardozo: A Study in Reputation 125-43 (1990).]
8. John C. P. Goldberg, The Life of the Law, 51 Stan. L. Rev. 1419, 1475 (1999).
9. Wood v. Lucy, 118 N.E. 214, 214 (N.Y. 1917).

only unjust but absurd results" was "irrelevant."[10] The term "formalism" today is often used as a pejorative, perhaps in large part because of
such cavalier attitudes towards justice. Cardozo himself was not such an
extremist. For example, in *Allegheny College* he expressed a preference
for precedent that, like the special treatment of charities, is "supported
by so many considerations of public policy and reason" over the "symmetry of a concept [the classical formulation of the consideration
doctrine] which itself came into our law, not so much from any reasoned
conviction of its justice, as from historical accidents of practice and
procedure."

Stated less extremely, however, formalism's insensitivity to results
may be more palatable. Frederick Schauer argued that the central feature
of formalism is the claim that legal decision-makers are in some sense
constrained by rules. At least in this limited sense, Cardozo was a formalist. At the very least, his opinions displayed a respect for the
formalities of contract law, even when he had to hold his nose to do
it. For example, in *Sun Printing*,[11] a controversial case about a contract
with allegedly indefinite terms, Cardozo noted that: "[t]he defendant is
trying to squirm out of a contract on very technical grounds. We sustained its position, though with avowed reluctance. If there is any
reasonable way of holding its complaint good, I am sure we shall be
glad to take advantage of it." Thus, Cardozo considered himself bound
to the formal rules of contract even in some cases where they seemed to
give an unjust, or at least unhappy, result.

But there is an even more formalistic and abstract version of contract
law. According to this version, the rules of contract law not only bind
judges even though the results may seem unfair, but they are also completely insensitive to particular facts. One account called this variety of
classical contract doctrine "pure" contract law. As Lawrence Friedman
put it:

> [T]he "pure" law of contract is an area of what we can call abstract
> relationships. "Pure" contract doctrine is blind to details of subject
> matter and person. It does not ask who buys and sells, and what is bought

---

10. C. C. Langdell, A Summary of the Law of Contracts 20-21 (2d ed. 1880). . . .
11. Sun Printing and Publ'g Ass'n v. Remington Paper and Power Co., 139 N.E. 470
(N.Y. 1923).

and sold. . . . The abstraction of classical contract law . . . is a deliberate renunciation of the particular.[12]

This "one size fits all" approach to contract was first popularized by Langdell, who thought that the law could be reduced to a surprisingly small number of legal principles: "[T]he number of fundamental legal doctrines is much less than commonly supposed; the many different guises in which the same doctrine is constantly making its appearance, and the great extent to which legal treatises are a repetition of each other, being the cause of much misapprehension."[13] Presumably one could learn these few fundamental principles and grind out results without much regard for the idiosyncrasies of particular sets of facts.

Although Cardozo considered himself bound to some degree by the formalities of contract law, he could never be said to have been "blind to the details of subject matter and person," and thus was not a formalist in this stronger sense. Cardozo *always* asked "who buys and sells, and what is bought and sold." He did not ask who the participants were merely to decide the case (i.e., in order to favor a charity or to account for unequal bargaining power), but rather to understand better the nature of the transaction. If Langdell was right that there were few fundamental rules of contract, Cardozo nevertheless found many variations of those fundamental rules and applied them when appropriate to various factual scenarios. Cardozo's own stance toward the allegedly fundamental nature of these rules was obviously ambivalent at best: the "half-truth" is that the consideration doctrine requires a bargained-for exchange, but the "whole-truth" is that what counts as a bargained-for exchange will depend a great deal on "who buys and sells, and what is bought and sold."

He was, therefore, not out to undermine or erode the formalities of contract law. Instead, what we have seen in *Allegheny College*, as well as in *Wood* . . . , is an insistence that these formalities be applied sensibly, with an understanding of the context in which the exchanges took place. The question is whether the parties, understanding their actions in

---

12. Lawrence M. Friedman, Contract Law in America: A Social and Economic Case Study 20 (1965).

13. C. C. Langdell, A Selection of Cases on the Law of Contracts: With References and Citations 11 (1871), quoted in William Twining, Karl Llewellyn and the Realist Movement 11 (1973).

light of the appropriate context, manifested an intention to be mutually bound to an agreement the court could enforce. We are not to choose between rigid formalities on the one hand and vague, open-ended justice on the other, but instead are to understand agreements the way the parties themselves understood them and then decide if such agreements meet the formal requirements of the law of contract.

11

SHOULD THE "INTENTION TO CREATE LEGAL RELATIONS" BE A CRITERION OF ENFORCEABILITY?

A manifested intention to be legally bound is widely thought by American contract scholars to be neither a necessary nor a sufficient ground for enforcing a private commitment. In other words, the existence of such a manifestation of intention is not needed to enforce a commitment, and the presence of such a manifested intent will not, by itself, support enforcement. Indeed, the first Restatement of Contract §20, whose Reporter was the great Harvard contracts professor Samuel Williston, stipulated that "neither mental assent to the promises in the contract, nor real or apparent intent that the promises shall be legally binding is essential."

Nevertheless, English law acknowledges the intention to create legal relations — whether proved directly or inferentially — to be an essential element of a contract. And Williston himself strongly urged

the Commissioners on Uniform State Laws to adopt the Uniform Written
Obligations Act, which reads:

> A written release or promise, hereafter made and signed by the person
> releasing or promising, shall not be invalid or unenforceable for lack of
> consideration, if the writing also contains an additional express statement,
> in any form of language, that the signer intends to be legally bound.

Finally, §21 of the Restatement (Second) of Contracts (the successor to §20)
appears to be hedging its bets: "Neither real nor apparent intention that a
promise be legally binding is essential to the formation of a contract, but a
manifestation of intention that a promise shall *not* affect legal relations
may prevent the formation of a contract." It may be that the intention to
be legally bound is harder to ignore than is generally thought.

In my article, *A Consent Theory of Contract*, I argue that the manifested intention to be legally bound is a legal principle that could be
used to understand and rationalize a wide variety of legal doctrines. For
example, as is suggested by Lon Fuller's analysis, we enforce contracts
with consideration because the existence of a bargain in a commercial
context is a good indication of an intention to be legally bound.
However, outside the commercial context the existence of a reciprocal
bargaining is not sufficient to show an intention to be legally bound. And
in both commercial and noncommercial settings, bargaining is not the
only reliable evidence of such an intention. (I explain why consensual
transfers — and the requirement of a "manifested intention to be legally
bound" — are essential to handling the social problems of knowledge,
interest and power in *The Structure of Liberty: Justice and the Rule of
Law* (Oxford University Press, 1998).)

Professor Jean Braucher of the University of Arizona strongly dis-
agrees with my contention that consent should be at the heart of contract
law. In *The Regulatory Role of Contract Law*, she contends that conception of consent I employ is often fictitious and unrealistically narrow
insofar as it ignores the differentials in wealth, power, knowledge, and
judgment, as well as the possibility of consenting to oppression. Contract
law, she argues, is inherently regulatory and, like all regulations, should
be chosen by regulators to accomplish desirable social purposes that
should not be inhibited by a concept so limited and artificial as that
of "consent." In her view, true freedom is actually thwarted rather
than facilitated by a "consent theory of contract."

Next, we read a story by Columbia law professor Patricia Williams from her article, *Alchemical Notes: Reconstructing Ideals From Deconstructed Rights*, that illustrates how the power to manifest a commitment to be legally bound can be a vital means of establishing trust in some contractual contexts. Finally, in an excerpt from his 2005 book, *From Promise to Contract*, Dori Kimel of Oxford University explains the significance of William's story and relates it to the debate (discussed in Chapter 9) over the relationship between contract and promise.

STUDY GUIDE: *Why should a nonbargained-for promise on which the promisee has not relied be enforced just because the promisee has manifested an intention to be legally bound? How might a willingness to enforce such promises lead to instances of overenforcement? Does the following approach require that parties be aware of what commitments the legal system will enforce? If so, how realistic is this assumption?*

A CONSENT THEORY OF CONTRACT*

Randy E. Barnett

INTRODUCTION

The mere fact that one man promises something to another creates no legal duty and makes no legal remedy available in case of non-performance. To be enforceable, the promise must be accompanied by some other factor. . . . The question now to be discussed is what is this other factor. What fact or facts must accompany a promise to make it enforceable at law?[1]

Which interpersonal commitments are properly enforceable as contracts? When contract theorists and philosophers treat this question, they commonly assume that the institution of contract somehow depends on the institution of promise-keeping. They think that contractual duties are

---

*From Randy E. Barnett, Rights and Remedies in a Consent Theory of Contract, in Liability and Responsibility 135 (R. G. Frey & Christopher W. Morris, eds. 1991).
   1. 1 A. Corbin, Corbin on Contracts §110, at 490 (1963).

species of the general duty to keep one's promise. I think this approach is wrong, both descriptively and normatively. I think that Arthur Corbin was right to insist that to "be enforceable, the promise must be accompanied by some other factor. . . ." The other factor, by assumption, is extraneous to the promise itself. Moreover, if by a "promise" we mean a commitment to act or refrain from acting at some time in the future, then a contractual duty can exist even where there is no promise — as with an immediate transfer of entitlements.

In this essay, I identify this factor as the "manifested intent to alienate rights" which I shall refer to as "consent." Consequently, I call this a "consent theory of contract." A consent theory posits that contractual obligation cannot be completely understood unless it is viewed as part of a broader system of legal entitlements. Such a system specifies the substance of the rights individuals may acquire and transfer, and the means by which they may do so. Properly understood, contract law is that part of a system of entitlements that identifies those circumstances in which entitlements are validly transferred from person to person by their consent. . . .

I.   ENTITLEMENT THEORY AND CONTRACT

A.   Entitlements as the Foundation of Contractual Obligation

The function of an entitlements theory based on individual rights is to define the boundaries within which individuals may live, act, and pursue happiness free of the forcible interference of others. A theory of entitlements specifies the rights that individuals possess or may possess; it tells us what may be owned and who owns it; it circumscribes the individual boundaries of human freedom. Any coherent theory of justice based on individual rights must therefore contain principles that describe how such rights are initially acquired, how they are transferred from person to person, what the substance and limits of properly obtained rights are, and how interferences with these entitlements are to be rectified.

These constituent parts of an entitlements theory comport substantially with the traditional categories of private law. The issue of initial acquisition of entitlements in real and chattel resources is dealt with primarily in property law; tort law concerns the protection of and proper limits on resource use; and contract law deals with transfers of rights between rights-holders. Each category contains its own principles of rectification for the breach of legal obligations. Viewing contract law as part of a more general theory of individual entitlements that specifies how resources may be rightly acquired (property law), used (tort law), and transferred (contract law) is not new. And, of course, the actual historical development of these legal categories has not perfectly conformed to the conceptual distinctions that an entitlements approach suggests. But this approach has long been neglected as a way of resolving some of the thorniest issues of contract theory and doctrine.

According to an entitlements approach, rights may be unconditionally granted to another (a gift), or their transfer may be conditioned upon some act or reciprocal transfer by the transferee (an exchange). Contract law concerns the ways by which rights are transferred or alienated. Accordingly, the enforceability of all agreements is limited by the rights people have and by the extent to which these rights are capable of being transferred from one person to another. Whether a purported right is genuine or can be legitimately transferred is not an issue of contract theory only, but is one that may also require reference to the underlying theory of entitlements. The explanation of the binding nature of contractual commitments is derived from more fundamental notions of entitlements and how they are acquired and transferred.

The subject of most rights-transfer agreements are entitlements that are indisputably alienable. In such cases the rules of contract law are entirely sufficient to explain and justify a judicial decision. However, . . . in rare cases — such as agreements amounting to slavery arrangements or requiring the violation of another's rights — contract law's dependence on rights theory will be of crucial importance in identifying appropriate concerns about the substance of voluntary agreements. For example, agreements to transfer inalienable rights — rights that for some reason cannot be transferred — or to transfer rights that for some reason cannot be obtained, would not, without more, be valid and enforceable contracts.[2] The process of contractual transfer cannot be completely comprehended, therefore, without considering more fundamental issues, namely the nature and sources of individual entitlements and the means by which they come to be acquired.

---

2. Other bases of obligation are possible besides contractual obligation, however, such as those recognized under the law of tort and restitution.

B.   The Social Function of Individual Rights

Legal obligations may be enforced by the use or threat of legal force and this dimension of force requires moral justification. The principal task of legal theory, then, is to identify circumstances when legal enforcement is morally justified. Entitlements theories seek to perform this task by determining the individual legal rights of persons — that is, those claims of persons that may be justifiably enforced.

Any concept of individual rights must assume a social context. If the world were inhabited by only one person, it might make sense to speak of that person's actions as morally good or bad. Such a moral judgment might, for example, look to whether or not that person had chosen to live what might be called a "good life." Yet it makes no sense to speak about this person's rights. The need for rights arises from the moment individuals live in close enough proximity to one another to compete for the use of scarce natural resources. Some scheme of specifying how individuals may acquire, use, and transfer resources must be recognized to handle the conflicts over resource use that will inevitably arise. Certain facts of human existence make certain principles of allocation ineluctable. For example, it is a fundamental human requirement that individuals acquire and consume natural resources, even though such activity is often inconsistent with a similar use of the same resources by others.

"Property rights" is the term used to describe an individual's entitlements to use and consume resources — both the individual's person and her external possessions — free from the physical interference of others. Today, the term "property rights" tends to be limited only to rights to external resources. Traditionally, however, it referred to the moral and legal jurisdiction a person has both over her body and over external resources.[3] The exact contours of a proper theory of rights need not be specified here. We need only recognize that *some* allocation of rights to resource possession and use is an unavoidable prerequisite of human survival and of human fulfillment and that, once allocated, at least some rights must be alienable.

---

3. See, e.g., J. Locke, An Essay Concerning the True Original Extent and End of Civil Government, in Two Treatises of Civil Government ch. V §27 (1690) ("every man has a *property* in his own *person*").

A theory of contractual obligation is the part of an entitlements theory that focuses on liability arising from the wrongful interference with a valid rights transfer. Until such an interference is corrected — by force if necessary — the distribution of resources caused by the interference is unjust. Justice normally requires that this situation be corrected to bring resource distribution into conformity with entitlements. In sum, contract law, according to an entitlements approach, is a body of general principles and more specific rules the function of which is to identify the rights of individuals engaged in transferring entitlements. These rights are then used to justify physical or legal force to rectify any unjust interference with the transfer process.

C.   Consent as the Moral Component of Contract

To identify the moral component that distinguishes valid from invalid rights transfers, it is first necessary to separate moral principles governing the rightful acquisition and use of resources from those governing their transfer. Rights are the means by which freedom of action and interaction is facilitated and regulated in society, and thus the rights we have to acquire previously unowned resources and to use that which we acquire must not be subject to the expressed assent of others. Although societal acquiescence may be a practical necessity for rights to be legally respected, no individual or group need actually consent to our appropriation of previously unowned resources or their use for our rights to morally vest. Similarly, principles governing rights transfer should be distinguished from principles governing resource use. Tort law concerns obligations arising from interferences with others' rights. A tortfeasor who interferes with another's rights (rather than obtaining a valid transfer of those rights to herself) is liable because of that interference, not because she consented to be held liable for her actions. A tortfeasor can be said to forfeit (as opposed to alienate or transfer) rights to resources in order to provide compensation to the victim of the tort.

In contrast, contract law concerns enforceable obligations arising from the valid transfer of entitlements that are *already vested* in someone, and this difference is what makes consent a moral prerequisite to contractual obligation. The rules governing the transfer of property rights perform the same function as rules governing their acquisition and those specifying their proper content: facilitating freedom of human action and interaction in a social context. Freedom of action and interaction would be seriously impeded, and possibly destroyed, if legitimate rights-holders who have not acted in a tortious manner could be deprived of their rights by force of law without their consent.

Of course, I can only summarize here the many reasons why viewing consent as the moral basis of contractual obligation — a view that is sometimes called "freedom of contract" — is so important to the operation of the enterprise of entitlements. These reasons cluster around two distinct dimensions of the consent requirement. The first dimension of consent may be called "freedom *to* contract." Viewing the rights-holder's consent as normally sufficient to transfer alienable rights enables persons to exchange entitlements to resources when, on their judgment, they can put the resources they obtain to better use than the resources they transfer. It also permits persons to make gratuitous transfers when they judge that under the circumstances the recipient can put the resource to better use than they can.

The second aspect of consent may be called "freedom *from* contract." Rights to resources may not be taken without obtaining the consent of the rights-holder. By rendering persons' control over resources immune from forced transfers, the requirement of consent permits persons to plan and act in reliance on their future access to their rightfully held resources. Moreover, the requirement of consent mandates that others take the interests of the rights-holder into account when seeking to obtain her rights. Only a requirement of consent can ensure that the welfare of the rights-holder is properly included in another's allocational decisionmaking. And the requirement of consent at the level of individuals is what makes possible the generation of market prices that convey invaluable information about relative scarcity and competing uses for resources in a form that may — indeed must — be taken into account when choices concerning scarce resources are made.

Although it is not altogether novel to suggest that consent is at the heart of contract law,[4] this view did not ultimately prevail among modern contract theorists and philosophers who largely adopted a promissory

---

4. See M. Ferson, The Rational Basis of Contracts and Related Problems in Legal Analysis 60 (1949). . . .

definition of contract.[5] Perhaps because promising is but a special instance of consent,[6] the prevailing equation of contract with promise is what has blinded the profession to the more fundamental theoretical role of consent. Moreover, that contractual obligation arises from a consent to alienate rights and is thereby dependent on a theory of entitlements or property rights is also largely overlooked. Yet it is certainly a commonly held and plausible conception of ownership that owning resources gives one the right to possess, use, and consensually transfer the rights to them free from the forcible coercion of others. . . .

III. DETERMINING CONTRACTUAL OBLIGATION IN A CONSENT THEORY

A. Establishing the Prima Facie Case of Consent

Richard Epstein has suggested that legal principles used to determine obligation can best be thought of as presumptive in nature.[7] Any such presumption of obligation, however, may be rebutted if other facts are proved to have existed that undermine the normal significance of the prima facie case. Such responses or "defenses" to the prima facie case are themselves only presumptively compelling. They in turn may be rebutted by still other facts alleged by the person seeking relief. In this way the principles or elements that determine legal obligation come in "stages."

In a consent theory, absent the assertion of a valid defense, proof of consent to transfer alienable rights is legally sufficient to establish the existence of a contractual obligation. Consent is prima facie binding

---

5. See, e.g., Restatement (Second) of Contracts §1 (1979) ("A contract is a promise or a set of promises for the breach of which the law gives a remedy, or the performance of which the law in some way recognizes as a duty."). . . .

Because a consent theory embraces more than the enforcement of promises, the most appropriate terms to describe contracting parties might be "transferor" and "transferee." For convenience, however, the more conventional terms "promisor" and "promisee" will still occasionally be used here.

6. See P. Atiyah, Promises, Morals, and Law 177 (1981) ("Promising may be reducible to a species of consent, for consent is a broader and perhaps more basic source of obligation.").

7. See Espstein, Pleadings and Presumptions, 40 U. Chi. L. Rev. 556 (1973).

both because of its usual connection with subjective assent (which protects the autonomy of the promisor) and because people usually have access only to the manifested intentions of others (which protects the reliance of the promisee and others as well as the security of transactions). There are two ways to manifest one's intention to be legally bound. The first is to deliberately "channel" one's behavior through the use of a legal formality in such a way as to convey explicitly a certain meaning — that of having an intention to be legally bound — to another. This is the formal means of consenting. The second and, perhaps, more common method is by indirectly or implicitly conveying this meaning by other types of behavior. This is the informal means of consenting.

1. Formal Consent. For a considerable part of the history of the common law, the principal way of creating what we now think of as a contractual obligation was to cast one's agreement in the form of a sealed writing. The emergence of assumpsit as the principal action of contractual enforcement required the development of a doctrinal limitation on the enforcement of commitments — that is, the doctrine of consideration.[8] This development eventually resulted in the ascendancy of the bargain theory of consideration, which had the unintended consequence of creating doctrinal problems for the enforcement of formal commitments where there was no bargained-for consideration. Notwithstanding their ancient history, formal commitments, such as those under seal, came to be thought of as "exceptions" to the "normal" requirement of consideration. Expressions such as "a seal imports consideration" or is "a substitute for consideration" became commonplace. In a climate of opinion dominated by notions of "bargained-for consideration" and "induced reliance," when there is no bargain and no demonstrable reliance to support enforcement, formal promises have had an uncertain place in the law of contract.

A consent theory of contract, however, provides the missing theoretical foundation of formal contracts and explains their proper place in a well-crafted law of contract. The voluntary use of a recognized formality by a promisor manifests to a promisee an intention to be legally

---

8. The Statute of Frauds, passed in 1677, was another such limitation. . . .

bound in the most unambiguous manner possible. Formal contracts ought to be an "easy" case of contractual enforcement, but prevailing theories that require bargained-for consideration or induced reliance would have a hard time explaining why. For example, when there is no separate bargained-for consideration for making an offer irrevocable for a certain period of time, a bargain theory of consideration would have a difficult time explaining the enforceability of "firm offers" which require neither consideration nor detrimental reliance for enforcement to be obtained. In a consent theory, by contrast, there need be no underlying bargain or demonstrable reliance for such a commitment to be properly enforced.

The same holds true for nominal consideration and for false recitals of consideration. A consent theory acknowledges that, if properly evidenced, the exchange of one dollar or a false recital by the parties that consideration exists may fulfill the channeling function of formalities, whether or not any bargained-for consideration for the commitment in fact exists. If it is widely known that the written phrase "in return for good and valuable consideration" means that one intends to make a legally binding commitment, then these words will fulfill a channeling function as well as, and perhaps better than, a seal or other formality. The current rule that the falsity of such a statement permits a court to nullify a transaction because of a lack of consideration is therefore contrary to a consent theory of contract.

2.   *Informal Consent.*   Consent to transfer rights can be express or implied. Formal contracts expressing consent to transfer alienable rights pose no problem for a consent theory. The enforcement of informal commitments where evidence of legally binding intentions is more obscure, however, has plagued contract law for centuries. In such agreements courts must infer assent to be legally bound from the circumstances or the "considerations" or "causa" that induced the parties' actions.

(a) *Bargaining as evidence of consent.*   Within a consent theory, the fact that a person has received something of value in return for a promise may indeed indicate that this promise was an expression of intention to transfer rights. Moreover, in some circumstances where gratuitous transfers are unusual, the receipt of a benefit in return for a promise should serve as objective notice to the promisor that the promise has been interpreted by the other party to be legally binding.[9]

Although the existence of a bargain or other motivation for a transaction may be good evidence of the sort of agreement that has been made, in a consent theory the absence of consideration does not preclude the application of legal sanctions if other indicia of consent are present. So if it can be proved, for example, that a party voluntarily consented to be legally bound to keep an offer to transfer rights open, to release a debt, to modify an obligation, or to pay for past favors, the lack of bargained-for consideration will not bar enforcement of these kinds of commitments in a consent theory.

Where bargaining is the norm — as it is in most sales transactions — there is little need for the law to require explicit proof of an intent to be legally bound, such as an additional formality, or even proof of the existence of a bargain. In such circumstances, if an arm's-length agreement to sell can be proved, there presumptively has been a manifestation of intent to be legally bound. For this reason, the Uniform Commercial Code's stricture that "[a] contract for the sale of goods may be made in any manner sufficient to show agreement, including conduct by both parties which recognizes the existence of such a contract,"[10] is entirely consonant with a consent theory.

(b) *Reliance as evidence of consent.* A consent theory also identifies those circumstances where the presence of reliance provides an adequate substitute for the traditional requirement of consideration. If the primary function of consideration is to serve as one way of manifesting assent to be legally bound, and not as a necessary element of the prima facie case of contractual obligation, then reliance and consideration may sometimes be functionally equivalent. Expenditures made by a promisee in reliance on the words and conduct of the promisor may prove as much about the nature of this transaction as the existence of consideration, especially where the reliance is or should be known to the promisor.

Suppose that *A* makes a substantial promise to *B* — for example, a promise to convey land. The promise, while clear, may be ambiguous as

---

9. The duties, if any, the receipt of a nongratuitous benefit imposes on the recipient are beyond the scope of this essay, except to note that such receipt may manifest the recipient's intent to be legally bound to a contemporaneous commitment.

10. U.C.C. §2-204 (1977).

to its intended legal effect. Does *A* intend to be bound and subject to legal enforcement if she reneges, or is she merely stating her current view of her future intentions? Now suppose that *B* announces to *A* his intention to rely on *A*'s promise in a substantial way — for example, by building a house on the land — and that *A* says nothing. Suppose further that *B* commences construction and observes *A* watching in silence. It would seem that under such circumstances *A*'s ambiguous legal intent has been clarified. By remaining silent in the face of reliance so substantial that *B* would not have undertaken it without a legal commitment from *A* — *A* could not reasonably have believed that *B* intended to make a gift to her of the house — *A* has manifested an intention to be legally bound.[11]

In this manner, a promisor's silence while observing substantial reliance on the promise by the promisee can manifest the promisor's assent to the promisee. In a consent theory, if consent is proved, then enforcement is warranted even if a bargain or a formality is absent. In sum, bargained-for consideration and nonbargained-for reliance are equivalent to the extent that the existence of either in a transaction may manifest the intentions of one or both of the parties to be legally bound. In any case, the absence of either bargained-for consideration or reliance will not bar the enforcement of a transfer of entitlements that can be proved in some other way — for example, by a formal written document or by adequate proof of a sufficiently unambiguous verbal commitment.[12]

B.   Contract Defenses: Rebutting the Prima Facie Case of Consent

Consent, either formal or informal, is required to make out a prima facie case of contractual obligation. This means that, in the absence of an "affirmative" defense to the prima facie case of contractual obligation, the manifested intention of a party to transfer alienable rights will

---

11. See, e.g., Greiner v. Greiner, 293 P. 759 (Kan. 1930). . . .

12. It is not being suggested here that such prophylactic measures that serve an evidentiary function — such as a statute of frauds, a parol evidence rule, or certain formal requirements — are inappropriate in a consent theory. . . .

justify the enforcement of such a commitment. Traditional contract defenses can be understood as describing circumstances that, if proved to have existed, deprive the manifestation of assent of its normal moral, and therefore legal, significance. These defenses may be clustered into three groups, each of which undermines the prima facie case of consent in a different way.

The first group of defenses — duress, misrepresentation, and (possibly) unconscionability[13] — describes circumstances where the manifestation of an intention to be legally bound has been obtained improperly by the promisee. The manifestation of assent either was improperly coerced by the promisee or was based on misinformation for which the promisee was responsible. The second group — incapacity, infancy, and intoxication — describes attributes of the promisor that indicate a lack of ability to assert meaningful assent. The third group — mistake, impracticability, and frustration — stem from the inability to fully express in any agreement all possible contingencies that might affect performance. Each describes those types of events (a) whose nonoccurrence was arguably a real, but tacit assumption upon which consent was based, and (b) for which the promisee should bear the risk of occurrence.[14] Each type of defense thus is distinguished by the way it undermines the normal, presumed significance of consent. But all valid contract defenses describe general circumstances where the appearance of assent tends to lack its normal moral significance.

These traditional contract defenses function in a consent theory, as they do currently, to preserve the actual voluntariness of rights transfer in those comparatively rare cases where consent has been improperly coerced or where we are willing to acknowledge other circumstances, such as misinformation, that vitiate the presence of consent. This refusal to enforce some instances of apparent assent does not, however, reflect a retreat to a subjective will theory. It remains true that an objective manifestation of intent to be legally bound is sufficient to give rise to

---

13. For analyses of unconscionability that would place it in this category of defenses, see, e.g., Epstein, Unconscionability: A Critical Reappraisal, 18 J.L. & Econ. 293 (1975); Leff, Unconscionability and the Code — The Emperor's New Clause, 115 U. Pa. L. Rev. 485 (1967).

14. In this third group of defenses, the consent was not improperly induced by the promisee, and the person giving consent was capable of doing so. This, in part, may help explain why courts are quite receptive to arguments by the promisee that the promisor assumed the risk of the mistake, impracticability, or frustration. . . .

an enforceable commitment. The only qualification is that this objective manifestation must have been voluntary.

STUDY GUIDE: Professor Braucher contends that contract law is inherently regulatory. What does she mean by that? How does it differ from the conception of contract in the previous excerpt? Why does she put "consent" in quotes? How does "consent" differ from the "freedom" to which she refers at the end of this excerpt? Where do you think freedom of contract fits into her conception of freedom? Is this ultimately a debate over the source of contractual obligation: the parties or the legal system? Or is it a debate over which is the greater danger: the abuse of one party by the other party or the abuse of one or both parties by the legal system itself? What practical difference would it make in real world transactions and lawsuits to adopt one approach or the other? Finally, at the end of this excerpt, notice the critique of the "inalienable rights" rhetoric that was discussed above in Chapter 3B.

THE REGULATORY ROLE OF CONTRACT LAW*

Jean Braucher

Use of the concept of consent seems to be inevitable in explanations and justifications of the law of contract. Consent itself, however, is a conclusion based on a complex set of normative judgments; consent is not a simple description of fact. In the event of a dispute between contracting parties, some external power must first decide whether the parties have consented in a valid manner and, if so, determine the scope of the consent. Legal decisionmakers, serving collective societal norms, construct consent. This process is unavoidably a means of regulation, one which fosters one view or another of beneficial contractual relations. Consent will not work as a rationale to enforce contracts without also bringing in social control of the parties' affairs in the event of dispute. . . .

---

*From Jean Braucher, Contract Versus Contractarianism: The Regulatory Role of Contract Law, 47 Wash. & Lee L. Rev. 697 (1990). Sections have been renumbered.

There are three essential dimensions to the regulatory role of contract law. First, law and legal decisionmakers make interrelated determinations concerning the validity of consent and the limits of consent as a rationale for enforcement. Sometimes the law mandates or prohibits terms because of validity problems, because the social limits of consent as a rationale have been reached, or for both of these reasons in combination. Second, as part of the process of interpreting whether a contract was formed and, if so, the scope of contractual obligation, legal decisionmakers mold obligations along socially desired lines. Interpretation cannot be neutral, but must be done from some point of view. Third, the law must supply a great deal of the content of contractual obligation. No matter how detailed parties are in their planning, they will never plan for every contingency. (Nor is it necessarily desirable that the law encourage them to try to do so). Supplied terms reflect social views of the proper goals of contractual relations. . . .

I. LIBERTARIAN CONSENT THEORY OF CONTRACT

If not for Randy Barnett, I might be accused of creating a straw man in the form of the libertarian literal consent theorist. Here is Barnett's own summary of his consent theory of contract:

> A consent theory of contract requires that an enforceable contract satisfy at least two conditions. First, the subject of a contract must be a morally cognizable right possessed by the transferor that is interpersonally transferable, or "alienable." Second, the possessor of the alienable right must manifest his intention to be legally bound to transfer the right — that is, he must consent.

This theory conceives of consent as express, conscious and individually controlled. In addition, a contract is a "transfer," not a relation. A discrete exchange is Barnett's paradigm of contract. Barnett believes his version of consent serves freedom and individual autonomy by giving each party who consents control in dealings with other parties.

Barnett plays down two of the three inevitable external normative dimensions of contract law, and he initially missed the third. He thus ignores the complexity and the limits of consent.

First, Barnett gives scant attention to questions concerning validity of consent and believes that validity can be summed up in an easy on/off determination of "voluntariness." He also removes from the domain of contract law questions about whether entitlements affect the validity of consent. The legitimacy of entitlements is treated as a separate question, a matter of property law, which in his view determines how persons can acquire resources. He believes contract, in contrast, specifies how these entitlements defined by property law can be transferred. Barnett's analytical structure cuts off inquiry into whether entitlements bear on the legitimacy of consent to contract. Following Robert Nozick, Barnett rejects a patterned view of distributive justice, treating a historical basis for entitlements as the only appropriate approach, on the grounds that patterned theories "require constant interferences with individual preferences." This is circular reasoning—the individual preferences Barnett is concerned about protecting depend upon the particular set of entitlements, so protection of preferences cannot justify these entitlements. Furthermore, patterned distributive justice need not depend on contract rules. Taxes and transfer payments are a more effective primary means of maintaining a desired distributive pattern of entitlements. In addition, having adopted a historical approach to entitlements, Barnett immediately backpedals from the principle of rectification it entails.[1]

Second, Barnett views interpretation to determine the fact and scope of consent as a simple matter. He takes the position that consent is a "clear, common sense test of enforceability." Barnett adopts contract law's standard "objective" test of questions of formation and interpretation, but does not address the difficulties of applying it. At one point, Barnett treats application as uncomplicated: "If the word 'yes' ordinarily means *yes*, then a subjective and unrevealed belief that 'yes' means *no* is generally immaterial. . . ." Barnett's statement invites comparison with the proposition that, "No means no," which has not been treated as self-evident in the law of rape. In rape law, consent historically has been socially constructed from a male point of view, although there have been recent changes in the law suggesting the development of a new perspective. Consent to contract is no less socially constructed, no matter what perspective is chosen as appropriate. At another point, Barnett

---

1. Barnett sets the lifetimes of original wrongdoers and original owners as the statute of limitations for redress of wrongful takings of resources. . . .

recognizes that "[t]he hard work facing any legal system" includes determining "what acts constitute 'consent,'" but Barnett neglects to take on the job. What Barnett fails to recognize is that legal interpretation inevitably involves social control of contract parties.

A large flaw in Barnett's consent theory is its focus on formation, while ignoring the very real and practical problem that the law must supply terms where the parties are silent. Barnett has conceded that most "real-world" contractual disputes do not involve issues of alienability of rights or of whether the parties manifested consent to transfer rights.[2] More often, the content of obligation is at issue. Barnett has made another even more significant concession about his theory — that use of fictitious consent is necessary to complete it and to supply terms:

> Developing a consent theory's approach to construing contractual intent when parties are silent on an issue would require a lengthy and separate treatment. Such an effort would involve, among other topics . . . the presumption that the parties intended what most similarly situated parties would have intended ex ante, thus putting the onus on a minority of parties to express dissent.

Express consent was alluring to Barnett as a central concept because of a false promise of full individual control. His quest was driven by radical individualism and a libertarian view of human nature. Barnett believes that it is possible to separate an individual's decisions from context, which includes the influence of groups and the society of which the individual is a member.[3] But individuals internalize social norms

---

2. Even on the question of manifestation of consent to some sort of obligation, full party control is not possible because the objective test calls for external evaluation of the parties' words and actions by a legal decisionmaker, a process which inevitably imports social control. . . .

3. Barnett's consent theory derives from a conception of a primal scene of solitary existence:

> From the moment individuals live in close enough proximity to one another to compete for the use of scarce natural resources, some way of allocating those resources must be found.

The trouble with this story is that individuals never have lived apart from a social group. The individual only exists within groups and a social context (even during occasional separations such as Robinson Crusoe's), and the individual's choices can only be understood in this context.

and experience them to a significant extent as their own values. On the other hand, individuals experience all of their decisions and actions as constrained by social context to some degree. There is no such thing as absolute autonomy, so we need not worry about losing it (about dreaded "crossings" of our "boundaries"). Individuality itself is a social construction fostered by many institutions, including contract.[4] . . .

II. VALIDITY OF CONSENT AND THE LIMITS OF CONSENT

A. Differentials in Wealth, Power, Knowledge, and Judgment

"Consent" occurs in the context of a prior distribution of entitlements and abilities. Interrelated elements of wealth, power, knowledge, and judgment of the parties constitute the conditions in which they make choices or undertake relationships. Choices, relations, entitlements, and abilities cannot be separated. A focus on "consent" in the context of the conditions of the status quo suggests that these conditions are a legitimate basis for choice, which is not necessarily so. Giving consent involves a relative judgment; one consents to a change, not to the prior position or the resulting one.

Contract law must make judgments about validity of consent. The parties cannot determine for themselves what constitutes valid consent. If that were so, a man with a gun to his head and his assailant could decide that physical duress does not affect validity of consent. Validity depends on external normative choices. In an imperfect world, where the distribution of entitlements is unjust and where traits and abilities vary dramatically, consent is at best a relative justification for contract enforcement, not an absolute one. Contract law must draw lines concerning when the circumstances make consent "valid." Arguably, it is redundant to speak of "valid consent"; invalid consent is not consent. Yet there are many common expressions about consent that refer to conditions necessary to validity: voluntary consent, informed consent,

---

4. Barnett's focus on individual freedom is in keeping with a long practice of ignoring the implications of the fact that most contracts involve an organization on one or both sides. . . .

consenting adults. These expressions recognize that the significance of acts and words of apparent consent may be undercut by circumstances as well as by characteristics of the one consenting.

Legal categories that deal with the problem of validity of apparent consent include duress and undue influence, misrepresentation (or fraud), mistake, incapacity, and unconscionability.[5] Unconscionability can be understood as a residual invalidity category that picks up cases of quasi-duress and quasi-fraud[6] and of limited capacity as well as combinations of various borderline validity problems. These legal categories refer to problems of power (duress), knowledge (fraud and mistake), and judgment (incapacity) and to elements and combinations of these three problems (undue influence, unconscionability). Translating the invalidity categories in this way emphasizes their malleability and expandability. How much power, knowledge, and judgment are necessary to make consent valid? Each of the categories calls for normative refinement in application.

Contract doctrine has not explicitly addressed wealth imbalances as a separate validity category, although wealth is often a factor in the validity doctrines or in particular contract rules. Contract law's failure to embrace redistribution as a core goal can be justified on the grounds that contract cannot do this job well. Contract law rules are often a crude, temporary, and puny means of redistribution. For example, a contract rule that redistributes wealth from landlords to tenants is crude because it does not help the homeless or affect wealthy non-landlords, while it does affect relatively poor as well as rich landlords. Furthermore, this sort of rule is temporary in that increased costs of a rule frequently can be passed along (to the tenants), or investments can be shifted to avoid the costs of the rule. Finally, given the extremes of wealth and poverty in our society, contract rules are a small, slow way to achieve redistribution. Taxes and transfer payments are a better way to maintain a pattern of distributive justice.

---

5. Eisenberg says these doctrines deal with "quality" of consent. Eisenberg, The Bargain Principle and Its Limits, 95 Harv. L. Rev. 741, 742 (1982). Although this terminology makes sense logically, consent is generally taken to be an on/off matter in contract law, which is a reason to use the word "validity."

6. See Leff, Unconscionability and the Code — The Emperor's New Clause, 115 U. Pa. L. Rev. 485, 487-488 (1967).

Using taxes and transfer payments as the central method of redistribution answers one critique of a patterned conception of justice, that it requires constant interference in people's transactions. A transition problem remains for those who believe in the importance of equity in the pattern of distribution: It is hard to tolerate, at a minimum, extreme contractual advantage-taking by those rich in entitlements in their dealings with the relatively poor, so long as we fail to redistribute sufficiently through taxes and transfer payments. This is a reason for contract law to take wealth disparities into account.

What is at stake in the validity doctrines of contract law is defining the conditions necessary to freedom. Attempting to do so raises deep value conflicts. At one extreme, libertarians want very minimal conditions because they fear that freedom will be limited in the name of fostering it. Libertarians conceive of freedom in negative terms, rather than in terms of creating even minimum positive conditions to allow self-actualization. At the other extreme, freedom could be defined in terms of substantively fair distribution, because of fear that unequal distribution of wealth and other advantages at the outset of any supposedly free process makes the process merely a way for the advantaged to increase their advantages. While one extreme tends to mean freedom for the rich, powerful, informed, and shrewd at the expense of the poor, weak, ignorant, and naive, the other threatens the idea of some role for individual choice. These extremes coincide with Nozick's two categories of justice — a historical basis (and process orientation), as opposed to a time-slice, "patterned" conception.

Invalidity doctrines in contract law, a compromise of these distributive and process conceptions of justice, have historically been more responsive to the libertarian end of the spectrum of opinion, sharply limiting the situations in which apparent consent could successfully be challenged. Initially, for example, duress only invalidated "apparent" consent in cases of physical assault, physical imprisonment or threats of serious bodily harm. Gradually, the doctrine of duress expanded to cover economic pressure, and the law was forced to acknowledge and struggle with the inevitable relativity of the idea of duress.

The invalidity categories have expanded, but a great constraint on expansion of legally recognized conditions for free contractual choice remains. This is the bifurcation of the question of consent into apparent consent and validity. Rather than looking at the total context in which consent has supposedly been given (which would be a more relational approach), the law of contract has asked, first, are there words or acts of consent ("objectively" judged)? If so, then the one who apparently consented must prove that he or she did not validly do so. Where there are words or acts of consent, this bifurcated analysis tips the balance in favor of validation of questionable consent. One could ask, in what sense was there an "appearance" of consent where the promisee extracted consent to a contract with a threat of physical harm? Surely there was no appearance of valid consent to the promisee who made the threat. The same can be said of a promisee who drafts a harsh term into paragraph 25 of the tiny print in a form contract used in a consumer transaction; in what sense is the drafter-promisee misled by an appearance of consent to that term on the part of the consumer? Yet in both cases, the "apparent" promisor has to raise and prove lack of valid consent.

The concern in the bifurcated approach seems not to be with reasonable reliance by the promisee, but rather with cooked-up validity challenges threatening security of transactions. The bifurcated analysis and allocation of burden of proof to the promisor in validity challenges also seem designed to restrict the juristic dispensing power to let people out of bad bargains. The policy choice has been to favor security of transactions over concern for validity of consent. Often, this approach is unfair. (One might even argue that limited validity analysis is inefficient to the extent that contract enforcement in a context of invalid consent exceeds prevention of manufactured validity challenges; this argument, however, only demonstrates the circularity of efficiency analysis on distribution questions — in this case, questions about how much information, judgment and power are necessary for valid choice.) Validity analysis has used a narrow focus on an event of consent, with minimal, constrained attention to social context, sometimes viewed as a suspect basis for questioning obligation.

A recurrent debate in the law of validity of contractual consent is whether to examine the process by which consent is achieved, the substance of the resulting contract, or both. The difficulty of defining improper process led to greater attention to substantive fairness, but the difficulty of defining fair substance led back to a focus on procedural fairness. Neither focus works, procedurally or substantively, to avoid the difficult normative choices involved in determining validity of consent. Procedurally, the problem is that it is as difficult to define fair procedure as to define fair results. Substantively, an exclusive focus on "fair" process leads to an apology for oppressive results flowing from prior imbalances in traits and wealth. Requiring every promisee to prove "fair" substance, however, would threaten the very idea of individual choice and increase unpredictability about the enforceability of contracts. Difficult value choices about the conditions necessary for valid consent are inescapable. Looking at both procedure and substance to develop a compromise approach to making these choices seems to be the best the law can do.

B. Consent to Oppression

A question related to validity is: what are the limits of consent as a justification for oppressive results? The law prohibits some terms and makes others unenforceable (and makes some mandatory), in part because of the impossibility of designing procedures adequate to make consent valid; to avoid impositions by one party on another, the law withholds enforcement, prohibits some terms, and requires others. Oppressiveness as a reason to require, to prohibit or not to enforce a contract term is in part based on invalidity of consent and in part goes beyond a rationale of lack of consent.

The law prohibits or makes unenforceable certain harsh terms and contracts because of doubt that they can be validly entered into; the suspicion is that only knowledge, power and judgment problems (often combined with lack of wealth) could produce them. The harshness of the terms is evidence of validity problems. In addition, widespread regret over certain sorts of contracts casts doubt on the validity of consent.

In most, and arguably all, cases where indecency of a term or contract might be used as a ground for denying enforcement, the conditions surrounding apparent consent are dubious, so that the validity and oppressiveness rationales can be understood as complementary. Take the example of *In the Matter of Baby M.*[7] Although rejected in the trial court and not addressed by the Supreme Court, there were plausible

---

7. 109 N.J. 396, 537 A.2d 1227 (1988).

fraud[8] and unconscionability[9] arguments against enforcing the contract. Furthermore, as to surrogacy contracts generally, there is evidence of judgment-related problems in a disproportionate number of women who seek to act as surrogate mothers; for example, many of them consciously or unconsciously use surrogacy as a way to attempt to deal with unresolved feelings associated with prior losses of fetuses in abortions and prior losses of children through relinquishment for adoption.[10]

---

8. The contract provided: "The sole purpose of this Agreement is to enable WILLIAM STERN and his infertile wife to have a child which is biologically related to WILLIAM STERN." Mary Beth Whitehead was not told that Elizabeth Stern did not try to become pregnant for fear of exacerbating multiple sclerosis. The trial court construed "infertile" not to mean literal inability to conceive, and determined that the omission of information concerning Dr. Stern's multiple sclerosis was not material. In addition, Mrs. Whitehead underwent a psychological evaluation and was told that she "passed." An agency recommended her as a surrogate even though the evaluator said it would be important to explore with her in more depth whether she would be able to relinquish the child and noted Mrs. Whitehead had a tendency to deny her feelings. This basis for fraud was rejected when asserted against the Sterns on the grounds that the infertility center that conducted the evaluation was not proved to be the Sterns' agent. The Supreme Court did not address the fraud issue, holding the contract unenforceable as against public policy.

9. Substantively, the argument was that $10,000 was too low a price in view of the efforts and risks on the part of the surrogate. Procedurally, there were the information problems that also formed the basis of the fraud argument. Additionally, the Whiteheads had no lawyer when they entered into the contract with the Sterns. The lawyer who reviewed a similar contract document with them in connection with Mrs. Whitehead's work with another couple (not the Sterns) was under contract with the infertility center to act as counsel for surrogate candidates, a fact the Whiteheads used to suggest that the lawyer was not fully dedicated to their interests.

10. See Parker, Motivation of Surrogate Mothers: Initial Findings, 140 Am. J. Psych. 117, 118 (1983). In a sample of 125 women who applied to be surrogates, 44 had either had an abortion or had relinquished a child for adoption. Parker wrote:

> Some women believed these previous losses would help them to control and minimize any depressive feelings they might have in response to relinquishing the baby. A few consciously felt that they were participating in order to deal with unresolved feelings associated with their prior losses.

Id. at 118. Here are two chilling anecdotes from Parker's study:

> The only applicant who had been adopted had been "forced" at age 14 to relinquish her baby, and she wanted to repeat the experience of relinquishment and master it. One applicant who had had an abortion said that instead of "killing a baby" she wanted to give the gift of a live baby to a loving couple who wanted to have and raise a child.

Id. . . .

In addition, there seems to be a high risk of misunderstanding between the parties about the nature of the "deal"; the mother usually thinks, and is encouraged by those who promote surrogacy to think, of herself not merely as providing a paid service, but as giving a great gift, which merits abiding respect and gratitude, while the father and his wife often come to want her eliminated from their and the baby's consciousness, and they consider payment of money to settle their debt. The mother is cheated when she does not get the esteem she was encouraged to expect.

Oppressiveness as a reason not to enforce a contract also goes beyond a rationale of lack of valid consent. Denying enforcement of oppressive terms is based on respect for an underlying value that consent is thought to serve — freedom. Whether contracts are conceived of as exchanges or as relations, the point is to restrict future freedom to some extent, so it only makes sense to talk of "freedom of contract" as referring to the freedom to get the advantages of restricting one's future freedom. Where someone else will pay for a restriction on future freedom, it can be considered "an opportunity." Yet there is a stock qualification — that we refuse to take this reasoning to the extreme of allowing a person to sell herself into slavery.

There are very few modern instances of people selling themselves into slavery, so the widespread use of this hypothetical, in addition to its pedigree, seems due to where it leads. The next question, almost inevitably, is: what is sufficiently "like" slavery also to be impermissible in the name of consent and freedom?[11] One can attempt to account for limits on consent as a justification for enforceability by creating the category of "inalienable rights"[12] or, more precisely, "market inalienability."[13] But the language of inalienable rights tends to suggest that consent is a sufficient rationale for enforceability except in the most dire, extreme sorts of cases. This is argument by label.

Many sorts of deals or terms are currently unenforceable, or prohibited by law. Denial of enforcement is a mild legal response to

---

11. . . . Barnett concedes the illegitimacy of slavery contracts and the legitimacy of extension of this idea by analogy, referring to "agreements amounting to slavery arrangements."

12. [Barnett states] that contract theory must be situated in entitlements theory, and that one can only contract away alienable, as opposed to inalienable, rights.

13. See Radin, Market-Inalienability, 100 Harv. L. Rev. 1849, 1854 (1987).

contracts considered socially undesirable; it means the law refuses to foster a market in that sort of deal. Where promises restrict freedom in questionable ways, refusal by the state to enforce them means that consent of the promisor must be continuing (consent in the past is not enough). Keeping up good relations then becomes the only way to get mutual advantages, since external enforcement is unavailable. . . .

There are numerous examples of the law's response to contracts or contract terms considered socially undesirable in themselves. A contract term waiving the statutory right to discharge in bankruptcy is not enforceable. Wage assignments and blanket household goods security interests in consumer credit are not merely unenforceable, they are prohibited, with the lender subject to civil sanction for putting these terms in a contract. It is a crime to engage in loansharking, offering credit at very high interest rates with implicit agreed remedies such as knee-breaking, or to offer sexual services for money. Is it helpful, when drawing lines such as these, to think in terms of "inalienable rights"? This sort of "rights talk" seems designed to stop thought rather than to help get a feel for the limits the law should put on prior consent as a rationale for current enforcement. . . .

In sum, validity of consent and oppressiveness of the resulting deal are related reasons to deny enforcement. Drawing validity lines involves determining how much wealth, power, knowledge and judgment are necessary for an obligation arising from a contractual relation to be enforced against a now unwilling party. Drawing validity lines thus involves defining the conditions for freedom. In drawing these lines, it is helpful to look at both the procedure by which the obligation supposedly came into being and its substance. Rules denying enforcement of particular harsh terms and contracts are based in part on doubts about validity of consent. The rationale for these rules also goes beyond lack of consent, in order to serve the underlying value of freedom. The rules refuse enforcement where a contract places too great a restraint on freedom and puts a person too drastically in another's control.

STUDY GUIDE: *How does the following story illustrate the importance for "outsiders" of being able to legally bind oneself formally to an enforceable contract? What advantages and disadvantages of formalities are revealed by her story? Does it suggest anything for the relationship of contract and promise?*

WHEN ONLY A FORMAL CONTRACT WILL DO

*Patricia J. Williams**

Some time ago, Peter Gabel[1] and I taught a contracts class together. Both recent transplants from California to New York, each of us hunted for apartments in between preparing for class and ultimately found places within one week of each other. Inevitably, I suppose, we got into a discussion of trust and distrust as factors in bargain relations. It turned out that Peter had handed over a $900 deposit, in cash, with no lease, no exchange of keys and no receipt, to strangers with whom he had no ties other than a few moments of pleasant conversation.[2] Peter said that he didn't need to sign a lease because it imposed too much formality. The handshake and the good vibes were, for him, indicators of trust more binding than a distancing form contract. At the time, I told Peter I thought he was stark raving mad, but his faith paid off. His sublessors showed up at the appointed time, keys in hand, to welcome him in. Needless to say, there was absolutely nothing in my experience to prepare me for such a happy ending.[3]

I, meanwhile, had friends who found an apartment for me in a building they owned. In *my* rush to show good faith and trustworthiness, I signed a detailed, lengthily-negotiated, finely-printed lease firmly establishing me as the ideal arm's length transactor.

As Peter and I discussed our experiences, I was struck by the similarity of what each of us was seeking, yet in such different terms, and with such polar approaches. We both wanted to establish enduring relationships with the people in whose houses we would be living; we both wanted to enhance trust of ourselves and to allow whatever closeness, whatever friendship, was possible. This similarity of desire, however,

---

*From Patricia J. Williams, Alchemical Notes: Reconstructing Ideals From Deconstructed Rights, 22 Harv. C.R.-C.L. L. Rev. 401 (1987).

1. Peter Gabel was one of the first to bring critical theory to legal analysis; as such he is considered one of the "founders" of Critical Legal Studies.

2. The people from whom Peter sublet did not want their landlord to know what they were doing — a not uncommon feature of New York life; they told him they wanted to minimize the "proof."

3. In fact, I remain convinced that, even if I were of a mind to trust a lessor with this degree of informality, things would not have worked out so successfully for me; many Manhattan lessors would not have trusted me, a black person, enough to let me in the door in the first place — paperwork, references and credit check notwithstanding.

could not reconcile our very different relations to the word of law. Peter, for example, appeared to be extremely self-conscious of his power potential (either real or imagistic) as a white or male or lawyer authority figure. He therefore seemed to go to some lengths to overcome the wall which that image might impose. The logical ways of establishing some measure of trust between strangers were for him an avoidance of conventional expressions of power and a preference for informal processes generally.

I, on the other hand, was raised to be acutely conscious of the likelihood that, no matter what degree of professional or professor I became, people would greet and dismiss my black femaleness as unreliable, untrustworthy, hostile, angry, powerless, irrational and probably destitute. Futility and despair are very real parts of my response. Therefore it is helpful for me, even essential for me, to clarify boundary; to show that I can speak the language of lease is my way of enhancing trust of me in my business affairs. As a black, I have been given by this society a strong sense of myself as already too familiar, too personal, too subordinate to white people. I have only recently evolved from being treated as three-fifths of a human,[4] a subpart of the white estate.[5] I grew up in a neighborhood where landlords would not sign leases with their poor, black tenants, and *demanded* that rent be paid in cash; although superficially resembling Peter's transaction, such "informality" in most white-on-black situations signals distrust, not trust. Unlike Peter, I am still engaged in a struggle to set up transactions at arm's length, as legitimately commercial, and to portray myself as a bargainer of separate worth, distinct power, sufficient *rights* to manipulate commerce, rather than to be manipulated as the object of commerce.

Peter, I speculate, would say that a lease or any other formal mechanism would introduce distrust into his relationships and that he would suffer alienation, leading to the commodification of his being and the degradation of his person to property. In contrast, the lack of a formal relation to the other would leave me estranged. It would risk a figurative isolation from that creative commerce by which I may be recognized as whole, with which I may feed and clothe and shelter myself, by which I

---

4. *See* U.S. Const. art. I, §2.

5. As opposed to being a real part of the white estate. The lease of which I speak was for an apartment in Brooklyn; my search had started in Long Island, where two realtors had refused even to show me apartments in Port Washington and Roslyn.

may be seen as equal — even if I am stranger. For me, stranger-stranger relations are better than stranger-chattel.

STUDY GUIDE: How does Professor Kimel relate the intention to be legally bound to the "contract as promise" model? How does he think Professor William's anecdote illustrates the difference between contract and promise?

INTENTION TO CREATE LEGAL RELATIONS*

Dori Kimel

As textbooks uniformly inform us, "an intention to create legal relations . . . is recognised by English law as *a separate requirement* for the formation of contracts." And yet . . . textbooks and theoretical accounts alike tend to dedicate very little attention to the intention requirement. As far as textbooks are concerned, the main explanation for this neglect is probably the relatively little attention that the intention requirement receives in courts, itself the result of the casual (and, in the most common types of contractual dispute, largely justified) use of factual presumptions (to the effect that the requisite intention was present), coupled with obvious evidential difficulties. When it comes to theoretical accounts, however, the neglect may be owed to more substantial considerations.

In the framework of "contract as promise" theories in particular, the requirement of an intention to create legal relations appears to be rather trivial, if not altogether superfluous. For the "separate requirement" of an intention to create legal relations to be significant or even explicable, it should be possible to think of a reason why not to have such an intention in the relevant circumstances, or at least why not to ascribe it systematically to rational agents (in these circumstances) even allowing that they may not have actively or consciously entertained it. (When someone starts crossing the road, for instance, we can normally ascribe to her the intention to reach the other side of the road safely, regardless of whether or not we think that she is actively or consciously

---

*From Dori Kimel, From Promise to Contract: Towards a Liberal Theory of Contract (2005).

entertaining a specific thought to the effect.) And if it is thought that there is no pertinent difference between contractual and promissory relations, and even more so if the former are thought to be but an improved version of the latter — if contracts are understood to offer all the benefits of promises (or exchanges of promises) with the additional bonus of enforceability — then the chances of finding such reasons look rather slim.

With one exception, of course. A party who is not sufficiently serious, sincere, or clear about the obligation she is undertaking, would understandably prefer (or should prefer) the undertaking not to be legally binding. With such cases in mind, and in the context of "contract as promise" theories, the intention requirement can simply be understood as one way of making sure that the obligation in question was undertaken sincerely, seriously, or indeed intentionally at all. Thus understood, however, the intention requirement is rather trivial indeed. Obligations that have not been undertaken seriously or sincerely may sometimes be the subject of protective legal doctrines such as promissory estoppel or estoppel by representation, but are clearly not the normal case of making contracts, nor the normal case of promising. Similarly, people who are not entirely clear about what they are doing cannot normally be described as voluntarily undertaking an obligation of whatever kind, legal or non-legal. The "intention to create" requirement, in other words, pertains, under this interpretation, to the act of undertaking an obligation as such, and not to the distinct *legal* nature of the obligation; the seriousness it demands is seriousness about entering a binding agreement per se, with the intention to create *legal* relations accounted for as but an inevitable implication thereof.

The approach to contract I outlined in this work offers another way of ascribing significance to the intention requirement — a way which takes it to be a distinct condition, distinguishable from insisting on the seriousness or voluntariness of the undertaking of an obligation as such. With its account of the difference in terms of intrinsic function and value between contract and promise, and with the ensuing notion that there is something to lose, and not just gain, in opting for legal rather than non-legal relations, this theory allows for an understanding of the contractual intention requirement as a reminder that the scope for voluntariness or seriousness in making a contract may not be exhausted by the voluntariness or seriousness which is required in the context of exchanging promises. It recommends an understanding of the contractual intention requirement as stipulating that making a *legally binding* agreement should be voluntary; that the parties must be serious not just about undertaking an obligation, but about undertaking a legal obligation. For this theory comfortably accommodates the possibility that a person may be perfectly serious about doing the former, while not at all intending to do the latter; in (seriously, voluntarily) making agreements with others, people may opt not to enjoy the kind of reassurance that only the law can provide, in order not to lose the qualities which are often lost in the transition from non-legal to legal relations. They may wish to leave more room for the operation — and the transparency — of the "right" motives. They may think it worthwhile to sacrifice some confidence (inasmuch as added confidence is felt to be significant or even possible in the circumstances) for the sake of enhancing personal trust, knocking down barriers to potential closeness, increasing the likelihood of developing personal bonds, or reinforcing existing ones. And it should be appreciated that such a preference need not make sense only where the subject matter of the agreement at stake or the circumstances surrounding it are distinctly private or intimate by nature, or where parties have some unique ideological stance that militates against entering the legal framework. To varying degrees of likelihood and intensity, the preference not to sacrifice the qualities that the legal framework tends to compromise may be pertinent in all circumstances of making agreements.

Patricia J Williams, in the book *The Alchemy of Race and Rights*,[1] provides a vivid illustration for such a preference in a beautifully told anecdote comparing the experiences of two protagonists engaged in apartment-hunting in New York. One of the protagonists ends up concluding a lease deal informally — deposit in cash, no lease, no receipt — saying that "he didn't need to sign a lease because it imposed too much formality. The hand-shake and the good vibes were for him indicators of trust more binding than a form contract." In the circumstances, this seemed the best strategy for him to adopt in order to "establish enduring relationships with the [landlords], . . . to enhance trust . . . and to allow whatever closeness was possible."

I will want to return to this anecdote's second protagonist later. For now, we can see how, from my explanation of the possible rationale

---

1. Patricia J. Williams, The Alchemy of Race and Rights (1991).

behind the preference not to establish *legal* relations, a justification emerges for why such a preference should, as a matter of legal policy, be allowed. Precisely because something valuable may be lost, and not just gained, in establishing relations within the legal framework, the option of staying outside it — the ability to exchange promises or make agreements with others without necessarily being "captured" by the legal version of this practice — emerges as a meaningful freedom. It emerges as a negative freedom that serves a very significant kind of positive freedom: the freedom to develop and reinforce personal relationships through exchanging promises, or in other words the freedom to make use and enjoy the benefits of the intrinsic function of promise.

Of course, a fraudulent or a manipulative use of this negative freedom need not be allowed. A legal policy that sets out to protect it must still guard, for instance, against its cynical use as an easy way out of a regretted deal. But little seems to militate against a policy of allowing people to enjoy the freedom from contract in an honest way, in their activity within the legitimate bounds of the freedom of contract — or, as may be more appropriate here, the freedom of agreement.

The normative argument of the last paragraph may be valid from the perspective of one creed of political morality but not of others. What should be clear, however, is how naturally the freedom from contract fits with the liberal approach. We have seen that by allowing more scope for people to utilise the intrinsic function of promise, the freedom from contract is conducive to the pursuit of personal relationships. Thus it serves one of the central aspects of personal autonomy, however, is even stronger than this. For . . . the contrasting intrinsic functions of promises (enhancing personal relations) and contracts (promoting personal detachment) are both valuable for autonomy, and moreover . . . the value of personal relations and the value of personal detachment tend to be mutually-reinforcing when the ability to maintain detachment and the ability to have relationships co-exist as viable options in people's lives. Allowing people to enjoy the freedom from contract is one way of safeguarding the availability of this very option. And as a policy that helps sustain the conditions in which two autonomy-enhancing values reinforce each other, its place in a liberal frame of reference should be secure.

As I have hinted already, the practical legal implications of respect for the freedom from contract must not be exaggerated. As far as rules of evidence are concerned, for instance, the argument thus far need not be understood as advocating a radical departure from existing practices. Particularly when it comes to standard commercial transactions, employing the presumption that parties have intended to create legal relations, and asking the party who claims otherwise to satisfy the relevant burden of proof, seems to me to be a perfectly sensible approach, and in other contexts, more lenient rules of evidence already apply, and the presumption that the parties intended to create legal relations is employed more carefully, or not at all.

More substantially, it should be noted that the argument in support of respect for the freedom from contract does not entail that parties to agreements (or receivers of promises) that were not intended to be legally binding should never be entitled to any kind of legal protection. A person who suffers loss as a result of honest reliance on an unjustifiably-broken promise should, in principle and in the right circumstances, be able to have her loss recovered. In the absence of an intention to create contractual relations — and hence in the absence of a contract — she would not be entitled to contractual remedies as such; but while performance remedies may, as a result, be excluded, nothing I said here militates against the award, possibly in tort, or (the equivalent of) reliance damages, to redress the actual loss. This suggestion should not be seen as incompatible with the preceding argument. . . . Just as contractual relations are not the only source of liability for harm caused to others in general, likewise there is no reason to see such relations as the only possible source of liability for harm caused through an unjustified failure to discharge a voluntarily undertaken obligation. Only those who (like Atiyah) think that contractual obligations arise strictly out of reliance or that reliance damages should be the standard response to a breach of contract, are likely to see the possibility of awarding such damages *in the absence of a contract* as mounting some distinct theoretical challenge; and only those who (like Fried) fail to recognise the differences between contract and promise — and therefore the significance of the contractual intention requirement — are likely to struggle in explaining the award of *no more* than reliance damages *despite the presence of an agreement.* . . .

At this point let me return to Patricia Williams' apartment-hunting anecdote. We saw that the actions of its first protagonist — who is, I should now add, a white male lawyer — illustrated the possibility and the possible merits of a preference to enter a binding and yet non-legal agreement. But the anecdote presses home yet another point, one that hints at the often greater complexities involved in choosing a strategy for making an agreement. For its second protagonist, Patricia Williams herself — also a lawyer, but black and female — the strategy of eschewing legal formalities did not seem viable. Despite the "similarity of desire" between her and her white, male colleague, the only option open to her in the circumstances was to deal "at arm's length," speak "the language of lease," and make a formal contract.

For current purposes, I think we can draw several distinct (though not unrelated) lessons from this part of the anecdote. First, it simply serves as a reminder of those differences between contract and promise that have been one of the main themes of this work. It illustrates how contract can serve as a genuine substitute for promise when it comes to these practices' similar instrumental functions. Indeed, as far as renting the apartment is concerned, it could be said that contract, unreliant (or anyway less reliant) on personal relationship and trust as it is, saved the day: it provided the only framework in which this particular tenant and these particular landlords could strike a mutually-advantageous deal. Yet when it comes to the intrinsic function that contract, as a practice, fulfils, this part of the anecdote illustrates yet another point that has emerged in earlier discussions. For the striking feature of the comparison between the two protagonists' experiences is not that one sought relationship and the other detachment; it is that one had the choice whereas the other did not. And the case of the latter illustrates the notion that personal detachment and personal relationships are valuable, and at that mutually-reinforcing, particularly when they co-exist as options in peoples' lives. The second protagonist's case illustrates that *dependence* on personal detachment is itself not so much a thing of value but a predicament. In this respect, there is a symmetry . . . between personal relationship and personal detachment. When a person depends on one or the other for the realisation of any given goal, naturally she is better off having it than not having it — when a black woman needs to rent an apartment from (presumably) white, racist, sexist (or any combination thereof) landlords, she is better off having rather than not having the option of dealing at arm's length — but real value becomes a prospect particularly inasmuch as and to the extent that one-dimensional dependence is replaced by the freedom that comes with choice.

12

WHAT ROLE SHOULD FORMAL CONTRACTS PLAY IN CONTRACT LAW?

Formal contracts are not to be confused with "form contracts" discussed in Chapter 8. The problem raised by form contract, sometimes called "contracts of adhesion," concerns whether it is a good idea to enforce a written contract that is prepared by one party, the terms of which the other party usually cannot negotiate and often may not have read. Formal contracts, in contrast, raise the issue of which promises the law ought to enforce.

Before there was a doctrine of consideration, the only contracts that received reliable enforcement at common law were those in writing and under seal. With the rise of the writ of Assumpsit and the doctrine of consideration, the function of formal contracts under seal became uncertain. Although the Statute of Frauds has long required that some contracts be in writing to be enforceable, these contracts must still be supported by bargained-for consideration. In most jurisdictions, the seal is no longer a substitute for consideration. As we read in Chapter 10, Lon Fuller argued that contracts supported only by "nominal consideration" of, say, one dollar should not be enforced, as consideration is a mere pretense.

In this chapter, we consider whether the value of formal contracts has been overly discounted. First, we read a piece by Joseph Siprut, written while he was a law student at Northwestern University, in which he contends that contracts supported only by nominal consideration should be enforceable even in the absence of bargained-for consideration. In a portion of his article that is omitted from this excerpt, he establishes that, despite legal folklore to the contrary, contracts supported by nominal consideration are generally unenforceable, with the exception of option and guaranty contracts. But why, he asks, limit the enforceability of formal contracts to these particular types?

We then read from "Intent to Contract," an article by Georgetown law professor Gregory Klass in which he examines various common law rules that condition the enforcement of an agreement on the parties' manifested intent to contract. He employs the theory of default and opt-out rules developed by Ayres and Gertner (discussed in Chapter 2) to address the following question: Assuming arguendo that the law sometimes wants to condition the legal enforcement of an agreement on the parties' manifest intent that it be enforceable, what rules should the law use to do so? In general he concludes that heightened formalities are sometimes advisable to show an intent to contract, especially in social circumstances in which persons ordinarily make promises they have no desire to see and do not expect to be enforced as contracts.

STUDY GUIDE: *In the next piece, what reasons are offered for enforcing "gratuitous contracts"? Notice that he is not proposing enforcing all gratuitous contracts. Why does he think that those promises supported by nominal consideration should be treated differently?*

WHY NOMINAL CONSIDERATION SHOULD BE BINDING*

Joseph Siprut

Suppose a wealthy uncle wishes to convey a portion of his real estate holdings to his nephew. Although very pleased to hear the good news, the nephew asks whether his uncle might put the promise in writing.

---

*From Joseph Siprut, The Peppercorn Reconsidered: Why a Promise to Sell Blackacre for Nominal Consideration Is Not Binding, But Should Be, 97 Nw. U. L. Rev. 1809 (2003).

To satisfy his nephew's skepticism, the uncle drafts a document stating that "for valuable consideration of $1, receipt of which is hereby acknowledged," he promises to pledge "Blackacre" to the nephew. The purported consideration of $1 is never paid. The uncle signs and notarizes the document, affixes his own personal seal to it (handily ordered off of the internet for $99), and writes in block letters at the top of the document: "THIS PROMISE IS A LEGALLY ENFORCEABLE OBLIGATION." The nephew promptly takes the document to an attorney and asks if the promise is indeed binding. . . . Should a gratuitous promise be binding if the promisor so desires? And if so, through what mechanism? . . .

SELF-INTERESTED ALTRUISM

Although it is commonly presumed that gratuitous promisors are motivated by altruism, some evidence suggests otherwise. . . . Readers may well ask themselves whether the last time they stopped to give change to someone on the street they felt good about themselves afterward. They might then wonder about the degree to which that feeling of self-righteousness motivated the act of giving itself. . . . Today, however, most significant gifts are made either to someone in one's circle of friends or family, or to a charity. Those who make them are not motivated solely or even primarily by altruism.

Farnsworth . . . cite[s] professional fundraisers who argue that the merits of donor behavior models favor exchange over pure altruism: "To say that one asks for nothing in return is not to say that one expects nothing in return."[1] There are certainly other (self-interested) reasons why a donor might make a gift.

> [A]n expectation of an enhanced reputation is only one of many reasons for making a gift. In the case of a gift to charity, one might expect to gain tax advantages. In the case of a gift to a relative or friend . . . one might hope for love and affection or, if death seems near, better treatment in the hereafter. A decision to give often results from a complex mixture of these and other motives that sometimes are difficult to identify.

---

1. [E. Allan Farnsworth, Promises and Paternalism, 41 Wm. & Mary L. Rev. 385, 387-388 (2000).]

Although one may get something in return for one's gift, one does not get it as the result of a swap. Despite the exchange, there is no bargain.[2]

The foregoing suggests there is something amiss in the law of consideration. The Restatement (Second) majority rule that would have courts police exchanges for a bargain "in fact" neglects that many exchanges, which are not regarded as bargains by the Restatement (Second) and most courts, still satisfy the reciprocity element of Restatement (Second) §71. . . .

LON FULLER'S LEGACY AND GRATUITOUS BEHAVIOR BENEATH THE SURFACE

Commentators generally agree as a basic rule that society should foster exchange, though the justifications commonly offered differ somewhat. Most would concur, however, that if economic actors behave as rational agents, then no one enters into an exchange unless it makes them better off. A "regime of enforceable promises" is therefore justified because it increases the likelihood of beneficial exchange.

However, making more than nominal consideration a necessary condition for enforcement of a promise — i.e., policing for a bargain in fact — implies that only bargain promises play a role in increasing utility through exchange. This assumption is unjustified, yet finds itself enshrined in common contractual knowledge.

For the past fifty years, Lon Fuller's *Consideration and Form* has represented the standard account of the presumed nonenforceability of gratuitous promises (absent reliance). Fuller offered a functional defense of the consideration doctrine and argued that consideration was not merely a historical relic of English common law. His view posits that a promise should be enforced only if it satisfied the "evidentiary," "cautionary," and "channeling" functions of a formality such as the seal. Accordingly, "the bargain context . . . provided an 'informal satisfaction' of the 'desiderata' of the formal requirements (the evidentiary,

---

2. *Id.* at 388-389 (internal citations omitted) (emphasis added). . . .

cautionary, and channeling functions) after the formalities themselves were no longer available."[3]

Fuller goes further, however, and surmises that "[w]hile an exchange of goods is a transaction which conduces to the production of wealth and the division of labor, a gift is, in Bufnori's words, a 'sterile transaction.' " Thus, the legacy of Fuller's seminal piece is that the consideration doctrine serves the purpose of determining whether the interaction between parties is productive, and therefore worthy of the judicial effort of enforcement. Of course, because only bargain promises are upheld under the consideration doctrine, the implication is that gratuitous promises are not "productive."

In fact, however, the conclusion that a gratuitous transfer produces less utility than an otherwise comparable, but bargained-for, transaction lacks support. As explained in the previous section, unless a voluntary gratuitous transaction is beneficial to both parties, it will not take place. Moreover, no doubt based on this reasoning, the American legal system does not otherwise discriminate against gratuitous transfers once executed (*i.e.*, once the gift is delivered).

Wherever the law provides a facility for private ordering — the possibility of making an enforceable promise; of transferring property by sale, gift, lease, or will; of creating a trust, appointing an agent, or forming a corporation — as a general rule, it will permit and uphold any lawful undertaking on the same terms, without inquiring into its importance or wisdom.

What is more, if a contractual system that enforces bargain promises is justified because it increases the likelihood of beneficial exchange, then the same argument accordingly applies with equal force to gratuitous promises: gifts have a wealth redistribution effect (*i.e.*, wealth is redistributed to persons who have more utility for the goods or the money than do the donors).

The argument that gratuitous promises do not merit enforcement, therefore, cannot depend merely on the belief that the gratuitous transfer is itself of insufficient social importance. And if the apparent prejudice against gratuitous transfers is actually focused on the absence of a

---

3. Andrew Kull, Reconsidering Gratuitous Promises, 21 J. Leg. Stud. 39, 46 (1989).

"channeling" or "evidentiary" function, that would merely be an argument in favor of using formalities in the context of gratuitous transfers, but not for removing gratuitous transfers from the scope of enforceability altogether.

We have thus far seen that donors are often motivated to make gratuitous promises, not by the force of purely altruistic motives, but by the same self-interested purposes that underlie bargain promises. Moreover, contrary to the central tenet of Fuller's *Consideration and Form*, if the consideration doctrine serves the purpose of determining whether the interaction between parties is productive, and therefore worthy of judicial enforcement, then consideration satisfies what should be a sufficient, but not necessary, condition to enforceability. The presence of consideration might signal a productive promise and may evidence deliberation (thus satisfying Fuller's conception of the functional role of consideration), but the *absence* of consideration does not necessarily mean the promise is any *less* productive or that the promisor deliberated any less carefully than he might have with consideration present.

Accordingly, economic-based arguments that the non-enforceability of gratuitous promises is justified because enforcement would be an overly costly use of judicial resources misses the mark. Surely there are gratuitous promises whose enforcement would be cost-prohibitive — e.g., "a case where a man promised to take a woman to dinner but later reneged." But suppose the same woman promised to give the man a dance lesson in exchange for dinner, and that he ultimately reneged. Such a bargain would satisfy the classical consideration requirement, and yet suing to enforce the agreement would be an absurdity every bit as much as suing to enforce the gratuitous promise (if it were enforceable) would be. Likewise, the case of the wealthy uncle promising to give his nephew Blackacre involves a very significant monetary sum: "Why should we suppose that the cost/benefit comparison is necessarily unfavorable to enforcement?"

With this theoretical underpinning in place, this Comment now discusses more explicitly why having some means available by which to bind an otherwise gratuitous promise literally raises the value of the promise to both parties.

WHY GRATUITOUS PROMISES SHOULD BE ENFORCED

A gratuitous promisor may have a self-interested preference in making the promise to give a gift binding. In the case of any gratuitous promise to make a gift (but in which, for whatever reason, the promisor chooses to defer delivery), the promisor might wish to alleviate the promisee's potential uncertainty about its conveyance. The promisor, in other words, might wish to counteract the promisee's fears of non-completion. In so doing, the promisor enhances the value of the prospect of his gift by committing himself.

This point is more powerfully illustrated by way of example. Suppose an academic think-tank has organized a series of academic lectures throughout the country. The extent of the tour (i.e., the number of cities visited, the number of lectures per city, and the length of the tour) is contingent on funding. It happens that this particular organization, and most others like it, survives primarily on donations and pledges.

Now suppose that the business manager of this organization is informed that a donor has promised to give $10,000 to help fund the lecture series. Clearly, the business manager cannot open up the accounting books and record a $10,000 deposit immediately thereafter. In other words, the organization cannot plan $10,000 worth of lectures because there is no guarantee that the donor will actually make the payment. Therefore, the standard practice of any business in like circumstances is to plan future events based only on the pledge amount multiplied by the probability that the pledge will actually be executed. If past history suggests that comparable pledges are fulfilled only half the time, the organization will accordingly plan only $5,000 worth of events.

By contrast, if the organization knew the promise was legally binding, then the promise would be worth more than the amount the think-tank could otherwise record in the books. It might cost $1,000 to enforce a $10,000 promise, and there might be a risk of insolvency. But even so, the resulting entry will likely be higher than the alternative $5,000. Thus, the value of the promise to the promisee is literally increased the moment that the promise becomes binding. Perhaps less obviously, but of great importance here, because the promise actually equates to more dollars on the organization's books, the promisor will himself benefit in like manner. That is, if a promisor derives satisfaction from the degree of happiness experienced by the promisee because of the promise, it stands to reason that, if the promisee derived a greater degree of happiness from the promise (because the promise is enforceable), so too would the promisor derive greater satisfaction. . . .

Skeptics may still find unsatisfactory a legal rule that would enforce a gratuitous promise for a promisee who has "neither incurred a detriment nor conferred a benefit" and who would therefore "receive a morally undeserved windfall" from enforcement of the promise. Two responses may be offered to this criticism. First, as we have already seen, it is simply not the case that enforcement of a gratuitous promise — or the prospect of enforcement — would demure benefits to the promisee and not the promisor. Promisors may have a self-interest in making, and will enjoy the benefits that flow from, a binding gratuitous promise. Second, if preventing a "windfall" is a concern, it should be noted that the promisor stands in equal stead with the promisee in this regard. "Having made a promise in order to capture a benefit for himself, the [promisor] cannot fairly be allowed to enrich himself by breaching the promise. In other words, a strong element of potential unjust enrichment is present."[4]

MENDING THE BRIDGE: FROM NOMINAL CONSIDERATION TO GRATUITOUS PROMISES

Although this Comment has demonstrated that a promisor may have a self-interest in making a binding gratuitous promise yet lack the means to do so, "[m]any of us indeed would shudder at the idea of being bound by every promise, no matter how foolish, without any chance of letting increased wisdom undo past foolishness. Certainly, some freedom to change one's mind is necessary for free intercourse between those who lack omniscience."[5] Fortunately, this Comment has not proposed that all promises should be binding, but rather, that if a promisor seeks to

---

4. Melvin A. Eisenberg, The World of Contract and the World of Gift, 85 Cal. L. Rev. 821, 848 (1997).

5. Morris R. Cohen, The Basis of Contract, 46 Harv. L. Rev. 553, 573 (1933). It is also unclear why a yearning for "letting increased wisdom undo past foolishness" should reflect poorly on enforcing gratuitous promises. As noted, many enforceable bargains have also led some unfortunate contracting parties, reflecting in the wisdom experience brings, to lament their foolishness.

make a binding gratuitous promise, he ought to be able to do so.[6] The only task remaining, therefore, is to choose a formality by which to signal this intention.

Although use of a formality is necessary for purely evidentiary reasons, formalities . . . serve many of the additional ends that consideration serves. Legal formalities, such as a formal promise under seal, "facilitate in varying degrees at least seven functions: ceremonial, evidentiary security, cautionary, deterrent, channeling or earmarking, clarification and certainty, and economic efficiency."[7] Therefore, even if one remains committed to paternalism — i.e., if gratuitous promises are unenforceable for the "promisor's own good" — it is not clear why consideration rather than an appropriate formality would suffice to make the promise binding.

Carving out a doctrinal role for formalities quickly leads to the question of which formality should be adopted for the purpose of binding gratuitous promises. The seal, it may be said, had its day in the sun but failed to survive the test of time. The Model Written Obligations Act was a nearly uniform disaster, at least if acceptance by legislatures is the standard for measuring success.

Nominal consideration, however, could effectively fill this formality role in the context of enforcing gratuitous promises. This is so for several reasons.

Ultimately, the doctrine of consideration is one part of a larger system of rules and principles. Indeed, "jettisoning the doctrine of consideration from the common-law system of contracts might create enormous and unpredictable strains elsewhere in the system."[8] Adopting nominal consideration to enforce gratuitous promises, therefore, would not disrupt the "seamless web" of contract law, and consideration law specifically. In fact, using nominal consideration in this regard would make consideration doctrine more internally consistent. Although courts would have the world believe that they "will not

---

6. Opponents of the theory that a gratuitous promise should be binding if the promisor so desires, therefore, attack a straw man with assertions that enforcing all promises will have undesirable consequences. . . .

7. [Eric Mills Holmes, Stature and Status of a Promise Under Seal as a Legal Formality, 29 Willamette L. Rev. 617, 626 (1993).]

8. [Mark B. Wessman, Retaining the Gatekeeper: Further Reflections on the Doctrine of Consideration, 29 Loy. L.A. L. Rev. 713, 840 (1996).]

inquire as to the adequacy of consideration," . . . this is not true. Courts do inquire into the adequacy of consideration when they police for bargains that are "mere pretense." Attempting to determine whether consideration was "genuinely bargained for" is nothing less than inquiring into the adequacy of consideration, irrespective of whether courts disguise the essence of this endeavor with different language. Thus, to that extent, adopting nominal consideration to enforce promises would be a move toward greater doctrinal consistency.

Second, . . . nominal consideration already functions as a formality in contexts other than gratuitous promises, as demonstrated by the second Restatement's explicit acknowledgment of nominal consideration's role as a formality in guaranty and option contracts. Thus, the path to nominal consideration serving as a formality in the context of gratuitous promises has already been paved.

Third, many courts and commentators (and practitioners) apparently believe that the doctrine of nominal consideration already does function as a formality in the context of gratuitous promises — or even that it always has. Thus, introduction of the "peppercorn doctrine" into contracts law — in the context of gratuitous promises — would presumably be more seamless than introducing an entirely new legal apparatus.

Fourth, modern English law does accept nominal consideration as a formality in the context of gratuitous promises. Therefore, the common law of England, particularly the case law of the last fifty years, provides an empirical analysis of how using nominal consideration for this very purpose would work in practice.

Fifth, nominal consideration "represents a partially successful *judicial* effort to create a formality."[9] Courts at the highest state level are presumably empowered to accept the doctrine of nominal consideration as legally binding whenever they wish. Thus, the fate of nominal consideration need not turn on approval by state legislatures, as it might, for example, for the seal.

---

9. [1 Samuel Williston & Richard A. Lord, A Treatise on the Law of Contracts 983 (4th ed. 1990).]

CONCLUSION

That the legal adage "a peppercorn is sufficient consideration" has achieved cocktail-party popularity belies its true power as a legal formality. Nominal consideration is an operative formality only in the context of options and guaranty contracts. What is more, . . . nominal consideration has never been used as a formality to bind gratuitous promises. . . . Hence, the time has come to rethink the rigid delivery requirement of gift law. If a formality is to be adopted to enforce a gratuitous promise, nominal consideration is not only well-suited for the job, but it would also shore up the somewhat embarrassing doctrinal wrinkle in contract law caused by the current rules pertaining to adequacy of consideration questions and the general bar against enforcing gratuitous promises.

STUDY GUIDE: Notice how Professor Klass uses the concept of default rule we examined in Chapter 2 and opt-out rules to evaluate (a) when intent to contract should be presumed unless the parties say otherwise, and (b) when there should be a presumption of nonenforcement unless the parties expressly manifest their intent to contract. What three considerations does he think are especially salient to interpreting parties' intent to contract? How do they apply in the contexts of gratuitous promises and preliminary agreements? Note: when he refers to the "stickiness" of a default rule, he means the difficulty of opting out of it. The more "sticky" the rule, the harder it is to opt out; the less "sticky" the rule, the easier to opt out.

INTENT TO CONTRACT*

Gregory Klass

There is a remarkable difference between black-letter contract laws of England and the United States. In England, as in most civil law countries, the existence of a contract depends, at least in theory, on the parties' intent to be bound. The rule dates to the Court of Appeal's

---

*From Gregory Klass, Intent to Contract, 95 Va. L. Rev. (forthcoming).

1919 refusal to enforce a husband's promise to his wife, on the grounds that "the parties did not intend that [the agreement] should be attended by legal consequences."[1] Section 21 of the Second Restatement of Contracts adopts something like the opposite rule: "Neither real nor apparent intention that a promise be legally binding is essential to the formation of a contract." In neither England nor the United States is an intent to be legally bound sufficient to create a contract. An agreement must, for example, be supported by consideration. But in England such an intent is said to be necessary, while the Second Restatement says that it is not.[2]

But a closer look reveals a more complex picture. The enforcement of a preliminary agreement in the United States "depends on whether [the parties] intend to be bound."[3] In Pennsylvania, a written gratuitous promise is enforceable if it "contains an additional express statement, in any form of language, that the signer intends to be legally bound."[4] The comments to section 21 suggest that in the case of domestic agreements and social arrangements, "some unusual manifestation of intention is necessary to create a contract."[5] And the Minnesota Supreme Court has refused to enforce a reporter's confidentiality promise to a source because it was "not persuaded that in the special milieu of media news-gathering a source and a reporter ordinarily believe they are engaged in making a legally binding contract."[6] Nor is the requirement of an intent to contract in England so meaningful in practice. A presumption that commercial agreements are intended to be legally binding, together with other evidentiary rules, mean that, as Atiyah observes, in most cases it "is more realistic to say that no positive intention to enter into legal relations needs to be shown."[7] . . .

---

1. Balfour v. Balfour [1919] 2 K.B. 571, 578.

2. While section 21 accurately represents the rule in almost all U.S. jurisdictions, the United States is a signatory to the United Nations Convention on Contracts for the International Sale of Goods (CISG). Article 14(1) of the CISG establishes something like the English rule for contracts for the international sale of goods: "A proposal for concluding a contract addressed to one or more specific persons constitutes an offer if it . . . indicates the intention of the offeror to be bound in case of acceptance."

3. Alan Farnsworth, Precontractual Liability and Preliminary Agreements: Fair Dealing and Failed Negotiations, 87 Col. L. Rev. 217, 255 (1987).

4. 33 PA. STAT. §6 (1997).

5. Second Restatement §21 cmt. c.

6. Cohen v. Cowles Media Co., 457 N.W.2d 199, 203 (Minn. 1990).

7. P. S. Atiyah, An Introduction to the Law of Contract 153 (5th ed. 1995).

The parties' contractual intent is also of obvious theoretical interest. It is much easier to justify holding a person legally liable for the violation of a legal duty she chose to undertake than it is for one that she incurred by accident. Randy Barnett goes so far as to argue that liability for breach of contract is justified only if the parties manifested an intent to be bound.[8] Or there is Dori Kimel's argument that the English rule is necessary to protect from legal interference the special relationships morally binding promises create.[9] And the parties' contractual intent should be highly relevant from the perspective of economic theory. . . . Whether or not the parties intended legal liability is relevant to the incentives the law creates, for legal incentives have traction only on parties who expect legal liability. And the parties' intent to be legally bound is also strong evidence of the efficiency of legal enforcement, as informed parties will choose incentives that create the most value for them.

This Article examines various common law rules that condition the enforcement of an agreement on the parties' intent to contract. It treats the question of contractual intent primarily as a design problem: Assuming arguendo that the law sometimes wants to condition the legal enforcement of an agreement on the parties' manifest intent that it be enforceable, what rules should the law use to do so. Rules for determining whether the parties, at the time of formation, intended to contract are rules of interpretation, and I recommend evaluating them using the familiar theory of contractual default and opt-out rules described by Ian Ayres and Robert Gertner.[10] . . .

---

8. Thus Randy Barnett's theory consent theory of contract:

> In a system of entitlements where manifested rights transfers are what justify the legal enforcement of agreements, any such manifestation necessarily implies that one intends to be "legally bound," to adhere to one's commitment. Therefore, the phrase "a manifestation of an intention to be legally bound" neatly captures what a court should seek to find before holding that a contractual obligation has been created.

Randy E. Barnett, A Consent Theory of Contract, 86 Colum. L. Rev. 269, 304 (1986) (footnotes omitted). See also Randy E. Barnett, The Sound of Silence: Default Rules and Contractual Consent, 78 Va. L. Rev. 821, 861 (1992) ("To make a contract according to this approach . . . a party must explicitly or implicitly manifest an intent to be legally bound.").

9. Dori Kimel, From Promise to Contract: Toward a Liberal Theory of Contract 136-42 (2003).

10. See especially Ian Ayres & Robert Gertner, Filling Gaps in Incomplete Contracts: An Economic Theory of Default Rules, 99 Yale L.J. 87 (1989); Ian Ayres and Robert Gertner, Majoritarian vs. Minoritarian Defaults, 51 Stan. L. Rev. 1591 (1999).

[There are] three considerations that are especially salient to interpreting parties' intent to contract. The first concerns the relative stickiness of different interpretive defaults. . . . If the goal is to condition legal liability on the parties' intent to contract, and if the law uses an express opt-out rule, an enforcement default will be systematically stickier than a nonenforcement default. Express opt-outs work only for parties who know what the default is, what it takes to contract around it and, most importantly for present purposes, that the rule applies to them. If, for example, the parties have not thought about legal liability . . . or mistakenly think that there is no contract for other reasons . . . , they do not know enough to expressly opt-out of enforcement. Parties who intend legal enforcement, on the contrary, are at least aware that it is in the offing. Consequently, where the law adopts an express opt-out, a nonenforcement default is more likely to give parties who intend enforcement a reason to reveal that intent than an enforcement default is to give parties who do not intend to be legally bound an incentive to reveal theirs. In short, enforcement defaults are systematically stickier.

The asymmetry exists only if the opt-out rule requires an express statement of intent, such as adherence to a legal formality or saying that one intends enforcement. If an enforcement default is instead combined with a manifest-intent opt-out rule — if it instructs courts to examine the totality of the circumstances to determine the objectively reasonable interpretation of the parties' intent — parties might avoid legal liability despite their ignorance of the rule or of the possibility of enforcement. Because under a manifest-intent opt-out rule the parties need not undertake special acts to avoid the default interpretation, opting-out does not presuppose knowledge of the rule or its applicability. And while it is true that the risk of court error under a manifest-intent rule might cause sophisticated parties to expressly state their intent where unsophisticated parties might remain silent, the incentive to do so is the same whether a sophisticated party's preferences match the default or not. Absent additional empirical assumptions, there is no reason to think that, with a manifest-intent opt-out rule, an enforcement default will be systematically stickier than a nonenforcement default.

The second point concerns the potential value of sticky defaults and therefore also costly opt-out rules. Up to this point, the analysis has largely assumed that the only goal in interpreting the parties' intent with respect to legal liability is to better enable them realize their preferences — to enforce their agreements when the parties want to be bound and to withhold enforcement when they want no legal liability. That is, the above discussion has generally assumed that contract law's sole function is to give parties the power to undertake new legal obligations when they wish. It is far from obvious, however, that this is the law of contracts' only function.[11]

There is little doubt that contract law is designed to give parties greater control over their legal obligations to one another. In H.L.A. Hart's terms, contract law is a sort of private power-conferring rule. That fact does not preclude, however, additional and equally important duty imposing functions. The law sometimes imposes liability on breaching promisors not because they entered into their agreements expecting or wanting enforcement, but because the promisor purposively induced a promisee to rely on an act she then failed to perform, because she accepted a present benefit in exchange for her future performance, or because there is a social interest in supporting the practice of undertaking and performing voluntary obligations. Stickier defaults, and by implication costlier opt-outs, serve such duty-imposing functions. More to the point, they can mediate between the sometimes conflicting interests the law has in, on the one hand, granting parties the power to control the scope of their legal obligations and, on the other, imposing liability on parties because of extralegal wrongs they have committed, harms they have caused or other considerations. . . .

If the law has an interest, for example, in compensating promisees who have been wronged by a breach, it has that interest even in cases where one or even both parties might, at the time of formation, have preferred no enforcement, or where, in the absence of transaction costs, one party would have traded away her right to enforcement. This is not to say that a contract law supported by such principles must be entirely indifferent to party preferences. By combining an enforcement default

---

11. A more thorough discussion of the themes in this and the following paragraphs can be found in Gregory Klass, Three Pictures of Contract: Duty, Power and Compound Rule, 83 N.Y.U. L. Rev. 1726 (2008). The pluralist theory of contract law I describe in that article is something like a reinvention of Lon Fuller's wheel. See Duncan Kennedy, From the Will Theory to the Principle of Private Autonomy: Lon Fuller's "Consideration and Form," 100 Colum. L. Rev. 94 (2000).

with a relatively costly opt-out rule, we can permit sophisticated and sufficiently motivated parties to avoid legal obligations they would otherwise owe one another without significantly impairing the duty-imposing functions of contract law. If contract law serves both a duty-imposing and a power-conferring function, rules for interpreting the parties' contractual intent as a condition of contractual validity can mediate conflicts between those functions. . . .

The final observation concerns a special cost to the parties of express opt-out rules. Something like the idea can be found in Lisa Bernstein's description of why parties sometimes choose not to provide in their contracts for all foreseeable eventualities.

> Transactors may also fail to include written provisions dealing with a particular contingency because each may fear that the other will inter-pret a suggestion that they do so as a signal that the transactor proposing the provisions is unusually litigious or likely to resist flexible adjustment of the relationship if circumstances change. These potential relational costs of proposing additional explicit provisions may result in aspects of a contracting relationship being allocated to the extralegal realm, parti-cularly in contexts where the post-contract-formation relationship between the transactors is highly relational in nature so that transactors' perceptions of the value of the transaction will be strongly affected by the attitudinal signals sent during pre-contractual negotiation.[12]

. . . [S]ignificant relational costs would seem to apply to expressly opting-out of enforcement or nonenforcement altogether. An expressed preference for legal liability early in the transaction might be taken, for example, as evidence of distrust or a propensity to litigate. An expressed preference for no legal liability might be taken as evidence that the party might not perform, or that she does not trust the other side not to engage in opportunistic litigation. A requirement that parties who want, or who do not want, a legal guarantee of performance say so will in many contexts involve such relational costs. . . .

Viewed in the abstract, the design problem can appear intractable. There are many variables, we know very little about the values of some, and it is difficult to agree on the values of others. If the project were to

---

12. [Lisa Bernstein, Merchant Law in a Merchant Court: Rethinking the Code's Search for Immanent Business Norms, 144 U. Pa. L. Rev. 1765, 1789-90 (1996).]

discover a single rule for the broad range of agreements that qualify as contracts, the cost-benefit equation might well be insoluble. There is simply too little information and too much diversity to determine a single best generic interpretive rule. The design question is easier to answer with respect to specific transaction types, where our sense of the salient costs and benefits is clearer, and the values at stake less contested. . . .

A. GRATUITOUS PROMISES

. . . Many courts will not enforce a gratuitous promise in the absence of promisee reliance. This is so even if the promise is supported by nominal consideration, though the exchange of a peppercorn clearly expresses the parties' preference for enforcement. In the familiar words of Judge Woolsey, "The parties may shout consideration to the house-tops, yet unless consideration is actually present, there is not a legally enforceable contract."[13] As Williston and others have noted, this is an odd rule. "It is something, it seems to me, that a person ought to be able to do if he wishes to do it. — to create a legal obligation to make a gift. Why not? . . . I don't see why a man should not be able to make himself liable if he wishes to do so."[14] If one agrees with Williston, the design question is how the law should determine when a gratuitous promisor wishes to make herself legally liable for a breach of her promise.

The answer will include both an interpretive default and an opt-out rule. There are three reasons to prefer a nonenforcement default for gratuitous promises. The first is an empirical sense that nonenforcement is the majoritarian default. Most parties who make gratuitous promises neither want nor expect legal liability. Second, if the law adopts an express opt-out (and I will argue it should), there is the asymmetry in stickiness. A gratuitous promisor who intends her promise to be binding knows enough to at least ask what the law requires to make it so; the gratuitous promisor who does not intend that her promise be enforced because the idea hasn't occurred to her, or because she mistakenly

---

13. In re Greene, 45 F.2d 428, 430 (S.D.N.Y. 1930).
14. Handbook of the National Conference of Commissioners on Uniform State Laws and Proceedings 194 (1925).

believes that it is unenforceable for other reasons, does not. Third, there are general reasons to prefer less rather than more enforcement of gratuitous promises. One is courts' inability to adequately judge the defenses appropriate for gratuitous promisors. Melvin Eisenberg makes this argument with respect to improvidence and ingratitude:

> An inquiry into improvidence involves the measurement of wealth, life-style, dependents' needs, and even personal utilities. An inquiry into ingratitude involves the measurement of a maelstrom, because many or most donative promises arise in an intimate context in which emotions, motives, and cues are invariably complex and highly interrelated. Perhaps the civil-law style of adjudication is suited to wrestling with these kinds of inquiries, but they have held little appeal for common-law courts, which traditionally have been oriented toward inquiry into acts rather than into personal characteristics.[15]

Alternatively or in addition, one might see a risk that widespread enforcement will erode the value of gratuitous promises. Eisenberg makes this point as well:

> Making simple affective donative promises enforceable would have the effect of commodifying the gift relationship. Legal enforcement of such promises would move the gifted commodity, rather than the affective relationship, to the forefront and would submerge the affective relationship that a gift is intended to totemize. Simple donative promises would be degraded into bills of exchange, and the gifts made to perform such promises would be degraded into redemptions of the bills. It would never be clear to the promisee, or even the promisor, whether a donative promise that was made in an affective sprit of love, friendship, affection, gratitude, or comradeship, was also performed for those reasons, or instead was performed to discharge a legal obligation or avoid a lawsuit. Affective moral values are too important to be trumped by the value of autonomy, and would be undermined if the enforcement of simple affective donative promises was mandated by law.[16]

---

15. Melvin A. Eisenberg, The Principles of Consideration, 67 Cornell L. Rev. at 662 (footnote omitted).

16. Melvin A. Eisenberg, The Theory of Contracts, in The Theory of Contract Law: New Essays 206, 230 (Peter Benson ed. 2001).

Though enforcement is the stickier default, some promisors who prefer enforcement will fail to contract around a nonenforcement default. This residual stickiness is a good thing given the social preference for not enforcing gratuitous promises.

What of the opt-out rule? If Eisenberg's arguments are correct, we should also prefer an opt-out rule that is more costly to the parties, which will in turn increase the stickiness of the nonenforcement default. This will be an express opt-out, rather than an all-things-considered examination of the parties' manifest intent. But greater stickiness is not the only or most significant reason for an express opt-out. Such a rule also avoids the verification costs associated with manifest-intent rules, which include both the cost of judicial resources and the cost of judicial error. The risk of error might be of special concern in the case of gratuitous promises, for reasons Eisenberg describes.

The relational costs of requiring gratuitous promisors who want enforcement to state that preference are minimal. These are not cases where enforcement is requested as the price of a return promise or performance. Rather, a gratuitous promisor's declaration that her promise shall be enforceable is freely given along with the promise. In most cases, such an additional gift would not undermine the purpose of the gratuitous promise as a whole, or otherwise erode the parties' trust in one another.

If we agree with Williston that gratuitous promisors should have the power to legally bind themselves, the sensible rule is a nonenforcement default combined with an express opt-out rule. . . . This is precisely what the Model Written Obligations Act (drafted by Williston) proposed: "A written release or promise, hereafter made and signed by the person releasing or promising, shall not be invalid or unenforceable for lack of consideration, if the writing also contains an additional express statement, in any form of language, that the signer intends to be legally bound." Since its promulgation in 1925, only Pennsylvania and Utah have adopted the Model Act, and only Pennsylvania has retained the rule. Perhaps the problem of gratuitous promises is less important in practice than it is to the theory of contract law. Or perhaps there is a deeper resistance to the Act's premise: that promisors should be able to choose when they shall be legally bound to perform. The latter would also explain the law's refusal to enforce promises for nominal consideration, for a peppercorn is also an expression of the parties' intent to be bound. The explanation is not, however, that the Model Act is poorly drafted, or that it picks out the wrong rule for interpreting the parties' contractual intent.

B. PRELIMINARY AGREEMENTS

Turning to preliminary agreements, . . . courts will enforce a preliminary agreement only if the plaintiff can show that the parties intended it to be enforceable. To quote Judge Leval in *Teachers Insurance* . . . :

> There is a strong presumption against finding binding obligation in agreements which include open terms, call for future approvals and expressly anticipate future preparation and execution of contract documents. Nonetheless, if that is what the parties intended, courts should not frustrate their achieving that objective or disappoint legitimately bargained contract expectations.[17]

This approach is essentially that of the English rule . . . : it adopts a nonenforcement default combined with an opt-out rule instructing courts to look to the totality of the circumstances to determine whether the parties intended legal liability. In *Teachers Insurance*, those circumstances included the language of agreement, the context of negotiations, with particular attention to the parties' motives, the number of open terms, the extent to which the agreement had been performed, and usage of trade. Farnsworth lists yet more factors courts consider, including "the kind of parties involved, the importance of the deal and the nature of the transaction,"[18] all of which are generally verifiable only by way of extrinsic evidence. The result of this wide-ranging inquiry into the parties' contractual intent mirrors experience with strict applications of the English rule without the strong presumption of intent or other evidentiary rules: a high degree of indeterminacy in case outcomes. Thus Alan Schwartz and Robert Scott observe that "[a]ny list of relevant factors confines a court's discretion to some extent, but [courts' approach to preliminary agreements] leaves the decision process largely obscure when, as with these factors, courts fail to attach weights

---

17. Teachers Ins. and Annuity Ass'n of America v. Tribune Co., 670 F.Supp. 491, 498-99 (S.D.N.Y. 1987).

18. [Farnsworth, supra, at 261.]

to the factors or to specify the relationship among them."[19] Farnsworth is more succinct: "It would be difficult to find a less predictable area of contract law." . . .

If the problem with the existing rule for preliminary agreements is that the manifest-intent opt-out provides too little certainty or predictability, the simpler solution is an express opt-out. Rather than attempting to tailor the default, we should simply require parties who want legal liability for their preliminary agreements to say so, informing courts of their considered preferences. The parties at the time they enter into a preliminary agreement are in a better position to know whether they will benefit from legal liability than a court is during subsequent litigation. By conditioning legal liability on an express contemporary statement of that preference, the law can give the parties a reason to share that information with the court — to generate simple and reliable evidence of their intent. . . .

What of the other variables relevant to determining the best rule for interpreting the parties' contractual intent? A few facts bear mention. Most preliminary agreement cases involve sophisticated parties represented by lawyers in negotiations over high-value transactions. The negotiations are typically lengthy, complex and relatively adversarial. And in most cases that reach the courts, the preliminary agreement has been reduced to writing. Taken together, these facts suggest that it is generally clear to the parties that they are moving toward a legally enforceable agreement. What remains uncertain is whether they have yet reached one.

These observations suggest that neither the out-of-pocket costs of an express opt-out nor party error costs should be especially worrisome. Particularly where there is already a writing, the costs of adding words to the effect of "This is a legally enforceable agreement" are minimal. And if the parties are sophisticated players represented by counsel, the chance that they will forget to add them or expect enforcement in their absence is minimal. Nor are the relational costs particularly high. In most preliminary agreements, the scope of legal liability is among the issues under discussion. Legal enforcement is already on the table. This

---

19. Alan Schwartz & Robert E. Scott, Precontractual Liability and Preliminary Agreements, 120 Harv. L. Rev. 661 (2007).

diminishes the relational costs of having to say precisely when enforcement shall attach.

The above arguments all go to the value of an express opt-out. There are two reasons to prefer a nonenforcement default. First, that default corresponds to the more general aleatory view of negotiations in U.S. law. There is no obligation to negotiate in good faith, and parties are free to walk away from negotiations for any or no reason. Unless or until there is a shift in U.S. law in this area, an enforcement default for preliminary agreements would be anomalous and potentially confusing. The second reason lies in the temporal structure of contracting. Parties enter negotiation from the position no contract and eventually reach a point where legal obligations attach. An enforcement default would require some test for when the parties had reached sufficient agreement to flip the default from nonenforcement to enforcement. The nonenforcement default leaves it to the parties to tell courts when they have crossed that line.

Taken together, these facts recommend . . . a nonenforcement default together with an express opt-out. A preliminary agreement should not be enforced unless the parties said they meant it to be. Unlike the argument with respect to gratuitous promises, the reason for such a rule is not majoritarian, but turns on the value of an information forcing default. We can achieve greater accuracy at a minimal cost by requiring parties who want to be bound to their preliminary agreements to say so. . . .

CONCLUSION: FURTHER THOUGHTS ON THE RESTATEMENT RULE

. . . The above discussion provides new material for the interpretation of the generic rule described in section 21 of the Second Restatement. I have suggested elsewhere two possible readings of the Restatement rule. On the first, the rule expresses a principled commitment to sometimes imposing contractual duties for reasons other than the parties' contractual intent. Contract law requires neither "real nor apparent intention that a promise be legally binding" because our interests in holding breaching promisor's legally liable do not all assume party choice. On the second reading, the Restatement rule is not a statement of principle, but reflects a judgment about the epistemic limits of judicial institutions and the practical requirements of contracting parties. Even if the only function of contract law is to give parties the power to alter their legal obligations when they wish, the English experience has shown that, absent formalities such as the seal, the parties' manifest intent to contract is often difficult or impossible to verify, and therefore unsuitable as a condition of contractual validity. The Restatement rule, on this power conferring reading, establishes a majoritarian default, leaving it up to parties who do not intend legal liability to inform courts of that fact. . . .

Contract law is somewhat like tort law, in that both impose legal duties on persons not only because they expect, want or intend them. Unlike the tort law, however, contract law is also designed to give persons the power to purposively undertake new obligations to one another. The Restatement rule functions to balance these different and sometimes divergent interests.

13

HOW DOES PROMISSORY ESTOPPEL FIT WITHIN THE STRUCTURE OF CONTRACT LAW?

In his 1974 monograph, *The Death of Contract*, Grant Gilmore tells the story of how Professor Arthur Corbin of Yale presented Harvard professor Samuel Williston, the Reporter for the first Restatement of Contracts, with a set of cases in which recovery was granted but bargained-for consideration was lacking. Unable to square these cases with the bargain theory as then-embodied in §75 Williston and the American Law Institute, being, in Gilmore's words, "honorable men," were compelled to add reliance-based §90 to pick up the slack. Thus was introduced into the first Restatement the antithesis of the doctrine of bargained-for consideration. "We have become accustomed to the idea that the universe includes both matter and anti-matter," Gilmore wrote. "Perhaps what we have here is Restatement and anti-Restatement or Contract and anti-Contract." Or so the story was told to him by Professor Corbin.

The words of §90 bear out the prevailing theory that promissory estoppel is a doctrine designed to protect detrimental reliance upon unbargained-for commitments. The problem with such a reliance theory, however, was pointed out by Morris Cohen in *The Basis of Contract* over fifty years ago: "Clearly, not all cases of injury resulting from reliance on the word or act of another are actionable, and the theory before us offers no clue as to what distinguished those that are."

The first reading in this chapter questions whether the doctrine of promissory estoppel is primarily about the protection of detrimental reliance. In *The Promissory Basis of Promissory Estoppel*, the late Edward Yorio and his colleague Steve Thel, both of Fordham University, joined a growing chorus of contracts scholars who, in the 1980s and 1990s, had begun to question whether the doctrine of promissory estoppel was really about protecting reliance in the absence of a bargain. Instead, they contended, as had Samuel Williston, that promissory estoppel was really about enforcing promises in the absence of a bargain. If so, then promissory estoppel represented merely a modest expansion of contractual obligation (to address the underenforcement of the bargain-theory of consideration) rather than a radical reliance-based alternative to breach of contract as a cause of action.

In 1996 Professor Eric Mills Holmes of the Appalachian School of Law published a massive study of how the doctrine of promissory estoppel varies from state to state. He identifies a pattern of "doctrinal evolution," which consists of four distinct stages. The fourth of these, the "Equity Stage," transcends the previous Contract and Tort Stages, leaving Professor Holmes to conclude that contracts scholars should themselves transcend the debate over whether promissory estoppel is really a contract or a tort doctrine.

STUDY GUDIE: In what sense have Professors Yorio and Thel shown that promissory estoppel is not concerned with protecting detrimental reliance? Is there a difference between compensating for expenses incurred in reliance on the statements of another and protecting a right to rely on another's commitment? Or is their point that the doctrine of promissory estoppel is no more (and no less) about reliance than is the doctrine of consideration? Why do you suppose that so many contracts scholars have for so long spilled so much ink on this issue? Could this controversy be a symbol of a deeper disagreement about the proper role of freedom of contract?

THE PROMISSORY BASIS OF SECTION 90*

Edward Yorio
Steve Thel

INTRODUCTION

As conceived and drafted, Section 90 of the *Second Restatement of Contracts* is based primarily on principles of reliance. It rests on the proposition that a person who has led another to rely on a promise ought to compensate the other for any harm suffered in reliance. This Article shows that the prominence of reliance in the text of Section 90 and in the commentary on the section does not correspond to what courts do in fact. Judges actually enforce promises rather than protect reliance in Section 90 cases.

Section 90 has been described as the *Restatement*'s "most notable and influential rule"[1] and as "perhaps the most radical and expansive development of this century in the law of promissory liability."[2] The section has had a profound influence on the law of contracts because it ratifies cases enforcing a promise in the absence of bargained-for consideration. By giving its imprimatur to those cases, the *Restatement* has encouraged courts to expand contractual liability beyond the traditional doctrinal limits of consideration.

Most commentators, like the *Second Restatement* itself, hold that the objective of Section 90 is to protect promisees from loss caused by reliance on a promise. Some commentators even argue that Section 90 has contributed to the replacement of promise with reliance as the basis of contractual liability. As this Article shows, however, these commentators are wrong about the way courts have decided Section 90 cases. Rather than using Section 90 to compensate promisees for losses suffered in reliance, judges use it to hold people to their promises by granting specific performance or by awarding expectation damages. . . .

---

*From Edward Yorio and Steve Thel, The Promissory Basis of Section 90, 101 Yale L.J. 111 (1991).

1. E. Allan Farnsworth, Contracts §2.19, at 95 (2d ed. 1990).

2. Charles L. Knapp, Reliance in the Revised Restatement: The Proliferation of Promissory Estoppel, 81 Colum. L. Rev. 52, 53 (1981).

II. THE REMEDY FOR BREACH OF A
SECTION 90 PROMISE

[A]s frequently happens in promissory estoppel cases, the value of the
plaintiff's detrimental reliance need not be identical with, or equated to,
the value of the defendant's promise. The cases hold that the appropriate
remedy lies in the enforcement of the defendant's promise. The promise
here . . . consisted of the defendant's commitment that it stood liable
under the policy for the amount of the judgment against the plaintiff.
The measure of damages must therefore be the amount of the judgment.[3]

This passage from a California opinion evidences what Williston
discovered and reported in the 1920's: the remedy routinely granted in
Section 90 cases is enforcement of the promise either by expectation
damages or by specific performance. The passage also supports
Williston's simple explanation: for breach of promise, the proper remedy
is to put the promisee in the same position in which she would have been
had the promise been kept.

The *Second Restatement* and an array of academic commentators
disagree with Williston and the California opinion. They argue that a
reliance measure of damages is appropriate in Section 90 cases because
the promisee's right of action is founded on detrimental reliance. In
support of that proposition, they proffer cases in which courts awarded
reliance damages for claims based on Section 90.

This part examines the cases and concludes, with Williston, that
the remedy routinely granted is either specific performance or expectation damages. Those rare instances in which courts award reliance
damages involve either a problem with the promise or a difficulty in
assessing expectation damages. Some courts (like the California
Supreme Court in the quoted passage) explain an expectancy measure
by expressly tying the remedy to the promise; more often, courts grant
specific performance or expectation damages without analysis or discussion. That courts enforce promises rather than compensate reliance
under Section 90 is powerful evidence that the basis of the section in
the courts is promise.

---

3. Tomerlin v. Canadian Indem. Co., 394 P.2d 571, 578 (Cal. 1964).

A.   Expectation Is the Routine Remedy under Section 90

1.   The Reported Cases

Although the *Second Restatement of Contracts* sanctions reliance as the measure of recovery in Section 90 cases, the cases it cites in explaining Section 90 reveal that expectation is the normal measure of relief. The reporter's note references twenty-nine cases in which the promisee was afforded relief; twenty-four cases that awarded expectancy relief in the form of specific performance, expectation damages, or an injunction; and only five cases that awarded reliance damages or restitution. In the few cases granting a nonexpectancy measure of relief, an award of expectation damages was inappropriate for one of the following reasons: there was no promise; the alleged promise was not proved; the case was decided under a legal principle different from breach of promise; or, expectation damages were difficult to prove.

Recent surveys confirm that expectancy is the routine measure of relief in Section 90 cases. A 1984 canvass of cases decided during the preceding fifteen years found that the typical monetary remedy was expectation damages and that specific performance was granted whenever it would have been available in a comparable cause of action involving a bargain.[4] A 1985 survey of every case in the preceding ten years that cited Section 90 of either *Restatement* found that five-sixths of the cases that addressed the issue of the extent of recovery granted full expectation relief and only one-sixth limited recovery to reliance damages.[5] A 1987 article concluded that courts routinely award expectancy relief.[6] In cases of donative promises, the remedy is specific performance or expectation damages; in cases of commercial promises, the remedy is expectation damages unless speculative or otherwise unavailable under the normal limitations on contract damages.

---

4. See [Jay M. Feinman, Promissory Estoppel and Judicial Method, 97 Harv. L. Rev. 678, 687-688 (1984)].

5. See [Daniel A. Farber and John H. Matheson, Beyond Promissory Estoppel: Contract Law and the "Invisible Handshake," 52 U. Chi. L. Rev. 903, 907, 909 (1985)].

6. See [Mary E. Becker, Promissory Estoppel Damages, 16 Hofstra L. Rev. 131, 135 (1987)].

2. Explanations for the Prevalence of Expectancy Relief

These surveys strongly suggest that courts proceed from the assumption that the appropriate remedy for breach of a Section 90 promise is to put the promisee in the same position in which she would have been had the promise been kept. But the idea that reliance is the appropriate measure of recovery under Section 90 is so ingrained in the academic culture that commentators seem compelled to find nonpromissory explanations for the prevalence of expectancy relief. Some of these explanations are ad hoc rationalizations that need not be addressed textually. Others have a superficial plausibility belied by plainly inconsistent cases. All of the explanations share an almost total lack of support in the opinions: courts enforce promises by specific performance, expectation damages, or an injunction, without relying on (or even mentioning) any of the nonpromissory explanations for expectancy relief proffered by the academic commentators.

One common explanation links the prevalence of expectancy relief to expansion of the ambit of Section 90. Originally conceived as a vehicle for enforcing donative promises, Section 90 now is often used to enforce commercial promises. Commentators argue that the reasons for awarding expectation damages for breach of a commercial bargain led courts to grant identical relief for a commercial claim under Section 90: expectancy relief promotes beneficial economic activity or compensates for opportunities foregone in reliance on the transaction with the promisor.

This explanation for the prevalence of expectancy relief is seriously flawed. Section 90 originated precisely because courts were enforcing promises outside the commercial context in the absence of a bargain. The early cases on which the section was based delivered a critically important message: a promise may be enforced even if it does not further the process of economic exchange. Moreover, these early cases granted expectancy relief even though a donative promisee generally does not forego other opportunities. The early history of Section 90 thus belies the suggestion that courts award expectation damages to further economic activity or to compensate for foregone opportunities. Recent surveys also establish that expectancy relief is routinely granted in cases of purely donative promises. Of the twenty-four cases cited in the *Second Restatement* in which the promisee obtained expectancy relief under Section 90, eleven involved donative promises.

Another common explanation for the prevalence of expectancy relief is based on the difficulty of proving the amount of the reliance loss in many cases: the promisee may have suffered a nonquantifiable personal loss or may have incurred unprovable opportunity costs. Commentators argue that expectation damages in these circumstances are the best available surrogate for compensating for a reliance loss.

This explanation works reasonably well when reliance damages are difficult or impossible to calculate. As a general theory, however, it would be persuasive only if courts were to opt for reliance damages in cases presenting a choice between readily calculable expectation and reliance damages. The reported cases demonstrate the contrary: when they have a choice, courts choose expectation. . . .

Courts often face a clear choice between specific performance and reliance damages (or restitution) in cases involving improvements made to land. In the typical case, a promise is made to give a family member a parcel of real estate. The promisee then makes improvements on the property, and the promisor reneges. These facts present several remedial alternatives: reliance damages measured by the amount the promisee expended improving the land; restitution measured by the value of the improvements to the promisor; or specific performance. Courts routinely grant specific performance. Difficulty in calculating reliance damages or restitution does not explain this outcome, for courts find it easy to calculate and award reliance damages or restitution when the plaintiff fails to prove that a promise was in fact made. While in some cases a change in location or lifestyle by the promisee may constitute a nonquantifiable reliance loss, courts grant specific performance in other cases in which the promisee continued to live in the same area and actually benefitted from rent-free use of the property before the promisor repudiated. Even when the plaintiff demonstrably suffered no reliance loss at all because the value of rent-free use of the land exceeded the cost of the improvements, specific performance is granted. In light of the disparity between reliance damages and expectancy relief in these cases, courts would limit the promisee's recovery to reliance damages if their objective was to protect reliance rather than to enforce promises.

3.   Flexibility of Remedies under Section 90

Several commentators suggest that courts take a flexible approach to remedies in Section 90 cases. Some read the *Second Restatement* — in particular the language allowing courts to limit the remedy as justice requires — as an endorsement of remedial flexibility. The commentators identify several reasons to limit the promisee to reliance damages, including: good faith on the part of the promisor, disparity between the value of the promise and the cost of reliance, ease of measuring the reliance loss, and difficulty in calculating expectation damages.

The claim for remedial flexibility sometimes goes beyond the normative argument that courts *ought* to devise flexible remedies to the descriptive proposition that courts *have in fact* adopted a flexible approach to remedies in Section 90 cases. The reported cases, however, do not support this proposition. Expectancy relief is granted in the overwhelming majority of cases. Moreover, as the following materials show, of the factors identified by proponents of flexibility as justifying reliance damages, only a difficulty in calculating expectation damages explains cases that award reliance, and this use of reliance merely represents a concession by courts to practical necessity, not a preference for remedial flexibility. The only other factor that may lead a court to grant reliance damages is a defect in the promise or in proof of the promise. Rather than exhibiting flexibility, the reported cases actually demonstrate that courts operate within a remedial straightjacket: so long as a promise is proven and expectancy relief is feasible, the promisee is put in the same position in which she would have been had the promise been kept.

B. Reliance Damages Are Awarded Only in Anomalous Cases

Unlike judges deciding Section 90 cases, commentators have long resisted the idea that the proper measure of relief is expectancy. As early as the 1926 American Law Institute proceedings on the *First Restatement*, Professor Williston failed to convince members of the audience of the propriety of expectancy relief. In 1932, Professor Gardner argued that the remedy for breach of a Section 90 promise should be limited to compensation for loss suffered in reliance. Four years later Fuller and Perdue, after quoting extensively from Williston's remarks at the 1926 proceedings, argued that the reasons for awarding expectation damages for breach of promises arising in commercial contexts do not extend to gratuitous promises. Almost contemporaneously, Professor Shattuck argued that recovery should be restricted to reliance damages because the basis of the promisee's claim is injurious reliance on the promise.

In the early 1950's, Section 90 was examined in a number of articles that presumed that the purpose of the section was to protect reliance by the promisee. From that premise, the authors concluded that reliance damages were the theoretically correct measure of relief in Section 90 cases. These articles helped lead the drafters of the *Second Restatement* to shape Section 90 in terms of reliance.

The most obvious effect of the academic assault on expectancy relief is the addition of language to Section 90 which allows courts to limit the remedy as justice requires. This language is intended to sanction the use of reliance damages in Section 90 cases. Comment (a) to the new section asserts that reliance is a principal basis for enforcing promises even in the context of a bargain, and comment (d) goes on to state:

> [T]he same factors which bear on whether any relief should be granted also bear on the character and extent of the remedy. In particular, relief may sometimes be limited . . . to damages or specific relief measured by the extent of the promisee's reliance rather than by the terms of the promise.

The preceding discussion shows that the *Second Restatement* moves significantly towards making reliance the appropriate measure of relief in Section 90 cases. If reliance is the basis for enforcing Section 90 promises (as comment (a) indicates), and if the remedy is to be linked to the reason for judicial intervention (as comment (d) indicates), it follows that reliance damages are an appropriate (and perhaps required) remedy in every Section 90 case. Although a reliance measure is the logical conclusion of its entire approach, the *Restatement* itself equivocates by stating that "a promise binding under this section is a contract, and full-scale enforcement by normal remedies is often appropriate."[7]

The *Second Restatement*'s equivocation may represent a concession to the fact that the reported cases award expectancy relief. Professor Eisenberg nevertheless faults the *Restatement* for not providing explicitly that "[a] promise that is reasonably relied upon is enforceable to the extent of the reliance."[8] Without specifically criticizing the *Restatement* for not fully embracing reliance damages, other commentators endorse the general principle that reliance damages are appropriate. Sometimes

---

7. See Restatement (Second) of Contracts §90 cmt. d (1981). . . .
8. [Melvin A. Eisenberg, Donative Promises, 47 U. Chi. L. Rev. 1, 32 (1979).]

they qualify their endorsement of reliance damages to allow for expectation damages or specific performance when the promisor has acted in bad faith or when reliance damages would be difficult to quantify. But these commentators agree that reliance is the preferable measure of relief for breach of a Section 90 promise. . . . [T]his position is not supported by the reported cases. . . .

1. The Cases Cited by the *Second Restatement*

The *Second Restatement* uses five illustrations, each based on the facts of an actual case, to demonstrate the propriety of partial relief — particularly reliance damages — in Section 90 cases. The reporter's note cites three additional cases to support the same proposition. Commentators use the same cases to exemplify reliance as the measure of recovery. As the foundation for a reliance-based theory, these cases merit careful scrutiny.

The first of the *Restatement*'s illustrations is based on Goodman v. Dicker, in which the defendants, local distributors for Emerson Radio, encouraged the plaintiffs to apply to Emerson for a dealer franchise. The defendants induced the plaintiffs to incur expenses in preparing to establish a franchise by representing that Emerson had accepted the plaintiffs' application and would deliver thirty to forty radios. Emerson neither delivered the radios nor granted the franchise. The plaintiffs sued the defendants for breach of contract. The trial court found that the plaintiffs did not prove the existence of a contract, but held that the defendants were estopped from denying the contract by reason of statements and conduct upon which the plaintiffs relied. The trial court awarded $1,500 in damages, covering cash outlays by the plaintiffs of $1,150 and $350 in anticipated profits on the sale of thirty radios. On appeal, the court affirmed but modified the award by denying the lost profits on the ground that the "true measure of damage is the loss sustained by expenditures made in reliance upon the assurance of a dealer franchise."

Commentators often cite *Goodman* as support for a reliance measure of damages in Section 90 cases. However, a prerequisite for the application of Section 90 was missing: the defendants did not promise to grant the plaintiffs a franchise, nor did they promise anything else. They simply represented that the plaintiffs' franchise application had been accepted by Emerson. Although the appellate court refers twice to the defendants' conduct in terms of promise, its summary of the trial court's findings of fact describes the defendants' behavior as "statements," "conduct," and "representations," but never "promise." In limiting the plaintiffs to reliance damages, the appellate court itself describes the defendants' statements as "assurance." While *Goodman* is sometimes assumed to be a contracts case, the defendants were not in a position to make a promise. They were not employees or agents of Emerson, but merely distributors. Therefore, it is inconceivable that they were promising on Emerson's behalf to grant the plaintiffs a franchise or that the plaintiffs reasonably interpreted the defendants' statements as a promise. This may explain why the appellate court held for the plaintiffs on the ground of equitable estoppel. It may also explain why the court did not cite or rely on Section 90, an omission found odd by one advocate of reliance damages. But because *Goodman* is a case of misrepresentation,[9] the appellate court's failure to allude to Section 90 is not at all odd. Its decision to deny expectation damages and to limit the plaintiffs to a tort remedy (reliance damages) is a natural response to a claim based on misrepresentation rather than promise. . . .

The next illustration [of an award of reliance damages] is based on Hoffman v. Red Owl Stores. Hoffman, who sought a grocery franchise from Red Owl, was assured by a Red Owl agent that Red Owl would grant a franchise if Hoffman invested $18,000 in capital in the grocery. Relying on statements by the agent, Hoffman took various steps preparatory to operating a Red Owl franchise, including selling his bakery and purchasing and operating another grocery to gain experience. Negotiations broke down when Red Owl subsequently insisted that Hoffman invest a greater amount of capital, and Hoffman brought suit for damages under Section 90. On a special verdict, the jury awarded various items of reliance damages. The trial court sustained the verdict except for one item of damages. Red Owl appealed the entire judgment; Hoffman appealed the decision to set aside the one item of damages. Adopting Section 90 and applying it to the facts, the Supreme Court of Wisconsin affirmed the trial court on all issues.

---

9. See [Randy E. Barnett & Mary E. Becker, Beyond Reliance: Promissory Estoppel, Contract Formalities, and Misrepresentations, 15 Hofstra L. Rev. 443, 488 n.212 (1987)] ("[I]t is likely that the *Goodman* court based liability on tortious misrepresentation of fact, rather than on promissory estoppel.").

Red Owl is one of the most cited and discussed cases arising under
Section 90. The outcome conforms superficially to reliance theory:
Hoffman did not recover the profits he would have earned in a Red
Owl franchise. . . . [However, the] summary of facts referred to the statements of Red Owl's agent as "assurances," never as "promises." The
trial court repeatedly described the agent's statements as "representations," not as "promises." The supreme court itself conceded that the
agreement lacked the terms necessary for a binding contract, but found
the agent's statements sufficiently definite to constitute a Section 90
promise. The court may have found a promise, however, because it
saw no other basis on which to hold for Hoffman, shoehorning the
facts into Section 90 in order to afford Hoffman some relief for what
the trial judge apparently regarded as (negligent) misrepresentation by
Red Owl's agent.

Even if the court really did regard Red Owl's liability as based on
promise, Hoffman's failure to recover expectation damages is entirely
consistent with a promise-based view of Section 90. To begin with,
Hoffman apparently did not seek expectation damages, nor did he appeal
the trial judgment on the ground that he was entitled to expectation
damages. Because the issue was not raised on appeal, the opinion in
Red Owl is hardly an endorsement of reliance as the measure of recovery
in Section 90 cases. Moreover, expectation damages, if sought, would
have been impossible to determine for two reasons. First, the parties had
not negotiated terms essential to assessing expectation damages. Second,
profits of a new business like the Red Owl franchise are generally too
uncertain to be awarded even in cases of consummated bargains. For
these reasons, Red Owl may not be read as a rejection of expectancy as
the measure of recovery (where feasible) in Section 90 cases. . . .

C. Summary

The notion that the appropriate measure of relief for breach of
a Section 90 promise is reliance damages permeates academic
commentary. . . . The reported cases tell a very different tale. The routine remedy for breach of a Section 90 promise is specific performance
or expectation damages. Reliance damages are awarded in rare cases,
but only if no promise is made or proven or if expectation damages are
difficult to determine. Otherwise, courts grant expectancy relief.

The impulse to enforce Section 90 promises by expectancy relief is so strong that courts have resisted an academic consensus in support of reliance damages. Reliance theorists offer no persuasive explanation for the fact that judges routinely grant expectancy relief. It is telling that courts grant expectation damages even when the value of the promise greatly exceeds the promisee's reliance, an outcome inconsistent with the conventional, reliance-based view of Section 90. It is also revealing that the only substantive explanation for judicial decisions awarding reliance damages is a defect in the promise or in the defendant's proof of the promise. That expectancy relief (if measurable) yields to reliance damages in cases of defective promise but prevails in cases of relatively insignificant reliance confirms that in the courts, Section 90 is about enforcing promises, not protecting reliance. . . .

[In addition, courts] sometimes deny recovery under Section 90 even though the promisee has relied to her detriment on a promise. This outcome is usually justified on the ground that reliance was not foreseeable by the promisor at the time of the promise. If reliance were the basis of Section 90, harm suffered by the promisee would mandate a remedy and foreseeability by the promisor would not matter. In contrast, the courts' insistence on foreseeability is entirely consistent with a theory of Section 90 based on serious promise. The promisee's behavior is not central in a promissory theory. The prospect of reliance is enough to make a promise binding, even if reliance does not in fact follow, and action in reliance is not enough if the reliance was not foreseeable. . . .

In their influential article, Fuller and Perdue offer two possible explanations for the prevalence of expectancy relief in Section 90 cases: "[E]ither the expectation interest is preferred as a measure of recovery because of its greater definiteness . . . or the factor of reliance serves to release the impulse to compel men to make good their promises. . . . " Although they argue that there is no way of demonstrating which is the "true" explanation, they concede that if the "definiteness" explanation prevailed, we might expect the award of reliance damages whenever the reliance interest offered a relatively certain standard for computing damages. If, however, reliance is merely the catalytic agent that stimulates the impulse to hold people to their promises, then ease of measuring the reliance interest is irrelevant, and expectation damages will be awarded in any event.

We now know that, even when they are readily calculable, reliance damages are not awarded in Section 90 cases. We also know that expectancy is the routine measure of relief. Fuller and Perdue's alternate explanation for the prevalence of expectancy relief comes fairly close to the thesis of this Article. Reliance plays a role under Section 90, but it is at most the role of directing courts to a more fundamental objective: enforcing certain types of promises. Various circumstances can make a promise enforceable, including a bargain or meeting the requirements set out by courts under Section 90. In the collection of factors that make a promise enforceable, there is nothing special about reliance. Some nonbargain promises are enforced in the absence of actual inducement or detriment. Some nonbargain promises are not enforced despite detrimental reliance by the promisee. And even when reliance contributes to making a promise binding, it triggers a judicial impulse to enforce the promise with expectation damages or specific performance, rather than merely to compensate for reliance.

IV.   THE IMPORTANCE OF PROMISE

. . . The critical and difficult question about Section 90 in the courts is not whether to protect reliance, but whether to enforce the promise at issue. It is neither sufficient nor necessary that the promise induce the promisee to rely to her detriment. Every promise may influence the promisee's behavior, and yet not every relied-upon promise is enforceable. What distinguishes enforceable from unenforceable promises is the quality of the commitment made by the promisor.

Separating serious from frivolous promises is one of the functions of the doctrine of consideration. This function was served in Section 90 of the *First Restatement* by the requirement that the promisor reasonably expects the promise to induce definite and substantial action (or forbearance). Although the *Second Restatement* dropped this requirement, in *every* case it cites under subsection 1 of Section 90 that grants relief, the promise was expected to induce particular and substantial action (or forbearance).

The promisor's contemplation of particular and substantial reliance is important not in and of itself, but because it signals the quality of her commitment. Other circumstances may establish that a promise was sufficiently well considered for legal intervention. Thus, a promisor who expects a benefit in return for her promise is fairly charged with the seriousness of the promise. The promisee's situation may also indicate that the promisor's commitment was well considered. In cases of marriage settlements, for example, promises may be enforced even in the absence of actual inducement because of the possibility, foreseen by the promisor, that the promisee might change her behavior in reliance on the promise. Alternatively, promises made in the marriage context may be regarded as inherently serious because they involve what is traditionally viewed as a very important part of personhood.

The central importance of promise under Section 90 is well illustrated by charitable pledges and by promises to procure insurance. Pledges are often enforced when there is no reliance. Indeed, even the normal Section 90 foreseeability requirement may not be satisfied by a pledge to a general fund campaign of a charity because the promisor does not contemplate any particular act by the charity in reliance on the pledge. Yet many courts enforce this type of charitable subscription. Other courts pointedly reject the *Restatement*'s invitation to enforce pledges outside of the normal requirements of Section 90. These courts emphasize the lack of consideration and the fact that the pledge was not directed to a specific project expected to be undertaken by the charity.

Although courts differ somewhat on the enforcement of pledges, the likelihood of enforcement generally varies with the quality of the promisor's commitment. Perhaps the easiest case is a pledge made in exchange for consideration furnished by the charity, such as naming a building for the donor. Somewhat more problematic — but still routinely enforced — are pledges made not in return for consideration, but with the promisor's knowledge that the charity might use the pledged funds for some particular and substantial project. If the promisor does not receive consideration or contemplate reliance by the charity, the risk is greater that the pledge was not seriously considered. Not surprisingly, therefore, some courts refuse to enforce such a pledge. Other courts apparently regard every promise made to a charitable institution engaged in good work as a promise that ought to be enforced. While it may seem wrong to break any promise, it may seem more wrong for someone to break a promise to support the work of an organization that she has recognized (by her promise) selflessly does good work.

Like charitable pledges, promises to procure insurance may be enforced in the absence of reliance by the promisee. Here, too, enforcement depends on the quality of the promisor's commitment. The *Second Restatement* states that courts should be cautious about enforcing insurance promises because of the severe consequences to the promisor: for failing to pay a small premium, she may be liable for the amount of a very large policy. Despite its warning, the *Restatement* proceeds to catalogue various factors that may justify enforcement even absent actual reliance, including the formality of the promise, part performance by the promisor, a commercial setting, or potential benefit to the promisor.

If the objective of Section 90 were to protect reliance, the formality of a promise could not substitute for reliance. On the contrary, formality matters only as evidence of the promisor's seriousness. Similarly, partial performance indicates that the promise was made with the intention of performing. Promises made in a commercial setting or with the expectation of obtaining a potential benefit are more likely to be serious than promises made in a purely donative context. Thus, each of the factors adduced by the *Restatement* indicates that the promise was likely to have been well considered; none relates to reliance by the promisee.

In addition, the promisor's commitment is generally likely to be serious because of the possibility, even if remote, that the promise might keep the promisee from obtaining insurance. This possibility should alert the promisor to the potentially severe consequences of making and breaching her promise. Thus, the *Restatement*'s argument for caution in enforcing these promises actually cuts the other way: a promise to procure insurance is almost certainly serious because performance involves relatively little cost and the consequence of not performing may be substantial loss to the insured.

Cases that fall within subsection 1 of Section 90, cases of charitable pledges and cases of insurance promises, all involve nonbargain promises. Enforcement depends not on the promisee's reliance, but on the seriousness of the promisor's commitment. The central importance of commitment is also shown by the many cases in which a fault with the promise leads the court to deny the plaintiff any relief. In nine of the ten cases cited by the *Second Restatement* in which the plaintiff does not obtain any relief, the outcome turns largely on a problem with the promise. When the plaintiff obtains partial relief, virtually the only substantive explanation is a defect in the promise or in the defendant's proof of the promise.

When courts award reliance damages in cases of defective promise or misrepresentation, they are vindicating the plaintiff's interest in not being harmed by the defendant's conduct. The wrong resembles that done by driving an automobile negligently and injuring a pedestrian.

By putting the plaintiff in the same position as before the deficient statements were made, reliance damages serve the same objective served by damages awarded to compensate for injury caused by negligence.

The theory of liability in these cases differs radically from that in the typical Section 90 case. Courts enforce promises under Section 90 when they view the promises as serious and deserving of enforcement qua promise; they do not enforce them out of solicitude for promisees. The promisor's commitment may be shown to be sufficiently serious by her contemplation of particular and substantial reliance, by the formality of the promise, by the situation of the promisee, or by a chance of benefit to the promisor. The importance to courts of promise explains why the remedy for breach of a Section 90 promise is invariably expectancy relief (if measurable); why the absence of inducement and detriment is irrelevant; why some promises are not enforced despite detrimental reliance; and why the outcome (in terms of both liability and remedy) generally turns on some aspect of promise.

CONCLUSION

The central question of contract law is: Which promises ought to be enforced? Fuller and Perdue assumed that the legal rules used to sift out promises for enforcement were based on interests of promisees, and many other scholars agree. Promisees have legitimate interests in promises being kept, and studying those interests can be very enlightening. In the context of Section 90 promises, however, those interests neither determine which promises are enforced nor the extent to which they are enforced. Judges respond instead to "the impulse to hold men to their promises."[10]

Conventional wisdom maintains that Section 90 holds promisors liable because a person who makes a promise causing another to act in reliance should compensate the other for her injury. However, when courts routinely grant specific performance or expectation damages, they do more than simply protect promisees from harm. Similarly, when courts grant relief despite convincing evidence that the promise neither induced reliance nor caused detriment, and when they deny relief despite

---

10. [Lon L. Fuller & William R. Perdue, Jr., The Reliance Interest in Contract Damages (pts. 1-2), 46 Yale L.J. 52, 70 (1936-1937).]

detrimental reliance, their motivation cannot be to protect promisees from injury caused by reliance on a promise.

Like the rest of contract law, Section 90 is about promises. What distinguishes enforceable promises from unenforceable ones under Section 90 are the proof and quality of the promisor's commitment. Whenever the criteria for a serious commitment by the promisor are satisfied, the promisee obtains full expectancy relief (if feasible) for the breach. Issues of both liability and remedy under Section 90 turn on promise, not reliance.

Section 90 has greatly expanded the scope of civil liability in twentieth-century American law. Contrary to received wisdom, that expansion has occurred in the contractual context of promise rather than the tort-related context of reliance. Far from evidencing the death of contract, the application of Section 90 by the courts demonstrates that promise is more vital than ever.

STUDY GUIDE: *In what sense does Professor Holmes' case research undermine the thesis of Professors Yorio and Thel? Do Yorio and Thel claim that promissory estoppel is waning? Professor Holmes contends that Equity Stage Four is the highest and best form of promissory estoppel. Do you agree? Can you see advantages to Contract Stage Two or Tort Stage Three? Is "evolution" always a good thing? For example, is the "evolution" from limited government to expansive government necessarily an improvement?*

THE FOUR EVOLUTIONARY STAGES OF PROMISSORY ESTOPPEL*

Eric Mills Holmes

INTRODUCTION

Promissory estoppel, it is said, is waning. As Twain might observe, that report appears greatly exaggerated. For instance, this Article

---

*From Eric Mills Holmes, Restatement of Promissory Estoppel, 32 Willamette L. Rev. 263 (1996). Sections have been renumbered.

establishes for the first time that all American jurisdictions (including American Samoa, Guam, Puerto Rico, and the Virgin Islands) have adopted and apply a doctrine of "promissory estoppel" grounded in Section 90 of the *Contracts Restatements*. Moreover, two jurisdictions (Georgia and Louisiana) have adopted promissory estoppel by statute. Furthermore, an evolving body of federal common law of promissory estoppel, predicated primarily on Section 90 of the *Restatement (Second) of Contracts*, has arisen in the 1990s. Federal courts apply this evolving federal common law of promissory estoppel under sundry federal acts. . . .

Rather than waning, the law of promissory estoppel is, as naturally as birth and death, subject to the evolutionary process by which our system of law develops. Far from death, promissory estoppel steadfastly has evolved in the common-law tradition for over five centuries. . . .

As an overview, promissory estoppel evolved in the American cases in four developmental stages: (1) *Estoppel Phase*, consisting initially of "defensive equitable estoppel" to estop contract defenses based on statutes of limitations and of frauds, and perhaps the parol evidence rule. In the second part of this first phase, courts extended "estoppel" based on representations of facts to "promissory" representations and enforced the promissory basis of the representation that created an affirmative theory of relief. Thus, this first stage consisted of defensive equitable (promissory) estoppel, and then offensive equitable (promissory) estoppel. (2) *Contract Phase*, in which promissory estoppel developed as a consideration substitute that courts used to validate promises and to award traditional-contract expectation damages, including lost profits. (3) *Tort Phase*, in which courts recognized a promisee's right to rely and a promissor's duty to prevent (or not cause) reasonably foreseeable, detrimental reliance. During this third phase, courts applied promissory estoppel as an offensive doctrine (independent of contract) for awarding reliance damages. (4) *Equity Phase*, in which courts assimilate the earlier three phases (estoppel, contract, and tort) and apply promissory estoppel as an equitable theory to rectify wrongs by awarding corrective relief based on the discrete facts of each case. The remedy is discretionary, with no mechanical bright line. Courts equitably fashion the remedy for each case to "fit the crime," which can include the full range of remedies (expectation, reliance, restitution, specific performance, and sometimes exemplary).

1. Estoppel Stage One: Defensive and Offensive Equitable Estoppel

Commencing with cases in the nineteenth century, this initial stage evidences promissory estoppel in its American genesis, an assimilation of two developmental attributes from the equitable principle of estoppel. First, estoppel provided the doctrine with a defensive reliance shield to estop contract defenses (e.g., statutes of limitations and frauds, and the parol evidence rule) from being raised. Second, estoppel gave promissory estoppel an offensive sword, empowering courts to award affirmative remedies. Estoppel's basis for affirmative relief arose when courts characterized promises as representations of fact for the application of equitable estoppel. All American jurisdictions have decisions that assimilate these attributes into their earliest common law of promissory estoppel. The doctrine thereafter continued seasonably to evolve. Only North Carolina and Virginia . . . arguably can be described as mired in this first stage of evolution.

a. Defensive Equitable "Promissory" Estoppel

The defensive reliance shield of estoppel arose historically when parties (who suffered losses in reliance on contracts that were unenforceable due to the Statute of Frauds or a statute of limitations) defensively declared that the other party was "estopped" to claim the statute as a defense. Initially, the courts estopped the other party from claiming the statute only if the doctrine of equitable estoppel applied, which required reliance on a misrepresentation of past or present fact. At that time, however, equitable estoppel did not apply to representations of future fact, or intentions regarding the future, or executory promises.

Gradually, the "equitable" basis of estoppel was extended judicially to include reliance on oral promises and on contracts. . . . In response to these early cases, the *Restatement (Second) of Contracts* added a new section that recognizes promissory estoppel as a shield to block a defense under the Statute of Frauds. Most, but not all, jurisdictions recognize promissory estoppel as a defensive reliance aegis to statutes of limitations and statutes of frauds (both general and UCC). Surprisingly, even North Carolina, which declares it does not adopt promissory estoppel as an affirmative cause of action, warmly embraces promissory estoppel as a bastion against the Statute of Frauds.

Courts apply the defensive nature of promissory estoppel throughout the other three evolutionary stages in five contexts: (1) to estop another from raising a statute of frauds and (2) statute of limitations, (3) the lack of consideration (i.e., as a consideration substitute explained in the next Stage Two), (4) indefinite promises, and (5) the parol evidence rule. . . . Thus, Part II of this Article will not discuss the defensive reliance shield further, with one important exception — the parol evidence rule.

. . . Two lines of cases apparently hold that promissory estoppel cannot "estop" the application of the parol evidence rule. First, a paucity of cases directly hold that promissory estoppel cannot operate in the face of the parol evidence rule because the prior or contemporaneous promise is not integrated in the written agreement. Second, there are decisions, which do not mention the parol evidence rule and presumably do not recognize the issue, holding: "Promissory estoppel is not a doctrine designed to give a party to a negotiated commercial bargain a second bite at the apple in the event it fails to prove a breach of contract."[1] In effect, these decisions hold that promissory estoppel cannot apply when there is a written contract validated for bargained-for consideration. In contrast, a strong line of decisions initially applied equitable estoppel, and later promissory estoppel, to block or end-run the parol evidence rule by holding that collateral oral statements failed to merge into a written contract.

In a significant decision under Florida law, the Fifth Circuit Court of Appeals applied promissory estoppel to enforce an insurance agent's statement made to the insured (a soldier later killed in Viet Nam) that the policy would not contain a war exclusion clause. The court held:

> Prudential argues that under no theory may this Court take cognizance of the agent's promise and its inequitable conduct because of the Florida rule that any matters transpiring prior to or contemporaneous with the signing of an application for insurance are waived or merged into the application. The rule is nothing more than an embodiment of the parol evidence rule. [The jury's verdict for the insured] recognized a duty of Prudential, dehors the writing, to act in an honorable and upright way in accordance with its agent's promise. Thus, application of promissory estoppel in no way trammels upon the parol evidence rule. Involved here

---

1. Walker v. KFC Corp., 728 F.2d 1215, 1220 (9th Cir. 1984) (applying California law). Arguably, such decisions hold that promissory estoppel is inapplicable when bargained-for consideration is present. . . .

is a separate enforceable promise and not a variance or modification of the terms of the policy.[2]

b.   Offensive Equitable "Promissory" Estoppel

The pivotal decision in *Prudential Insurance* naturally leads to the final trait of promissory estoppel in Stage One, the progression of decisions from adapting equitable estoppel to adopting promissory estoppel as an affirmative theory of recovery. Selected insurance cases will illustrate that progression. Consider this straightforward example: A party asks an insurance agent if a particular matter is covered by a certain kind of insurance policy. Although the written policy does not cover the matter, the agent responds: "We've got you covered," or "We cover you for $7,500, and you are fully covered," or similar assurances. Did the insurance agent make a representation of fact or a promise regarding coverage? In reality, it makes little difference as long as estoppel is applied affirmatively to enforce the agent's statement. Thus, whereas earlier decisions applied defensive equitable estoppel, modern decisions — felicitously following the principles of good faith, conscience, and equity underpinning estoppel — apply promissory estoppel as an affirmative cause of action to validate and enforce the agent's promise.

The transition from equitable to promissory estoppel underwrites the transition to Contract Stage Two in the evolution of promissory estoppel. In evolving to Contract Stage Two, promissory estoppel adapts the defensive nature of estoppel and puts estoppel's equitable basis of recovery on more accurate, affirmative grounds. . . .

2.   Contract Stage Two: Promissory Estoppel
as Consideration Substitute

The second historical stage finds courts applying promissory estoppel as a consideration substitute to validate and enforce promises (not

---

2. Prudential Ins. Co. v. Clark, [456 F.2d 932, 937 (5th Cir. 1972)] (citations omitted).

purchased or bargained for) and awarding contractual expectation damages. The early twentieth-century cases led to the adoption of Section 90 in the first Restatement of Contracts, which led to the general acceptance of promissory estoppel as a substitute for consideration. In legally binding promises, these decisions use a technique of "estoppel to deny consideration" to justify a traditional contract expectation judgment. While older decisions speak of "estoppel" or "equitable estoppel," as explained in Stage One, modern decisions say "promissory estoppel." This classic defensive use of estoppel (from Estoppel Stage One) to deny consideration commonly is understood as making promissory estoppel synonymous with, and the equivalent of, consideration *(locum tenens)*. Conceptually at Stage Two, promissory estoppel is a defensive shield (protecting a contract right) but is not an offensive sword (creating a new right).

That the consideration substitute was the second stage may elicit wonder given a general assumption that detrimental-reliance-damage cases came second in time. However, . . . American jurisdictions have consideration substitute cases that typically follow (or occur contemporaneously with) Estoppel Stage One. If a study were made of only those abundant decisions, one would deduce that promissory estoppel is a contract theory with its basis grounded in promises and classical benefit-ofthe-bargain remedies.[3] Most jurisdictions, however, have advanced beyond this consideration substitute stage.

Nonetheless, approximately sixteen jurisdictions linger, some resolutely, at Contract Stage Two.[4] Indeed, jurisdictions that have not progressed beyond this contract stage focus their promissory estoppel law on the requirement of a "promise." To trigger Section 90, they hold that the promise must be clear, definite, and unambiguous (i.e., an

---

3. See, e.g., Edward Yorio and Steve Thel, The Promissory Basis of Section 90, 101 Yale L.J. 111, 111 (1991) ("This Article shows that the prominence of reliance in the text of Section 90 and in the commentary on the section does not correspond to what courts do in fact. Judges actually enforce promises rather than protect reliance in Section 90 cases.").

4. Given our common-law system of gradually evolving decisions on a common subject, it is difficult to draw precise border lines. With that disclaimer, these jurisdictions have not evolved beyond Stage Two: Arizona, Georgia, Idaho, Iowa, Kansas, Kentucky, Maine, Maryland, Michigan, Missouri, Montana, Nevada, New Hampshire, North Dakota, Rhode Island, and West Virginia. If reasonable minds may differ, Kansas and Missouri conceivably could be at Tort Stage Three.

"offer"). Based on this heightened requirement of promise qua offer, the sixteen jurisdictions draw legal conclusions such as: "An expression of an intention to do something is not a promise."[5] Such holdings ignore the *Restatement (Second)*'s definition: "A promise is a manifestation of intention to act or refrain from acting in a specified way, so made to justify a promisee in understanding that a commitment has been made." However, the requisite promise typically is elevated in sixteen state courts to the stature of an "offer" to "presentiate" a contract. As a consequence, promissory estoppel is held inapplicable in most of their court opinions. Some of the sixteen restrict the doctrine even further. Idaho, Iowa, Wyoming, and perhaps Georgia hold that the first element of promissory estoppel is a "clear and definite agreement." As the Idaho Supreme Court explained: "Under contract law, promissory estoppel, when proven, acts as a consideration substitute in the formation of a contract. While promissory estoppel may provide consideration for a contract, there must be a sufficiently definite agreement to have an enforceable contract."[6] . . .

Finally, the majority of approximately thirty-four jurisdictions do not restrict the equitable doctrine of promissory estoppel to the status of a contractual consideration substitute. In the renowned 1938 opinion of Fried v. Fisher,[7] the Pennsylvania high court explained that the promissory estoppel "doctrine is not so much one of contract, with a substitute for consideration, as an application of the general principle of estoppel." As a fitting transition to Tort Stage Three, the South Carolina Supreme Court ruled that promissory estoppel is not the legal equivalent of a contract even when used as a consideration substitute. Rather, it is the application of an equitable principle:

> The circumstances which may trigger the application of promissory estoppel in this case cannot be tortured into the requisite elements of a traditional contract. A contract and promissory estoppel are two

---

5. School Dist. No. 69 v. Altherr, 458 P.2d 537, 544 (Ariz. Ct. App. 1969).
6. Black Canyon Racquetball Club, Inc. v. Idaho First Nat'l Bank, 804 P.2d 900, 907 (Idaho 1991) (citation omitted).
7. 196 A. 39, 41-42 (Pa. 1938). . . .

different creatures of the law; they are not legally synonymous; the birth of one does not spawn the other.[8]

In accord, most courts progressed by providing corrective relief for the litigating parties based on the harm suffered. Again, the affirmative heart of estoppel (good faith, conscience, and equity) was the prime source for this development in the doctrine's evolution.

3. Tort Stage Three: Independent Claim for Detrimental Reliance

This stage is most familiar. When cases arose with defects in contract formation, courts held classical contract relief inapplicable, as explained in the Contract Stage Two opinions. Yet, some courts perceived the necessity for corrective justice between the parties. Conceptually, those courts adopted and applied promissory estoppel as an offensive theory creating a new right independent of classical bargained-for contract theory protecting the expectation interest. Rather than focusing on the promise as an element of mutual assent, courts at this developmental stage turned to the notion of a promissory commitment and focused on the promisee's right to rely and the promisor's duty to prevent (or not cause) reasonably foreseeable harmful reliance.

Courts at this stage recognize the distinction between a "promise," which connotes commitment, and an "offer," which connotes bargain. Thus, the required "promise" is not viewed in terms of a "clear and definite" offer/promise. An Oregon decision explains that "if a promise is not sufficiently definite to be enforceable, estoppel might permit the party who reasonably relies on that promise to obtain reliance damages. Thus, we implicitly recognized that a person can reasonably and foreseeably rely on a promise that is not sufficiently definite to be enforced."[9] Based on objective reasonable expectations of the promisor and promisee, a promise is an invitation for the promisee to rely. The right to rely arises from promissory statements, assurances, and

---

8. Duke Power Co. v. S.C. Pub. Serv. Comm'n, 326 S.E.2d 395, 406 (S.C. 1985).
9. Franklin v. Stern, 858 P.2d 142, 145 (Or. Ct. App. 1993). . . .

representations that show sufficient commitment to induce reasonable reliance in another. Any reliance is evaluated objectively for both reasonableness and foreseeability.[10] Customarily, the jury evaluates reasonableness and foreseeability as issues of fact given all the surrounding circumstances. Rather than awarding the value of the promise, the judgment seeks to rectify the harm caused (the detrimental reliance) by molding an equitable remedy within the judge's discretion (i.e., as justice requires). Typically called reliance damages, the remedy generally restores the harmed party to a pre-promise posture.

Approximately twenty jurisdictions[11] have evolved to Tort Stage Three. Those twenty jurisdictions (plus the thirteen jurisdictions at Equity Stage Four) evidence that the majority of American jurisdictions approve and adopt promissory estoppel as a theory, independent of contract, for awarding reliance damages. Acknowledging the defects in contract formation and validation on discrete facts, these courts, as a consequence, perceive the correlative rights and duties as distinct from contract. Courts focus on the promisor's promissory commitment that assuringly creates a reasonable reliance expectation in the promisee. Courts also cite and apply the *Restatement (Second)* definition: "A promise is a manifestation of intention to act or refrain from acting in a specified way, so made as to justify a promisee in understanding that a commitment has been made." The harm suffered by the promisee in exercising the right to rely is promissorily caused. Because the harm suffered (detrimental reliance) was reasonably expected and caused by the promissory commitment, it could have been prevented by the promisor. The promisor, having breached the duty to prevent the reasonable expectation, must rectify the harm suffered. Because no offer or contract can be validated, courts fashion remedies at this stage based solely on

---

10. The states at this third stage rectify foreseeable and reasonable detrimental reliance by their courts molding a corrective remedy that achieves justice between the litigating parties. Reasonable foreseeability, but not actual foreseeability, is required. . . .

11. The Stage Three jurisdictions are: Alabama, Alaska, Connecticut, Delaware, District of Columbia, Florida, Hawaii, Illinois, Massachusetts, Mississippi, Nebraska, New Jersey, New Mexico, Ohio, Oklahoma (but generally awards "full contractual remedies"), Oregon, South Carolina, Tennessee, Utah, Vermont, and Wyoming. To avoid a turf dispute, conceivably Mississippi may still be at Contract Stage Two and Alaska, Nebraska, and Vermont may have matured to Equity Stage Four. . . .

the extent of the promisee's reliance. Furthermore, because these decisions do not validate and enforce promises but rather compensate for the reliance harm caused, the damages have been perceived as tort damages imposed to right wrongs.

. . . However, although detrimental reliance damages appear *ex delicto* in nature, promissory estoppel does not have to be classified as a tort. As explained in Stage Four below, the more accurate classification for promissory estoppel is "equity," which assimilates and applies the earlier three phases (Estoppel Stage One, Contract Stage Two, and Tort Stage Three) as the facts in each case demand in good faith, conscience, and justice.

At Stage Two, reliance and expectation damages tend to equate when promissory estoppel is used as a consideration substitute. But Stage Three demonstrates that courts use promissory estoppel to award reliance damages, which equate more with tort damages by restoring the promisee to a pre-promise status. That tort-like restoration is not necessarily paradoxical when courts recognize that one branch of promissory estoppel's family tree lies in tort.

Ostensibly, promissory estoppel could be asserted as an independent tort theory of detrimental reliance. For instance, Colorado courts recently confronted a claim for tortious promissory estoppel. The court, however, held that a claim for promissory estoppel cannot lie in tort. Moreover, a few courts hold that promissory estoppel is not a basis for a punitive damages award. One reason for this lies in the doctrine's ancient "Mother Mold" of equity. Punitive damages are not recoverable under South Carolina law, for instance, because promissory estoppel is an equitable doctrine that, in good faith and conscience, properly points to Stage Four in the doctrine's evolution. By assimilating the three prior developmental stages of estoppel, contract, and tort in its family tree, the modern doctrine of promissory estoppel has seasoned and matured as courts return to its historical taproot in ancient equity and to its precursor equitable estoppel.

4. Equity Stage Four: Equitable Promissory Estoppel — Duties, Rights, and Remedies

The remedy identified in Stage Four is discretionary, arising from equitable rights and duties that encompass the promisee's right reasonably to rely on promissory commitments, and the promisor's duty to prevent foreseeable reliance by the promisee. Courts in the 1980s and 1990s, reverting to the spirit of 1349 in Edward III's mandate to the Lord Chancellor, forthrightly are reclaiming the "prerogative of Grace" based on the principles of "Conscience, Good Faith, Honesty and Equity." For some reason, unknown to this writer, over the centuries we either forgot or merged three of these principles (good faith, conscience, and honesty) and use only one — Equity. We speak of equitable principles, rather than chancery principles. Modern courts cognitively call out and apply that "chancery" root in administering promissory estoppel.

> The name "promissory estoppel" has been adopted as indicating that the basis of the doctrine is not so much one of contract, with a substitute for consideration, as an application of the general principle of estoppel to certain situations. [The doctrine's evolution] is an attempt by courts to keep remedies abreast of increased moral consciousness of honesty and fair representations in all business dealings.[12]

Thus, grounded on the four chancery principles and standards for evaluating conduct, modern courts reaffirm their chancery powers and apply promissory estoppel to rectify wrongs with discretely designed corrective relief. For instance, under California, New York, Texas, and Utah law, promissory estoppel is definitely held to be an equitable doctrine recognizing equitable rights and remedies. As the California Supreme Court noted:

> Treatise writers and commentators have confirmed the generally equitable nature of promissory estoppel in enforcing a promise which otherwise would be unenforceable. (Citation omitted) The available authorities generally concur, however, that as of 1850 assumpsit would not lie to enforce a gratuitous promise, where the promisee's detrimental reliance was not requested by the promisor. . . . The equitable character of promissory estoppel is confirmed by a close scrutiny of the purpose of the doctrine, namely, that "injustice can be avoided only by enforcement of the promise." . . . Both historically and

---

12. People's Nat'l Bank v. Linebarger Constr. Co., 240 S.W.2d 12, 15 (Ark. 1951).

functionally, the task of weighing such equitable considerations is to be performed by the trial court, not the jury. We conclude that the trial court properly treated the action as equitable in nature, to be tried by the court with or without an advisory jury as the court elected.[13]

In thirteen jurisdictions, the common law of promissory estoppel has progressed to the unabridged, equitable stage.[14]

. . . [T]his author proffers one final impression about the equitable right and remedy of promissory estoppel. . . . The primary equitable right is the promisee's right to rely. That right arises from the objective, reasonable expectations that were created and foreseeable by the promisor. The promissory "statements" must evidence objectively a sufficient commitment or assurance on which a reasonable person would rely. . . .

The remedy for promissory estoppel is discretionary. No rigid or mechanical remedy rule applies. The remedy is not necessarily co-extensive with damages for contract breach, but is equitably molded ad hoc for each case according to the dictates of good faith, conscience, and justice. With their reliance sabers, courts award the full range of remedies based on specific performance, restitution, expectation, reliance, exemplary (seldom), or some other appropriate relief to achieve corrective justice between the parties in the context of their distinct litigation.

---

13. [C & K Eng'g Contractors v. Amber Steel Co., 587 P.2d 1136, 1138-1139, 1141 (Cal. 1978)].

14. Promissory estoppel does not languish in the contract/tort shadowland but rests, stably rooted in equity, in the following jurisdictions: Arkansas, California, Colorado, Indiana, Louisiana, Minnesota, New York (in federal Second Circuit opinions because the high court of New York authoritatively neither has accepted nor rejected Section 90 as an affirmative claim), Pennsylvania, Puerto Rico, South Dakota, Texas, Vermont, Washington, and Wisconsin. Conceivably, Vermont may not have sufficient decisions to place it at Stage Four. . . .

IV

PERFORMANCE AND BREACH

14

WHAT CONSTITUTES GOOD FAITH PERFORMANCE?

In the fifties and sixties contract scholars rejected so-called "conceptualist" or "formalist" approaches that attempted to dictate the outcome of cases with concepts and rules. Contract scholarship was dominated by "realist" inquiries into the complexities of actual commercial practice seeking to identify the multiple factors or considerations that judges should take into account when deciding cases. Usually it was denied that these factors could or should be weighted or organized in some manner in advance of a legal dispute. To explain the implied duty of good faith performance, for example, Professor Robert Summers of Cornell proposed a series of six categories of bad faith performance: evasion of the spirit of the deal, lack of diligence and slacking off, willfully rendering only "substantial" performance, and interference with or failure to cooperate in the other party's performance. Although he did not rule out the possibility of developing rules to guide judicial decision making, he denied that a unifying theory of good faith performance explaining these categories was possible.

In the seventies and eighties, contract scholarship came to be dominated by scholars — often those influenced by economic analysis, but also by philosophy, political theory, and other disciplines — seeking unified theories of legal doctrine in a variety of subjects. University of Iowa professor Steven Burton's article, *Breach of Contract and the Common Law Duty to Perform in Good Faith*, represents this generational shift. In it, Professor Burton presents a comprehensive theory of good faith performance. According to Burton, the problem of good faith performance arises when a contract gives one party a degree of discretion in performing, and this discretion is then used by that party to recapture an opportunity foregone at contract formation. So to determine whether a party has acted in bad faith, one must identify both an opportunity "objectively" foregone and a "subjective" intention to recapture it.

In the excerpt from *The General Duty of Good Faith — Its Recognition and Conceptualization*, Professor Summers criticizes Burton's theory of good faith performance on the grounds that it is neither as clear as Burton claims nor as comprehensive as Summers thinks it needs to be to explain the doctrine embodied in Restatement (Second) of Contracts §205.

STUDY GUIDE: In what respect is Professor Burton's theory "economic"? What is the relationship between his conception of "good faith" and the parties' intentions? How well does his theory of "foregone opportunities" explain the situations in which good faith performance problems arise? Would it apply to noneconomic motivations as well as economic ones?

BREACH OF CONTRACT AND THE COMMON LAW DUTY TO PERFORM IN GOOD FAITH*

Steven J. Burton

A majority of American jurisdictions, the Restatement (Second) of Contracts, and the Uniform Commercial Code (U.C.C.) now recognize the duty to perform a contract in good faith as a general principle of

---

*From Steven J. Burton, Breach of Contract and the Common Law Duty to Perform in Good Faith, 94 Harv. L. Rev. 369 (1980).

contract law. The conduct of virtually any party to any contract accordingly may be vulnerable to claims of breach stemming from this obligation. Yet neither courts nor commentators have articulated an operational standard that distinguishes good faith performance from bad faith performance.[1] The good faith performance doctrine consequently appears as a license for the exercise of judicial or juror intuition, and presumably results in unpredictable and inconsistent applications. Repeated common law adjudication, however, has enriched the concept of good faith performance so that an operational standard now can be articulated and evaluated.

The good faith performance doctrine establishes a standard for contract interpretation and a covenant that is implied in every contract. The good faith question often arises because a contract is an exchange expressed imperfectly and projected into an uncertain future. Contract parties rely on the good faith of their exchange partners because detailed planning may be ineffectual or inadvisable. Therefore, express contract terms alone are insufficient to determine a party's good faith in performance.

Even so, the courts employ the good faith performance doctrine to effectuate the intentions of parties, or to protect their reasonable expectations. Standards expressed in these terms, however, are of little aid in applying the doctrine. They direct the inquiry away from duties imposed upon the parties irrespective of their assent.[2] But they direct

---

1. See generally . . . Summers, "Good Faith" in General Contract Law and the Sales Provisions of the Uniform Commercial Code, 54 Va. L. Rev. 195 (1968). Professor Summers does not purport to identify the criteria that judges use or ought to use in deciding whether particular conduct is in bad faith. Instead, he asserts that

> good faith is an "excluder." It is a phrase without general meaning or (meanings) of its own and serves to exclude a wide range of heterogeneous forms of bad faith. In a particular context, the phrase takes on specific meaning but usually this is only by way of contrast with the specific form of bad faith actually or hypothetically ruled out. . . .

2. The good faith performance doctrine should be distinguished sharply from the doctrine of unconscionability, which governs the formation of a contract. . . . Unconscionability gives courts latitude to refuse to enforce all or part of an agreement that is not a product of meaning choice by both parties or is so one sided in its terms as to favor one party unreasonably. E.g., Williams v. Walker-Thomas Furniture Co., 350 F.2d 445, 449 (D.C. Cir. 1965); U.C.C. §2-302(1). Unconscionability thus is a limitation on

attention to the amorphous totality of the factual circumstances at the time of formation, and fail to distinguish relevant from irrelevant facts within that realm. The analysis would be advanced further by an operational standard that respects the autonomy of contract parties and calls the relevant facts to the foreground of the totality of the circumstances.

This requires a better understanding of the contractual expectation interest. Traditionally, the expectation interest is viewed as comprising the property, services, or money to be received by the promisee. This Article suggests that it also encompasses the expected cost of performance to the promisor. This expected cost consists of alternative opportunities foregone upon entering a particular contract. . . .

. . . Good faith limits the exercise of the discretion in performance conferred on one party by the contract. . . .

Bad faith performance occurs precisely when discretion is used to recapture opportunities foregone upon contracting — when the discretion-exercising party refuses to pay the expected cost of performance. Good faith performance, in turn, occurs when a party's discretion is exercised for any purpose within the reasonable contemplation of the parties at the time of formation — to capture opportunities that were preserved upon entering the contract, interpreted objectively. The good faith performance doctrine therefore directs attention to the opportunities foregone by a discretion-exercising party at formation, and to that party's reasons for exercising discretion during performance. . . .

I. CONTRACT BREACH BEHAVIOR: A COST PERSPECTIVE . . .

The economic cost of any action — including the act of contracting, the act of performing, and the act of breaching a contract — should be

---

freedom of contract that allows the courts to police the bargaining relationship and to override the manifested intention of the parties in the interest of justice. . . .

The good faith performance obligation, in contrast, typically is implied in contracts involving arm's-length transactions, often between sophisticated businesspersons. . . . Although the parties are not free to disclaim the obligation to perform in good faith as such, . . . they are free to determine by agreement what good faith will permit or require of them.

viewed descriptively as the value of the next best opportunity necessarily foregone by taking that action. Almost every action entails many foregone opportunities because resources, such as goods, services, money, or reputation, are scarce. . . .

A simple breach of an express contract consists of an attempt by one party to recapture opportunities foregone upon contracting. By hypothesis, a party enters a contract when it believes that no greater benefit can be derived by expending elsewhere the resources required for the contract performance. Events between the time of formation and the time of performance may prove this belief to have been erroneous. Before its own performance is rendered, a party with a losing contract may seek to recapture foregone opportunities to the extent possible. This can be accomplished *only* by redirecting the resources committed to the promised performance and therefore by failing to perform the promise.

A buyer of corn, for example, may fail to perform a contract for future delivery for a large number of reasons. If the market price falls the buyer will wish to recapture the opportunity of buying on the spot market or on a changed futures market. If the buyer gets a hot tip on the potato market, it may wish to redirect purchase money earmarked for the corn contract to enable it to purchase more potato contracts. If investor confidence in the commodities market slips, the buyer may wish to move its business into stocks or real estate or may wish to go out of business. These and other uses for the resources committed to the initial corn contract may be opportunities necessarily foregone when entering the corn contract.

An express promise therefore should be viewed as entailing representations as to the future, both regarding the resources to be received by the promisee and simultaneously regarding opportunities foregone by the promisor, even though the identity of opportunities foregone in any case is problematic. Consequently, one can describe simple breach of an express contract as a failure to do that which one promised to do or doing that which one promised not to do, and independently as a recapture of opportunities foregone upon entering the contract. The effect is identical in the simple case. The concept of recapturing foregone opportunities, however, is more general and can be employed also to embrace at least the implied covenant of good faith.

II.   A THEORY OF THE GOOD FAITH
PERFORMANCE DOCTRINE

A breach of contract by failing to perform in good faith is both like and unlike a breach of contract by failing to perform a simple express promise. From the cost perspective, it is similar analytically in that the key fact establishing a breach is a party's recapture of opportunities foregone upon entering the contract. It is different in that an observer cannot know whether a party acted to recapture foregone opportunities by determining that the other party did not receive the property, services, or money to be transferred under the contract. This Part introduces the concept of discretion in contract performance as a means of examining the specific problem governed by the good faith performance doctrine. The theory developed here is that a party fails to perform in good faith when it uses such discretion to recapture foregone opportunities.

A.   The Problem: Legitimate and Illegitimate Uses
of Discretion in Contract Performance

The standard doctrinal formulation of the good faith performance duty was first articulated in 1933 by the New York Court of Appeals in Kirke La Shelle Co. v. Paul Armstrong Co.:

> In every contract there is an implied covenant that neither party shall do anything which will have the effect of destroying or injuring the right of the other party to receive the fruits of the contract, which means that in every contract there exists an implied covenant of good faith and fair dealing.

Because it adopts the traditional focus on the benefit to be received by the promisee and fails to focus on the problem of discretion in performance, however, this early effort to articulate the good faith principle conceals more than it reveals.

1. Discretion in Performance. — Discretion in performance arises in two ways. The parties may find it to their mutual advantage at formation to defer decision on a particular term and to confer decision-making authority as to that term on one of them. Discretion also may arise, with similar effect, from a lack of clarity or from an omission in the express contract.[3] In either case, the dependent party must rely on the good faith of the party in control. Only in such cases do the courts raise explicitly the implied covenant of good faith and fair dealing, or interpret a contract in light of good faith performance.[4] This will be illustrated by examining the cases involving discretion as to quantity, price, time, and conditional aspects of a contract.

Deferred decisions as to quantity take the form of requirements and output contracts, in which specific agreement typically is reached on all terms except the quantity of goods bought or sold. A buyer under a requirements contract and a seller under an output contract have effective control of the quantity exchanged because they can manipulate their apparent requirements or output by modifying their methods of marketing or production. At the time of formation, the dependent party could have insisted on fixed quantity terms in the contract or required agreement on detailed provisions governing the other party's method of doing business. The flexibility and simplicity of a requirements or output contract, however, often compensate for the risk of such manipulations. Both at common law and under the U.C.C., a buyer's requirements or a seller's output means such actual quantities as occur in good faith.

Deferred decisions as to price may take two forms. In most jurisdictions at common law, agreement as to price is an essential term and must be set or be ascertainable for a contract to be formed. There is, however, some authority at common law for enforcing a contract in which the price is to be set by an appraisal by one party. In that case, the price must be set in good faith.[5] In addition, the price term more commonly may be left open to vary with sales, production, or other factors through a formula in the contract for determining the price when payment is due.

---

3. It is the potential for a lack of clarity and completeness that necessitates the implication of the good faith covenant in every contract. Contracting parties typically will presuppose a measure of cooperation from each other. Express language accordingly will fail to set forth all of the specific undertakings of the parties. . . .

4. The analysis in this Article is based on a survey of over 400 cases in which courts explicitly refer to good faith in performance.

5. . . . There also is some authority for enforcing an agreement to agree on price, in which case the parties must negotiate the price in good faith . . . . See also U.C.C. § 2-305(1); Knapp, Enforcing the Contract to Bargain, 44 N.Y.U. L. Rev. 673 (1969).

Good faith performance is required when one party controls the factors that determine the price.

Deferred decisions as to the time of performance may allow one party to determine when it shall perform, when the other party shall perform, or when the contract shall terminate. Often such decisions must be made in good faith. A final decision as to the binding effect of a contract promise on one party similarly may be deferred when the contract is subject to a condition. When that condition is within one party's effective control, that party must act in good faith. For example, a party whose performance is conditioned on governmental approval of its plans or on other related contracts may be required to act in good faith to secure the fulfillment of the condition. Similarly, a party benefiting from a condition of satisfaction must act at least in good faith in claiming that it is dissatisfied with the proffered performance.

The good faith performance doctrine thus may be used to protect a "weaker" party from a "stronger" party. Unlike the unconscionability doctrine, however, weakness and strength in this context do not refer to the substantive fairness of the bargain or to the relative bargaining power of the parties. Good faith performance cases typically involve arm's-length transactions, often between sophisticated business persons. The relative strength of the party exercising discretion typically arises from an agreement of the parties to confer control of a contract term on that party. The dependent party then is left to the good faith of the party in control.

   2. Distinguishing Legitimate and Illegitimate Uses of Discretion. — The problem of good faith in contract performance can be clarified in terms of a party's reasons for exercising discretion. The *Kirke La Shelle* formulation of the implied covenant of good faith and fair dealing is misleading. It suggests on its face that there are but two issues: whether one party received the fruits of the contract and, if not, whether the other party caused the harm. That the dependent party does not receive anticipated benefits, however, is not dispositive. A party with discretion may withhold all benefits for good reasons. The cases therefore carry the inquiry further and establish that the state of mind of the discretion-exercising party is of central importance. The courts, mindful that good faith should not be used as a vehicle for judicial fiat, defer to a party who acts with no improper purpose.

   Consider, for example, a set of cases involving actions by lessees under commercial percentage leases in which the implied covenant of good faith and fair dealing was applied. The leases provided for rentals to be paid primarily as a percentage of the gross receipts of the lessee's business on the premises. In each case, the lessee altered its business in a way that reduced sales from the leased premises and therefore the amount owed as rent: by moving a lucrative part of the business to other premises leased from the same lessor on a flat rental basis;[6] by opening competing stores in the same neighborhood;[7] or by diverting customers to another store.[8]

The lessor lost in two of the three cases, even though the lessee in each instance reduced the actual rent received by the lessor under the contract formula. Where the lessee opened competing stores in the same neighborhood, the court observed simply that large chains usually kept adding to the number of their stores.[9] When the lessee moved a lucrative part of its business to other premises in the same building, where a flat rental applied, the court held that the lessee was free to decide on which floor to locate that part of its business, absent fraud, trickery, or express terms to the contrary.[10] However, where the lessee diverted business for the "sole purpose"[11] of bringing gross receipts down at the leased premises, a "direct violation"[12] of the covenant was established.

The fact that a discretion-exercising party causes the dependent party to lose some or all of its anticipated benefit from the contract thus is insufficient to establish a breach of contract by failing to perform in good faith. The *Kirke La Shelle* dictum, although still widely employed, fails to reflect the subsequent common law experience. The cases suggest that the purpose of the discretion-exercising party is a key factor.

---

6. Mutual Life Ins. Co. v. Tailored Woman, Inc., 309 N.Y. 248, 128 N.E.2d 401 (1955).

7. Food Fair Stores, Inc. v. Blumberg, 234 Md. 521, 200 A.2d 166 (1964). See also Stop & Shop, Inc. v. Ganem, 347 Mass. 697, 200 N.E.2d, 248 (1964).

8. Goldberg 168-05 Corp. v. Levy, 170 Misc. 292, 9 N.Y.S.2d 304 (Sup. Ct. 1938), *modified and aff'd*, 256 A.D. 1086, II N.Y.S.2d 315 (1939).

9. Food Fair Stores, Inc. v. Blumberg, 234 Md. 521, 535, 200 A.2d 166, 174 (1964).

10. Mutual Life Ins. Co. v. Tailored Woman, Inc., 309 N.Y. 248, 128 N.E.2d 401 (1955).

11. Goldberg 168-05 Corp. v. Levy, 170 Misc. 292, 294, 9 N.Y.S.2d 304, 306 (Sup. Ct. 1938), *modified and aff'd*, 256 A.D. 1086, II N.Y.S.2d 315 (1939).

12. Id.

B.   Breach of Contract By Failing to Perform in Good Faith

1.   Good Faith: The Reasonable Contemplation of the Parties. —
The results in the percentage lease cases, as in most good faith performance cases, have intuitive appeal. A few courts have sought to
articulate this intuition in terms of the reasonable contemplation of the
parties. The good faith performance doctrine may be said to permit the
exercise of discretion for any purpose — including ordinary business
purposes — reasonably within the contemplation of the parties. A contract thus would be breached by a failure to perform in good faith if a
party uses its discretion for a reason outside the contemplated range — a
reason beyond the risks assumed by the party claiming a breach.

The contemplation standard of good faith performance is helpful
because it distinguishes in principle the duty to perform in good faith
from duties imposed on the parties either for reasons of public policy or
to avoid unjust enrichment. Moreover, it suggests two specific questions
for determining good faith: (1) what was the discretion-exercising
party's purpose in acting; and (2) was that purpose within the reasonable
contemplation of the parties?[13] . . .

However, the contemplation standard alone leaves much room for
manipulation and fiction. It provides little guidance for determining
which of the plausible expectations at formation and which of the
plausible motives at performance manifest good faith or bad faith
performance. The contemplation standard only directs one to consult the
parties' intentions and reasonable expectations — an amorphous totality

---

13. The percentage lease cases may be explained in this light. Where a lessee
opened competing stores in the same neighborhood, the court said there is nothing
"unusual" about large retail chains adding to the number of their stores . . . and so held
that the act was undertaken in good faith. The implication was that the defendant's
action was within the ordinary course of business and therefore was reasonably within
the contemplation of the parties. When a lessee moved part of its business to a different
floor of the building where a flat rental applied, . . . the rearrangement of the merchant's
wares within the rented space was similarly seen as a normal business practice. However, where a lessee diverted customers to other premises for the sole purpose of bringing down gross receipts at the leased premises, . . . the lessee's reason for acting lay
outside the bounds of the contract. The lessor reasonably contemplated that variations
in the percentage rent would result from market factors affecting the volume of business at
the lessee's location. But it may be inferred reasonably that neither party contemplated
at formation that the lessee would interfere with the flow of customers in order to reduce
its own sales at the leased premises.

of the circumstances at the time of formation. In contrast, the cost perspective on contract breach behavior makes it possible to identify with greater particularity the relevant expectations and motives that have been held to constitute bad faith.

2. Bad Faith: Recapturing Foregone Opportunities. — Bad faith performance consists of an exercise of discretion in performance to recapture opportunities foregone at formation. The dependent promisee's expectations encompass both the subject matter to be received under a contract, and the expected costs of performance by the other party. A recapture by one party of foregone opportunities necessarily harms the other. A reasonable person accordingly would enter a contract that confers discretion on the other party only on the belief that the discretion will not be used to recapture foregone opportunities.[14]

Like the contemplation approach to good faith performance, . . . the foregone opportunities approach has both objective and subjective aspects. The identity of foregone opportunities is determined by an objective standard, focusing on the expectations of reasonable persons in the position of the dependent parties. Whether a particular discretion-exercising party acted to recapture foregone opportunities is a question of subjective intent. The two approaches are consistent. If a discretion-exercising party uses its control to recapture a foregone opportunity, it follows that it is not acting for a purpose within the contemplation of the parties. If such a party acts for a reason contemplated by the parties, it is not recapturing a foregone opportunity.

The foregone opportunities approach, however, advances the analysis further than the contemplation approach. It narrows the field of relevant intellectual inquiry by isolating with greater particularity the factors that must be considered in determining good or bad faith performance. The totality of the circumstances contemplated or expected by

---

14. The economic motive to be described is not the only motive that is beyond the reasonable expectations of a dependent party. Some noneconomic motives, such as spite or ill will, are likely to run afoul of the good faith performance doctrine or otherwise to result in liability for breach of contract. See Monge v. Beebe Rubber Co., 114 N.H. 130, 316 A.2d 549 (1974) (bad faith of employer found when employee under at will contract was fired after refusing sexual advances of her boss). . . . Noneconomic factors so rarely are evidenced in the reported cases, however, that the focus of the theory must be on economic motives.

the parties includes both benefits to the promisee (the traditional focus) and costs to the promisor (foregone opportunities). For the purpose of the good faith performance doctrine, the relevant and distinct set of facts is that subset of the totality of circumstances (1) at formation, bearing on the expected costs to a discretion-exercising promisor; and (2) at performance, bearing on whether the promisor exercised its discretion in performance to recapture a foregone opportunity. That the dependent promisee did not receive benefits under the contract as it had hoped simply is not dispositive.

C.   Justification of the Good Faith Performance Doctrine

There are two potential justifications of the good faith performance doctrine — legal and economic.[15] In traditional legal terms, it can be argued that the security of contractual transactions is enhanced by the good faith performance doctrine. Because contracting parties do not contract with those they do not trust to some extent, a dependent party will have reason to rely on the good faith of a discretion-exercising party. Such reliance plausibly is based on the simple belief that the party with discretion in performance will keep the contract, and therefore will not use its discretion to recapture foregone opportunities. Requiring a party who recaptures foregone opportunities to compensate the other increases the reliability of flexible contracts and therefore the security of such transactions. . . .

The good faith performance doctrine may be said to enhance economic efficiency by reducing the costs of contracting. The costs of exchange include the costs of gathering information with which to choose one's contract partners, negotiating and drafting contracts, and risk taking with respect to the future. The good faith performance doctrine reduces all three kinds of costs by allowing parties to rely on the law in place of incurring some of these costs.

---

15. For a classic exposition on the relationship between juristic and economic justifications of contract law, see Fuller & Purdue, [The Reliance Interest and Contract Damages (pt. 1), 46 Yale L.J. 52, 60-66 (1936)].

Many contracting parties investigate the market in part to identify and select those prospective contract partners whose reputations for business integrity reduce the risk of disappointing contract performance. Such information never will be wholly complete or trustworthy. A choice is presented if the law offers a prospect of compensation to a contract party who may incur losses due to the other party's lack of business integrity. Contract parties who wish to reduce uncertainty as to their prospective partners' integrity either may gather more information before contracting or may substitute the legal information before contracting or may substitute the legal incentive for honorable behavior — and the prospect of recovering damages — for some such information. The economically rational person presumably would choose the less costly alternative at the margin.

The good faith performance doctrine similarly reduces the costs of negotiating and drafting contracts. After selecting each other as probably contract partners, the parties will choose the amount of detail to include in their express contract. The alternatives to detailed planning are (1) relying on legal rules that supply a set of normal terms that otherwise would be negotiated, or (2) in the absence of such terms, bearing the cost of uncertainty. The good faith performance doctrine provides such a set of legal rules and gives parties who wish to reduce uncertainty the choice of engaging in more detailed planning or substituting good faith at the margin. The good faith performance doctrine thus makes the short contract, one that requires relatively more interpretation and implication, less risky and therefore less costly.

Finally, the good faith performance doctrine induces the parties to minimize the joint costs of the contract by negotiating and drafting clauses that will reduce the prospect of losses should a party after formation wish to redirect resources. Theoretically, the joint costs of the contract will be minimized if liability is placed on the party who can more cheaply cover the contingency by express terms — the party best able to protect itself. By hypothesis, that party will be the discretion-exercising party, who would have far better information concerning its own alternative opportunities, and the probability that a later opportunity will prove more attractive. On the other hand, for the dependent party to protect itself, it must secure a lengthy series of express promises as to those alternative opportunities that the other party may not pursue. This would involve a costly process of eliminating hypothetical contingencies. The joint cost of contracting therefore would be less when a party with discretion is required to protect itself. All it need do is include a condition that preserves particular alternative opportunities under specified circumstances.[16]

STUDY GUIDE: *Why does Professor Summers find Burton's approach to be inadequate? Are these the sorts of difficulties that inhere in any attempt at a unified legal theory?*

THE GENERAL DUTY OF GOOD FAITH — ITS RECOGNITION AND CONCEPTUALIZATION*

Robert S. Summers

The text of section 205 of the Restatement (Second) of Contracts, adopted by the American Law Institute in 1979 and published in final form in 1981, provides:

§250. *Duty of Good Faith and Fair Dealing.*   Every contract imposes upon each party a duty of good faith and fair dealing in its performance and its enforcement.[1]

This section, together with its accompanying Comment and Reporter's Note, recognizes and conceptualizes a general duty of good faith and fair dealing in the performance and enforcement of contracts in American

---

16. . . . [H]owever, the economic argument is not conclusive on the ultimate question whether the good faith performance doctrine is a good thing. It is costly for the legal system to present the parties with the less costly alternative of relying on the good faith of their contract partners rather than on more information concerning their partners' reputations or on more detailed contracts. There is no empirical basis at present for concluding that the legal system is more efficient than the market alternatives at enhancing the reliability of contracts at the margin, though such a conclusion seems intuitively sound. Suffice it to say that this uncertainty is common to any economic analyses of the common law that compare the alternative of no doctrine with an existing doctrine.

In addition, like any theoretical justification, this argument is vulnerable to the legal realist's claim that capability problems so impede the legal system's operation in fact that the theory is insufficiently reflective of reality. . . .

*From Robert S. Summers, the General Duty of Good Faith — its Recognition and Conceptualization, 67 Corn. L. Rev. 810 (1982).

1. Restatement (Second) of Contracts §205 (1979).

law. In addition, a number of other sections and Comments particularize the bearing of this general duty in various ways.[2]

The first Restatement of Contracts, which appeared in 1932, did not include a section comparable to section 205. This new section reflects one of the truly major advances in American contract law during the past fifty years.

The late Robert Braucher, then Professor of Law at Harvard Law School, was the Reporter for the Restatement Second during the years when section 205 was in embryo, and he drafted it. Professor Braucher acknowledged that an article I wrote on the subject published in 1968 substantially influenced the recognition and conceptualization of good faith in section 205.[3] . . .

C.   The General Indefinability of Good Faith

Many commentators suggest that they are willing to accept that good faith cannot, as such, be usefully defined in terms of a single, general, positive meaning, but most of them still find this state of affairs rather difficult to live with. At one point or another, in text or in footnote, they try their hand at what seems to be tendered as a general definition. Here are some of the results:

— Good faith is an "absence of intention to harm a legally protected pecuniary interest."[4]

— Good faith performance "occurs when a party's discretion is exercised for any purpose within the reasonable contemplation of the parties at the time of formation — to capture opportunities that were preserved upon entering the contract, interpreted objectively."[5]

— Good faith and fair conduct consists of action "according to reasonable standards set by customary practices and by known individual expectations."[6]

---

2. See, e.g., Restatement (Second) of Contracts §§34, 74, 157, 172, 176, 188, 228, 241, 248, 251, 257, 259, 264, 265, 277 (1979).

3. The article is Summers, "Good Faith" in General Contract Law and the Sales Provisions of the Uniform Commercial Code, 54 Va. L. Rev. 195 (1968). . . .

4. [Burton, Breach of Contract and the Common Law Duty to Perform in Good Faith, 94 Harv. L. Rev. 369, 372-373 n.17 (1980).]

5. Id. at 373.

6. Holmes, A Contextual Study of Commercial Good Faith: Good Faith Disclosure in Contract Formation, 39 U. Pitt. L. Rev. 381, 452 (1978).

My view is that all such efforts to define good faith, *for purposes of a section like 205*, are misguided. Such formulations provide little, if any, genuine *definitional* guidance. Moreover, some of them may restrictively distort the scope of the general requirement of good faith. For example, the factors relevant in the context may not be confined to what "custom" and communicate "expectations" dictate. In addition, such formulations may lead judges and lawyers to ponder and argue over *the* meaning of good faith and in this or other ways divert focus away from the issue of whether a claimed form of bad faith really is, in light of all relevant circumstantial detail, to be so characterized. Finally, the very idea of good faith, if I am right, is simply not the kind of idea that is susceptible of such a definitional approach.

All this is not to say that some of the phrases appearing in the foregoing proffered definitions have no relevant utility. As fragments of statements of *rationales* for the requirement of good faith, they plainly do. But to provide a rationale for a requirement is one thing; to define the ideas that figure in the requirement itself is another. . . .

Professor Burton, in a most interesting essay in the Harvard Law Review, recently proposed a model decision procedure for the resolution of novel cases posing of good-faith *performance*. The essence of his model is as follows. One of the two parties will always have what Professor Burton calls "discretion to perform." At the time of contracting, that party will have given up some of his freedom of action, which Professor Burton calls "foregone opportunities" (to that party, a "cost" of contracting). Bad-faith contractual activity is then defined as "exercising discretion" to recapture one or more of the opportunities foregone upon entering a contract. To determine whether an opportunity was in fact foregone, it is necessary to inquire into the reasonable expectations of the "dependent party" (the other party). The party with discretion to perform acts in good faith if he does not attempt to recapture a foregone opportunity. Professor Burton also argues that "whether a particular discretion-exercising party acted to recapture foregone opportunities is a question of subjective intent" — a "subjective inquiry." Moreover, the "objective inquiry" into the dependent party's reasonable expectations is not alone "dispositive." Indeed, Professor Burton stresses that instead the inquiry into state of mind is "of central importance." . . .

Professor Burton makes a number of claims on behalf of his approach, as opposed to what he calls the "traditional" approach (born not so long ago in the history of the common law and including, presumably, that of section 205). First, he says that his approach provides more analytical focus. It isolates "with greater particularity the factors that must be considered in determining good or bad-faith performance." Instead of an "amorphous totality of factual circumstances," we have an inquiry into reasonable expectations of the "dependent party" and the subjective intent of the "discretion-exercising" party — all to determine precisely whether the discretion-exercising party has acted to recapture foregone opportunities so as to constitute bad faith. Is this analysis necessarily any more focused than that of section 205 in novel good-faith performance case? Does it focus on the right things? Does it go far enough? These are large questions, and I cannot now do full justice to them. . . . It is true that Professor Burton's model introduces new terminology and appears to reduce to two questions; but I do not see that anything turns on this. Why, for example, should it "advance the analysis" to inquire whether the discretion-exercising party is seeking to "recapture foregone opportunities," rather than whether his actions fall outside the reasonable expectations of the dependent party in light of the various factors in the circumstances that legitimately shape those expectations? Or why does it help (if it does) in our foregoing lease illustration to inquire whether the tenant, in diverting customers, was trying to recapture costs incurred in entering the contract, rather than whether what the tenant did was, all things considered, contrary to the spirit of the deal?

One may also question whether the Burton model really focuses on the right things. For example, does the subjective inquiry into the discretion-exercising party's state of mind really have the central importance that is claimed? Part of the claim, as I understand it, is that this inquiry is *typically* relevant, not just contingently so. This does not accord with section 205. Moreover, in a great many well-decided performance cases, courts give little or no consideration to this factor. Indeed, its independent significance in the Burton model is at least in some areas problematic. Consider . . . the lease illustration. If the court decides that the reasonable expectations of the landlord rule out the tenant's acts of diverting customers to his other store, what if anything would it add to inquire into the tenant's state of mind? It is said (a) that the "traditional analysis" focuses mainly on benefits due the promisee under the agreement and (b) that this is inadequate because the promisor may be "entitled" to withhold something in good faith. Whether or not

(a) is true, (b) does not follow. If what is due the promisee really does exclude what the promisor wants to withhold, then that will be dispositive. What one is "entitled" to withhold depends on what is due the promisee. (This is not to say that an inquiry into the promisor's state of mind can never have independent significance in good-faith performance cases.)

Further, in my view the Burton model does not go far enough. That is, it does not provide as much focus as section 205 of the Restatement Second and the general case law permit. I suspect that it is now possible to develop useful lists of factors generally relevant to the determination of good-faith performance in a number of different performance contexts. Professor Burton seems content, for example, to leave the general test of reasonableness of expectations relatively unanalyzed. . . . Nothing in the excluder conceptualization embodied in section 205 is inconsistent with the articulation of such criteria. A general requirement of good faith can rule out forms of bad faith identifiable by reference to these criteria.[7] Indeed, as I have already suggested, some such criteria in some contexts may now be ripe for formulation in rules.

Professor Burton claims that, in addition to more focus, his model provides more generality than other approaches and thus is more "law-like." In particular, he thinks it is less a "license" for the exercise of ad hoc judicial intuition. Again, I fail to see why there is any less generality in the Restatement Second approach. Certainly each "context" to which Professor Braucher referred in the Comments consists of more than "the discrete case." Indeed, he adopted a number of *general* categories for the classification of general types of bad faith — categories well populated with actual decisions. Moreover, there is no reason why the legal generalities emergent in these contexts cannot take account of factors that vary with the stage in the contracting process at which the issue of good faith arises.

Finally, Professor Burton claims that his model provides a useful new "perspective and policy framework" within which good-faith performance issues are more manageable. Close analysis suggests,

---

7. Professor Burton has suggested that I once believed the contrary. Thus, he suggests that in my earlier article I purported to offer the excluder analysis "instead" of criteria of decision. . . . He states that I "was led effectively to deny that any general principle or principles could be articulated as criteria for judicial decision." . . . I plead not guilty to both charges.

however, that it is less general than Professor Burton makes it seem, and that it introduces economic ideas and terminology that may breed uncertainty or confusion. I will say something further only about the first of these observations. The model is less general because it is in truth drawn mainly from those cases in which contracting parties have in fact conferred on one of the parties some genuine discretionary power in matters of performance. Many good-faith performance cases are not of this kind; they do not confer *discretion* to perform in some way. It is not difficult to discern the likely motive here behind the Burton model. The maneuver of adopting a conceptual framework in which one party is always considered to have discretion felicitously generates the *possibility* that the "discretion-exercising" party might have failed to perform in good faith, and thus seems to give pervasive point to the "subjective inquiry" of such central importance in the model. After all, "a party with discretion may withhold all benefits for good reasons." In many cases posing issues of good-faith performance, however, there will be no such discretion and therefore no such possibility. And even when this is not so, the subjective inquiry may lack independent significance.

15

WHEN IS A BREACH MATERIAL?

The effort to explicate the concept of material breach, like that of good faith performance, long took the form of identifying a list of factors to be taken "into account" in reaching a decision. For example, in determining whether a failure to perform is material, the Restatement (Second) of Contracts §241 identifies the following "circumstances" as "significant":

> (a) the extent to which the injured party will be deprived of the benefit which he reasonably expected; (b) the extent to which the injured party can be adequately compensated for the part of that benefit of which he will be deprived; (c) the extent to which the party failing to perform or to offer to perform will suffer forfeiture; (d) the likelihood that the party failing to perform or to offer to perform will cure his failure, taking account of all the circumstances including any reasonable assurance; (e) the extent to which the behavior of the party failing to perform or to offer to perform comports with standards of good faith and fair dealing.

How these factors are to be weighed or organized and *why* they are indicia of a material breach is not explained.

To fill this gap, Professor Eric Andersen, perhaps not coincidentally a colleague of Steven Burton at Iowa, proposed a general theory of material breach in *A New Look at Material Breach in the Law of Contracts*. According to Andersen, to understand material breach we must first appreciate the problem that this concept is intended to handle. Material breach is used to decide when a party is justified in cancelling any further performance from the other party and in seeking damages for any costs incurred in obtaining a substitute performance. Andersen contends that a promisee is justified in cancelling performance when the promisor's words or actions have undermined what he calls the promisee's "interest in future performance." This is the interest that all contracting parties have before and during the performance phase of the contract in receiving performance from the other side in the future. Cancellation is justified when the words or conduct of one party undermine the reasonable expectation that future performance will be satisfactory.

STUDY GUIDE: *How does Professor Andersen's theory explicate the "factors" specified by §241 of the Restatement? What is the difference between the interest in future performance and the interest in present performance? What is the difference between cancellation damages and compensatory damages? What relationship does this theory reveal between the concept of material breach and that of anticipatory repudiation? What differences does it reveal between the concept of material breach and the substantial performance doctrine?*

A NEW LOOK AT MATERIAL BREACH IN THE LAW OF CONTRACTS*

Eric G. Andersen

Every year beginning law students embark on a tour of the basic principles of contract law. The journey may be hurried through a single semester or extended across the entire first year, but inevitably the course encounters the topic of material breach. Inquiring minds want to know the difference between a material breach and any other breach of contract.

---

*From Eric G. Andersen, A New Look at Material Breach in the Law of Contracts, 21 U.C. Davis L. Rev. 1073 (1988).

The instructor has a ready answer: any breach entitles the victim to a remedy, usually damages. But a *material* breach has additional consequences. It constitutes the nonoccurrence of a constructive condition of exchange, which gives the victim the power to treat the breach as total. The exercise of that power brings the contract to an end, discharges all executory duties of both parties and gives the victim a right to damages in lieu of the future performance of the other. Using the terminology of the Uniform Commercial Code, the victim is entitled to "cancel" the contract.[1]

Some students are not satisfied. They understand that they have been given an explanation of the consequences of a material breach, but not of its substance. They insist on knowing what makes a breach material or not.

The instructor, beginning to feel uncomfortable, responds that "[t]here is no simple test to ascertain whether a breach is material."[2] It depends on "whether on the whole it is fairer"[3] to permit the victim to cancel than not to permit cancellation. "It is always a question of fact, a matter of degree, a question that must be determined relative to all the other complex factors that exist in every instance. The variation in these factors is such that generalization is difficult and the use of cases as precedents is dangerous."[4]

The students persist: surely the law can do better than that. Even if no mathematically precise test for materiality exists, there must be a standard, an approach of some kind that governs so important a question.

The instructor is relieved to direct them to the First and Second Restatements of Contracts,[5] in which careful attention is devoted to the meaning of materiality. The Restatements set out a number of "circumstances" to be considered to determine whether a breach is material. Some students may accept this approach to materiality, especially when assured that scores of courts have dutifully noted or quoted the Restatement factors and applied them to resolve disputes. Others are

---

1. U.C.C. §2-106(4) (1987).
2. J. Calamari & J. Perillo, Contracts §11-22, at 459 (3d ed. 1987).
3. S. Williston, 6 A Treatise on the Law of Contracts §841, at 159 (3d ed. 1962).
4. A. Corbin, 3A Corbin on Contracts §704, at 318 (1960).
5. See Restatement of Contracts §275 (1932) . . . ; Restatement (Second) of Contracts §241 (1979). . . .

more skeptical; to them the relevant Restatement provisions seem enigmatic at best.

Then the students become lawyers and encounter the material-breach case law in practice. Any confidence they may have had that those cases reflect a basic coherence and rationality is likely to be shaken. They soon discover that many courts that purport to follow the Restatements actually ignore them when the time comes to decide the materiality question. Others seem to pick and choose among the stated factors without justifying their choices. Still others do not even attempt to apply the "circumstances" of the Restatements, but follow tests under which materiality is simply "a question to be decided on 'the inherent justice of the matter.' "

A close look at the relevant Restatement provisions makes it difficult to blame the courts for falling into confusion or completely bypassing them. The provisions resemble a list of ingredients rather than a recipe; no real guidance is provided on the order or proportions in which to combine the provisions. Indeed, a careful analysis suggests that some of the Restatement factors are substantively irrelevant or misleading as elements of the materiality analysis. In a cynical moment, the lawyer — whether practitioner, jurist, or academic — may wonder whether a paraphrase of Professor Gilmore's quip about the inclusion of section 90 in the First Restatement might also apply to the materiality factors in the Restatements: An attentive study leads to the despairing conclusion that no one has any idea what the damn things mean.[6]

This Article proposes a new perspective on material breach. It argues that materiality is best understood in terms of the specific purpose of the cancellation remedy that material breach entails. That remedy is designed to secure and enhance the likelihood that *future* duties will be properly performed. It does so by enabling the victim of a breach to acquire elsewhere the performance (or its economic equivalent) of the future duties that were to have been rendered by the other party. A breach should be considered material only when, given the particular facts of the case at hand, the victim needs that ability. Although this perspective does not eliminate doubt or uncertainty, it has the advantage of a simple and internally coherent theory. It remains for the courts to exercise judgment, but by using the approach proposed by this Article

---

6. G. Gilmore, The Death of Contract 64-65 (1974).

the courts are aided by a clear view of the questions they must answer. . . .

II.　A REMEDIAL APPROACH TO MATERIAL BREACH

Material breach is best understood on the basis of the cancellation remedy it invokes. Remedies for breach of contract are subject to, or at least influenced by, a number of important policies. A primary policy is to protect the victim's expectation interest without imposing unnecessary costs on the party in breach. A useful approach to material breach emerges when the cancellation remedy is examined in light of that policy.

For present purposes, the contractual expectation interest may be understood as consisting of two distinct components. This Article refers to them as the *interest in present performance* and the *interest in future performance*. The purpose and effect of the cancellation remedy is to protect the interest in future performance, not the interest in present performance. In keeping with remedial policy, the cancellation remedy should be made available — that is, a breach is material — only when that remedy would protect the victim's interest in future performance without imposing unnecessary costs on the other side.

A.　Material Breach and Remedial Policy

Characterizing a breach of contract as material is equivalent to saying that the cancellation remedy, in addition to compensatory damages, should be made available to the victim of the breach. That remedy includes the power to withhold one's own performance for the period (if any) during which cure is permitted, and thereafter to bring the contract to an end, discharging the remaining duties of both parties. Thus, if a builder pours a defective foundation for a new house, and the breach is considered material, the owner has not only a cause of action for the damages to remedy the defective work, but also the power to fire the builder and a right to damages in lieu of the future work the builder will not be permitted to perform. When the owner takes advantage of that power and seeks those additional damages, the material breach has been treated as total.

Materiality is most usefully approached by focusing not on the specifics of the breach, but on the appropriateness of making the cancellation remedy available to the victim under the circumstances of the particular case. That appropriateness is based on the fundamental remedial policy that seeks to accommodate two competing goals: (1) the victim's expectation interest — the benefit of the bargain — should be protected, (2) but without imposing on the party in breach costs unnecessary to doing so.

That policy is not the only one bearing on contract remedies, of course. But it plays a distinct and crucial role in contract enforcement. In contrast to the rules on foreseeability and certainty, which establish boundaries on the nature and extent of the legally cognizable expectation interest, the policy of avoiding needless costs governs the means by and extent to which that interest will be protected. That policy, therefore, is pivotal to understanding the meaning of materiality because the effect of characterizing a breach as material is precisely to make available to the victim certain important means for protecting the expectation interest. . . .

B.   The Interests Impaired When a Contract Is Breached

The most obvious interest of a party to a contract is in receiving the promised performance when due from the other party. When that interest is impaired because performance is wrongfully delayed, withheld, or imperfectly rendered, the victim is injured in the sense that what was received (if anything) is less valuable than what was promised. For example, when a landowner contracts to have a commercial building constructed, direct financial interests are impaired if the building is completed late or imperfectly. The owner may lose rent from tenants, be liable to tenants for delays, or be required to spend money repairing defects. The interest in receiving proper performance when due is the interest in present performance. This interest comes into existence at the time performance is due. It is impaired by nonfeasance or malfeasance of the performance promised by the other side.

Impairments of the interest in present performance routinely are remedied through compensatory damages. The victim of the breach is entitled to a judgment sufficient to pay for the loss of value that breach causes. To be sure, difficult issues can and do arise in connection with determining the amount of money required to compensate for a failure to perform properly[7] or with the decision to award specific relief rather than damages. Nevertheless, an award of damages to compensate for missing or imperfect performance is a standard and well-understood part of the remedial landscape.

The interest in present performance is not a party's only interest, however. A breach may impair another distinct and important interest. The moment a contract is formed each party acquires an interest in the likelihood that the contract will be performed in the future as agreed. The most important element of that interest is the probability that the other party will perform as and when agreed. To the extent that probability of performance exists, a sense of security about the future arises upon which plans may be based and commitments made. That security is one of the primary benefits to individuals participating in contractual relationships.

As John Rawls put it, one person must have confidence in the word of another "to set up and to stabilize small-scale schemes of coopera- tion, or a particular pattern of transactions."[8] These schemes or transactions do not come into existence or are unstable unless each person has confidence that the other will perform. That confidence arises by "putting oneself under an obligation to carry through later. Only in this way can the scheme be made secure so that both can gain from the benefits of their cooperation. The practice of promising exists for pre- cisely this purpose."

Charles Fried, in keeping with his view that the moral obligation created by a promise is the basis of contract, describes the confidence that another will perform a promise as "my conviction that you will do what is right."[9] That "trust becomes a powerful tool for our working our mutual wills in the world. So remarkable a tool is trust that in the end we

---

7. One of the best known is the problem whether to base damages on the cost of repairs or completion as opposed to the diminution in value to the victim as a result of the breach when the former significantly exceeds the latter. This issue is reflected in such venerable cases as Jacob & Youngs, Inc. v. Kent, 230 N.Y. 239, 129 N.E. 889 (1921), Groves v. John Wunder Co., 205 Minn. 163, 286 N.W. 235 (1939), and Peeveyhouse v. Garland Coal Co. 382 P.2d 109 (Okla.), *cert. denied*, 375 U.S. 906 (1963). In each case, the issue is not whether to award damages sufficient to put the victim of the breach in the same position as if the contract had been performed, but how to measure or define that position.

8. J. Rawls, A Theory of Justice 346 (1971).

9. C. Fried, Contract as Promise 8 (1981).

pursue it for its own sake; we prefer doing things cooperatively when we might have relied on fear or interest or worked alone."

The importance of the interest in the likelihood of future performance is recognized in section 2-609 of the Uniform Commercial Code, which provides an innovative remedy — the right to demand assurances — when that interest is impaired, although not to a degree sufficient to warrant cancellation. The official comment to that section states:

> [A] continuing sense of reliance and security that the promised performance will be forthcoming when due[ ] is an important feature of the bargain. If either the willingness or the ability of a party to perform declines between the time of contracting and the time for performance, the other party is threatened with the loss of a substantial part of what he has bargained for.

The likelihood of future performance usually is demonstrably important to the individual entering a particular agreement. The owner who contracts for the construction of a building needs the confidence that the building will be built by the time agreed. On the basis of that confidence, the owner is willing to make commitments to the building's future tenants that it would be unwilling to make without that confidence.

A party's interest in the likelihood of future performance is not limited to the probability that the other side will perform properly and on time. A party may have an important interest in the opportunity to perform its own future duties. A construction company under contract to erect a building, for example, may act in important ways, such as marshalling its resources in a particular manner, because of its confidence that it will be participating in the project in the future. Moreover, public awareness that the company will engage in that performance may enhance the company's reputation and prospects for other employment.

A party's interest in a sense of confidence or security about the future performance of a contract is the interest in future performance. It comes into being when the contract is formed and exists until the time for performance arrives.[10] Although its value could be quantified in

---

10. When performance comes due, the interest in future performance disappears and is replaced with the interest in present performance. For example, when the building is due to be completed and the tenants are ready to move in, the owner's need no longer is for the confidence to plan and make commitments for the future; it is to have the building available and properly constructed.

many cases, it is sufficient for present purposes to establish its existence as an important benefit of the bargain under a contract. For reasons to be discussed, it is not necessary to determine its precise economic value.

Understanding the nature of the interest in future performance is aided by emphasizing what it is not. It is not simply the economic benefit that future performance will bring, discounted to present value. It may encompass but goes well beyond the value of preparations to perform or receive performance that might or might not be cognizable under the rules governing compensatory damages.[11] It is not the idiosyncratic sense of comfort that a particular person might enjoy on account of an agreement, the impairment of which might cause that individual some degree of emotional distress. On the contrary, the interest in future performance is based on the objective theory of contract. It is the value of the confidence and security that a reasonable person in the position of the relevant party would enjoy at the time the contract was made if it were assumed that the other side would be ready, willing, and able to perform at the appointed time.

Specific examples help give life to the idea of the interest in future performance and its relation to the interest in present performance.

Example 1:

> A and B make an agreement under which A is to accompany B and act as B's courier on a forthcoming trip to the European Continent. After the contract is formed, but well in advance of the trip, B informs A that B does not intend to take A on the trip or to pay the agreed price.

A has suffered no impairment of the interest in present performance because that interest has not yet come into existence. But the interest in future performance has been seriously undermined. Prior to B's repudiation, A could prepare to perform, forgo opportunities for other employment or commitments, or make other plans on the assumption that the trip would take place. After the repudiation, A obviously no longer enjoys that confidence. B's statement has injured A in a demonstrable way.

---

11. Such losses might be excluded from recovery in damages under the rules relating to certainty and foreseeability. . . .

Example 2:

> A contracts to build a house for B. The contract price, to be paid in a
> series of progressive payments, includes the drilling of a water well on
> B's property to a depth of 150 feet. The contract states that B will pay an
> agreed price per foot if a greater depth is required to achieve an adequate
> flow of water. While the house is under construction, A drills to a depth
> of 250 feet before an adequate flow is achieved and includes the per-foot
> charge for the extra 100 feet in the next bill to B. Before the payment is
> due, B writes to A that the charge for the extra well depth is "in dispute"
> and will not be paid, but that the remainder of the bill, as well as future
> progress payments, will be timely paid.

When B's letter is received, A has suffered no impairment of the
interest in present performance, because the progress payment in question is not yet due. A's interest in future performance has been impaired.
In contrast to Example 1, however, that impairment extends only to A's
confidence about receiving the payment for the extra drilling. A's confidence that B will make the rest of the progress payment, as well as
those that are to follow, is undisturbed. The harm caused A by the
impairment of the interest in future performance is relatively insignificant.

Example 3:

> A and B enter a contract under which B is to do earthmoving and grading
> work on a building site at which A is the general contractor. While
> driving a bulldozer close to a building under construction by A, B's
> employee seriously damages the building in breach of a term of the
> agreement requiring B to perform in a "workmanlike manner." The
> cost of repairing the damage is more than twice the amount of the
> next progress payment.

A has suffered an injury to the interest in present performance.
Proper performance by B would have left the building unharmed.
From the facts given, it cannot be ascertained whether A's interest in
future performance has been impaired. If, for example, B promptly
replaced the errant employee with someone of known skill and judgment, or if the remainder of the work to be done under the contract
involved no work close to any other structure and B's work had been

entirely satisfactory in every other respect, then *A* might have no grounds for lack of confidence that future performance would be rendered properly and timely. In that case, *A*'s interest in future performance might remain unimpaired.

By contrast, if the work remaining to be done required using earth-moving equipment in close proximity to twenty other buildings under construction, and if it were clear that the same employee would be using the same bulldozer to do that work, *A* might be unable to assume with any confidence that the remainder of the job would be carried out without further mishap. The interest in future performance would be seriously impaired.

Example 4:

> *B* is under contract to construct a house for *A*. When *B* states that the work has been completed and requests final payment, *A* discovers that *B* has used a different kind of sewer pipe than called for in the contract. The pipe used is grossly inferior to that specified and can be expected to corrode and leak within a few years.

The impairment of *A*'s interest in present performance is obvious. The house as delivered is significantly less valuable than that promised. *A* has suffered no impairment of the interest in future performance, however, because that interest has ceased to exist. When *A* acted on the breach, *B* had completed the job, although with major imperfections. At that point in time, *A* had no need for confidence in the likelihood of proper performance by *B* in the future because *B* had nothing left to do. Although the harm to *A* is serious, it is restricted entirely to the interest in present performance.

The preceding examples underscore the conceptual separateness of the interest in present performance and the interest in future performance. They also illustrate that the impairment of the latter is not simply a function of the magnitude of a breach, whether measured by the cost of repairs or the harm or inconvenience imposed upon the victim. As shown by Examples 2, 3, and 4, a breach may injure the victim demonstrably, yet harm the interest in future performance only slightly or not at all. The proper inquiry is a specific one. It must focus on that period of time between promising and performing during which one is entitled to assume that, as far as the contract is concerned, the future is organized securely. A breach of contract may or may not seriously disrupt that assumption. If it does, however, an injury has been caused that warrants a particular remedy.

C.   The Burden of the Material Breach Doctrine: Protecting the Interest in Future Performance

The preceding discussion shows that the expectation interest consists of two distinct components: the interest in present performance and the interest in future performance. Although the goal of contract enforcement is to protect the expectation interest, the remedies for breach protect each component of that interest in a distinct way. Example 3 above illustrates the point. When the subcontractor negligently injured the building in breach of a contract term requiring performance in a workmanlike manner, the general contractor suffered an impairment of the interest in present performance and therefore became entitled to damages sufficient to repair the harm done to the building. In this Article, that remedy is referred to as *compensatory damages*. Although it often is used in a somewhat broader sense, the term here means the damages to which the victim of a breach is entitled to compensate for a defective or missing performance.

As noted, the general contractor's interest in future performance also was impaired if the circumstances indicated that the subcontractor was likely to commit other breaches of contract in the future. The payment of compensatory damages does nothing to remedy the general contractor's loss of confidence in the subcontractor's ability or commitment to perform its executory duties properly. The remedy for that loss is cancellation, which is made available by a finding of material breach.

Cancellation actually consists of two separate but complementary remedies. The first is the discharge of all remaining executory duties of both parties. The second is an entitlement to damages in lieu of the discharged, executory duties of the party in breach. Thus, if the cancellation remedy is properly invoked, the general contractor is entitled both to fire the subcontractor and to be awarded damages sufficient to hire another person to finish the work. This Article refers to the damages arising in connection with cancellation as *cancellation damages*. . . .

The distinct purposes and effects of compensatory damages and cancellation can be seen clearly by comparing an anticipatory repudiation with breach by nonperformance, either of which may be material. As illustrated by Example 3 above, a breach by nonperformance always injures the interest in present performance. It may or may not impair the interest in future performance, but it will be a material breach only if it does so. By contrast, an anticipatory repudiation always impairs *only* the interest in future performance and not the interest in present performance. By definition, the person committing an anticipatory breach has not failed to perform a duty when due, but has manifested either an unwillingness or an inability to perform future duties.

Breach by anticipatory repudiation is thus a "pure" example of material breach. Because only the interest in future performance is affected, the repudiation is either material, justifying cancellation, or no breach at all. Compensatory damages, as the term is used here, never are appropriate.

When a breach by nonperformance harms both the interest in present performance and the interest in future performance, compensatory damages and cancellation are concurrently available. In theory, at least, the combination of the two remedies fully protects the victim's expectation interest. It is crucial to recognize, however, that the victim's interest in future performance is protected by discharge and cancellation damages. Compensatory damages cannot do so.

D. A Proposed Standard for Material Breach

The essential conclusions of Part II are: (1) that a finding of material breach can be understood as a decision that cancellation should be made available to the victim of a breach of contract in addition to compensatory damages; and (2) that the effect of cancellation is to protect the victim's interest in future performance. Those conclusions, when considered in light of the basic principle of contract remedies that the expectation interest of the victim should be protected at the least cost to the breaching party, produce a workable standard for material breach. A breach is material only if the cancellation remedy is necessary to protect the victim's interest in future performance. . . .

III.   APPLYING THE PROPOSED MATERIALITY STANDARD . . .

B.   Cases in Which an Interest in Future Performance Is Lacking . . .

The materiality analysis often is applied unnecessarily to another category of cases — those in which the victim has no interest in future performance at all. Perhaps the most typical and important example of such cases is the construction contract in which the builder completes performance, but does so imperfectly. The analysis that follows is set in the context of that factual setting, although the principles involved apply more broadly. The builder will seek to recover the contract price, less damages for any breach, under a claim of "substantial performance," which means simply the absence of material breach. The owner may resist the claim that anything further is owed under the contract on the basis that substantial performance was not rendered — meaning that the builder's breach was material — and that the owner's duty to make further payments under the contract therefore is discharged. In such cases, the application of the material breach doctrine is pointless.

Analysis of the category of cases described — indeed the very existence of the category — depends upon the distinction between incomplete and imperfect performance. The difference may seem elusive. Suppose that a contractor breaches a contract to install a new roof by using tiles of uneven color, so that when all the tiles are in place, the roof has a patched and streaked appearance instead of a uniform color. It may not be immediately apparent why it matters whether one considers the work to be incorrectly performed as opposed to unfinished. When material breach is concerned, however, it matters very much whether the job is considered to be only imperfect or also incomplete.

In approaching this distinction, it helps to bear in mind the reason for making it in the first place. The purpose of the cancellation remedy is to protect the owner's interest in future performance. Arming the owner with the potential power to discharge the builder — to deprive the builder of the right to perform, and be paid for, future duties under the contract — is the best way of protecting the owner's interest in the likelihood that those duties will be performed without serious shortcomings — if not by the builder, then by someone else.

The time may come under the contract when, notwithstanding any flaws in the builder's past performance, the builder will have no further executory duties. At that point, therefore, the owner no longer has an interest in future performance. Discharging the builder becomes meaningless because the builder has no executory duties to discharge. Moreover, the compensation owed the victim cannot include an element of cancellation damages, because those damages consist of the value to the victim of the discharged, executory duties of the breaching party. . . .

Despite the irrelevance of the cancellation remedy when the breaching party has completed performance, the material-breach doctrine routinely is applied in such cases. Some courts, no doubt sensing the inconsistency between the material breach (or, as it is referred to in this context, the substantial performance) doctrine and the expectancy principle in such cases, solve the problem by granting restitution to the party in breach on the uncritical assumption that the value of the work performed is equal to the contract price less compensatory damages. In the absence of a good reason to apply the materiality analysis, the proper approach is simply to disregard the material breach doctrine and consider recovery to be "on the contract." . . .

V

DEFENSES TO
CONTRACTUAL
OBLIGATION

16

WHEN SHOULD A COURT REFUSE TO ENFORCE A CONTRACT?

Finding that a contract existed and was breached does not exhaust the inquiry into its enforceability. The elements of a contract — mutual assent and enforceability — only justify the enforcement of a promise *if* the promisor does not assert the existence of circumstances that undermine the normal significance of what is referred to as the "prima facie" case of contract. Circumstances that have been accepted as valid reasons for refusing to enforce a contract are called legal *defenses*. The writings in this chapter focus on just a few of the many defenses that have been recognized by courts.

In *Unconscionability: A Critical Reappraisal*, Professor Richard Epstein of the University of Chicago introduces the subject with his discussion of the common law defenses of duress, fraud, and incompetence. He then argues that the principles underlying these defenses can be used to explain (and limit) the application of the defenses of unconscionability and undue influence. In *The Bargain Principle and its Limits*, Professor Melvin Eisenberg of the University of California at Berkeley argues that unconscionability has a broader application than Epstein maintains. He suggests it applies to whole classes of cases in which the assumptions on which the "bargain principle" rests do not hold.

In his article, *American Mutual Mistake: Half-Civilian Mongrel, Consideration Reincarnate*, Val Ricks of the South Texas College of Law offers a historical account of the doctrine of mutual mistake that links it to the old "benefit-detriment" conception of consideration. He contends that, when the bargain theory prevailed, the need arose for an expanded, though still limited, defense of error in entering into the bargain, which evolved into today's defense of mutual mistake. In *Mistake in Contract Law*, Melvin Eisenberg provides a more normative take on the doctrine. His account emphasizes the pervasiveness of "tacit assumptions" held by both parties that are as much a part of every bargain as the terms that are expressed or implied in fact.

This chapter concludes with an issue that lies at the intersection of the defenses of unilateral mistake and material misrepresentation: When does one party have a duty to disclose information that would correct a mistake being made by another party? In *Mistake, Disclosure, Information, and the Law of Contracts*, Professor Anthony Kronman, formerly the Dean of Yale Law School, argues that parties must disclose information they obtained casually, but may withhold information that was "deliberately acquired."

A.   DURESS, UNDUE INFLUENCE, AND UNCONSCIONABILITY

STUDY GUIDE: How does Professor Epstein view the relationship between the common law defenses of duress, fraud, and incompetence and the doctrines of unconscionability and undue influence? Why does he reject the defense of "economic duress"? What analogy does he draw between unconscionability doctrine and the statute of frauds? Does his conception of unconscionability address all the circumstances thought to be covered by this doctrine? Does it address all the problems that should be handled by the doctrine?

UNCONSCIONABILITY: A CRITICAL REAPPRAISAL*

Richard A. Epstein

I. INTRODUCTION

The classical conception of contract at common law had as its first premise the belief that private agreements should be enforced in accordance with their terms. That premise of course was subject to important qualifications. Promises procured by fraud, duress, or undue influence were not generally enforced by the courts; and the same was true with certain exceptions of promises made by infants and incompetents. ... Yet even after these exceptions are taken into account, there was still one ground on which the initial premise could not be challenged: the terms of private agreements could not be set aside because the court found them to be harsh, unconscionable, or unjust. The reasonableness of the terms of a private agreement was the business of the parties to that agreement. ...

This general regime of freedom of contract can be defended from two points of view. One defense is utilitarian. So long as the tort law protects the interests of strangers to the agreement, its enforcement will tend to maximize the welfare of the parties to it, and therefore the good of the society as a whole. The alternative defense is on libertarian grounds. One of the first functions of the law is to guarantee to individuals a sphere of influence in which they will be able to operate, without having to justify themselves to the state or to third parties: if one individual is entitled to do within the confines of the tort law what he pleases with what he owns, then two individuals who operate with those same constraints should have the same right with respect to their mutual affairs against the rest of the world.

Whatever its merits, however, it is fair to say that this traditional view of the law of contract has been in general retreat in recent years. That decline is reflected in part in the cool reception given to doctrines of laissez-faire, its economic counterpart, since the late nineteenth

*From Richard A. Epstein, Unconscionability: A Critical Reappraisal, 18 J.L. & Econ. 293 (1975).

century, or at least since the New Deal. The total "hands off" policy with respect to economic matters is regarded as incorrect in most political discussions almost as a matter of course, and the same view is taken, moreover, toward a more subtle form of laissez-faire that views all government interference in economic matters as an evil until shown to be good. Instead, the opposite point of view is increasingly urged: market solutions — those which presuppose a regime of freedom of contract — are sure to be inadequate, and the only question worth debating concerns the appropriate form of public intervention. That attitude has, moreover, worked its way (as these things usually happen) into the fabric of the legal system, for today more than ever, courts are willing to set aside the provisions of private agreements.

One of the major conceptual tools used by courts in their assault upon private agreements has been the doctrine of unconscionability. That doctrine has a place in contract law, but it is not the one usually assigned it by its advocates. The doctrine should not, in my view, allow courts to act as roving commissions to set aside those agreements whose substantive terms they find objectionable. Instead, it should be used only to allow courts to police the process whereby private agreements are formed, and in that connection, only to facilitate the setting aside of agreements that are as a matter of probabilities likely to be vitiated by the classical defenses of duress, fraud, or incompetence. . . .

II.   TRADITIONAL COMMON LAW DEFENSES

A.   Duress

We begin our examination of contractual limitations with duress. In its simplest form the defense of duress allows *A*, a promisor, to excuse himself from performance of his part of the bargain because the promisee, *B*, used force or the threat thereof in order to procure his consent. The defense makes perfectly good sense even in a regime that respects the freedom of contract once it is recognized that the initial distribution of rights under the tort law protects both a person's physical integrity and his private property. Duress is an improper means of obtaining *A*'s consent because it requires him to abandon one of these two initial rights ("your money or your life") in order to protect the other. *A*'s case is crystal clear where, for example, he transfer[s] goods, under a threat of force to his person; and it is but an easy extension to the next case where force is used to procure not the transfer of goods, but the promise thereof. The defense of duress allows *A*, as defendant in a contract action, to vindicate *both* his initial entitlements, even though he has yielded to the force of the moment. *A*'s consent has been given, but there is good reason to set it aside.

The issue of duress is important in another class of cases, those involving the so-called problem of the "duress of goods." Suppose that *B* has agreed to clean *A*'s clothes for $10. After the work is done, *B* tells *A* that he will return the clothes only if *A* pays, or promises to pay, him $15. If *A* pays the $15, it is quite clear that he has an action to recover the $5 excess. *B* has put him to a choice between *his* clothes and *his* money. As in the case of duress by the threat of force, *B* has required *A* to abandon one of his rights to protect another, and the action to recover the $5 is designed to make certain that *A* will be able to protect them both. . . .

The defense of duress, though capable of extension is also subject to limitations, the most important of which concerns the question of "economic duress." Suppose that *B* at the outset refuses to clean *A*'s clothes unless *A* pays him $15, even when *B*'s previous price had been $10. There is no doubt that *A* is worse off on account of *B*'s decision to make a "take it or leave it" offer, but it would be the gravest mistake to argue that *B*'s conduct constitutes actionable duress because it puts *A* to an uncomfortable choice. Indeed the case is sharply distinguishable both from the threats or use of force and from the duress of goods. In those two cases of duress, *B* puts *A* to the choice between two of his entitlements. In this situation he only puts *A* to the choice between entitlement and desire, between *A*'s money, which he owns, and *B*'s services, which he desires. It is the very kind of choice involved in all exchanges. *A* could not complain if *B* decided not to make him any offer at all; why then is he entitled to complain if *B* decides to make him *better off* by now giving him a choice when before he had none? If *A* does not like *B*'s offer, he can reject it; but to allow him to first accept the agreement and only thereafter to force *B* to work at a price which *B* finds unacceptable is to allow him to resort (with the aid of the state) to the very form of duress that on any theory is prohibited. There is no question of "dictation" of terms where *B* refuses to accept the terms desired by *A*. There is every question of dictation where *A* can repudiate his agreement with *B* and hold *B* to one to which *B* did not consent; and that element of dictation remains even if *A* is but a poor individual and *B* is a large and powerful corporation. To allow that to take place is to indeed countenance an "inequality of bargaining power" between *A* and *B*, with *A* having the legal advantage as he is given formal legal rights explicitly denied *B*. The question of duress is not that of the equality of bargaining power in a loose sense that refers to the wealth of the parties. It is the question of what means are permissible to achieve agreement. Where, as with force, the means themselves are improper, the threat to use them is improper as well; where those means are proper, so too is the threat to use them.[1] It is a mistake to assert that the law of duress is designed to protect "freedom of the will" without specifying those things from which it should be free. "Economic duress" is not a simple generalization of the common law notions of duress; it is their repudiation. The integrity of the law of contract can be preserved only if that notion is flatly and fully rejected, and the role of duress limited to the case where one party puts the other to a choice between two of his entitlements by means, such as force or the breach of contracts that in and of themselves are valid.

B.   Fraudulent Misrepresentations

The case against fraudulent misrepresentation is easy to make out.[2] As a moral matter, a person should not profit by his own deceit at the expense of his victim; and as a general matter, no social good can derive

---

1. But note the opposite opinion of Holmes: "When it comes to the collateral question of obtaining a contract by threats, it does not follow that, because you cannot be made to answer for the act, you may use the threat." Silsbee v. Webber, 171 Mass. 378, 381, 50 N.E. 555, 556 (1898).

2. I put aside in this discussion the treatment of "innocent" misrepresentations, whether or not carelessly made. In those cases in which the representation is made in order to assist the representee, no liability should attach, absent agreement to the contrary, because the representee may be fairly said to take the risk that the information is in error. Where, however, the representation is made in order to induce the representee to act for the benefit of the representor, he should be held if the representation is false; such happens, for example, when a purchaser of real estate is allowed either rescission or damages when the seller makes a material, but innocent, misrepresentation about the property sold. The "benefit test" in effect seeks to estimate the ways in which the parties would have allocated the risks if the matter had been brought to their attention. Fraud is the easy case because the allocation of risks is easy, given the deliberate nature of the defendant's conduct.

from the systematic production of misinformation. It is quite true that a person is in a better position to defend himself against fraud than against force, if only because he can check out the representations from his own sources or walk away from their maker without adverse legal consequences. But the carelessness of a victim does not excuse, much less justify, the perpetration of fraud. Where a promise induced by fraud is yet to be performed, the fraud is good defense against an action for breach. Where the promise has been performed, the fraud is good reason to give the promisor the remedy of rescission, or where that is inappropriate, money damages. As with duress, the agreement is not respected because of the process of its formation. The reasonableness of the terms are of no concern to the court, and the same is true of the market position of the parties. (A monopolist can be a plaintiff in a fraud action.) The conduct of the promisee alone is sufficient to allow the promisor to repudiate the agreement.

There are strong common law limitations on the reach of fraud doctrines, similar to those applied to duress. True, it has been always possible at common law to maintain actions for concealment (as with the man who papers over cracks in the walls of a house to hide evidence of termites from a prospective purchaser). Yet, by the same token, a contract cannot be set aside on account of the simple *nondisclosure* of facts, which if known might have put the other party off the agreement that was in fact reached. This position has, of course, come under attack, as many have advocated the imposition of affirmative duties to disclose in a wide variety of contexts. Yet that course is fraught with difficulties of its own. First, it is difficult to determine as a matter of public policy what information must be disclosed because it is "material." It is most likely much cheaper and more effective to allow the parties in question to ask for the information that *they* regard as material, after which the general rules governing fraud and misrepresentation may be applied to the responses that are given. Second, disclosure requirements are always awkward because the party subject to them will have to act as a fiduciary toward someone with whom he wishes to deal at arm's length. Why must A be required to reveal to B at no cost information that he possesses no matter what its cost to him? The common law has been reluctant to impose affirmative duties to speak, just as it has been reluctant to impose affirmative duties to act. The undistinguished record of legislative disclosure laws, be it in truth-in-lending or in securities regulation, suggests that the traditional common law response to the problem was indeed a sound one, which insured that the prohibition against fraud was not by artifice allowed to swallow the basic premise in favor of freedom of contract.

C. Defense of Incompetence: Infancy, Insanity, and Drunkenness

Before we can turn to the question of unconscionability, we must, within the framework of the classical model, deal with questions of infancy, insanity, drunkenness, and the like, all going to the competence of the contracting parties. With [this] competence thereby called into question, it becomes difficult to argue that the consent, even if given, is in the best interests of the party who has given it, or that the punctual enforcement of the agreement is likely to advance the public good. The important question is, how can we minimize the cost associated with the rules governing incompetence? These costs are of two sorts: first, enforcing contracts that should not be enforced and, second, not enforcing those that should be enforced. The rules fashioned to minimize them should, I believe, take into account three considerations. First, they should attempt to identify broad classes of individuals who in general are not able to protect their own interests in negotiation. A case-by-case analysis of incompetence is for the most part too costly to administer, and it generates too much uncertainty in all transactions. Second, the rules should be designed to allow third parties to identify persons in the protected class in order that they may steer clear of contractual arrangements with them. It is one thing to prohibit exploitation of incompetents; it is quite another to say that people must deal with them, even to their own disadvantage. Third, the rules in question should not create artificial incentives for parties to lower the level of competence they bring into the marketplace. It is dangerous to allow people to plead their own incompetence in any transaction that they wish, with the benefit of hindsight, to repudiate.

These considerations suggest that the refusal to enforce contracts against infants is in general appropriate.[3] It is quite likely that most, though not all, infants will be unable to protect their own interests in

---

3. The arguments about insanity and drunkenness closely parallel those about infancy. One possible difference is that it may be more difficult for an outsider to

negotiation, even in transactions not vitiated by fraud. Those who deal with infants will, moreover, usually be on notice of their special status and can therefore take steps to protect themselves. They can refuse to deal with the infant at all, or they can demand that he be represented by a guardian of full age and capacity in any transaction. Finally, it is likely that most, but not all, infants will not be able to manipulate the legal rules to their conscious advantage.[4]

The recognition of the infancy defense in light of these considerations is not without its costs, as the rule in question will either block or increase the costs of certain transactions for infants who are quite capable of protecting themselves. In order to minimize the dislocations it is possible to recognize certain exceptions to the general rule consistent with its major purposes. Take for example a case of a merchant who has delivered necessaries to an infant who has consumed them. To refuse to enforce the contract will require the merchant to lose both his goods and the price for them, while leaving the infant enriched at his expense. To avoid this outcome, courts properly have allowed the merchant an action for the reasonable value of the goods consumed, a figure that may well be lower than the contract price. The rejection of the contract price represents a degree of judicial intervention that prevents *both* exploitation by the merchant and the unjust enrichment by the infant, and as such is preferable to a simple refusal to give any action to the merchant. Take another instance: suppose the infant represents to the merchant that he is of full age in circumstances where that is believable. If goods have been delivered and consumed, it is again proper to protect the merchant by allowing him to recover the reasonable value of his goods, or, given the infant's fraud, even the benefit of his bargain.

---

know of the insanity (though not the drunkenness) of the person with whom he deals. If that point could be set to one side, as seems likely, then these situations could be governed by most of the same rules that apply to the contracts of infants.

4. In dealing with these factors, it is important to choose the right age for the infancy defense to apply. Traditionally, that age has been twenty-one. However, many teenagers leave the direct control of their parents at eighteen, either to go to college or to join the work force; and there is little reason to suppose any major increase in competence between ages eighteen and twenty-one. Eighteen has therefore in recent years been adopted in many jurisdictions as the age of majority, a sound result.

III.   UNCONSCIONABILITY APPLIED

The merits of these exceptions to the general rule in favor of contractual enforcement is one question; their proof in particular cases is quite another. The courts could place upon the defendant a burden of proving fraud, duress or incompetence, say by the preponderance of the evidence. That approach would tend to insure that each of these defenses will be established only where the facts of the case so warrant. There is, however, a cost created by putting this burden upon the defendant. Solely because he cannot meet the appropriate standard of proof, he may not be able to establish a contractual defense in a case where it in fact applies. If this last form of error results in substantial costs, then it should be appropriate to modify the rules of evidence in a manner that makes it easier for the defendant to establish fraud, duress or incompetence. It may well be that the relaxation of the standard of proof required to make out any defense will increase the number of instances where the undeserving defendant is able to defeat the plaintiff's legitimate contractual expectations. But if the costs thereby created are low, then the change in the rules of proof is justified on the grounds that it reduces the total error in enforcement, even though all error is not thereby eliminated.

The legal system has long used this rationale to justify some restrictions on the freedom of contract. The Statute of Frauds, which requires that certain kinds of agreements be put in writing, has the prevention of fraud as one of its chief objects. Yet its application necessarily insures the nonenforcement of certain untainted oral transactions. The parol evidence rule, which prohibits the use of oral evidence to vary or contradict the provisions of an "integrated" written contract, is also designed to control fraud; and it, too, frustrates the enforcement of legitimate consensual arrangements. One can attack either of these two rules on the ground that the control of fraud comes at too high a price (measured by the number of proper transactions nullified), given the alternative means of its control and prevention. But neither rule can be attacked on the ground that it is directed toward an illegitimate end.

The doctrine of unconscionability, properly conceived and applied, serves the same general end as the Statute of Frauds and the parol evidence rule. Ideally, the unconscionability doctrine protects against fraud, duress and incompetence, without demanding specific proof of any of them. Instead of looking to a writing requirement to control against these abuses, it looks both to the subject matter of the agreements and to the social positions of the persons who enter into them.[5] The difficult question with unconscionability is not whether it works towards a legitimate end, but whether its application comes at too great a price.

The traditional case of undue influence, though not always so classified, falls under the general rubric of unconscionability. It involves cases in which one person brings to bear psychological pressure of considerable force and duration against the will of another individual who, while of full legal capacity, may be irresolute, feeble or weak. Any agreement between the party who exerts the influence and the party who yields to it is not likely to work in the interests of both; it is much more likely to be the doing of the stronger party even if the formal expression of both. While the weakness of the party under the influence might not be easy for a stranger to detect, it is doubtless known to the party who takes advantage of it. In general the judicial position that allows agreements to be set aside if procured by undue influence seems unexceptionable, even though some cases will, no doubt, fall close to the line. Those who wish to deal with persons who might be subject to such influence are well advised to be sure that independent advice is provided them in order to forestall any possible abuse. And once that is done, whatever agreement is reached can then be enforced under the general rules of contract law. . . .

One of the strengths of the unconscionability doctrine is its flexibility, an attribute much needed because it is difficult to identify in advance all of the kinds of situations to which it might in principle apply. One recent case, for example, that appears to warrant the application of unconscionability rules, involves recently returned prisoners of the Vietnam war. After receipt of accumulated back pay, these men were approached by experienced salesmen who proceeded to sell them unattractive municipal bonds. These transactions should as a class be set aside at the option of the buyers. We have here a narrow class of purchasers, vulnerable by reason of their long captivity, given sudden

---

5. Rules governing incompetence, for example, can be regarded as a special case of those governing unconscionability, particularly since they are a suitable means of preventing fraud and duress. They represent an effort to minimize the errors in the administration of the law of contracts, with as much precision as the judicial process admits.

control over substantial funds. Opposite them are salesmen who know how to exploit them. Proof of fraud is apt to be difficult in this case, even if the fraud itself is likely. Setting aside the transaction gives the shrewd buyer a chance to repudiate an arm's length deal he does not like, but it is highly unlikely that many buyers took conscious advantage of this legal benefit. It is also possible that some proper transactions will be set aside, but again those costs are apt to be small, measured against the gains derived. But the limits of the principle must be noted. The case should go the other way if, for example, these men on their own initiative went to a brokerage house to purchase these same bonds.

The limitations on the use of conscionability doctrines are as important as their application. Should, for example, the doctrine be used to protect those who are poor, unemployed, on welfare, or members of disadvantaged racial or ethnic groups? The perils of this course are great. First, it is difficult, if not impossible, to assert that the persons who fall into any or all of these classes are not in general competent to fend for themselves in most market situations. They are not infants, impressionable heirs, or gullible prisoners of war. Second, the subject matter of the transactions is for the most part standard consumer goods that are sold in generally competitive markets, and not interests in trust funds or real estate difficult to value even under the best of circumstances. The costs of setting these transactions aside, moreover, are apt to be quite great, for it will be more expensive for members of the "protected" class to contract on their own behalf within a complex web of legal rules. In addition, there will no doubt be both opportunity and incentive for many to take advantage of the rights conferred upon them by law to manipulate the system to their own advantage. The absence of protective rules will have costs, measured by the tainted transactions given full legal effect, but these costs, all things considered, are apt to be lower than those incurred by demanding proof of fraud to set the transactions aside.

In consumer transactions, therefore, it will be necessary to take great care in specifying the circumstances where protective rules should be adopted in order to prevent fraud or duress. One possible case that might warrant the use of such protective rules involves door-to-door salesmen, who often rely on both high pressure tactics and outright fraud to complete a sale. Yet I suspect that the unconscionability doctrine functions at best as a very blunt instrument in cases of this sort, and that it is better to adopt some legislative solution to control the problem. Here for example it is possible to specify a short "cooling off" period in which the buyer is allowed as a matter of positive law to disaffirm the contract of sale at his own option without a showing of fraud or duress. In this context, moreover, it might even be desirable, given the costs of such a rule upon honest merchants, for the legislature to adopt one rule for encyclopedias and quite another for beauty products, particularly if different levels of abuse are involved in the two cases. We are not faced with an elegant question of legal theory or with a moral question of great urgency. The only issue is what combination of common law doctrine and legislative enactment will work to minimize the abuses in consumer transactions.

IV. SUBSTANTIVE UNCONSCIONABILITY

In this last section we shall deal with the doctrine of unconscionability in a way that first puts to one side all the considerations about fraud, duress, and incompetence. Instead, our attention shifts to the cases in which courts will strike down either whole contracts or, more frequently, particular clauses on the ground that they are, as a *substantive* matter only, unfair and unconscionable. It is difficult in the abstract to insist that no contract language invites invalidation for these reasons.[6] But the crucial point is that most clauses that do *in fact* appear in agreements cannot be fairly challenged on those grounds. It is difficult to know what principles identify the "just term," and for the same reasons that make it so difficult to determine the "just price." And the problem with substantive unconscionability is further increased because the clauses so attacked are, at the time of formation, arguably in the interests of both parties to the agreement.

---

6. In this context I think it is dangerous to begin the analysis of unconscionability by talking about *hypothetical* clauses that have never appeared in any commercial agreement, particularly if the hypothetical case is then used as an argument in support of real control. As an instance of such clause: "The parties hereby agree that during the first year of operation of this automobile, should the automobile be operated on any Tuesday afternoon by a party wearing a red necktie, all rights in the automobile will be forfeited by the owner and ownership of the auto will revert to the seller." John E. Murray, Jr., Murray on Contracts 746 (1974). It is difficult to see how the clause so invented could ever be used; one would not expect, for example, to find it in jurisdictions that make no use of the unconscionability principle. . . .

STUDY GUIDE: *What rationale does Professor Eisenberg offer for the "bargain principle"? Are you satisfied with this account? What relationship does he see between this principle and the doctrine of unconscionability? Why does he reject the "procedural" unconscionability approach of Arthur Leff and Richard Epstein? To what degree is he successful in articulating an approach that is substantive as opposed to procedural?*

THE BARGAIN PRINCIPLE AND ITS LIMITS*

Melvin Aron Eisenberg

I. THE BARGAIN PRINCIPLE

. . . Suppose . . . that the defendant resists all but restitutionary damages, on the ground that the terms of the bargain were unfair, in the sense that the value of the performance he promised to render exceeded the value he was to receive in exchange.

Generally speaking, the answer of the common law has been to invoke what I have called the bargain principle, which is commonly expressed by such catchphrases as "courts do not inquire into the adequacy of consideration" or "mere inadequacy of consideration will not void a contract." When stated in this way, the principle appears to be substantive, but in large part it is a rule about remedies. What it means is that damages for unexcused breach of a bargain promise should invariably be measured by the value the promised performance would have had to the plaintiff, rather than, and regardless of, the cost or value of the performance for which the defendant's promise was exchanged — a formulation that can be expressed by the concept that a bargain promise should be enforced to its full extent.

If this principle were to be rigorously applied, bargain promises could never be reviewed for fairness of terms. A number of arguments can be made, on the bases of fairness and economic efficiency, that the principle should be so applied, at least in the context of a half-completed bargain.

---

*From Melvin Aron Eisenberg, The Bargain Principle and Its Limits, 95 Harv. L. Rev. 741 (1982).

First. The idea of reviewing a bargain for fairness of terms implies that an objective value can be placed upon a bargained-for performance. It can be argued, however, that objective value of a bargained-for performance is not a meaningful concept, because the value of such a performance is that which the parties assign to it. A related argument is that a party who has received a bargained-for performance cannot legitimately object to paying a price that reflects its value to him, and his agreement shows that he valued the performance at least as high as the promised price.

Second. If A has rendered a bargained-for performance to B, we know that A was willing to render that performance to B for the agreed-upon price. We cannot know whether A would have rendered that performance to B for any lesser price. It can therefore be argued that, having rendered the performance, A cannot legitimately be required to accept any lesser price. Such a requirement would unfairly convert A from a voluntary to an involuntary actor, because had he known in advance that the price would be reduced, he might not have contracted and performed.

Third. The extent to which private actors are willing to engage in credit transactions (that is, bargains involving exchanges over time) and make plans on the basis of those transactions depends partly on the probability that bargain promises will be kept. It can therefore be argued that failure to enforce bargain promises to their full extent would subvert efficiency by diminishing the willingness of private actors to enter into and plan upon the basis of credit transactions.

Fourth. The contract price is normally the most efficient price, in the economist's sense of that term, because permitting the price of a commodity to be determined by the interaction of buyers and sellers will normally move the commodity to its highest-valued uses, as expressed by the amounts competing buyers are willing to pay, and will best allocate the factors necessary for the commodity's production.

These arguments find their fullest justification in what might be called the exemplary case for application of the bargain principle — that is, a half-completed bargain in a perfectly competitive market. Such a market involves four elements: a homogeneous commodity (which may consist of either goods or services); a marketplace at which perfect cost-free information concerning price is readily available (hereinafter referred to as a homogeneous marketplace); productive resources that are sufficiently mobile that pricing decisions readily influence their allocation; and participants whose market share is so small that none can affect the commodity's price, so that each takes the market price as given by outside forces. . . .

In short, in the exemplary case the bargain principle is supported by considerations of both fairness and efficiency. Indeed, the bargain principle may well have been formulated on the premise that real cases did not materially differ from the exemplary case. In practice, however, such differences frequently arise, and the balance of this Article considers the strength of the bargain principle when the assumptions of the exemplary case are relaxed. . . .

II. THE PRINCIPLE OF UNCONSCIONABILITY

Each of the arguments supporting the bargain principle has considerable force, even outside the context of the exemplary case. Each, however, overstates its claim when it is extended beyond that case. The argument that objective value is neither a meaningful nor an appropriate concept can be countered by observing that the law often measures objective value in bargains that are not made in a perfectly competitive market. For example, off-market contracts between a beneficiary and his trustee or between a fiduciary and his corporation are customarily subject to review for objective fairness. If the mechanism by which a contract price was generated is inferior, in a normative way, to some other mechanism available to a court — such as measurement based on market price, cost, or benefit conferred — then resort to the other mechanism may well be in order. This point also helps answer the related argument that a promisor who has received a bargained-for performance cannot legitimately object to paying a price that reflects the value he placed on the performance. A promisee is not necessarily entitled to capture a surplus representing the excess of the promisor's subjective value over a price set in an objectively desirable manner.

The argument that revising a bargained-for price may unfairly convert a party who has rendered a bargained-for performance into an involuntary actor can be countered by a similar objection. If the price was not set by a mechanism that is regarded as fair, such as a competitive market, it may not be unfair or undesirable to revise it judicially. Many rules of law induce some form of involuntary behavior.

The argument based on the need to facilitate credit transactions and private planning depends for its weight on the strength of the policy behind facilitation, which in turn depends in part on the quality of the market in which the contract is made. In any event, not all types of credit transactions are necessarily to be encouraged, not all bargains involve planning, and in some transactions occurring off competitive markets a party might not be deterred from contracting by the prospect of a reduction in price.

The argument based on the efficiency of contract price is fully effective only to the extent that the relevant market does not materially differ from a perfectly competitive market. In fact, however, many contracts are made in markets that are highly imperfect.

In short, while the arguments supporting the bargain principle are weighty and suggest that limits on the principle should be imposed cautiously, they are not conclusive. Always, therefore, there has been a strong countercurrent against the bargain principle. Equity courts have long reviewed contracts for fairness when equitable relief has been sought. Within recent years the principle has emerged — first in section 2-302 of the Uniform Commercial Code, then in the cases,[1] and later in section 208 of the Restatement (Second) of Contracts, other uniform acts, and the Restatement (Second) of Property — that law courts too may limit or deny enforcement of a bargain promise when the bargain is "unconscionable." . . .

When the concept of unconscionability was first made explicit by the Uniform Commercial Code, the initial effort was to reconcile it with the bargain principle. A major step in this direction was a distinction, drawn in 1967 by Arthur Leff, between "procedural" and "substantive" unconscionability.[2] Leff defined procedural unconscionability as fault or unfairness in the bargaining *process*; substantive unconscionability as fault or unfairness in the bargaining *outcome* — that is, unfairness of terms. The effect (if not the purpose) of this distinction, which

---

1. See, e.g., Williams v. Walker-Thomas Furniture Co., 350 F.2d 445 (D.C. Cir. 1965).

2. [See Leff, Unconscionability and the Code — The Emperor's New Clause, 115 U. Pa. L. Rev. 485, 486-487 (1967).]

influenced much of the later analysis,[3] was to domesticate unconscionability by accepting the concept insofar as it could be made harmonious with the bargain principle (that is, insofar as it was "procedural"), while rejecting its wider implication that in appropriate cases the courts might review bargains for fairness of terms. Correspondingly, much of the scholarly literature and case law concerning unconscionability has emphasized the element of unfair surprise, in which a major underpinning of the bargain principle — knowing assent — is absent by hypothesis.

Over the last fifteen years, however, there have been strong indications that the principle of unconscionability authorizes a review of elements well beyond unfair surprise, including, in appropriate cases, fairness of terms. For example, comment c to section 208 of the Restatement (Second) of Contracts states that "[t]heoretically it is possible for a contract to be oppressive taken as a whole, even though there is no weakness in the bargaining process." Similarly, section 5.108(4)(c) of the Uniform Consumer Credit Code lists as a factor to be considered in determining whether a transaction is unconscionable "gross disparity between the price of the property or services . . . [and their value] measured by the price at which similar property or services are readily obtainable in credit transactions by like consumers." And a number of cases have held or indicated that the principle of unconscionability permits enforcement of a promise to be limited on the basis of unfair price alone. . . .

It is not the purpose of Part II to exhaust the concept of unconscionability. Quite the contrary: a basic thesis of this Article is that unconscionability is a paradigmatic concept that can never be exhaustively described. It is, however, a major purpose of Part II to suggest a methodology by which specific unconscionability norms should be developed. Accordingly, the norms described in this Part are important not only in themselves, but also as demonstrations of that methodology. Three general propositions underlie the methodology, and should be stated at the outset: (1) Since the bargain principle rests on arguments of fairness and efficiency, it is appropriate to develop and apply a specific unconscionability norm whenever a class of cases can be identified

---

3. See, e.g., Epstein, Unconscionability: A Critical Reappraisal, 18 J.L. & Econ. 293 (1975).

in which neither fairness nor efficiency supports the bargain principle's application. (2) The development and application of specific unconscionability norms is closely related to the manner in which the relevant market deviates from a perfectly competitive market. (3) The distinction between procedural and substantive unconscionability is too rigid to provide significant help in either the development or the application of such norms. . . .

B. Transactional Incapacity

Suppose that we vary the perfectly competitive market by assuming . . . that the subject matter of the bargain is highly complex, rather than homogeneous. The significance of this variation is that an individual may be of average intelligence and yet may lack the aptitude, experience, or judgmental ability to make a deliberative and well-informed judgment concerning the desirability of entering into a given complex transaction. I shall refer to such inability as transactional incapacity. Assume now that A, who knows or has reason to know of B's inability to deal with a given complex transaction, exploits that incapacity by inducing B to make a bargain that a person who had capacity to deal with the transaction probably would not make. . . .

. . . The maxim that a promisor is the best judge of his own utility can have little application: by hypothesis, the promisor is not able to make a well-informed judgment concerning the transaction. The promisee, on his part, has engaged in activity that the economic system has no reason to encourage. Indeed, quite the contrary. Economic theory is predicated in large part on the concept that knowledgeable consumers, contracting freely, will move commodities to their highest-valued uses. In cases involving the exploitation of transactional incapacity, the promisee may very well move the commodity, at least temporarily, *away* from the knowledgeable consumer who would value it most highly, and thereby frustrate the market mechanism. . . .

It might be argued against the doctrine of transactional incapacity . . . that its introduction would lead to uncertainty in contracting. That problem, however, is inherent in every contract defense. Admittedly, the principle of unconscionability introduces somewhat more uncertainty than many other defenses, but in accepting that principle contract law has in effect bargained away some of its certainty to augment its fairness. In reviewing that jurisprudential bargain, as it applies to the doctrine of transactional incapacity, it is therefore important to examine with precision the problem of uncertainty. So examined, the problem seems relatively minor. First, the doctrine would almost never be applicable to contracts between merchants concerning commodities in which they regularly deal, because a merchant can fairly presume that other merchants have capacity to practice their trade. Second, a promisee with a high regard for certainty could normally avoid application of the doctrine by advising an unsophisticated party to a complex transaction that he should get competent advice. Third, if, as seems to be the case, the courts even today often covertly apply something like a doctrine of transactional incapacity . . . , open recognition of the doctrine could actually increase certainty, by eliminating covert elements in judicial decision-making and thereby facilitating prediction by lawyers. . . .

The doctrine of transactional capacity is not limited to cases where a promisor lacks capacity to understand the value of the performances to be exchanged; it also applies to cases in which the promisor can understand the value of the performance called for but lacks capacity to understand the meaning of contractual provisions governing the parties' rights in the event of nonperformance. This application is most likely to occur in transactions involving form contracts prepared by relatively sophisticated sellers who deal regularly with relatively unsophisticated buyers. Such transactions raise a special problem. A wide range of buyers are likely to use any given form. Some will be capable of understanding virtually any provision, while others will not. Of those who do not, some might have refused to enter into the contract if they had understood the provision, while others would have gone ahead. Because the agent of the seller who deals with a given buyer may not know the category into which the buyer falls, how should the doctrine of transactional incapacity be applied in form contract cases?

The answer is, if a provision changes the rights that a buyer would otherwise have on nonperformance in a manner the seller knows or should know many buyers would probably not knowingly agree to, it is unconscionable to word the provision in language the seller knows or should know many buyers will lack capacity to understand. For example, in the well-known case of Williams v. Walker-Thomas Furniture Co., the buyer regularly purchased furniture and home appliances from the seller on installment credit. The purchase agreements were printed contracts in the form of chattel leases, which contained the following provision:

> [T]he amount of each periodical installment payment to be made by [purchaser] to the Company under this present lease shall be inclusive of and not in addition to the amount of each installment payment to be made by [purchaser] under such prior leases, bills, or accounts; and all payments now and hereafter made by [purchaser] shall be credited pro rata on all outstanding leases, bills and accounts due the Company by [purchaser] at the time each such payment is made.

The effect of this provision was that until the buyer was completely out of debt to the seller, no item she had ever purchased from it would be completely paid off, even though the balances due on some of the items might be worked down (as they were in *Williams*) to a few cents. As a result, no such item would be immune from procedures for summary recovery under replevin statutes, or would fall within the protection of statutes exempting defined classes of property from attachment to satisfy judgments. The seller certainly knew or should have known that many (indeed almost all) buyers would lack capacity to understand the effect of this provision, and probably knew or should have known that if buyers had understood that effect, many would have refused to sign. Under traditional legal rules, the provision would probably have nevertheless bound the buyer on the theory that she had a duty to read the contract and be aware of its contents. Indeed, this was just what happened in *Williams* in the lower court. If such a provision was inconspicuous, most modern courts would probably not enforce it, under the unconscionability norm of unfair surprise. Thus, in its opinion remanding the case, the United States Court of Appeals for the District of Columbia Circuit emphasized the importance of determining whether the term was "hidden in a maze of fine print." But such a provision should be deemed unconscionable, under the doctrine of transactional incapacity, even if it is conspicuous to the eye. Thus, in Gerhardt v. Continental Insurance Cos.,[4] the court struck down an obscurely worded exception to a comprehensive insurance policy on the ground that it was "neither conspicuous *nor* plain

---

4. 48 N.J. 291, 225 A.2d 328 (1966).

and clear."[5] In Weaver v. American Oil Co.,[6] involving a complex and legalistically phrased provision under which the operator of an Amoco gas station indemnified Amoco against Amoco's own negligence, the court said: "The party seeking to enforce such a contract has the burden of showing that the provisions were explained to the other party and *came to his knowledge* and there was in fact a *real and voluntary meeting of the minds and not merely an objective meeting.*"[7]

What should be the remedy in such cases? Ordinarily, the balance of the contract should stand, but the rights of the parties should be those that would have prevailed in the absence of the relevant term — unless the seller shows either that he explained the term, that it was conspicuous and the buyer had the capacity to understand its effect, or, perhaps, that if the buyer had understood it he would nevertheless have signed. The remedy hardly seems severe, since its only effect is that the parties are governed by a presumably fair rule of law, and the seller can avoid even this effect by writing the term in plain English and presenting it in a manner that avoids unfair surprise.

C.   Unfair Persuasion

In a perfectly competitive market, persuasion ordinarily plays little or no role in contract formation: buyers and sellers either take the uniform market price of a homogeneous commodity, or they do not. Away from such a market, however, persuasion may play an important role. This opens the possibility that a party who is normally capable of acting in a deliberative manner may be rendered temporarily unable to do so by unfair persuasion.

First, a definition: by "unfair persuasion" I mean the use of bargaining methods that seriously impair the free and competent exercise of judgment and produce a state of acquiescence that the promisee knows or should know is likely to be highly transitory. . . .

Although the principle of unconscionability allows the courts to adopt the doctrine of unfair persuasion on analytical grounds alone,

---

5. Id. at 298, 225 A.2d at 332 (emphasis added).
6. 257 Ind. 458, 276 N.E.2d 144 (1971).
7. Id. at 464, 276 N.E.2d at 148 (emphasis in original). . . .

some support for the doctrine can be found even in existing case law. A good example is Odorizzi v. Bloomfield School District,[8] decided by the California District Court of Appeal in 1966. According to the complaint, Odorizzi, an elementary school teacher, had been arrested on criminal charges of homosexual activity. After he had been questioned by the police, booked, released on bail, and gone forty hours without sleep, two school district officials came to his apartment. The officials advised Odorizzi that if he did not resign immediately he would be dismissed and his arrest would be publicized, jeopardizing his chances of securing employment elsewhere, but that if he resigned at once the incident would not be publicized. Odorizzi then resigned, and the criminal charges were later dismissed. The court held that on these facts Odorizzi was entitled to reinstatement. Undue influence, the court said, involves two aspects — undue susceptibility and undue pressure:

> Undue influence in its second aspect involves an application of excessive strength by a dominant subject against a servient object. Judicial consideration of this second element in undue influence has been relatively rare, for there are few cases denying persons who persuade but do not misrepresent the benefit of their bargain. Yet logically, the same legal consequences should apply to the results of excessive strength as to the results of undue weakness. Whether from weakness on one side, or strength on the other, or a combination of the two, undue influence occurs whenever there results "that kind of influence or supremacy of one mind over another by which that other is prevented from acting according to his own wish or judgment, and whereby the will of the person is overborne and he is induced to do or forbear to do an act which he would not do, or would do, if left to act freely."

Support for a doctrine of unfair persuasion can also be found in rules that permit a buyer who has made a contract in his own home to rescind during a specified "cooling-off" period, typically three days. Such rules have been adopted by a number of state legislatures, by the Commissioners on Uniform State Laws in the Uniform Consumer Credit Code, by the Federal Trade Commission, and by Congress with regard to home improvement contracts. The diverse agencies

---

8. 246 Cal. App. 2d 123, 54 Cal. Rptr. 533 (1966).

adopting these rules gave recognition to the problem of a transitory state of acquiescence produced by unfair means, and fixed a reasonable boundary line for determining the time within which such a state may be expected to lapse. The principle underlying these rules supports a comparable rule applicable to transactions outside the home.

Two objections might be made to the doctrine of unfair persuasion, as here defined. First, it might be argued that the doctrine would permit review of any contract induced by advertising, since advertising often relies on an appeal to non-deliberative elements. This argument need not detain us. Unfair persuasion exists only where the promisee creates and exploits a state of acquiescence that he knows or should know is only transitory. In the case of advertising, time must normally elapse between persuasion and purchase. Accordingly, advertisers would normally have no reason to believe that their advertising would be effective unless it produced a more-than-transitory effect.

A second possible objection is that under the doctrine of unfair persuasion the courts could review any consumer transaction entered into as an immediate result of sales talk. This objection has weight, but it must be put in perspective. In the overwhelming bulk of transactions involving sales talk, there is no use of bargaining methods that seriously impair the free and competent exercise of judgment. Application of the doctrine could also be cut down by limiting its scope to cases in which the consumer makes known his change of heart fairly soon after the bargain, both by analogy to the cooling-off rules and because late objection implies that the seller's persuasion had more than a transitory effect.

Assume, however, that in some cases it will be difficult to distinguish between normal sales talk and unfair persuasion, so that the doctrine of unfair persuasion would enable some consumers to back out of a transaction in which the persuasion was not actually unfair. Even under this assumption, the problem is not particularly worrisome. Observation suggests that reputable merchants commonly permit consumers to return unused merchandise for refund or credit. Accordingly, erroneous application of the doctrine of unfair persuasion in the consumer context would do no more than produce a result that is often obtainable from reputable merchants even without judicial intervention.

D.   Price-Ignorance

One condition of a perfectly competitive market is a homogeneous marketplace in which cost-free information concerning price is readily available. When this condition is not satisfied and marketplaces are differentiated, the price of a homogeneous commodity in a given marketplace may be strikingly higher than the price at which the commodity is normally sold. For example, the New York Times recently reported as follows on a group of Manhattan stores, most of them clustered on Fifth Avenue, which apparently specialize in one-shot sales, often to tourists:

> [S]uch shops . . . [offer] $40 radios for $80, $30 calculators for $95 and ivory and jade collectibles, so-called, at similarly inflated prices, according to cases cited by the New York City Department of Consumer Affairs. . . .
> . . . [A] lawyer representing some of the leading stores . . . acknowledged that marked prices in his clients' stores might be high . . . but he said that a knowledgeable [sic] shopper could easily negotiate a better deal. "My clients will not allow customers to walk out unless they insist on paying less than cost," he maintained, suggesting that a store that paid $50 for a radio and marked it to sell for $100 would be willing to sell it to a shrewd customer for $51. . . .
> In one shop, . . . [a salesman] offered a Sanyo RP-1900 AM radio for $80 (list price $39.95) and an RP-6700 AM-FM model for $100 ($59.95). . . .

Similarly, a number of cases have concerned door-to-door sales at a price more than twice as high as that charged for comparable commodities in conventional retail marketplaces. . . .

In analyzing whether the seller has acted wrongfully in such cases, we must first determine what accounts for the disparity between the contract price and the normal retail price. Let us begin with the Fifth Avenue stores described in the Times article. These sellers appear to offer little or no advantage over nearby stores that sell the same commodities at list price. Since no consumer would knowingly pay twice that price in the absence of such advantage, it seems clear that the price disparity in this case is based on the ignorance of some consumers concerning normal retail prices and on their assumption that further search is unnecessary because a merchant-seller's price for a homogeneous commodity is almost certainly representative of the prevailing price.

Accordingly, one method for dealing with such transactions would be to adopt a rule that a merchant who offers homogeneous commodities at fixed prices impliedly represents that the offered price is not strikingly disproportionate to its prevailing price at other readily accessible marketplaces — giving due weight to the merchant's tangible and intangible advantages over other merchants, its reputation, and the normal range of pricing variations. On every aspect of a sale transaction except price, the old doctrine of caveat emptor has given way to the doctrines that a seller will be held to his express representations and that the very act of sale gives rise to implied warranties. The theory of caveat emptor was that the obligation to ensure quality was on the buyer; to put it differently, that it was the buyer's task to search for defects in the product. The buyer therefore absorbed the loss if he did not search or searched inadequately. The theory of implied warranty, on the other hand, is that holding out a product for sale creates certain expectations in a buyer — for example, that the goods are fit for the ordinary purposes for which such goods are used — and that these expectations should be protected unless the seller has explicitly negated them.

Caveat emptor might be viewed as justified in its day if we assume that when this doctrine prevailed, buyers had little or no confidence in sellers and therefore had no expectation of quality beyond such expectations as arose from their own search. In a modern economy, however, buyers place confidence in merchant-sellers regarding a great variety of product attributes, and most merchants work hard to engender and maintain that confidence. So too with price. At one time, perhaps, buyers viewed every sale transaction as an occasion for haggling and had no expectations concerning price beyond those engendered by their own search. Today, however, haggling is the exception, not the rule, and it seems clear that in most consumer marketplaces the quotation of a price, like other statements made by a seller, is understood to convey information. This information, in turn, raises certain expectations and implicitly gives rise to certain representations. In particular, it would conform to modern understanding to adopt a rule that a merchant who offers a homogeneous commodity at a fixed price impliedly represents that the price is not strikingly disproportionate to that at which the commodity is normally sold in readily accessible marketplaces, giving due weight to the merchant's relevant advantages, reputation, and normal price variations.

... Application of the bargain principle to such cases is unsupported by either of that principle's two major props. Fairness does not support application of the principle, since the promisee has violated conventional morality by making a kind of misrepresentation and by exploiting the promisor's ignorance of a body of cheaply acquired and readily available knowledge (as opposed to knowledge that is generated by the promisee's own skill and diligence). Efficiency considerations are at worst neutral: since the commodity is by hypothesis selling at a much lower price in comparable marketplaces, it hardly seems likely that the higher price is required to move the commodity to its highest-valued uses or to allocate properly the factors necessary for its production. Indeed, it is arguable that by reducing wasteful search, a prohibition on exploitation of price-ignorance would lead to greater efficiency than would enforcing the bargain to its full extent. A consumer who knows that the law prohibits a merchant from charging a price for a homogeneous commodity that the merchant knows or should know strikingly exceeds the prevailing price in comparable marketplaces can make a more or less informed decision on whether the likelihood of finding a moderately lower price justifies the cost of searching for such a price. In contrast, a consumer who knows that the law does not prohibit such behavior may feel constrained to search several marketplaces for every purchase, lest he be exploited in the first marketplace. ...

IV.   CONCLUSION ...

Placing limits on the bargain principle is not cost-free. A major advantage of that principle, at least in theory, is its conceptual simplicity and the ease with which it can be administered. To apply the principle, it need only be determined whether a bargain was made, and if so, what remedy is required to put the innocent party in the position he would have been in had the bargain been performed. Development of specific unconscionability norms and limitations on the full reach of the bargain principle in certain types of executory contracts makes the doctrine more complex by singling out certain transaction-types for special treatment. Administration is also made more complex and problematical by requiring decisions on such issues as whether a given course of conduct was exploitive or whether a given price was unfairly high.

The simplicity of the bargain principle, however, is partly a mirage. Concepts of fairness were smuggled into contract law even when the principle seemed most secure, through doctrines such as the legal-duty rule and the principle of mutuality. Partly because these doctrines are allowed to achieve their ends only in a covert fashion, they operate in an extremely technical manner and are riddled with legalistic exceptions. Furthermore, an increase in the complexity of some areas of law may be desirable, if it accurately mirrors the increased complexity of social and economic life. Placing limits on the bargain principle involves costs of administration. Failure to place such limits, however, involves still greater costs to the system of justice.

B. MUTUAL MISTAKE

STUDY GUIDE: *When reading the next two excerpts, consider whether and how these rationales for the doctrine of mutual mistake differ from each other. Which do you find more persuasive? Is it fair to call the rationale offered by Professor Ricks "paternalistic"? Is either account more compatible with "freedom of contract"? Can they be reconciled? How do they explain the requirement that a mistake in present existing fact be mutual?*

MUTUAL MISTAKE: CONSIDERATION REINCARNATE*

Val D. Ricks

Many law students learn about the American doctrine of mutual mistake by studying the "cow case." Walker promised to sell Rose 2d of Aberlone, a cow, to Sherwood. Walker had purchased Rose as a breeder for $850; as a breeder she was worth $750 to $1,000, he said. But Walker thought Rose's breeding days had ended. He and Sherwood bartered for Rose as if she were only beef, setting a price at about

---

*From Val D. Ricks, American Mutual Mistake: Half-Civilian Mongrel, Consideration Reincarnate, 58 La. L. Rev. 663 (1998).

$78. After the bargain was struck, Walker discovered Rose was pregnant. The court allowed Walker to keep the cow because Walker and Sherwood entered the contract believing that Rose was barren when she was actually a breeder. They made a mutual mistake.

The *Sherwood* court required, as would courts today, that Walker prove three things in order to merit relief from his contract: (i) that a mistake of fact occurred, (ii) that both parties to the contract made that mistake, and (iii) that the mistake was serious enough to justify relief. ... Courts and commentators have found this requirement of seriousness difficult to understand and apply. ... [C]ommentators have called the element troublesome and imprecise. The Restatement (Second) of Contracts (and Professor Farnsworth's hornbook) opts to give examples of the requirement's application rather than any definition or guiding principle.

However, a review of the case law establishes some consistent patterns of application. Courts employ American mutual mistake to resolve a gamut of cases which might appear unrelated at first glance. Mutual mistake applies to warrant relief (or in other words, a factual assumption is found to be basic, essential, etc.) most often when the mistake results in present impossibility or impracticability of performance, present frustration, or a gross undercutting of the equivalence of the parties' exchange. Though not previously explicated in such short form, these three categories explain most of the case law. ...

Mutual mistake is distinct from other mistake-related doctrines such as misunderstanding,[1] mistake in performance or payment, mistake in transcription, and unilateral mistake. The rationales and policies which animate these other doctrines differ from those guiding mutual mistake, and these doctrines generally apply to fact scenarios other than those covered by mutual mistake. Moreover, these doctrines have a different history than mutual mistake. They, therefore, lie outside the scope of this article. The volume and complexity of material covered here requires a narrower scope.

Mutual mistake's ambiguous doctrine and broad, seemingly unconnected applications have prompted a number of courts and commentators

---

1. The doctrine of misunderstanding is exemplified by the case of the ships Peerless: Raffles v. Wichelhaus. ...

to theorize as to mutual mistake's rationale. Most recently, American mutual mistake has been deconstructed and subjected to economic analysis. Economic analysis yields inconclusive results as to mutual mistake's efficiency: the doctrine can be applied efficiently or not. Some have suggested that relief for mutual mistake must be available in contract law, even though sometimes applied inefficiently overall, to lower the potential risks of transacting or at least to bolster the perception that courts will sanction the reasonable actions of contracting parties. . . . Commentators have been only a little more helpful. Most commentators have only stated broadly that the presence of a mutual mistake undercuts the policies for enforcement of a contract. . . .

The plethora of rationales offered indicates that no one knows the "true rationale" for mutual mistake or that one does not exist. Some commentators decry this lack of rationale. Others are content to report cases and decline to try to explain mutual mistake's widely varying applications. Even so, no one has suggested doing away with mutual mistake. Most agree the doctrine is salutary, even though they cannot explain precisely why we have it.

MUTUAL MISTAKE AND CONSIDERATION

Mutual mistake's genealogy and current use lead to the surprising conclusion that mutual mistake plays in our law a role played by consideration, particularly benefit-based consideration, in the older common law. . . . Briefly reviewing some history of consideration, to see its tandem development away from the role now played by mutual mistake, makes this conclusion clearer.

When contract law first formed in assumpsit actions, consideration doctrine kept parties from error, as St. Germain said:

> But yf hys promyse be so naked that there is no maner of consyderacyon why yt sholde be made/ than I thynke hym not bounde to perfourme it / for it is to suppose that there was som errour in the makyng of the promyse. . . .

Under this notion of consideration, what would look like a mistake was actually void for lack of consideration. To take an example of the older form of consideration that has survived, if one party promises a payment of money in exchange for another's forbearance from suit, consideration exists for the first's promise only if the second's claim has some actual validity or reasonable basis. If the claim is completely invalid, then no reason exists for the promise; indeed, the promisor gains no benefit and the promisee no detriment from the forbearance. Without a valid claim, the purpose of the promised payment would be frustrated. Consideration doctrine keeps the promisor from error.

As contract law developed, consideration's function remained the same but its mechanism changed. This change happened gradually throughout the eighteenth and nineteenth centuries. Originally, a doctrine which made sure good reason existed for making a promise, consideration came to disregard the reasons for a promise. Instead, it came to let the parties evaluate the reasons for themselves and examined only the form in which a promise was made or contained. The form, later recognized as the "bargain" or "bargained-for exchange" was supposed to insure that no error occurred, though consideration had (and probably developed during that time) other functions.[2] . . .

Powell could, by 1791, find consideration sufficient in a sealed, formal writing. By the end of the eighteenth century, Holmes could argue that "[c]onsideration is a form as much as a seal," and that mere form was sufficient. Legislation later held that a writing would raise a presumption of consideration. By 1931, the American Law Institute omitted any reasons for promising from its first restatement definition of consideration and instead held a promise actionable merely if the prescribed bargain form of deliberation had occurred. . . .

Consideration as form no longer protected against error, so common law lawyers found cases of error arising in already-formed contracts. Doctrines of failure of consideration and mistake arose in the late 1600s and early 1700s to reach a just result in these cases, at least those in which one party had already transferred money. During the same period, litigants would occasionally obtain relief in equity. By the nineteenth century, as consideration doctrine looked more and more to the form of the promise rather than the reasons for it, failure of consideration and mistake had already filled in largely where consideration no longer

---

2. See, e.g., Lon L. Fuller, *Consideration and Form*, 41 Colum. L. Rev. 799 (1941) (separating to some extent consideration's evidentiary and "channeling" functions from its cautionary function).

supplied, at least when they took account of frustration of contract and undercutting of the parties' exchange. Cases of mistake multiplied, both in England and America.

In the 1990s mutual mistake protects parties in somewhat the same way the older doctrine of consideration did (particularly benefit-based consideration), but from a different procedural posture. This function of mutual mistake accounts for the various descriptions of the seriousness requirement, the most telling of which actually requires a showing that the mistake was as to "the substance of the whole consideration" or the "*sine qua non* or efficient cause" of the agreement. Inasmuch as this older consideration doctrine is unclear to us now (or, additionally, to the extent it was unclear at common law), we will remain unclear about which mistakes meet the seriousness requirement.

Mutual mistake doctrine can be applied to the actual cases to which consideration doctrine was once applied. If a benefit or detriment to one of the parties was a principle reason or purpose for making a promise, then such benefit or detriment is probably a basic assumption, or material, fundamental, substantial, essential, or vital fact. If that reason or purpose is frustrated or its fulfillment is impossible, then mutual mistake doctrine will allow the party whose purpose it was to rescind. When a perceived mutual benefit provides reasons for a bilateral contract, a mutual mistake that grossly undercuts the parties' exchange will frustrate that purpose and remove the benefit, and the injured party may rescind. Originally a good reason for making a promise was both necessary and sufficient for enforcement; it remains necessary under mutual mistake doctrine.

We should not be surprised by the connection between mutual mistake and the older understanding of consideration. The civil law analogue of consideration is cause, and the civil law contains a doctrine called error in the principal cause, which means to mistakenly think cause exists when it does not. F.H. Lawson, a British commentator reviewing English mutual mistake cases, opined that:

> the natural and rational explanation of the effect given to *error in substantia* is that the law is prepared in certain cases to save a party from the results of a mistaken motive. The three leading continental systems have been unable to avoid subjective tests. Once they are adopted, *error in substantia* really glides into *error in causa*, and whatever causa may have been in the past, it now contains a strong admixture of motive, and when it is worth considering is almost indistinguishable from it.

Lawson suggested that the requirement that the mistake be mutual acts as a check to prevent the law of contract from entirely disintegrating into concern for subjective motives.

The relationship of mutual mistake to reasons for promising prompts questions about the evolution of consideration doctrine. Professor Atiyah has noted the paternalism that existed under the older consideration law. The courts' saying they will enforce only those promises made with good reason seems paternalistic. Now our consideration doctrine allows parties to make their own bargains; reason is not considered in contract formation. But if the law will undo a promise which does not comply roughly with the older notions of consideration, has the law become less paternalistic? Of course, mutual mistake never took account of a promise to pay for forbearance to sue when the claim later turned out to be invalid. In allowing such a promise to bind without a valid claim, but on a good faith claim only, the law may become less paternalistic. Moreover, accompanying mistake doctrine has always been a host of corollaries assigning the risk of some mistakes to the parties. Assumption of risk doctrine had no place in the substance-based doctrine of consideration. Perhaps free market assumptions allowing reasonable persons to determine their own fate show up more in our assumption of risk doctrines than in our newer consideration doctrine. Even more importantly for mutual mistake, when courts allocate risk that the parties have not expressly or impliedly allocated themselves, as they occasionally do, courts preclude an examination of the substantive reasons for promising and instead force parties to allocate those risks in the future. Paradoxically, this move, more than any other relating to mutual mistake, perhaps indicates judicial promotion of personal autonomy in contract law.

On the other hand, perhaps Americans do not want less paternalism. Or maybe we want the possibility of paternalism to remain with us. No one has yet suggested we do away with mutual mistake. Moreover, as noted above, commentators continue to suggest rationales supporting its existence and (at least occasional) use. We want our courts to protect us not just from other parties but also from the inherent unpredictability of the world. Perhaps only on this basis can our trust in our society and each other continue to the degree necessary to maintain that society. . . .

Of course, I do not suggest mutual mistake could take the place of the older consideration doctrine. Its different procedural posture makes that impossible. Also, *mistake* as a concept can only be stretched so far. It does not cover future events, generally, nor does it cover events about which the parties have assumed the risk. Wise parties explicitly allocate risks of which they are aware, making mutual mistake inapplicable. Surely other limitations exist which prohibit it from replacing exactly the older doctrine. These limitations do not mean mutual mistake does not fulfill the same function, however, in this more limited manner. Other doctrines, namely frustration and impracticability, deal with future contingencies. I am also not suggesting that replacing the older doctrine of consideration is mutual mistake's only function, though it appears to function that way very often. . . .

Of course, the original rationale for mutual mistake may have changed but a new, yet undiscovered reason might justify the rule's use. I think this possible in the case of mutual mistake. The market economy rationales that seem to underlie much of bargain theory break down in a mutual mistake case. Free market justifications for contract law presume that people act rationally and have access to perfect information. Neither rational action nor access to perfect information occurs when parties act under a mutual mistake. That courts' application of mutual mistake takes place without concern for efficiency suggests that these ideas, however, do not animate mutual mistake doctrine. Even if they did, any explanation of mutual mistake should account for the decline of the principles which created the need for mutual mistake in the first place. Historically, these needs appear to have been the same principles that created the need for the original doctrine of consideration. Only a look back to them will resolve conclusively why we keep mutual mistake in service today.

STUDY GUIDE: Notice the role played by tacit assumptions in Professor Eisenberg's treatment of mistake. The importance of tacit assumptions was also stressed in my article on default rules and contractual consent in Chapter 2. Does this signal that there is something different about the defense of mistake than the defenses of misrepresentation or duress? Hint: Do some defenses provide reasons not to enforce terms to which the parties manifested their consent while other defenses attempt to discern the scope and limits of their consent?

MISTAKE IN CONTRACT LAW*

Melvin A. Eisenberg

Suppose that *A* and *B* enter into a contract that is either based on or reflects some kind of mistake made by *A*, or by *A* and *B* jointly. After the mistake is discovered, *A* claims that because of the mistake, the contract should either be unenforceable, if it has not been performed, or reversible, if it has been.

The problems raised by claims of this kind have been a source of persistent difficulty in contract law. In part, this difficulty results from the complex nature of the underlying issues: intuitively, there seems to be a serious tension between the concept that a mistake may be a ground for relief in contractual transactions and such basic ideas of contract law as risk-shifting, the security of transactions, and rewards for knowledge, skill, and diligence. Much of the difficulty, however, results from the use of legal categories and doctrinal rules that are not sufficiently based on a functional analysis. In this Article, I develop the legal rules that should govern mistake in contract law. These rules are intended to be normative rather than descriptive, but by and large, they are consistent with the results in existing cases and often explain the cases better than existing doctrine does. . . .

SHARED MISTAKEN FACTUAL ASSUMPTIONS

Another important type of mistake in contract law consists of a mistaken factual assumption about the present state of the world outside the mind of the actor who holds the assumption. Mistaken factual assumptions differ from evaluative mistakes both because they do not concern evaluations of future states of the world and because they are made by an actor who is, by hypothesis, not well-informed. They differ from mechanical errors because they do not involve blunders that result from transient errors in a party's mental or physical machinery. They differ from mistranscriptions, because they do not turn on whether a writing is erroneous. They differ from interpretive mistakes, because they do not turn on the meaning of an expression.

---

*From Melvin A. Eisenberg, Mistake in Contract Law, 91 Cal. L. Rev. 1573 (2003).

A mistaken factual assumption may either be shared by both parties to a contract or held by only one of the parties. . . . Traditionally, shared mistaken factual assumptions have been treated under the heading of *mutual mistake*, meaning a mistake that is shared by both parties. This terminology fails to differentiate shared mistakes according to their functional characteristics. Some kinds of shared mistakes should provide a basis for relief, while others should not. Even shared mistakes that should provide a basis for relief fall into different categories that require differing treatment. For example, in mistranscription cases, the parties both mistakenly believe that the writing properly transcribes the bargain. In many interpretive-mistake cases, the parties both mistakenly believe that an expression is unambiguous or that each party attaches the same meaning to the expression.

In short, that a mistake is shared is relevant but it is not critical. What is critical is the character of the shared mistake. That character is captured in the term shared mistaken factual assumptions. . . .

THE GENERAL PRINCIPLE

In analyzing shared assumptions from the perspective of mistake, it is useful to begin with shared assumptions that are made explicit in a contract. If a contract is explicitly based on a shared assumption that turns out to have been mistaken, normally the mistake should furnish a basis for relief under a relatively straightforward interpretation of the language of the contract. This point can be illustrated by hypothetical variations on two leading cases, *Griffith v. Brymer* and *Lenawee County Board of Health v. Messerly*.

In *Griffith v. Brymer*, Edward VII was to be crowned in Westminster Abbey on June 26, 1902, following a coronation procession from Buckingham Palace to the Abbey. Brymer had a room on St. James's Street that overlooked the route of the procession. On June 24, Griffith entered into an oral agreement with Brymer's agents to take the room for the purpose of viewing the procession, at the price of £100, and handed over his check for that amount. Unbeknown to either party, that morning Edward's physicians had decided that he required surgery, and as a result the coronation and procession had been postponed. Griffith sued to recover the £100.

The contract in this case did not specifically spell out the parties' assumption that the coronation and procession was still on. But suppose it did. In particular, suppose that the contract explicitly stated, "This agreement is made on the assumption that the coronation and procession are still on as of this moment." It could then be concluded, under a straightforward interpretation of the language of the contract, that if the assumption was incorrect, Griffith would recover his payment. (Interpretation, although straightforward, would be required because the hypothetical provision does not explicitly state that Griffith will recover his payment if the assumption is incorrect.)

In *Lenawee County Board of Health v. Messerly*, the Messerlys owned a three-unit apartment building, located on a 600-square-foot property, which they used as an income-producing investment. Unbeknown to the Messerlys, a predecessor in interest had installed a septic tank on the property without a permit and in violation of the applicable health code. The Messerlys offered the apartment building for sale, and Carl and Nancy Pickles bought it for $25,500, under an installment contract, as an income-producing investment. Five or six days later, when the Pickleses went to introduce themselves to their tenants, they discovered raw sewage seeping out of the ground. Tests conducted by a sanitation expert indicated that the sewage system was inadequate. Subsequently, the County Board of Health condemned the property and obtained a permanent injunction proscribing habitation until the property was brought into conformance with the County sanitation code. Even assuming ideal soil conditions, 750 square feet of property was mandated for a septic system for a one-family home and 2,500 square feet was mandated for a three-family dwelling. Therefore, it was impossible to remedy the illegal septic system within the confines of the 600-square-foot parcel on which the apartment building was located. As a result, the only way the apartment building could be put to residential use was to pump and haul the sewage, which would have cost twice the income that the property generated. Accordingly, the value of the supposed income-producing property was negative: the property could not possibly produce income in excess of costs.

When the Pickleses learned these facts, they stopped making payments. The Messerlys then sought foreclosure, sale of the property, and a deficiency judgment. The Pickleses countersued for rescission. The contract did not explicitly refer to whether the apartment building could legally be used as an income-producing property. But suppose it did. Specifically, suppose that the contract had explicitly provided that "This agreement is based on the assumption that the apartment building constitutes a lawful income-producing property." Again, relief would have been justified under a relatively straightforward interpretation of the language of the contract.

Now suppose a shared mistaken assumption is tacit rather than explicit. The concept of a *tacit assumption* has been explicated as follows by Lon Fuller:

> Words like "intention," "assumption," "expectation" and "understanding" all seem to imply a *conscious* state involving an awareness of alternatives and a deliberate choice among them. It is, however, plain that there is a psychological state that can be described as a "tacit assumption," which does not involve a consciousness of alternatives. The absent-minded professor stepping from his office into the hall as he reads a book "assumes" that the floor of the hall will be there to receive him. His conduct is conditioned and directed by this assumption, even though the possibility that the floor has been removed does not "occur" to him, that is, is not present in his conscious mental processes.[1]

A more colloquial expression that captures the concept of tacit assumptions is the phrase "taken for granted." As this expression indicates, tacit assumptions are as real as explicit assumptions. Tacit assumptions are not made explicit, even where they are the basis of a contract, just because they are taken for granted and therefore don't need to be

---

1. Lon L. Fuller & Melvin Aron Eisenberg, Basic Contract Law 744 (7th ed. 2001); see also Randy E. Barnett, Contracts: Cases and Doctrine [1027 (3d ed. 2003)]:

> As computer researchers struggling to develop "artificial intelligence" have painfully realized, beginning in infancy every person learns far more about the world than she could possibly articulate — even to herself. Any parent can testify to the untold number of questions that children ask eliciting information that adults unconsciously take for granted. Until subjected to the barrage, one cannot fully appreciate the immense store of knowledge one possesses. One is also struck by one's inability to articulate what one knows perfectly well.
>
> Each of us brings [virtually infinite] knowledge and skill to every interpersonal interaction and much, perhaps most, of this knowledge we hold in common. For example, even persons who have never conceived of the concept of gravity know that to build a tower out of toy blocks we have to begin at the bottom, not at the top. (An elaborately programmed computer used for one artificial intelligence experiment did not "realize" this basic fact and responded to a command to stack blocks by starting at the top. It then had to be reprogrammed with this basic assumption.) This vast repository of shared knowledge about the world and how it works is often referred to as "common sense." Common sense makes communication by means of a common language possible.

expressed. They are so deeply embedded that it simply doesn't occur to the parties to make them explicit — any more than it occurs to Fuller's professor to think to himself, every time he is about to walk through a door, "remember to check my assumption that the floor is still in place."

The general principle that should govern such cases is that if a mistake concerning a shared factual assumption would provide a basis for relief to the adversely affected party if the assumption was explicit, so too should the assumption provide a basis for relief to the adversely affected party if the assumption is tacit, provided that the assumption is material (by which I mean, for this purpose, an assumption that is the basis or foundation of the contract or, as an opinion in the House of Lords put it, "an underlying assumption without which the parties would not have made the contract they in fact made"). The reason for this principle is that in such cases the contract implicitly allocates away from the adversely affected party the risk that the assumption was mistaken. By the *adversely affected party*, I mean a party who would suffer a loss if the contract was enforced, because due to the mistake, either (1) the performance he is to receive is worth much less than he agreed to pay and reasonably expected the performance would be worth, or (2) his own performance would cost much more than the price he is to be paid and the costs he reasonably expected to incur.

So, for example, it is pretty clear that the parties in *Griffith v. Brymer* operated on the tacit assumption — took for granted — that the coronation and procession were still on when they made their contract, and that this assumption was material. Accordingly, if relief would have been justified if the parties had made this assumption explicit, so too was it justified when, as was actually the case, the assumption was tacit. Indeed, this was just the result. The court held that Griffith was entitled to a return of his money on the ground that "the agreement was made on the supposition by both parties that nothing had happened which made performance impossible. This was a missupposition of the state of facts which went to the whole root of the matter."

Similarly, in *Lenawee*, it is pretty clear that the parties operated on the tacit assumption — took for granted — that the property could be used for income-producing purposes, and that this assumption was material. If relief would have been justified if the parties had made that assumption explicit, so too would it have been justified if the assumption was tacit. Accordingly, the court held that but for a clause in the contract, which the court interpreted to put the risk on the Pickleses

("Purchaser has examined this property and agrees to accept same in its present condition"), rescission would have been appropriate:

> [R]escission is indicated when [a] mistaken belief relates to a basic assumption of the parties upon which the contract is made, and which materially affects the agreed performances of the parties. . . .
> All of the parties to this contract erroneously assumed that the property . . . was suitable for human habitation and could be utilized to generate rental income. The fundamental nature of these assumptions is indicated by the fact that their invalidity [frustrated, indeed precluded, the Pickleses'] intended use of the real estate. . . . Thus, the parties' mistake as to a basic assumption materially affects the agreed performances of the parties.

Accordingly, shared mistaken tacit assumptions are unlike mechanical errors not only in the character of the mistake, but in the way the mistake plays out. In the case of a mechanical error, the party who seeks relief wants to be excused from, or reverse a performance that he rendered pursuant to, a contract that he has actually made. In contrast, in the case of a shared mistaken tacit assumption, the party who seeks relief wants to depart only from the literal words of the contract, not from the contract itself, which includes the tacit assumption.

It is sometimes suggested that shared mistaken assumptions that are not explicitly spelled out in the contract should not justify legal relief because contracts should be interpreted literally. This argument is incorrect for several reasons.

First, a literalist approach undermines the purpose of contract law. That purpose is to effectuate the objectives of parties to promissory transactions, provided that appropriate conditions, such as enforceability, are satisfied, and subject to appropriate constraints, such as unconscionability. The objectives of contracting parties, and the contracts in which these objectives are embodied, are not limited to the words that the parties utter or write. As modern contract law recognizes, a contract is "the total legal obligation which results from the parties' agreement"[2] — which means "the agreement of the parties in fact as found in their language or by implication from other circumstances."[3]

---

2. U.C.C. §1-201(11) (2002).
3. *Id.* §1-201(3).

Among these circumstances are the parties' shared tacit assumptions. . . .

Second, literalism is an incoherent theory, because it cannot possibly be applied to all expressions, and there are no metaprinciples that could tell us which expressions can sensibly be literally interpreted and which cannot. The classic explication of this point is Lieber's famous passage, "fetch some soupmeat":

> Let us take an instance of the simplest kind, to show in what degree we are continually obliged to resort to interpretation. . . .
>
> Suppose a housekeeper says to a domestic: "fetch some soupmeat," accompanying the act with giving some money to the latter; he will be unable to execute the order without interpretation, however easy and, consequently, rapid the performance of the process may be. Common sense and good faith tell the domestic, that the housekeeper's meaning was this: 1. He should go immediately, or as soon as his other occupations are finished; or, if he be directed to do so in the evening, that he should go the next day at the *usual* hour; 2. that the money handed him by the housekeeper is intended to pay for the meat thus ordered, and not as a present to him; 3. that he should buy such meat and of such parts of the animal, as, to his knowledge, has commonly been used in the house he stays at, for making soups; 4. that he buy the best meat he can obtain, for a fair price; 5. that he go to that butcher who usually provides the family, with whom the domestic resides, with meat, or to some convenient stall, and not to any unnecessarily distant place; 6. that he return the rest of the money; 7. that he bring home the meat in good faith, neither adding any thing disagreeable nor injurious; 8. that he fetch the meat for the use of the family and not for himself. Suppose, on the other hand, the housekeeper, afraid of being misunderstood, had mentioned these eight specifications, she would not have obtained her object, if it were to exclude all *possibility* of misunderstanding. For, the various specifications would have required new ones. Where would be the end? We are constrained then, always, to leave a considerable part of our meaning to be found out by interpretation, which, in many cases must necessarily cause greater or less obscurity with regard to the exact meaning, which our words were intended to convey.[4]

Lieber's illustration makes clear that even the simplest expression cannot sensibly be limited to the words that comprise it. So, for example,

---

4. Francis Lieber, Legal and Political Hermeneutics 17-19 (3d ed. 1880).

under literalist theory the servant would be obedient to the instruction "fetch some soupmeat" if, for example, he went for the soupmeat a week later, purchased soupmeat of a kind the family never used, or fetched soupmeat and ate it himself.

Or take an illustration that is even more directly applicable to shared mistaken tacit assumptions. Suppose that Jesse is an Orthodox Jew, who keeps strictly Kosher, and Rebecca is a Reform Jew, who does not. Rebecca knows that Jesse keeps strictly Kosher. Jesse and Rebecca meet periodically for dinner at the Star Delicatessen, a Kosher restaurant. On Monday, they agree to meet for dinner at the Star on Wednesday night. Unbeknown to either of them, on the previous Thursday the local Rabbinate had declared that the Star's method of preparing food did not satisfy Kosher rules. Jesse learns of this development on Tuesday, calls Rebecca, explains the situation, and says, "I can't have dinner with you at the Star. Let's have dinner somewhere else." Rebecca replies, "No, you agreed to have dinner at the Star; if you don't meet me there tomorrow you will be breaking your promise." Isn't it clear that Rebecca's position is untenable? Jesse has not broken his promise, because the agreement, and therefore his promise, was based on the shared mistaken tacit assumption that the Star was Kosher.

Or suppose that Albert, a ballet dancer, meets Brenda at an early-afternoon art opening in New York City, and they agree to go jogging together in Central Park in two days. Unbeknown to Albert, he has a tiny stress fracture, which is discovered later that afternoon when his foot begins to hurt and he sees an orthopedist. The orthopedist tells Albert that jogging once for a short time would not necessarily make the fracture worse; in fact, many people with stress fractures don't realize the cause of their pain and therefore continue their normal activities. However, jogging would be at least somewhat painful. Moreover, the most important treatment for a stress fracture is six to eight weeks of rest, and continued stress on the foot could possibly lead to a complete fracture and even to improper healing and consequent bone deformation. That evening, Albert calls Brenda, explains the situation, and says, "I can't go jogging with you the day after tomorrow. Let's have breakfast instead." Brenda replies, "No, you agreed to go jogging in the Park the day after tomorrow, and from what you tell me it isn't impossible for you to do so. If you don't go jogging with me tomorrow morning you will be breaking your promise." Isn't it clear that Brenda's position is untenable? Albert has not broken his promise, because the agreement, and therefore his promise, was based on the shared mistaken tacit assumption that both Albert and Brenda had no physical affliction that would make jogging painful and risky.

Griffith v. Brymer and *Lenawee* do not differ from these cases. Griffith's promise was based on the tacit assumption, which he shared with Brymer, that the coronation was on. The Pickleses' promise was based on the tacit assumption, which they shared with the Messerlys, that the apartment building was suitable for human habitation and legally capable of producing income. Neither Jesse, nor Albert, nor Griffith, nor the Pickleses broke a promise when each insisted that their contracts included the shared tacit assumption.

In short, every contract includes explicit terms, implied terms, implicit terms, usages, and tacit assumptions, and every contract must be interpreted in the context of the purpose for which, and the circumstances in which, the contract was made. Where a tacit assumption is material, the agreement also includes an implied understanding that, subject to certain limitations, the risk that the assumption is mistaken is allocated away from the adversely affected party. Accordingly, the principle that a shared mistaken tacit assumption normally provides a basis for relief does not undercut the agreement of the parties. Rather, that principle, if properly applied, *carries out* the agreement of the parties. So in *Griffith v. Brymer*, if the agreement is construed to include the parties' shared tacit assumption that when the contract was made the coronation was on, then the agreement itself justifies relief for Griffith. If, in a situation like *Lenawee*, the agreement is construed to include the parties' shared tacit assumption that when the contract was made there was no existing legal barrier to using the property to produce income, then the agreement itself justifies relief for the purchaser. . . .

Of course, if actors had infinite time and no costs, then they could ransack their minds to think through every one of their tacit assumptions and make each of those assumptions explicit. But actors do not have infinite time and they do have costs. It would be irrational to take the time and incur the costs to determine and make explicit every tacit assumption, because the time and costs of doing so would often approach or exceed the expected profit from the contract. It would also normally be virtually impossible to make such a determination. As Randy Barnett has stated:

> [When we add] to the infinity of knowledge about the present world the inherent uncertainty of future events . . . we immediately can see that the seductive idea that a contract can . . . articulate every contingency

that might arise before . . . performance is sheer fantasy. For this reason, contracts must be silent on an untold number of items. And many of these silent assumptions that underlie *every* agreement are as basic as the assumption that the sun will rise tomorrow. They are simply *too* basic to merit mention.

In short, in contracting, as in other parts of life, some things go without saying. And a central characteristic of things that go without saying is — they are not said.

All of this can be put more generally. A contract consists of the promises of which it is comprised. Promise is a social institution, not a legal institution. The law may or may not enforce a promise, but it does not make the promise. If a contract consists in part of a promise that is expressly qualified, the contract should not be enforced if the qualification has come into play. The same thing is true if a contract consists in part of a promise that is implicitly qualified, whether by usage, tacit assumptions, or other elements. One way to determine the meaning of a promise is to ask, if the promisor does not perform according to the literal words of the promise and the promisee requests an explanation, what answer would the promisor give? If the promisor's only answer is, "my preferences changed," or "my valuations of the performances due under the contract changed," he has not offered an adequate justification. If the promisor thinks these are sufficient reasons not to perform, he doesn't understand what a promise is. But if the promisor's answer is, "my promise was implicitly conditioned on the tacit assumption, which we shared, that the present state of the world was X, and in fact the state of the world was not-X," most people would think this was an adequate justification, at least prima facie. Indeed, most people would go further, and say that the person who is acting improperly in such a case is not the promisor, but the promisee, for trying to hold the promisor to the literal words of a promise when, under a tacit assumption shared by both parties, the literal words were not the whole promise. To think differently is to approach the world in the totemic way that children sometimes do, looking only at the literal meaning of words.[5]

---

5. A popular children's book series, Amelia Bedelia, draws on children's literalistic approach to language. Amelia Bedelia goes to work for Mr. and Mrs. Rogers. When Amelia is asked to dust the furniture, she sprinkles dust on the furniture. When she is asked to draw the curtains, she sketches the curtains. When she is asked to measure two cups of rice, she determines that two cups of rice measure 4 inches. And so forth. Peggy Parrish, Amelia Bedelia (1963).

C. Unilateral Mistake and the Duty to Disclose

STUDY GUIDE: *What reason does Professor Kronman give for affirming the normal presumption that a party must bear the cost of her own mistake? How does his analysis of the duty to disclose information differ from that of Richard Epstein? Why draw a distinction between casually and deliberately acquired information?*

MISTAKE, DISCLOSURE, INFORMATION, AND THE LAW OF CONTRACTS*

Anthony T. Kronman

I. MISTAKE AND THE ALLOCATION OF RISK

Every contractual agreement is predicated upon a number of factual assumptions about the world. Some of these assumptions are shared by the parties to the contract and some are not. It is always possible that a particular factual assumption is mistaken. From an economic point of view, the risk of such a mistake (whether it be the mistake of only one party or both) represents a cost. It is a cost to the contracting parties themselves and to society as a whole since the actual occurrence of a mistake always (potentially) increases the resources which must be devoted to the process of allocating goods to their highest-valuing users. . . .

Information is the antidote to mistake. Although information is costly to produce, one individual may be able to obtain relevant information more cheaply than another. If the parties to a contract are acting rationally, they will minimize the joint costs of a potential mistake by assigning the risk of its occurrence to the party who is the better (cheaper) information-gatherer. Where the parties have actually assigned the risk — whether explicitly, or implicitly through their adherence to trade custom and past patterns of dealing — their own allocation

---

*From Anthony T. Kronman, Mistake, Disclosure, Information, and the Law of Contracts, 7 J. Leg. Stud. 1 (1978).

must be respected. Where they have not — and there is a resulting gap in the contract — a court concerned with economic efficiency should impose the risk on the better information-gatherer. This is so for familiar reasons: by allocating the risk in this way, an efficiency-minded court reduces the transaction costs of the contracting process itself.

The most important doctrinal distinction in the law of mistake is the one drawn between "mutual" and "unilateral" mistakes. Traditionally, courts have been more reluctant to excuse a mistake promisor where he alone is mistaken than where the other party is mistaken as to the same fact. Although relief for unilateral mistake has been liberalized during the last half-century (to the point where some commentators have questioned the utility of the distinction between unilateral and mutual mistake and a few have even urged its abolition), it is still "black-letter" law that a promisor whose mistake is not shared by the other party is less likely to be relieved of his duty to perform than a promisor whose mistake happens to be mutual.

Viewed broadly, the distinction between mutual and unilateral mistake makes sense from an economic point of view. Where both parties to a contract are mistaken about the same fact or state of affairs, deciding which of them would have been better able to prevent the mistake may well require a detailed inquiry regarding the nature of the mistake and the (economic) role or position of each of the parties involved. But where only one party is mistaken, it is reasonable to assume that he is in a better position than the other party to prevent his own error. . . .

In the past, it was often asserted that, absent fraud or misrepresentation, a unilateral mistake never justifies excusing the mistaken party from his duty to perform or pay damages. This is certainly no longer the law, and Corbin has demonstrated that in all probability it never was. One well-established exception protects the unilaterally mistaken promisor whose error is known or reasonably should be known to the other party. Relief has long been available in this case despite the fact that the promisor's mistake is not shared by the other party to the contract.

For example, if a bidder submits a bid containing a clerical error or miscalculation, and the mistake is either evident on the face of the bid or may reasonably be inferred from a discrepancy between it and other bids, the bidder will typically be permitted to withdraw the bid without having to pay damages (even after the bid has been accepted and in some cases relied upon by the other party). . . .

A rule of this sort is a sensible one. While it is true that . . . the mistaken party is likely to be the one best able to prevent the mistake from occurring in the first place (by exercising care in preparing his bid or in reading the proposed contract which has been submitted to him), the other party may be able to rectify the mistake more cheaply in the interim between its occurrence and the formation of the contract. At one moment in time the mistaken party is the better mistake-preventer (information-gatherer). At some subsequent moment, however, the other party may be the better preventer because of his superior access to relevant information that will disclose the mistake and thus allow its correction. This may be so, for example, if he has other bids to compare with the mistaken one since this will provide him with information which the bidder himself lacks. . . .

The cases in which relief is granted to a unilaterally mistaken promisor on the grounds that his mistake was known or reasonably knowable by the other party appear, however, to conflict sharply with another line of cases. These cases deal with the related problems of fraud and disclosure: if one party to a contract knows that the other is mistaken as to some material fact, is it fraud for the party with knowledge to fail to disclose the error and may the mistaken party avoid the contract on the theory that he was owed a duty of disclosure? This question is not always answered in the same way. In some cases, courts typically find a duty to disclose and in others they do not. It is the latter group of cases — those not requiring disclosure — which appear to conflict with the rule that a unilateral mistake will excuse if the other party knows or has reason to know of its existence.

In the cases not requiring disclosure, one party is mistaken and the other party knows or has reason to know it. Can these cases be reconciled with those which stand for the proposition that a unilateral mistake plus knowledge or reason to know will excuse the mistaken party? More particularly, can the apparent divergence between these two lines of cases be explained on economic grounds? . . .

II. THE PRODUCTION OF INFORMATION
AND THE DUTY TO DISCLOSE

A. General Considerations

It is appropriate to begin a discussion of fraud and nondisclosure in contract law with the celebrated case of Laidlaw v. Organ.[1] Organ was a New Orleans commission merchant engaged in the purchase and sale of tobacco. Early on the morning of February 19, 1815, he was informed ... that a peace treaty had been signed at Ghent by American and British officers, formally ending the War of 1812. ...

Knowledge of the treaty was made public in a handbill circulated around eight o'clock on the morning of the nineteenth. However, before the treaty's existence had been publicized ..., Organ ... called on a representative of the Laidlaw firm and entered into a contract for the purchase of 111 hogsheads of tobacco. Before agreeing to sell the tobacco, the Laidlaw representative "asked if there was any news which was calculated to enhance the price or value of the article about to be purchased." It is unclear what response, if any, Organ made to this inquiry.

As a result of the news of the treaty — which signalled an end to the naval blockade of New Orelans — the market price of tobacco quickly rose by 30 to 50 percent. Laidlaw refused to deliver the tobacco as he had originally promised. Organ subsequently brought suit to recover damages and to block Laidlaw from otherwise disposing of the goods in controversy. Although the report of the case is unclear, it appears that the trial judge directed a verdict in Organ's favor. The case was appealed to the United States Supreme Court which in an opinion by Chief Justice Marshall remanded with directions for a new trial. The Court concluded that the question "whether any imposition was practiced by the vendee upon the vendor ought to have been submitted to the jury" and that as a result "the absolute instruction of the judge was erroneous." Marshall's opinion is more famous, however, for its dictum than for its holding:

> The question in this case is, whether the intelligence of extrinsic circumstances, which might influence the price of the commodity, and

---

1. Laidlaw v. Organ, 15 U.S. (2 Wheat.) 178.

which was exclusively within the knowledge of the vendee, ought to have been communicated by him to the vendor? The court is of opinion that he was not bound to communicate it. It would be difficult to circumscribe the contrary doctrine within proper limits, where the means of intelligence are equally accessible to both parties. But at the same time, each party must take care not to say or do anything tending to impose upon the other.

News of the treaty of Ghent affected the price of tobacco in New Orleans. Price measures the relative value of commodities: information regarding the treaty revealed a new state of affairs in which the value of tobacco — relative to other goods and to tobacco-substitutes in particular — had altered. An alteration of this sort is almost certain to affect the allocation of social resources. If the price of tobacco to suppliers rises, for example, farmers will be encouraged to plant more tobacco and tobacco merchants may be prepared to pay more to get their goods to and from market. In this way, the proportion of society's (limited) resources devoted to the production and transportation of tobacco will be increased. . . .

From a social point of view, it is desirable that information which reveals a change in circumstances affecting the relative value of commodities reach the market as quickly as possible (or put differently, that the time between the change itself and its comprehension and assessment be minimized). If a farmer who would have planted tobacco had he known of the change plants peanuts instead, he will have to choose between either uprooting one crop and substituting another (which may be prohibitively expensive and will in any case be costly), or devoting his land to a nonoptimal use. In either case, both the individual farmer and society as a whole will be worse off than if he had planted tobacco to begin with. The sooner information of the change reaches the farmer, the less likely it is that social resources will be wasted. . . .

Allocative efficiency is promoted by getting information of changed circumstances to the market as quickly as possible. Of course, the information doesn't just "get" there. Like everything else, it is supplied by individuals (either directly, by being publicized, or indirectly, when it is signalled by an individual's market behavior).

In some cases, the individuals who supply information have obtained it by a deliberate search; in other cases, their information has been acquired casually. A securities analyst, for example, acquires information about a particular corporation in a deliberate fashion—by carefully studying evidence of its economic performance. By contrast, a businessman who acquires a valuable piece of information when he accidentally overhears a conversation on a bus acquires the information casually.

As it is used here, the term "deliberately acquired information" means information whose acquisition entails costs which would not have been incurred but for the likelihood, however great, that the information in question would actually be produced. These costs may include, of course, not only direct search costs (the cost of examining the corporation's annual statement) but the costs of developing an initial expertise as well (for example, the cost of attending business school). If the costs incurred in acquiring the information (the cost of the bus ticket in the second example) would have been incurred in any case—that is, whether or not the information was forthcoming—the information may be said to have been casually acquired. The distinction between deliberately and casually acquired information is a shorthand way of expressing this economic difference. . . .

If information has been deliberately acquired (in the sense defined above), and its possessor is denied the benefits of having and using it, he will have an incentive to reduce (or curtail entirely) his production of such information in the future. This is in fact merely a consequence of defining deliberately acquired information in the way that I have, since one who acquires information of this sort will by definition have incurred costs which he would have avoided had it not been for the prospect of the benefits he has now been denied. By being denied the same benefits, one who has casually acquired information will not be discouraged from doing what—for independent reasons—he would have done in any case. . . .

One effective way of insuring that an individual will benefit from the possession of information (or anything else for that matter) is to assign him a property right in the information itself—a right or entitlement to invoke the coercive machinery of the state in order to exclude others from its use and enjoyment. . . . The assignment of property rights in information is a familiar feature of our legal system. The legal protection accorded patented inventions and certain trade secrets are two obvious examples.

One (seldom noticed) way in which the legal system can establish property rights in information is by permitting an informed party to enter — and enforce — contracts which his information suggests are profitable, without disclosing the information to the other party. Imposing a duty to disclose upon the knowledgeable party deprives him of a private advantage which the information would otherwise afford. A duty to disclose is tantamount to a requirement that the benefit of the information be publicly shared and is thus antithetical to the notion of a property right which — whatever else it may entail — always requires the legal protection of a private appropriation. . . .

It is unclear, from the report of the case, whether the buyer in *Laidlaw* casually acquired his information or made a deliberate investment in seeking it out (for example, by cultivating a network of valuable commercial "friendships"). If we assume the buyer casually acquired his knowledge of the treaty, requiring him to disclose the information to his seller (that is, denying him a property right in the information) will have no significant effect on his future behavior. Since one who casually acquires information makes no investment in its acquisition, subjecting him to a duty to disclose is not likely to reduce the amount of socially useful information which he actually generates. Of course, if the buyer in *Laidlaw* acquired his knowledge of the treaty as the result of a deliberate and costly search, a disclosure requirement will deprive him of any private benefit which he might otherwise realize from possession of the information and should discourage him from making similar investments in the future.

In addition, since it would enable the seller to appropriate the buyer's information without cost and would eliminate the danger of his being lured unwittingly into a losing contract by one possessing superior knowledge, a disclosure requirement will also reduce the seller's incentive to search. Denying the buyer a property right in deliberately acquired information will therefore discourage both buyers and sellers from investing in the development of expertise and in the actual search for information. The assignment of such a right will not only protect the investment of the party possessing the special knowledge, it will also impose an opportunity cost on the other party and thus give him an incentive to undertake a (cost-justified) search of his own.

If we assume that courts can easily discriminate between those who have acquired information casually and those who have acquired it deliberately, plausible economic considerations might well justify imposing a duty to disclose on a case-by-case basis (imposing it where the information has been casually acquired, refusing to impose it where the information is the fruit of a deliberate search). A party who has casually acquired information is, at the time of the transaction, likely to be a better (cheaper) mistake-preventer than the mistaken party with whom he deals — regardless of the fact that both parties initially had equal access to the information in question. One who has deliberately acquired information is also in a position to prevent the other party's error. But in determining the cost to the knowledgeable party of preventing the mistake (by disclosure), we must include whatever investment he has made in acquiring the information in the first place. This investment will represent a loss to him if the other party can avoid the contract on the grounds that the party with the information owes him a duty of disclosure. . . .

A rule which calls for case-by-case application of a disclosure requirement is likely, however, to involve factual issues that will be difficult (and expensive) to resolve. *Laidlaw* itself illustrates this point nicely. On the facts of the case, as we have them, it is impossible to determine whether the buyer actually made a deliberate investment in acquiring information regarding the treaty. The cost of administering a disclosure requirement on a case-by-case basis is likely to be substantial.

As an alternative, one might uniformly apply a blanket rule (of disclosure or nondisclosure) across each class involving the same sort of information (for example, information about market conditions or about defects in property held for sale). In determining the appropriate blanket rule for a particular class of cases, it would first be necessary to decide whether the kind of information involved is (on the whole) more likely to be generated by chance or by deliberate searching. The greater the likelihood that such information will be deliberately produced rather than casually discovered, the more plausible the assumption becomes that a blanket rule permitting non-disclosure will have benefits that outweigh its costs.

In *Laidlaw*, for example, the information involved concerned changing market conditions. The results in that case may be justified (from the more general perspective just described) on the grounds that information regarding the state of the market is typically (although not in every case) the product of a deliberate search. The large number of individuals who are actually engaged in the production of such information lends some empirical support to this proposition. . . .

III. UNILATERAL MISTAKE AND THE
DUTY TO DISCLOSE

The rule that a unilaterally mistaken promisor will be excused when his mistake is known or should be known to the other party is typified by the mistaken bid cases and by those in which the mistaken party's error is the result of his having misread a particular document (usually, the proposed contract itself). In both instances, the special knowledge of the non-mistaken party (his knowledge of the other party's error) is unlikely to be the fruit of a deliberate search. Put differently, a rule requiring him to disclose what he knows will not cause him to alter his behavior in such a way that the production of information of this sort will be reduced.

A contractor receiving a mistaken bid, for example, usually becomes aware of the mistake (if he does at all) by comparing the mistaken bid with others that have been submitted, or by noting an error which is evident on the face of the bid itself. In either case, his knowledge of the mistake arises in the course of a routine examination of the bids which he would undertake in any event. The party receiving the bid has an independent incentive to scrutinize carefully each of the bids which are submitted to him: the profitability of his own enterprise requires that he do so. It is of course true that the recipient's expertise may make it easier for him to identify certain sorts of errors in bids that have been submitted. But the detection of clerical mistakes and errors in calculation is not likely to be one of the principal reasons for his becoming an expert in the first place. A rule requiring the disclosure of mistakes of this kind is almost certain not to discourage investment in developing the sort of general expertise which facilitates the detection of such mistakes.

17

SHOULD COURTS ADJUST CONTRACT TERMS TO HANDLE CHANGED CIRCUMSTANCES?

Contracts can never expressly cover every possible contingency. Human beings lack perfect foresight, and parties may consider it too expensive to negotiate and agree about those foreseeable contingencies that have only a small chance of occurring. Moreover, as was noted by Professor Eisenberg in his article on mistake in Chapter 16, all contracts are premised on certain tacit assumptions held by one or both parties — assumptions so numerous and so basic that they could not possibly all be articulated. How should a court treat a contract when an event occurs that is not covered by express terms? The authors in this section take two distinct approaches to this question.

In *Court Adjustment of Long-Term Contracts: An Analysis Under Modern Contract Law*, Professor Robert Hillman of Cornell suggests that courts should be permitted to supplement a contract by supplying terms to cover unexpected contingencies so as to preserve an ongoing contractual relationship. He argues that such modifications are sometimes justified as reflecting the tacit assent of the parties and sometimes are justifiably imposed on the parties when there are gaps in their agreement.

In her study of gain merchants contracts, University of Chicago law professor Lisa Bernstein came to identify two types of norms that existed between the parties: "relationship-preserving norms" and "end-game norms." Only the latter are intended to be legally enforceable. So while some adjustment of terms by parties who wished to continue their relationship was normal, when parties no longer wanted to do business with each other, they did not expect or desire adjustment of their contract terms but wanted them enforced as written. In this excerpt she considers a number of reasons why this would be the case.

Professor Robert Scott, the former dean of the University of Virginia School of Law, builds upon this empirical foundation and offers additional theoretical reasons why contracts should be enforced as written and not adjusted by courts. In his article, *The Case for Formalism in Relational Contracts*, he responds to both the efficiency and fairness rationales for court adjustment of contracts and concludes (tentatively) that the strict enforcement of the terms of the agreement is preferable.

STUDY GUIDE: *How does Professor Hillman justify judges modifying terms of a contract? How does he respond to the objection that this would be to impose terms on parties without their consent? Can you see any practical difficulties with his approach?*

COURT ADJUSTMENT OF
LONG-TERM CONTRACTS*

Robert A. Hillman

A manufacturer or utility, contemplating long-term energy needs, enters a twenty-year fuel supply agreement. The buyer and supplier agree on a base price, subject to periodic adjustment based on increased costs of production. The agreement initially is satisfactory to both parties. Then, due to an unanticipated event such as an oil embargo or high inflation, costs dramatically rise and outpace the price-adjustment provision. Because continued performance will result in substantial losses,

---

*From Robert A. Hillman, Court Adjustment of Long-Term Contracts: An Analysis Under Modern Contract Law, 1987 Duke L.J. 1 (1987).

the supplier proposes an adjustment of the price formula. The buyer refuses to adjust and the supplier, preferring the uncertain results of litigation to certain continuing losses, repudiates the agreement. The buyer then seeks specific performance.

A court may respond in a variety of ways to the problem posed by these facts. It can hold the supplier to the contract by granting the buyer specific performance or damages. Conversely, under the impracticability doctrine, the court can excuse the supplier from performing. Or, it can grant relief based on a party's restitution or reliance interest. In the alternative, the court can try to induce a settlement, for example, by deferring any holding and ordering the parties to bargain further. Finally, the court can adjust the contract, such as by modifying the terms of the agreement and conditioning specific performance on acceptance of the charges. Courts typically have followed the first approach, barring any relief to the supplier. The last approach, court adjustment, has enjoyed little judicial acceptance.[1] . . .

In this article, I analyze when, if ever, court adjustment is appropriate. I argue that the supplier is entitled to some form of relief in at least some situations, that these situations can be identified with sufficient precision, that courts have adequate tools to shape appropriate relief, and that court adjustment is good policy in limited, but distinct, circumstances. . . .

I. RECOGNITION OF A DUTY TO ADJUST

A. The Agreement Model

Because most contracting parties are aware that conditions may change during the course of their agreement and that allocating all risks is impossible, too costly, or unnecessary, many long-term contracts expressly require adjustment of terms in light of changed circumstances. For example, some coal contracts include a "gross inequities adjustment provision," which requires the parties to negotiate in good faith to resolve "inequities" resulting from economic conditions that the parties

---

1. Only one court has adjusted a long-term contract in a situation similar to the one described in the opening problem. See Aluminum Co. of Am. (Alcoa) v. Essex Group, Inc., 499 F. Supp. 53 (W.D. Pa. 1980). . . .

did not contemplate at the time they made their agreement. Alternatively, the parties may expressly agree that the price or other provision is merely a projection and is subject to further negotiation. In either case, when the supplier seeks negotiation under the flexibility-preserving term, the supplier is attempting to perform the contract, not avoid it. The buyer's refusal to bargain would be a breach.

Even if the supply contract contains no express agreement to adjust, the circumstances existing at the time of contracting may demonstrate that the parties intended such a duty. Consider the following typical backdrop to long-term contracting. The parties enjoy relatively equal bargaining strength, are familiar with each other, and have previously dealt with each other. The subject matter of the contract, although not involving a standardized commodity, is also not unusual (for example, the sale of coal). The parties are therefore comfortable with little formality. In addition, the parties want to continue to deal with each other because they are aware of the costs of finding a market substitute after investing in a relationship and after forming understandings that lower the cost of doing business. In short, the parties want to continue a profitable relationship and maintain their goodwill and reputation in their industry.

Such parties to long-term contracts also are interested in ensuring a supply or a market at a reasonable price, not in making wagers about market shifts. Although they expect disruptions during the course of the agreement, the parties do not attempt to plan for nebulous risks, and they may even fail to allocate some foreseeable but remote risks because allocation costs too much or may rock the boat. Put another way, both parties can increase mutual gains from the contract by remaining flexible after signing the contract, thereby saving costs related to planning for risks and bickering after contract breakdown.

With these relational realities explicit, the issue is whether the agreement, although silent on the duty to adjust in exigent circumstances, includes such a duty. In some situations, the answer is "yes." First, the circumstances may support a finding of a trade custom of adjustment,[2] or previous adjustments between the buyer and the supplier may

---

2. A trade custom is "any practice or method of dealing having such regularity of observance . . . as to justify an expectation that it will be observed." U.C.C. §1-205(2) (1977). A trade custom need not be "ancient or immemorial"; a new custom observed regularly in the trade is sufficient because it is likely to be adopted by the parties. . . .

constitute a course of dealing[3] or a course of performance.[4] The Uniform Commercial Code encourages resort to such evidence in interpreting the parties' agreement on the theory that, unless excluded, the parties intended to incorporate the trade custom, course of dealing, or course of performance. Thus, although silent on adjustment, an agreement may require it. Again, a refusal to adjust would be a breach.[5]

Apart from any duty based on trade custom, course of dealing, or course of performance, a party may have a good-faith duty to adjust. In problems of performance, good faith requires "cooperation on the part of one party to the contract so that another party will not be deprived of his reasonable expectations." In our example, then, performance by the buyer contrary to the supplier's reasonable expectations is in bad faith. The supplier's argument is that, as a result of the circumstances at or after the time of contracting, each party reasonably expected the other to act consistently with its interests by being flexible and cooperating to preserve the relationship when serious trouble arose.

Adjustment often may be precisely what the parties expect. The best way to maintain an informal, harmonious relationship, preserve goodwill and reputation, and protect one's investment is to remain flexible and avoid disputes and litigation. Indeed, disagreements in long-term settings are most often settled without pursuing legal remedies. Contracting parties view their obligations as growing not only out of the contract, but also out of the norms of their relationship such as cooperation and compromise. As Karl Llewellyn long ago pointed out, the written contract is only a "rough indication around which [real working] relations vary."[6] For example, when confronted with large

---

3. A course of dealing is defined as a "sequence of previous conduct between the parties to a particular transaction which is fairly to be regarded as establishing a common basis of understanding for interpreting their expressions and other conduct." U.C.C. §1-205(1) (1977). . . .

4. U.C.C. §2-208(1) (1977) provides:

> Where the contract for sale involves repeated occasions for performance by either party with knowledge of the nature of the performance and opportunity for objection to it by the other, any course of performance accepted or acquiesced in without objection shall be relevant to determine the meaning of the agreement.

5. Evidence of trade custom and the like can supplement agreements, explain them, or even change the literal meaning of express terms. . . .

6. Llewellyn, What Price Contract? — An Essay in Perspective, 40 Yale L.J. 704, 737 (1931).

cost increases, one coal supplier recently requested relief from more than forty utilities. Only two utilities balked, and the contract of one of those that refused had less than a year to run.

Obviously, not every contract raises a duty to adjust if something goes awry. If the scenario is not what I have described — for example, if the agreement is a large one-time deal involving a standardized commodity — a reasonable party might not expect the other to adjust. In addition, even if adjustment of terms in the face of unanticipated circumstances is customary in the trade, the parties have adjusted in the past, or the parties expect to adjust in the future, they may view adjustment as a matter of comity — i.e., as a "favor" that may be returned, not as something required under the law of their contract. In short, these parties may believe they have the legal right to refuse to adjust, although in practical terms they believe they will adjust. The parties view contract law as a club held in reserve but infrequently used.

When the parties view adjustment only as a matter of comity, a buyer would have the right to refuse to adjust. Suppose, however, that the parties contract under circumstances creating an expectation of flexibility, without acknowledging the contract club. Under traditional objective assent theory of contract formation,[7] the club is lost, and a duty to adjust arises if, at the time of contracting or thereafter,[8] a party reasonably believes that no legal club is available. Courts should not overlook the possibility of such reasonable expectations in the long-term contract setting by uniformly holding a party to a written price (or other) term.

A duty to adjust, therefore, can override express contract terms such as fixed-price terms or even price-adjustment formulas, provided that the parties reasonably expect those terms to yield to the implied duty. The amount of bargaining over a particular express provision and the parties'

---

7. See Embry v. Hargadine, McKittrick Dry Goods Co., 127 Mo. App. 383, 388, 105 S.W. 777, 778 (1907) ("In so far as their intention is an influential element, it is only such intention as the words or acts of the parties indicate; not one secretly cherished which is inconsistent with those words or acts.").

8. If a party's reasonable expectations of adjustment are based on circumstances arising after contract formation, such as repeated instances in which the other party does not insist on performance according to the letter of the contract, the express term may be waived or a course of performance established. As to the former, a waiver is an intentional relinquishment of a right. Some courts require consideration to support a waiver, . . . while others do not. . . .

purpose in including the provision are obviously critical in determining whether adjustment trumps an express provision. For example, in Missouri Public Service Co. v. Peabody Coal Co.,[9] a coal supplier sought in contract negotiations to use the Consumer Price Index as an index for adjusting the price for increased production costs. The electrical utility insisted on using the Industrial Commodity Index. The parties adopted the Industrial Commodity Index, but it failed to keep pace with the supplier's costs. The price formula selected by the parties was thus a dickered term, suggesting that the parties did not intend to change the term later.

Even in such situations, the parties may not have intended a price formula to govern adjustment when the cost increase is extreme, especially if the index used does not appear to work the way the parties intended. The parties may have designed the formula to ensure the supplier a recovery of its costs plus a reasonable profit, and to protect the utility from uncapped price increases under foreseeable conditions. Thus, both parties may have used such a feature to limit their risks. But when costs dramatically outpace the price formula, and the formula does not limit the supplier's risks, the provision may not apply because the parties did not intend it to apply. Instead, assuming the circumstances otherwise support a reasonable expectation of adjustment, the parties have a duty to adjust the price provision.

Although it fails to discuss the adjustment duty, Aluminum Co. of America (Alcoa) v. Essex Group, Inc.[10] is an example of a case in which a price formula apparently failed to achieve the parties' goal of limiting their risks. The parties agreed to refer to the Wholesale Price Index-Industrial Commodities (WPI) to adjust the nonlabor production costs borne by Alcoa in converting alumina to aluminum for Essex. The price formula included a ceiling on how much Essex would be required to pay, but no floor. The WPI failed to reflect unanticipated cost increases due to oil price inflation and pollution control, causing Alcoa a projected loss of over sixty million dollars for the remainder of the contract. Alcoa argued that the WPI did not work as the parties intended and that relief was appropriate.

---

9. 583 S.W. 2d 721 (Mo. Ct. App.), *cert. denied*, 444 U.S. 865 (1979).
10. 499 F. Supp. 53 (W.D. Pa. 1980).

The district court agreed. In its view, the issue was whether the parties intended the WPI to apply regardless of the circumstances, or whether they intended the index to apply only within a range of potential cost fluctuations, with additional adjustments to be made through further bargaining when the range was exceeded. Weighing all the circumstances, the court found that the parties intended the latter. Especially persuasive to the court was the fact that the parties were "huge industrial enterprises" with highly trained, sophisticated managements. Such parties plainly sought to limit their risks, as evidenced by other contract provisions such as the "elaborate 'force majeure' clauses" and the "care and expense" of the negotiations and drafting. In addition, Alcoa proposed the WPI only after determining that the WPI had "closely tracked" Alcoa's nonlabor production costs for years and was likely to do so in the future. Some of this evidence may not be highly persuasive, and perhaps when a court encounters a detailed price provision the initial assumption should be that the parties intended it to apply in all circumstances. Nevertheless, the court should not preclude the supplier from showing otherwise. . . .

B.   The "Gap" Model

The principal justification for an adjustment duty under the agreement model derives from the principle of freedom of contract.[11] There is often a fine line, however, between enforcing the parties' intentions and judicial gap filling, especially when those intentions are gleaned from the circumstances rather than an express agreement. An independent justification exists, however, for an adjustment duty in some cases in which the evidence is insufficient to find an express or implied agreement to adjust. The duty is based on the desirability of requiring the parties to share unallocated losses.

The realities of planning suggest that a particular risk, such as an oil embargo or runaway inflation, may be unallocated. If parties explicitly or implicitly agree not to deal with such a problem because it is too remote, too costly to provide for, or too likely to upset the deal, there is

---

11. Freedom of contract protects the parties' autonomy, and maximizes both the parties' and society's welfare. . . .

little reason based on the agreement for placing the risk solely on either party. Although contracts are entered for the purpose of ensuring performance in an unpredictable future, reasonable parties often do not expect a promisor to act as an insurer by performing regardless of calamitous circumstances. This is true even in contracts containing price-adjustment features, if these features are designed to deal only with a certain magnitude and species of risk.

Suppose, for example, that unforeseen circumstances increase a supplier's costs of supplying a utility more than 100 percent, that the price-adjustment feature fails to keep pace, and that the supplier faces severe losses over the remaining term of the contract. Suppose further that the supplier acted reasonably; the losses are not attributable to the supplier's own failure to bargain for an appropriate price formula, to stockpile inventories, to expand its supply sources, or to use less expensive methods of production. In fact, suppose that the supplier's own sources of raw materials all insisted on short-term agreements only. Because the particular risk of cost increases was unforeseen and because the supplier acted reasonably and now faces calamitous losses, the situation appears ripe for supplier relief under UCC section 2-615.

The effect of cessation on the utility also needs to be considered, however. The utility may have relied on a long-term supply of fuel by building a new power station, by failing to oppose a long-term rate structure based on preinflation prices, or by forgoing other market opportunities.

The traditional approach to this problem is all or nothing: either the supplier is excused[12] or the utility is entitled to performance under the contract. Courts rarely favor the supplier in such cases. Instead, they retreat to a "finding" that the supplier promised to perform and therefore assumed the risk of even an oil embargo. In reality, confronted with the adage that courts should not make contracts for the parties and with remedial inflexibility in the face of strong interests on both sides, the court may simply opt for a facile solution.

Does the all-or-nothing approach make sense? In a gap situation, where the parties' agreement does not justify a refusal to adjust and where both parties have strong contradictory interests, it would be better

---

12. Typically each party would be entitled to restitution of any benefit conferred. . . .

to recognize a duty to adjust and enforce the duty through appropriate remedies. First, an adjustment duty is even-handed. Both parties have significant interests worthy of protection in a situation in which there is little reason to favor either one completely. An adjustment duty also avoids unexpected gain by one party at the cost of catastrophe for the other, when neither is earned. Moreover, an adjustment duty helps both parties ultimately to benefit from their contract. Finally, in an atmosphere of flexibility and cooperation, an adjustment duty may reflect what the parties would have agreed to at the time of contracting had they addressed the problem of changed circumstances.

II. COURT ADJUSTMENT

Assuming the court finds a duty to adjust and the parties have failed to adjust, the question of fashioning an appropriate remedy confronts the court. When the buyer's bad faith is the cause of the failure to adjust, one approach would be to find that adjustment is an implied condition precedent to the supplier's performance and to excuse the supplier. Modeled after the general contract law approach to breaches of contract, this response would be appropriate whenever the buyer's particularly unreasonable response to the exigent circumstances casts doubt on the buyer's future satisfactory performance. Because determining whether the buyer is acting in bad faith will often be very difficult — requiring the court to weigh adjustment offers and other potentially ambiguous conduct of the parties — and because cessation is typically onerous and wasteful, the court should rarely excuse the supplier.

A less severe approach would be to order the parties to engage in good faith bargaining, mediation, or other dispute resolution techniques. Such an order may prompt the parties to reach some reasonable agreement. If the parties still do not reach agreement, or if the court believes such an approach would be fruitless, a third approach would be for the court itself to adjust the contract. . . .

B. Judicial Competence to Adjust Long-Term Contracts

Some commentators argue that adjusting long-term contracts, which requires determining whether risks were allocated, understanding and applying complex accounting data, and foreseeing the future, is simply too complex for judges. These commentators believe that judges lack both the parties' expertise concerning the subject matter and prior training or experience in creating contract terms. The argument is not overly persuasive. The problem of complex cases is not unique to the performance of long-term contracts. Consider, for example, the substantive and remedial complexities of securities, patent, and antitrust cases. The judicial incompetence argument casts doubt on our entire judicial system. Furthermore, the argument erroneously impugns all judicial adjustment, and overlooks the practicality of a modest adjustment such as specific performance for a limited duration or a cash buy-out designed to recoup the buyer's reliance expense. . . .

Commentators also ignore, or unfairly malign, the fact that a judge has the benefit of hindsight. Hindsight provides judges with accurate, current information that not only helps them to adjust the contract to reflect present conditions, but also provides clues as to the likelihood of future events. In addition, a judge can turn to special masters, magistrates, expert witnesses, and the parties and their lawyers for help in crystallizing the potential remedies.[13] With such aid, a judge should be able to reform the contract to reflect the parties' goals under new circumstances.

Furthermore, even if a judge opts for a price adjustment rather than a more modest approach, adjustment does not require the judge to alter the fundamental nature of the parties' long-term agreement. Realistically, the agreement will continue to require flexibility and cooperation, and the new, judicially prescribed price formula may even require additional adjustment as circumstances change. In short, judges cannot do more than the parties could do in allocating future risks, but judges should do what can be done. Otherwise, the supplier suffers the entire loss in a situation in which the parties agreed to adjust (the agreement model) or in which there is little reason for placing the entire loss on either party and fairness calls for sharing (the gap model).

---

13. For example, the court can require the parties to assist it in fashioning relief by submitting proposed orders and supporting briefs. . . .

C.   Judicial Adjustment as a Restriction
of the Parties' Autonomy

Critics also argue that court adjustment restricts the parties' autonomy and, in effect, remakes the contract for the parties. But assume that a court *can* approximate the adjustment the parties should have made. Under the agreement model, the parties reasonably expect adjustment; court adjustment is therefore a form of specific performance that supports, rather than defeats, the parties' expectations.

Similarly, court adjustment under the gap model does not impinge on the parties' freedom because the parties have created no law to govern their rights and duties. A buyer could, of course, enter a contract in which the supplier expressly insures performance regardless of the circumstances. Or the supplier could expressly provide for release from the contract under onerous circumstances (for example, when costs are equal to or greater than the contract price). In such cases, ignoring the contract allocation of risk would impinge on freedom of contract. But if such an agreement was not made, neither party is contractually entitled to any particular resolution of the problem when an unallocated risk arises. Nevertheless, because the parties are joined in an enterprise that encourages reliance and creates expectations, neither party should have the unilateral right to insist on performance or to walk away from the deal. Of course, the parties are free after contract breakdown to agree on a new approach to govern their affairs. The parties' failure to set their own agenda at that time or at the time of initial contracting constitutes implicit consent to the court's intervention to adjust the agreement for them. . . .

A related argument against court adjustment is that it forces parties to perform in an unhappy marriage that would be better terminated. Parties in litigation have demonstrated their inability to perform without a costly breakdown, the argument goes, and it is therefore unlikely that they would do better in the future even under a more equitable arrangement. Limiting adjustment to the duration term reflects this concern and minimizes this problem. But if a court does opt to adjust the price, thus removing an inequity in the agreement, perhaps the parties *will* do better. In addition, the buyer need not be forced to perform under the adjusted regime. The court could grant the buyer specific performance, conditioned on the buyer's acceptance of the adjustment. Thus the buyer would have the choice to either end the deal or accept performance of the adjusted contract. The supplier should not be heard to complain if the buyer chooses specific performance because the adjustment would largely obviate the supplier's reasons for seeking a release in the first place.

Ultimately, the criticism that court adjustment is an impermissible interference into the parties' freedom of contract fails to recognize that courts under current doctrine often "make" contracts for the parties. The UCC, for example, sets forth statutory gap-fillers, instructs the courts to carve up unconscionable contracts, and authorizes orders of specific performance under terms the court views as "just." In fact, a UCC comment authorizes precisely the approach suggested in this article.[14] In addition, courts, using their equity powers, have a tradition of adjusting contracts. For example, courts have long whittled away at covenants not to compete, adjusting the duration, area, and substance of such promises. . . .

III. CONCLUSION

I neither argue that court adjustment is always proper, nor that parties cannot contract out of it. Court adjustment, however, is appropriate in some circumstances that are sufficiently identifiable. The "relational" realities of modern-day, long-term contracting suggest that when an unanticipated disruption causes calamitous losses to a party, a duty to adjust may arise. Further, if the court finds a duty to adjust, the court can, in some circumstances and often in modest ways, adjust the contract for the parties. Although these "relational" facts support the recognition of an adjustment duty, this does not mean that we must find a radical, new way of looking at contract.[15] We must only pay closer attention to the more accurate factual premises of the relational view as seen in business practice, and we must be willing to show greater courage in fashioning appropriate remedies.

---

14. [U.C.C.] §2-615 comment 6 ("In situations in which neither sense nor justice is served by either answer when the issue is posed in flat terms of 'excuse' or 'no excuse,' adjustment under the various provisions of this Article is necessary. . . ."). . . .

15. "[O]ne can be a soldier in the relational contract army without urging a repudiation of existing doctrine." Kidwell, A Caveat, 1985 Wis. L. Rev. 615, 621-622.

STUDY GUIDE: *What is the difference between a "relation-preserving norm" and an "end-game norm"? Of what value is this distinction in understanding the virtue of judicial adjustment of contracts? Why would parties not want all their relation-preserving norms enforced upon breach? Why does Professor Bernstein contend that the existence of enforceable end-game norms in a written contract facilitates coopera-tion between parties in a long-term relation? Does her analysis undermine in any way that of Professor Hillman? Can you see any commonality between her approach and that of a "consent theory of contract" discussed in Chapter 11?*

RELATION-PRESERVING VS. END-GAME NORMS*

Lisa Bernstein

When courts apply the Code's trade usage provision and look at how a majority of market transactors deal with an issue, or apply the course of dealing or course of performance provisions and look at how partic-ular transactors have dealt with an issue, they will, in many instances, be observing the norms that transactors choose to follow when they cooperatively resolve disputes among themselves and want to preserve their relationship ("relationship-preserving norms," or "RPNs"). Some RPNs are "performance norms," which reflect the implicit extralegal terms transactors have agreed to abide by as long as they continue to trust one another and/or value potential future dealings. Other RPNs are "dispute-resolution norms," norms that transactors follow in attempting to cooperatively resolve disputes in a manner that will not jeopardize future dealings. Even when these RPNs are clear and well-developed, they may be quite different from the terms of transactors' written con-tracts, which contain the norms that transactors would want a third-party neutral to apply in a situation where they were unable to cooperatively

---

*From: Lisa Bernstein, Merchant Law in a Merchant Court: Rethinking the Code's Search for Immanent Business Norms, 144 U. Pa. L. Rev. 1765 (1996).

resolve a dispute and viewed their relationship as being at an end-game stage ("end-game norms," or "EGNs").[1]

There are two types of end-game stages. The first is an absolute end-game where the parties, perhaps because of the action giving rise to the alleged breach, have decided not to deal with one another again. The second is an end-game round, a situation where the parties are in a long-term contractual relationship that they wish to maintain, but where one or both of them have committed to following a strategy that binds them to seek application of EGNs under certain circumstances.[2] A transactor might follow a strategy of seeking application of EGNs in an end-game round in order to maintain the credibility of his threat to do so in similar situations in the future. In some contracting contexts, particularly those characterized by repeat dealing or long-term relationships, maintaining a credible threat to invoke EGNs in appropriate circumstances may actually facilitate cooperation.

There are a number of reasons that RPNs are likely to diverge from the EGNs contained in written contracts. First, RPNs may reflect adherence to an aspect of the transactors' agreement that they deliberately allocated to the extralegal realm, perhaps because the obligation that they sought to create conditioned on information that was observable but not verifiable, or because the legal system costs associated with memorializing the obligation in a legally enforceable provision would have been prohibitively high. Second, RPNs may reflect patterns of adjustments that transactors are willing to make at some stages of their

---

1. Even when transactors act in accordance with RPNs, the terms of their legally enforceable contract may influence their behavior. Because the provisions of the contract define the maximum amount that the promisee can recover in the event that she chooses to treat a particular breach as an end-game breach, these provisions will affect whether she finds it worthwhile to treat a particular breach as an end-game breach.

2. My study of grain and feed disputes found that traders who arbitrated against one another often viewed their relationship as being at an absolute end-game. However, it also found that when the disputing traders worked for medium or large companies, the companies they worked for did not view themselves as being in an absolute end-game. Rather, they viewed themselves as being in an end-game round — they were willing to deal with one another again in the future, but the plaintiff-company nevertheless fought hard for the application of EGNs. As one grain company executive explained and others confirmed, companies sometimes seek strict enforcement of the trade rules and contractual provisions (EGNs) in order to maintain the credibility of their threat to do so in the future, a threat that may be quite important to their ability to maintain long-term cooperative relationships and their ability to routinely obtain reasonable settlements without going to arbitration.

contracting relationship but that they are nonetheless unwilling to promise to make. Third, RPNs and EGNs may also diverge because RPNs whose effectiveness depends on social or reputational sanctions imposed by members of a particular market or social group tend to be simpler than the explicit contractual provisions that cover the same aspects of the transaction. In addition, these RPNs often have special features that are designed to enable members of the relevant group to determine whether the norms have been violated. These features may be both unnecessary and excessively costly if mechanisms for third-party fact finding, dispute resolution, and enforcement of judgments are available. Fourth, because the best norm to govern a particular situation often depends on transactors' perception of the likelihood of opportunism, transactors who are in the midst of a cooperative relationship will often find it desirable to follow norms that would be highly undesirable if they thought the likelihood of opportunism was high. Finally, RPNs may diverge from EGNs because there are many adjustments that transactors would be willing to make to preserve a profitable relationship that they would be unwilling to make in the absence of the prospect of future gain.

There is empirical evidence from a variety of contracting contexts that suggests that merchants behave in ways that reflect an implicit understanding of the distinction between end-game and relationship-preserving norms and that they do not necessarily want the RPNs they follow during the cooperative phase of their relationship to be used to resolve disputes when their relationship is at an end-game stage.

In the grain and feed industry, when disputes arise between merchandisers with a long-standing trading relationship, they will ordinarily just "split the difference" in an effort not to damage their relationship. This is an example of a relationship-preserving dispute-resolution norm. NGFA arbitrators, however, rarely "split the difference." This aspect of the tribunal's adjudicative approach is widely praised by traders and appears to be the desired EGN. Similarly, while smaller feed merchandisers who transact primarily on a local or regional basis often include official weight provisions in their contracts, they routinely accept one another's unsupervised in-house weights. Official weights are expensive, so this practice results in significant transaction cost savings. The norm of accepting in-house weights is a relationship-preserving performance norm that exists alongside a flatly contradictory explicit contractual provision embodying the desired EGN — a provision requiring official weights.

Stewart Macaulay's 1963 study of the contracting practices of manufacturing firms provides additional evidence that merchants implicitly distinguish between relationship-preserving and end-game norms.[3] For example, Macaulay's study found that although buyers and sellers entered into contracts that entitled the seller to recover expectation damages (an EGN) if the buyer failed to take the quantity of goods ordered, buyers "expected to be able to cancel orders freely subject to only an obligation to pay for the seller's major expenses," a norm closely approximating reliance damages. Sellers confirmed that in settling such disputes in situations where lawyers had not yet become involved, they routinely accepted these reliance-type payments in complete satisfaction of their claims. Reliance damages seem to be the transactors' preferred RPN.

The study also found that businessmen "will negotiate a solution when a problem arises apparently as if there had never been any original contract," with the dominant attitude being that " '[y]ou can settle any dispute if you keep the lawyers and accountants out of it.' " This suggests that transactors negotiate primarily, though not exclusively, in the shadow of RPNs when their relationship is not at an end-game. As one businessman explained, "if something comes up you get the other man on the telephone and deal with the problem. You don't read legalistic contract clauses at each other if you ever want to do business again." In those infrequent instances where "relatively contractual methods are used to make adjustments in ongoing transactions and to settle disputes," this is usually done because the "[d]emands of one side . . . are deemed unreasonable by the other . . . [in which case they] occasionally are blocked by reference to the terms of the agreement between the parties." This suggests that when one transactor observes the other transactor deviating from implicit RPNs, he may respond by invoking or threatening to invoke an EGN. In sum, Macaulay's study suggests that the terms of a written contract are viewed as relevant primarily when transactors have decided not to deal again, that is, when their relationship is at an end-game.

The legislative history of the Code provides more explicit evidence that merchants do not necessarily want RPNs to be applied by courts in

---

3. [Stewart Macaulay, Non-Contractual Relations in Business: A Preliminary Study, 25 Am. Soc. Rev. 55, 61-21 (1963).]

end-game situations. In an early draft of the Code, Llewellyn proposed replacing the perfect tender rule with a rule of substantial performance that made a price adjustment, rather than rejection, the consequence of nonconforming tender. Llewellyn defended his proposal on the ground that it reflected the ways that merchants generally dealt with nonconforming tender and would "impose the better practice of the marketplace as a rule of law."[4] The New York Merchants Association, however, took the position that "the price adjustments that merchants made when goods 'are not entirely up to standard' — 'the give and take of ordinary mercantile life,' should not be made obligatory in the law." It lobbied for retaining the perfect tender rule, explaining that while the rule did create a risk that buyers would opportunistically reject goods in a falling market, this type of opportunism could "take care of [itself] 'mighty quick' through [other] merchant practices," such as sellers demanding cash in advance from buyers with a reputation for this sort of behavior. The Association further explained that a rule of substantial performance would not only create a risk that sellers would opportunistically "unload all their shopworn and defective goods," but would also give juries a vast amount of discretion that would lead to erratic and error-prone decisions. In the merchants' view, the combination of the perfect tender rule and nonlegal sanctions was more advantageous than a rule of substantial performance with judicial discretion.

Thus, merchants recognize the distinction between relationship-preserving and end-game norms, and do not necessarily want RPNs to be used to resolve end-game disputes. However, courts applying the Code's usage of trade, course of dealing, and course of performance provisions routinely take RPNs into account in deciding cases where the transactors' relationship is at an end-game stage. This adjudicative approach may impose an efficiency loss on transactors not only because it prevents them from selecting their preferred mix of legal and extra-legal provisions, but also because in many contexts the content of RPNs is likely to be different from the content of efficient EGNs.

---

4. Zipporah B. Wiseman, The Limits of Vision: Karl Llewellyn and the Merchant Rules, 100 Harv. L. Rev. 465, 525 (1987).

STUDY GUIDE: What does Professor Scott mean by "formalism"? Does it resemble the "contextual formalism" described by Curtis Bridgeman (in Chapter 10)? What sorts of considerations does Professor Scott think support formalism in contract law? What weaknesses does he see in the ex ante efficiency rationale for selecting "default rules"? What draw-backs does he see for the ex post efficiency rationales for the adjustment of contract terms? Does his approach undermine the arguments of Professor Hillman? How does his case depend on the relative compe-tence of contracting parties on the one hand and judges on the other?

THE CASE FOR FORMALISM IN RELATIONAL CONTRACT*

Robert E. Scott

Complete contracts (to the extent that they exist in the real world) are rarely, if ever, breached since by definition the payoffs for every relevant action and the corresponding sanctions for nonperformance are prescribed in the contract. In the case of incomplete (or relational) con-tracts, however, parties have incentives to breach by exploiting gaps in the contract. Making the verifiable terms of the contract legally enforce-able and regulating incompleteness in a consistent manner reduces, but does not eliminate, these incentives to breach. There still remains the fundamental question: should the law seek to complete the contract for the parties? And, if so, from what vantage point should the contractual gaps be filled? Determining the answers to these questions has preoc-cupied contract law scholars for the past twenty-five years.

In this Article, I . . . outline the core arguments for (and difficulties with) three alternative strategies for interpreting relational contracts. . . . One strategy is for the state to seek to achieve *ex ante efficiency*. This strategy is designed to protect (and even improve) the utility of the set of contractual signals for future parties. It requires courts to ignore the litigating parties' subjective intentions and fill con-tractual gaps objectively — that is, according to assumptions about the

---

*From Robert E. Scott, The Case for Formalism in Relational Contract, 94 Nw. U. L. Rev. 847 (2000). Some sections have been renumbered.

risks that parties similarly situated would plausibly have agreed to bear at the time the contract was made. This is the default rule paradigm that has occupied much of the agenda of the law-and-economics branch of relational theory. . . .

There is a second strategy. Rather than attempt to specify default rules that fill the gaps ex ante, the courts can seek to direct the *ex post efficient* result. That is, they can fill in the "right" result or the "right relational" result by imposing an equitable adjustment that takes all of the relational and contextual factors into account as they appear at the time of adjudication. This has been the solution most frequently suggested by the law-and-society branch of relational contract scholars. Here, the argument proceeds from the claim that relational contracts create reciprocal "relational" duties. Courts should enforce these duties when the parties cannot agree.[2] For example, in relational contexts, changed circumstances that materialize after the contract was made will sometimes threaten to impose severe losses on a disadvantaged party. The severity of the available contractual remedies — whether specific performance or damages — implies that the disadvantaged party did not fully consent to the losses that enforcement would cause. In this situation, Richard Speidel has argued, a court-imposed solution would do "little damage to the requirement of consent in contract law."[3] There is simply a "gap in the agreement or risk allocation" that a court can fill based upon information available to it at the time of adjudication. In sum, courts should fill such gaps by creating contract terms that are fair ex post.

There is a third strategy. . . . [that] borrows from the physician's classic injunction, "first, do no harm," and resolutely declines to fill any gaps at all. Under this *formalist* approach, courts are instructed not to create ex ante defaults or undertake any ex post adjustments, but to enforce the (facially unambiguous) express terms of the contract literalistically or "as written." To be sure, a formalist strategy does not absolutely preclude courts from functional interpretation of a given contract, but it does require the parties expressly to signal ex ante their preference for more aggressive modes of interpretation of the contract terms. . . .

---

2. Robert Hillman, Court Adjustment of Long-Term Contracts: An Analysis Under Modern Contract Law, 1987 Duke L.J. 1.

3. Richard E. Speidel, Court-Imposed Price Adjustments Under Long-Term Supply Contracts, 76 Nw. U. L. Rev. 369 (1981).

These, then, are the principal strategic choices the state faces when called upon to adjudicate disputed contracts. The particular strategy that is selected will necessarily affect the method of contractual interpretation that courts employ (and vice versa). If the state selects the "wrong" interpretive strategy or performs its regulatory function in an inconsistent manner, the costs of contracting will rise. Thus, the central question for contract law scholars remains: which strategic objective is best?

In evaluating this question, it is critically important to emphasize what the debate is and is not about. The debate that divides the academics who think about these questions is not over the nature of *contract* as an institution. We are all relationalists now. In that sense Macneil and Macaulay have swept the field. Contract, we now know, is complex and subjective and synthetic in every sense of those terms. The debate, rather, is over the proper nature of *contract law*. All contracts are relational, complex and subjective. But contract law, whether we like it or not, is none of those things. Contract law is formal, simple, and (returning to Macneil's terminology) *classical*. . . .

THE BARRIERS TO EX ANTE EFFICIENCY

The traditional assumption made by many scholars that the state can achieve ex ante efficiency by incorporating default rules from the commercial context into incomplete relational contracts is, at best, simplistic and, at worst, seriously misleading. To the extent that the efficiency norm purports to embrace both predictable interpretations of incomplete contracts as well as the standardization of contract terms, it is subject to a fundamental dilemma: the process of incorporating useful defaults often leads to misinterpretation of the express terms of the contract, while seeking predictability in interpretation undercuts the process of standardization.[8] For example, courts often fill gaps by incorporating

---

8. Courts typically interpret the meaning of express terms in an agreement by looking to precisely the same commercial and legal context they use to identify and incorporate default terms. Unfortunately, by giving custom and usages of trade interpretive priority over the express terms in the contract, courts may unwittingly misinterpret the meaning of the express terms the parties have used. Thus, if the law treats the words used to opt out of an otherwise applicable custom or usage as themselves highly elastic and context-relative, attempts to escape those default understandings become problematic.

context evidence to show that apparently determinate terms in a contract are subject to "reasonable variations" or are only "estimates." On the one hand, official "recognition" of these default understandings may assist future parties in better designing their contractual relationship. But, on the other hand, the act of incorporating these defaults as an aid to interpretation of the litigated contract will also have the effect of conditioning the explicit price and quantity terms in the contract, terms that otherwise appeared fixed and determinate on their face. . . .

AN ALTERNATIVE STRATEGY: EX POST EFFICIENCY

A plausible alternative goal for the state is for courts not to develop default rules to promote ex ante efficiency but rather for courts to direct the ex post efficient result. Here the argument is quite straightforward. If there are to be tradeoffs, why not trade off the chimera of ex ante certainty in favor of ex post efficiency (or fairness). . . .

There are [two] objections to the argument for ex post efficiency. First, the unfairness of enforcing the terms of the contract as written apparently stems from the belief that unforeseeable events caused the promisor to incur large losses. Thus, the ex post strategy requires courts to answer the vexing questions of foreseeability and causation in order to decide how much of the loss the disadvantaged party should bear. There is significant evidence that courts have so much difficulty with these questions that they opt for full enforcement in the great majority of cases involving frustration and excuse. The ex post strategy may thus be assuming a level of competency that courts cannot reasonably achieve. In short, reaching "fair" results may simply be too difficult to implement in specific cases. Second, there is the distributional justice problem of deciding what is a "fair" adjustment. Moral philosophy does not appear to provide criteria with which to answer such microdistributional questions. . . .

A FORMALIST STRATEGY OF INTERPRETATION

Both of these two familiar strategies — seeking ex ante efficiency or ex post efficiency — presuppose a role for courts in filling gaps in incomplete contracts. The principal difference is whether gaps are filled from an ex ante or an ex post perspective. But . . . there is a third strategy for courts to consider: decline to fill gaps at all. From this formalist perspective, the legal terms in relational contracts would be subject to a literalistic interpretation; courts would enforce verifiable express terms as written and decline the invitation to complete the contract. The benefits of this strategy are obvious. If correct interpretation is indeed an important value and if this requires interpretation that is transparent and predictable, then it follows that restricting the role of legal enforcement to the enforcement of facially unambiguous express terms will (over time) generate better and more accurate interpretations of those portions of disputed contracts that the parties choose to reduce to formal, legal terms.

The costs of the formalist strategy are equally obvious. A return to a formalist conception of contract law . . . will increase the number of disputed contracts in which enforcement is denied because the contract is found to be fatally incomplete and/or ambiguous. Moreover, contracting parties now will be required to incur the costs of developing standard-form prototypes for expressly allocating common risks that contract law might otherwise have assigned by default. . . .

Given these tradeoffs, the formalist strategy is more or less attractive depending on the competency of courts to perform both core functions — correct interpretation of contractual text and incorporation of the customs and understandings that are immanent in the contractual context — at the same time. If these are functions that courts can (and do) perform with relative competence, then one or the other of the activist interpretive strategies is preferable to formalism. If these are functions that courts do not perform well together, then leaving contextual and other relational norms to be enforced by extralegal sanctions might actually improve the efficiency of the legal regulation of relational contracts. . . .

THE (TENTATIVE) CASE FOR FORMALISM

The lesson from theory and experience points toward legal modesty as the superior strategy for courts seeking to regulate relational contracts. Successful incorporation of context, whether to specify efficient default rules ex ante or achieve efficient adjustment ex post, requires that a key empirical condition — *competent courts and incompetent parties* — be satisfied. Comparing the efforts of courts instructed to engage in activist incorporation with courts instructed to follow constrained modes of interpretation suggests some skepticism about the plausibility of this condition. . . .

The activist interpretive approach embodied in the [Uniform Commercial] Code has had several significant effects. One important effect is the observed practice of groups of commercial parties opting out of the Code entirely in important classes of cases. One of the principal reasons for the National Grain and Feed Association's decision to abandon the Code was its desire to have written express terms subject to a formalist and objective interpretive methodology and not to be trumped by evidence of course of dealing or usage of trade. Lisa Bernstein suggests that the explanation for this practice lies in the parties' desire to separate the legal norms that govern their written agreements from the informal social norms that govern their actions. An alternative (and complementary) explanation, however, is that opting out of the Code permits the grain and feed merchants to secure the economic benefits of legal formalism by substituting a private common-law process for the legal activism of the Code.

In any case, what is clear from the data is that the antiformalist approach embodied in the Code is premised on a notion of trade custom that, in the words of David Charny, relies on "a nostalgia for an idealized, perhaps mythical premodern age — for the intimate local communities of shared value and custom, enforced by knowledge, reputation, and ties of affectional loyalty."[13] What we see instead is the evolution of intermediaries and the development of custom by trade association rulemaking. Moreover, the rules developed by these intermediaries are themselves formalist. The approach to dispute resolution generated by these local "customs" reveals a preference for literal interpretation of express contract terms and a rejection of context-specific "situation sense" analysis of particular contractual relationships. . . . [T]he evidence that incorporation does not work is sufficiently striking to undermine the uncritical assumption of the academic and professional proponents of the Code that an activist role in regulating

---

13. David Charny, The New Formalism in Contract, 66 U. Chi. L. Rev. 842, 846 (1999) (declaring that "Llewellyn's antiformalism is a flop").

relational contracts is a priori preferable to the more modest objectives for the state embodied in the common law.

To be sure, building the case against incorporation does not establish the case for formalism. Nevertheless, the objections that have been mounted to date against formalism have largely missed their mark. Formalist interpretation is not an inflexible and wooden application of arid first principles — the criticism launched so successfully at the early formalists. Formalism in relational contract is an interpretive strategy that deserves careful scrutiny to the extent that it is a superior method for reducing the costs of contracting for most parties to commercial contracts.

Thus, nothing in the case for formalism would preclude judicial policing of firms seeking to use literal language as a vehicle to exploit consumers or other "occasional" contractors. Such a limitation on formal modes of interpretation would be consistent with other, familiar limitations on freedom of contract. For example, one might fear that large firms with high volume and well-developed bureaucratic structures would benefit from formalism in their dealings with smaller firms (or consumers) that contract only occasionally. Reliance on formal terms managed by a bureaucratic infrastructure could be a form of rent-seeking in which rivals were disadvantaged by the higher cost to them of formal adherence to the legal norms. There are many responses to this possibility. Industry-specific rules for traders as well as social norms of trust and reciprocity deter much of this behavior, at least among repeat players. Well-developed doctrines of unconscionability are available to police rent-seeking by powerful entities. Moreover, the tools of formal language can be used as a sword against rentseeking as well as a shield. One familiar response to the risk of exploitation is legislatively mandated boilerplate — such as the language required to disclaim warranty liability under the Code — that generates (over time) standardized invocations for shifting common legal risks. . . .

CONCLUSION

The central claim of this Article can be stated quite clearly. Formalist modes of interpretation are justified because, and only because, they offer the best prospect for maximizing the value of contractual relationships, *given the empirical conditions that seem to prevail*. The apparent failure of the grand experiment in functional inter-pretation under the Code does not prove that the incorporation project was misguided in principle. It merely suggests that implementing such a project may require a more complex institutional design than courts are able to handle competently.

Thus, at bottom the case for formalism in relational contract turns on the relative implausibility of the empirical conditions necessary for ac-tivist incorporation: *competent courts and incompetent parties*. The evidence from the cases adjudicating contract disputes under both the Code and the common law is that the more likely empirical condition is *competent parties and incompetent courts*. The common-law interpre-tive methodology is grounded on the implicit assumption that courts function well when they operate within tightly constrained, formal modes of analysis. Courts will perform poorly, on the other hand, where they attempt the typically legislative tasks of harmonizing value conflicts and actively regulating complex economic activity. This Article offers some evidence of the wisdom of the common law.

18

WHAT IS THE RELATIONAL THEORY OF CONTRACT?

In the previous chapter, Robert Scott referred to long-term contracts as "relational contracts," a term coined by Professor Ian Macneil of Northwestern University as part of what has been come to be called his "relational theory of contract."[1] Relationalists stress that contracts must be viewed within a complex web of relations that color and influence their meaning. Many of the insights of relational contract theory have been widely — indeed universally — accepted by contract scholars. But, as we shall see, many who identify themselves as "relationalists" would go farther.

Some contracts professors take a relational approach throughout their course, while others consider relational contract theory separately as a rival to more traditional approaches. In this chapter we consider whether relational contract theory represents a radical but valid alternative to the sort of contract law you have studied in your course. We begin with an article by Professor Feinman in which he further explains the theory and its applications both past and prospective. In it, he

---

1. In Randy E. Barnett, Conflicting Visions: A Critique of Ian Macneil's Relational Theory of Contract, 78 Va. L. Rev. 1175 (1992), I summarize Macneil's distinctive approach to relationalism and respond to his challenge to basing contract law on consent.

contrasts a relational approach with what Ian Macneil called "classical" and "neoclassical" contract law.

We then turn to an article by Professor Melvin Eisenberg who both criticizes the deficiencies of "classical" contract law (everyone's favorite target) and contends that relationalism is susceptible to some of the very same weaknesses. While affirming the contributions made by relational theory, Eisenberg denies that this theory justifies any distinctive *law* of relational contracts.

Next we read a summary and defense of relationalism by Ethan Leib of the University of California, Hastings College of Law that responds to Professor Eisenberg's critique, along with the analyses of Professors Bernstein and Scott that appear in Chapter 17. Finally, we conclude with an evaluation of relational contract theory by Dori Kimel, who cautions against the blurring of useful distinctions between arms-length contracts among strangers, and contracts in which a relational element exists.

In reading all of the contributions to this chapter, it is useful to keep in mind a distinction — employed by each contributor in his own way — between a relational *theory* of contract law and a relational *law* of contract. Confusion can be avoided by paying attention to which of these two ideas is being discussed at any particular juncture.

STUDY GUIDE: According to Professor Feinman, how do classical, neoclassical, and relational contract approaches differ? Why are the accommodations made by neoclassical contract theory to relational insights inadequate? What does Professor Feinman mean by the "fragmenting" of contract law? (You may recall a similar idea mentioned by Duncan Kennedy in Chapter 11.) Why does Professor Feinman think this fragmentation will continue apace but that relationalism will not supplant traditional neoclassical doctrines of contract law?

RELATIONAL CONTRACT THEORY
IN CONTEXT*

Jay M. Feinman

When one struggles against ancient concepts — and their labels — it seems almost impossible to avoid being misunderstood, even by very perceptive people.

> Ian R. Macneil

INTRODUCTION

In this Article, I want to situate Macneil's relational contract theory within the story of the development of contract law, to describe the parallel developments in the law, and to draw out some of the implications of the theory and the developments. Macneil's scholarship inhabits the broader realm of social theory as well as the narrower realm of contract law, but it is only the narrower realm that I consider here. . . .

I.   CLASSICAL AND NEOCLASSICAL
CONTRACT LAW

Relational contract is one of the latest steps in the scholarly project of responding to the inadequacies of classical contract law, so the appropriate starting point is the familiar story of classical law, along the three dimensions of scope, method, and substance. The scope of contract law as conceived by classical scholars and judges was very broad. Classical contract law was the realm of consensual relations, as distinguished from the nonconsensual relations governed by tort law. All consensual relations of any kind were within the realm of contract. A single body of law could govern such a wide range of transactions because of its method. The classical method involved the application of relatively clear rules of legal doctrine, typically framed at a high level of generality and

---

*From Jay M. Feinman, Relational Contract Theory in Context, 94 Nw. U. L. Rev. 737 (2000).

presenting dichotomous choices. The scope and method served the substance; as the realm of consensual relations, contract law simply set ground rules for self-maximizing private ordering.

By the time of its enshrinement in Williston's treatise and the original Restatement of Contracts, classical contract law already was under attack. The essence of the criticism of classical law and its reconstruction through succeeding scholarly generations was contextualization; the more classical contract law was placed in context, the less sense it made. The contextualization took two forms, one internal and the other external to the body of law itself. The internal criticism compared the ostensible rules with the results in the cases, finding that the rules did not explain the cases and that no formal, general rules ever could. The external criticism situated the rules in the world of actual contracting practice, arguing that the law's approach needed to be changed to serve the objectives of contract law.

Neoclassical contract law — the law of the Uniform Commercial Code, the Restatement (Second) of Contracts, and today — is the product of this criticism. It is "neoclassical" because it addresses the shortcomings of classical law rather than offering a wholly different conception of the law. The scope of neoclassical law is residual and fragmented. There is still a unitary body of contract principles (the rules of formation, validation, performance, and remedies), but the law is residual in that it no longer attempts to encompass all consensual transactions. Labor law and corporate law, for example, are no longer within the scope of contract. The law also is fragmented, in that the unitary principles are not necessarily applied in the same way in all types of cases. We have seen the recognition of transaction types — for example, the law of sales is part of the general law of contract but marked off for separate treatment.

Neoclassical method is a mix of rules and standards. This is still doctrine, by and large, but it is doctrine of a much softer sort than in classical law. This softening is best captured in the preference for rules in the original Restatement as compared to the preference for standards in the Restatement (Second). The substantive core of neoclassical law is based on the assumption that parties act out of self-interest set within a context of trade custom and balanced by social values. Contract is still fundamentally about achieving one's own ends, but those ends are understood largely in terms of the context out of which they arise. In some cases, moreover, these ends may be subordinated to external social policies.

II. THE NEOCLASSICAL ACCOUNT OF RELATIONAL CONTRACT

As the mainstream conception of modern contract law, neoclassical law has a tremendous capacity to deal with new theories and developments. New approaches or insights can be redescribed, absorbed, or marginalized as necessary in order to maintain the integrity of the subject. This is what has happened to relational contract theory. Rather than being viewed as a fundamental challenge to neoclassical law, relational contract has been described in terms of scope, method, and substance that allow it to be comfortably accommodated within the mainstream.

In the neoclassical conception, relational contract theory adds a theoretical insight about the unity underlying various types of exchange transactions. This insight buttresses contract law's claim to a general scope, but this is largely of scholarly interest. A much more important contribution that relational contract theory has made is its description of the relational-discrete continuum. Macneil's work brought to light the importance of considering relational contracts — extensive, long-term relationships — as a distinctive form of contracting. Relational contracts, like sales contracts, can be governed by the core principles of contracts, as long as the courts applying the principles are sensitive to the factual differences in context.

Relational method has also been seen as consistent with neoclassical method. Macneil's structure of contract norms is an elegant if unnecessarily detailed account of the need to contextualize, and of the desirability of using vague standards that make it easy for the courts to accomplish such contextualization. Similarly, the substance of relational contract theory has been seen as a refinement of neoclassical contract law. In relational contracts, greater attention needs to be paid to the desirability of fairness and cooperation; in relational contracts, short-term self-interest sometimes needs to be subordinated to long-term self-interest.

From the neoclassical perspective, then, relational contract theory has one central insight: there exists a class of relational contracts that deserve treatment as a special subcategory of the general contract law. This is an important, previously unrecognized insight, but it is also one that easily can be absorbed into the scope, method, and substance of neoclassical law. This insight is seen as accounting for most of the contribution that relational contract theory has to make to the law.

Beyond that contribution, relational contract is seen as an interesting, if perhaps excessively detailed sociological theory that is not particularly useful to the project of formulating and applying contract doctrine.

III.   A DIFFERENT VIEW OF
RELATIONAL CONTRACT

The neoclassical account of relational contract theory is, I believe, widely held. It also is too limited. Relational contract is much more complex, and presents a much greater challenge to neoclassical contract law, than this account suggests. . . . Here is a different account of relational contract theory and of what a truly relational contract law would look like. . . .

Begin with the scope of relational contract. Relational contract simultaneously dramatically broadens and dramatically fragments the scope of contract law as compared to neoclassical law. Macneil begins with the "primal roots of contract,"[2] and this beginning leads him to broad definitions of "contract" and "exchange": "[C]ontract encompasses all human activities in which economic exchange is a significant factor."[3] "Exchange," in turn, is not limited to defined monetizable exchange, but also includes other interactions in which reciprocity is a dominant element. Accordingly, the scope of relational contract is very general, in some respects even more general than was classical contract law. It brings back within the field of contract law some of the topics that were spun off in the development of neoclassical law; labor relations is a prominent example. It breaks down doctrinal boundaries further by potentially bringing tort and property law topics within the definition of contract. And it brings within the scope of contract relations those activities that have economic aspects but that are not primarily economic, such as family relations. Relational contract, therefore, is willing to treat an astonishingly wide range of transactions as subject to the same body of theory.

---

2. Ian R. Macneil, The New Social Contract: An Inquiry into Modern Contractual Relations 1 (1980).

3. [Ian R. Macneil, Relational Contract Theory: Challenges and Queries, 94 Nw. U. L. Rev. 877, 894 n.2 (2000).]

At the same time, however, relational contract is aimed at fragmenting in a more earnest way than neoclassical law. Neoclassical law recognizes that there are contexts in which the same rules will be applied differently because of factual differences — differences between contracts for sales of goods as compared to construction contracts, for example. Relational contract almost begins by looking through the other end of the telescope. The contract norms are stated at a high degree of generality, but they direct our attention to features particular to the contract at issue and to the relational context out of which it arises. These elements of relational analysis argue for much more developed contextualization. This contextualization results not only in locating relations along the relational-discrete continuum, but also in distinguishing contracts according to more familiar categories, such as standardized consumer transactions and long-term relationships involving sophisticated commercial parties. The result is a relational contract law that contains much more generalization across different settings at the same time as it accentuates the differences between settings.

It is much harder to describe briefly the method of relational contract law. The insight about the fragmentation of contract law is a beginning. Relational analysis is contextual with a vengeance, immersing itself in the facts of the particular contract and of the contexts from which it arises. But here is a crucial and often misunderstood point: context is not enough. Facts are essential, but facts do not dictate solutions. It is not possible to immerse oneself in the facts of a situation and come to the correct solution that is immanent in those facts.

Instead, facts are filtered through the structure of the relational method. The key to this structure is the concept of contract norms. The normative structure begins with ten common contract norms, such as role integrity, reciprocity, and implementation of planning. Macneil identifies these norms as arising out of study of all types of contracting behavior, employing the broad definition of contract noted earlier. These norms can be used in the analysis of any contract. However, different norms are of different value depending on the nature of the contract. For example, implementation of planning and effectuation of consent are especially important in contracts with strong discrete elements, while role integrity, preservation of the relation, and harmonization of relational conflict are particularly important in contracts with especially relational characteristics.

The relevant normative structure also includes external norms. These obviously include values of the society defined by law that may or may not be reflected in the particular relation. In addition to positive law, relevant external norms include customs of an industry or other relevant group, rules of a trade association or professional organization, and norms generated by any group intersecting with the relation at issue.

It is crucial to understand the multiple levels of this normative structure, because misunderstanding it leads to misunderstanding all of relational contract theory. The normative structure includes what we ordinarily think of as norms relevant to the understanding of a contract under neoclassical law. In a sales case involving a particular trade, for example, there may be norms internal to the contract and norms of a trade, relevant to such issues as interpretation or waiver under principles of course of performance, course of dealing, or trade usage. These types of norms are, of course, included in a relational analysis. But the contract norms also embody norms developed through the observation of many different contract settings unrelated to the context at issue; the results of this observation, and the theorizing about these results, are the sources of the contract norms. And the use of external norms makes clear that social values beyond the relation at issue also must be considered relevant.

The use of this normative structure in analyzing contracts leads substantially, if not totally, to a rejection of doctrinal method as it is ordinarily practiced, in favor of a method that looks much more like policy analysis. From this perspective, doctrine consists of rules and standards taking a deductive form about legal consequences (e.g., "substantial performance satisfies a constructive condition") while policy consists of arguments in a consequential form (e.g., "contract terms should be interpreted to avoid forfeiture"). In analyzing a relation, we find facts that, when seen through the structure of norms internal and external to the relation, suggest that the law ought to reach a certain result. This analysis is aimed at determining the benefits of acting in a certain way, however, not at formulating rules or principles that dictate results independent of the norms.

The substantive core of relational contract theory proceeds from two propositions: that contract is fundamentally about cooperative social behavior, and that contracts containing significant relational elements are the predominant form of contracting. This suggests that there is a baseline of obligation in contracting, one that arises out of the contract norms. This position is distinguished from the classical position that there is a baseline of no obligation, or the neoclassical position that there is a core of self-interest affected at the periphery by custom and regulation. The precise content of the obligation is determined by the application of relational method.

This is not to suggest that relational contract necessarily dictates cooperation or communitarianism. (Certainly not for Macneil.) If we think of relational contract as a reaction to neoclassical contract, the emphasis on cooperation is a corrective to neoclassical law's retention of the core classical position of self-interest. More generally, the recognition that different contracts have different contexts and values — in particular, that contracts can have strongly discrete or strongly relational elements — gives balance to the concepts of cooperation and competition, or, in Macneil's terms, of reciprocity and the restraint of power.

IV. PARALLEL DEVELOPMENTS IN THE LAW

In my view, therefore, relational contract theory presents a substantial alternative to neoclassical contract law. . . . Interestingly, while the mainstream of contract law and contract law scholarship has been proceeding without the benefit of relational contract theory, developments in particular kinds of cases have suggested its relevance. Following the three dimensions of scope, method, and substance, in this Part I will bring those developments to light.

Relational contract is both more general and more fragmented than neoclassical law, as discussed above. The generalizing tendency has not been pursued in the law, but the fragmenting tendency has. For at least the past forty years (coincidentally, the span of Macneil's career), the traditional doctrinal structure in private law has been in decline. There are many reasons for this, and some of them relate to the shift away from classical law discussed previously. A particular element of the decline has been the spinning off of subfields that have become relatively independent of their parent subject. This has both diminished the scope of the traditional fields and established a new structure that makes the traditional trivium of contract-tort-property increasingly tenuous. We can see this in three examples, one from each traditional field: insurance law, which has seceded from contract; landlord-tenant law, which has seceded from property; and products liability, which has seceded from tort. . . .

Insurance is a contractual relationship, but courts and legislatures have developed a body of insurance law that is distinct from the mainstream of contract. For example, the doctrine of reasonable expectations has bled over somewhat from insurance contracts to standard form contracts generally, but it still creates a rule of interpretation and construction in insurance cases that is profoundly different from the rule applied in run-of-the-mill contract cases. The obligation of good faith applies in every contract, but it generally gives rise to a tort cause of action and extracontractual remedies only in insurance cases. Waiver and estoppel are applied more generously against insurance companies than against other contracting parties, while misrepresentations by the insured are often treated more leniently. And so on.

Landlord-tenant law presents a different picture. It originated, of course, in the law of property. Here, part of the story is the use of contract principles as the field was carved out of property law. The tenant's inability to avoid a lease when ousted from quiet enjoyment of the premises was cured by supplementing the conveyance concept of the lease with the concept of conditions from contract law. But the law of contract regarding tenancies is very different from the general law of contract. As in contract law, there are implied warranties, but the implied warranty of habitability is broader than any contract law warranty, essentially nondisclaimable, and protected by unique remedies.

Products liability law is still more different, having mixed contract and tort origins. Over time, the doctrinal origins in contract have mostly disappeared, but the basis in expectations has not. Yet the area has not been absorbed by tort. Instead, it has become an independent field, deserving of its own Restatement, with principles that developed and then influenced both its parent fields.

The method of analysis used in developing these fields and then applying the law in them is to a considerable degree nondoctrinal, in the same sense that relational analysis is nondoctrinal. The fields are defined without reference to doctrinal categories. Instead, the key to definition is contextualization. The areas are defined by factual similarities among the cases that fall within them. . . . Once the field is defined, principles are developed and cases decided through a normative analysis not dissimilar to the analysis of contract norms. The type-situation, when thought of as a relation, is redescribed as exhibiting a normative structure. External social values are brought to bear as well. The analysis by the courts in well-known cases . . . all speak of reciprocity, propriety of means, restraint of power, and the like within the relation and within relations of the type, and they all apply supracontract norms to reshape the law. Even after these areas have matured, judicial opinions often have a strikingly relational cast.

Developments in these areas have been to a considerable extent pro-consumer, but by no means uniformly so. This suggests the substance of these developments. Although they all are contractual settings, they all involve settings in which there are characteristically (though not always) relations of inequality. Accordingly, the law of contract, built around a paradigm of relative equality, is not particularly well suited to deal with them. As such, they demonstrate a baseline of obligation independent of the terms of the contract. But like the substance of relational contract, the law in these areas does not run only in one direction.

V.   IMPLICATIONS

The development of these subfields provides some evidence of the power of relational contract theory. But what are the implications of these developments for where relational theory might go next?

First, I think it is clear that if any progress is to be made, it will be made in the direction of further fragmenting analysis rather than extending Macneil's project of creating a more general theory of contract. Therefore, we can identify and develop additional subfields that can operate as independent relational contexts, as do insurance, landlord-tenant, and products liability law. It would be particularly interesting to develop subfields in which there are not the obvious levels of inequality. . . .

One possibility is family economic relations. . . . Old chestnuts like *Hamer v. Sidway* and *Kirksey v. Kirksey* and newer classics like *Marvin v. Marvin* [can be] brought together to consider how contracts and contract law are used in family settings and how we should think about contracting in the context of intimate relations.

Another possibility is commercial construction contracting. Here we have a setting in which contracts, including form contracts, are widely used by a mix of repeat players and occasional players of different size and sophistication, in which interactions take place over time in a variety of settings, and in which problems always arise. . . .

A quite different possibility concerns long-term, extensive relationships between large economic entities. There was a moment when there seemed to be a prospect of extending relational analysis to these situations, which many people think of as the paradigm of a relational contract. The Westinghouse uranium cases and *Aluminum Co. of America v. Essex Group* produced a flurry of literature about the desirability of judicially mandated adjustments in long-term contracts. Given this literature, . . . one would think that this would be a natural area for the application of relational theory, but it has not turned out that way. The likely reason for this is that the scholarly literature outweighs the volume of litigated disputes. The cases were sparked in some part by unusual events, including the unusual inflation of the time, and as the economic circumstances that gave rise to them passed, so did litigation of this type. There also may be a tendency to avoid litigating these problems, or at least to avoid bringing the litigation to conclusion, because of all that is stake.

Second, is it possible that relational contract theory can reshape the core of contract doctrine — the traditional doctrinal structure of rules and principles of formation, performance, etc.? . . . While . . . I was once optimistic about the project, I now believe that the relational norms will not supplant the more familiar doctrines anytime soon, much less replace the even more fundamental doctrines such as indefiniteness, conditions, or parol evidence.

I believe, however, that a version of relational contract theory can have real influence as a counterweight to the still-powerful discrete, maximizing tendencies of neoclassical contract law. If we think of doctrine as a structure of argument rather than a set of rules, then it becomes clear that neoclassical contract and relational contract generate competing general accounts of the sources and nature of obligation in contract law. . . . Neoclassical contract emphasizes the autonomy of individuals and the limited liability that autonomy necessitates. It focuses, therefore, on the agreement process as an exercise of autonomy to create liability, and tries to construct the expectations of the parties from their agreement and the context that gives their agreement meaning. In contrast, relational contract emphasizes the interdependence of individuals in social and economic relationships. Because its paradigmatic unit of inquiry is the extensive relation rather than the discrete transaction, relational contract focuses on the necessity and desirability of trust, mutual responsibility, and connection. Not all of these bonds should be legally enforceable, but beginning analysis by recognizing them is likely to produce a broader set of obligations.

STUDY GUIDE: According to Professor Eisenberg, what are the deficiencies of "classical contract law"? Do all or some of these deficiencies apply to the "formalist" approach defended by Professor Scott in Chapter 17? How do their approaches differ? Notice Professor Eisenberg's reliance on empirical psychology, as opposed to economics. (His discussion of this research has been highly truncated for this excerpt.) Most importantly, why does he think that the empirical insights of relational contract theory do not lead to a law of relational contracts?

WHY THERE IS NO LAW OF RELATIONAL CONTRACTS*

Melvin A. Eisenberg

The identification of relational contracts as a critical construct and an important field of study has led to important insights concerning the economics and sociology of contracting. It has not, however, led to a body of relational contract law: that is, we do not have a body of meaningful and justified contract law rules, either in place or proposed, that apply to, and only to, relational contracts. In this Article, I will show why this is so.

I.   CLASSICAL CONTRACT LAW

Like most modern contract theories, relational contract theory can only be understood against the backdrop of the school of classical contract law, to which it stands in opposition. I will therefore begin with a brief tour of that school.

---

*From Melvin A. Eisenberg, Why There Is No Law of Relational Contracts, 94 Nw. U. L. Rev. 805 (2000).

A. The Characteristics of Classical Contract Law

Classical contract law was marked by several characteristics. It was axiomatic and deductive. It was objective and standardized. It was static. It was implicitly based on a paradigm of bargains made between strangers transacting on a perfect market. It was based on a rational-actor model of psychology.

1. The Axiomatic and Deductive Nature of Classical Contract Law

Classical contract law was axiomatic in nature. Axiomatic theories of law take as a premise that fundamental doctrinal propositions can be established on the ground that they are self-evident. At least in their strictest versions, such theories allow no room for justifying doctrinal propositions on the basis of social propositions — that is, propositions of morality, policy, and experience. So, for example, Langdell, speaking to the question of whether an acceptance by mail was effective on dispatch, said:

> The acceptance . . . must be communicated to the original offerer, and until such communication the contract is not made. It has been claimed that the purposes of substantial justice, and the interests of contracting parties as understood by themselves, will be best served by holding that the contract is complete the moment the letter of acceptance is mailed; and cases have been put to show that the contrary view would produce not only unjust but absurd results. The true answer to this argument is that it is irrelevant. . . .[1]

. . . Classical contract law . . . conceived of contract law as a set of fundamental legal principles that were justified on the ground that they were self-evident, and a second set of rules that were justified on the ground that they could be deduced from the fundamental principles. For example, it was an axiom of classical contract law that in principle only a bargain promise had consideration — that is, was enforceable — although exceptions were recognized for certain kinds of promises

---

1. C. C. Langdell, A Summary of the Law of Contracts 15, 20-21 (2d ed. 1880).

that were enforceable on purely historical grounds. The issue then arose whether a firm offer — an unbargained-for promise to hold an offer open — was legally enforceable. The conclusion of classical contract law was, no.[3] This conclusion was justified by deduction alone. The major premise was that only bargains had consideration. The minor premise was that a promise to hold a firm offer open is not bargained for. The conclusion was that a firm offer was not enforceable.

Another axiom of classical contract law was that bargains were formed only by offer and acceptance. The issue then arose whether an offer for a unilateral contract — an offer to be accepted by the performance of an act — was revocable before performance had been completed, even if the offeree had begun to perform. The conclusion of classical contract law was, yes.[4] This conclusion too was justified by deduction alone. The major premise was that an offeror could revoke an offer at any time prior to acceptance unless he had made a bargained-for promise to hold the offer open. The minor premise was that an offer for a unilateral contract was not bargained for and was not accepted until performance of the act had occurred. The conclusion was that an offer for a unilateral contract was revocable before performance had been completed, even after the offeree had begun to perform.

Langdell's view that an acceptance can be effective only on receipt was also based on deductive reasoning. By axiom, a bargain can be formed only by offer and acceptance. By axiom, an expression cannot be an acceptance unless it is communicated to the addressee. By deduction, an acceptance can be effective only on receipt.

2.   The Objective and Standardized Nature of Classical Contract Law

The principles of contract law can be ranged along various spectra according to the kinds of variables on which the application of any given principle depends. One such spectrum runs from objectivity to subjectivity. A principle of contract law lies at the objective end of this spectrum if its application depends on a directly observable state of the world, and at the subjective end of the spectrum if its application

---

3. See, e.g., Dickinson v. Dodds, 2 Ch. D. 463 (1876).
4. See, e.g., Petterson v. Pattberg, 161 N.E. 428 (N.Y. 1928).

depends on a mental state. For example, application of the plain-meaning rule of interpretation depends on a determination of observable meanings attached to words by established communities. In contrast, application of the rule that if both parties attach the same meaning to an expression, that meaning prevails, depends on a determination of the parties' mental states.

A second spectrum of principles runs from standardization to individualization. A principle of contract law lies at the standardized end of this spectrum if its application depends on an abstract variable that is unrelated to the intentions of the parties or the particular circumstances of the transaction, and it lies at the individualized end of the spectrum if its application depends on situation-specific variables that relate to intentions and other individual circumstances. For example, application of the doctrine that adequacy of consideration will not be reviewed depends on a single variable — the presence of a bargain — that is deliberately designed to screen out all information concerning individual circumstances. In contrast, application of the doctrine of unconscionability depends on a number of situation-specific variables that are wholly concerned with individual circumstances.

The rules of classical contract law lay almost wholly at the objective and standardized end of these spectra. So, for example, classical contract law adopted such standardized rules as the bargain principle, the parol evidence rule, and the objective theory of interpretation, and it rejected such individualized rules as unconscionability, the duty to negotiate in good faith, and subjective principles of interpretation.

3.   The Static Nature of Classical Contract Law

Another characteristic of classical contract law is that it was static rather than dynamic. Classical contract law focused almost exclusively on a single instant in time — the instant of contract formation — rather than on dynamic processes such as the course of negotiation and the evolution of a contractual relationship.

4.   The Implicit Paradigm of Classical Contract Law

Next, classical contract law was implicitly based on a paradigm of bargains made between strangers transacting in a perfect market. So, for example, classical contract law rejected principles of unfairness, which typically have their fullest application in transactions that occur either off-market or on very imperfect markets and have little application to contracts made between strangers on perfect markets.

5. The Rational-Actor Model of Psychology

Finally, classical contract law was based on a rational-actor model of psychology, under which actors who make decisions in the face of uncertainty rationally maximize their subjective expected utility, with all future benefits and costs discounted to present value. In particular, the rules of classical contract law were implicitly based on the assumptions that actors are fully knowledgeable, know the law, and act rationally to further their economic self-interest. This model accounts in part for such rules as the duty to read, whose operational significance was that actors were conclusively assumed to have read and understood everything that they signed. It also accounts in part for the rule that bargains would not be reviewed for fairness: if actors always act rationally in their own self-interest, then, in the absence of fraud, duress, or the like, all bargains must be fair.

B. A Brief Critique of Classical Contract Law

Mary McCarthy once said of Lillian Hellman that every word Hellman wrote was dishonest, including "and" and "the." Something similar could be said of classical contract law. Every aspect of that school of law was incorrect.

1. Law Must be Justified by Social Propositions

To begin with, axiomatic theories of law cannot be sustained. No significant doctrinal proposition can be justified on the ground that it is self-evident. Doctrinal propositions can ultimately be justified only by propositions of morality, policy, and experience. A distinction must be drawn here between the justification of a doctrine and the justification for following a doctrine. Once a doctrine has been adopted it may justifiably be followed, either in the interest of stability, reliance, and the like, or because of social reasons for following rules that have been adopted in a certain way. However, those elements only justify following the doctrine; they do not justify the doctrine itself.

Deductive theories are no more sustainable than axiomatic theories. A doctrine, even if normatively justified, cannot alone serve as the premise of deductive reasoning, because all doctrines are always subject to as-yet-unarticulated exceptions based on social propositions. Such an exception may be made because the social propositions that support the doctrine do not extend to a new fact pattern that is within the doctrine's scope. Alternatively, such an exception may be made because a new fact pattern that is within the doctrine's stated scope brings into play other social propositions that require the formulation of a special rule for that fact pattern. . . .

Accordingly, the applicability of a doctrine to a fact pattern that falls within the doctrine's stated scope is always dependent on a conclusion that social propositions, on balance, do not justify creating an exception for the fact pattern. Correspondingly, even an application of a doctrine that seems perfectly straightforward and easy is such not as a matter of deductive logic alone, but because social propositions do not justify the creation of an exception to cover the case at hand. The concept, implicit and often explicit in classical contract law, that contract law can be developed axiomatically and deductively, cannot be sustained.

2.   Many Rules of Contract Law Should be Individualized, Subjective, or Both

The basic principle that should determine the content of contract law is that the law should effectuate the objectives of parties to a promissory transaction if appropriate conditions are satisfied and subject to appropriate constraints. Because the objective of contract law should be to further the interests of the contracting parties, the rules of contract law must often be formulated so that their application will turn on the particular circumstances of the parties' transactions and, in certain cases, on the parties' subjective intentions. Whether a given rule of contract law should be objective or subjective, and whether it should be standardized or individualized, are matters that must be decided on a rule-by-rule basis. The overriding preference of classical contract law for objective, standardized rules was incorrect.

3. Contract Law Should Take Account of the Dynamic Aspects of the Contracting Process

Promissory transactions seldom occur in an instant of time. They have a past, a present, and a future, and often it is not easy to say where the past ends and the present begins (because, for example, the process of concluding a deal is often a rolling process) or where the present ends and the future begins (because, for example, the contract is partly what it was at the time of contract formation and partly what it becomes thereafter). Because promissory transactions seldom occur in an instant of time, contract law, if it is to effectuate the objectives of parties to promissory transactions, must reflect the reality of contracting by adopting dynamic rules that parallel that reality, rather than static rules that deny that reality.

4. The Paradigmatic Case of Classical Contract Law Is an Abnormal Case

The implicit empirical predicate of classical contract law, that the paradigm contract is one made by strangers transacting on a perfect market, was also flawed. Contracts are seldom made on perfect markets, and seldom made between strangers. . . .

5. Rational-Actor Psychology Does Not Adequately Explain the Behavior of Contracting Parties

A great body of theoretical and empirical work in cognitive psychology within the last thirty or forty years has shown that rational-actor psychology, under which actors who make decisions in the face of uncertainty rationally maximize their subjective expected utility, with all future benefits and costs discounted to present value, often lacks explanatory power. Although rational-actor psychology is the foundation of the standard economic model of choice, the empirical evidence shows that this model often diverges from the actual psychology of choice, because it fails to take into account the limits of cognition. . . . In contrast to rational-actor psychology, cognitive psychology recognizes the limits of cognition. For purposes of contract law, three kinds of limits of cognition are especially salient: bounded rationality, irrational disposition, and defective capability.

a. Bounded Rationality.   To begin with, the substantive action that would maximize an actor's utility may not even be considered by the actor, because actors set process limits on their search for and their deliberation on alternatives.

b. Irrational Disposition.   In addition, actors are, as a systematic matter, unrealistically optimistic. (Lawyers don't realize this, because they are trained to be systematically pessimistic.) . . .

c. Defective Capability.   Finally, cognitive psychology has established that actors use certain decisionmaking rules (heuristics) that yield systematic errors. . . . For example, actors systematically make decisions on the basis of data that is readily available to their memory, rather than on the basis of all the relevant data. Furthermore, actors systematically give undue weight to instantiated evidence as compared to general statements, to vivid evidence as compared to pallid evidence, and to concrete evidence as compared to abstract evidence. Similarly, actors are systematically insensitive to sample size and erroneously take small samples as representative samples.

Another defect of capability concerns the ability of actors to make rational comparisons between present and future states. . . . Actors also systematically give too little weight to future benefits and costs as compared to present benefits and costs. . . . [E]mpirical evidence shows that actors often not only underestimate but also ignore low-probability risks.

In sum, cognitive psychology has established that cognition is limited in ways that are not accounted for by rational-actor psychology. Classical contract doctrines, which assumed that parties to contracts are rational actors, often did not reflect the actual circumstances of contract formation.

II.   RELATIONAL CONTRACT THEORY

Relational contract theory, fathered by Ian Macneil, stands as a mirror image of classical contract law. Classical contract law was axiomatic and deductive; relational contract theory is open and inductive.

Classical contract law was standardized; relational contract theory is individualized. Classical contract law was based on the paradigm of strangers transacting on a perfect market; relational contract theory is based on the paradigm of transactions by actors who are in an ongoing relationship, and often in a bilateral monopoly. Classical contract law was static; relational contract theory is dynamic. Classical contract law was based on rational-actor psychology; relational contract law is not. . . .

This rejection of the basic approaches and assumptions of classical contract law is all to the good. However, constructing a body of relational contract law requires more than rejecting the approaches and assumptions of classical contract law. It also requires the formulation of a new body of legal rules based on approaches and assumptions that are justified by morality, policy, and experience. This is a place to which relational contract theory has not gone and cannot go. To begin with, it is impossible to locate, in the relational contracts literature, a definition that adequately distinguishes relational and nonrelational contracts in a legally operational way — that is, in a way that carves out a set of special and well-specified relational contracts for treatment under a body of special and well-specified rules.

One approach to the problem of definition has been to define relational contracts as those contracts that are not "discrete." This approach, of course, requires a definition of discrete contracts. Vic Goldberg has defined a discrete contract as a contract "in which no duties exist between the parties prior to the contract formation. . . ."[15] However, even in the case of a relational contract no duties can exist *under the contract* prior to its formation. (Of course, the parties may be under other duties to each other prior to formation, but that is true whether the contract is relational or discrete.) Similarly, although a duty may arise, prior to the formation of a contract, to negotiate the terms of a contract in good faith, that duty arises as a result of a preliminary commitment, or on the basis of preliminary actions taken by one or both parties, not under the terms of the contract.

---

15. Victor Goldberg, Towards an Expanded Economic Theory of Contract, 10 J. Econ. Issues 45, 49 (1976). . . .

Macneil sometimes treats discreteness as an end of a spectrum rather than as a definition of a body of contracts. Under this approach, a contract is characterized as lying at the discrete end of the spectrum if it has less of certain characteristics — for example, less duration, less personal interaction, less future cooperative burdens, less in the way of units of exchange that are difficult to measure — and as lying at the relational end of the spectrum if it has more of the relevant characteristics.

A spectrum approach is certainly acceptable if we view relational contracts only from a sociological and economic perspective. However, the enterprise of contract law entails the formulation of rules, and a spectrum approach is inadequate to that enterprise, because it cannot be operationalized. Under such an approach, many or most contracts will have both relational and discrete elements. Accordingly, except for the relatively few cases that lie at one end of the spectrum, or that satisfy or fail to satisfy every item on the checklist, there would be no way to know whether the general rules of contract law or special rules of relational contract law should be applied in any given case. Rules whose applicability depended on where a contract is located in a spectrum — that is, on how many relational indicia the contract has and of what kind — would be rules in name only.

Therefore, if there is to be a body of contract-law rules to govern relational contracts, it is imperative to establish a definition of relational contracts that centers on one or more characteristics that meaningfully distinguish relational and discrete contracts, and the definition must do so in a way that justifies the application of a special body of contract rules to relational contracts as so defined. One characteristic on which such a definition might turn is duration. . . . But . . . this variable won't do the job. . . . For example, a long-term fixed-rent lease in which the tenant is responsible for maintenance, insurance, and taxes may involve little relationship between landlord and tenant. Similarly, a long-term lease of capital equipment, like aircraft, may require almost no contact between the parties so long as periodic payments are made. In contrast, a two-week contract to remodel a room may be highly relational, as may be a one-day contract between a photographer and a portrait sitter.

Although long duration is not a defining characteristic of relational contracts, it might be treated as an independent variable in contract law, so that there would be special rules for all long-term contracts, regardless of whether they are relational. . . . But whether or not there should be special rules for contracts of long duration, long duration does not of itself make a contract relational, and short duration does not of itself make a contract discrete. . . .

What is especially striking about the numerous efforts to define relational contracts, and the failure of all these efforts, is that a straight-forward definition of relational contracts is readily at hand. The obvious definition of a relational contract is a contract that involves not merely an exchange, but also a relationship, between the contracting parties. Correspondingly, the obvious definition of a discrete contract is a contract that involves only an exchange, and not a relationship. Macneil himself has sometimes favored such a definition. For example, in *The New Social Contract*, Macneil defines a discrete contract as "one in which no relation exists between the parties apart from the simple exchange of goods." Such a definition not only can be operationalized, but also reflects the everyday, common sense meaning of the term "rela-tional." It also highlights a major shortcoming of competing definitions: any definition of a relational contract that fails to turn on whether the contract involves a relationship is bound to be incongruent with the ordinary meaning of the term it purports to define.

Once such a definition has been adopted, however, we can see that discrete contracts are almost nonexistent, because virtually all contracts either create or reflect relationships. Discrete contracts — contracts that are not relational — are almost as imaginary as unicorns. A contract to build something as simple as a fence creates a relationship. A contract to sell almost any commercial product is likely to either create or reflect a relationship. Consumer contracts commonly involve ongoing relation-ships even when they are made with huge bureaucratic organizations: most shoppers at Macy's have shopped there before and expect to shop there again. Neither Macy's nor the shoppers perceive each individual exchange as an isolated nonrelational transaction. Even contracts on perfect spot markets are likely to involve traders or brokers who have continuing relationships of some sort.

Trying, at least for the sake of argument, to imagine a discrete contract, Macneil is quite naturally driven to extremes:

[A]t noon two strangers come into town from opposite directions, one walking and one riding a horse. The walker offers to buy the horse, and after brief dickering a deal is struck in which delivery of the horse is to be made at sundown upon the handing over of $10. The two strangers expect to have nothing to do with each other between now and sundown;

they expect never to see each other thereafter; and each has as much feeling for the other as has a Viking trading with a Saxon.[21]

... In the end, Macneil admits that a discrete contract is "an impossibility," and characterizes discrete contracts as "entirely fictional."

One reason for the overthrow of classical contract law is that it was tacitly based on the empirically incorrect premise that most contracts were discrete. Ironically, however, relational contract theory has made an empirical mistake comparable to that made by classical contract law: insofar as relational contract theory supports the idea that there should be a body of special rules to govern relational contracts, it is tacitly based on the incorrect premise that relational contracts are only a special subcategory of contracts as a class. Once relational contracts are properly defined, however, and it is recognized that all or almost all contracts are relational, it is easy to see that relational contracts are not a special subcategory of contracts, and therefore should not and cannot be governed by a body of special contract-law rules. There can be no special law of relational contracts, because relational contracts and contracts are virtually one and the same.

Consider, in this connection, the special rules proposed for relational contracts in some of the relational contract literature. These include the following: (1) Rules that, in the case of relational contracts, would soften or reverse the bite of the rigid offer-and-acceptance format of classical contract law, and the corresponding intolerance of classical contract law for indefiniteness, agreements to agree, and agreements to negotiate in good faith. (2) Rules that would impose upon parties to a relational contract a broad obligation to perform in good faith. (3) Rules that would broaden the kinds of changed circumstances (impossibility, impracticability, and frustration) that constitute an excuse for nonperformance of a relational contract. (4) Rules that would give content to particular kinds of contractual provisions that may be found in relational contracts, such as best-efforts clauses or unilateral rights to terminate at will. (5) Rules that would treat relational contracts like partnerships, in the sense that such contracts involve a mutual enterprise and should be construed in that light. (6) Rules that would keep a relational contract

---

21. [Ian R. Macneil, Contracts: Exchange Transactions and Relations 13 (2d ed. 1978).]

together. (7) Rules that would impose upon parties to a relational contract a duty to bargain in good faith to make equitable price adjustments when changed circumstances occur, and would perhaps even impose upon the advantaged party a duty to accept an equitable adjustment proposed in good faith by the disadvantaged party. (8) Rules that would permit the courts to adapt or revise the terms of ongoing relational contracts in such a way that an unexpected loss that would otherwise fall on one party will be shared by reducing the other party's profits.[23] Because there is no significant distinction between contracts as a class and relational contracts, these rules, and others like them, can be separated into two broad classes: those that are good for all contracts and therefore should be general principles of contract law, and those that are not good for any contracts.

For example, the relational contract literature is correct in pointing to the deficiencies of classical contract law concerning the rigid offer-and-acceptance format of classical contract law and, more particularly, the intolerant treatment, in classical contract law, of such issues as indefiniteness, agreements to agree, and agreements to negotiate in good faith. If parties believe they have a deal, indefiniteness should rarely be a good defense. And if parties agree to agree or to negotiate in good faith, that is a deal. All this holds true, however, for all contracts. Correspondingly, there should be an obligation to perform contracts in good faith, but this obligation should also apply to all contracts.

Similarly, the principles that determine when changed circumstances should serve as an excuse should be applicable to all contracts. Indeed, some of the best-known impossibility, impracticability, or frustration cases, like *Taylor v. Caldwell* and *Krell v. Henry*, involved contracts that were of very short duration and entailed little in the way of a relationship. Rules that give content to terms like best-efforts or termination-at-will provisions should also apply to all contracts. Finally, the conception that contracts are mutual enterprises, and can be analogized to partnerships, is also applicable to all contracts.

On the other hand, the concepts that parties have an obligation to negotiate in good faith to make equitable price adjustments when circumstances change, and that the courts can revise the terms of ongoing

---

23. See, e.g., . . . Robert A. Hillman, Court Adjustment of Long-Term Contracts: An Analysis Under Modern Contract Law, 1987 Duke L.J. 1 (1987).

contracts, are highly questionable for any contracts. There are a variety of ways to contract for the possibility of price adjustments — for example, the use of hardship or equitable-adjustment provisions. In the case of long-term contracts, where such adjustments would be most plausible, normally both parties will be sophisticated and well-advised, and will have the capacity to make use of such a provision if they chose to do so. Therefore, the omission of such a provision in a long-term contract should normally be viewed as a deliberate decision. (A corollary of this position, of course, is that the courts should liberally enforce such provisions when they are utilized.)

Similarly, although the rules of contract law should operate to prevent one party from opportunistically using an insubstantial breach or the nonfulfillment of an insignificant condition as a contrived excuse for breaking a deal, the concept that legal rules can keep a living relationship together is quixotic. Association compelled by law against the wishes of a party is not a living relationship, or at best is a highly impoverished relationship.

Moreover, the concept that parties should be legally forced to stay locked into a thick long-term contractual relationship — that is, an intensive long-term contractual relationship that involves personal elements and extends over a significant portion of the parties' lives — ignores the teachings of cognitive psychology. By virtue of the nature of such relationships, it will be almost impossible to predict, at the time the contract is made, what contingencies may affect the relationship's future course. Furthermore, at the time such a contract is made, each party is likely to be unduly optimistic about the likelihood of the relationship's long-term success and about the willingness of the other party to avoid opportunistic behavior during the course of the relationship. Finally, the parties to such a contract are likely to give undue weight to the state of their relationship as of the time the contract is made, which is vivid, concrete, and instantiated; to erroneously take the state of their relationship at that point as representative of the relationship's future state; and to give too little thought to, and place too little weight on, the risk that the relationship will go bad. Rules that would compel the continuation of such relationships only invite opportunistic exploitation. The solution to the problems presented by such contracts is not to hold the relationship together, but to allow either party to readily dissolve the relationship on fair terms, even if the right to dissolve is not written into the contract. . . .

CONCLUSION

Relational contract theory has helped to bring home two of the fundamental weaknesses of classical contract law — its static character, and the flawed nature of its implicit empirical premise that most contracts are discrete. Relational contract theory has also greatly illuminated the economics and sociology of contracting. Finally, relational contract theory has excelled in its treatment of specific types of contracts, like franchise agreements, and specific types of express or implied terms, like best-efforts provisions. As a result of all these contributions, relational contract theory has been a highly important factor in the formulation of modern contract law.

What relational contract theory has not done, and cannot do, is to create a law of relational contracts. Because there is no significant difference between contracts as a class and relational contracts, relational contracts must be governed by the general principles of contract law, whatever those should be. Of course, certain categories of contracts present special kinds of problems. These problems, however, derive not from the fact that the contracts in these categories are relational, but from more specific attributes. Long-term contracts, contracts to govern thick relationships, contracts that are both especially interactive and especially not well-specifiable, and other categories of contracts may each present special problems that stem from their special features. Even in these cases, for the most part the law of contract should be able to solve the relevant problems by the formulation of general principles that apply to all contracts, but are responsive to intentions and circumstances in particular cases. But relational contracts, as such, are not a special category of contract, because all or virtually all contracts are relational. That is why we do not have, and should not have, a law of relational contracts.

STUDY GUIDE: How does Professor Leib distinguish between the empirical, analytic and normative claims of relational contract theory?   How does Professor Leib respond to the critiques of a relational contract law offered by Professors Feinman, Bernstein and Scott?

RELATIONAL CONTRACT THEORY: A SYMPATHETIC RECONSTRUCTION*

Ethan Leib

As many have observed, it is a difficult business to summarize relational contract theory. There are many "relationalists," — and some who view themselves as relational contract theory's critics concede that "we are all relationalists now."[1] Still, for my purposes, a quick sketch should be sufficient.

At the center of relational contract theory is an empirical observation about the real world of contracting, a related effort to reorient the paradigm under which contract theory is organized and analyzed, and a set of normative and doctrinal prescriptions for how to apply contract law to disputing parties. It is probably fair to say that it is only the empirical observation (and a moderate form of it, to boot) that relational contract theory's critics are willing to concede. Yet other dimensions of the theory are embraced by those I describe as "relationalists," adherents of relational contract theory.

A.   THE EMPIRICAL CLAIM

The empirical observation around which consensus has formed is that many contracts in the real world involve long-term complex relationships and are not merely "one-shot" discrete transactions. In these "relational contracts," social norms often seem to play a larger role in controlling the parties' conduct than the threat of legal sanctions do.

---

*From Ethan J. Leib, Contracts and Friendships, 59 Emory Law Journal (forthcoming).

1. Although oft-credited to Robert E. Scott, The Case for Formalism in Relational Contract, 94 Nw. U. L. Rev. 847, 852 (2000), the phrase also appeared in an earlier comment on Ian Macneil's relational theory by Randy E. Barnett, Conflicting Visions: A Critique of Ian Macneil's Relational Theory of Contract, 78 Va. L. Rev. 1175, 1200 (1992). But see Richard E. Speidel, The Characteristics and Challenges of Relational Contracts, 94 Nw. U. L. Rev. 823, 845 n.86 (2000) (Scott now states that [w]e are all relationalists. . . . Nonsense. Those advocating the virulent strain of formalism are [not] relationalists and the sooner we say so the better.).

Trust and social solidarity tend to underwrite and support (and, in turn, tend to be unwritten and supported by) these types of contracts, and informal cooperation, coordination, and collaboration are typical in contractual relations. In these types of relationships, parties expect some form of loyalty.

Although contracts between strangers are, of course, possible, relational contract theory emphasizes that many contracts do not show this pattern of strangership; by contrast, relationalists highlight just how often contracts are formed between parties who are otherwise connected in pre-existing and on-going relationships. More, relationalists observe that when parties find themselves in such on-going relationships, contractual behavior tends to be driven by informal and implicit dimensions of their mutual understandings rather than by any "paper" deal that exists on account of formalities taken within the relationship, if any.

This isn't terribly controversial stuff, though it took a while for these insights to be fully understood by and incorporated into mainstream contracts thinking. To the extent that one sometimes hears that "we are all relationalists now," all it can mean is that most people have embraced the relationalists empirical observation. There are, nevertheless, two significant cleavages between relationalists and non-relationalists that have emerged from this now-widely accepted empirical observation, both of which are about what follows from the observation as a matter of general contract theory and as a normative and prescriptive matter within contract law.

B.   THE ANALYTIC CLAIM FOR A PARADIGM SHIFT IN CONTRACT THEORY

Relationalists contend that relational contracts are so prevalent in the real world that the general theory of contract must itself acknowledge this practical reality. That is, contract theory must be oriented in such a way as to put relational contracts at its center. This can mean several things.

First, owing to the recognition that many contracts (some relationalists would say *most* — if not *all* — contracts) are relational, relationalists argue that it would be useful to analyze contracts on some continuum or gradation from the most discrete to the most relational. By utilizing this method of analysis, one can differentiate more easily among types of contracts and apply the proper policy approach to each contractual context. Second, because relational contracts are so common, relationalists argue that the general theory of contracts needs to pay respect to the nature of real contracts in the world — and not operate with a presumption that the law of contracts is to be designed as a law for strangers, in which there is little background trust. Because the relationalists think that relational contracts are pervasive, they argue that orienting contract law as a method to provide trust for discrete and formal transactions is inappropriate. Rather, a new paradigm is needed to account for the degree to which relational contracts are central to the enterprise of contracting.

One can easily understand why relational contract theory's analytic move is more controversial than its underlying empirical claim. Some relationalists might think this analytical claim about reorienting contract theory follows from the empirical claim. But that isn't necessarily true. The empirical claim around which there is little controversy is actually a rather modest one: some contracts are deeply relational. All that follows from this claim, perhaps, is that general contract theory must make room for analyzing and respecting a class of relational contracts.[2] But that hardly requires the sort of paradigm shift in theory and law one tends to associate with the urgings of hard-core relationalists. At least part of the resistance to the analytical claim comes from the sense that the empirical claim can easily be accommodated by slight modifications of reigning contract theories. But this resistance generally works because non-relationalists simply do not buy the more aggressive empirical claims that most contracts are meaningfully characterized by relational properties and can be usefully analyzed based upon where they fall on the discrete-relational continuum.

The analytic claim becomes more pressing if the empirical claim is acknowledged to be deeper; if relational contracts are very pervasive (though the degree of pervasiveness to make the analytic claim plausible is very hard specify, of course), it becomes harder to embrace traditional contract theory, which presumes contracts between strangers as its paradigm. At least if one's meta-theoretical commitments require contract

---

2. For analysis of how the empirical claim was absorbed into mainstream "neo-classical" contract law, see generally Jay M. Feinman, Relational Contract Theory in Context, 94 Nw. U. L. Rev. 737 (2000). . . .

theories to "fit" the underlying practice of contracting, it becomes hard not to orient one's contract theory to match the reality of the social practice. Indeed, most relationalists explicitly or implicitly embrace a stronger form of the empirical claim than non-relationalists do.

The underlying empirical dispute, however, is actually pretty hard to resolve. It is virtually impossible to get a sense of what is happening in most contracts and it is very hard to say how pervasive a contract type needs to be to require reorienting the theory of contract. These difficulties are at least part of the reason we are unlikely to see much conciliation between the camps anytime soon.

Still, it should be noted that there are ways to contest a strong form of the empirical claim and nevertheless subscribe to a form of the analytic claim. One could concede that true relational contracts are actually a rather small class of contracts, all things considered, but that they are so normatively attractive in their foregrounding of cooperation, collaboration, and solidarity that we should want to model other contracts on that particularized, even if somewhat atypical, form of contracting. One could argue that modeling contracts on deep relationships of collaboration and solidarity would orient parties better in their transactions — and could even maximize their surplus. This is a way to defend the core relationalist analytical claim without needing to prove the empirical claim in any strong form.

The opposite is also true, however: one could concede the strong form of the empirical claim and still resist the analytical claim on normative grounds. One could say that preserving forms of strangership is essential to our economy and society and, accordingly, contracts should be modeled on personal distance, as traditional contract theory has been. If we design contracts and orient our contract theory as something categorically different from our personal relationships governed largely by moral and social norms — presumed to be "relational" at the extreme — we are most likely to avoid the juridification or contractualization of intimate personal relations.[3] Although we lose something in

---

3. Forms of this argument against the analytic claim are actually quite common among non-relationalists. See generally . . . Aditi Bagchi, Contract v. Promise (forthcoming); Melvin A. Eisenberg, Why There Is No Law of Relational Contracts, 94 Nw. U. L. Rev. 805, 820 (2000) ("This massive contractualization of human relationships [which is effected by relational contract theory] undesirably obscures critical differences between economic and affective relationships, between explicit and tacit reciprocity,

the fit of the theory (if the strong empirical claim is, after all, true), we gain some protection of the private sphere from the law — and that is, arguably, normatively desirable. . . .

But there is also another way of contesting the strong form of the empirical claim while still arguing for a version of the analytical claim. One could plausibly find orienting contract theory on the discrete-relational continuum so useful as a way of distinguishing among types of contracts that one could be relatively indifferent to how strong the empirical claim is and still want to use the classificatory apparatus from relational contract theory. Some relationalists — and Ian Macneil is exemplary on this score, delineating a laundry list of dimensions of relationality (or "common contract norms")[4] — have developed sophisticated ways of describing the relational features of contracts and have helped create categories of analysis that divide the real-world of contract practice in a way that might prove analytically useful.

The trappings of relational contract theory may be useful for categorical neatness, for theoretical integrity and exhaustiveness, or for more general philosophical reasons (apart from "fit"). Since the apparatus of the theory can accommodate promise-based liability, consent-based liability, reliance-based liability, and relationship- or status-based liability, its very pluralism may be attractive, especially to those who tire of seeking a fully coherent promissory or reliance-based theory of contractual obligation. So many other contract theorists use only a singular organizing principle to account for a social practice that is rather heterogeneous, and the appeal of relational theory may be its willingness to

---

between relationships that should be enforceable by both law and social norms and relationships that should be enforceable only by social norms."). . . .

It is worth noting that this type of argument — if it is right — goes a long way to helping address Seana Shiffrin's recent concern about contract norms' "divergence" from moral norms of promising. See Seana Valentine Shiffrin, The Divergence of Contract and Promise, 120 Harv. L. Rev. 708 (2007). If contracts are best designed as something different from promises in "private" life, there is less reason to worry that there is norm divergence. This argument is spelled out at length in Aditi Bagchi's very interesting paper.

4. The list changes from time to time and is not intended to be exhaustive. But here are the standard elements in Macneil's most recent articulation: role integrity (requiring consistency, involving internal conflict, and being inherently complex); reciprocity; implementation of planning; effectuation of consent; flexibility; contractual solidarity; the restitution, reliance, and expectation interests (the linking norms); creation and restraint of power; propriety of means; and harmonization of relational conflict with the social matrix and supracontractual norms.

welcome multifarious sources of obligation and deep fragmentation of the field of contract. Although, to be sure, Macneil's complicated matrices probably scare away more contract theorists than they invite into the fold, the approach of seeing contracts through their relational dimensions has proven to be a rich method of dividing the often too-unified world of contract theory. Relational contract theorists can win over adherents if contracts can be usefully mapped and ordered based on their relational elements, even if only a small fraction of contracts are actually of a "purely" relational type.

C.   THE NORMATIVE CLAIM ABOUT CONTRACT LAW

Whereas the first relationalist claim—the empirical one—is really sociological and the second—the analytic one—is really meta-theoretical, the third is a claim about what the law should be. And there is plenty of controversy about relational contract *law*. . . .

[R]elationalists respond to the reality of relational contracts and the centrality of relational contract to understanding the practice with a set of special doctrines that tend to be a set of loose standards rather than formalistic rules. Most importantly . . . , the key relationalist move on the doctrinal or legal front is to suggest that courts, when faced with disputing parties in relational contracts, should seek to apply the intrinsic norms of the relationship to settle the dispute even if an application of classical contract law to the parties' paper deal might lead to a different conclusion. Again, relationalists emphasize the implicit dimension of contractual undertakings and the unfolding nature of the contractual relationship, which develops and gets modified over time, even if the paper deal doesn't reflect such developments. Relationalists instruct judges to bring social norms to bear upon disputing parties, since the social norms are the real scaffolding for the parties relationship and must be given respect and effect to support relational contracting properly. This doesn't, however, mean that relationalists reject the application of all external norms; applying legal norms is always, in part, the application of external norms. Relationalists only require heightened sensitivity to calibration with internal norms as well.

In its most modest form, relationalists urge incorporating trade usages, courses of dealing, courses of performance, and a general good faith obligation. But this urging has largely already been adopted by modern contract law through the Uniform Commercial Code; the common law also already embraces these minimalist relationalist pre-scriptions. True adherents of relational contract theory believe that these modest incorporation strategies of letting the parties relational norms control as a legal matter do not go far enough. A much more substantial effort to mine parties' relationships for implicit understandings and social norms — and to analyze their relational properties to help resolve disputes between them — should follow from a strong commitment to relational contract theory. Note that these implicit understandings can play a role in adjudicating questions of formation, performance, mod-ification, interpretation, or remedies.

This set of normative claims relationalists offer about their preferred approach to contract law has met with substantial opposition. In the first place, it is very difficult for some to envision how to operationalize a special set of judicial principles to govern relational contracts; to oper-ationalize the principles successfully, one would seem to need an operationalized definition of the relational contract as a threshold matter. However, it is difficult, non-relationalists argue, to pin down with any degree of clarity which contracts should count as relational ones. Here is how Eisenberg puts it: "it is impossible to locate . . . a definition that adequately distinguishes relational and non-relational contracts in a le-gally operational way — that is, in a way that carves out a set of special and well-specified relational contracts for treatment under a body of special and well specified rules." Although duration is often the test used as a shortcut by relationalists, it is clearly an insufficient one: there are short-term transactions that trigger substantial interdependence and there are long-term transactions that still remain discrete and con-trolled primarily by legal documents and formalities. And once the test for what counts as a relational contract becomes so diluted as to encompass every contract (because every contract establishes some relationship), there is not, as Eisenberg has argued, much room for a special relational contract law.

But Eisenberg's critique of relational contract theory, . . . misses its mark in several ways. First, it is only one brand of the normative claim that seeks special treatment for a small class of relational contracts; more thorough-going relationalists might very well concede that there needn't be a special set of standards that would only apply to "relational contracts." These relationalists would have contract law develop a generalized law to apply to all or most contracts, in light of their relational nature. So Eisenberg's concern about the need for an operationalized legal definition of the relational contract may not be necessary after all, if the majority of contracts are relational.

Alternatively, if we take Macneil's most recent suggestion for the content of relational contract law — to apply internal relational norms to contractual disputes, whatever the relationship and whatever the contract — no complicated work needs to be done to separate the world into relational and non-relational contracts. Rather, to the extent there are any relational norms, the law should remain sensitive to them. That may not be an easy task, but it doesn't implicate Eisenberg's concern about differentiating relational and non-relational contracts.

More importantly, perhaps, Eisenberg fails to prove that there is no way to operationalize a law of relational contracts. Although he seems to think a "spectrum approach" (of seeing contracts along a spectrum from the discrete to the relational) is "acceptable . . . from a sociological and economic perspective," he concludes that a spectrum cannot be used within contract law because "many or most contracts will have both relational and discrete elements" and because "[r]ules whose applicability depended on where a contract is located in a spectrum — that is, on how many relational indicia the contract has and of what kind — would be rules in name only." Yet this entire argument hinges on a substantive view about the desirability of rules over standards, something relationalists tend to contest as part of their normative claim. Indeed, Eisenberg offers no *proof* that standards are not capable of being legally operationalized; he simply states that it would be hard to develop clear rules using a spectrum approach, betraying his preference for rules over standards. . . .

To be sure, one may want clear legal rules for all sorts of reasons and decide to reject relational contract theory because its spectrum approach relies too heavily on standards. Indeed, Macneil has already admitted that to be a good practitioner of relational contract analysis, we'd have to become "anthropologists, sociologists, economists, political theorists, and philosophers;"[5] a tall order indeed. Yet, Eisenberg's dispute is ultimately about the merits, not an explanation for the impossibility of a relational contract law. If relationalists told judges to apply the

---

5. [Ian R. Macneil, The New Social Contract 70 (1980).]

intrinsic norms between parties to a contract dispute, we could debate whether that is a good direction to give judges and whether a judge could ever carry out the direction well in light of evidentiary difficulties. But we couldn't really say with any certainty that such a direction is not capable of being legally operationalized. One can choose to be a non-relationalist because one likes rules over standards; yet liking rules over standards does not tell us, in the words of Eisenberg's title, "why there is no law of relational contracts."

There are two related substantive objections to directing judges in accordance with relational contract theory to apply relational norms to contractual disputes. One is an argument deriving from the path-breaking work of Lisa Bernstein, which tends to show that the law cannot easily incorporate trade usages and customs: few actually exist and few are generally observed.[6] This skepticism that the law can discover internal norms within relational contracts is quite relevant for relational contract theory: if relationalists are committed to the normative claim that the law should incorporate and seek internal norms between parties, evidence that tends to show that these norms are rarely mutually understood between parties and rarely embraced by parties surely complicates the viability of the relationalists' normative prescription.

Still, there is reason to believe that Bernstein's work can be read more as a cautionary note about evidence than as a decisive proof against relational contract theory as such. In short, Bernstein's empirical studies are obviously limited to a few areas of inquiry. And although they are fascinating windows into certain trade communities, it hardly follows that there are no immanent business norms that exist, that can be discovered, and that are followed and can be enforced by courts. Some had taken Bernstein's empirical findings to support the rejection of any incorporation strategy, whether of Karl Llewellyn's in the UCC or of the relationalists more generally. Yet, that seems an unnecessary jump to a conclusion about the viability and desirability of incorporation and it certainly isn't required by the available evidence. In any case, another

---

6. See generally Lisa Bernstein, Private Commercial Law in the Cotton Industry: Creating Cooperation Through Rules, Norms, and Institutions, 99 Mich. L. Rev. 1724 (2001); Lisa Bernstein, The Questionable Empirical Basis of Article 2's Incorporation Strategy: A Preliminary Study, 66 U. Chi. L. Rev. 76 (1999); Lisa Bernstein, Merchant Law in a Merchant Court: Rethinking the Code's Search for Immanent Business Norms, 144 U. Penn. L. Rev. 1765 (1996). . . .

plausible response to Bernstein's findings . . . is to find ways to get courts to send relational disputes into mediation, arbitration, and agency management, since these institutions are likely more capable than courts at discovering such norms anyway, if and when they exist.

A related concern that underwrites the argument against the normative claim stems from what Eric Posner calls the possibility and likelihood of "radical judicial error."[7] The worry here is slightly different from Bernstein's. Whereas she emphasizes that there may be no immanent norms between parties, Posner emphasizes that even if there were such norms, judges would not be competent to discover or apply them. . . .[8] The gist of his argument is that judges are going to resolve disputes essentially at random if they are stuck trying to figure out parties' internal norms. However, judges will be capable of engaging in formalistic decisionmaking — and they should stick to that task within their competence. . . .

This is clearly not the place to attempt to settle the age-old debates between formalists and non-formalists and between objectivists with respect to contract law who favor outward signals of agreement and meaning, and subjectivists for whom parties' intentions should always prevail. But a few observations seem appropriate in light of the recent effort to rejuvenate formalism in response to the relationalist challenge.

First, the assumption of radical judicial error is quite difficult to swallow. Admittedly, the empirical evidence available to settle the question of the error-proneness of judicial decision-making is remarkably thin. Yet the claim that judges would do no better than random at using their common sense to understand the underlying deals in contractual contexts seems like it is the one that should bear the burden of proof. Posner has not met that burden yet, so presuming that properly instructed judges can get it right much of the time (or at least on average better than random) is far from outlandish. Indeed, even if there is the possibility for radical judicial error in a class of cases, those are the cases in which formalism might be appropriate; relational norms can still be applied in

---

7. See Eric A. Posner, A Theory of Contract Law Under Conditions of Radical Judicial Error, 94 Nw. U. L. Rev. 749 (2000).

8. . . . Although Scott abjures from signing onto the radical judicial error hypothesis, concerns about judicial competence certainly animate his argument for formalism as well. . . .

other cases where the parties intentions can be made relatively clear through context and common sense.

Second, if judges are, in fact, so incompetent at divining business deals, there would be reason to suspect they would be similarly incompetent at the rigors of formalism. After all, formalism's contributions to contract law — consideration, the statute of frauds, the parol evidence rule, the plain meaning rule, offer-and-acceptance principles, indefiniteness rules — are hardly uniformly applied and can be unpredictable for parties and lawyers alike. Maybe it is somewhat easier to enforce a paper deal than it is to enforce a real deal, which is hard to discover — especially when parties have incentives to lie when the relationship breaks down. But it is still altogether plausible that judges wouldn't be very good at formalism either. They like their discretion and aren't any better at potentially undesirable acontextual rule application. If they aren't very good at formalism, formalism isn't a great alternative to the complexity of discovering relational norms. . . .

Third, formalism's premise that parties will be properly chastened and put all they want in their paper deals in anticipatory response to formalistic courts is not obviously viable. It is ultimately an empirical question whether formalism as a judicial strategy can actually succeed in getting parties to put all their important matters into formal arrangements, since the choice to use formalities is a complex one. Parties choose not to use formalities for many reasons. For example, contracting with forms is very costly and since few contracts actually result in legal disputes, it is a cost that is often not worth incurring because of the low risk of contractual failure. Moreover, in many cases, a longterm relationship will be presumed to require accommodation over time that cannot easily be anticipated at some moment of formal formation. Finally, in many cases of contractual relations, the relationship is premised on social and interpersonal ties (even though parties would want legal sanctions once the relationship ends); getting formalistic about the paper deal up front will lead parties not to cooperate at all, costing both parties the surplus they otherwise could have achieved from the relationship. Given these factors that contribute to the sort of incomplete and gap-ridden contracts we see in relational contracting, formalism might actually serve not to chasten parties at all but only to prevent these forms of cooperation altogether. . . .

Of course, formalists understand that there are real costs associated with formalism, but relationalists see those costs as so deeply undermining contract laws purpose and legit imacy that they can't stomach it. More practically, although formalists emphasize all the gains in predictability and "rule of law" that might result from a commitment to enforcing only clear paper deals that are bargained-for promises, relationalists focus on a different kind of "calculability:" the predictability for the parties' themselves rather than for their lawyers. The capitalist system — if that's one's point of departure for designing contract — can work better, they argue, if parties can bank on their real deals, not idiosyncratic paper deals that their adversarial lawyers draw up with little sensitivity to the underlying relationship between the parties.

STUDY GUIDE: Is Dori Kimel's objection to the "relational paradigm in contract theory" consistent with that of Professor Eisenberg? In other words, does Kimel wish to make a distinction that Professor Eisenberg denies is possible? Can these two critiques be reconciled or do they cancel each other out?

REFLECTIONS ON THE RELATIONAL MODEL*

Dori Kimel

Neither the phenomenon of the relational contract nor its theoretical exploration is . . . new. In one form or another, such arguments have been familiar for quite some time now, with much of the pioneering work having been done by Ian Macneil in the 1970s, and developed ever since by him as well as an ever-growing number of eminent followers. The starting point for much of the pioneering work — focusing primarily on complex, long-term commercial relationships such as ones involving long-term supply, distributorship, agency, franchise and the like — was the observation that those often encompass norms of conduct which are unaccounted for by "mainstream" contract theory, and which, potentially, pose unique practical, doctrinal and theoretical challenges.

I view that core observation as indisputable, and attempts to rise to such challenges as laudable; indeed, much of the controversy they generated in the early years of relational theory seems unwarranted today. The present contribution, accordingly, is by no means meant as an attack on relational theory as a whole. . . . Thus, I would not want to deny that

*From Dori Kimel, The Choice of Paradigm for Theory of Contract: Reflections on the Relational Model, 27 Oxford J. Legal Stud. 233 (2007).

there are relational contracts, or that there is possibly some scope for doctrinal reform related to relationality, or that one measure of success for any putative theory of contract is its ability to shed light on relational contracts just as much as it "fits" with discrete ones. I will, however, want to take issue with the view according to which contract law, as it is and as a whole, is "relationally constituted". . . . I would like to question the notion that the key to a sound theoretical grasp of the nature of contract and its social role lies in the adoption of the relational paradigm.

THE THEORETICAL CHARGE

. . . The gist of the [relational theoretical] argument . . . is that contract *theory* as we know it fails to account for the true nature of contractual relations, and hence of contract; so long as it is based around a discrete paradigm, or anyway so long as it fails to adopt a relational paradigm, it is bound to remain out of touch with reality and riddled with fiction, and thus fail to explain precisely what it sets out to explain. . . . More than any other line of argument, it is this sort of query, and the sort of analysis offered by relationists, that sustains the call for a change of paradigm in contract theory. . . .

I want to outline my response to the theoretical charge by way of a digression; that is, I want to look at what its implications might be in terms of our understanding of contract's alleged extra-legal counterpart, namely promise. . . . My point is this: if contracts are relational and that is something that should make us rethink our theoretical grasp of the institution as a whole, then promises are far more so. Promises, far more paradigmatically than contracts, are made or exchanged in the context of ongoing personal relationships. Much less controversially (at least) than is the case with contracts, promises *between strangers* can be seen, not only statistically but also logically speaking as the exception to a rule. So if the relationists are right about the fatal flaws of non-relational contract theory, their charge may be even more pertinent to the philosophical analysis of promise as we know it.

Accounts of promise as, say, a *voluntary* undertaking, usually performed by way of some *conventional speech act*, of a fairly well-defined *obligation* — one which, if undertaken successfully, is *owed to the promisee*, so that (other things being equal) she has *a right* to its performance alongside the unique *prerogative* to release the promisor, and so on — can be said to be at odds with promissory reality far more dramatically than mainstream contract theory may be at odds with the reality of contractual relations. After all, in promissory contexts much more routinely than in contractual ones, we find parties conducting themselves differently from what promissory logic on its own may lead us to expect. So perhaps the "logic" in question is pure outmoded fantasy? Perhaps the theory of promise, too, should be made relational? Perhaps here, too, precepts such as those italicized above should be eschewed as fiction, to be altogether replaced by the overarching theoretical aim of fully embedding promises in the broader context of those networks of social and personal interactions in which they typically occur?

The crux of my objection to this line of thought is as follows. It is true that the reality of promissory relations frequently appears to be at odds with pretty much all mainstream philosophical analysis of promissory obligation. But that is because the norms that feature in and around promissory events are often not promissory norms as such, but norms of the background relationship between promisor and promisee — be that a friendship, an intimate or a collegiate relationship, or as the case may be. In fact, norms of those relationships in the context of which promises are typically made or exchanged sometimes do not just supplement, but *compete with* promissory norms — compete, if not in terms of their very logic, at least in terms of their practical effect. Thus, for example — perhaps primarily in the context of particularly close or intimate interactions, as in loving relationships — certain norms of the background institution — those governing, say, the manner of verbal communication between the parties — may compete with those promissory norms that constitute the mode of undertaking, so as to militate against the relative formality of so doing by way of a dedicated, discrete speech act (let alone a linguistically conventional one). Or, to take an example pertaining to the normative implications of a promise once it has been made, a promisee who happens to be a friend of the promisor may have a *"friendship duty"* to release the promisor, yet (so long as she does not do so) also a *promissory right* to the performance of the promise; meanwhile the promisor may be under a *promissory obligation* to perform, while also bearing a *"friendship right"* to be released, and consequently *not* perform.

When it comes to a background institution such as friendship, in most cases — in the normal case, I would say — the norms generated by the background relationship will prevail in such a contest: the promisee-friend will release, the promisor-friend will not perform. That means that if we are not attuned to such distinctions and complications — distinctions between norms in terms, *inter alia*, of their precise source; complications in the shape of potential tensions between such different norms from different sources — we may simply observe that, "in reality," the promise is not binding, at least not in the sense upon which philosophers of promise or philosophers of obligation tend to insist; or, when it comes to the example pertaining to loving relationships, the resulting observation may be that promises are altogether excluded from such a context, or (at least) that a promise is not, or not paradigmatically, made by way of a distinct, conventional speech act.

Such reactions would amount, however, to regrettable over-simplifications. In fact, the very key to understanding such composite situations, with the particular nuances they encompasses, is in being able to tell the promissory logic and the norms it generates from the norms of that other institution with which it interacts, and their distinct sources and gravitational forces and relative weights. That both examples show that specific promissory norms involved in a contest of sorts with non-promissory ones — and, as the case may be, in one way or another being defeated by them — is the starting point, at least, for posing the next set of pertinent questions on the way to fully grasping what really goes on and what is really interesting in such scenarios. Opting instead for a "relational theory of promise" would thus lead not only to a great deal of distortion in our understanding of promise, but also of the background institution in question (friendship, loving relations, or as the case may be) — and finally of the way in which the two institutions interact and how contests between their respective norms arise and are resolved and what the normative aftermath of such resolutions is likely to be. The relational theory of promise is sure to be *complicated* — certainly more complicated than any theory of promise has been before — yet also uniquely blind to the truly important nuances and complications that its subject matter encompasses.

Going back to contract, my point would be that, that is also the case with relational theory here. There is a distinct clamour amongst relationists for a certain kind of analytical transparency; for a theoretical and a doctrinal canon that is truer to "the real world" and eschews fiction and simplification. However, what is offered as the remedy for alleged confusion and distortion in rival theories engenders deeper confusion and greater distortion, for it involves the blurring of lines that divide different social institutions, and missing out on an understanding of how such institutions function and interrelate in the context of diffcrent types of relationship while still preserving their distinct character, neither necessarily subsuming nor subsumed by these relationships in the process. The failure to grasp the precise boundaries between promise and the multitude of distinct types of social relationship in the context of which promise operates, would lead to analytical distortion far deeper and more pervasive than that involved in misconstruing this or that rule or sub-rule of promissory liability. The same is true of contract.

CONCLUSION

The general picture, as I see it, looks something like this. Contracts are often made at arm's length — outside the framework of an already existing, significant, personal relationship between the parties, and without necessarily a commitment by the parties to form such a relationship in future. The institution's ability to facilitate such exchanges is one of its distinct strengths. Sometimes contracts are also made in relational frameworks, or such frameworks develop in time around an existing contractual bond. The institution's propensity to facilitate arm's length transactions continues to play an important role with regard to such cases, too, for the modes of detachment it provides often form precisely the kind of background that is needed in order for the potential encapsulated in potentially relational contracts to be realised. In any event, when contract features in a relational context, it need not subsume the relationship in question any more than it need be subsumed by it. An analysis of the *contractual* dimension of relationships that aims to colonize every other dimension and treats it as, potentially, one more variable to be taken into account when a contractual dispute arises, not only misconstrues the proper function of contract and the nature of the relationship, but also fails to account for the legally binding exchange — indeed, the exchange in general — as but one component of human interaction. . . .

[W]hen Macaulay warns that given that "there is a text between the lines in most contracts," then "if we do not attempt to implement this implicit text, we are denying reasonable expectations,"[9] he seems unduly to deny both the ability to distinguish and the soundness of the distinction between the different kinds of expectation that a single relationship may involve. The expectation to have legal redress in case of disappointment does not and need not attach itself to every other expectation we may have of others with whom we have a relationship, even one that has a contractual dimension — let alone that the *reasonableness* of such an expectation need not depend solely on the reasonableness or otherwise of those other expectations to which it may or may not be attached. . . .

In a recent article, Ian Macneil . . . commented in passing . . . that "*all* human social relations are exchange relations."[10] Since I cannot quite imagine how this proposition could be credibly defended in the first place, I would not want to speculate either on the shape that a serious critique thereof may take. I suspect, however, that a defence of some such view — with its collapsing of all social relations into exchange, to be followed (as it did for Macneil) by that of exchange into contract — is precisely what is needed in order to establish the supremacy of the relational paradigm in contract theory.

---

9. [S. Macaulay, 'The Real and the Paper Deal: Empirical Pictures of Relationships, Complexity and the Urge for Transparent Simple Rules' in 'Introduction: The Research Agenda of Implicit Dimensions of Contracts' in D. Campbell, H. Collins and John Wightman (eds), Implicit Dimensions of Contract (Oxford: Hart Publishing, 2003), 51 at 102.]

10. Ian R. Macneil, 'Reflections on Relational Contract Theory after a New-Classical Seminar', in above n 1, 207 at 214. The full implications of this view for contract theory, in the context of Macneil's work, should be read in conjunction with his definition of "contract" as "relations among people who have exchanged, are exchanging, or expect to be exchanging in the future — in other words, exchange relations" [Ian R. Macneil, 'Relational Contract Theory: Challenges and Queries' (2000) 94 Nw. U. L. Rev. 877, at 878], and "exchange" as something that (as Feinman put it) "is not limited to defined monetizable exchange, but also includes other interactions in which reciprocity is a dominant factor." [J. M. Feinman, 'Relational Contract Theory in Context' (2000) 94 Nw. U. L. Rev. 737 at 741].